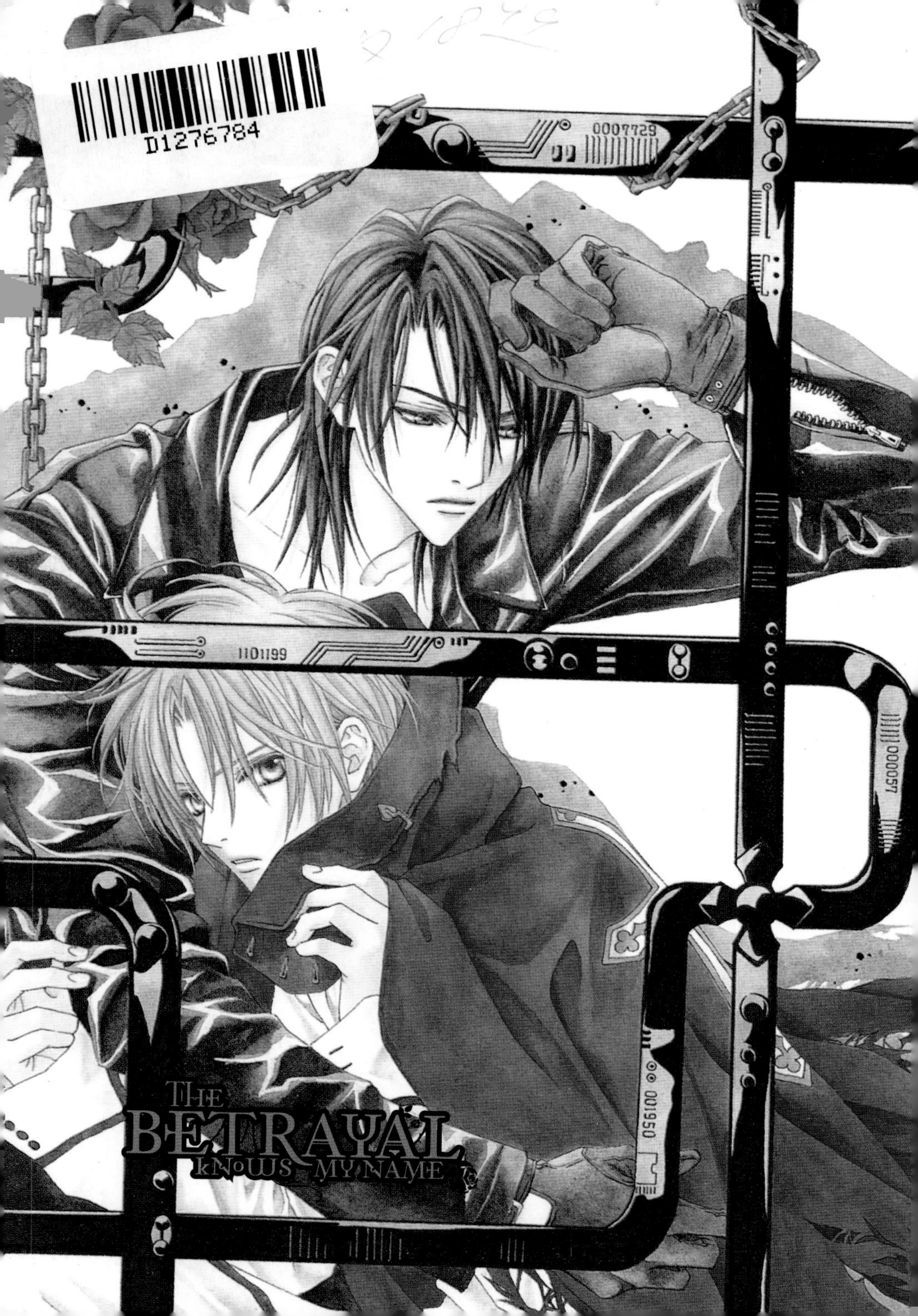
THE
BETRAYAL
KNOWS MY NAME
0007729
1101199
000057
001950

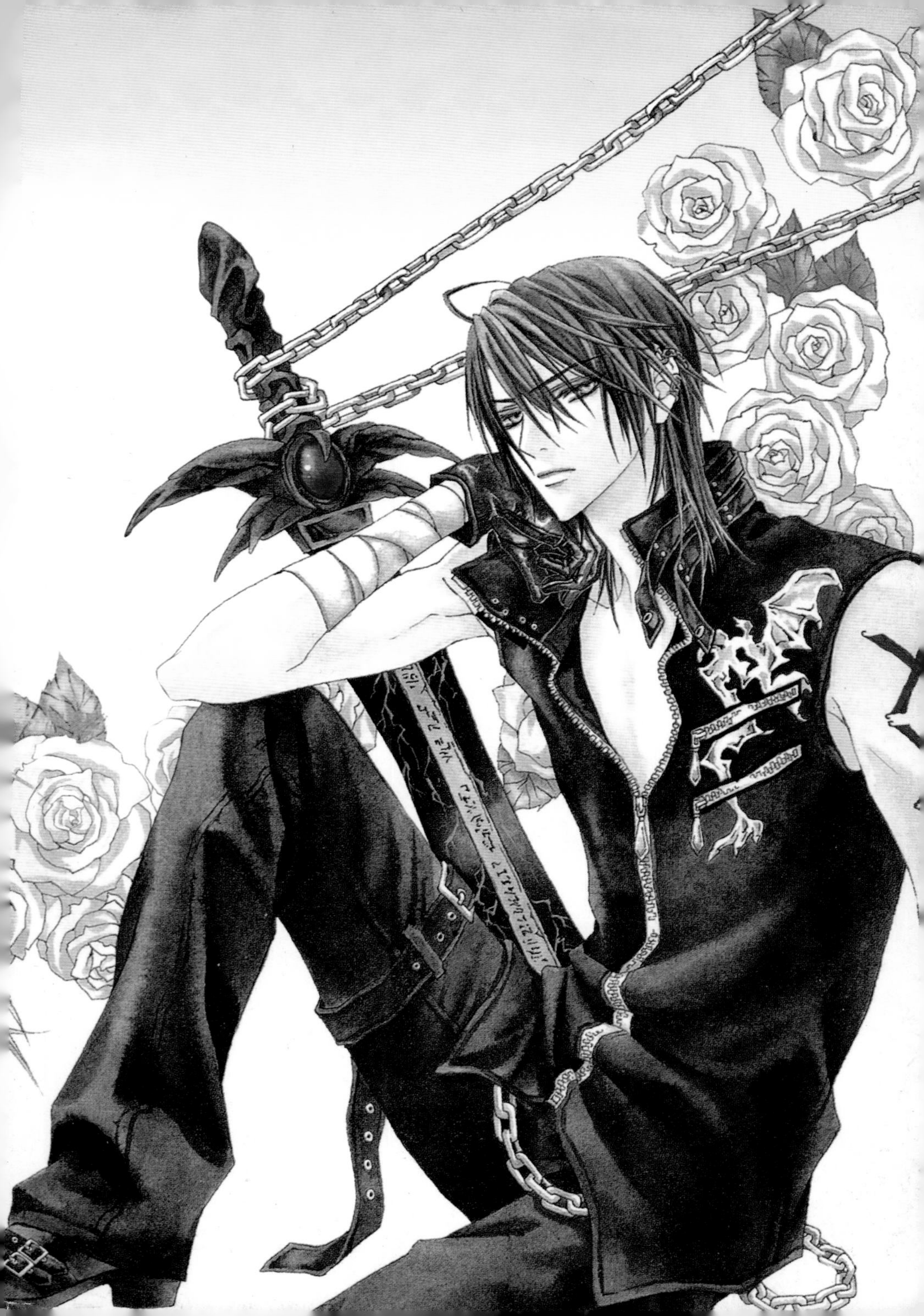

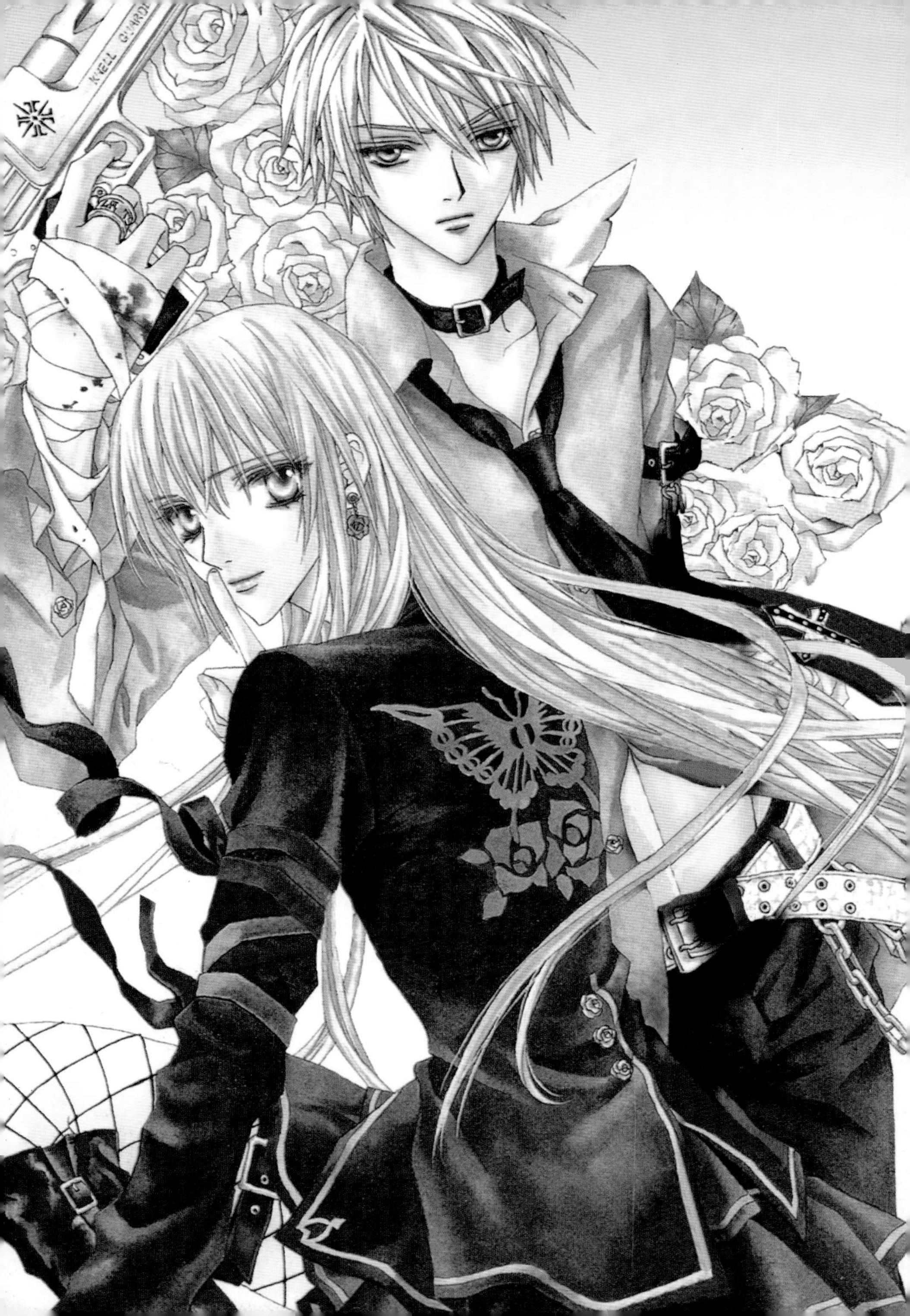

The Betrayal Knows My Name

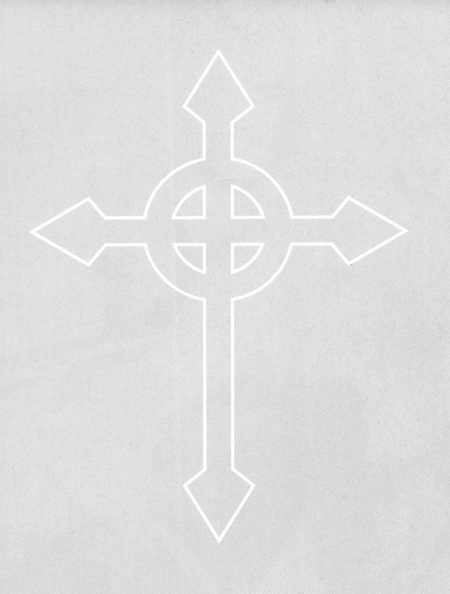

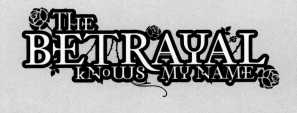

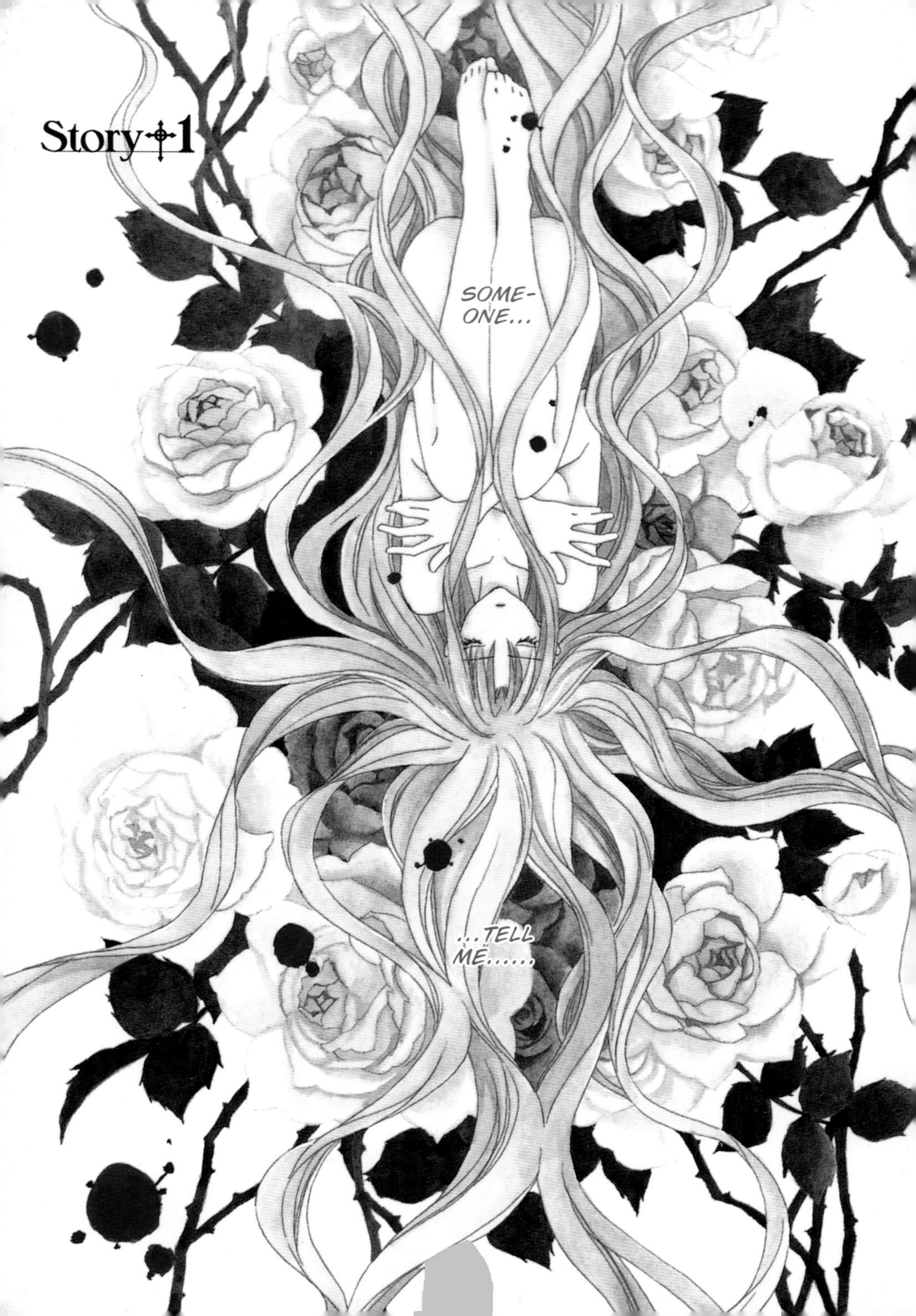
Story 1
SOME-
ONE...
...TELL
ME......

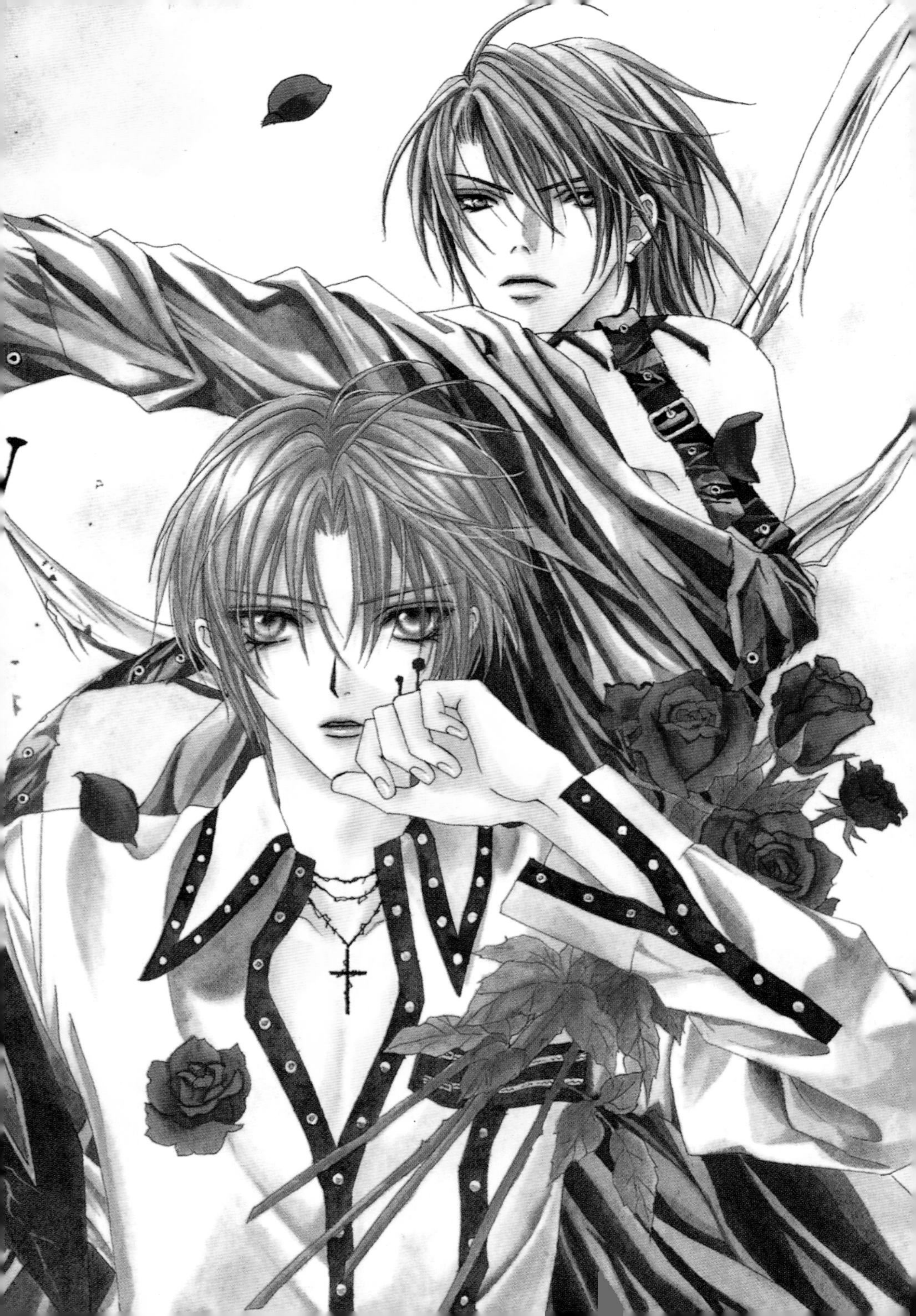

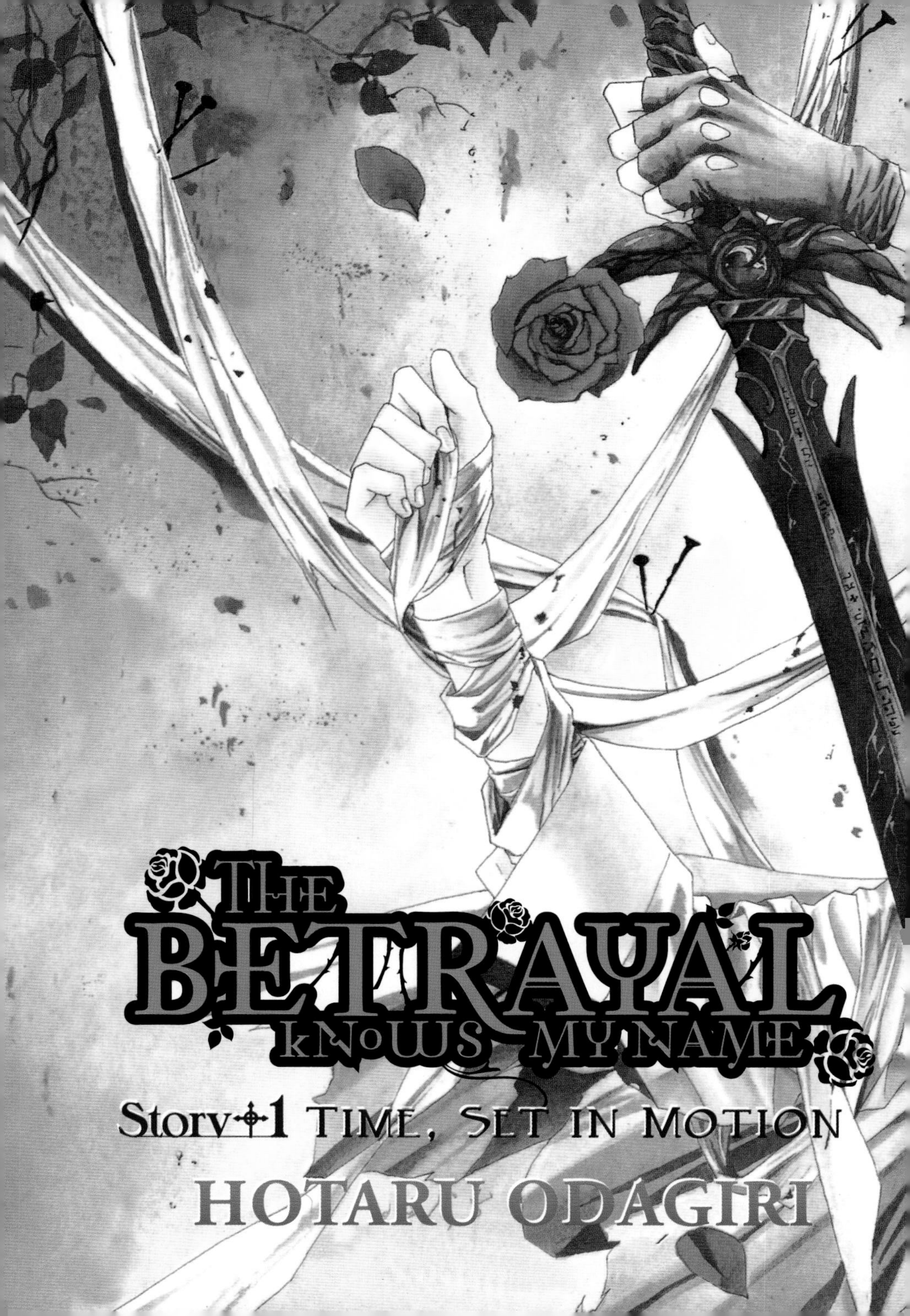
The Betrayal Knows My Name
Story 1 Time, Set in Motion
Hotaru Odagiri

1
Contents

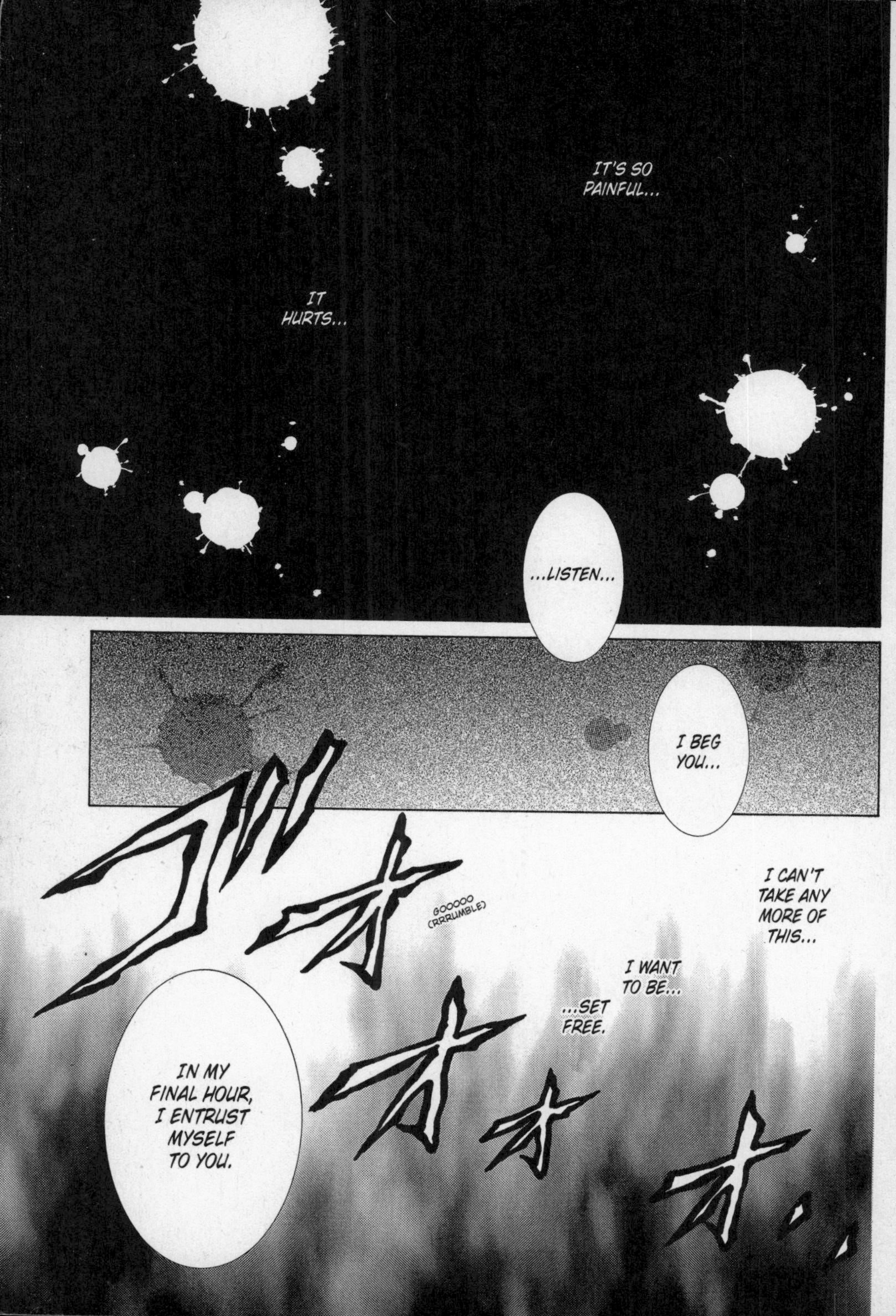
IT'S SO PAINFUL...
IT HURTS...
...LISTEN...
I BEG YOU...
I CAN'T TAKE ANY MORE OF THIS...
I WANT TO BE...
...SET FREE.
GOOOOO (RRRUMBLE)
IN MY FINAL HOUR, I ENTRUST MYSELF TO YOU.

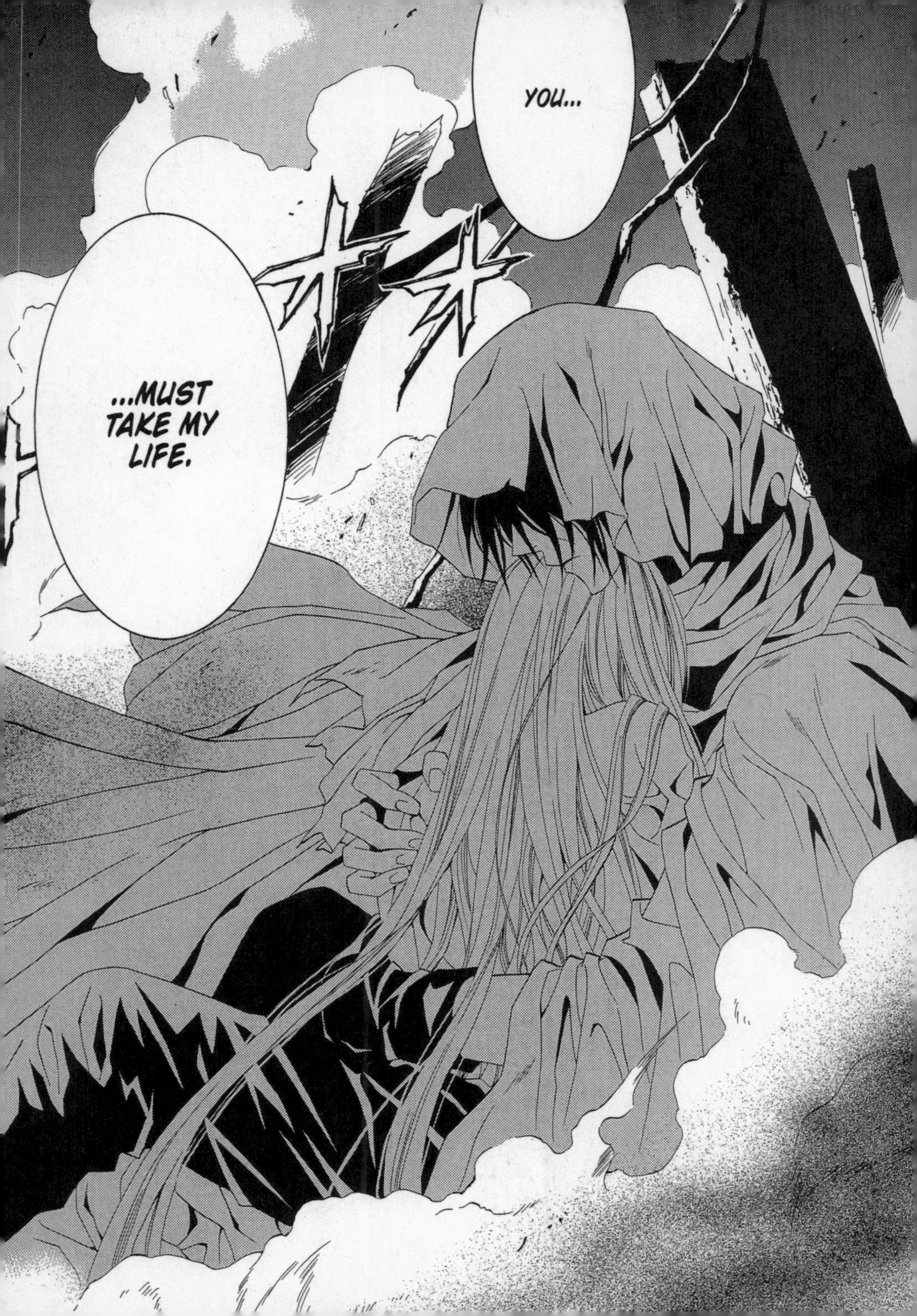
YOU...
...MUST TAKE MY LIFE.

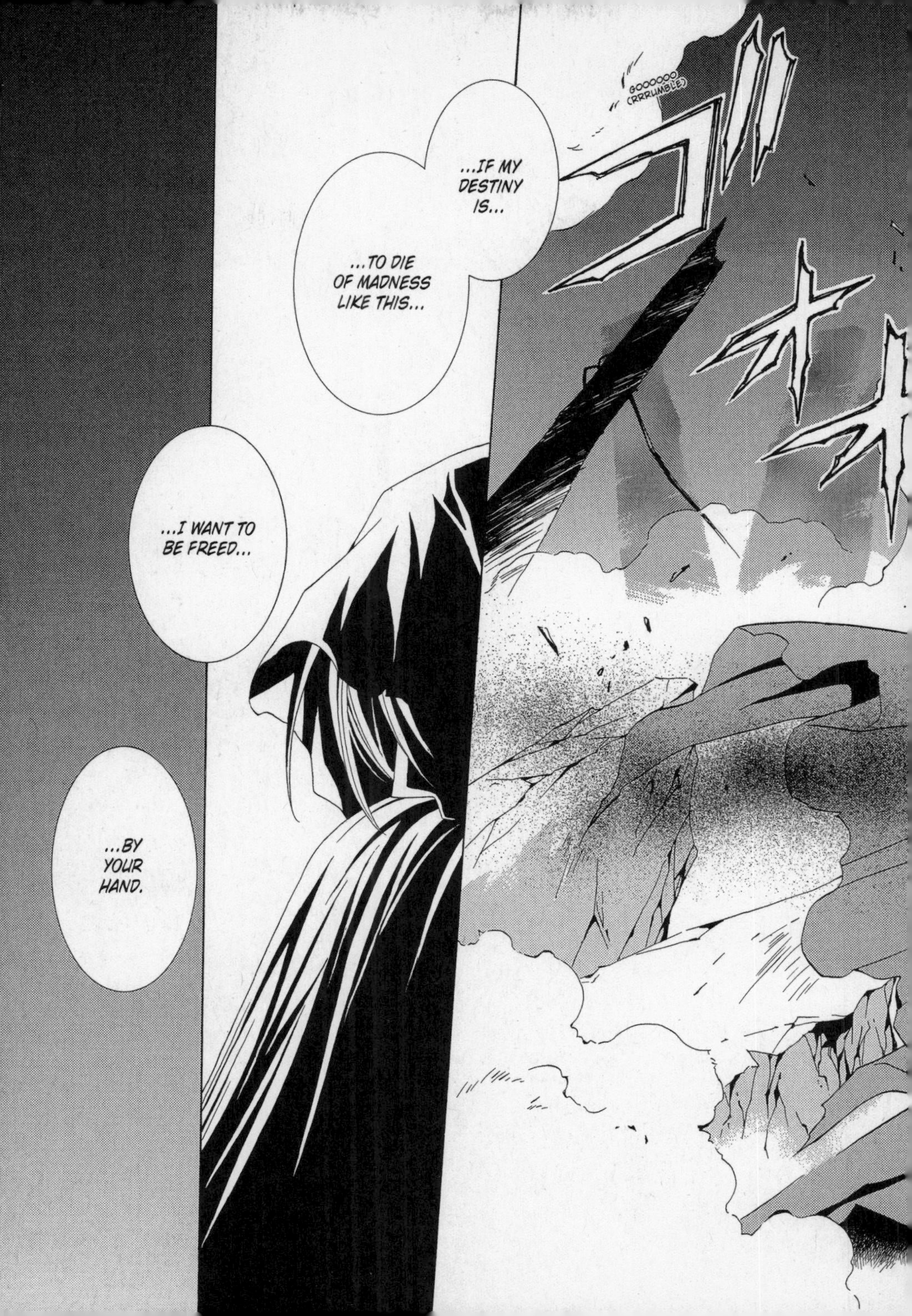
GOOOOOO (RRRUMBLE)
...IF MY DESTINY IS...
...TO DIE OF MADNESS LIKE THIS...
...I WANT TO BE FREED...
...BY YOUR HAND.

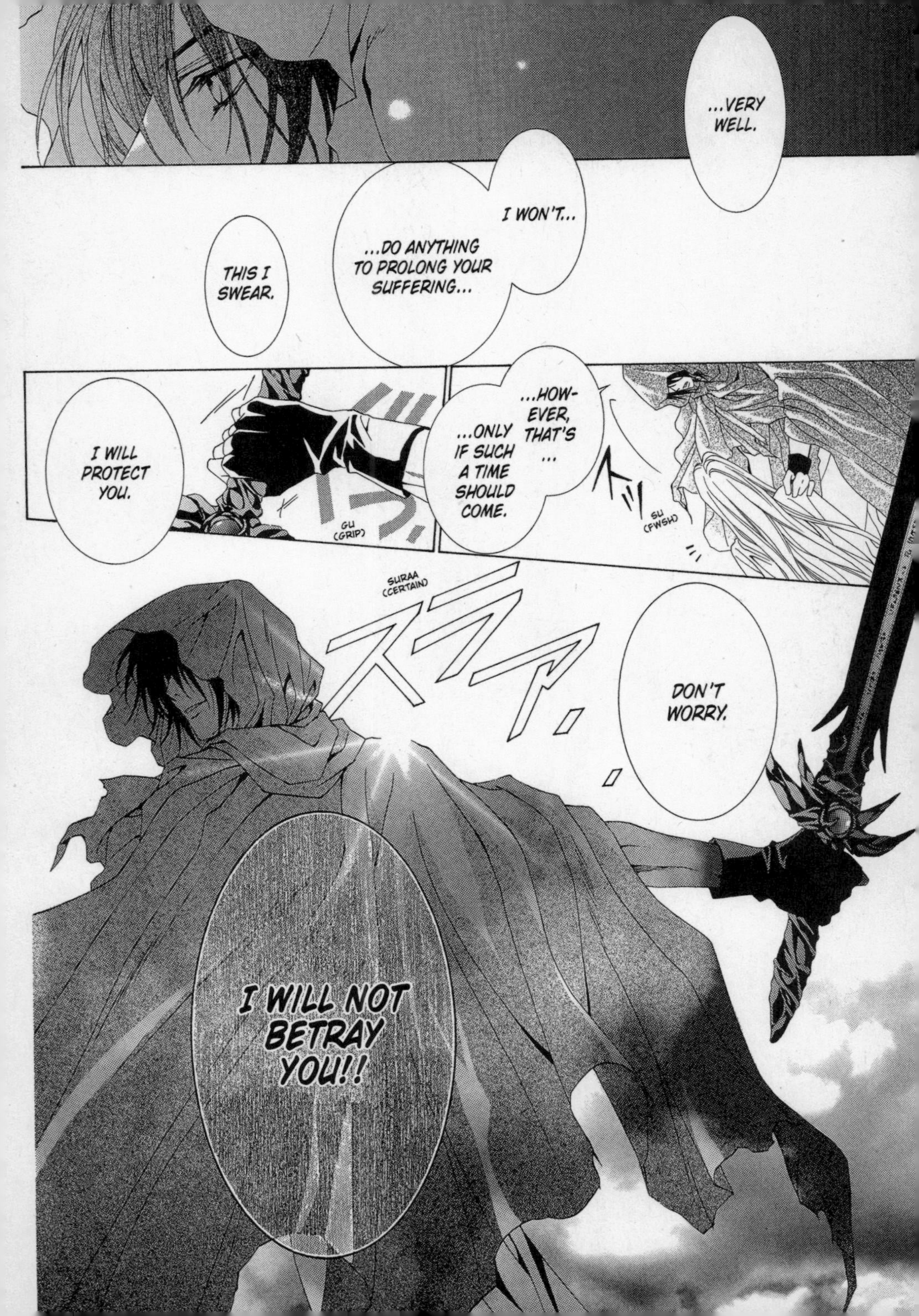
...VERY WELL.
I WON'T...
...DO ANYTHING TO PROLONG YOUR SUFFERING...
THIS I SWEAR.
SU (FWSH)
...HOW-EVER, THAT'S...
...ONLY IF SUCH A TIME SHOULD COME.
GU (GRIP)
I WILL PROTECT YOU.
SURAA (CERTAIN)
DON'T WORRY.
I WILL NOT BETRAY YOU!!

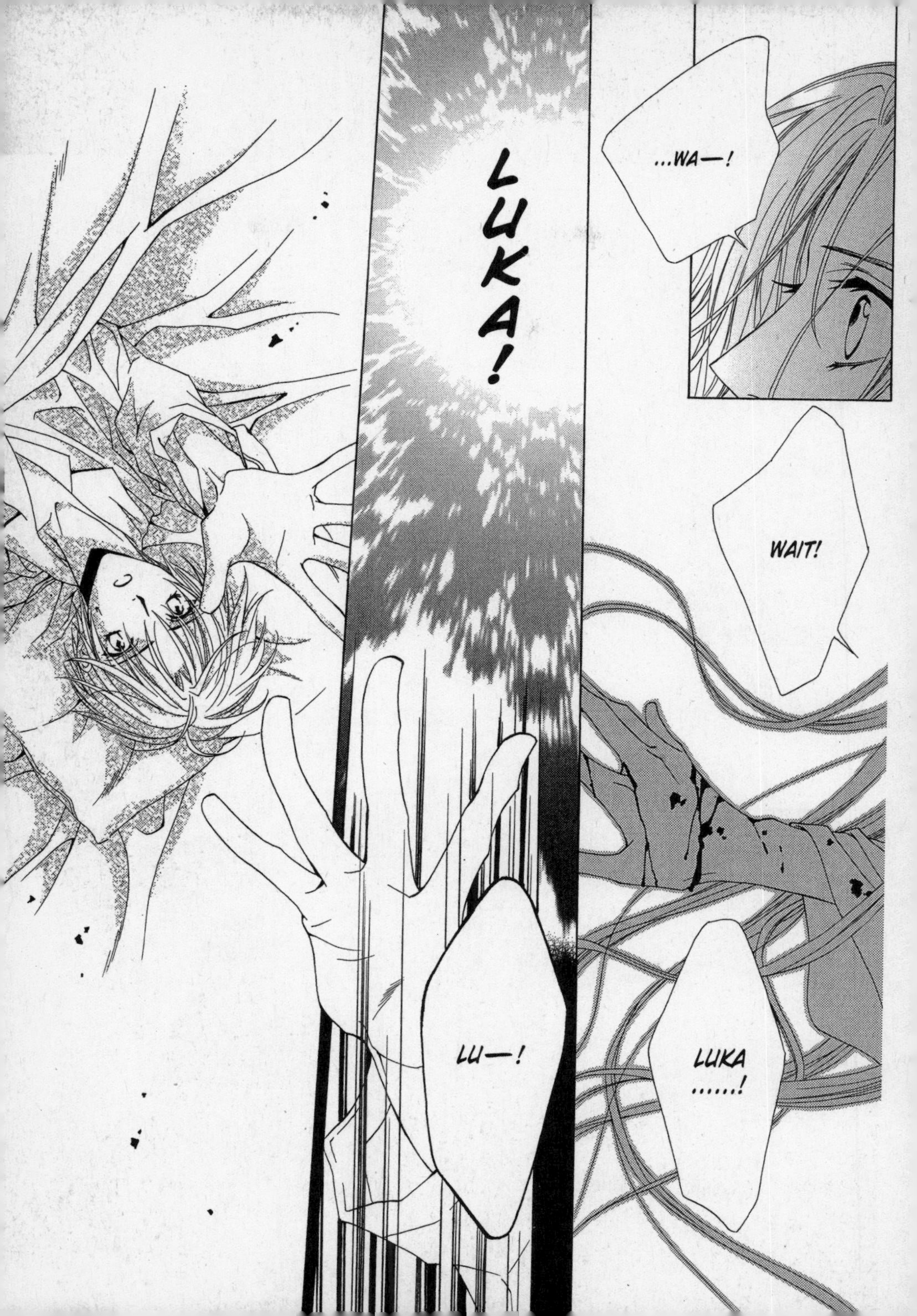
...WA—!
WAIT!
LUKA!
LUKA
......!
LU—!

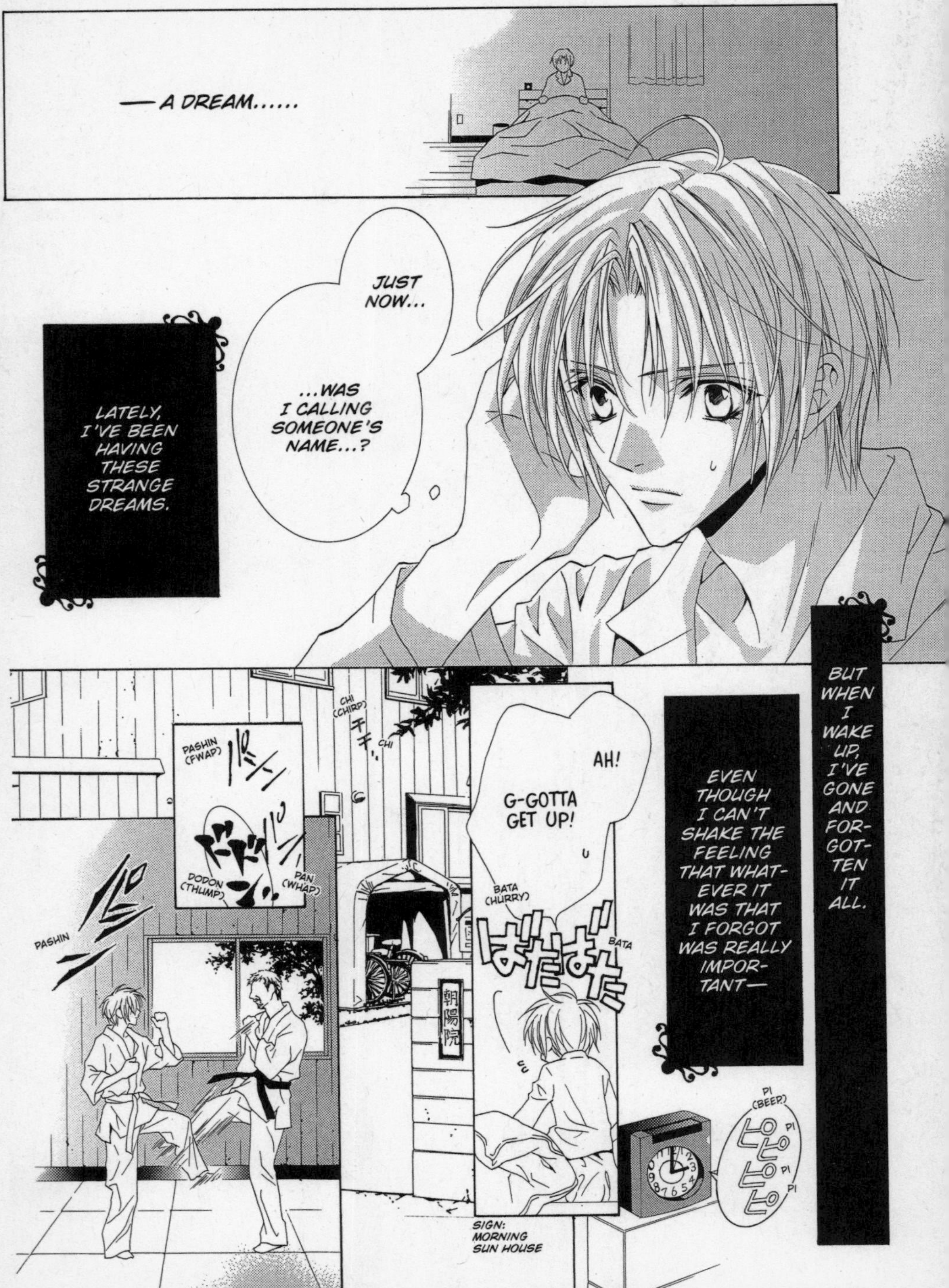
— A DREAM......
JUST NOW...
...WAS I CALLING SOMEONE'S NAME...?
LATELY, I'VE BEEN HAVING THESE STRANGE DREAMS.
BUT WHEN I WAKE UP, I'VE GONE AND FOR-GOT-TEN IT ALL.
EVEN THOUGH I CAN'T SHAKE THE FEELING THAT WHAT-EVER IT WAS THAT I FORGOT WAS REALLY IMPOR-TANT—
PI (BEEP) PI PI PI
AH!
G-GOTTA GET UP!
BATA (HURRY) BATA
SIGN: MORNING SUN HOUSE
朝陽院
CHI (CHIRP) CHI
PASHIN (FWAP)
DODON (THUMP)
PAN (WHAP)
PASHIN

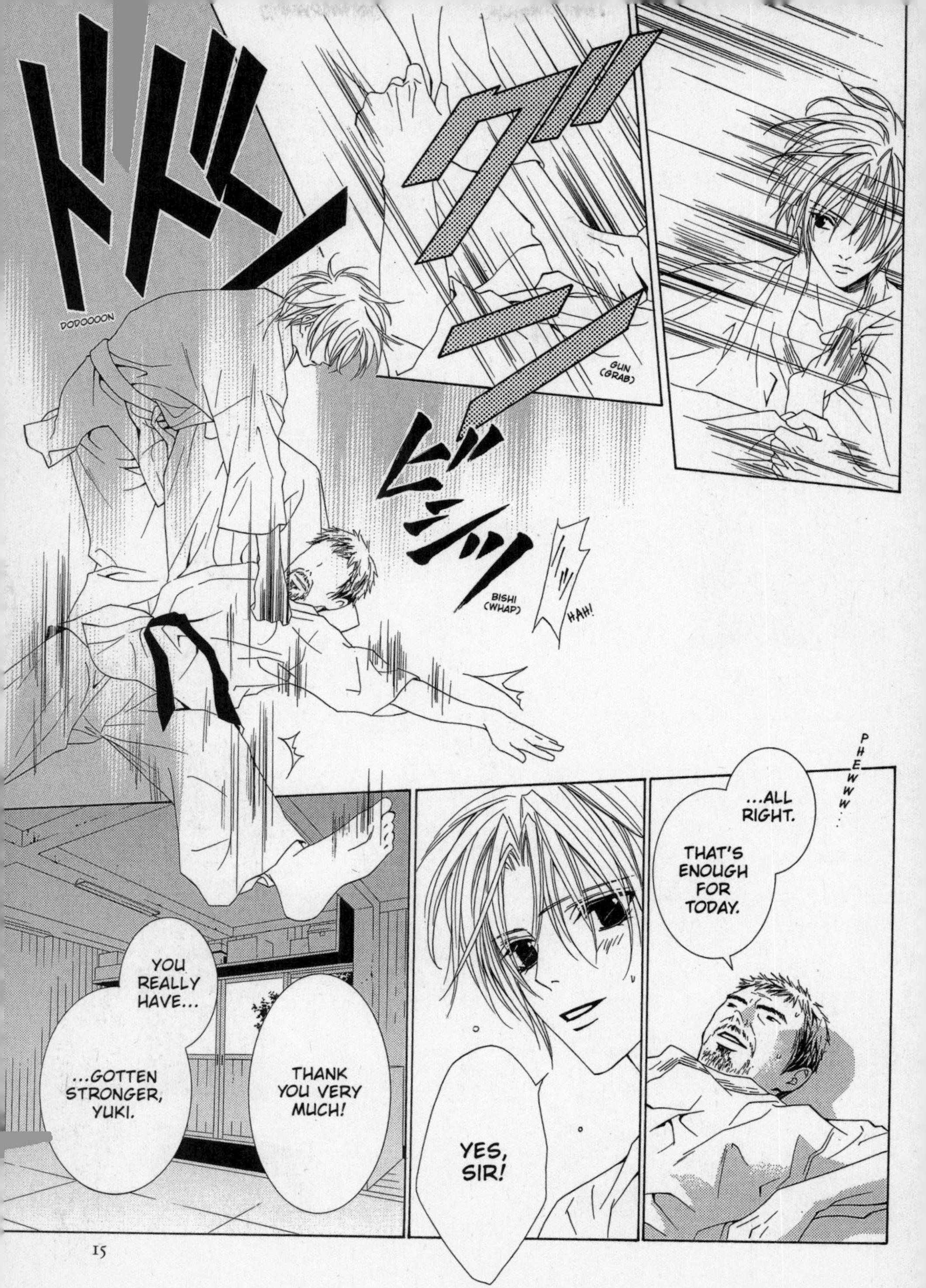
GUN (GRAB)
BISHI (WHAP)
HAH!
DODOOOON
PHEWWW...
...ALL RIGHT.
THAT'S ENOUGH FOR TODAY.
YES, SIR!
YOU REALLY HAVE...
...GOTTEN STRONGER, YUKI.
THANK YOU VERY MUCH!

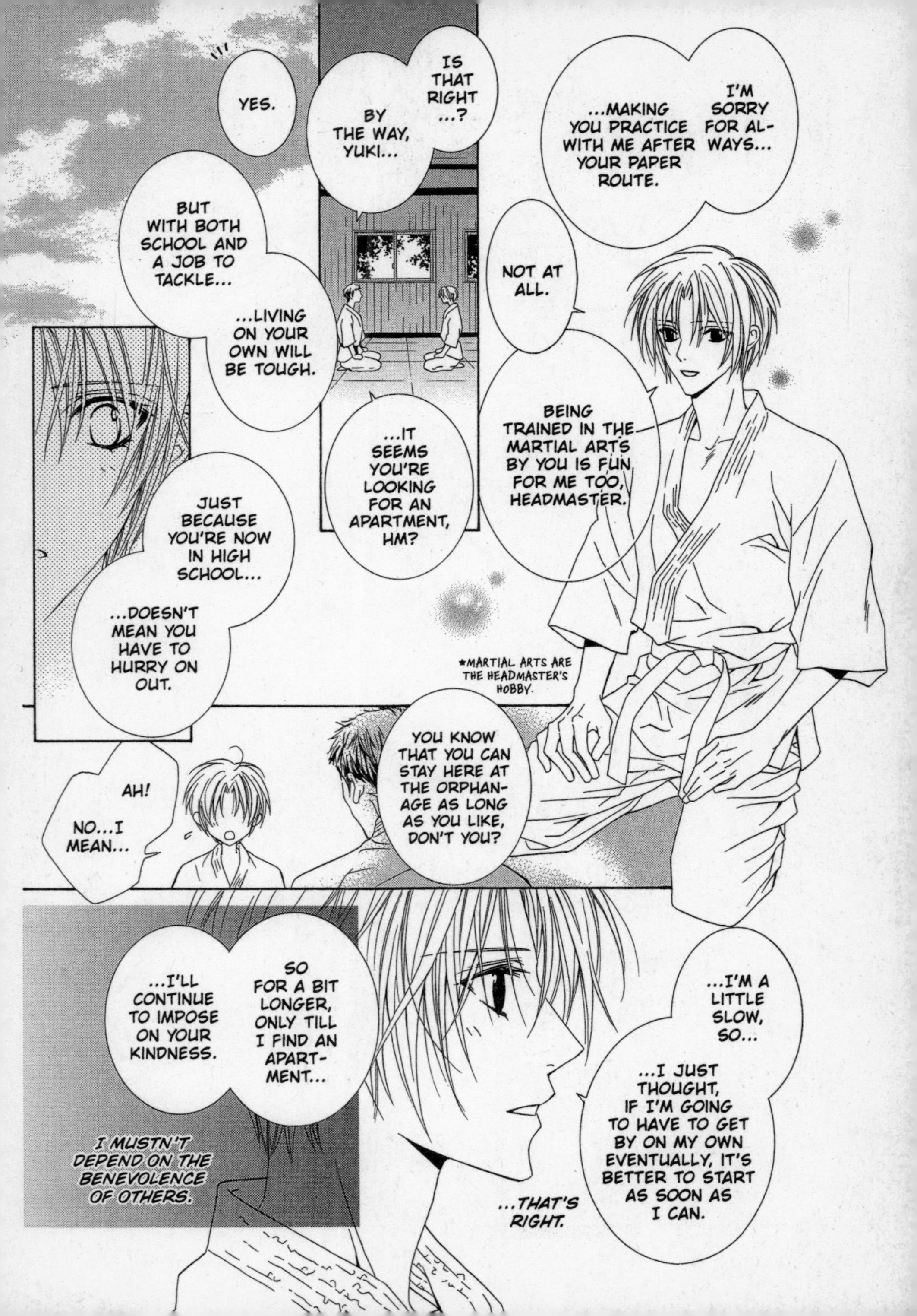
I'M SORRY FOR ALWAYS...
...MAKING YOU PRACTICE WITH ME AFTER YOUR PAPER ROUTE.
NOT AT ALL.
BEING TRAINED IN THE MARTIAL ARTS BY YOU IS FUN FOR ME TOO, HEADMASTER.
*MARTIAL ARTS ARE THE HEADMASTER'S HOBBY.
IS THAT RIGHT ...?
BY THE WAY, YUKI...
...IT SEEMS YOU'RE LOOKING FOR AN APARTMENT, HM?
YES.
BUT WITH BOTH SCHOOL AND A JOB TO TACKLE...
...LIVING ON YOUR OWN WILL BE TOUGH.
JUST BECAUSE YOU'RE NOW IN HIGH SCHOOL...
...DOESN'T MEAN YOU HAVE TO HURRY ON OUT.
YOU KNOW THAT YOU CAN STAY HERE AT THE ORPHANAGE AS LONG AS YOU LIKE, DON'T YOU?
AH!
NO...I MEAN...
...I'M A LITTLE SLOW, SO...
...I JUST THOUGHT, IF I'M GOING TO HAVE TO GET BY ON MY OWN EVENTUALLY, IT'S BETTER TO START AS SOON AS I CAN.
...THAT'S RIGHT.
SO FOR A BIT LONGER, ONLY TILL I FIND AN APARTMENT...
...I'LL CONTINUE TO IMPOSE ON YOUR KINDNESS.
I MUSTN'T DEPEND ON THE BENEVOLENCE OF OTHERS.

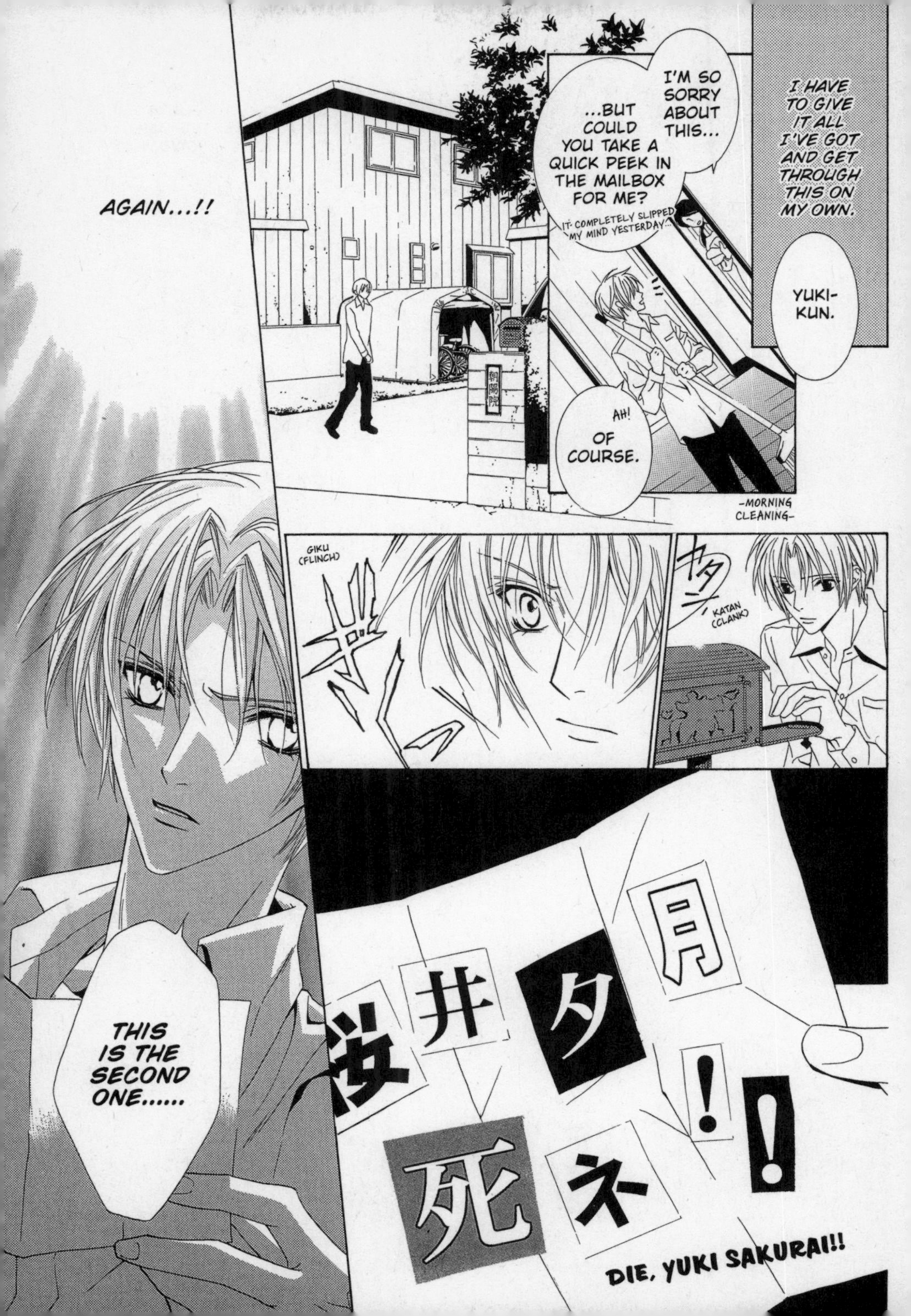

I HAVE TO GIVE IT ALL I'VE GOT AND GET THROUGH THIS ON MY OWN.
YUKI-KUN.
I'M SO SORRY ABOUT THIS...
...BUT COULD YOU TAKE A QUICK PEEK IN THE MAILBOX FOR ME?
IT COMPLETELY SLIPPED MY MIND YESTERDAY...
AH! OF COURSE.
-MORNING CLEANING-
AGAIN...!!
KATAN (CLANK)
GIKU (FLINCH)
DIE, YUKI SAKURAI!!
THIS IS THE SECOND ONE......

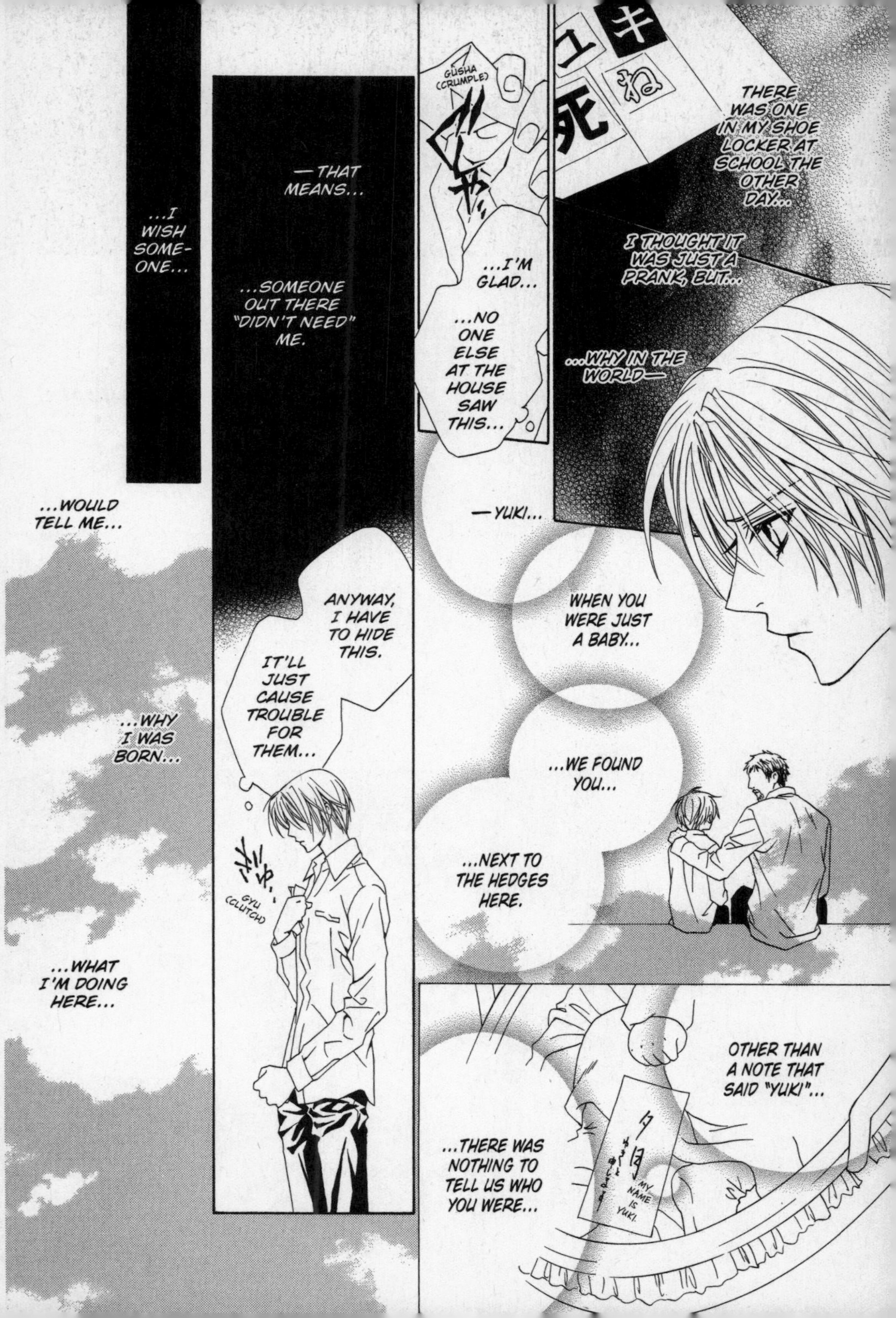
THERE WAS ONE IN MY SHOE LOCKER AT SCHOOL THE OTHER DAY...
I THOUGHT IT WAS JUST A PRANK, BUT...
...WHY IN THE WORLD—
GUSHA (CRUMPLE)
...I'M GLAD...
...NO ONE ELSE AT THE HOUSE SAW THIS...
—THAT MEANS...
...SOMEONE OUT THERE "DIDN'T NEED" ME.
...I WISH SOME-ONE...
—YUKI...
WHEN YOU WERE JUST A BABY...
...WE FOUND YOU...
...NEXT TO THE HEDGES HERE.
ANYWAY, I HAVE TO HIDE THIS.
IT'LL JUST CAUSE TROUBLE FOR THEM...
GYU (CLUTCH)
...WOULD TELL ME...
...WHY I WAS BORN...
...WHAT I'M DOING HERE...
OTHER THAN A NOTE THAT SAID "YUKI"...
...THERE WAS NOTHING TO TELL US WHO YOU WERE...
MY NAME IS YUKI.

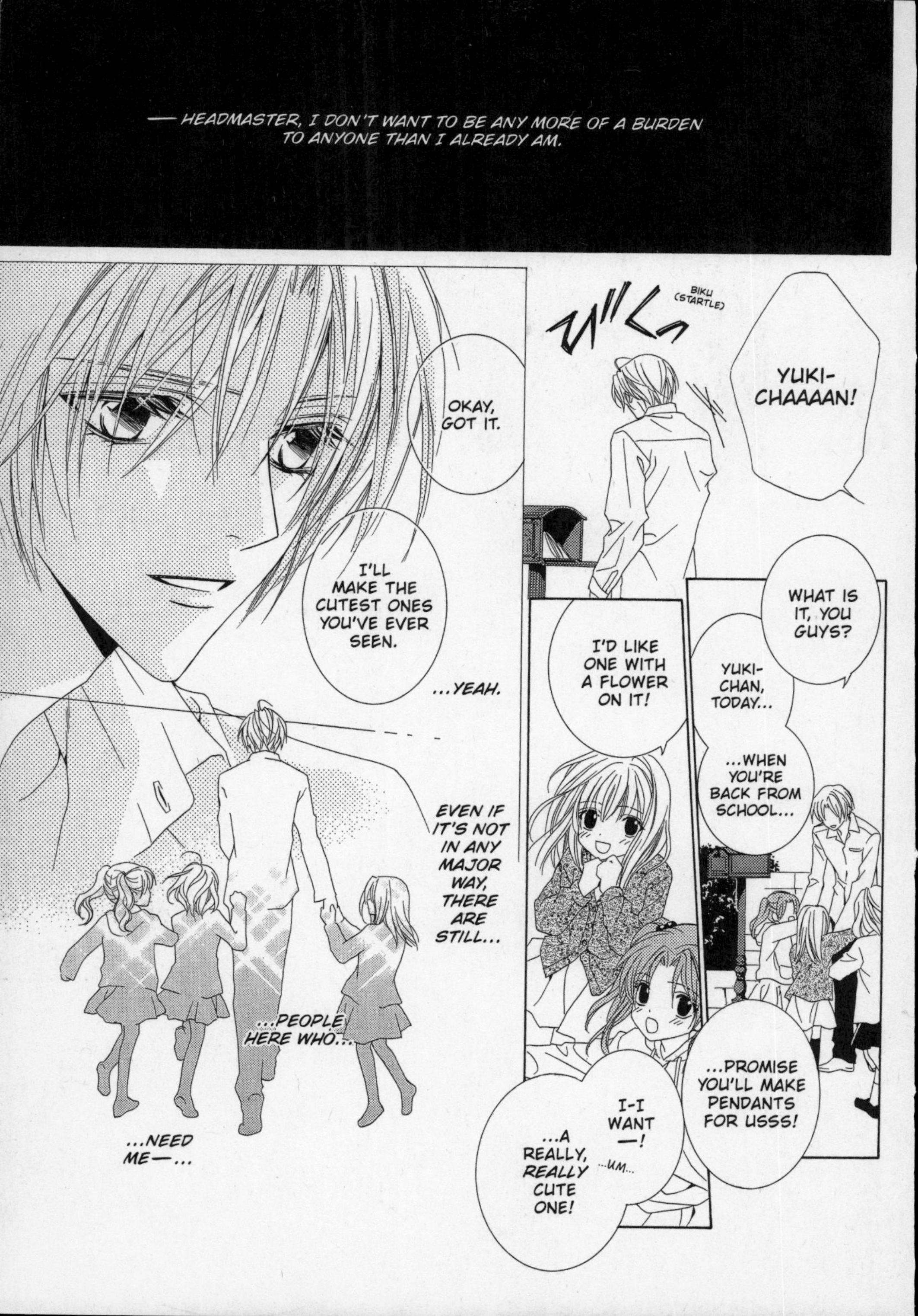
— HEADMASTER, I DON'T WANT TO BE ANY MORE OF A BURDEN TO ANYONE THAN I ALREADY AM.
YUKI-CHAAAAN!
BIKU (STARTLE)
WHAT IS IT, YOU GUYS?
YUKI-CHAN, TODAY...
...WHEN YOU'RE BACK FROM SCHOOL...
...PROMISE YOU'LL MAKE PENDANTS FOR USSS!
I'D LIKE ONE WITH A FLOWER ON IT!
I-I WANT—!
...UM...
...A REALLY, REALLY CUTE ONE!
OKAY, GOT IT.
I'LL MAKE THE CUTEST ONES YOU'VE EVER SEEN.
...YEAH.
EVEN IF IT'S NOT IN ANY MAJOR WAY, THERE ARE STILL...
...PEOPLE HERE WHO...
...NEED ME—...

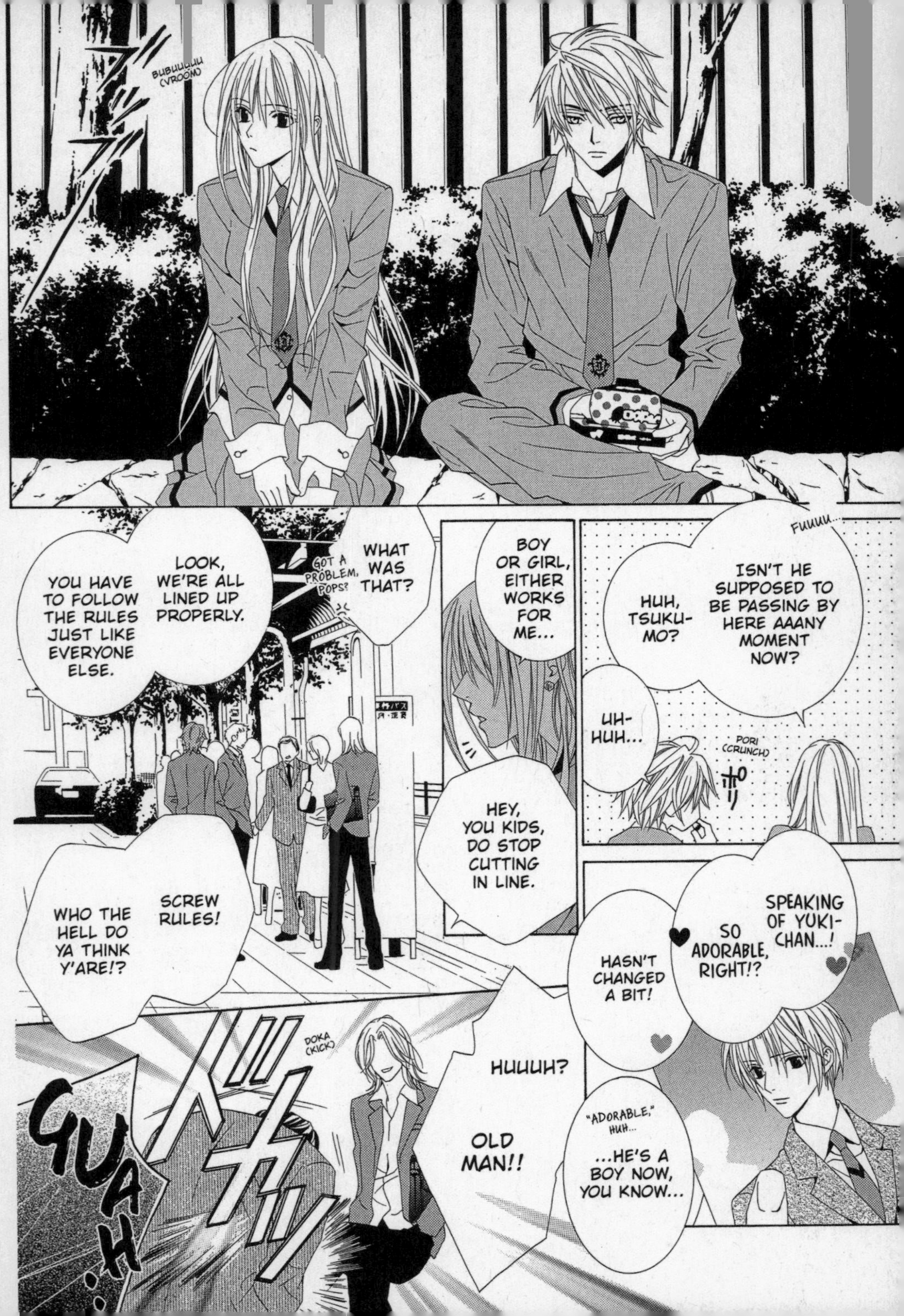
BUBUUUUU (VROOM)
FUUUU...
ISN'T HE SUPPOSED TO BE PASSING BY HERE AAANY MOMENT NOW?
HUH, TSUKUMO?
UH-HUH...
PORI (CRUNCH)
BOY OR GIRL, EITHER WORKS FOR ME...
WHAT WAS THAT?
GOT A PROBLEM, POPS?
LOOK, WE'RE ALL LINED UP PROPERLY.
YOU HAVE TO FOLLOW THE RULES JUST LIKE EVERYONE ELSE.
SPEAKING OF YUKI-CHAN...!
SO ADORABLE, RIGHT!?
HASN'T CHANGED A BIT!
HEY, YOU KIDS, DO STOP CUTTING IN LINE.
SCREW RULES!
WHO THE HELL DO YA THINK Y'ARE!?
"ADORABLE," HUH...
...HE'S A BOY NOW, YOU KNOW...
HUUUH?
OLD MAN!!
DOKA (KICK)
GUAH..!

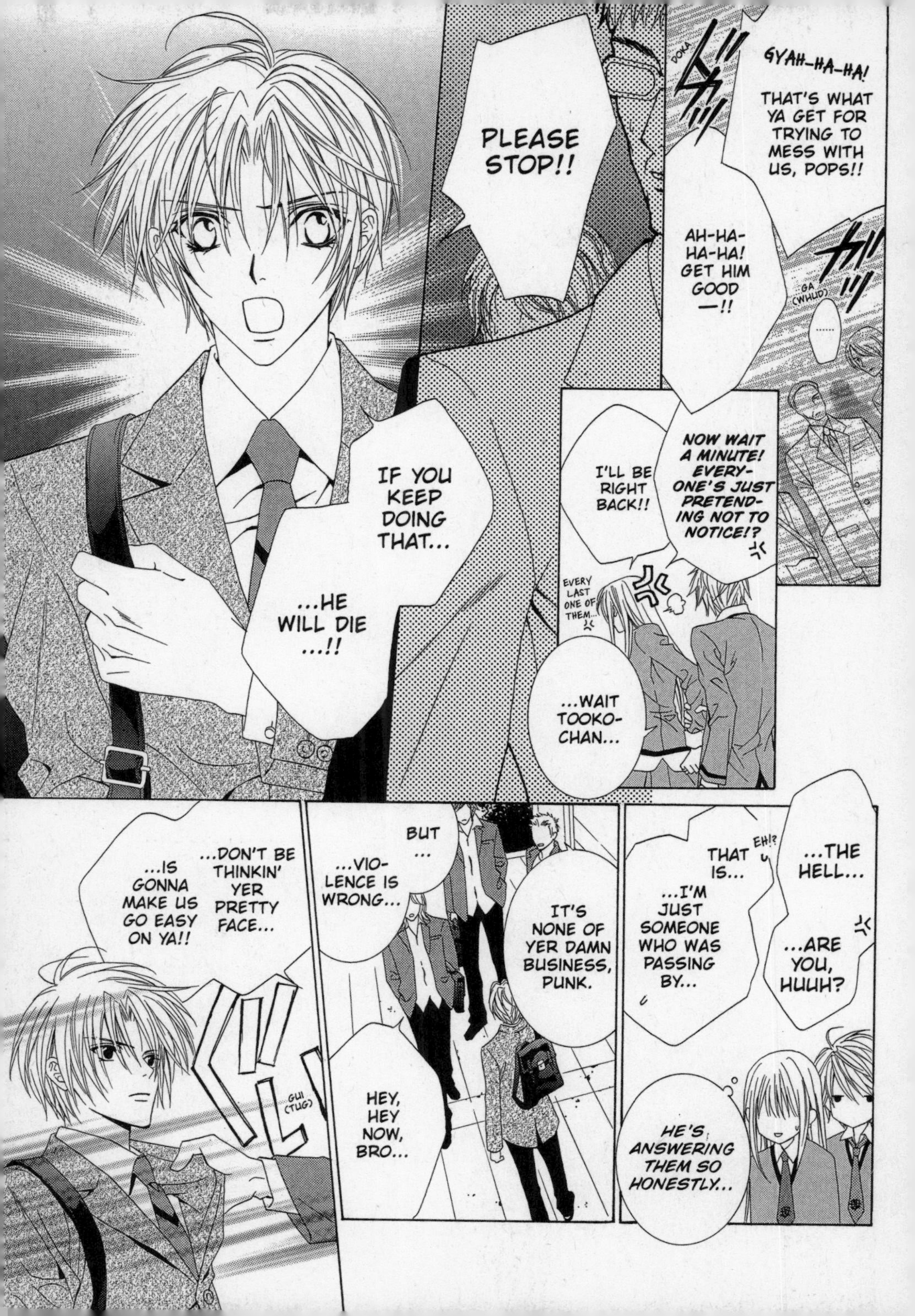

DOKA
GYAH-HA-HA!
THAT'S WHAT YA GET FOR TRYING TO MESS WITH US, POPS!!
AH-HA-HA-HA! GET HIM GOOD—!!
GA (WHUD)
......
NOW WAIT A MINUTE! EVERYONE'S JUST PRETENDING NOT TO NOTICE!?
EVERY LAST ONE OF THEM...
I'LL BE RIGHT BACK!!
...WAIT TOOKO-CHAN...
PLEASE STOP!!
IF YOU KEEP DOING THAT...
...HE WILL DIE ...!!
...THE HELL...
...ARE YOU, HUUH?
EH!?
THAT IS...
...I'M JUST SOMEONE WHO WAS PASSING BY...
HE'S ANSWERING THEM SO HONESTLY...
IT'S NONE OF YER DAMN BUSINESS, PUNK.
BUT...
...VIOLENCE IS WRONG...
HEY, HEY NOW, BRO...
...DON'T BE THINKIN' YER PRETTY FACE...
...IS GONNA MAKE US GO EASY ON YA!!
GUI (TUG)

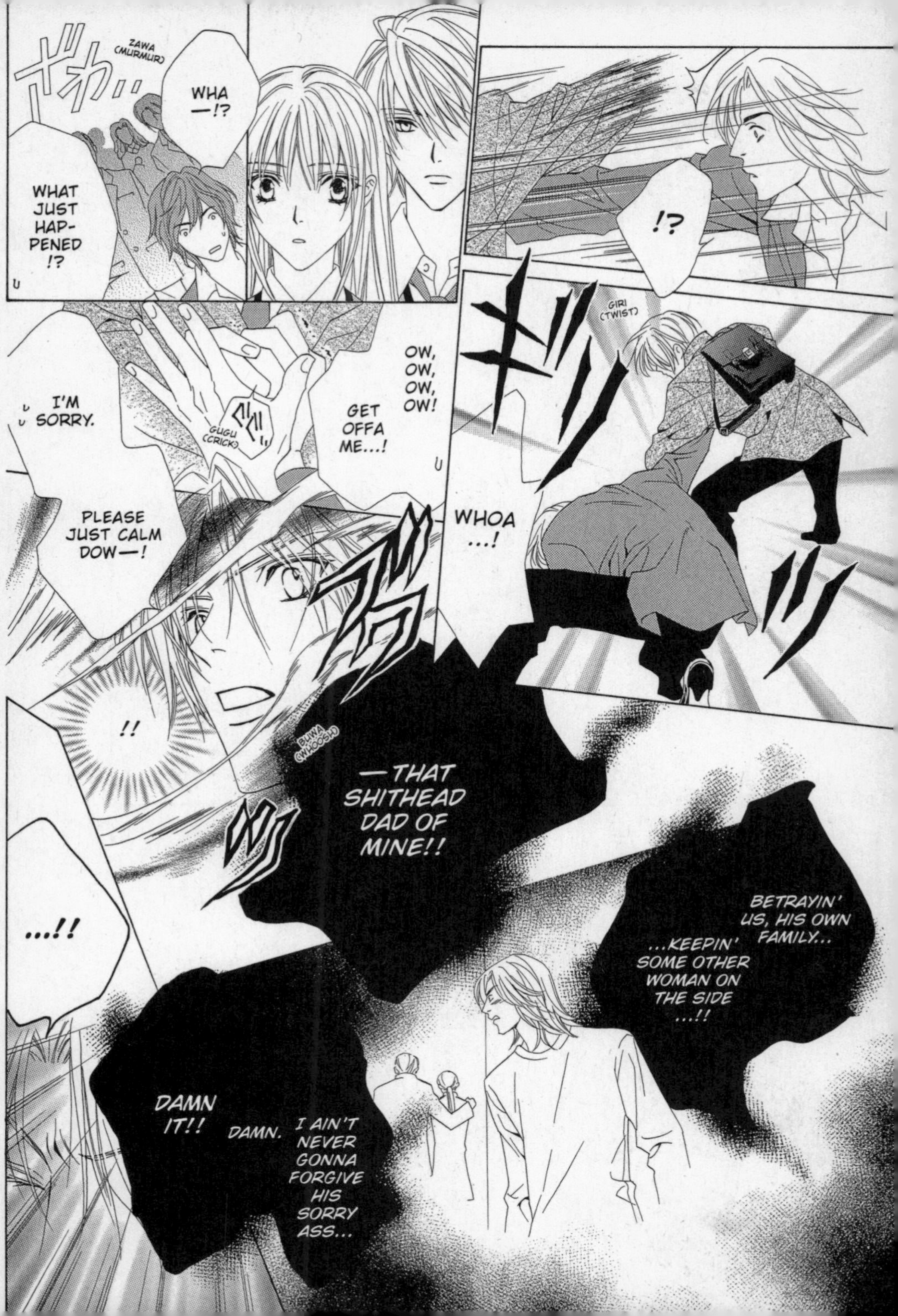

ZAWA (MURMUR)
WHA—!?
WHAT JUST HAPPENED!?
!?
GIRI (TWIST)
OW, OW, OW, OW!
GET OFFA ME...!
GUGU (CRICK)
I'M SORRY.
WHOA...!
PLEASE JUST CALM DOW—!
!!
BUWA (WHOOSH)
—THAT SHITHEAD DAD OF MINE!!
...!!
BETRAYIN' US, HIS OWN FAMILY...
...KEEPIN' SOME OTHER WOMAN ON THE SIDE...!!
DAMN IT!!
DAMN.
I AIN'T NEVER GONNA FORGIVE HIS SORRY ASS...

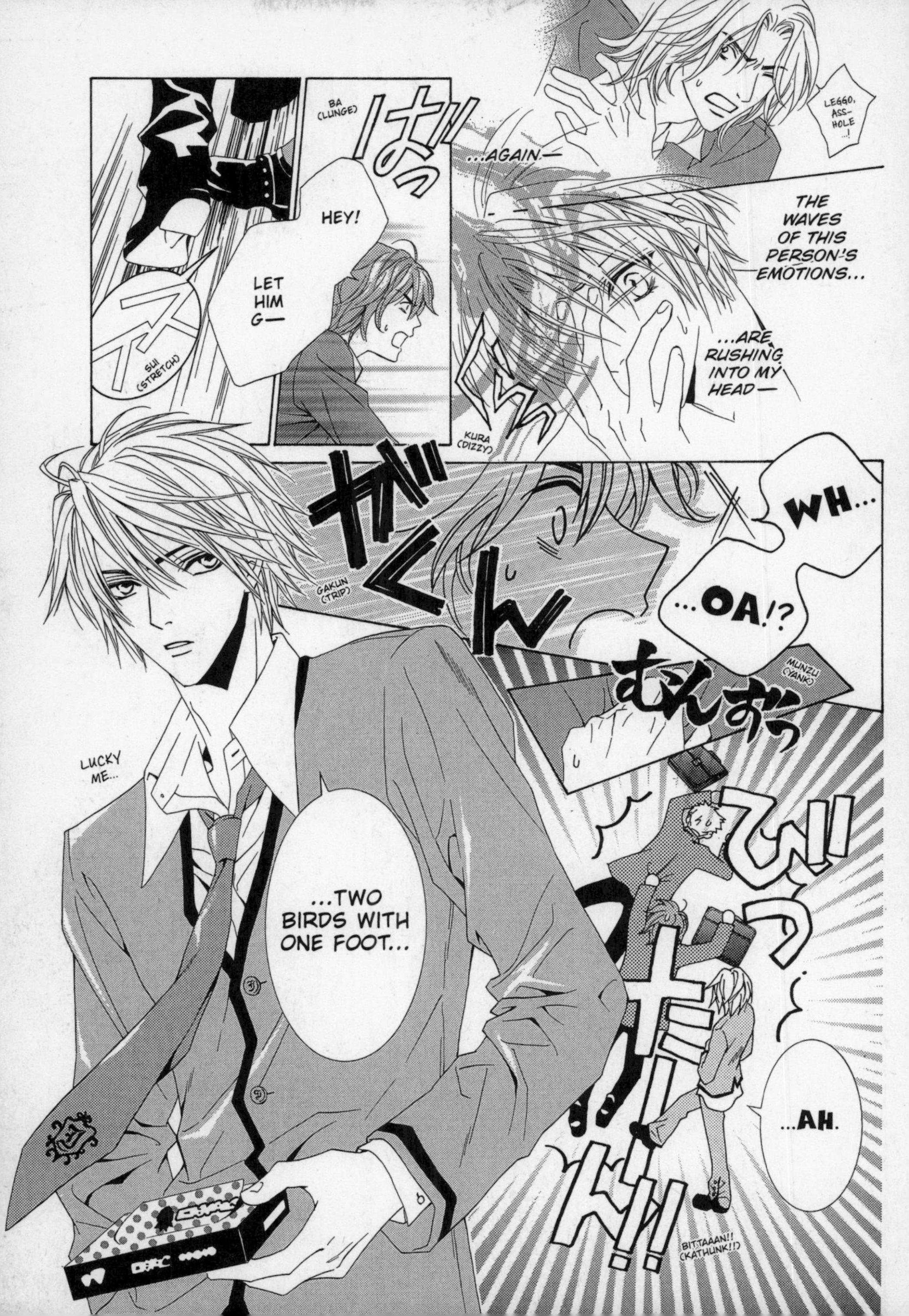
LEGGO, ASS-HOLE ...!
...AGAIN—
THE WAVES OF THIS PERSON'S EMOTIONS...
...ARE RUSHING INTO MY HEAD—
KURA (DIZZY)
BA (LUNGE)
HEY!
LET HIM G—
SUI (STRETCH)
WH...
...OA!?
GAKUN (TRIP)
MUNZU (YANK)
...AH.
BITTAAAN!! (KATHUNK!!)
LUCKY ME...
...TWO BIRDS WITH ONE FOOT...

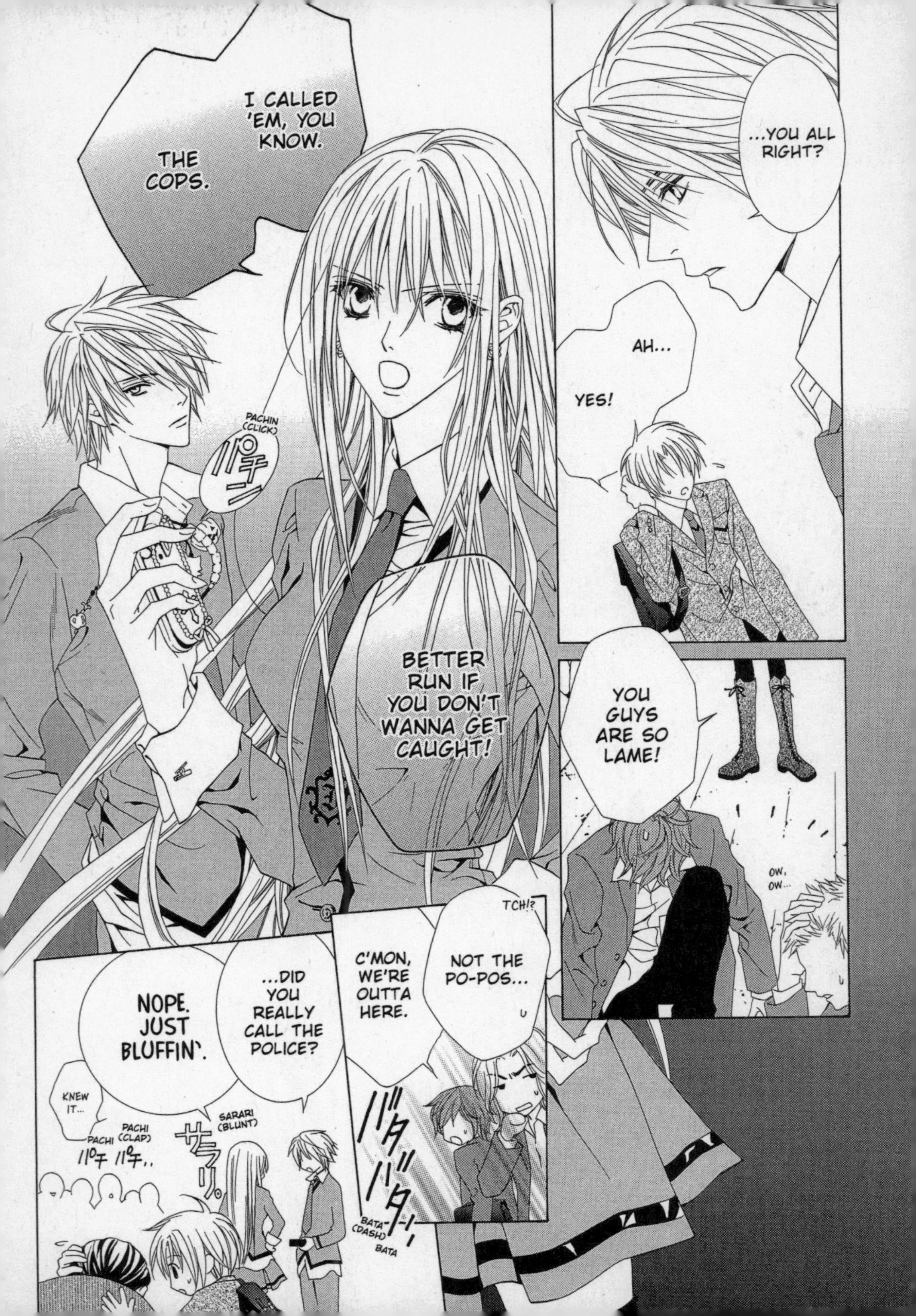
...YOU ALL RIGHT?
AH...
YES!
I CALLED 'EM, YOU KNOW.
THE COPS.
PACHIN (CLICK)
BETTER RUN IF YOU DON'T WANNA GET CAUGHT!
YOU GUYS ARE SO LAME!
OW, OW...
TCH!?
NOT THE PO-POS...
C'MON, WE'RE OUTTA HERE.
BATA (DASH) BATA
...DID YOU REALLY CALL THE POLICE?
NOPE. JUST BLUFFIN'.
SARARI (BLUNT)
KNEW IT...
PACHI (CLAP) PACHI

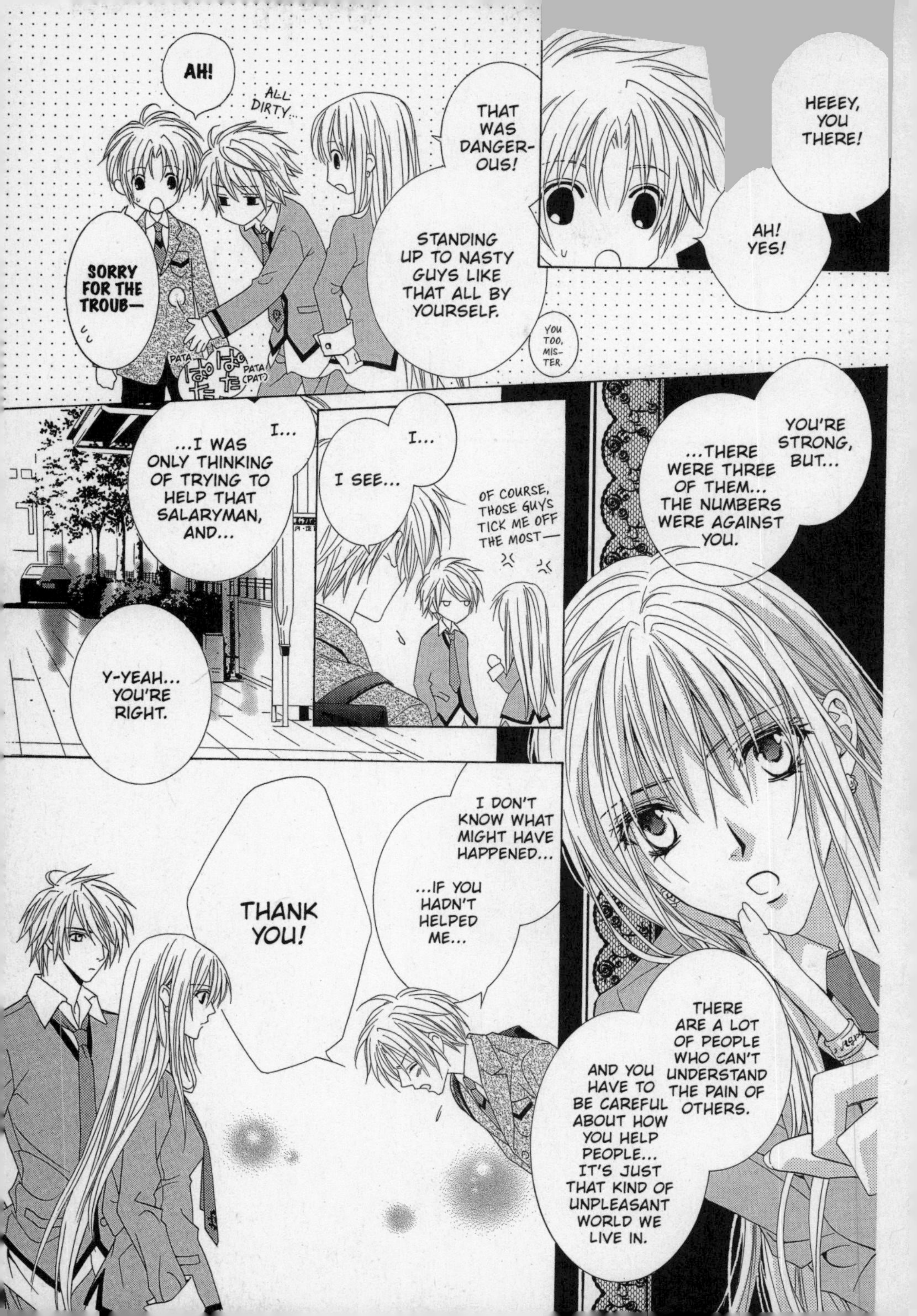
HEEEY, YOU THERE!
AH! YES!
THAT WAS DANGER-OUS!
STANDING UP TO NASTY GUYS LIKE THAT ALL BY YOURSELF.
YOU TOO, MIS-TER.
AH!
ALL DIRTY...
SORRY FOR THE TROUB—
PATA PATA (PAT)
YOU'RE STRONG, BUT...
...THERE WERE THREE OF THEM... THE NUMBERS WERE AGAINST YOU.
I...
I SEE...
OF COURSE, THOSE GUYS TICK ME OFF THE MOST—
I...
...I WAS ONLY THINKING OF TRYING TO HELP THAT SALARYMAN, AND...
Y-YEAH... YOU'RE RIGHT.
THERE ARE A LOT OF PEOPLE WHO CAN'T UNDERSTAND THE PAIN OF OTHERS.
AND YOU HAVE TO BE CAREFUL ABOUT HOW YOU HELP PEOPLE... IT'S JUST THAT KIND OF UNPLEASANT WORLD WE LIVE IN.
I DON'T KNOW WHAT MIGHT HAVE HAPPENED...
...IF YOU HADN'T HELPED ME...
THANK YOU!

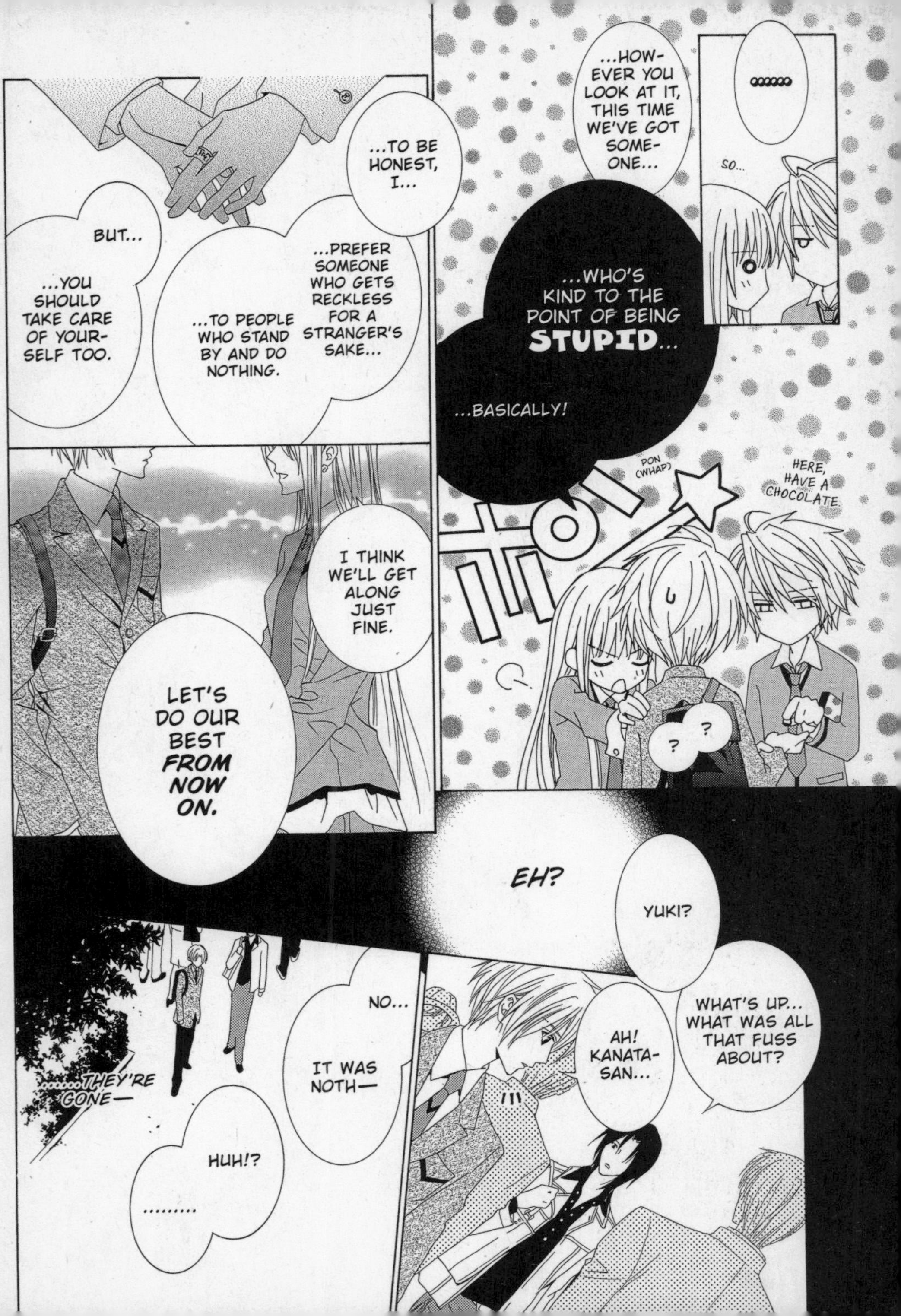
......
SO...
...HOW-EVER YOU LOOK AT IT, THIS TIME WE'VE GOT SOME-ONE...
...WHO'S KIND TO THE POINT OF BEING STUPID...
...BASICALLY!
PON (WHAP)
HERE, HAVE A CHOCOLATE.
?
?
...TO BE HONEST, I...
...PREFER SOMEONE WHO GETS RECKLESS FOR A STRANGER'S SAKE...
...TO PEOPLE WHO STAND BY AND DO NOTHING.
BUT...
...YOU SHOULD TAKE CARE OF YOUR-SELF TOO.
I THINK WE'LL GET ALONG JUST FINE.
LET'S DO OUR BEST FROM NOW ON.
EH?
YUKI?
WHAT'S UP... WHAT WAS ALL THAT FUSS ABOUT?
AH! KANATA-SAN...
NO...
IT WAS NOTH—
HUH!?
....
.......THEY'RE GONE—

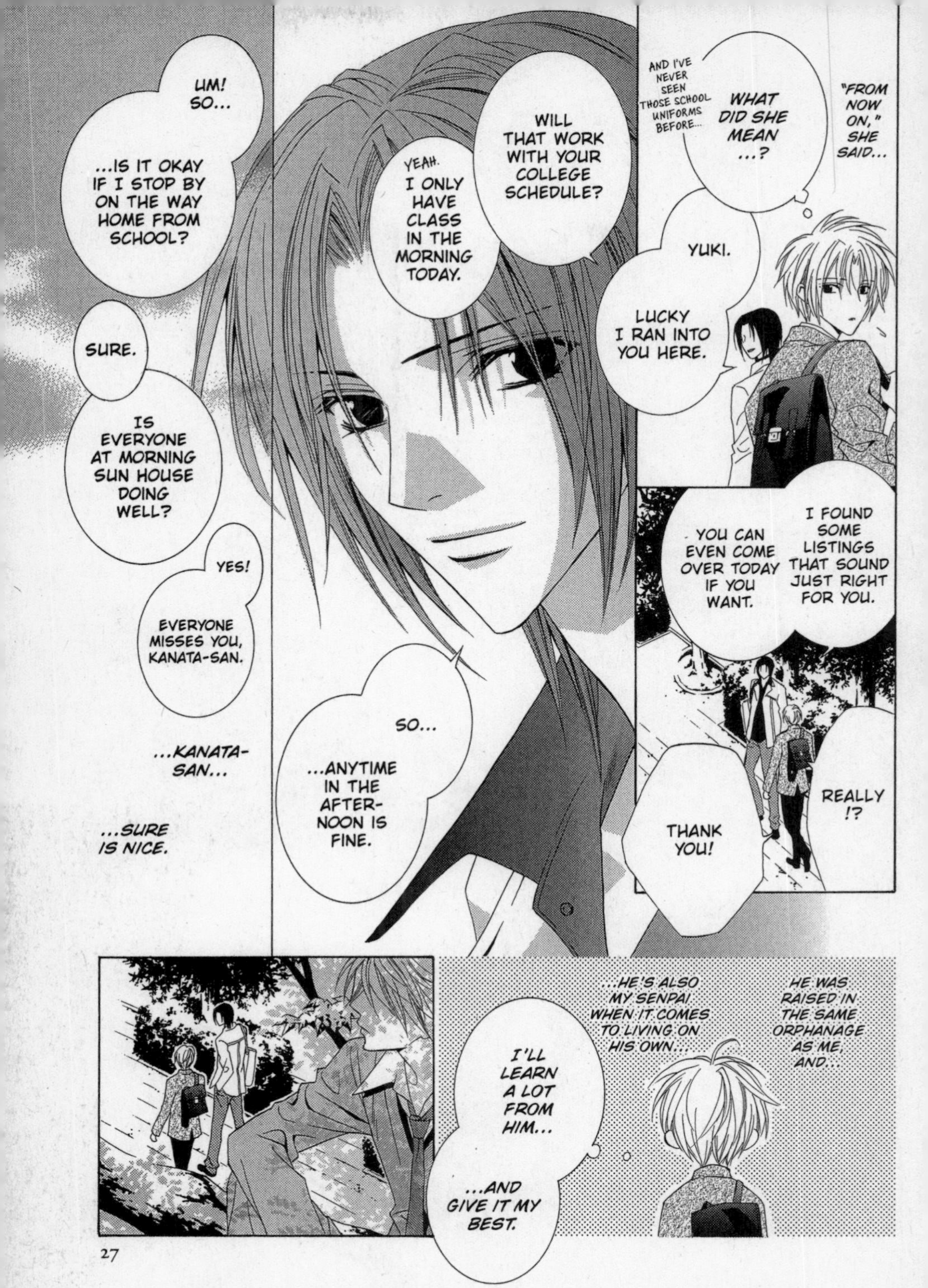
"FROM NOW ON," SHE SAID...
WHAT DID SHE MEAN ...?
AND I'VE NEVER SEEN THOSE SCHOOL UNIFORMS BEFORE...
YUKI.
LUCKY I RAN INTO YOU HERE.
I FOUND SOME LISTINGS THAT SOUND JUST RIGHT FOR YOU.
YOU CAN EVEN COME OVER TODAY IF YOU WANT.
REALLY !?
THANK YOU!
WILL THAT WORK WITH YOUR COLLEGE SCHEDULE?
YEAH. I ONLY HAVE CLASS IN THE MORNING TODAY.
SO...
...ANYTIME IN THE AFTER-NOON IS FINE.
UM! SO...
...IS IT OKAY IF I STOP BY ON THE WAY HOME FROM SCHOOL?
SURE.
IS EVERYONE AT MORNING SUN HOUSE DOING WELL?
YES!
EVERYONE MISSES YOU, KANATA-SAN.
...KANATA-SAN...
...SURE IS NICE.
HE WAS RAISED IN THE SAME ORPHANAGE AS ME, AND...
...HE'S ALSO MY SENPAI WHEN IT COMES TO LIVING ON HIS OWN...
I'LL LEARN A LOT FROM HIM...
...AND GIVE IT MY BEST.

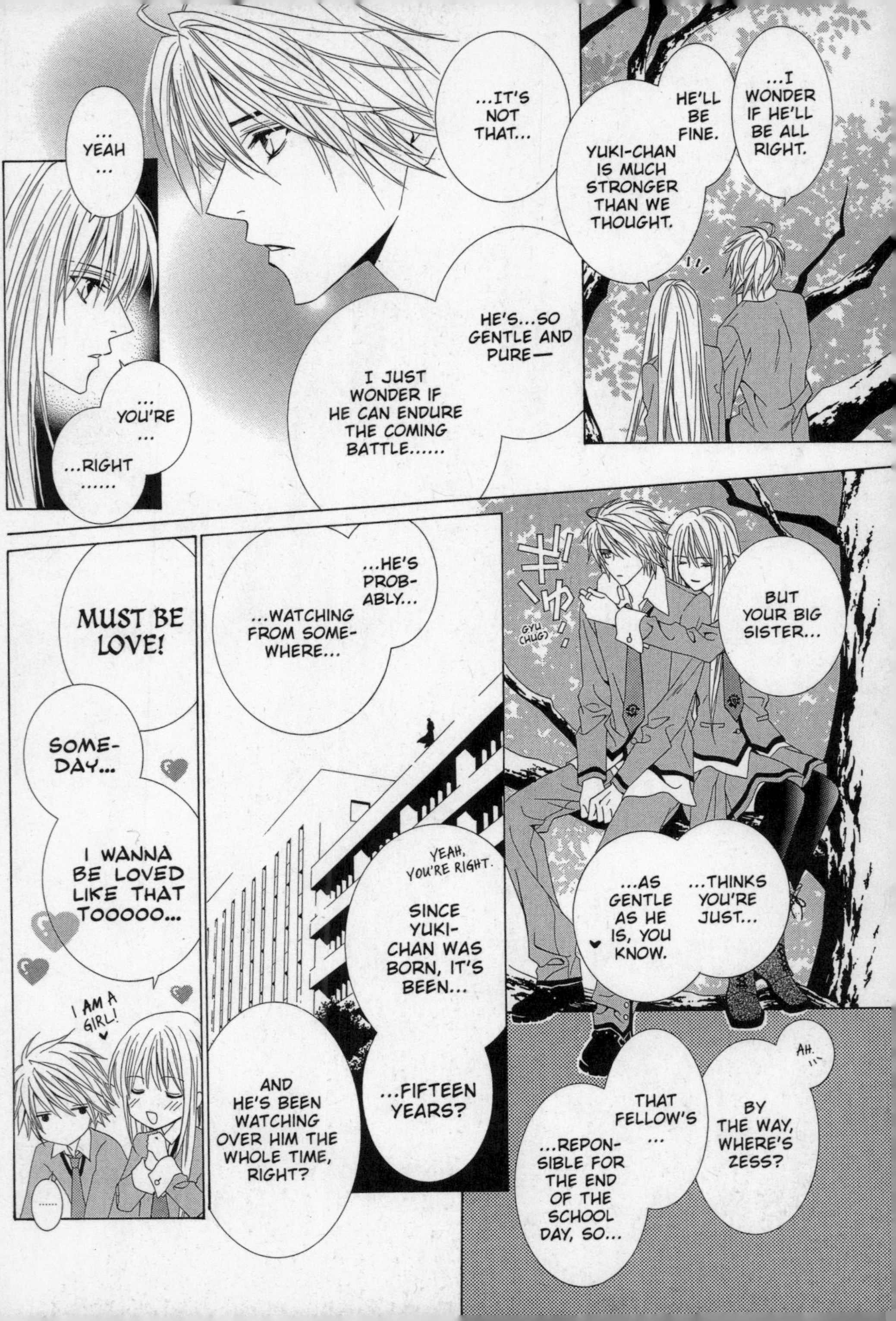
...I WONDER IF HE'LL BE ALL RIGHT.
HE'LL BE FINE.
YUKI-CHAN IS MUCH STRONGER THAN WE THOUGHT.
...IT'S NOT THAT...
HE'S...SO GENTLE AND PURE—
I JUST WONDER IF HE CAN ENDURE THE COMING BATTLE......
...YEAH...
...YOU'RE...
...RIGHT......
GYU (HUG)
BUT YOUR BIG SISTER...
...THINKS YOU'RE JUST...
...AS GENTLE AS HE IS, YOU KNOW.
AH.
BY THE WAY, WHERE'S ZESS?
THAT FELLOW'S...
...REPONSIBLE FOR THE END OF THE SCHOOL DAY, SO...
...HE'S PROBABLY...
...WATCHING FROM SOMEWHERE...
YEAH, YOU'RE RIGHT.
SINCE YUKI-CHAN WAS BORN, IT'S BEEN...
...FIFTEEN YEARS?
AND HE'S BEEN WATCHING OVER HIM THE WHOLE TIME, RIGHT?
MUST BE LOVE!
SOMEDAY...
I WANNA BE LOVED LIKE THAT TOOOOO...
I AM A GIRL!
......

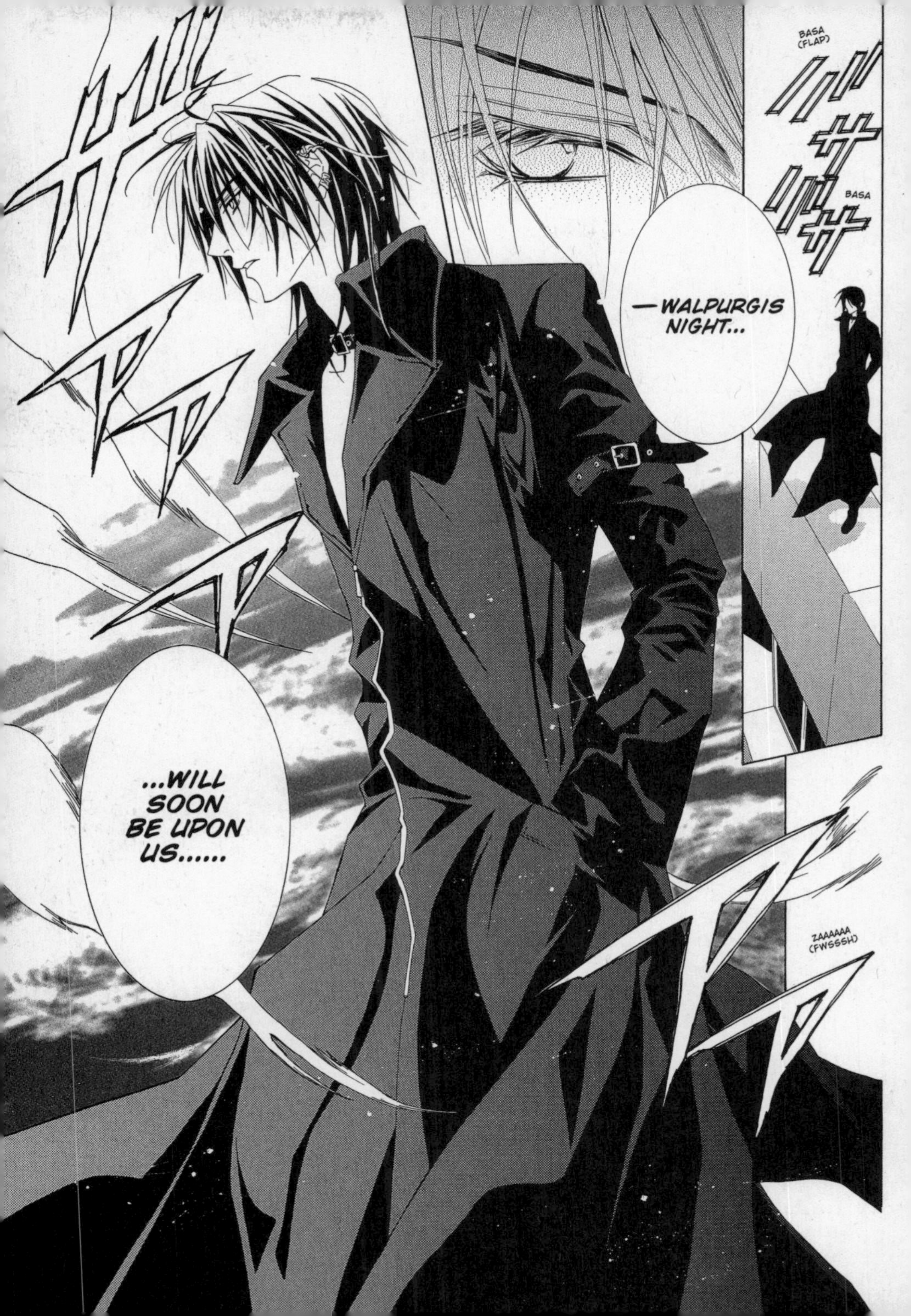
BASA (FLAP)
BASA
—WALPURGIS NIGHT...
...WILL SOON BE UPON US......
ZAAAAAA (FWSSSH)

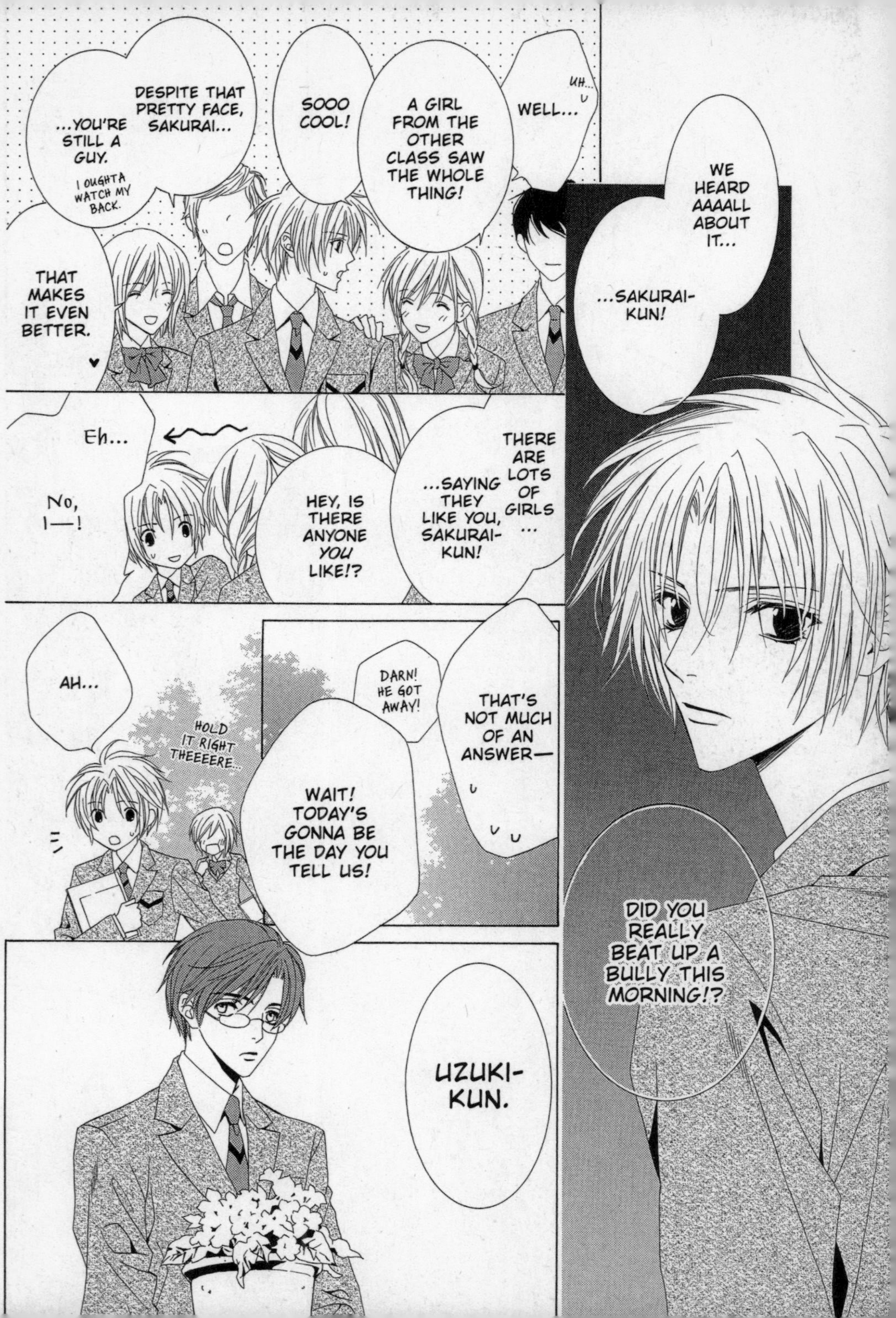
WE HEARD AAAALL ABOUT IT...
...SAKURAI-KUN!
DID YOU REALLY BEAT UP A BULLY THIS MORNING!?
UH...
WELL...
A GIRL FROM THE OTHER CLASS SAW THE WHOLE THING!
SOOO COOL!
DESPITE THAT PRETTY FACE, SAKURAI...
...YOU'RE STILL A GUY.
I OUGHTA WATCH MY BACK.
THAT MAKES IT EVEN BETTER.
THERE ARE LOTS OF GIRLS...
...SAYING THEY LIKE YOU, SAKURAI-KUN!
HEY, IS THERE ANYONE *YOU* LIKE!?
Eh...
No, I—!
THAT'S NOT MUCH OF AN ANSWER—
DARN! HE GOT AWAY!
WAIT! TODAY'S GONNA BE THE DAY YOU TELL US!
HOLD IT RIGHT THEEEERE...
AH...
UZUKI-KUN.

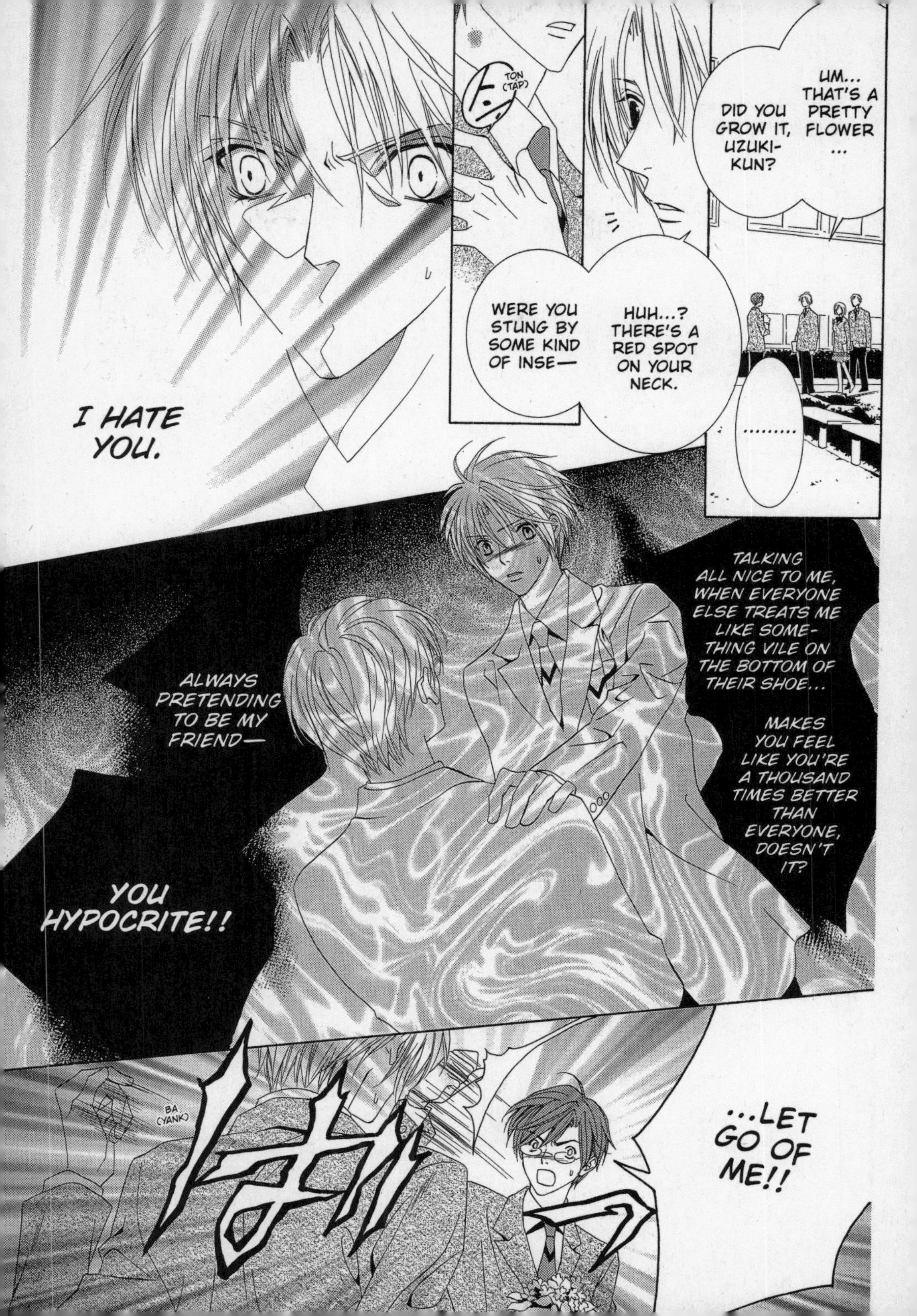
UM... THAT'S A PRETTY FLOWER...
DID YOU GROW IT, UZUKI-KUN?
....
TON (TAP)
HUH...? THERE'S A RED SPOT ON YOUR NECK.
WERE YOU STUNG BY SOME KIND OF INSE—
I HATE YOU.
TALKING ALL NICE TO ME, WHEN EVERYONE ELSE TREATS ME LIKE SOMETHING VILE ON THE BOTTOM OF THEIR SHOE...
MAKES YOU FEEL LIKE YOU'RE A THOUSAND TIMES BETTER THAN EVERYONE, DOESN'T IT?
ALWAYS PRETENDING TO BE MY FRIEND—
YOU HYPOCRITE!!
...LET GO OF ME!!
BA (YANK)

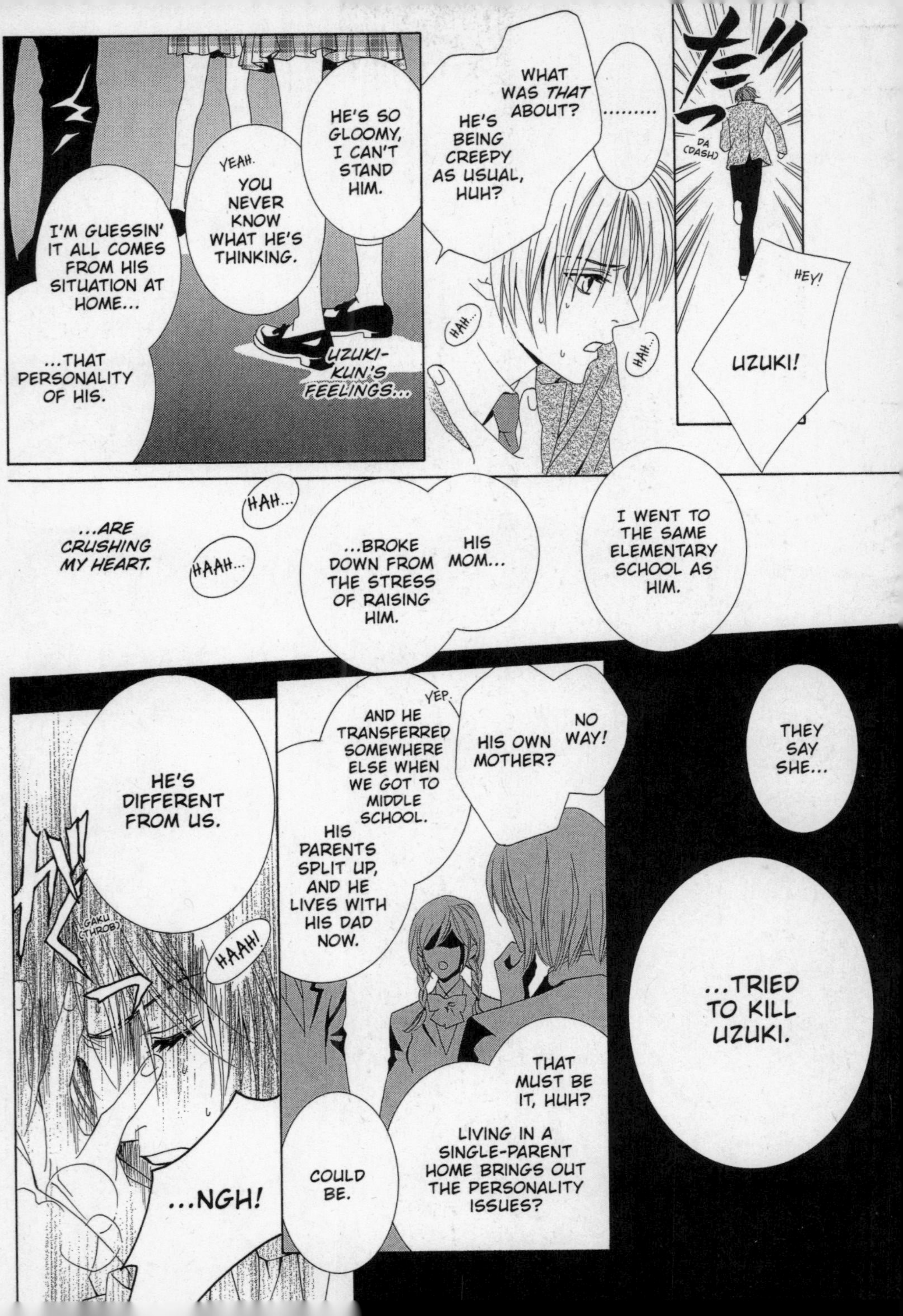
DA (DASH)
HEY!
UZUKI!
....
WHAT WAS THAT ABOUT?
HE'S BEING CREEPY AS USUAL, HUH?
HAH...
HAH...
HE'S SO GLOOMY, I CAN'T STAND HIM.
YEAH.
YOU NEVER KNOW WHAT HE'S THINKING.
I'M GUESSIN' IT ALL COMES FROM HIS SITUATION AT HOME...
...THAT PERSONALITY OF HIS.
UZUKI-KUN'S FEELINGS...
I WENT TO THE SAME ELEMENTARY SCHOOL AS HIM.
HIS MOM...
...BROKE DOWN FROM THE STRESS OF RAISING HIM.
HAH...
HAAH...
...ARE CRUSHING MY HEART.
THEY SAY SHE...
...TRIED TO KILL UZUKI.
NO WAY!
HIS OWN MOTHER?
YEP.
AND HE TRANSFERRED SOMEWHERE ELSE WHEN WE GOT TO MIDDLE SCHOOL.
HIS PARENTS SPLIT UP, AND HE LIVES WITH HIS DAD NOW.
THAT MUST BE IT, HUH?
LIVING IN A SINGLE-PARENT HOME BRINGS OUT THE PERSONALITY ISSUES?
COULD BE.
HE'S DIFFERENT FROM US.
GAKU (THROB)
HAAH!
...NGH!

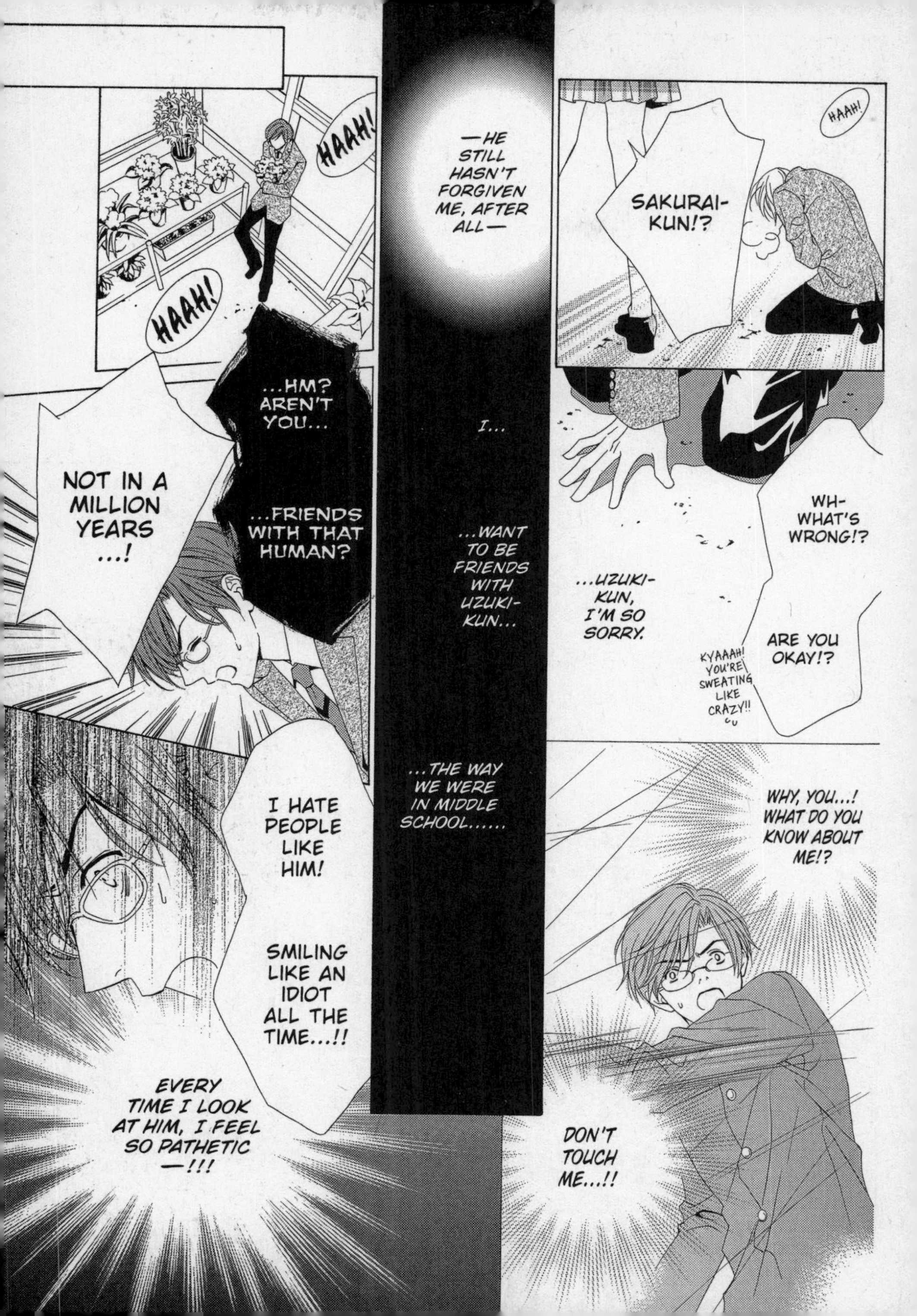
HAAAH!
SAKURAI-KUN!?
WH-WHAT'S WRONG!?
ARE YOU OKAY!?
KYAAAH! YOU'RE SWEATING LIKE CRAZY!!
...UZUKI-KUN, I'M SO SORRY.
—HE STILL HASN'T FORGIVEN ME, AFTER ALL—
I...
...WANT TO BE FRIENDS WITH UZUKI-KUN...
...THE WAY WE WERE IN MIDDLE SCHOOL......
WHY, YOU...! WHAT DO YOU KNOW ABOUT ME!?
DON'T TOUCH ME...!!
HAAAH!
HAAAH!
...HM? AREN'T YOU...
...FRIENDS WITH THAT HUMAN?
NOT IN A MILLION YEARS...!
I HATE PEOPLE LIKE HIM!
SMILING LIKE AN IDIOT ALL THE TIME...!!
EVERY TIME I LOOK AT HIM, I FEEL SO PATHETIC—!!!

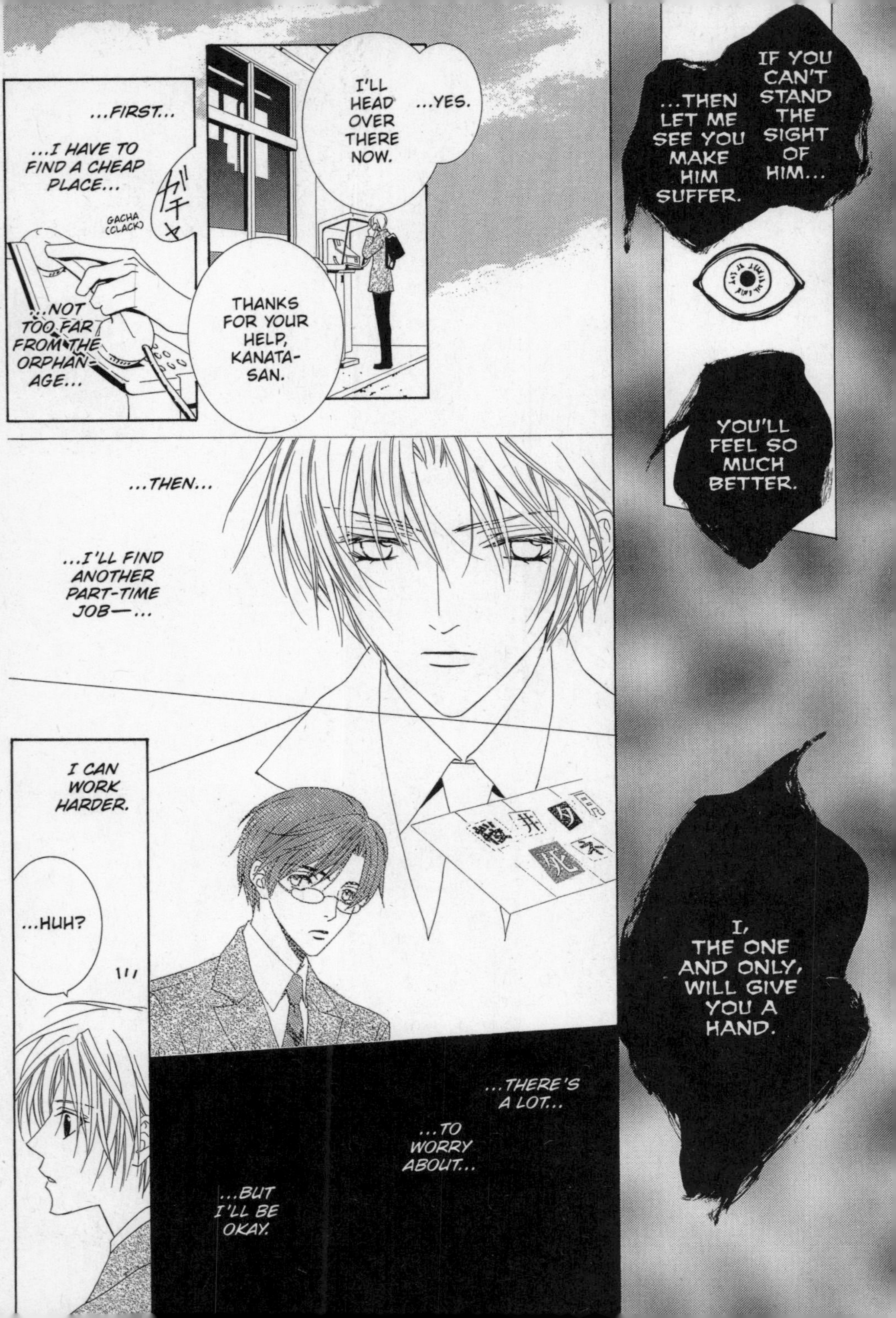

IF YOU CAN'T STAND THE SIGHT OF HIM...
...THEN LET ME SEE YOU MAKE HIM SUFFER.
...YES.
I'LL HEAD OVER THERE NOW.
THANKS FOR YOUR HELP, KANATA-SAN.
ガチャ
GACHA (CLACK)
...FIRST...
...I HAVE TO FIND A CHEAP PLACE...
...NOT TOO FAR FROM THE ORPHANAGE...
YOU'LL FEEL SO MUCH BETTER.
...THEN...
...I'LL FIND ANOTHER PART-TIME JOB—...
I CAN WORK HARDER.
...HUH?
I, THE ONE AND ONLY, WILL GIVE YOU A HAND.
...THERE'S A LOT...
...TO WORRY ABOUT...
...BUT I'LL BE OKAY.

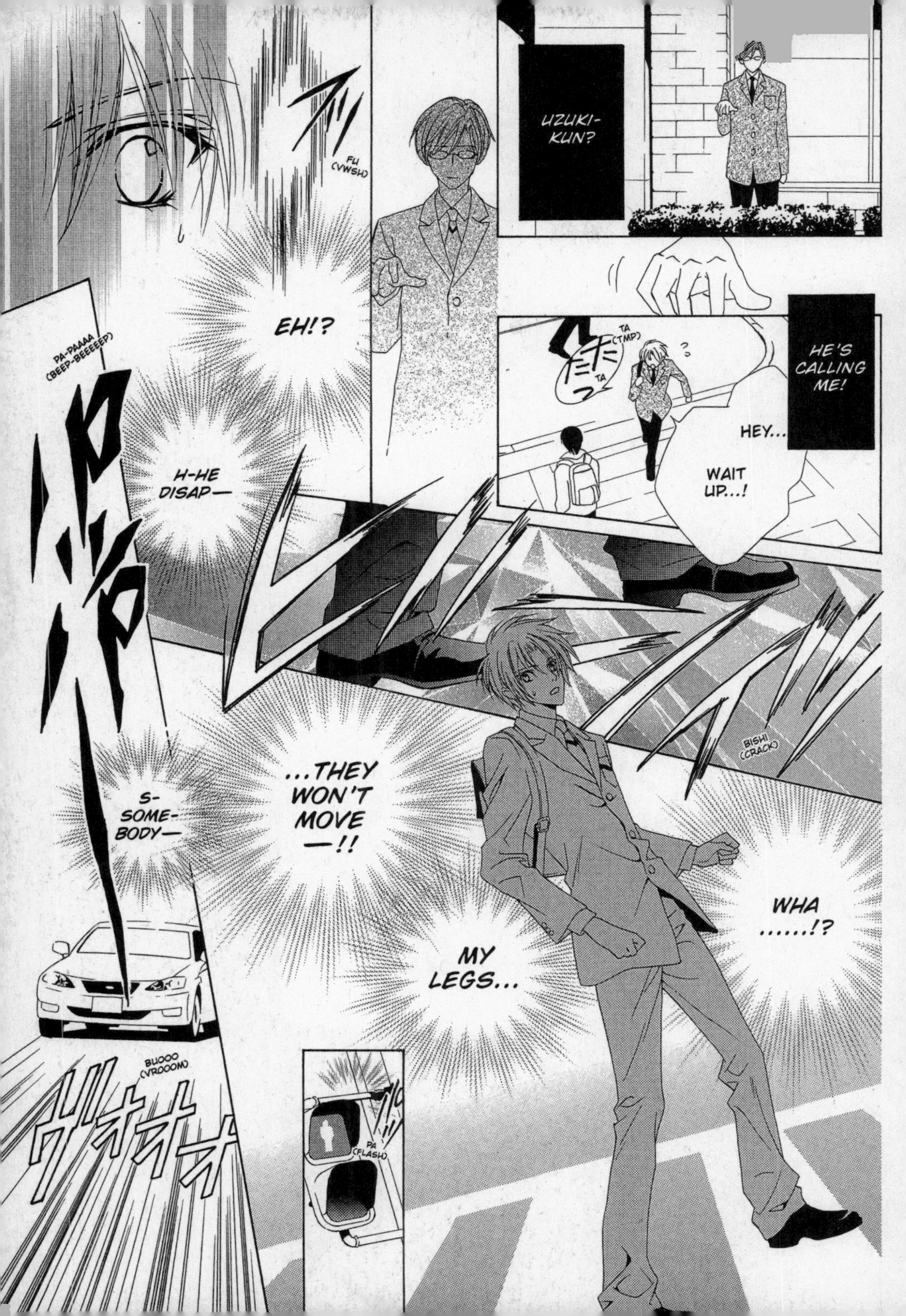
UZUKI-KUN?
HE'S CALLING ME!
HEY...
WAIT UP...!
TA (TMP)
TA
FU (VWSH)
EH!?
H-HE DISAP—
PA-PAAAA (BEEP-BEEEEEP)
BISHI (CRACK)
WHA ......!?
...THEY WON'T MOVE —!!
MY LEGS...
S-SOME-BODY—
PA (FLASH)
BUOOO (VROOOM)

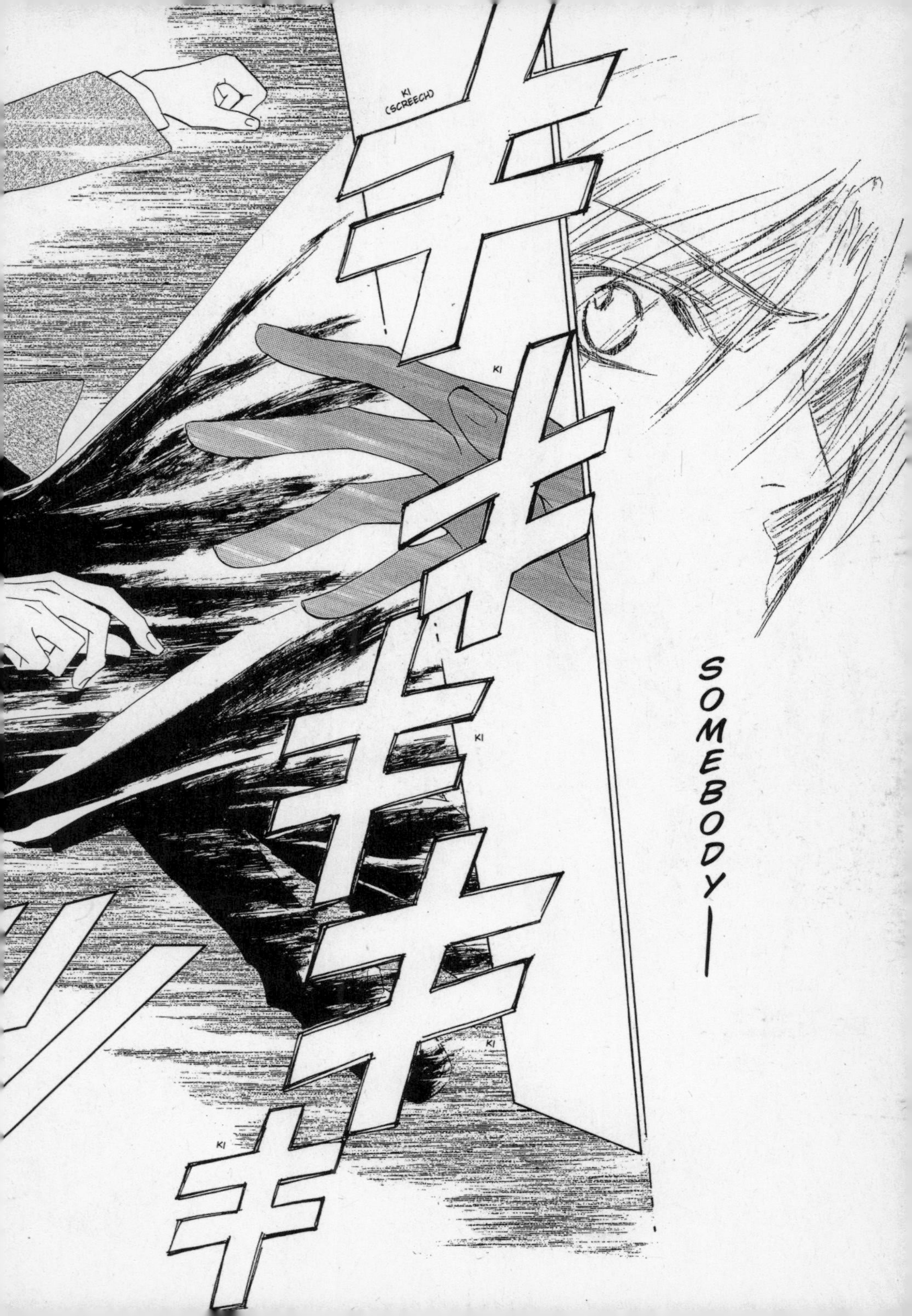
SOMEBODY—
KI
(SCREECH)
KI
KI
KI
KI

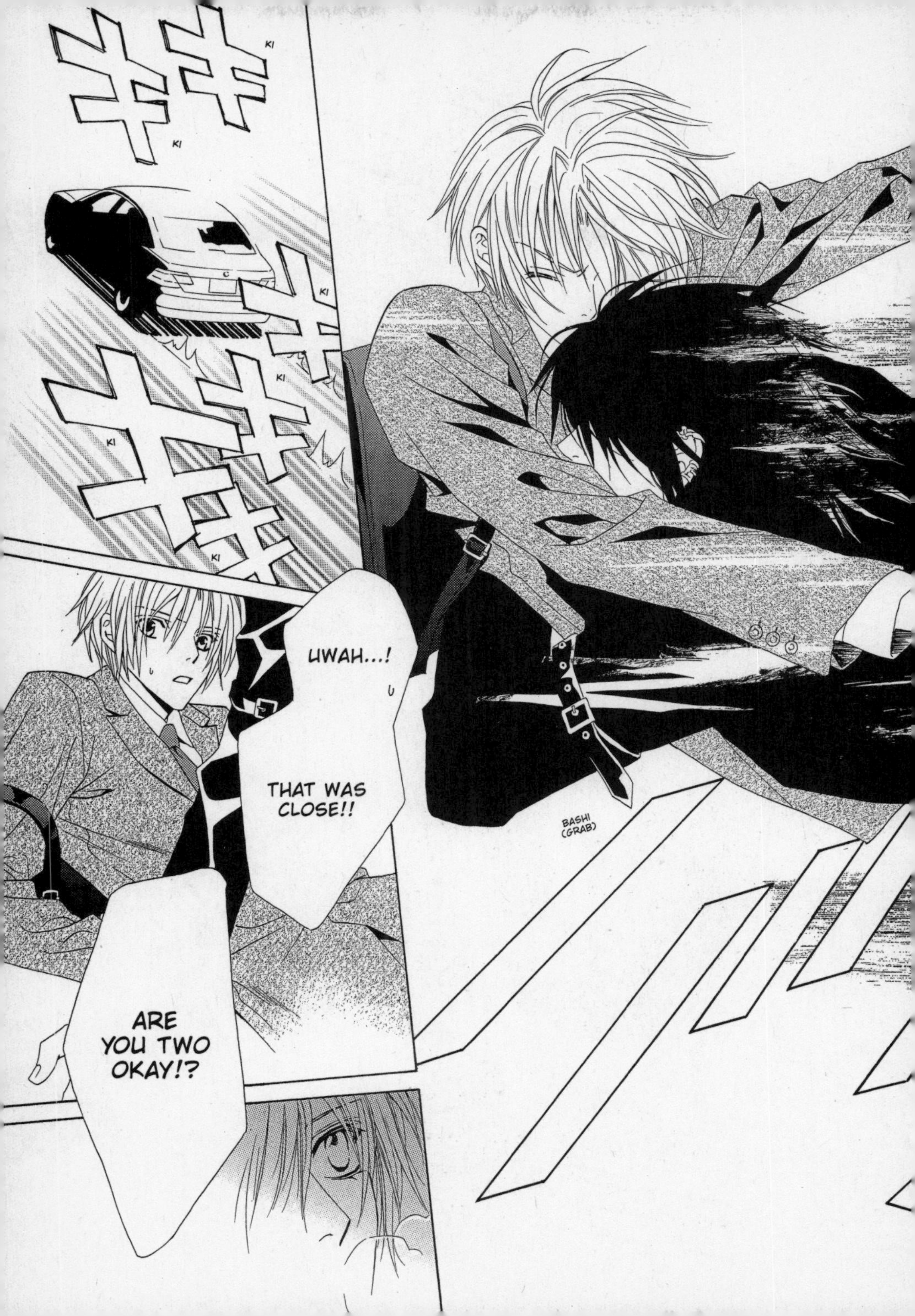

KI
KI
KI
KI
KI
KI
BASHI (GRAB)
UWAH...!
THAT WAS CLOSE!!
ARE YOU TWO OKAY!?

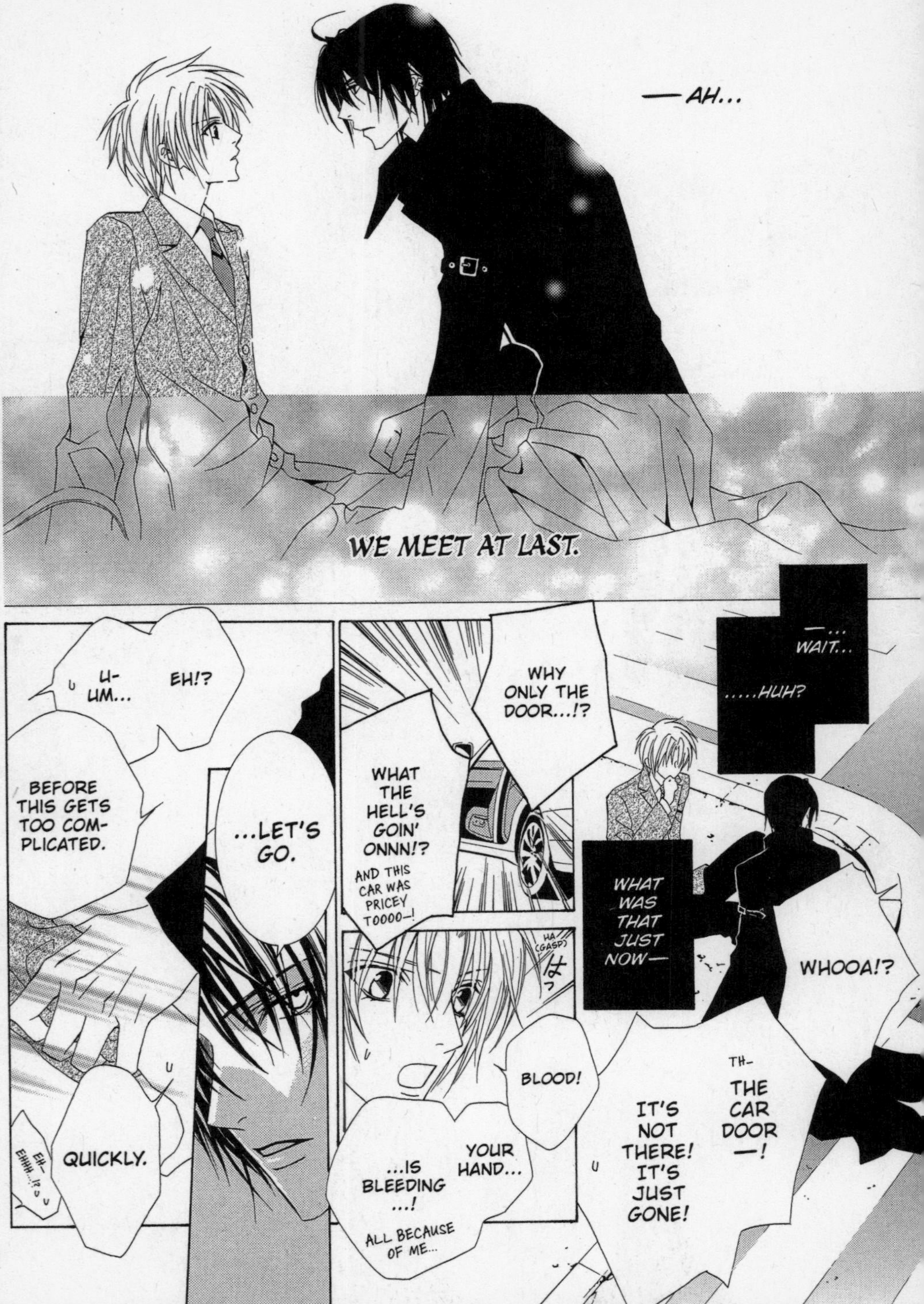
—AH...
WE MEET AT LAST.
—... WAIT...
.....HUH?
WHAT WAS THAT JUST NOW—
WHOOA!?
TH- THE CAR DOOR—!
IT'S NOT THERE! IT'S JUST GONE!
WHY ONLY THE DOOR...!?
WHAT THE HELL'S GOIN' ONNN!?
AND THIS CAR WAS PRICEY TOOOO—!
HA (GASP)
BLOOD!
YOUR HAND... ...IS BLEEDING ...!
ALL BECAUSE OF ME...
EH!?
U-UM...
BEFORE THIS GETS TOO COMPLICATED.
...LET'S GO.
QUICKLY.
EH—EHHH...!?

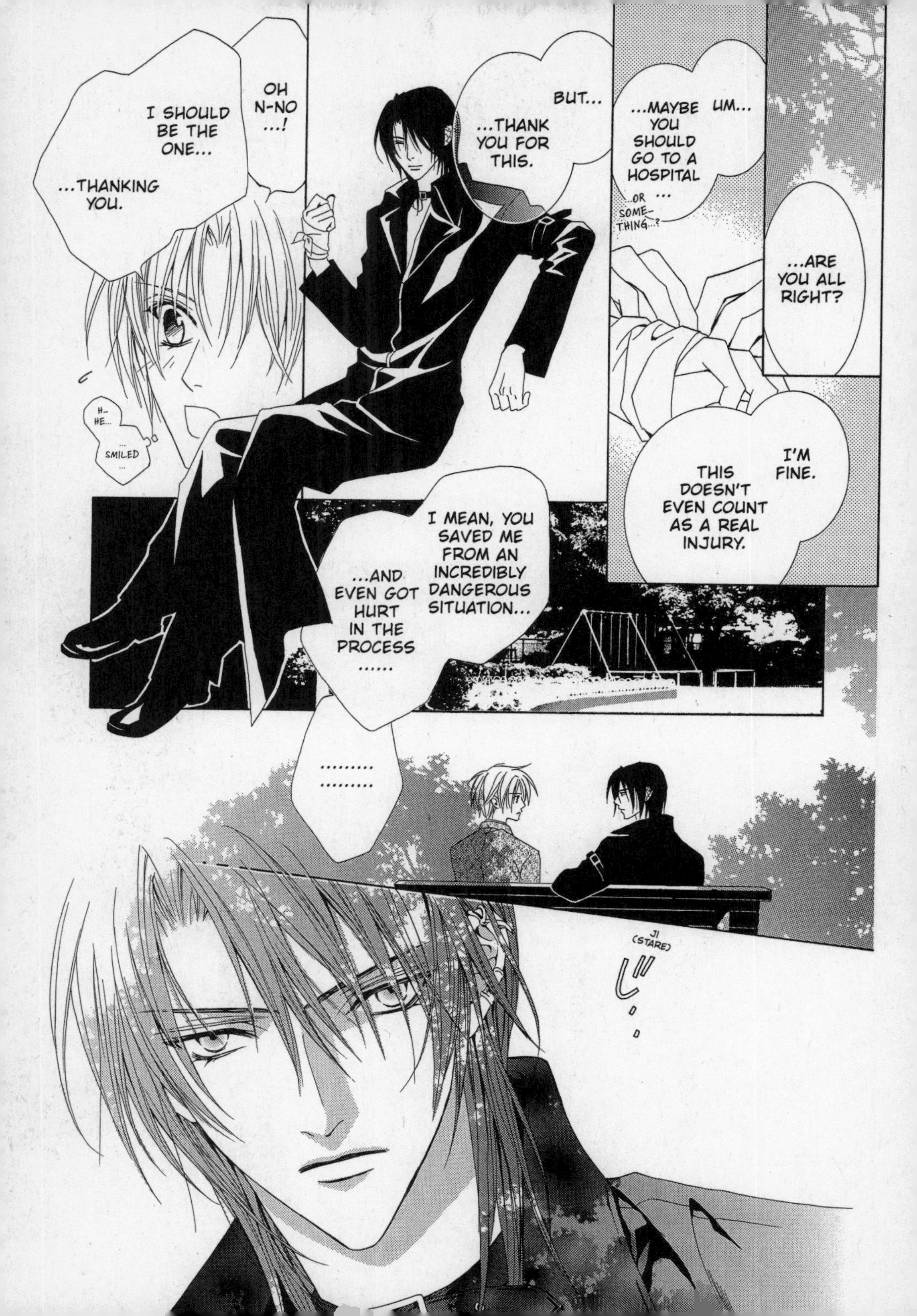
...ARE YOU ALL RIGHT?
UM...
...MAYBE YOU SHOULD GO TO A HOSPITAL ...
...OR SOMETHING...?
I'M FINE.
THIS DOESN'T EVEN COUNT AS A REAL INJURY.
BUT...
...THANK YOU FOR THIS.
I MEAN, YOU SAVED ME FROM AN INCREDIBLY DANGEROUS SITUATION...
...AND EVEN GOT HURT IN THE PROCESS ......
OH N-NO ...!
I SHOULD BE THE ONE...
...THANKING YOU.
H-HE... ...SMILED...
....
JI (STARE)

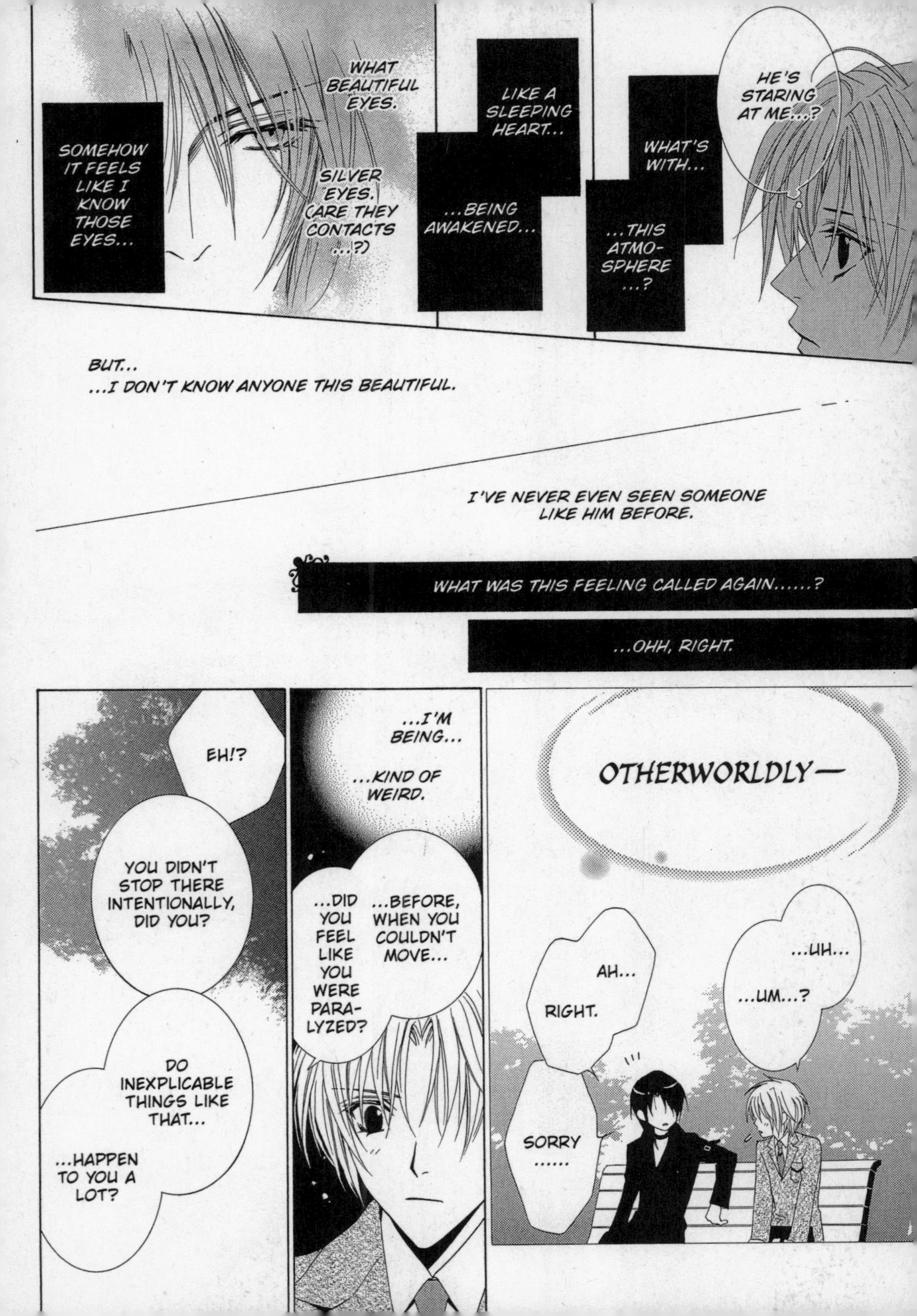
HE'S STARING AT ME...?
WHAT'S WITH...
...THIS ATMOSPHERE...?
LIKE A SLEEPING HEART...
...BEING AWAKENED...
WHAT BEAUTIFUL EYES.
SILVER EYES. (ARE THEY CONTACTS...?)
SOMEHOW IT FEELS LIKE I KNOW THOSE EYES...
BUT...
...I DON'T KNOW ANYONE THIS BEAUTIFUL.
I'VE NEVER EVEN SEEN SOMEONE LIKE HIM BEFORE.
WHAT WAS THIS FEELING CALLED AGAIN......?
...OHH, RIGHT.
OTHERWORLDLY—
...UH...
...UM...?
AH...
RIGHT.
SORRY......
...I'M BEING...
...KIND OF WEIRD.
...BEFORE, WHEN YOU COULDN'T MOVE...
...DID YOU FEEL LIKE YOU WERE PARALYZED?
EH!?
YOU DIDN'T STOP THERE INTENTIONALLY, DID YOU?
DO INEXPLICABLE THINGS LIKE THAT...
...HAPPEN TO YOU A LOT?

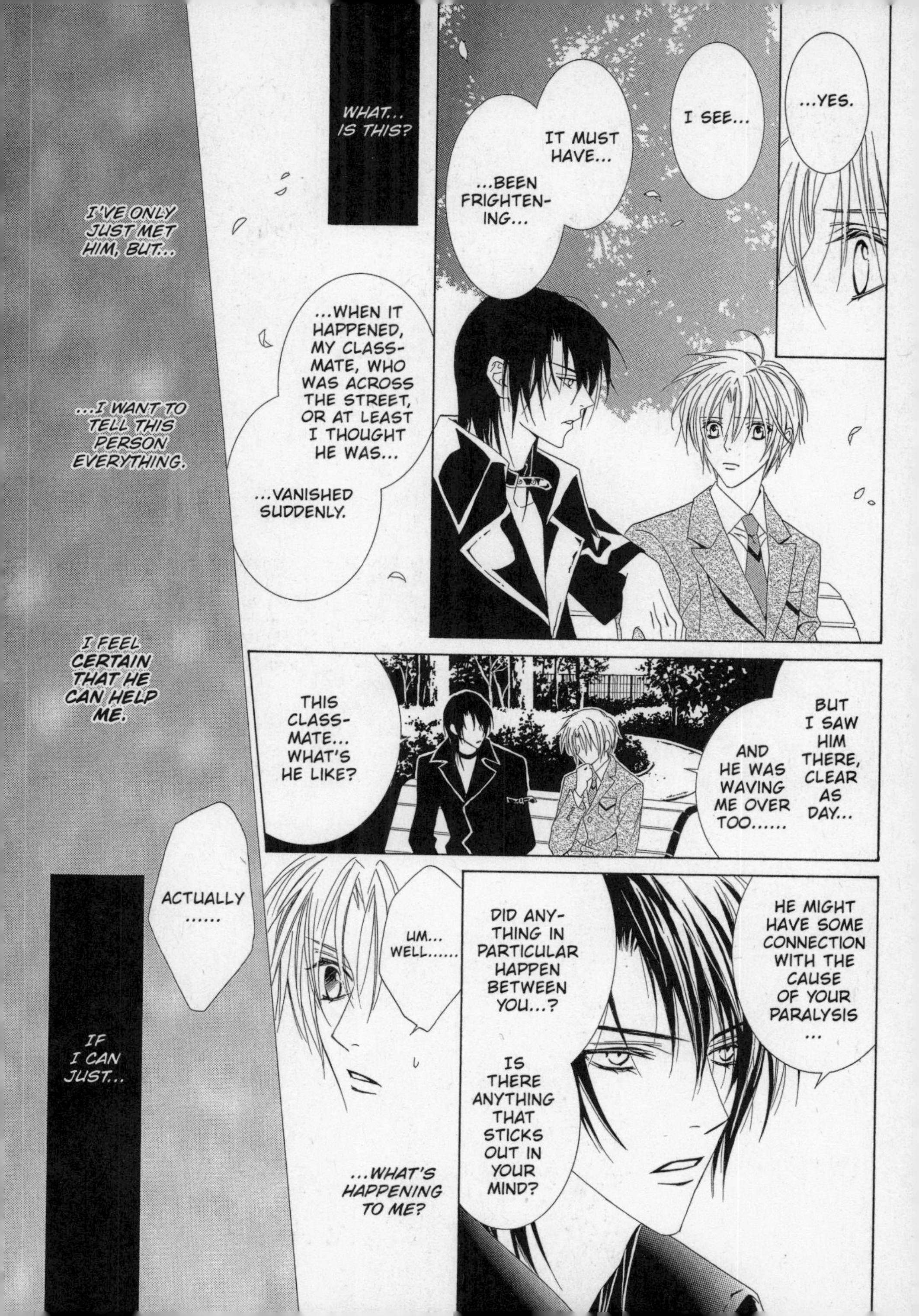
...YES.
I SEE...
IT MUST HAVE...
...BEEN FRIGHTENING...
WHAT... IS THIS?
...WHEN IT HAPPENED, MY CLASSMATE, WHO WAS ACROSS THE STREET, OR AT LEAST I THOUGHT HE WAS...
...VANISHED SUDDENLY.
I'VE ONLY JUST MET HIM, BUT...
...I WANT TO TELL THIS PERSON EVERYTHING.
BUT I SAW HIM THERE, CLEAR AS DAY...
AND HE WAS WAVING ME OVER TOO......
THIS CLASSMATE... WHAT'S HE LIKE?
I FEEL CERTAIN THAT HE CAN HELP ME.
HE MIGHT HAVE SOME CONNECTION WITH THE CAUSE OF YOUR PARALYSIS...
DID ANYTHING IN PARTICULAR HAPPEN BETWEEN YOU...?
IS THERE ANYTHING THAT STICKS OUT IN YOUR MIND?
UM... WELL......
ACTUALLY......
...WHAT'S HAPPENING TO ME?
IF I CAN JUST...

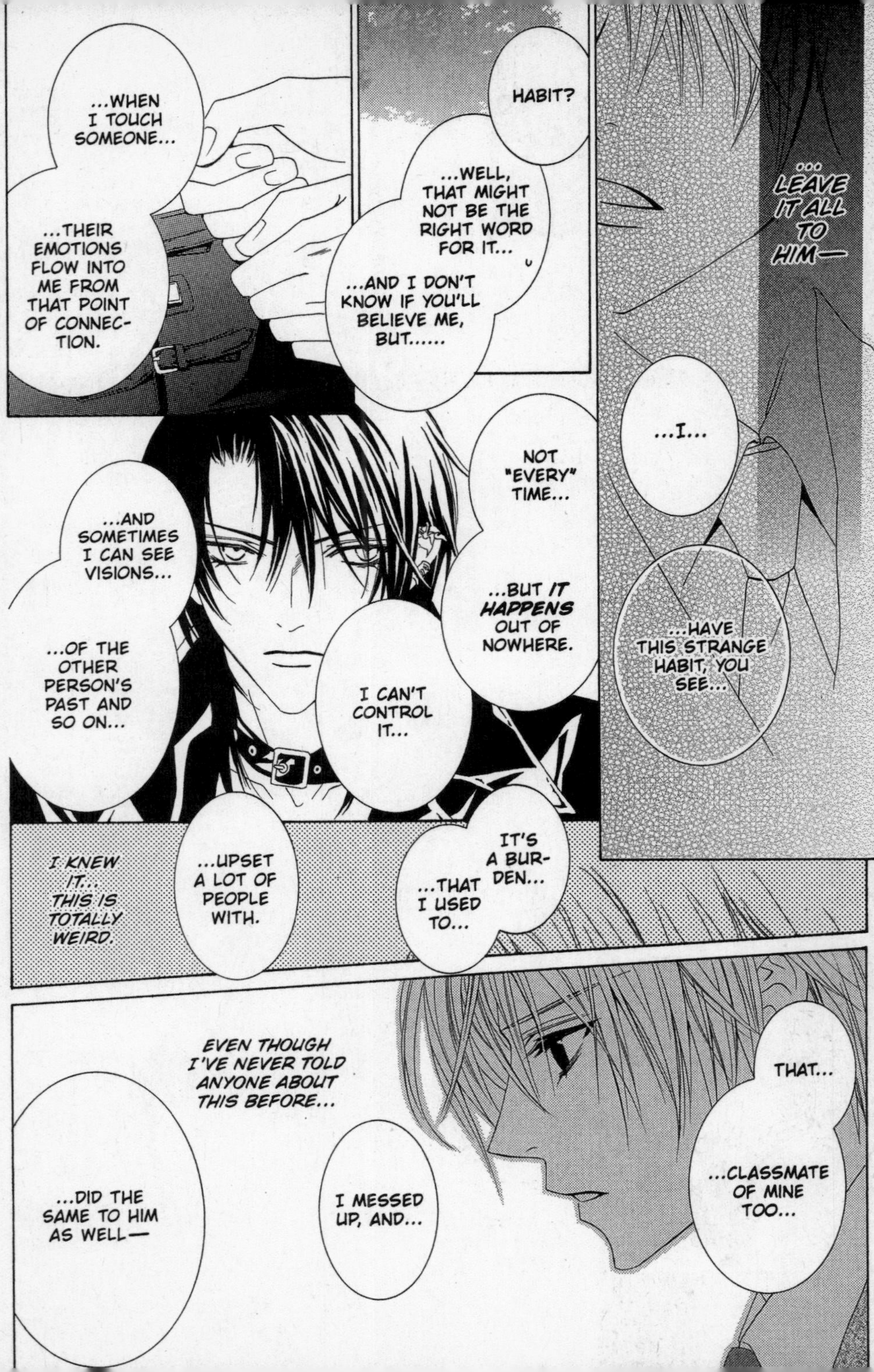
...LEAVE IT ALL TO HIM—
...I...
...HAVE THIS STRANGE HABIT, YOU SEE...
HABIT?
...WELL, THAT MIGHT NOT BE THE RIGHT WORD FOR IT...
...AND I DON'T KNOW IF YOU'LL BELIEVE ME, BUT......
...WHEN I TOUCH SOMEONE...
...THEIR EMOTIONS FLOW INTO ME FROM THAT POINT OF CONNECTION.
NOT "EVERY" TIME...
...BUT *IT HAPPENS* OUT OF NOWHERE.
I CAN'T CONTROL IT...
...AND SOMETIMES I CAN SEE VISIONS...
...OF THE OTHER PERSON'S PAST AND SO ON...
IT'S A BURDEN...
...THAT I USED TO...
...UPSET A LOT OF PEOPLE WITH.
I KNEW IT... THIS IS TOTALLY WEIRD.
THAT...
...CLASSMATE OF MINE TOO...
I MESSED UP, AND...
EVEN THOUGH I'VE NEVER TOLD ANYONE ABOUT THIS BEFORE...
...DID THE SAME TO HIM AS WELL—

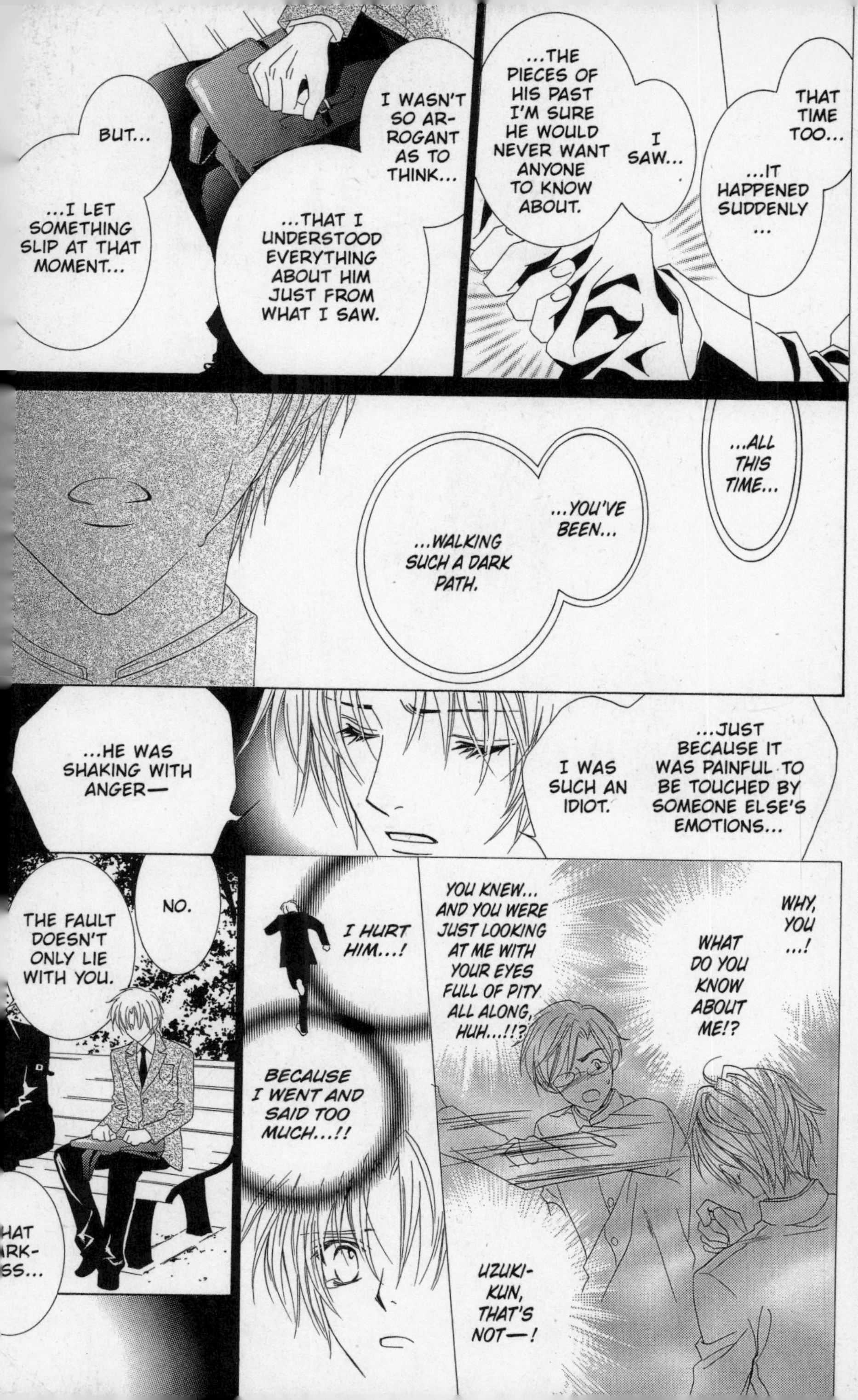
THAT TIME TOO...
...IT HAPPENED SUDDENLY...
I SAW...
...THE PIECES OF HIS PAST I'M SURE HE WOULD NEVER WANT ANYONE TO KNOW ABOUT.
I WASN'T SO AR-ROGANT AS TO THINK...
...THAT I UNDERSTOOD EVERYTHING ABOUT HIM JUST FROM WHAT I SAW.
BUT...
...I LET SOMETHING SLIP AT THAT MOMENT...
...ALL THIS TIME...
...YOU'VE BEEN...
...WALKING SUCH A DARK PATH.
...JUST BECAUSE IT WAS PAINFUL TO BE TOUCHED BY SOMEONE ELSE'S EMOTIONS...
I WAS SUCH AN IDIOT.
...HE WAS SHAKING WITH ANGER—
WHY, YOU ...!
WHAT DO YOU KNOW ABOUT ME!?
YOU KNEW... AND YOU WERE JUST LOOKING AT ME WITH YOUR EYES FULL OF PITY ALL ALONG, HUH...!!?
UZUKI-KUN, THAT'S NOT—!
I HURT HIM...!
BECAUSE I WENT AND SAID TOO MUCH...!!
NO.
THE FAULT DOESN'T ONLY LIE WITH YOU.

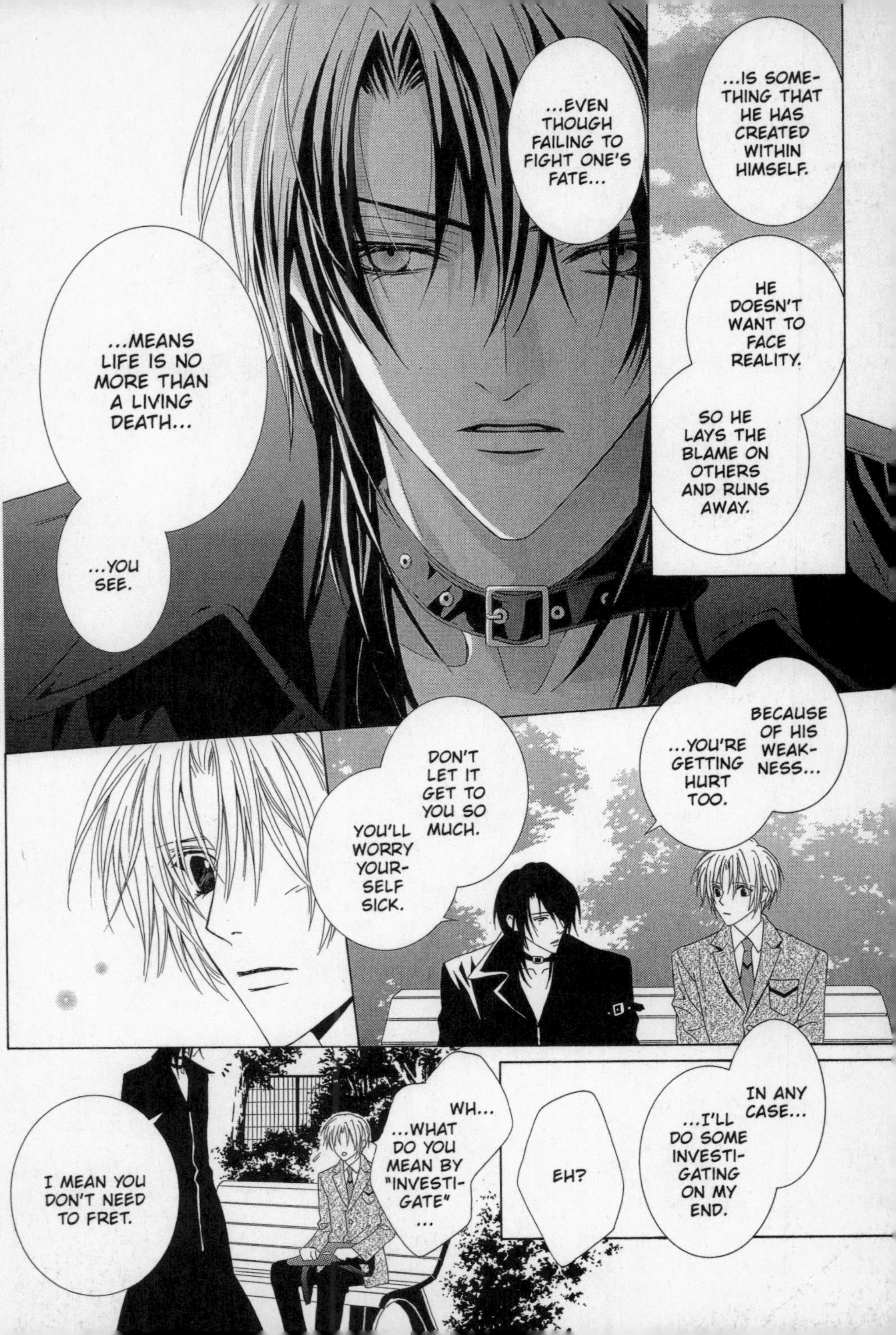
...EVEN THOUGH FAILING TO FIGHT ONE'S FATE...
...IS SOMETHING THAT HE HAS CREATED WITHIN HIMSELF.
HE DOESN'T WANT TO FACE REALITY.
SO HE LAYS THE BLAME ON OTHERS AND RUNS AWAY.
...MEANS LIFE IS NO MORE THAN A LIVING DEATH...
...YOU SEE.
BECAUSE OF HIS WEAKNESS...
...YOU'RE GETTING HURT TOO.
DON'T LET IT GET TO YOU SO MUCH.
YOU'LL WORRY YOURSELF SICK.
IN ANY CASE...
...I'LL DO SOME INVESTIGATING ON MY END.
EH?
WH...
...WHAT DO YOU MEAN BY "INVESTIGATE"...
I MEAN YOU DON'T NEED TO FRET.

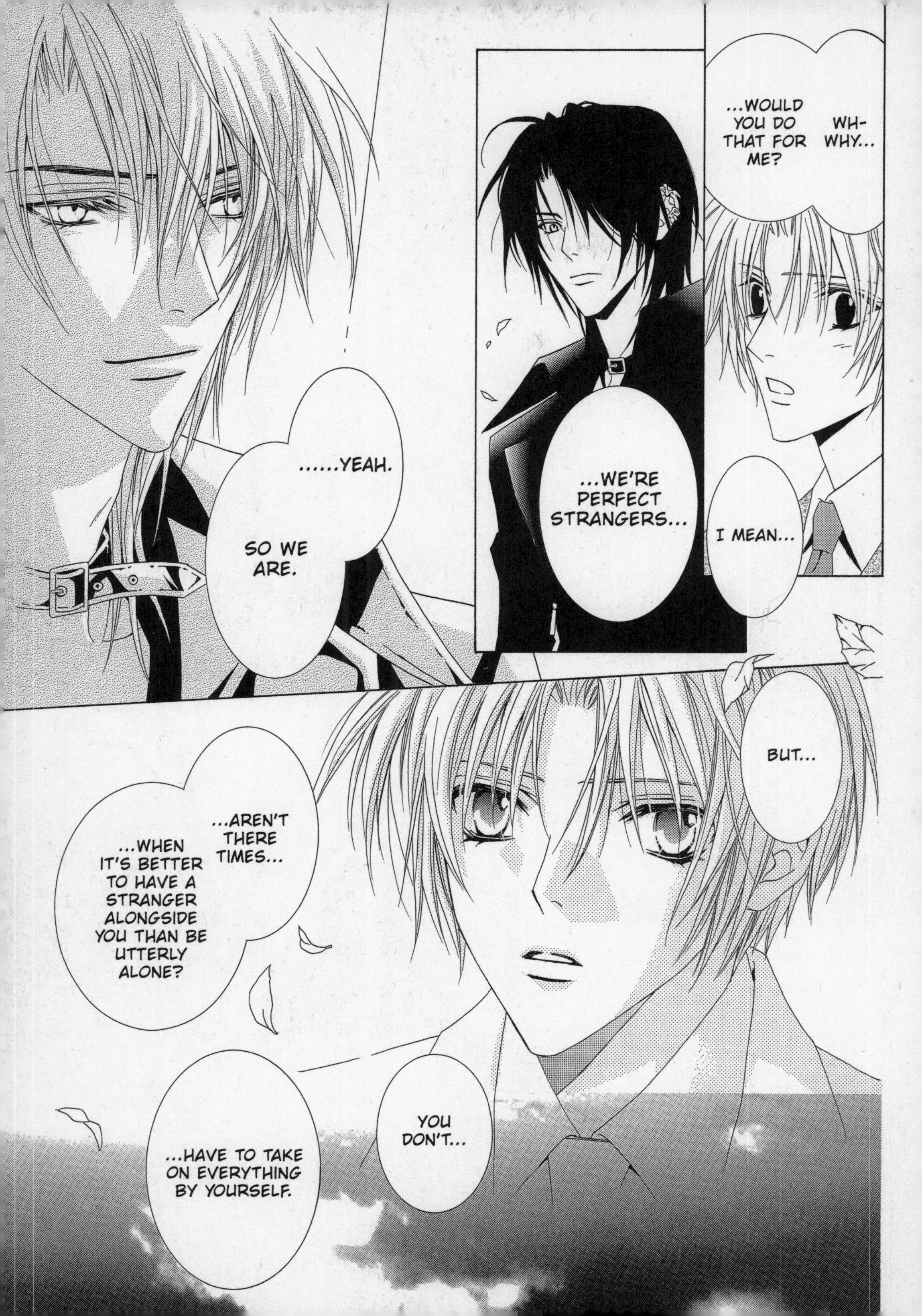
WH-WHY...
...WOULD YOU DO THAT FOR ME?
I MEAN...
...WE'RE PERFECT STRANGERS...
......YEAH.
SO WE ARE.
BUT...
...AREN'T THERE TIMES...
...WHEN IT'S BETTER TO HAVE A STRANGER ALONGSIDE YOU THAN BE UTTERLY ALONE?
YOU DON'T...
...HAVE TO TAKE ON EVERYTHING BY YOURSELF.

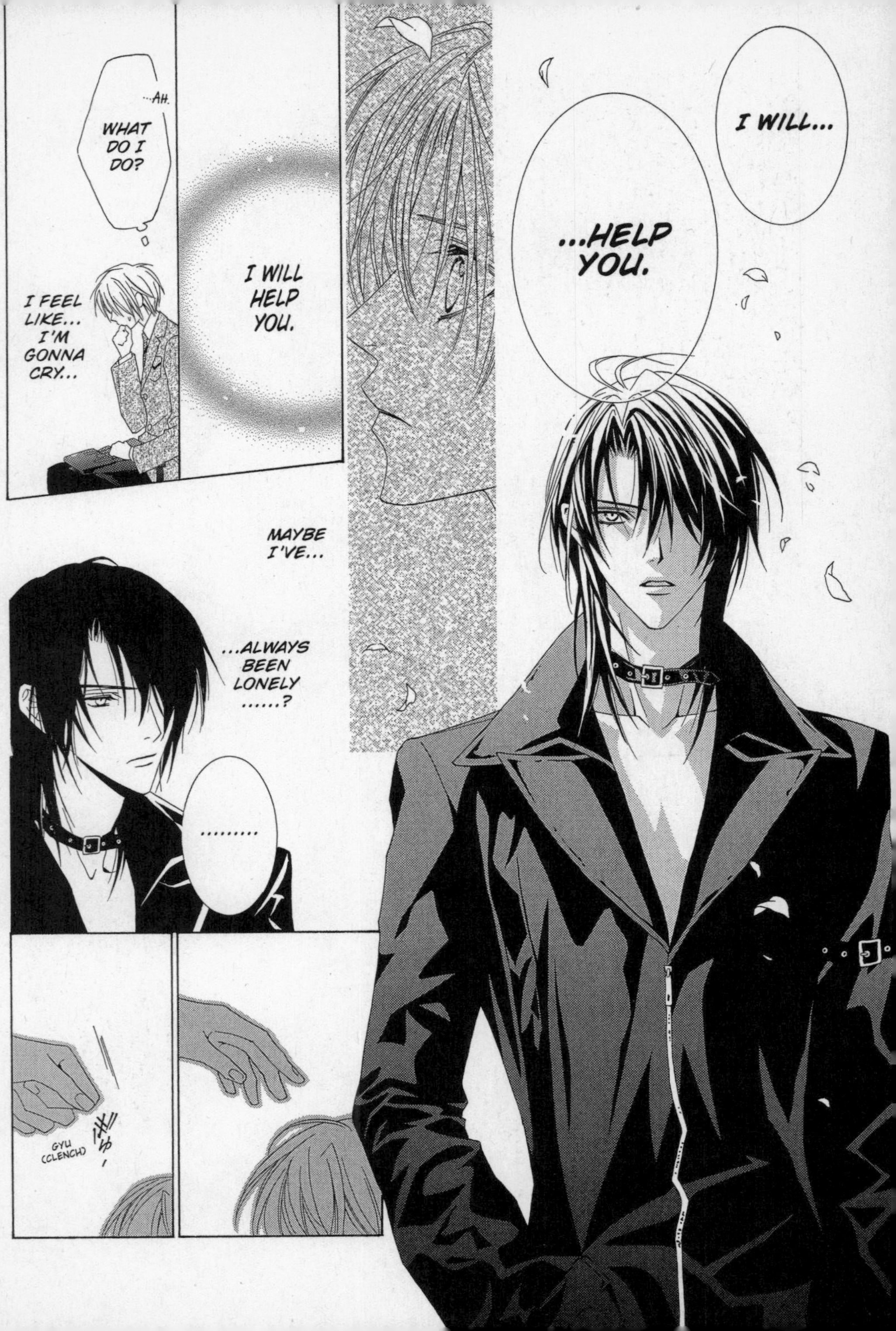

...AH.
WHAT DO I DO?
I FEEL LIKE... I'M GONNA CRY...
I WILL HELP YOU.
I WILL...
...HELP YOU.
MAYBE I'VE...
...ALWAYS BEEN LONELY ......?
....
GYU (CLENCH)

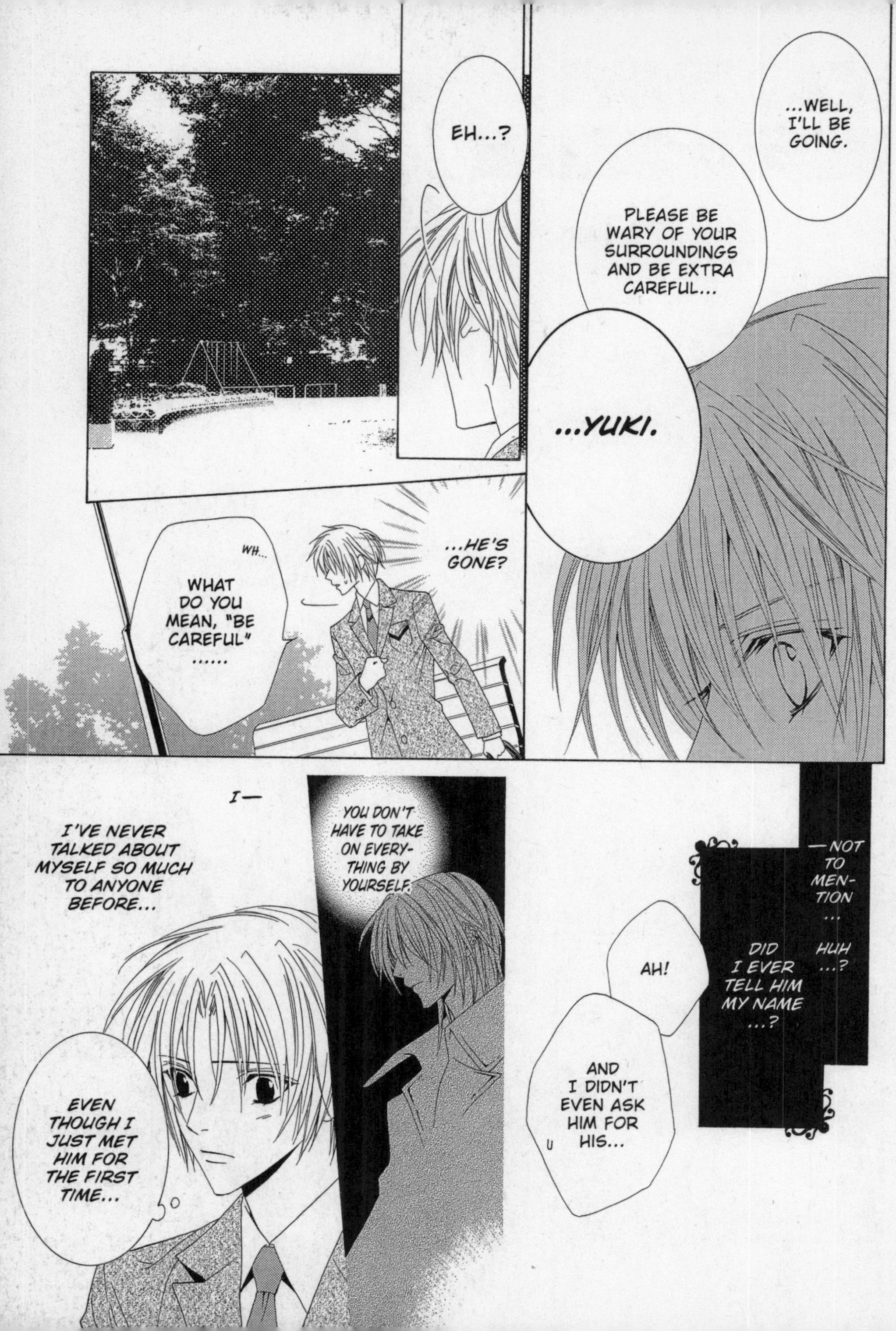
...WELL, I'LL BE GOING.
PLEASE BE WARY OF YOUR SURROUNDINGS AND BE EXTRA CAREFUL...
...YUKI.
EH...?
...HE'S GONE?
WH... WHAT DO YOU MEAN, "BE CAREFUL" ......
—NOT TO MENTION...
HUH...?
DID I EVER TELL HIM MY NAME...?
AH!
AND I DIDN'T EVEN ASK HIM FOR HIS...
I—
I'VE NEVER TALKED ABOUT MYSELF SO MUCH TO ANYONE BEFORE...
YOU DON'T HAVE TO TAKE ON EVERY-THING BY YOURSELF.
EVEN THOUGH I JUST MET HIM FOR THE FIRST TIME...

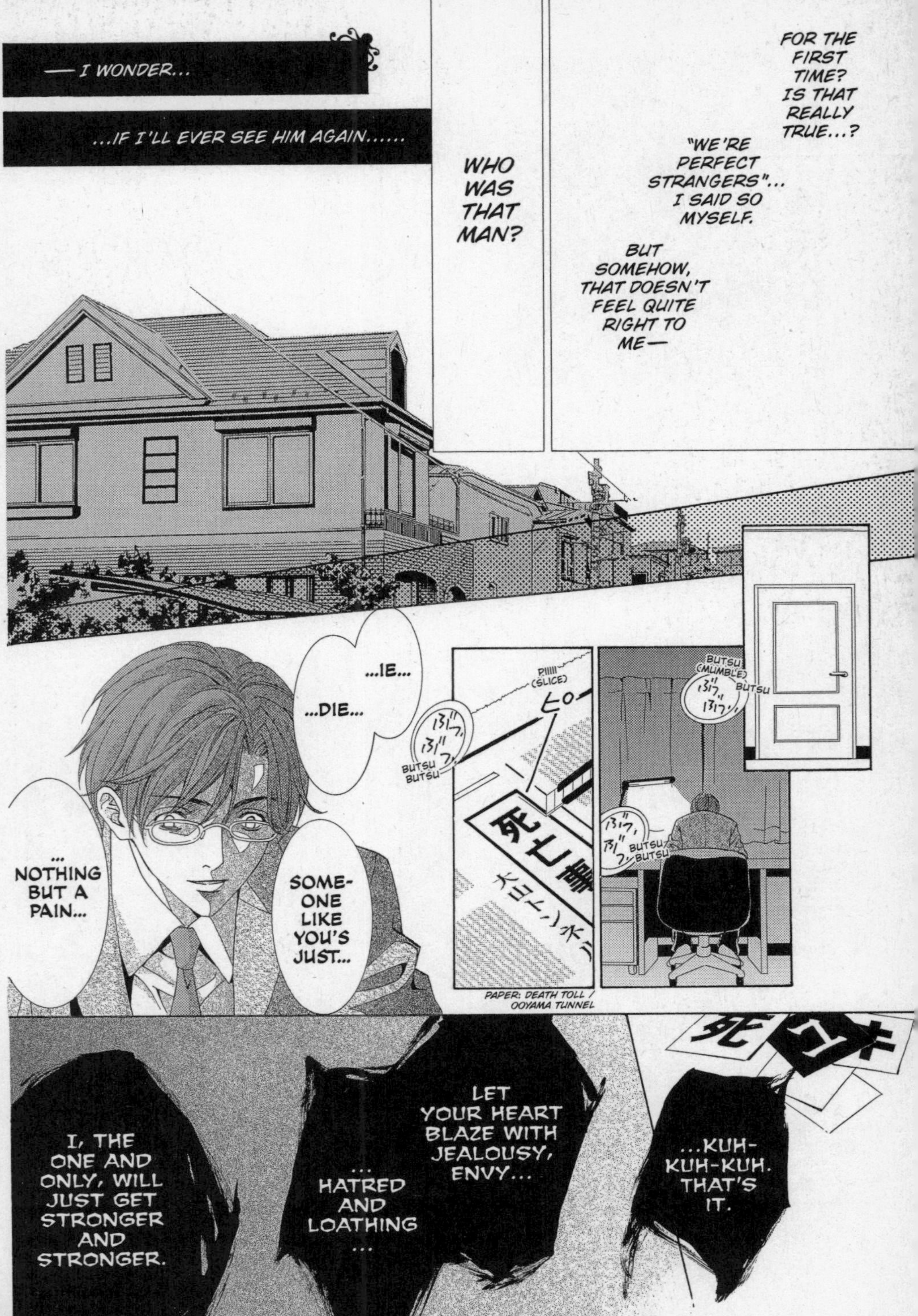
FOR THE FIRST TIME? IS THAT REALLY TRUE...?
"WE'RE PERFECT STRANGERS"... I SAID SO MYSELF.
BUT SOMEHOW, THAT DOESN'T FEEL QUITE RIGHT TO ME—
WHO WAS THAT MAN?
—I WONDER...
...IF I'LL EVER SEE HIM AGAIN......
BUTSU (MUMBLE) BUTSU
BUTSU BUTSU
P!!!!! (SLICE)
BUTSU BUTSU
PAPER: DEATH TOLL / OOYAMA TUNNEL
...IE...
...DIE...
SOME-ONE LIKE YOU'S JUST...
... NOTHING BUT A PAIN...
...KUH-KUH-KUH. THAT'S IT.
LET YOUR HEART BLAZE WITH JEALOUSY, ENVY...
... HATRED AND LOATHING ...
I, THE ONE AND ONLY, WILL JUST GET STRONGER AND STRONGER.

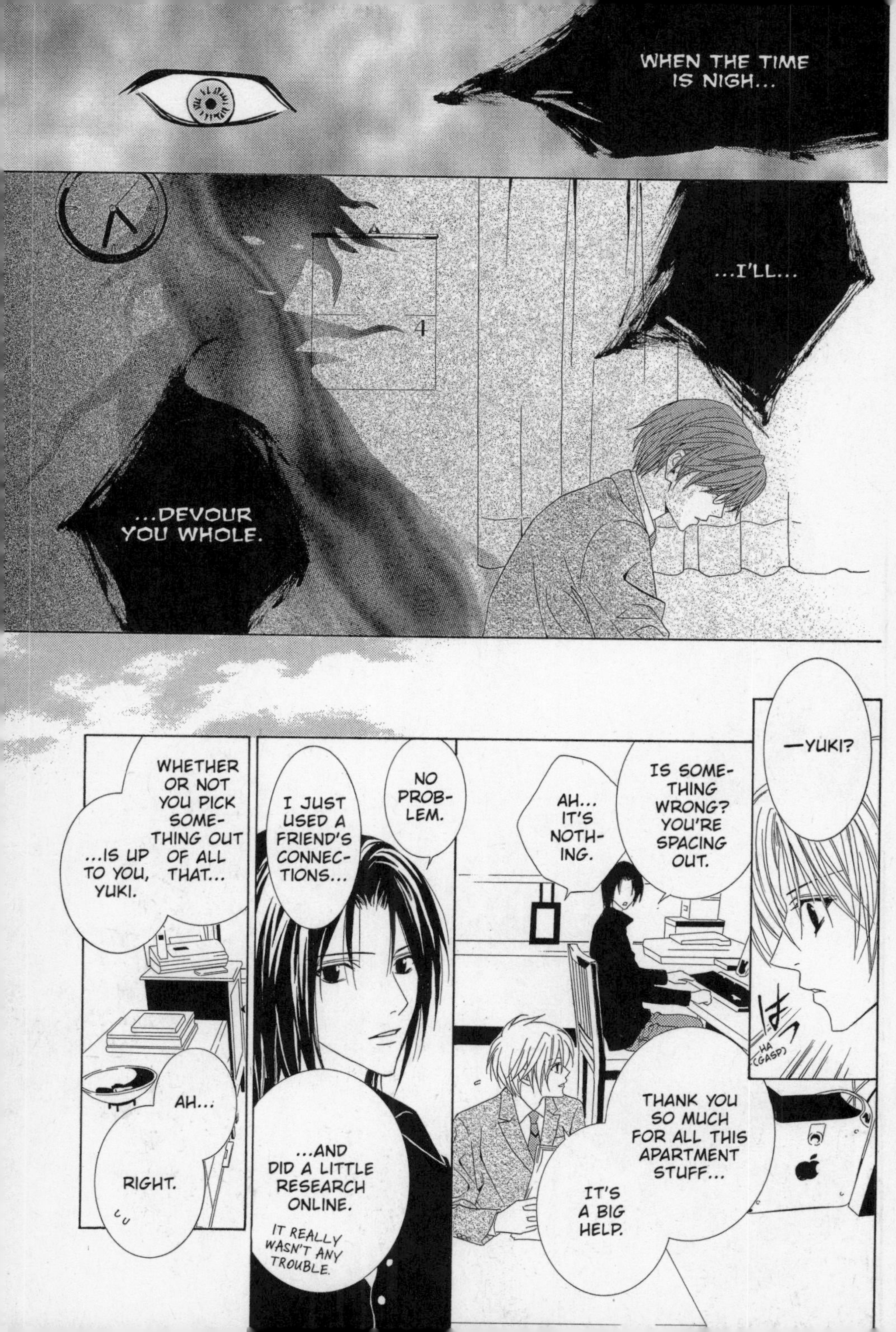
WHEN THE TIME IS NIGH...
...I'LL...
...DEVOUR YOU WHOLE.
—YUKI?
HA (GASP)
IS SOMETHING WRONG? YOU'RE SPACING OUT.
AH... IT'S NOTHING.
THANK YOU SO MUCH FOR ALL THIS APARTMENT STUFF...
IT'S A BIG HELP.
NO PROBLEM.
I JUST USED A FRIEND'S CONNECTIONS...
...AND DID A LITTLE RESEARCH ONLINE.
IT REALLY WASN'T ANY TROUBLE.
WHETHER OR NOT YOU PICK SOMETHING OUT OF ALL THAT...
...IS UP TO YOU, YUKI.
AH...
RIGHT.

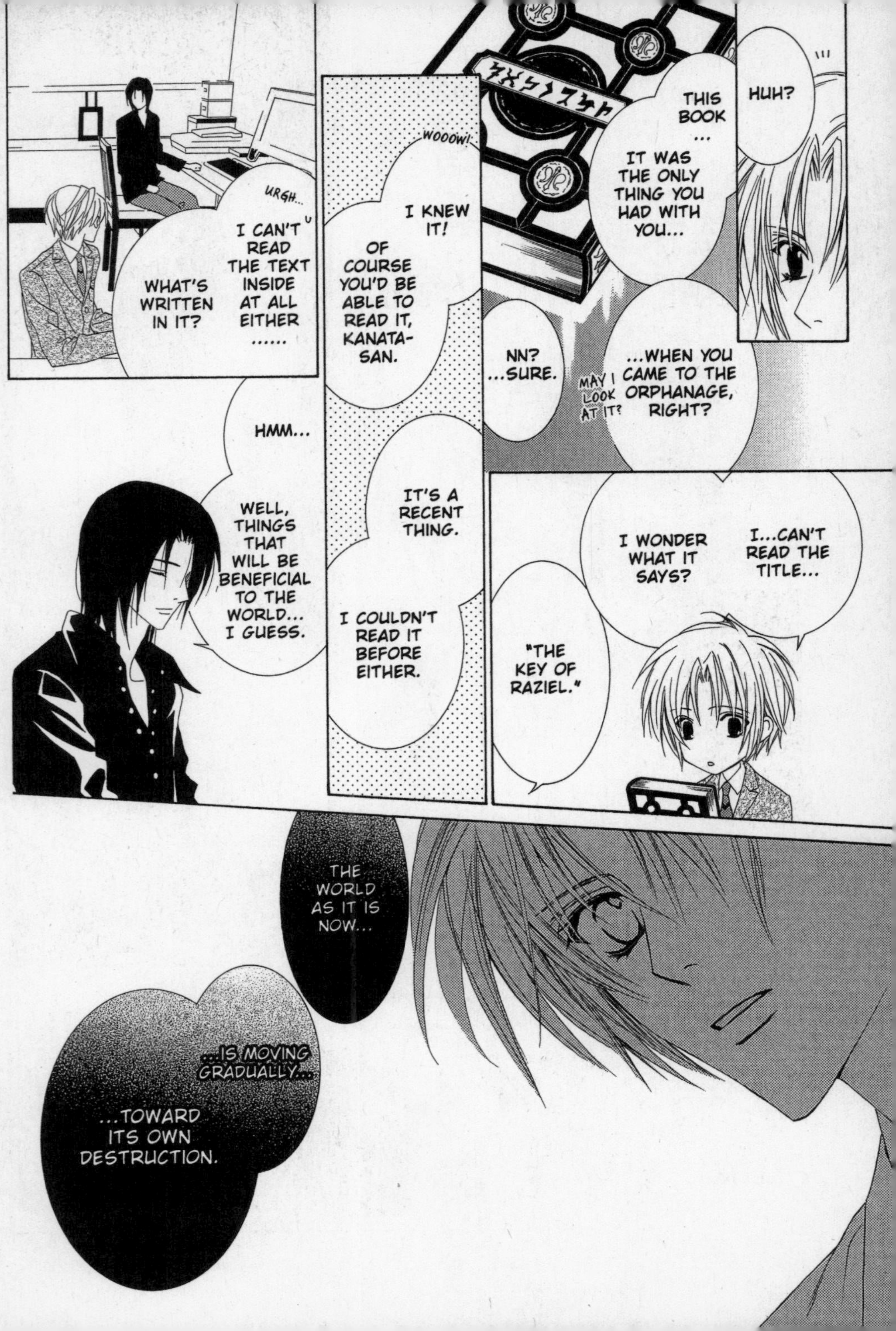
HUH?
THIS BOOK ...
IT WAS THE ONLY THING YOU HAD WITH YOU...
...WHEN YOU CAME TO THE ORPHANAGE, RIGHT?
MAY I LOOK AT IT?
NN? ...SURE.
WOOOW!
I KNEW IT!
OF COURSE YOU'D BE ABLE TO READ IT, KANATA-SAN.
URGH...
I CAN'T READ THE TEXT INSIDE AT ALL EITHER ......
WHAT'S WRITTEN IN IT?
I...CAN'T READ THE TITLE...
I WONDER WHAT IT SAYS?
"THE KEY OF RAZIEL."
IT'S A RECENT THING.
I COULDN'T READ IT BEFORE EITHER.
HMM...
WELL, THINGS THAT WILL BE BENEFICIAL TO THE WORLD... I GUESS.
THE WORLD AS IT IS NOW...
...IS MOVING GRADUALLY...
...TOWARD ITS OWN DESTRUCTION.

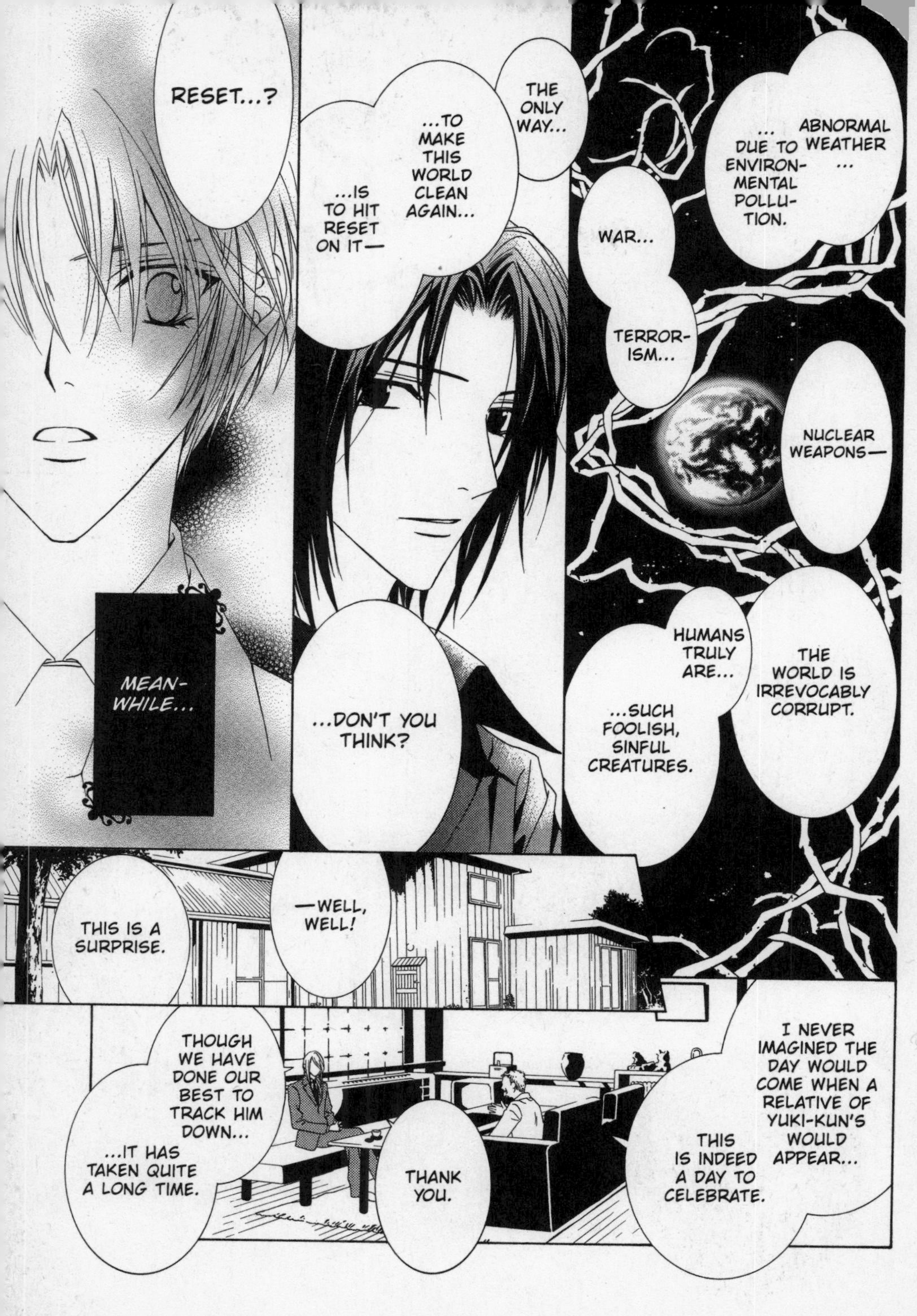
ABNORMAL WEATHER...
...DUE TO ENVIRONMENTAL POLLUTION.
WAR...
TERRORISM...
NUCLEAR WEAPONS—
THE WORLD IS IRREVOCABLY CORRUPT.
HUMANS TRULY ARE...
...SUCH FOOLISH, SINFUL CREATURES.
THE ONLY WAY...
...TO MAKE THIS WORLD CLEAN AGAIN...
...IS TO HIT RESET ON IT—
...DON'T YOU THINK?
RESET...?
MEAN-WHILE...
—WELL, WELL!
THIS IS A SURPRISE.
I NEVER IMAGINED THE DAY WOULD COME WHEN A RELATIVE OF YUKI-KUN'S WOULD APPEAR...
THIS IS INDEED A DAY TO CELEBRATE.
THANK YOU.
THOUGH WE HAVE DONE OUR BEST TO TRACK HIM DOWN...
...IT HAS TAKEN QUITE A LONG TIME.

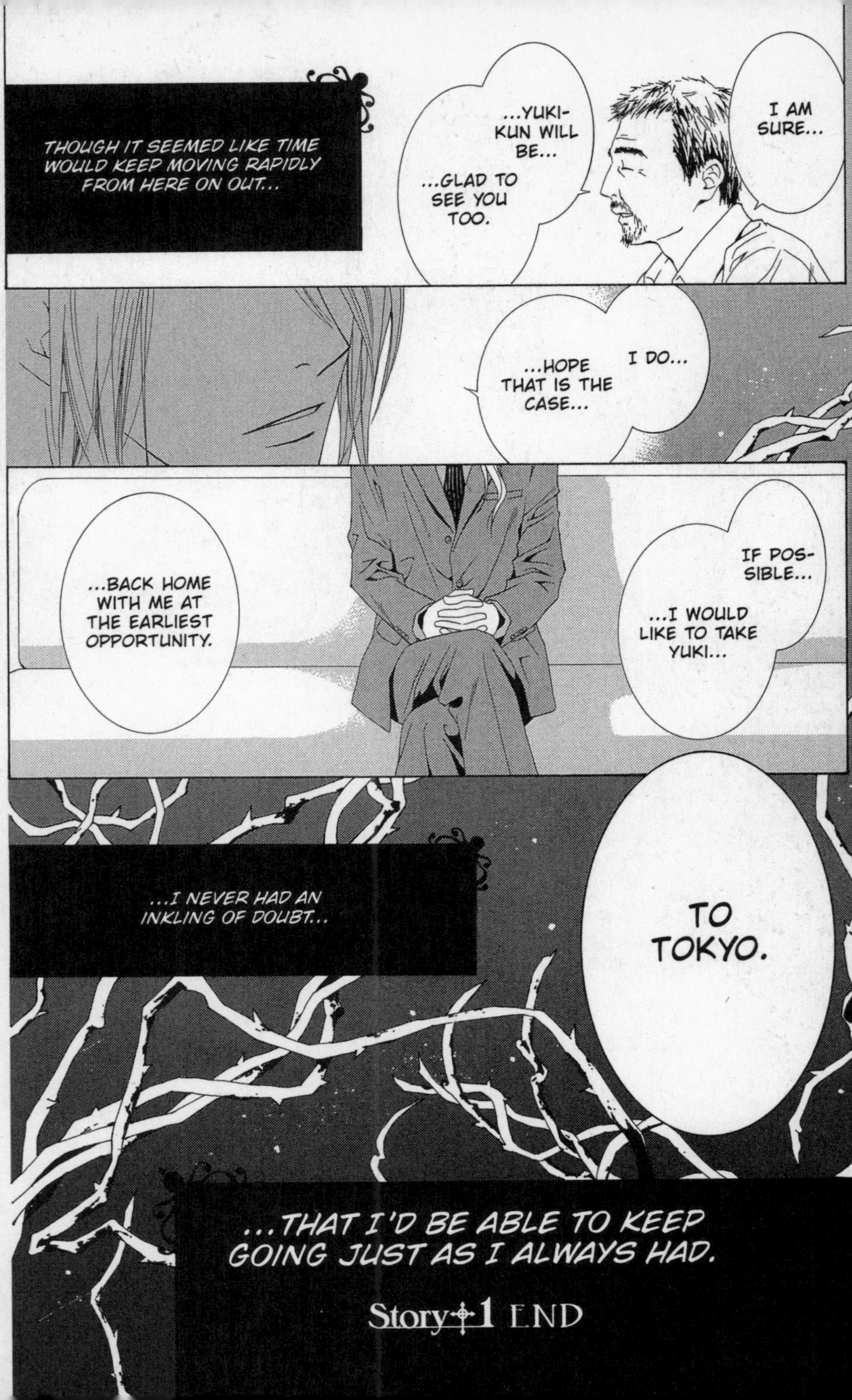
I AM SURE...
...YUKI-KUN WILL BE...
...GLAD TO SEE YOU TOO.
THOUGH IT SEEMED LIKE TIME WOULD KEEP MOVING RAPIDLY FROM HERE ON OUT...
I DO...
...HOPE THAT IS THE CASE...
IF POSSIBLE...
...I WOULD LIKE TO TAKE YUKI...
...BACK HOME WITH ME AT THE EARLIEST OPPORTUNITY.
TO TOKYO.
...I NEVER HAD AN INKLING OF DOUBT...
...THAT I'D BE ABLE TO KEEP GOING JUST AS I ALWAYS HAD.
Story 1 END

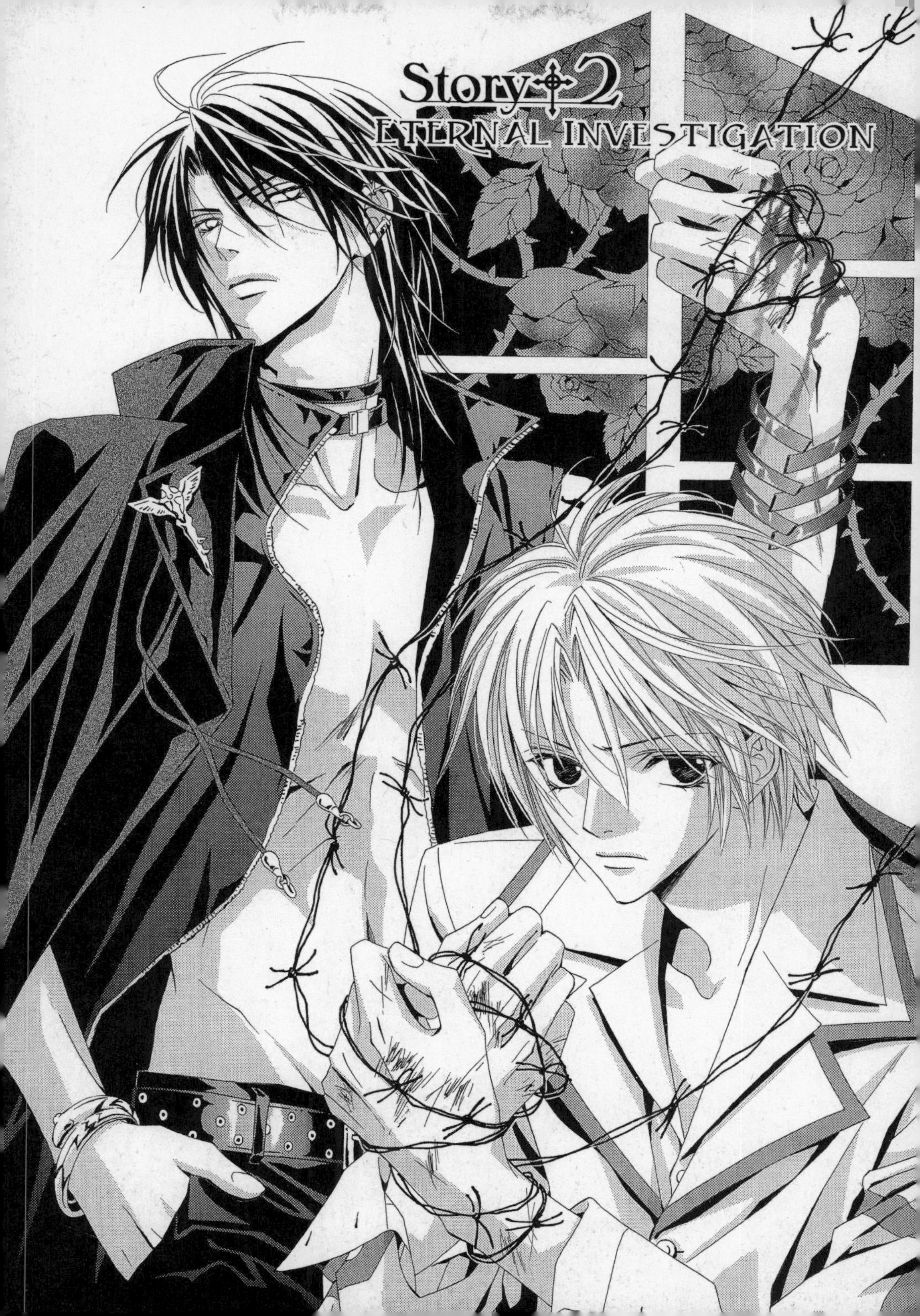
Story 2
ETERNAL INVESTIGATION

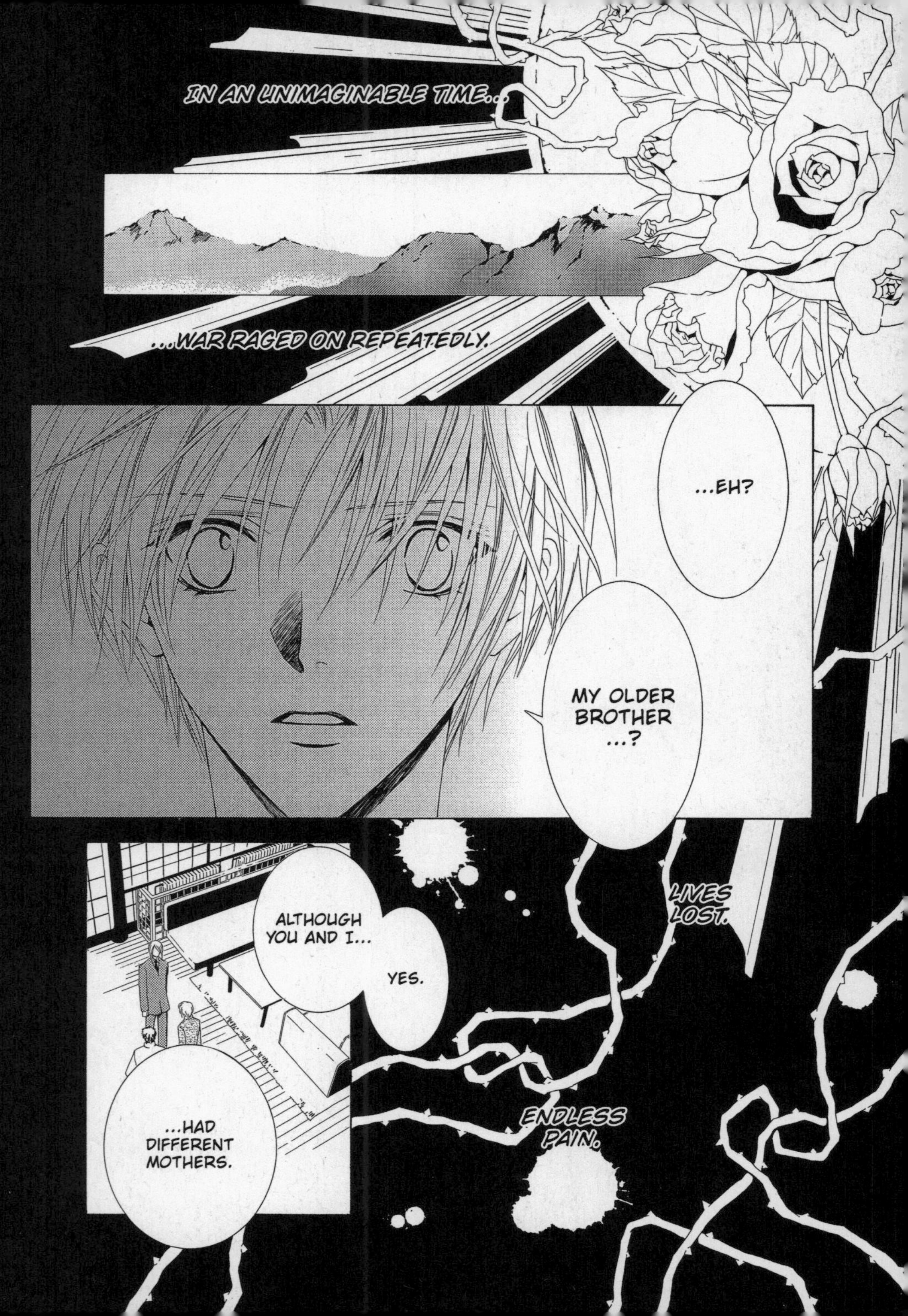
IN AN UNIMAGINABLE TIME...
...WAR RAGED ON REPEATEDLY.
...EH?
MY OLDER BROTHER ...?
LIVES LOST.
ALTHOUGH YOU AND I...
YES.
...HAD DIFFERENT MOTHERS.
ENDLESS PAIN.

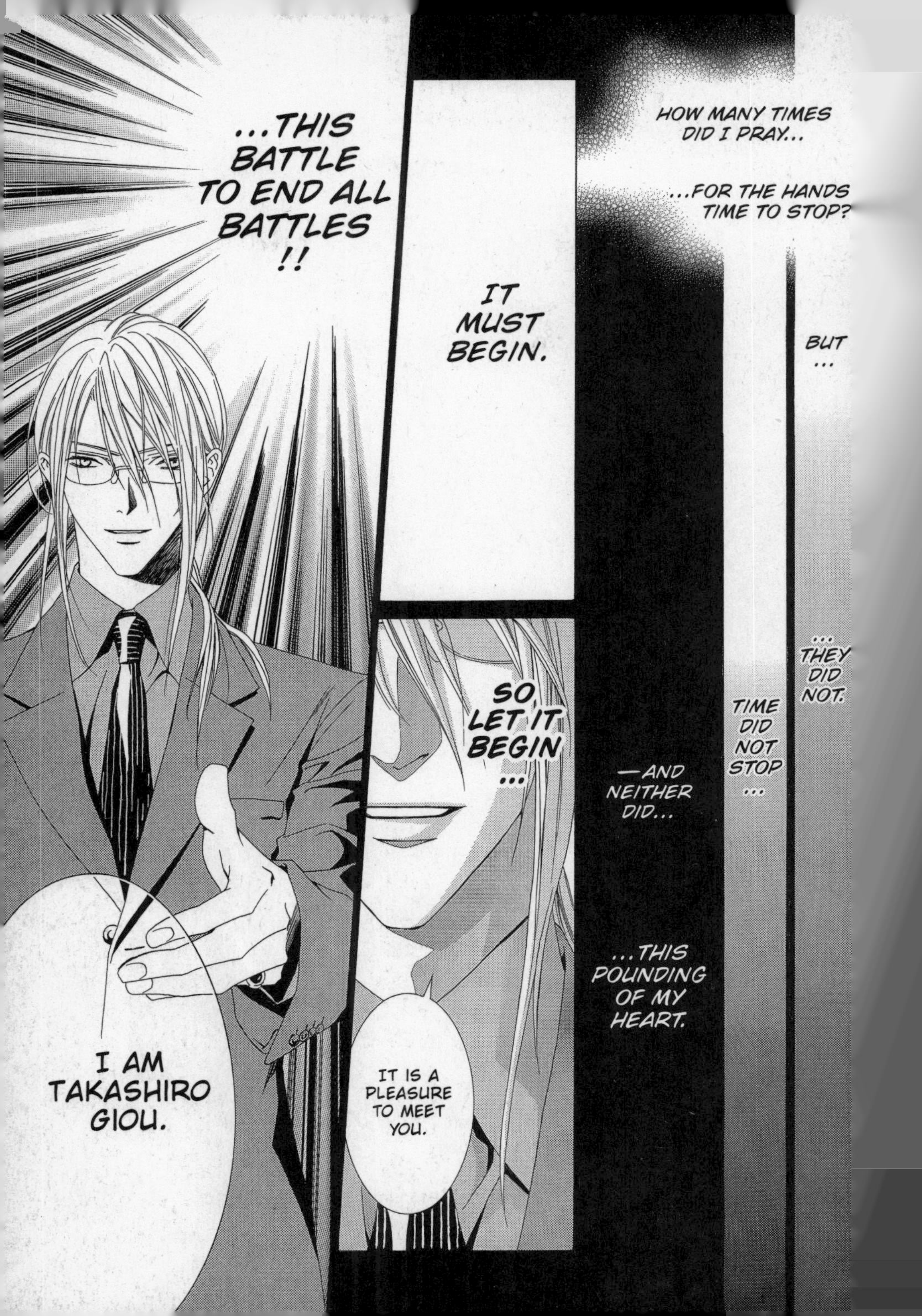
HOW MANY TIMES DID I PRAY...
...FOR THE HANDS TIME TO STOP?
BUT ...
...THEY DID NOT.
TIME DID NOT STOP ...
—AND NEITHER DID...
...THIS POUNDING OF MY HEART.
IT MUST BEGIN.
...THIS BATTLE TO END ALL BATTLES !!
SO, LET IT BEGIN ...
IT IS A PLEASURE TO MEET YOU.
I AM TAKASHIRO GIOU.

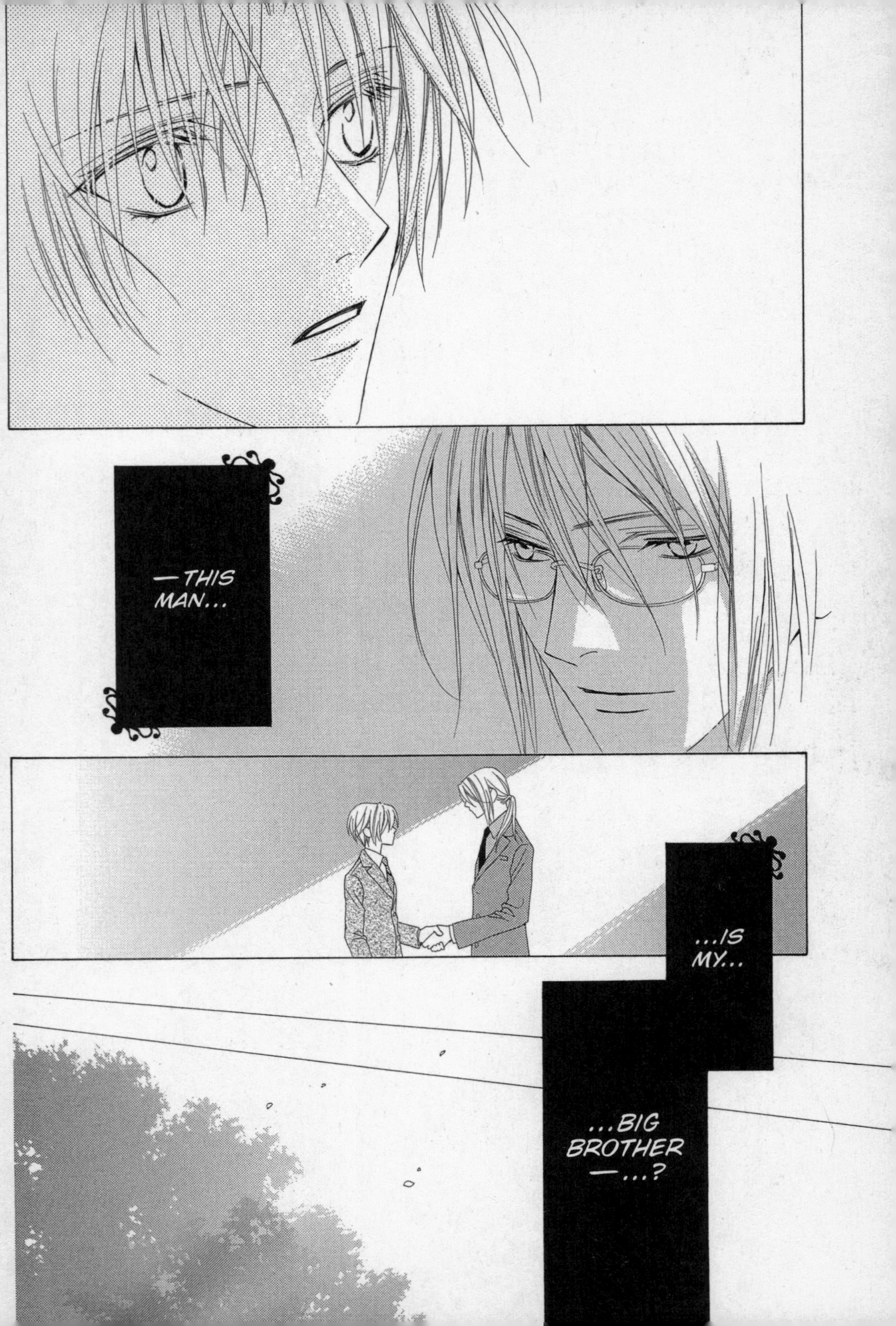
—THIS MAN...
...IS MY...
...BIG BROTHER—...?

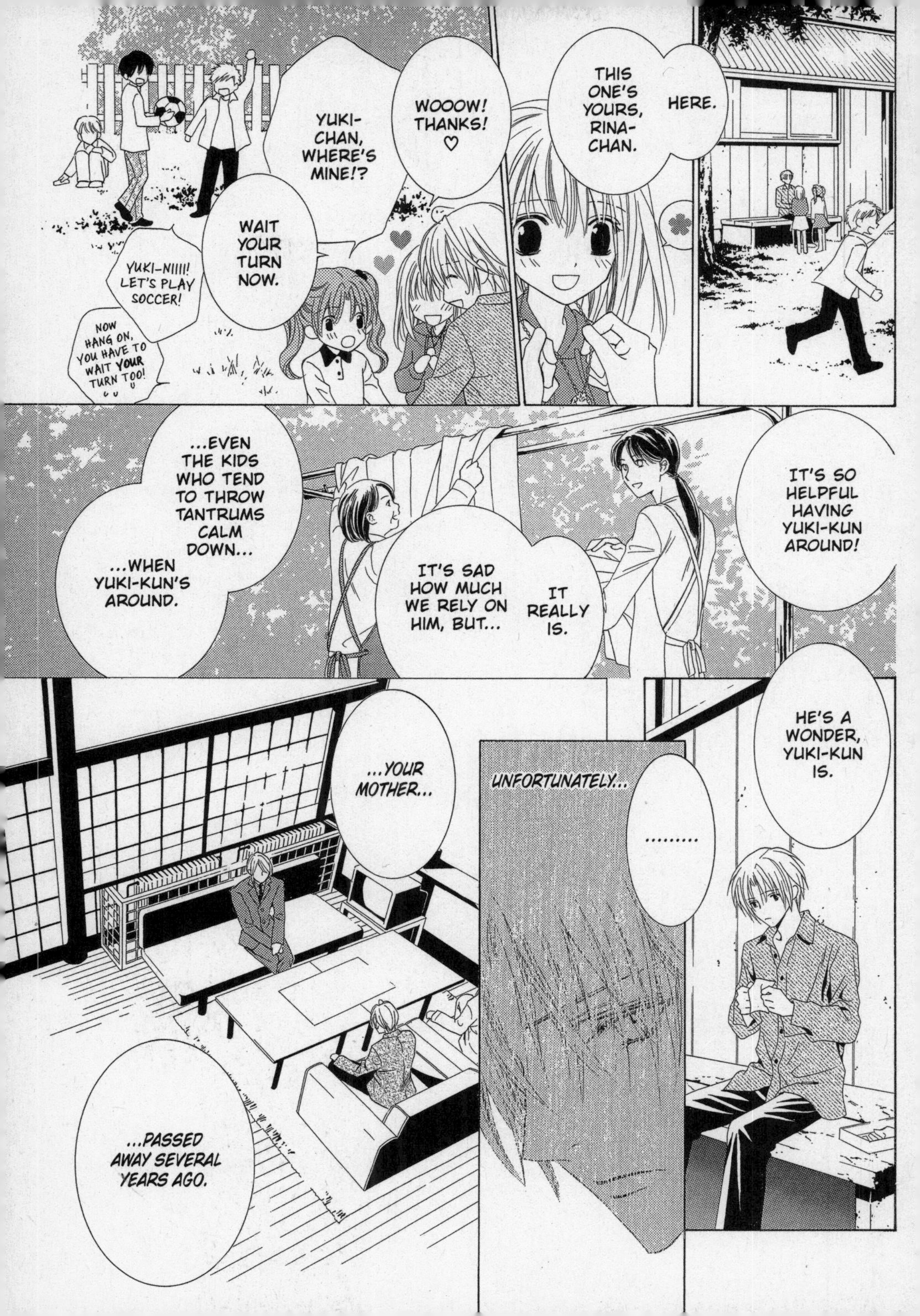
HERE.
THIS ONE'S YOURS, RINA-CHAN.
WOOOW! THANKS! ♡
YUKI-CHAN, WHERE'S MINE!?
WAIT YOUR TURN NOW.
YUKI-NIIII! LET'S PLAY SOCCER!
NOW HANG ON, YOU HAVE TO WAIT YOUR TURN TOO!
IT'S SO HELPFUL HAVING YUKI-KUN AROUND!
IT REALLY IS.
IT'S SAD HOW MUCH WE RELY ON HIM, BUT...
...EVEN THE KIDS WHO TEND TO THROW TANTRUMS CALM DOWN...
...WHEN YUKI-KUN'S AROUND.
HE'S A WONDER, YUKI-KUN IS.
....
UNFORTUNATELY...
...YOUR MOTHER...
...PASSED AWAY SEVERAL YEARS AGO.

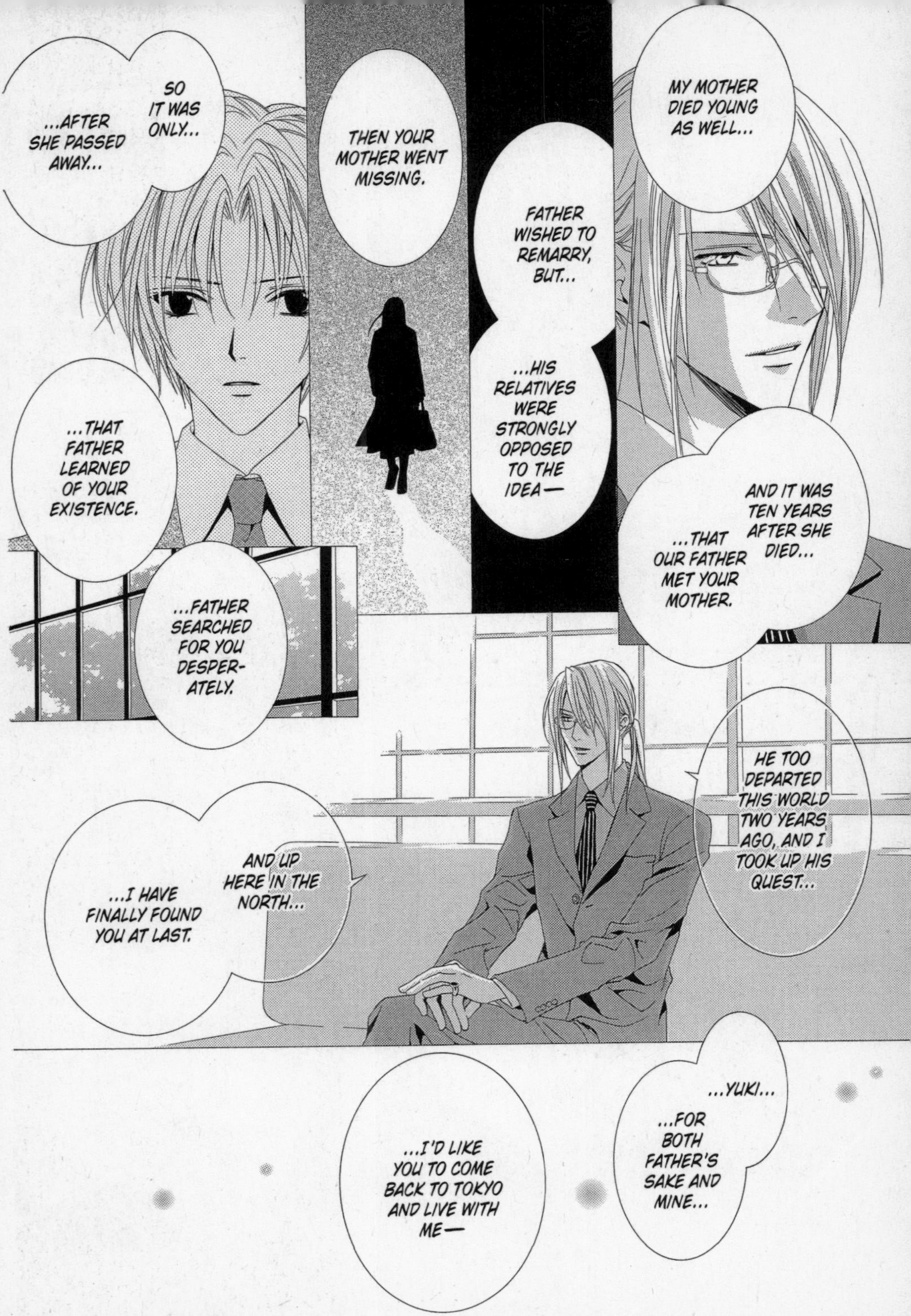
MY MOTHER DIED YOUNG AS WELL...
AND IT WAS TEN YEARS AFTER SHE DIED...
...THAT OUR FATHER MET YOUR MOTHER.
FATHER WISHED TO REMARRY, BUT...
...HIS RELATIVES WERE STRONGLY OPPOSED TO THE IDEA—
THEN YOUR MOTHER WENT MISSING.
SO IT WAS ONLY...
...AFTER SHE PASSED AWAY...
...THAT FATHER LEARNED OF YOUR EXISTENCE.
...FATHER SEARCHED FOR YOU DESPERATELY.
HE TOO DEPARTED THIS WORLD TWO YEARS AGO, AND I TOOK UP HIS QUEST...
AND UP HERE IN THE NORTH...
...I HAVE FINALLY FOUND YOU AT LAST.
...YUKI...
...FOR BOTH FATHER'S SAKE AND MINE...
...I'D LIKE YOU TO COME BACK TO TOKYO AND LIVE WITH ME—

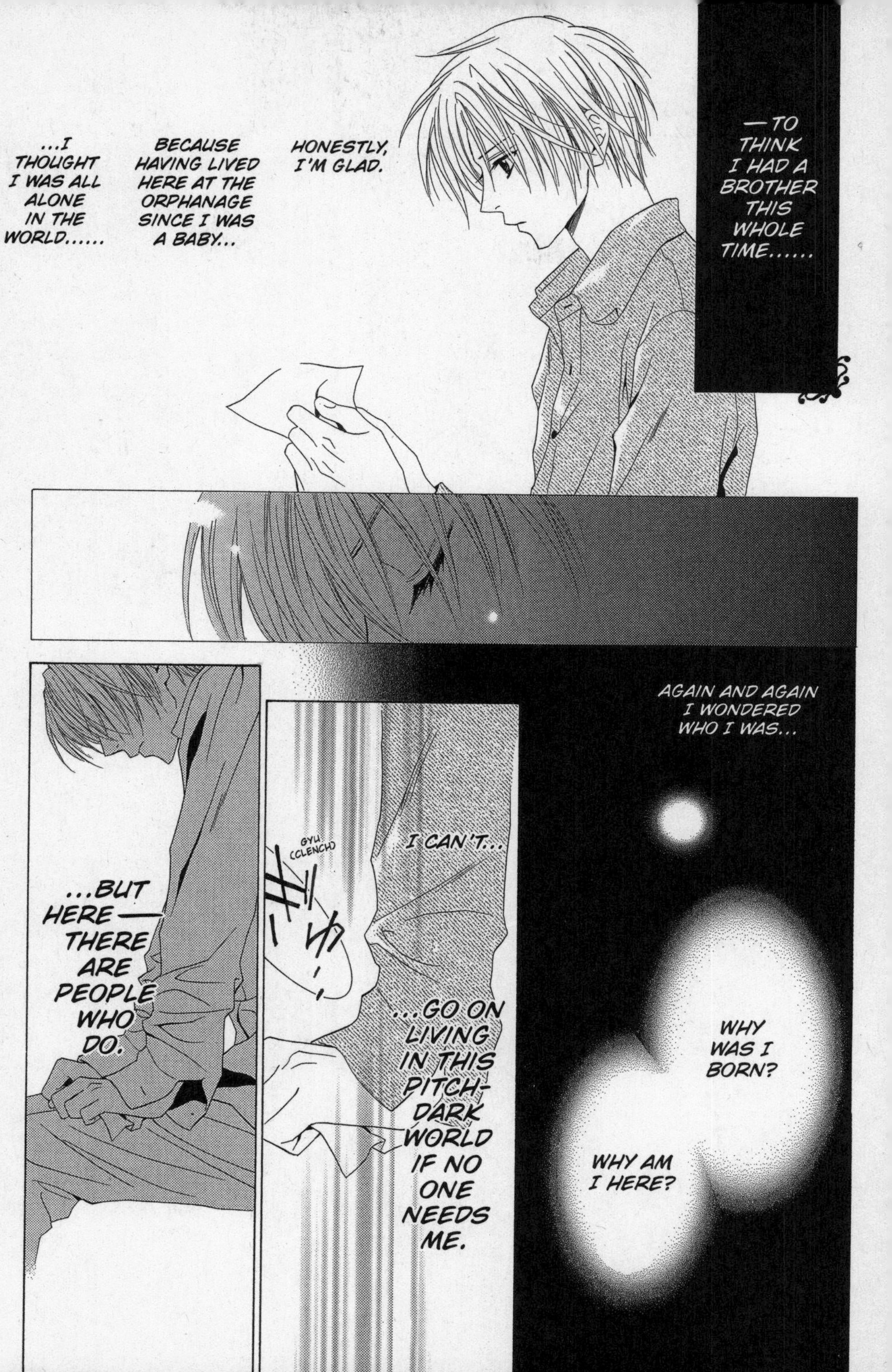
—TO THINK I HAD A BROTHER THIS WHOLE TIME......
HONESTLY, I'M GLAD.
BECAUSE HAVING LIVED HERE AT THE ORPHANAGE SINCE I WAS A BABY...
...I THOUGHT I WAS ALL ALONE IN THE WORLD......
AGAIN AND AGAIN I WONDERED WHO I WAS...
WHY WAS I BORN?
WHY AM I HERE?
I CAN'T...
...GO ON LIVING IN THIS PITCH-DARK WORLD IF NO ONE NEEDS ME.
GYU (CLENCH)
...BUT HERE— THERE ARE PEOPLE WHO DO.

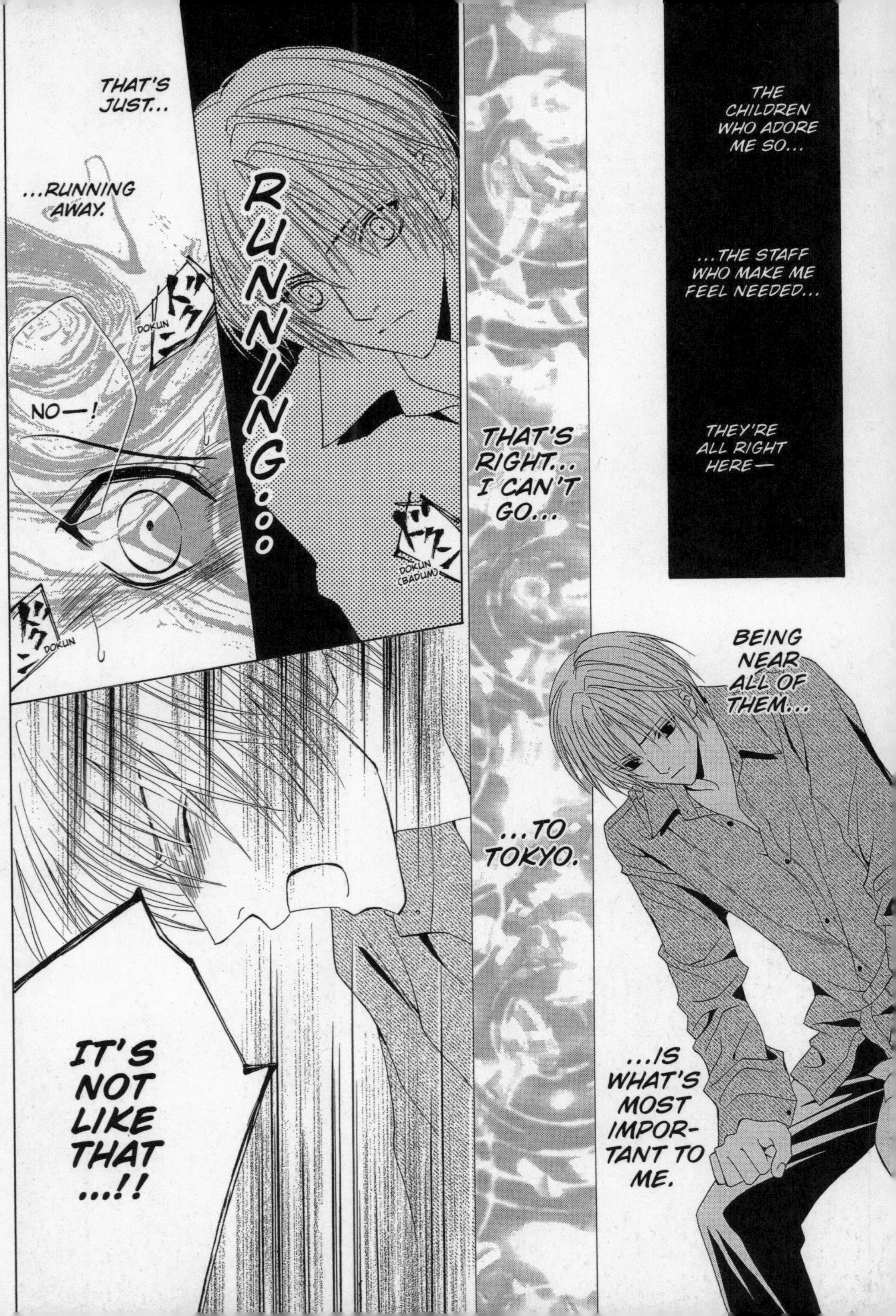
THE CHILDREN WHO ADORE ME SO...
...THE STAFF WHO MAKE ME FEEL NEEDED...
THEY'RE ALL RIGHT HERE—
BEING NEAR ALL OF THEM...
...IS WHAT'S MOST IMPORTANT TO ME.
THAT'S RIGHT... I CAN'T GO...
...TO TOKYO.
THAT'S JUST...
...RUNNING AWAY.
RUNNING...
DOKUN
NO—!
DOKUN (BADUM)
DOKUN
IT'S NOT LIKE THAT ...!!

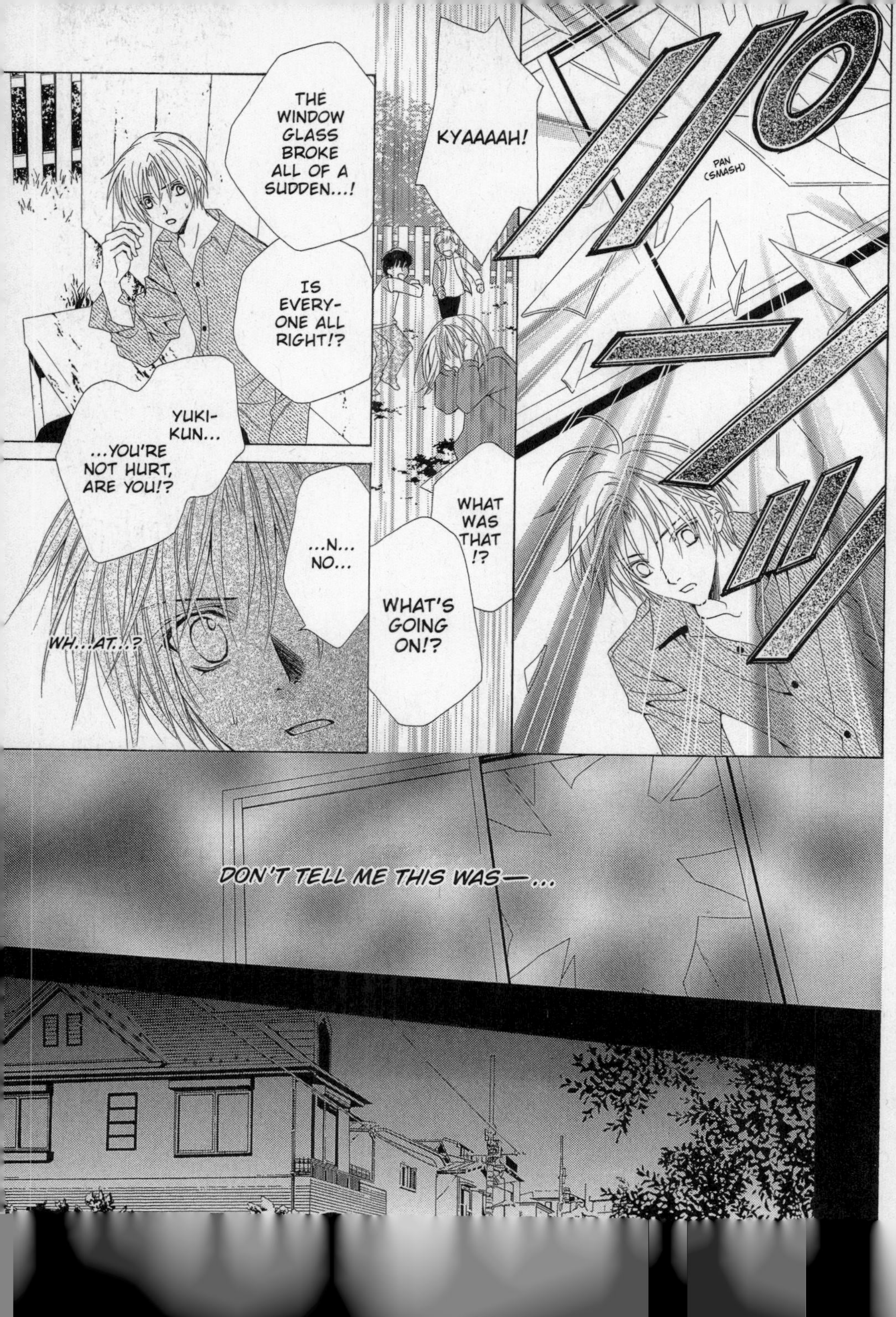
PAN (SMASH)
KYAAAAH!
THE WINDOW GLASS BROKE ALL OF A SUDDEN...!
IS EVERY-ONE ALL RIGHT!?
WHAT WAS THAT!?
WHAT'S GOING ON!?
YUKI-KUN... ...YOU'RE NOT HURT, ARE YOU!?
...N... NO...
WH...AT...?
DON'T TELL ME THIS WAS—...

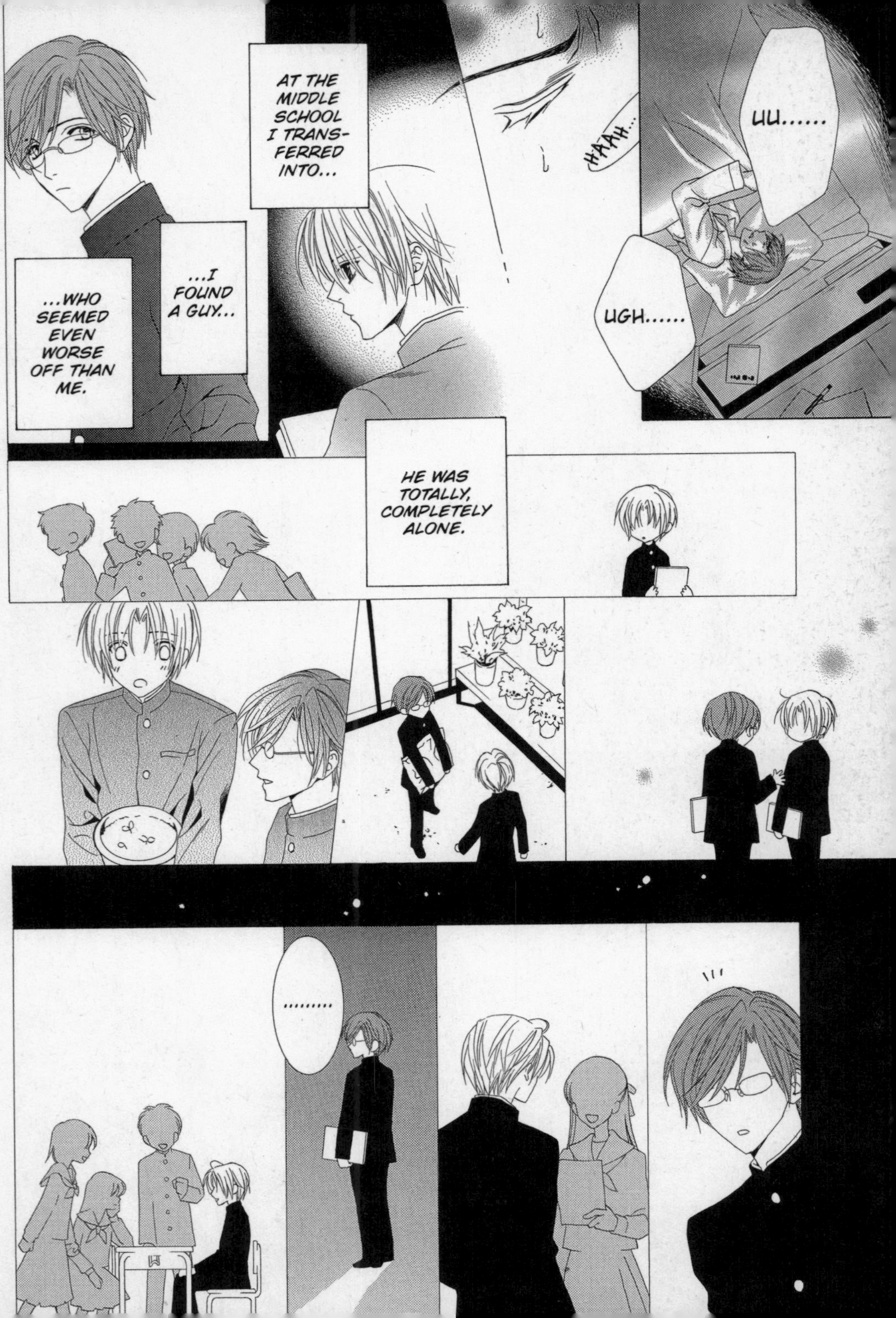
UU......
UGH......
HAAH...
AT THE MIDDLE SCHOOL I TRANS-FERRED INTO...
...I FOUND A GUY...
...WHO SEEMED EVEN WORSE OFF THAN ME.
HE WAS TOTALLY, COMPLETELY ALONE.
....

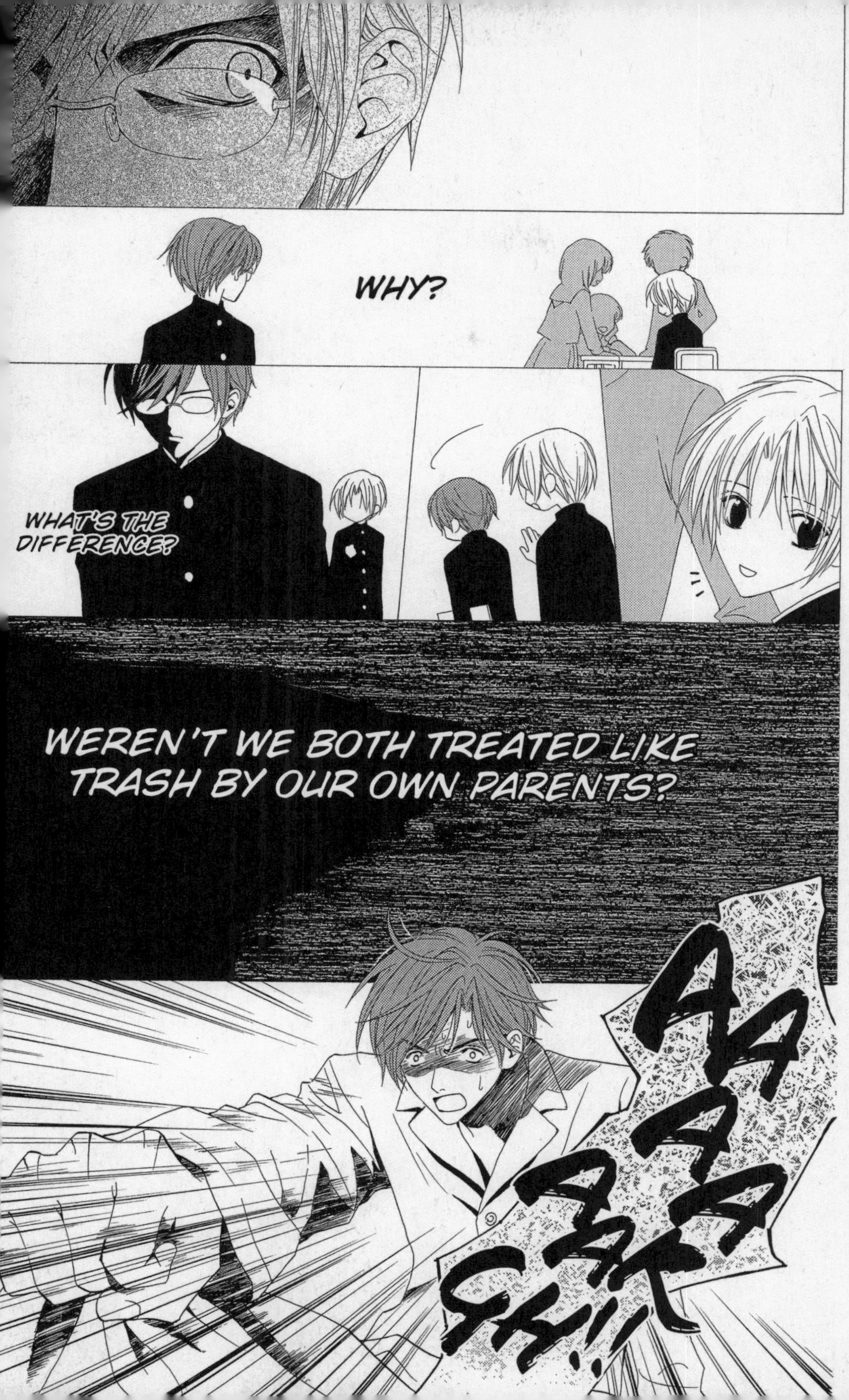
WHY?
WHAT'S THE DIFFERENCE?
WEREN'T WE BOTH TREATED LIKE TRASH BY OUR OWN PARENTS?
AAAAAAH!!

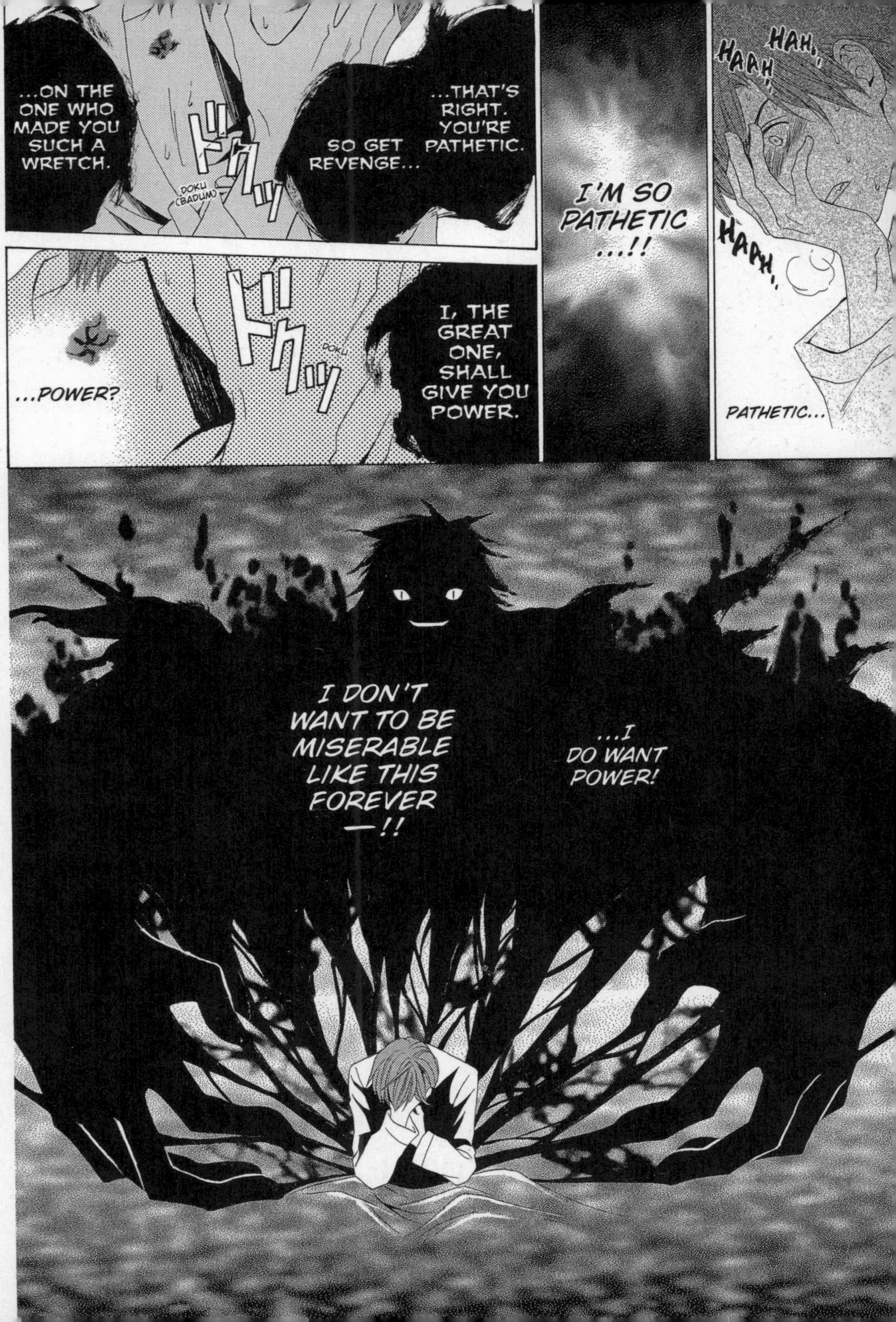

HAH, HAAH,
HAAH..
PATHETIC...
I'M SO PATHETIC ...!!
...THAT'S RIGHT. YOU'RE PATHETIC.
SO GET REVENGE...
...ON THE ONE WHO MADE YOU SUCH A WRETCH.
DOKU (BADUM)
I, THE GREAT ONE, SHALL GIVE YOU POWER.
DOKU
...POWER?
...I DO WANT POWER!
I DON'T WANT TO BE MISERABLE LIKE THIS FOREVER—!!

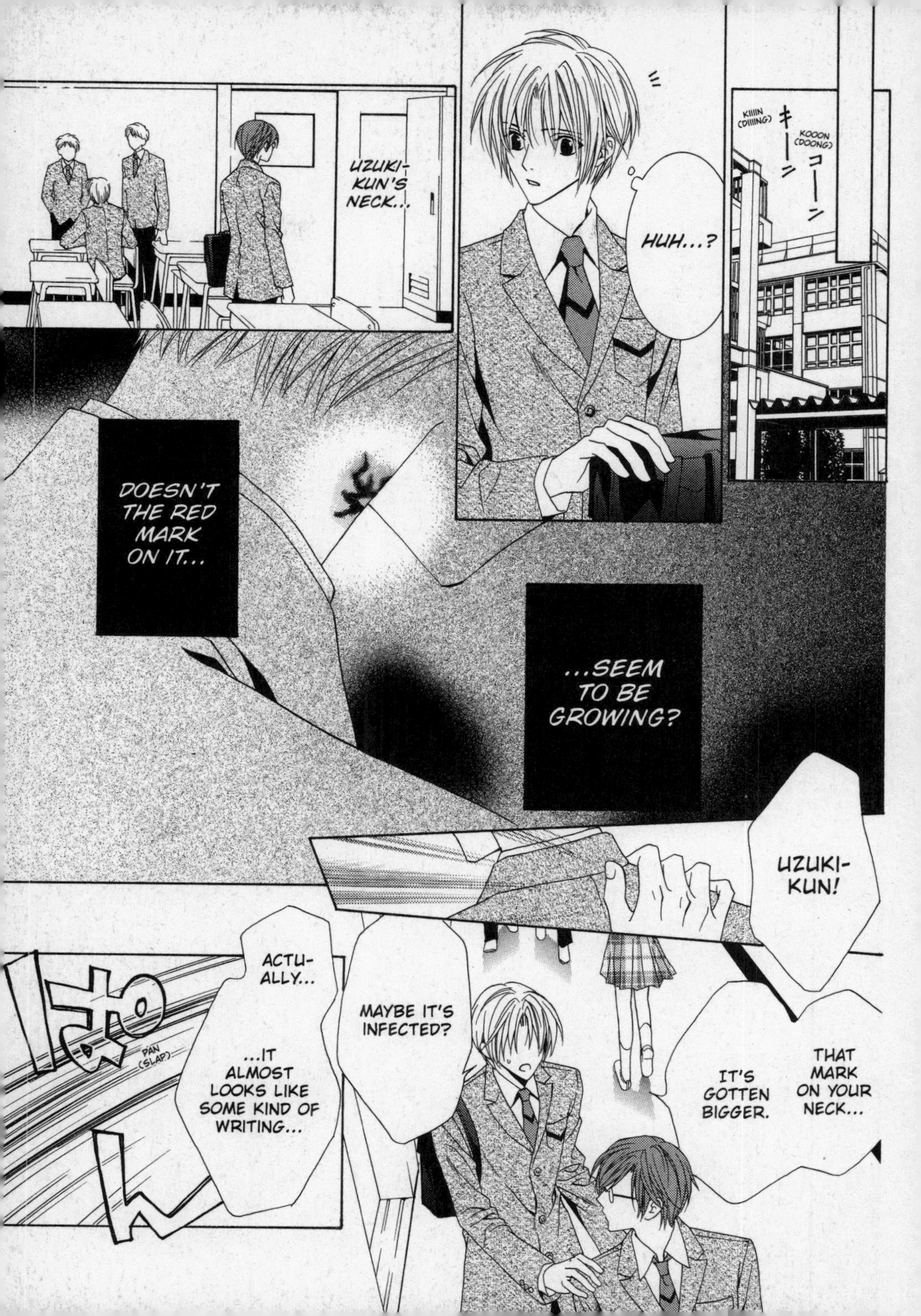

キーン
KIIIN (DIIIING)
コーン
KOOON (DOONG)
HUH...?
UZUKI-KUN'S NECK...
DOESN'T THE RED MARK ON IT...
...SEEM TO BE GROWING?
UZUKI-KUN!
THAT MARK ON YOUR NECK...
IT'S GOTTEN BIGGER.
MAYBE IT'S INFECTED?
ACTU-ALLY...
...IT ALMOST LOOKS LIKE SOME KIND OF WRITING...
ぱん
PAN (SLAP)

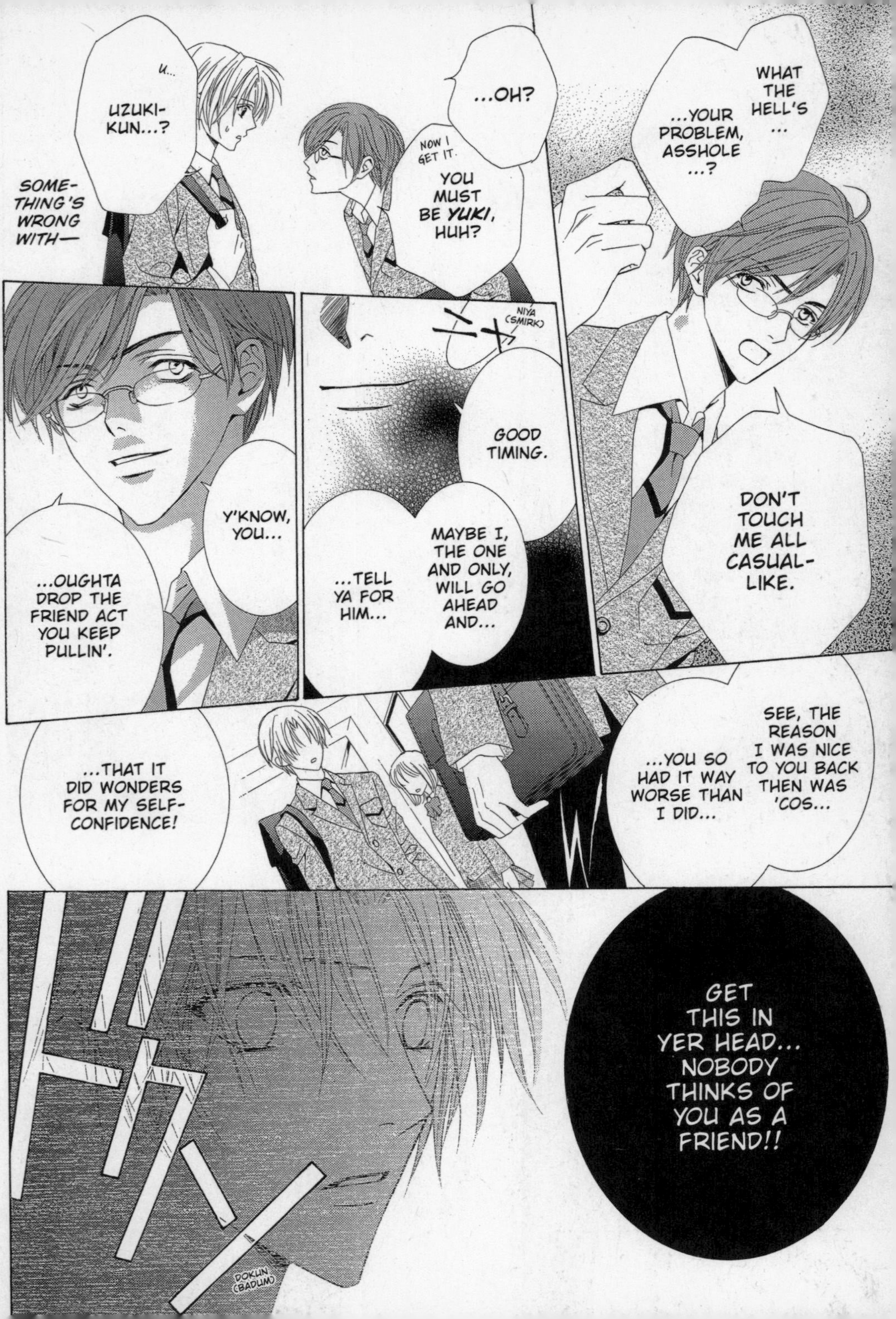

WHAT THE HELL'S ...
...YOUR PROBLEM, ASSHOLE ...?
DON'T TOUCH ME ALL CASUAL-LIKE.
U...
UZUKI-KUN...?
SOME-THING'S WRONG WITH—
...OH?
NOW I GET IT.
YOU MUST BE YUKI, HUH?
NIYA (SMIRK)
GOOD TIMING.
MAYBE I, THE ONE AND ONLY, WILL GO AHEAD AND...
...TELL YA FOR HIM...
Y'KNOW, YOU...
...OUGHTA DROP THE FRIEND ACT YOU KEEP PULLIN'.
SEE, THE REASON I WAS NICE TO YOU BACK THEN WAS 'COS...
...YOU SO HAD IT WAY WORSE THAN I DID...
...THAT IT DID WONDERS FOR MY SELF-CONFIDENCE!
GET THIS IN YER HEAD... NOBODY THINKS OF YOU AS A FRIEND!!
DOKUN (BADUM)

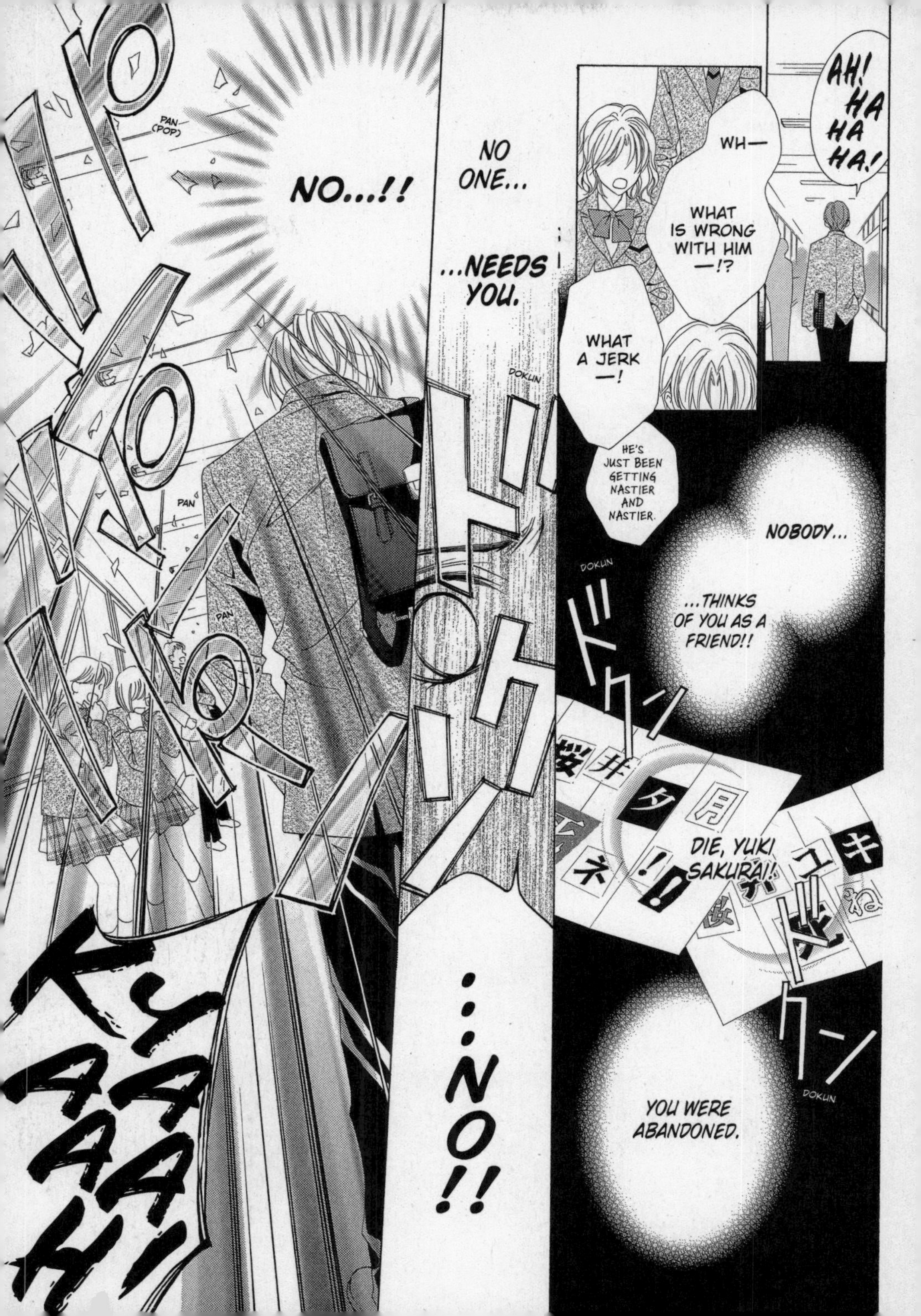
AH! HA HA HA HA!
WH—
WHAT IS WRONG WITH HIM—!?
WHAT A JERK—!
HE'S JUST BEEN GETTING NASTIER AND NASTIER.
NOBODY...
...THINKS OF YOU AS A FRIEND!!
DOKUN
DIE, YUKI SAKURAI!!
YOU WERE ABANDONED.
DOKUN
NO ONE...
...NEEDS YOU.
DOKUN
...NO!!
NO...!!
PAN (POP)
PAN
PAN
KYAAAAAAH!

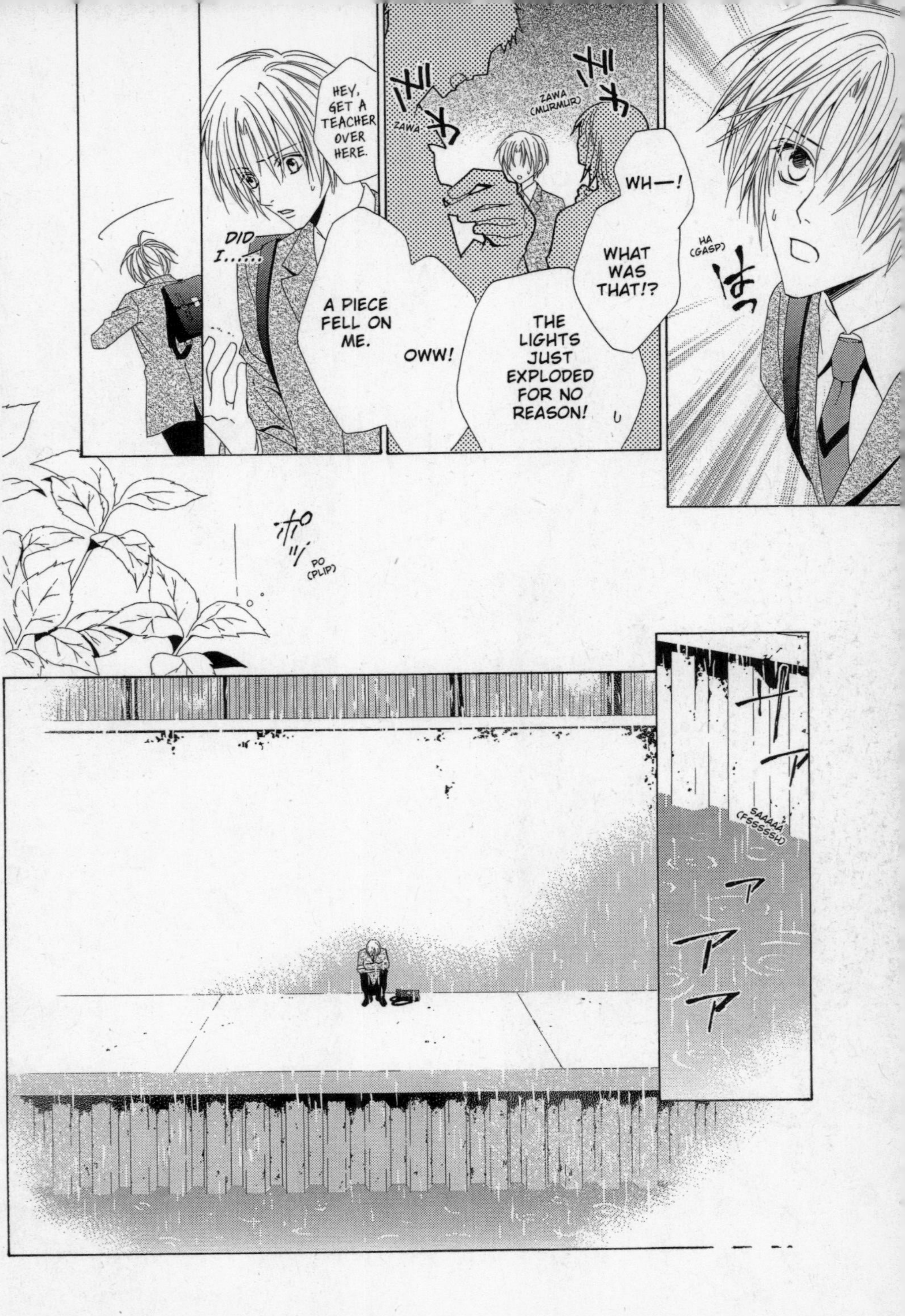
HA
(GASP)
WH—!
WHAT WAS THAT!?
ZAWA
(MURMUR)
ZAWA
THE LIGHTS JUST EXPLODED FOR NO REASON!
OWW!
A PIECE FELL ON ME.
HEY, GET A TEACHER OVER HERE.
DID I......
PO
(PLIP)
SAAAAA
(FSSSSSH)

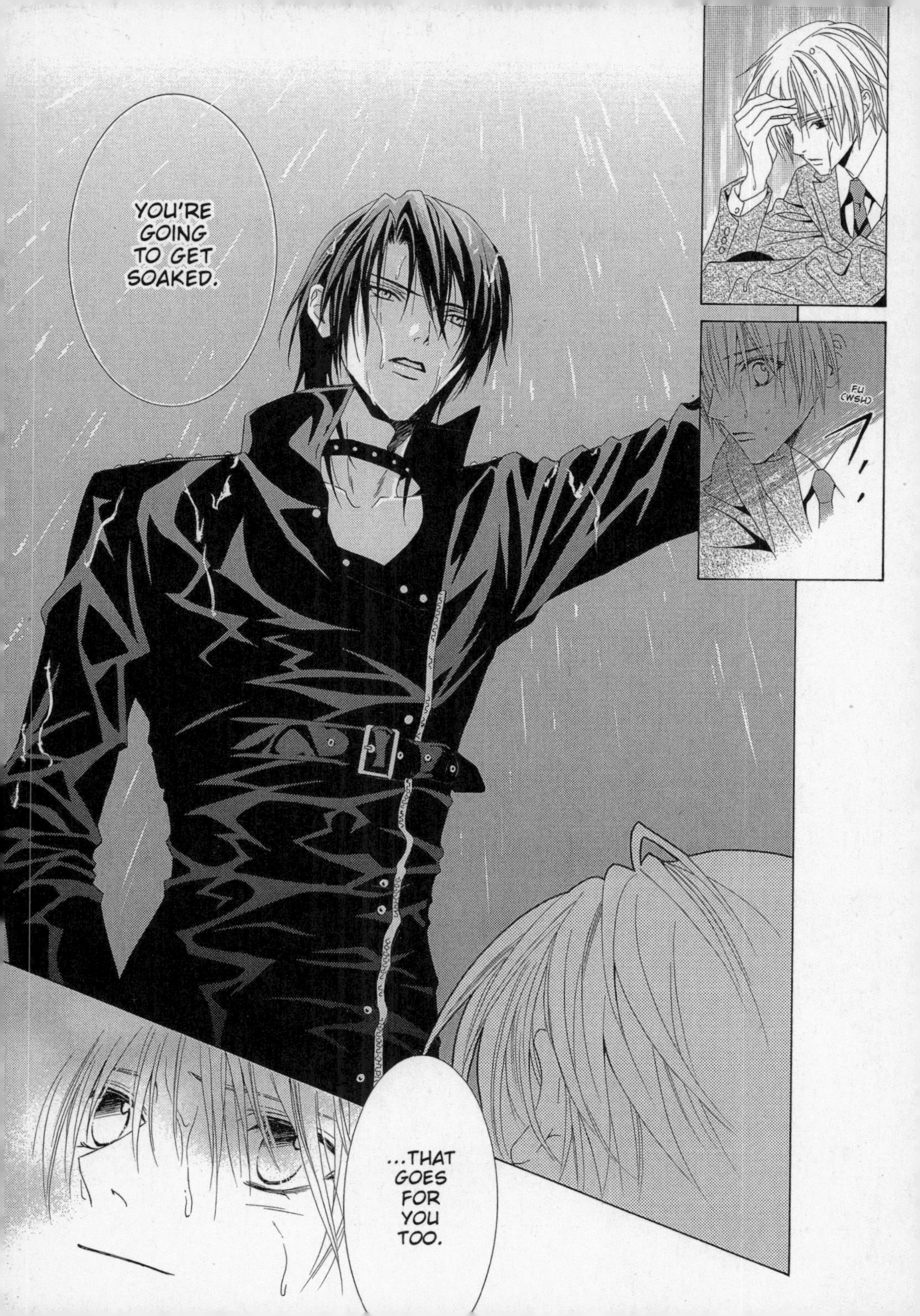
FU (WSH)
YOU'RE GOING TO GET SOAKED.
...THAT GOES FOR YOU TOO.

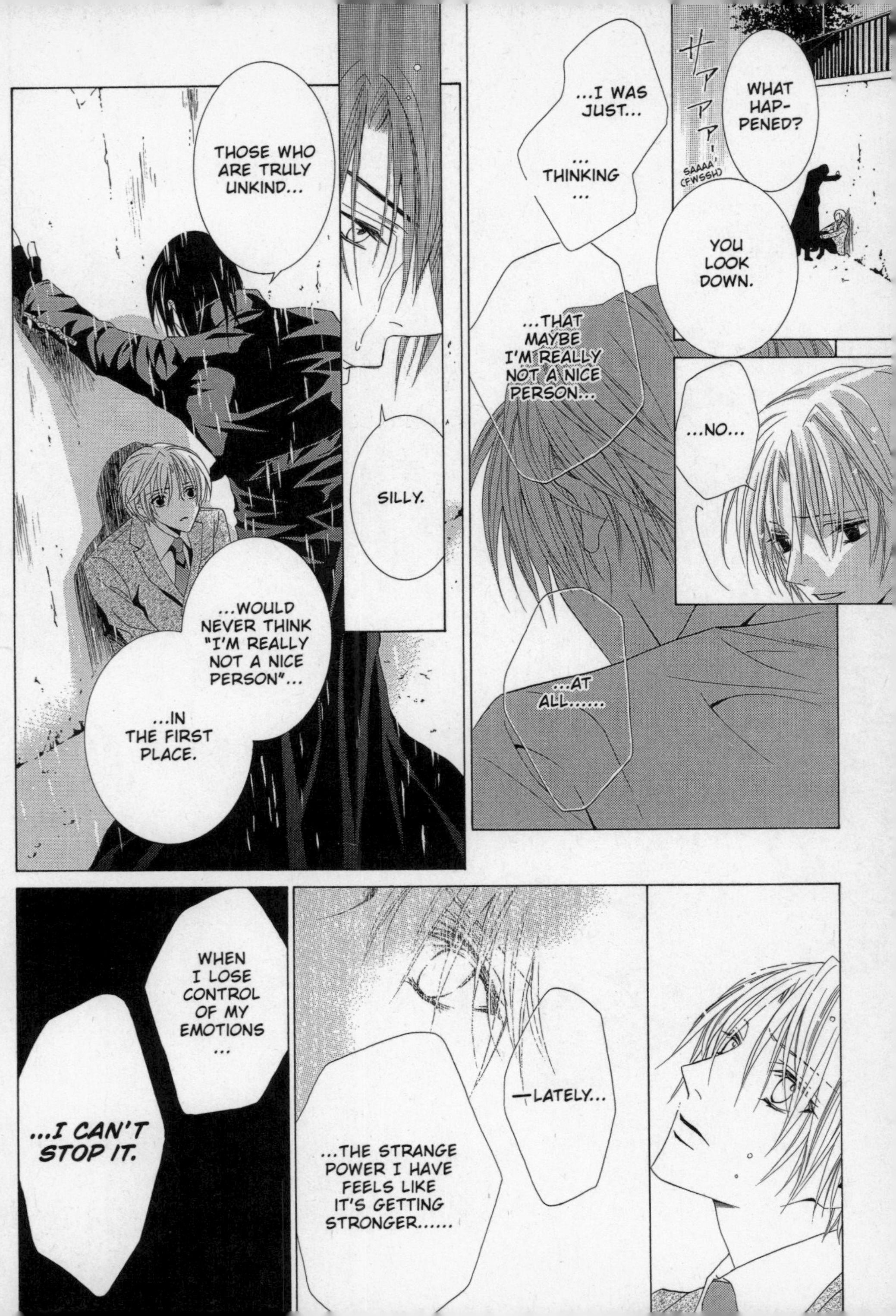
WHAT HAP-PENED?
SAAAA (FWSSH)
YOU LOOK DOWN.
...NO...
...I WAS JUST...
... THINKING ...
...THAT MAYBE I'M REALLY NOT A NICE PERSON...
...AT ALL......
SILLY.
THOSE WHO ARE TRULY UNKIND...
...WOULD NEVER THINK "I'M REALLY NOT A NICE PERSON"...
...IN THE FIRST PLACE.
—LATELY...
...THE STRANGE POWER I HAVE FEELS LIKE IT'S GETTING STRONGER......
WHEN I LOSE CONTROL OF MY EMOTIONS ...
...I CAN'T STOP IT.

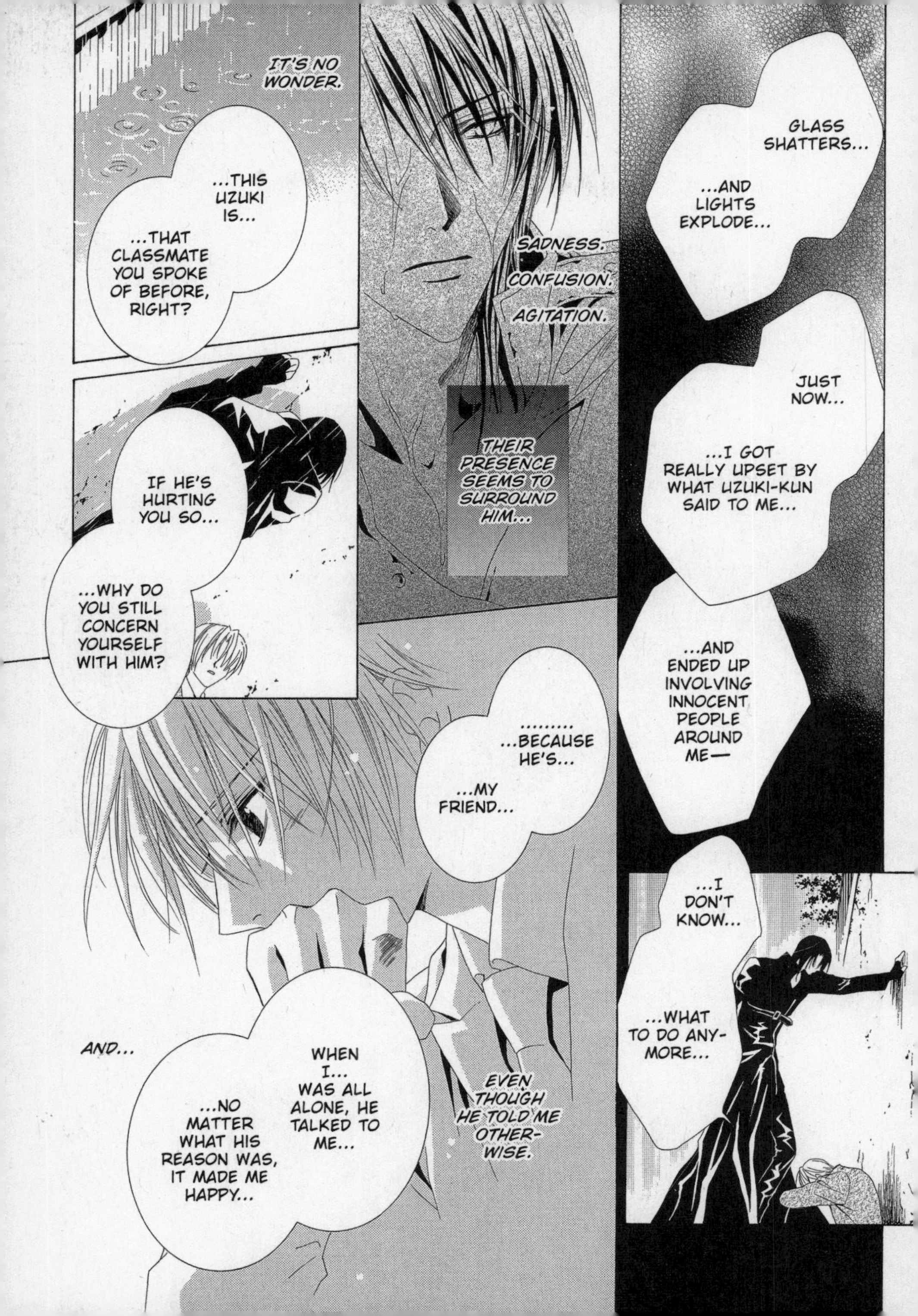
GLASS SHATTERS...
...AND LIGHTS EXPLODE...
JUST NOW...
...I GOT REALLY UPSET BY WHAT UZUKI-KUN SAID TO ME...
...AND ENDED UP INVOLVING INNOCENT PEOPLE AROUND ME—
...I DON'T KNOW...
...WHAT TO DO ANY-MORE...
SADNESS.
CONFUSION.
AGITATION.
THEIR PRESENCE SEEMS TO SURROUND HIM...
IT'S NO WONDER.
...THIS UZUKI IS...
...THAT CLASSMATE YOU SPOKE OF BEFORE, RIGHT?
IF HE'S HURTING YOU SO...
...WHY DO YOU STILL CONCERN YOURSELF WITH HIM?
....
...BECAUSE HE'S...
...MY FRIEND...
EVEN THOUGH HE TOLD ME OTHER-WISE.
WHEN I... WAS ALL ALONE, HE TALKED TO ME...
...NO MATTER WHAT HIS REASON WAS, IT MADE ME HAPPY...
AND...

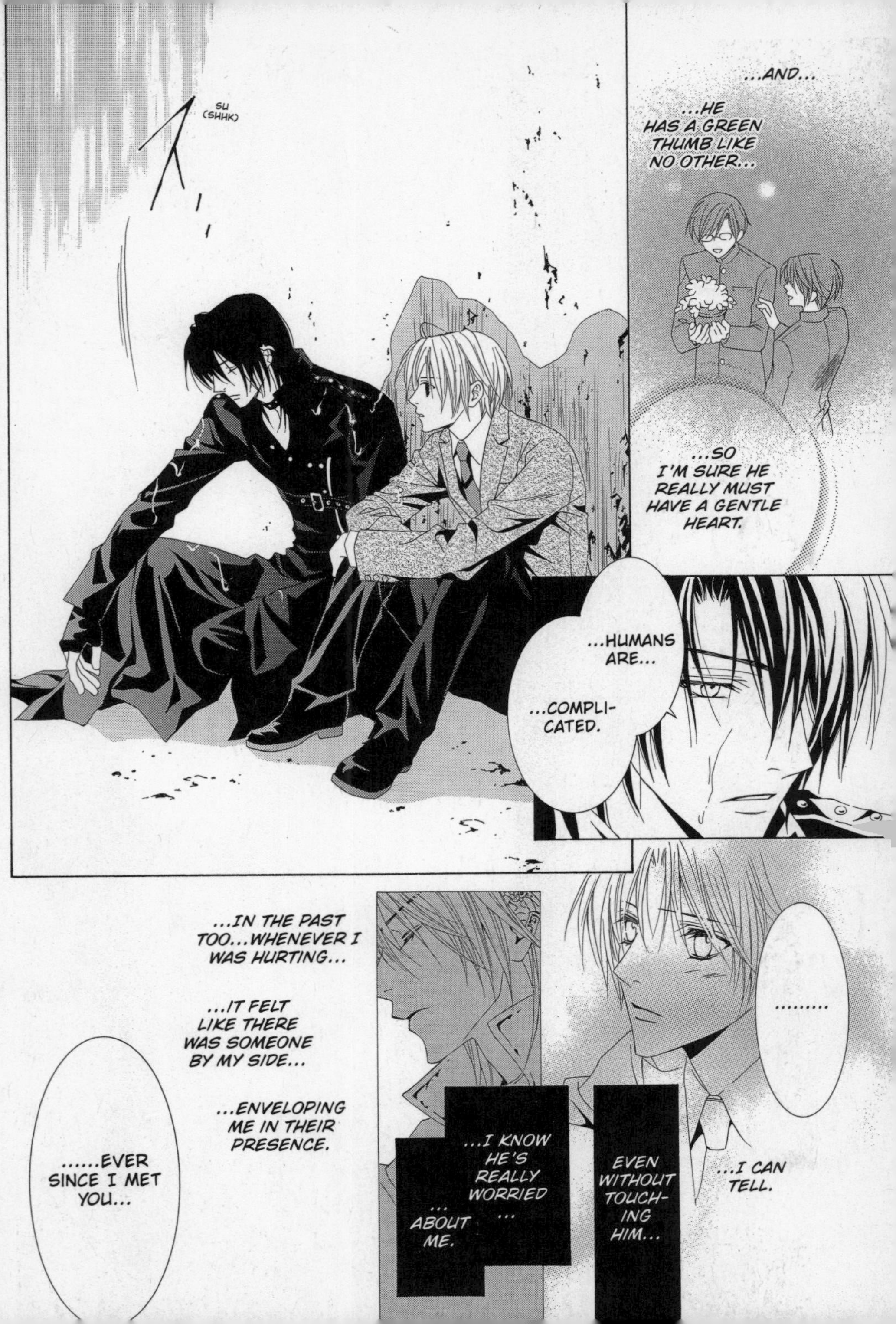

...AND...
...HE HAS A GREEN THUMB LIKE NO OTHER...
...SO I'M SURE HE REALLY MUST HAVE A GENTLE HEART.
SU (SHHK)
...HUMANS ARE...
...COMPLICATED.
....
...I CAN TELL.
EVEN WITHOUT TOUCHING HIM...
...I KNOW HE'S REALLY WORRIED...
...ABOUT ME.
...IN THE PAST TOO...WHENEVER I WAS HURTING...
...IT FELT LIKE THERE WAS SOMEONE BY MY SIDE...
...ENVELOPING ME IN THEIR PRESENCE.
......EVER SINCE I MET YOU...

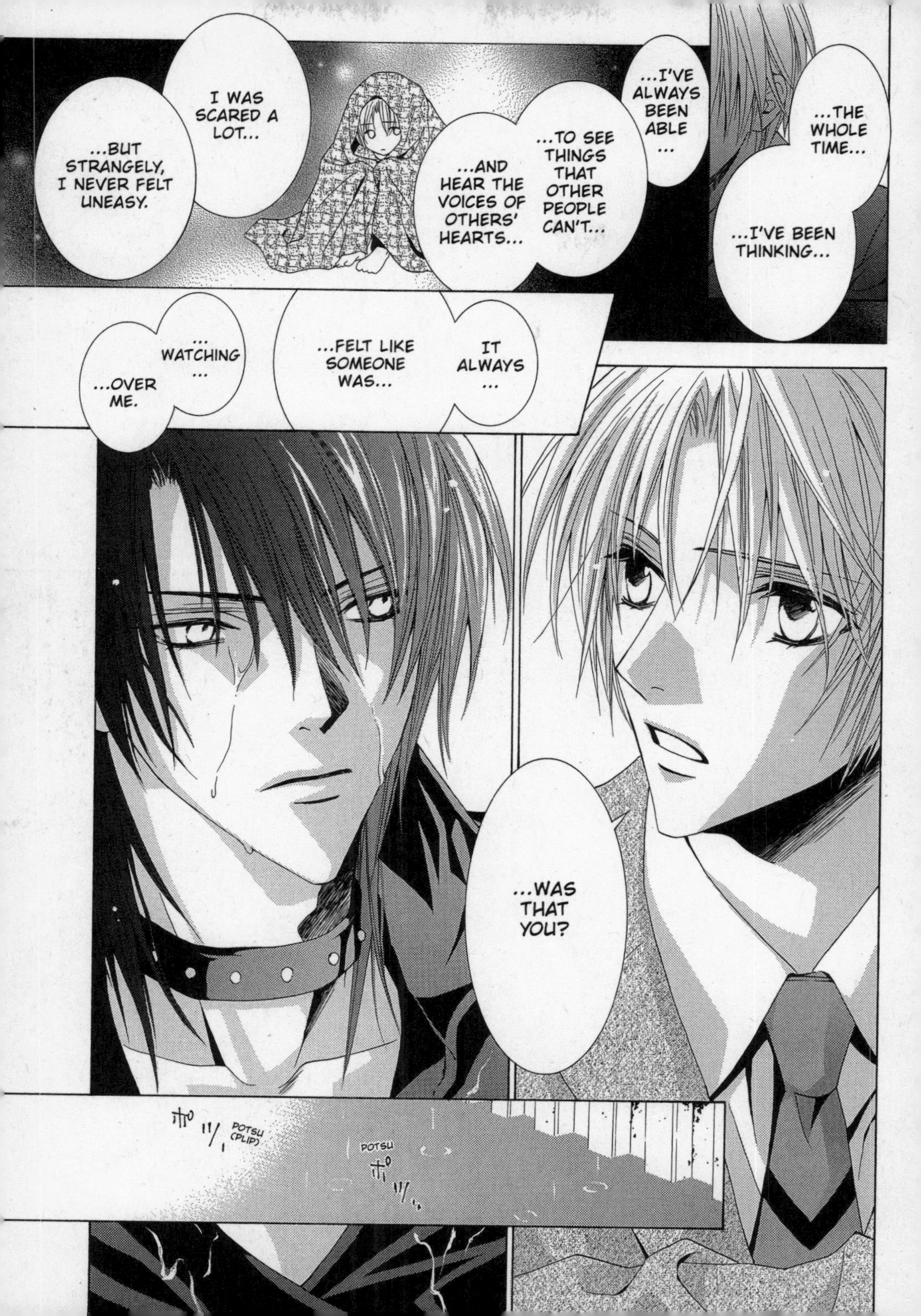
...THE WHOLE TIME...
...I'VE BEEN THINKING...
...I'VE ALWAYS BEEN ABLE...
...TO SEE THINGS THAT OTHER PEOPLE CAN'T...
...AND HEAR THE VOICES OF OTHERS' HEARTS...
I WAS SCARED A LOT...
...BUT STRANGELY, I NEVER FELT UNEASY.
IT ALWAYS...
...FELT LIKE SOMEONE WAS...
...WATCHING...
...OVER ME.
...WAS THAT YOU?
POTSU (PLIP)
POTSU

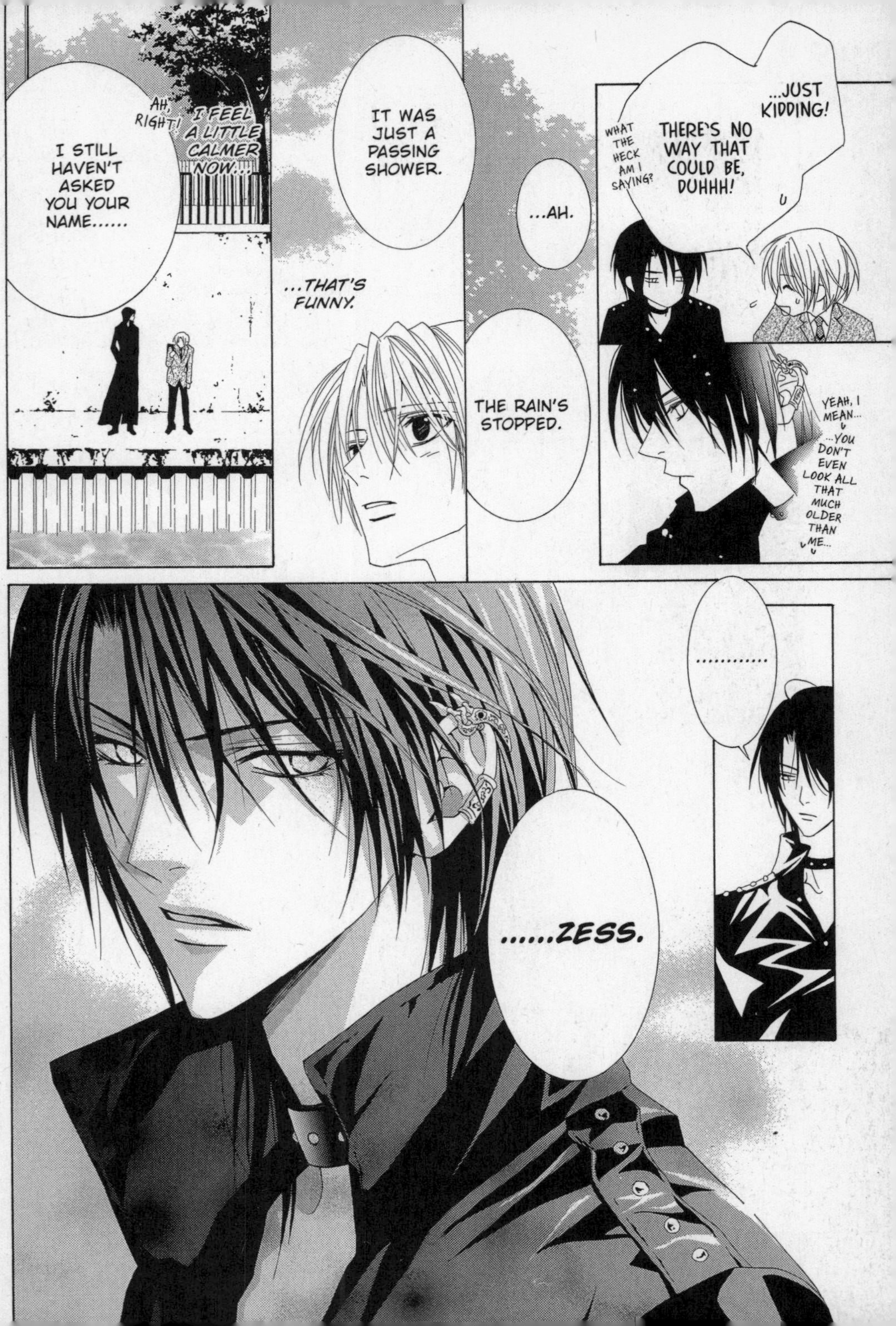
WHAT THE HECK AM I SAYING?
THERE'S NO WAY THAT COULD BE, DUHHH!
...JUST KIDDING!
YEAH, I MEAN... ...YOU DON'T EVEN LOOK ALL THAT MUCH OLDER THAN ME...
...AH.
THE RAIN'S STOPPED.
IT WAS JUST A PASSING SHOWER.
...THAT'S FUNNY.
AH, RIGHT!
I FEEL A LITTLE CALMER NOW...
I STILL HAVEN'T ASKED YOU YOUR NAME......
....
......ZESS.

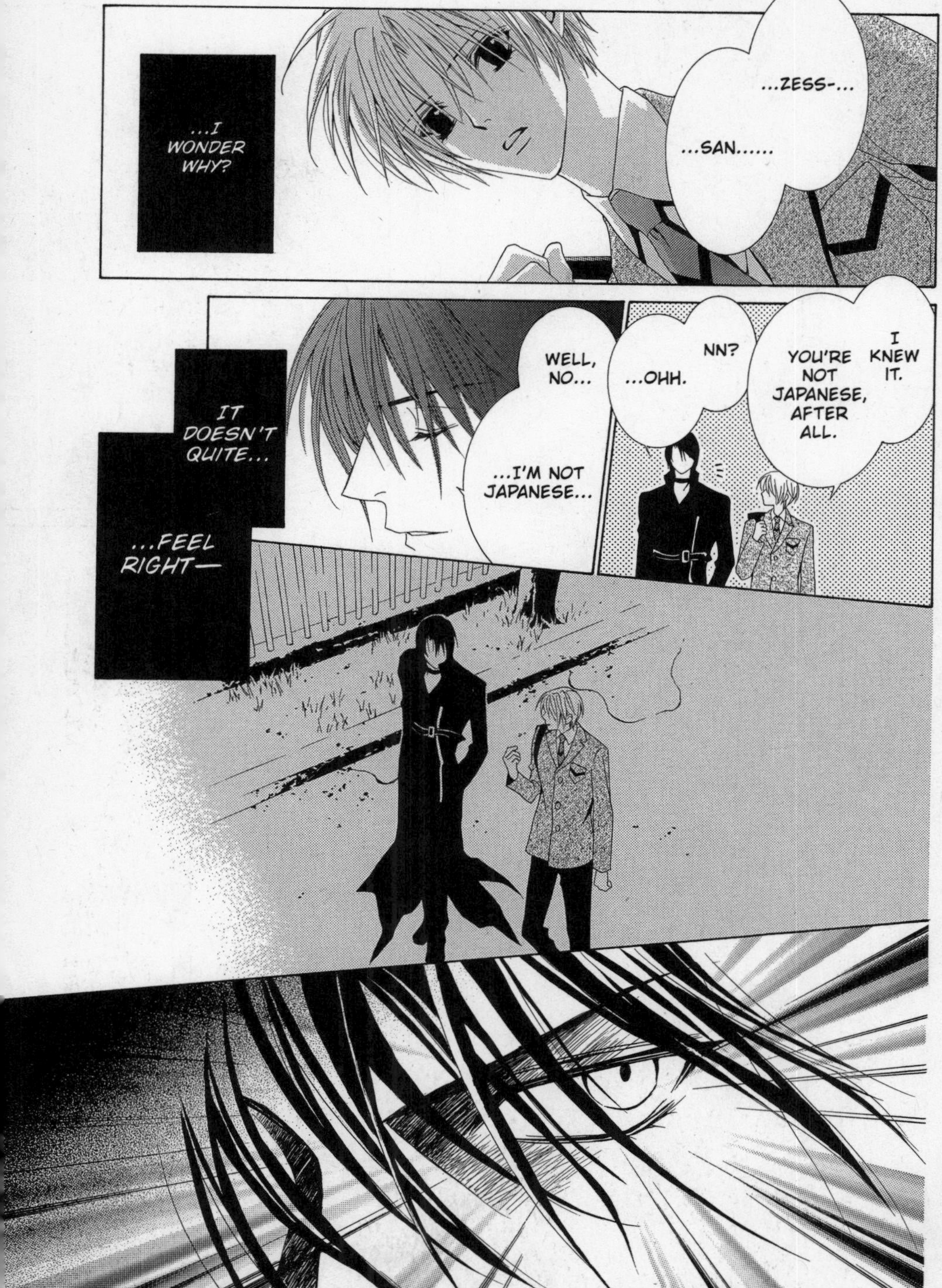
...ZESS-...
...SAN......
...I WONDER WHY?
I KNEW IT.
YOU'RE NOT JAPANESE, AFTER ALL.
NN?
...OHH.
WELL, NO...
...I'M NOT JAPANESE...
IT DOESN'T QUITE...
...FEEL RIGHT—

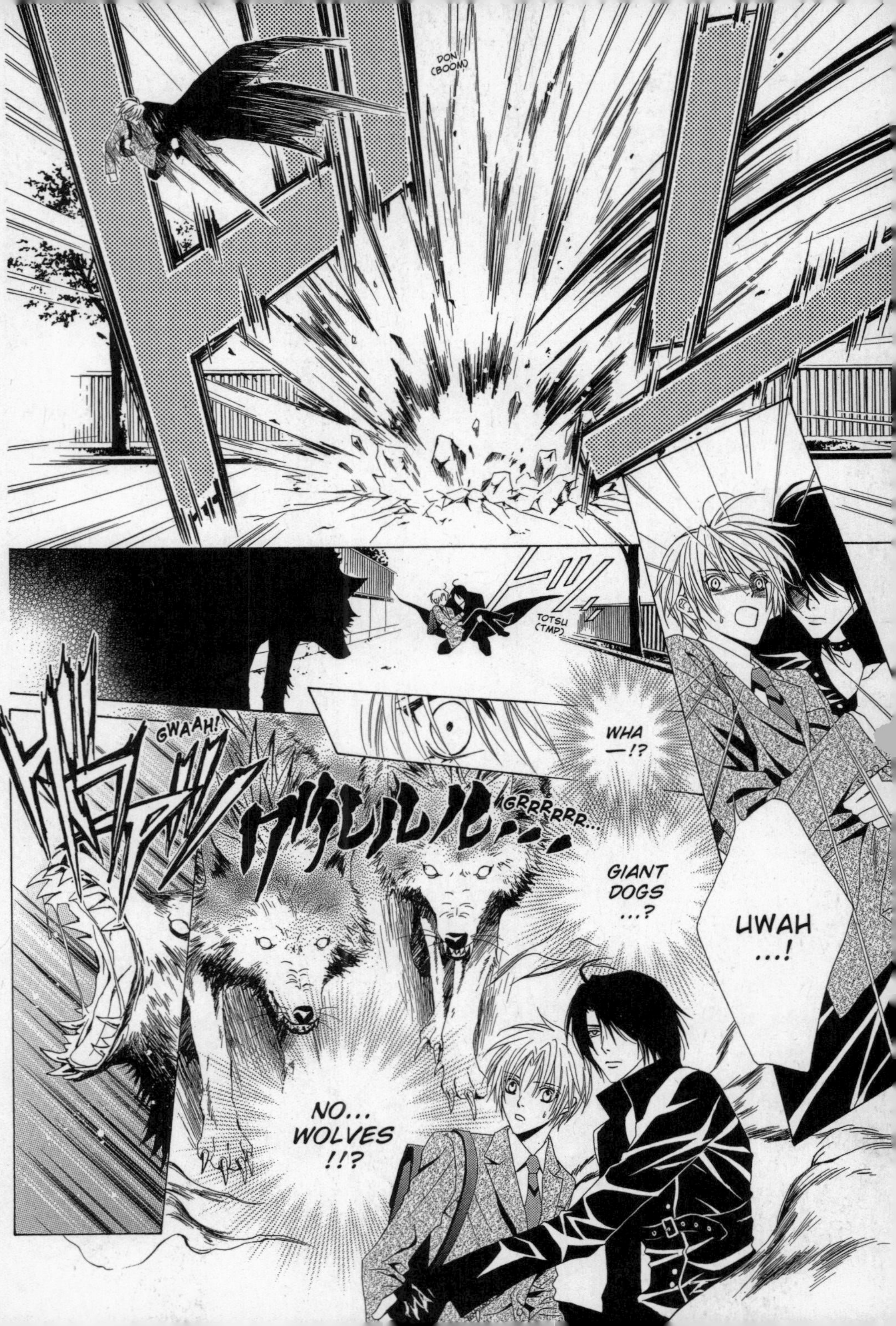
DON
(BOOM)
TOTSU
(TMP)
WHA —!?
UWAH ...!
GIANT DOGS ...?
GRRRRRR...
GWAAH!
NO... WOLVES !!?

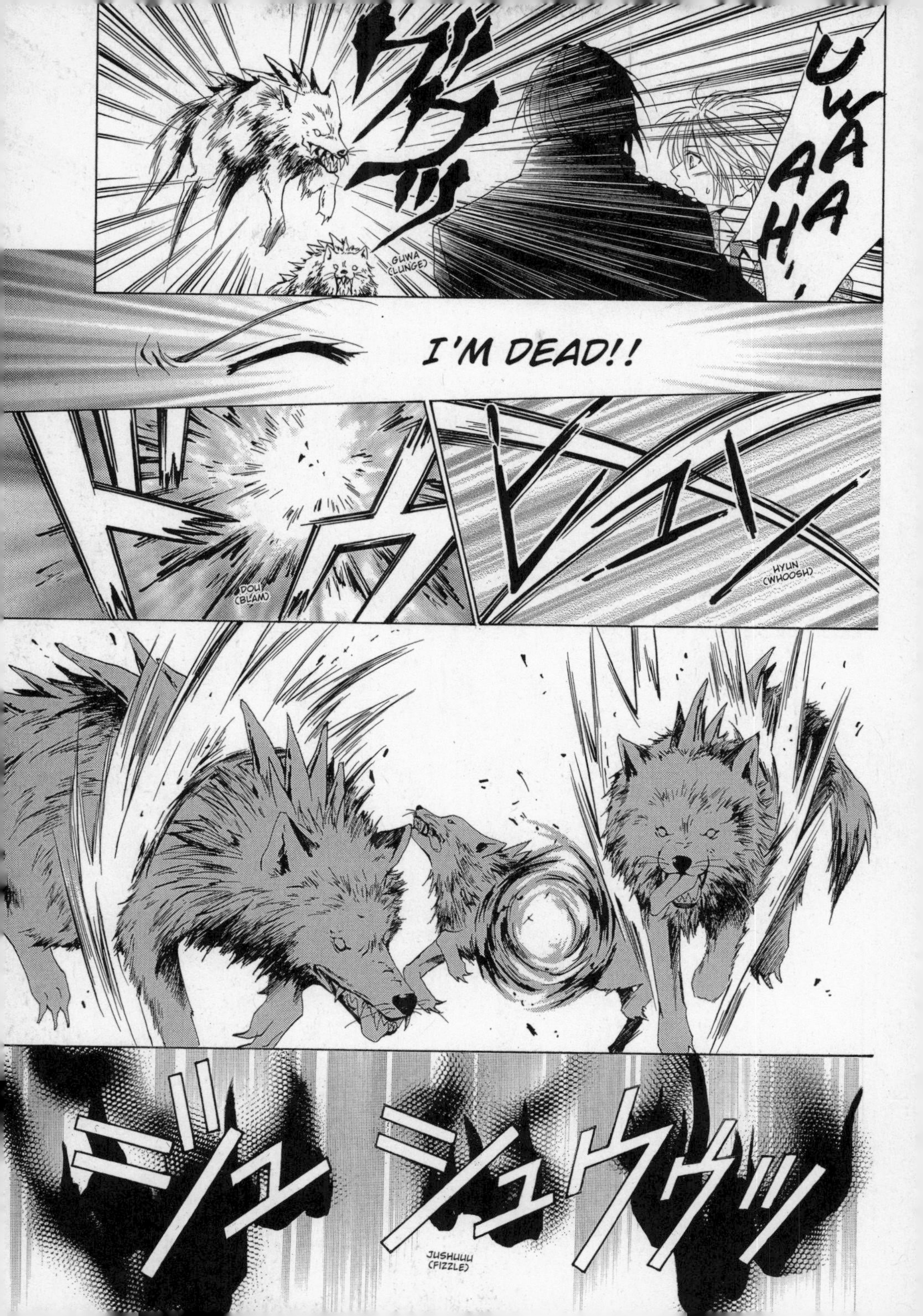
UWAAAAH...
GUWA (LUNGE)
I'M DEAD!!
HYUN (WHOOSH)
DOU (BLAM)
JUSHUUU (FIZZLE)

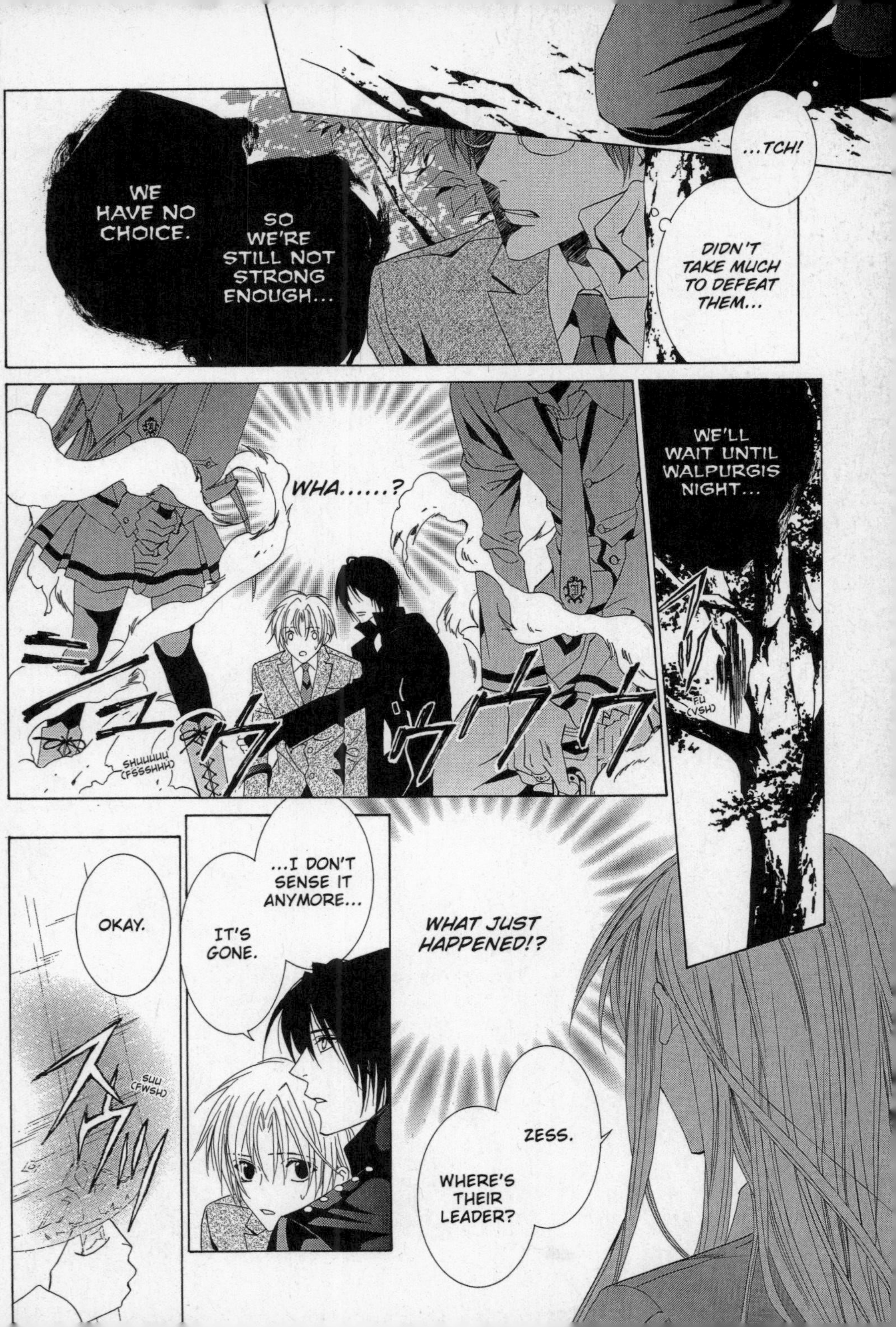
...TCH!
DIDN'T TAKE MUCH TO DEFEAT THEM...
SO WE'RE STILL NOT STRONG ENOUGH...
WE HAVE NO CHOICE.
WE'LL WAIT UNTIL WALPURGIS NIGHT...
FU (VSH)
WHA......?
SHUUUUU (FSSSHHH)
WHAT JUST HAPPENED!?
...I DON'T SENSE IT ANYMORE...
IT'S GONE.
OKAY.
SUU (FWSH)
ZESS.
WHERE'S THEIR LEADER?

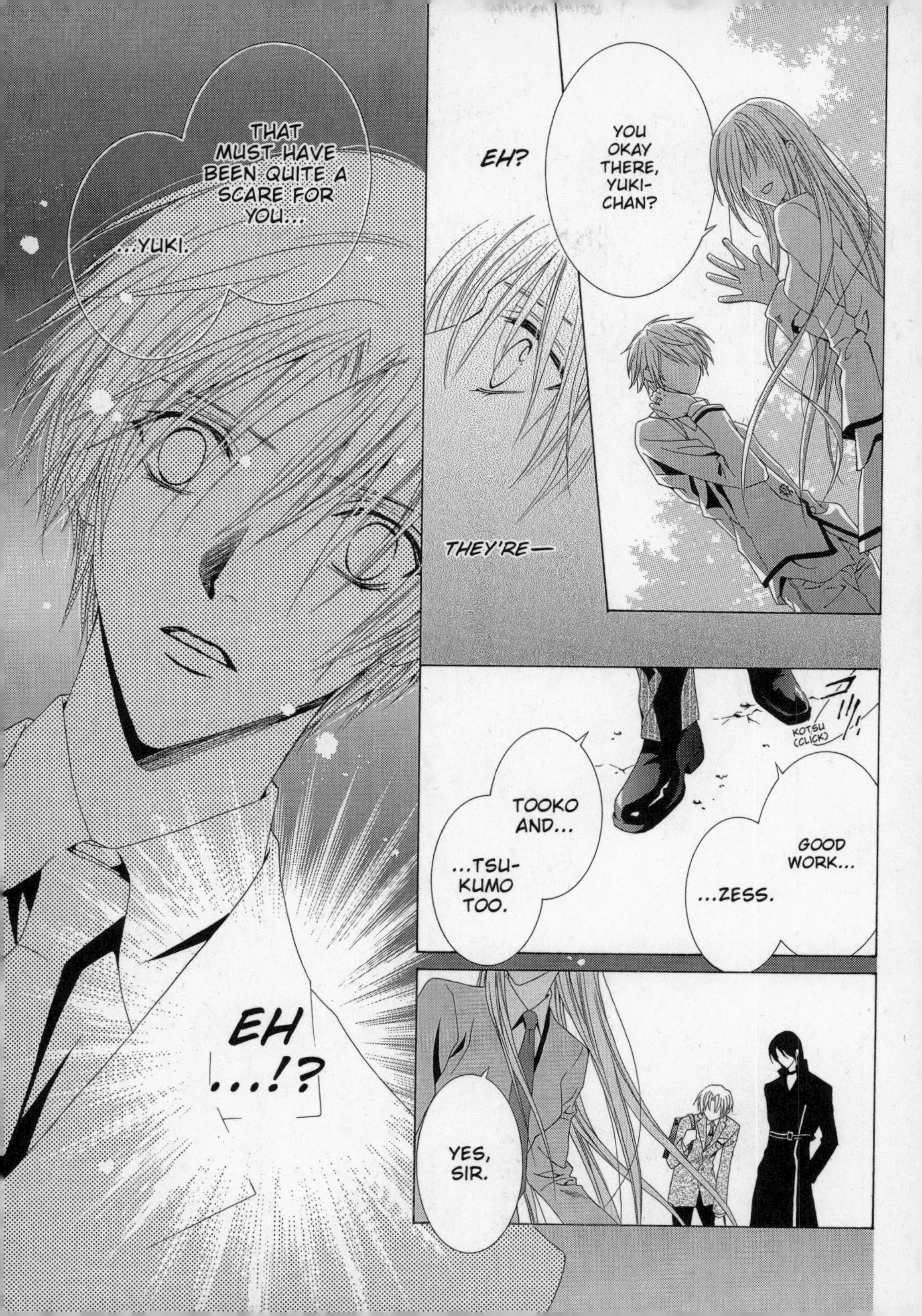
YOU OKAY THERE, YUKI-CHAN?
EH?
THEY'RE—
KOTSU (CLICK)
TOOKO AND...
...TSU-KUMO TOO.
GOOD WORK...
...ZESS.
YES, SIR.
THAT MUST HAVE BEEN QUITE A SCARE FOR YOU...
...YUKI.
EH ...!?

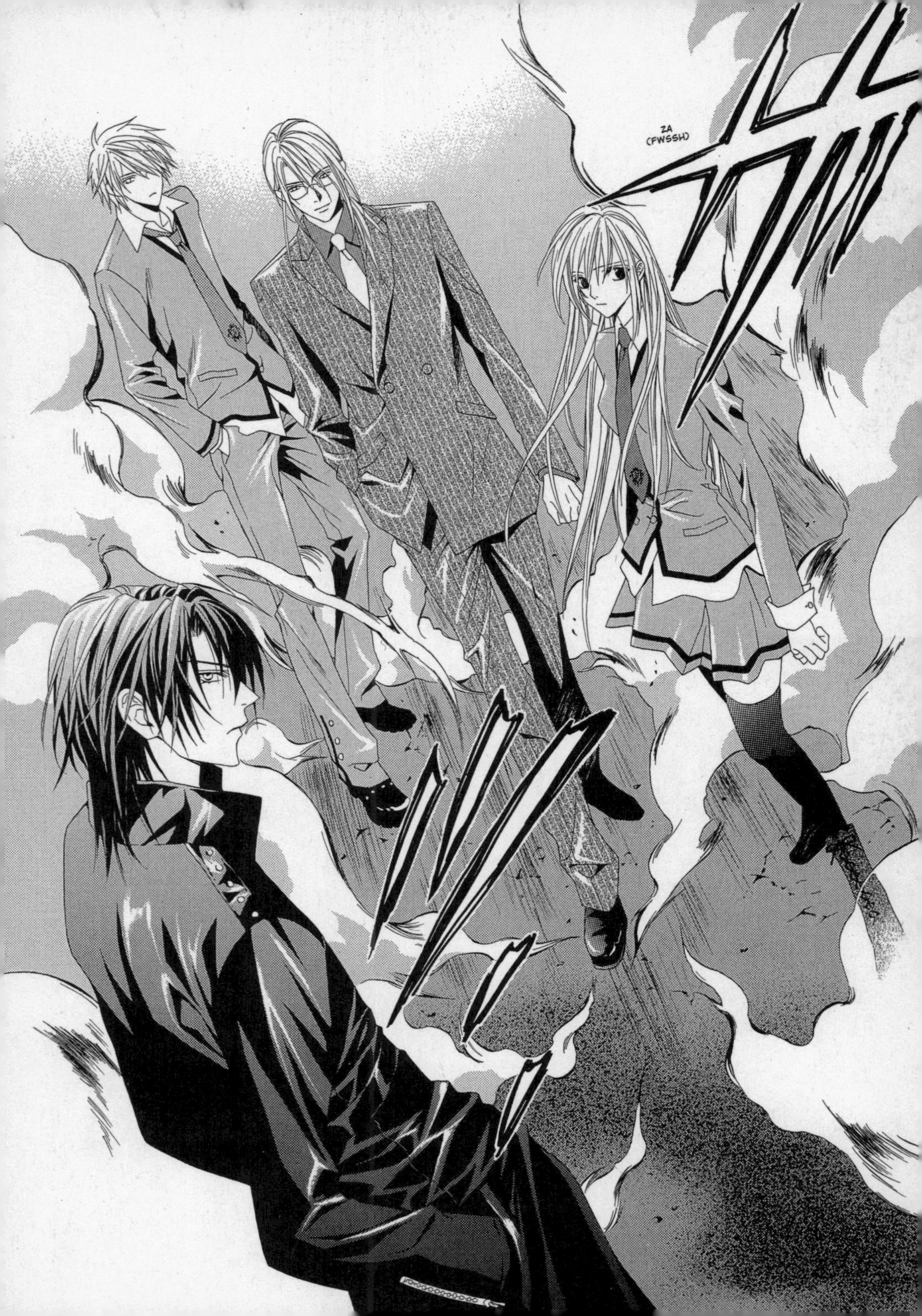
ZA
(FWSSH)

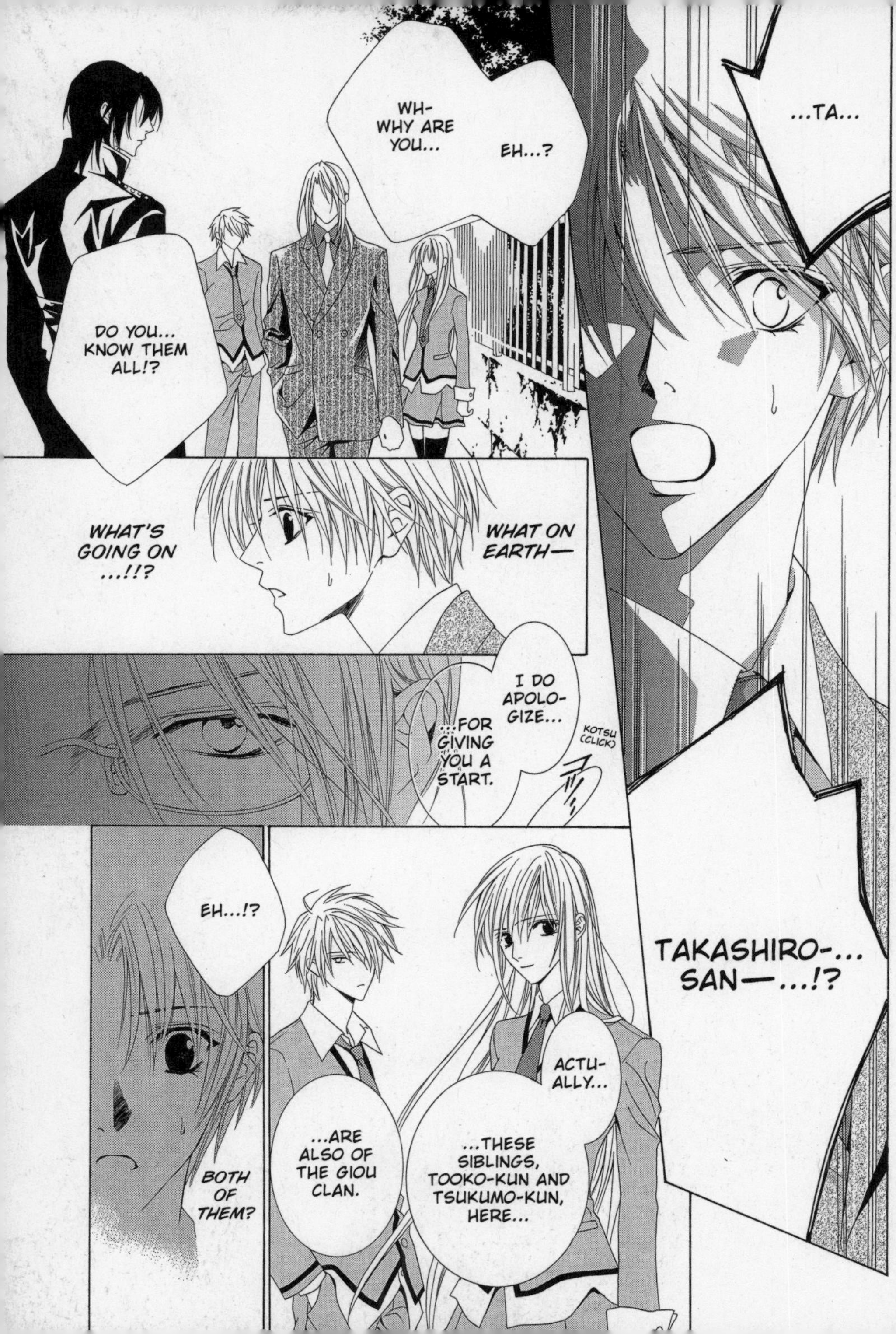
...TA...
TAKASHIRO-... SAN—...!?
EH...?
WH- WHY ARE YOU...
DO YOU... KNOW THEM ALL!?
WHAT ON EARTH—
WHAT'S GOING ON ...!!?
I DO APOLO-GIZE...
...FOR GIVING YOU A START.
KOTSU (CLICK)
ACTU-ALLY...
...THESE SIBLINGS, TOOKO-KUN AND TSUKUMO-KUN, HERE...
...ARE ALSO OF THE GIOU CLAN.
EH...!?
BOTH OF THEM?

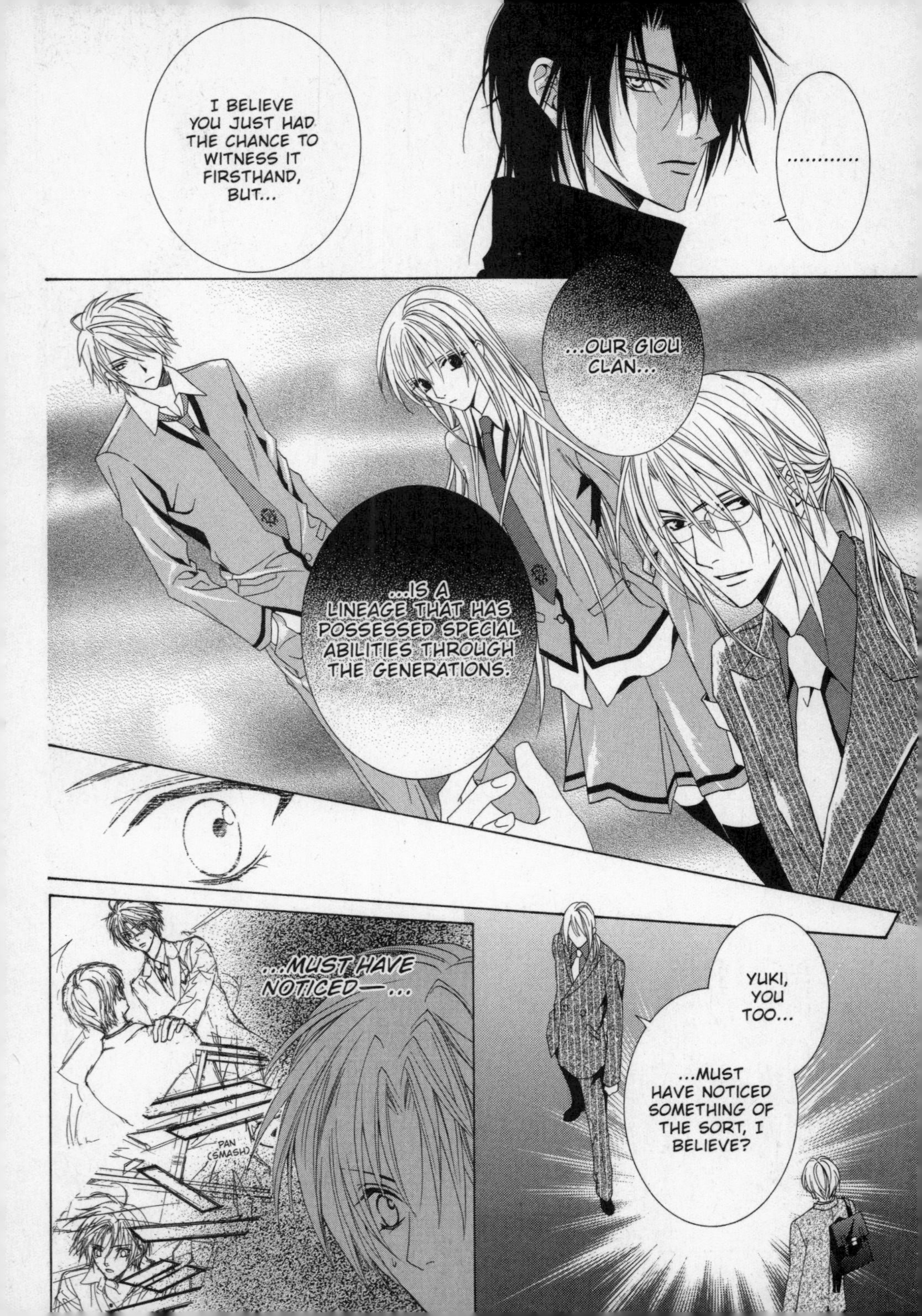
....
I BELIEVE YOU JUST HAD THE CHANCE TO WITNESS IT FIRSTHAND, BUT...
...OUR GIOU CLAN...
...IS A LINEAGE THAT HAS POSSESSED SPECIAL ABILITIES THROUGH THE GENERATIONS.
YUKI, YOU TOO...
...MUST HAVE NOTICED SOMETHING OF THE SORT, I BELIEVE?
...MUST HAVE NOTICED— ...
PAN (SMASH)

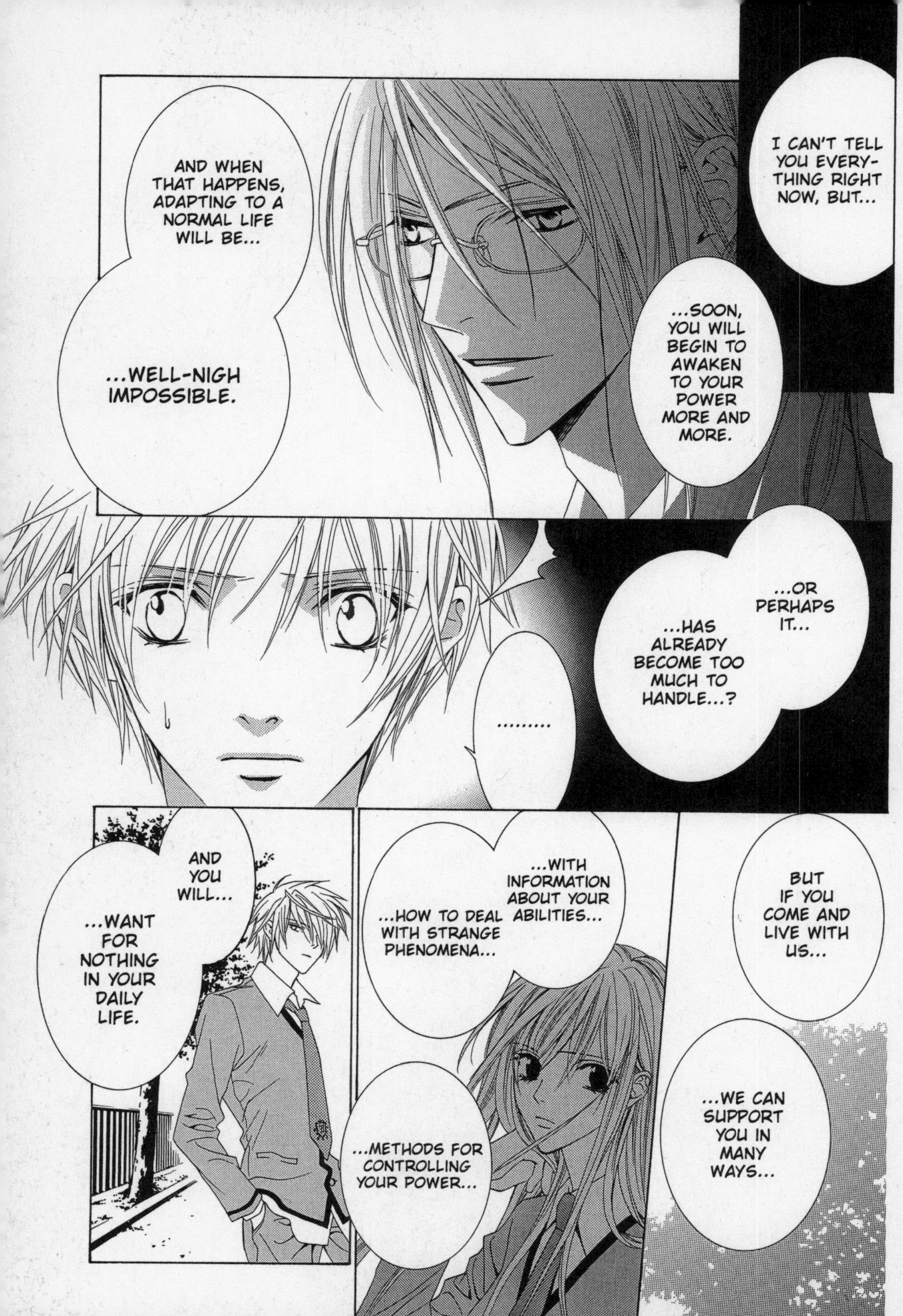
I CAN'T TELL YOU EVERY-THING RIGHT NOW, BUT...
...SOON, YOU WILL BEGIN TO AWAKEN TO YOUR POWER MORE AND MORE.
AND WHEN THAT HAPPENS, ADAPTING TO A NORMAL LIFE WILL BE...
...WELL-NIGH IMPOSSIBLE.
...OR PERHAPS IT...
...HAS ALREADY BECOME TOO MUCH TO HANDLE...?
....
BUT IF YOU COME AND LIVE WITH US...
...WE CAN SUPPORT YOU IN MANY WAYS...
...WITH INFORMATION ABOUT YOUR ABILITIES...
...HOW TO DEAL WITH STRANGE PHENOMENA...
...METHODS FOR CONTROLLING YOUR POWER...
AND YOU WILL...
...WANT FOR NOTHING IN YOUR DAILY LIFE.

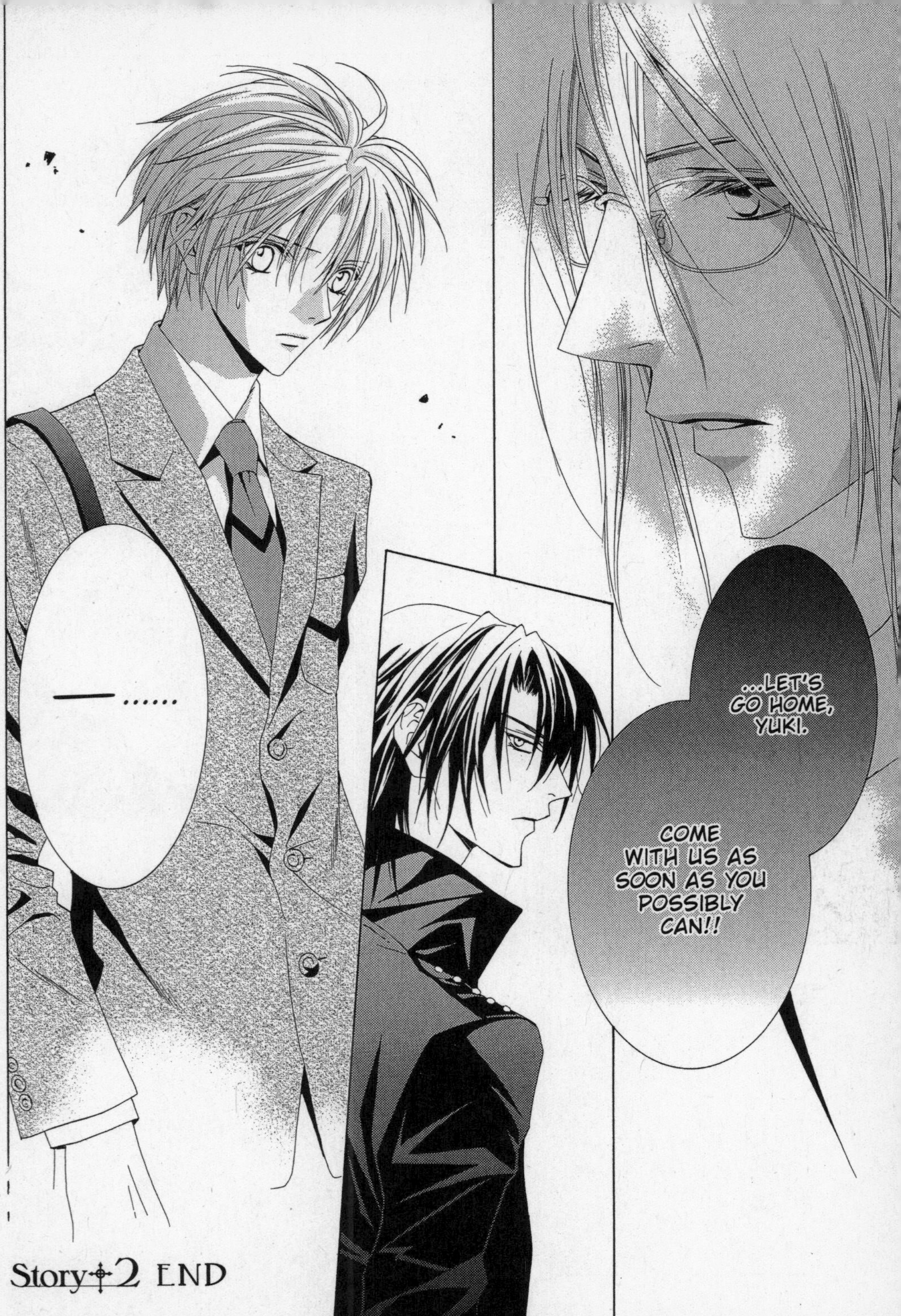
...LET'S GO HOME, YUKI.
COME WITH US AS SOON AS YOU POSSIBLY CAN!!
——......

Story 2 END

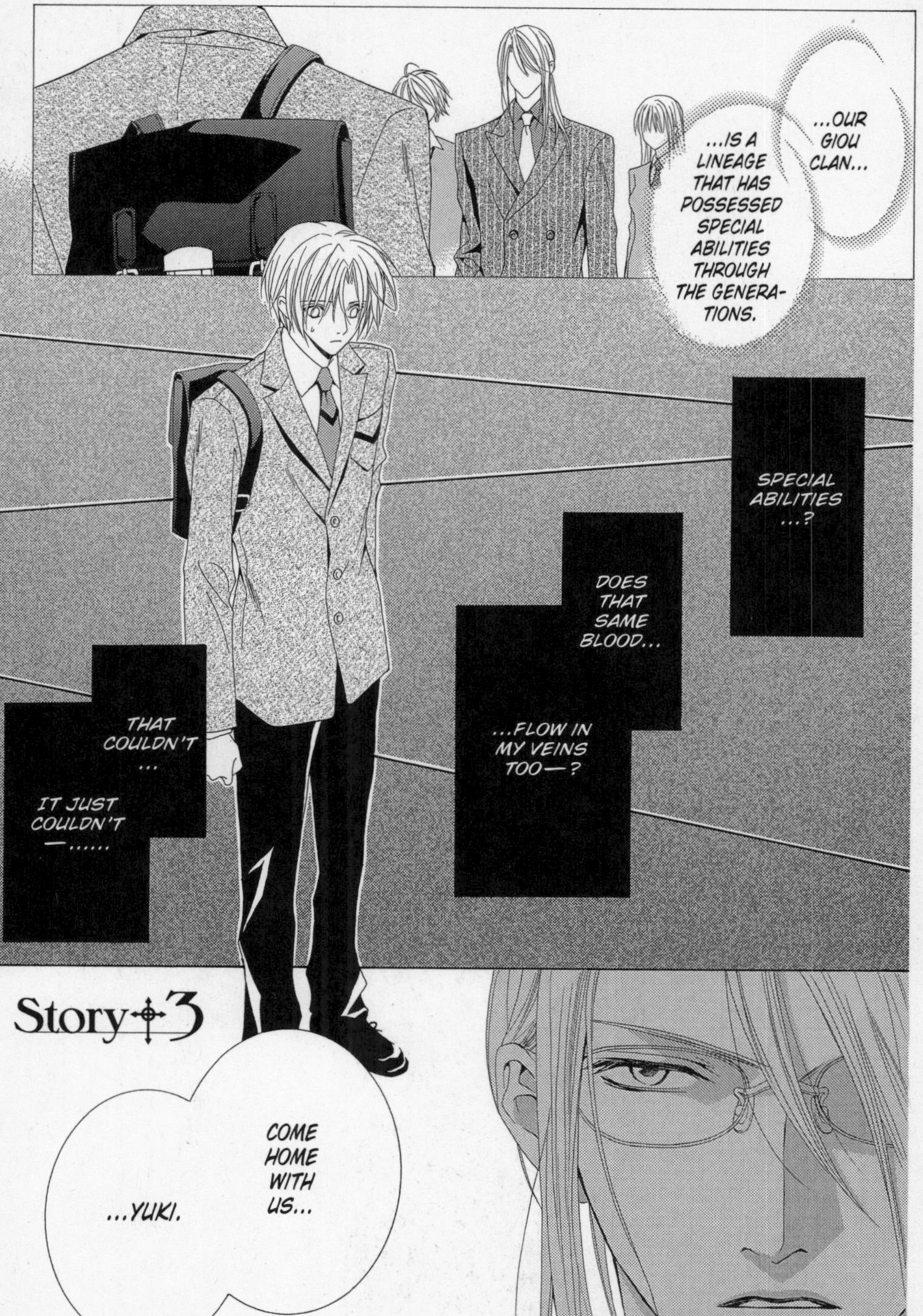
...OUR GIOU CLAN...
...IS A LINEAGE THAT HAS POSSESSED SPECIAL ABILITIES THROUGH THE GENERATIONS.
SPECIAL ABILITIES ...?
DOES THAT SAME BLOOD...
...FLOW IN MY VEINS TOO—?
THAT COULDN'T ...
IT JUST COULDN'T —......
Story 3
COME HOME WITH US...
...YUKI.

Story 3
WALPURGIS NIGHT

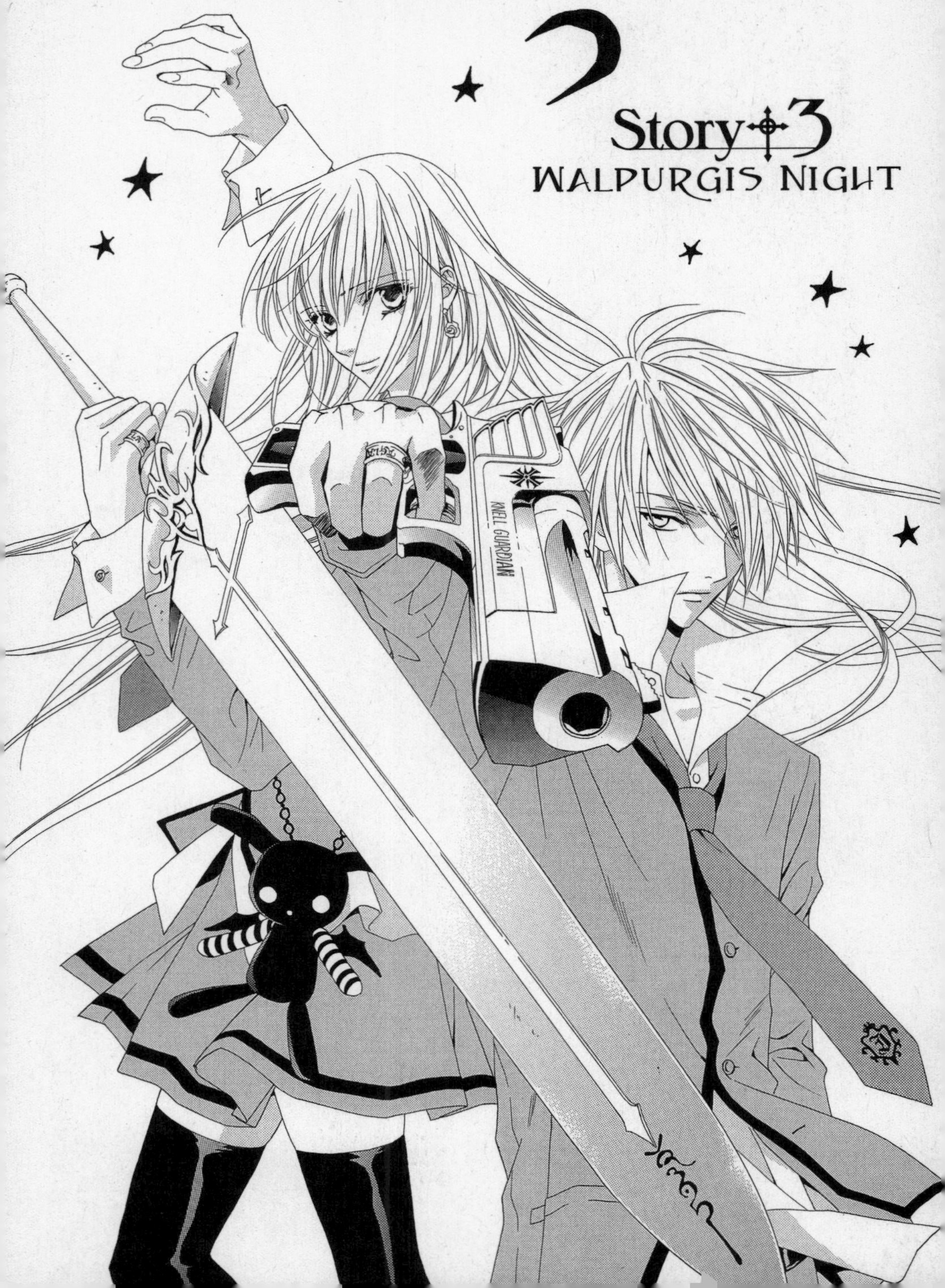
KNELL GUARDIAN

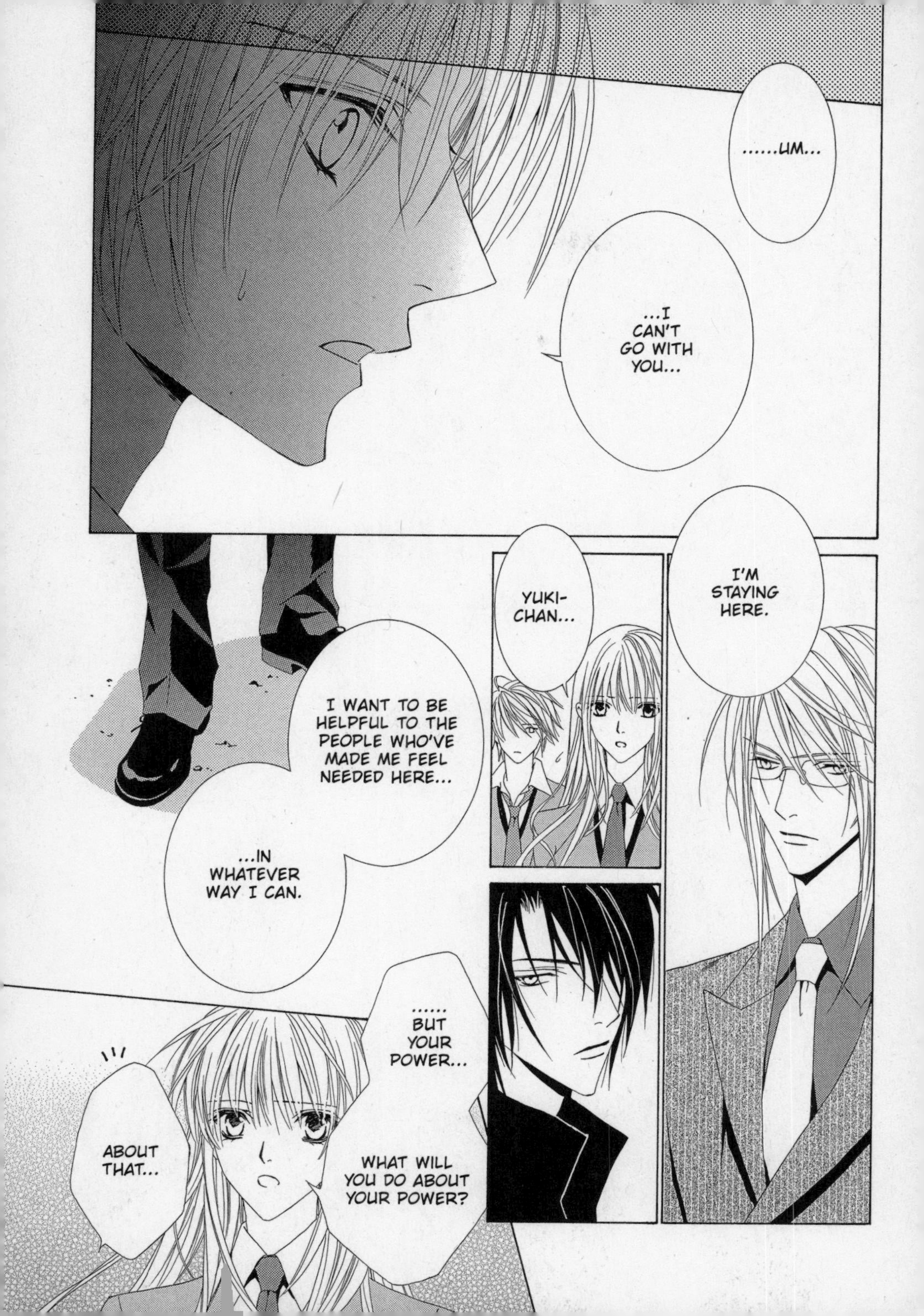

......UM...
...I CAN'T GO WITH YOU...
I'M STAYING HERE.
YUKI-CHAN...
I WANT TO BE HELPFUL TO THE PEOPLE WHO'VE MADE ME FEEL NEEDED HERE...
...IN WHATEVER WAY I CAN.
...... BUT YOUR POWER...
WHAT WILL YOU DO ABOUT YOUR POWER?
ABOUT THAT...

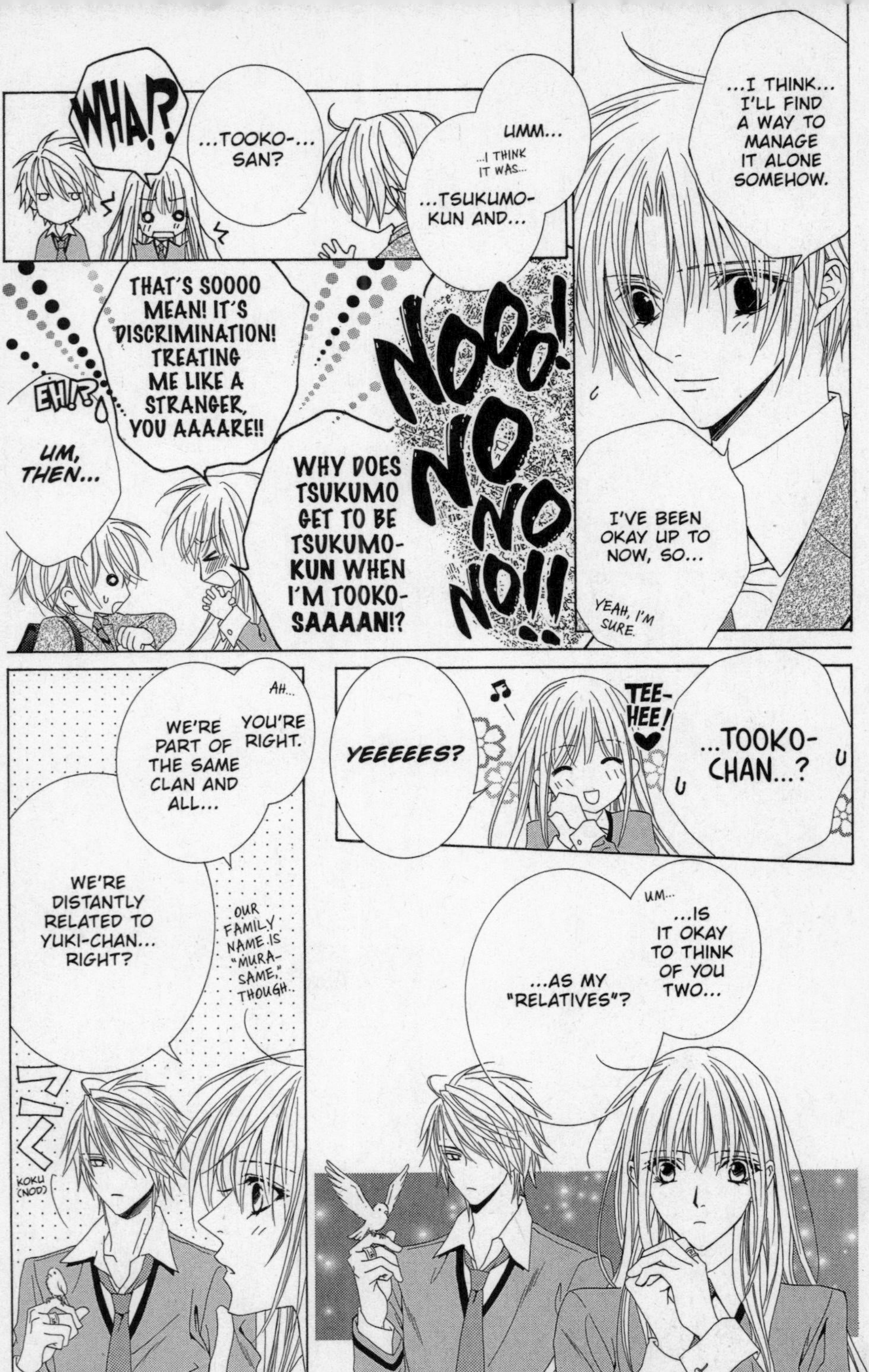
...I THINK... I'LL FIND A WAY TO MANAGE IT ALONE SOMEHOW.
UMM...
...I THINK IT WAS...
...TSUKUMO-KUN AND...
...TOOKO-... SAN?
WHA!?
I'VE BEEN OKAY UP TO NOW, SO...
YEAH, I'M SURE.
NOOO! NO NO NO!!
WHY DOES TSUKUMO GET TO BE TSUKUMO-KUN WHEN I'M TOOKO-SAAAAN!?
THAT'S SOOOO MEAN! IT'S DISCRIMINATION! TREATING ME LIKE A STRANGER, YOU AAAARE!!
EH!?
UM, THEN...
...TOOKO-CHAN...?
TEE-HEE!
YEEEEES?
AH...
YOU'RE RIGHT.
WE'RE PART OF THE SAME CLAN AND ALL...
UM...
...IS IT OKAY TO THINK OF YOU TWO...
...AS MY "RELATIVES"?
OUR FAMILY NAME IS "MURA-SAME," THOUGH...
WE'RE DISTANTLY RELATED TO YUKI-CHAN... RIGHT?
KOKU (NOD)

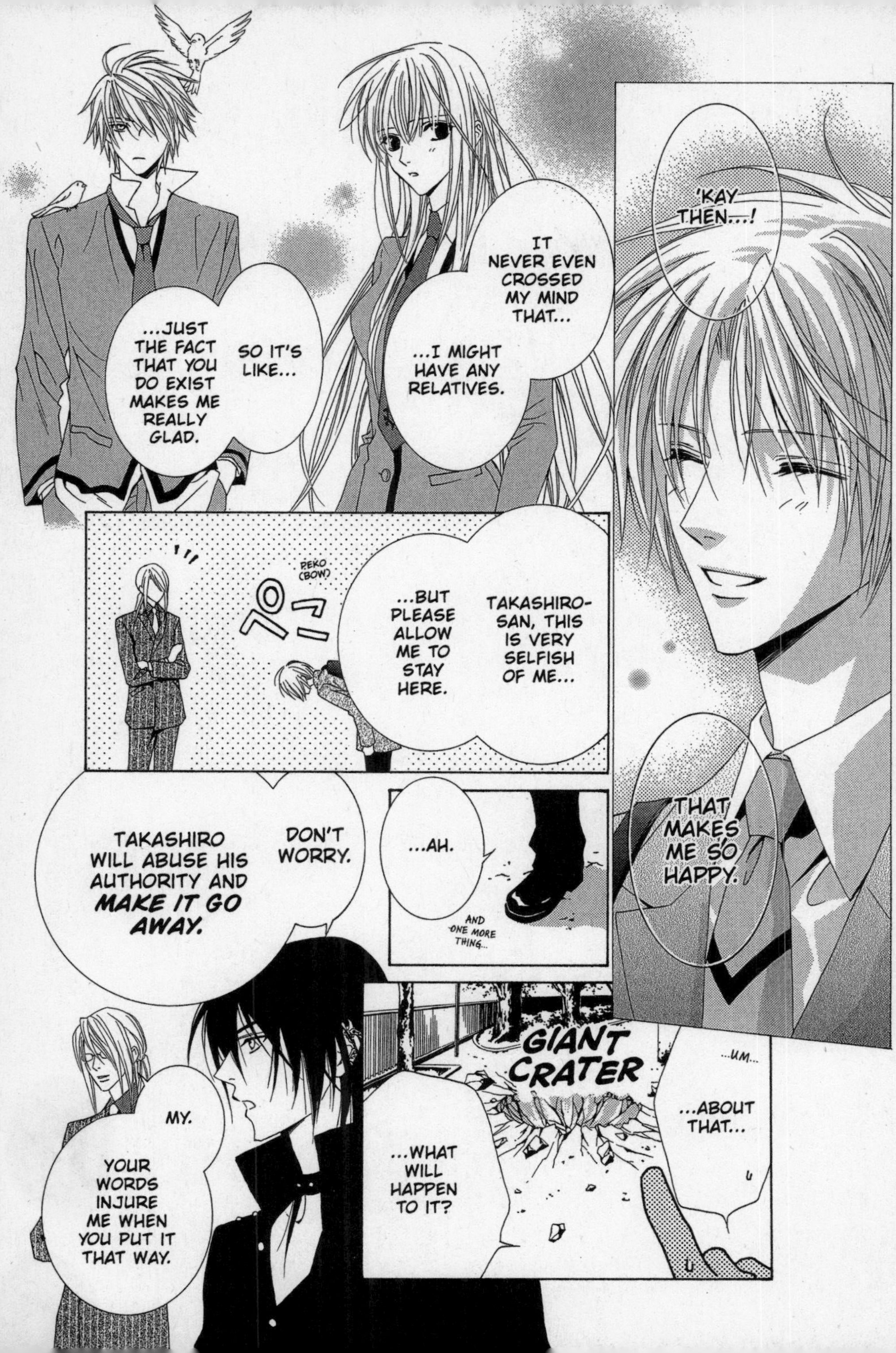
'KAY THEN...!
IT NEVER EVEN CROSSED MY MIND THAT...
...I MIGHT HAVE ANY RELATIVES.
SO IT'S LIKE...
...JUST THE FACT THAT YOU DO EXIST MAKES ME REALLY GLAD.
THAT MAKES ME SO HAPPY.
TAKASHIRO-SAN, THIS IS VERY SELFISH OF ME...
...BUT PLEASE ALLOW ME TO STAY HERE.
PEKO (BOW)
...AH.
AND ONE MORE THING...
DON'T WORRY.
TAKASHIRO WILL ABUSE HIS AUTHORITY AND MAKE IT GO AWAY.
...UM...
...ABOUT THAT...
GIANT CRATER
...WHAT WILL HAPPEN TO IT?
MY.
YOUR WORDS INJURE ME WHEN YOU PUT IT THAT WAY.

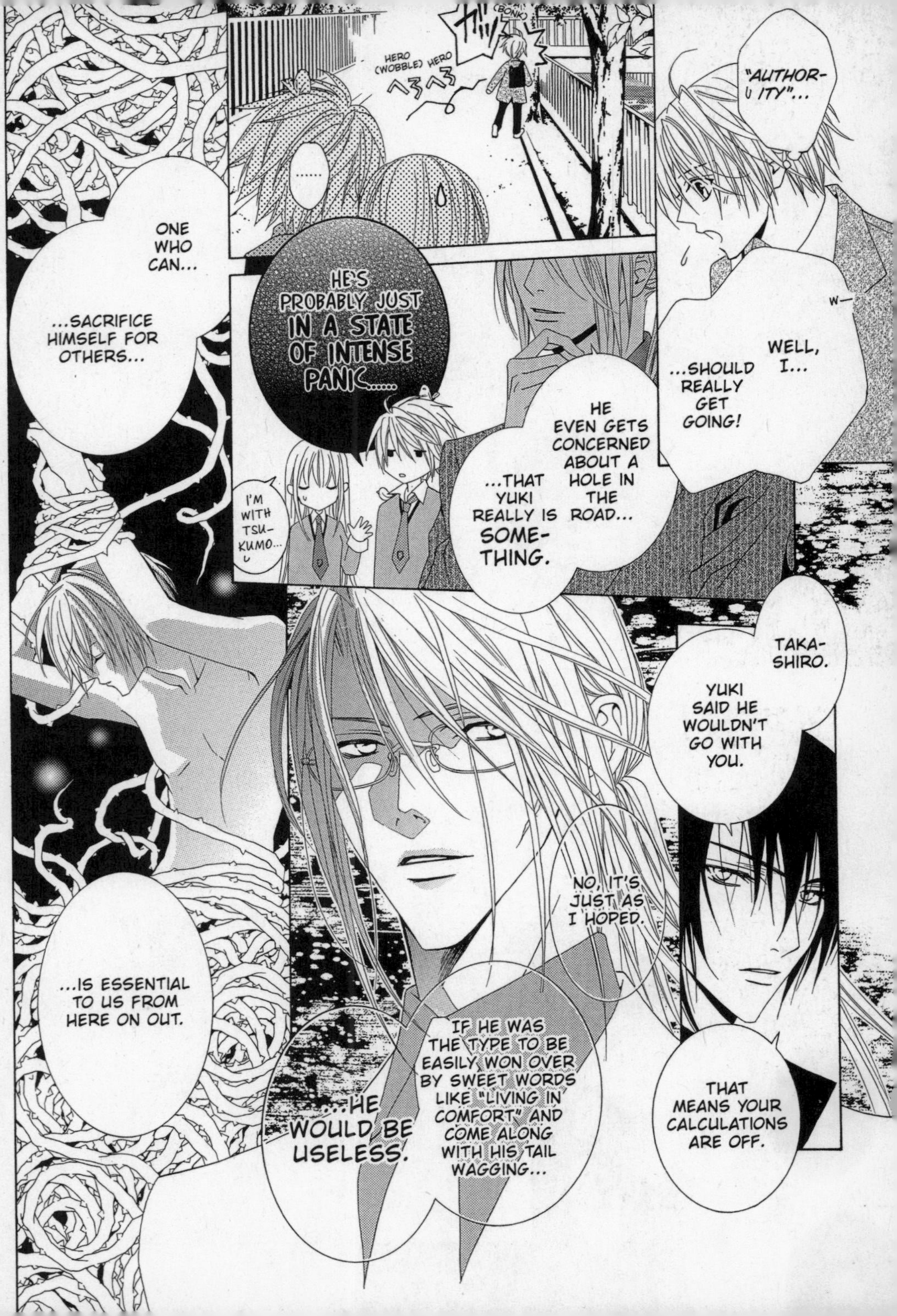
"AUTHOR- ITY"...
(BONK)
HERO (WOBBLE) HERO
へろへろ
......
W—
WELL, I...
...SHOULD REALLY GET GOING!
HE'S PROBABLY JUST IN A STATE OF INTENSE PANIC......
I'M WITH TSU- KUMO...
HE EVEN GETS CONCERNED ABOUT A HOLE IN THE ROAD...
...THAT YUKI REALLY IS SOME- THING.
ONE WHO CAN...
...SACRIFICE HIMSELF FOR OTHERS...
TAKA- SHIRO.
YUKI SAID HE WOULDN'T GO WITH YOU.
NO, IT'S JUST AS I HOPED.
THAT MEANS YOUR CALCULATIONS ARE OFF.
IF HE WAS THE TYPE TO BE EASILY WON OVER BY SWEET WORDS LIKE "LIVING IN COMFORT" AND COME ALONG WITH HIS TAIL WAGGING...
...HE WOULD BE USELESS.
...IS ESSENTIAL TO US FROM HERE ON OUT.

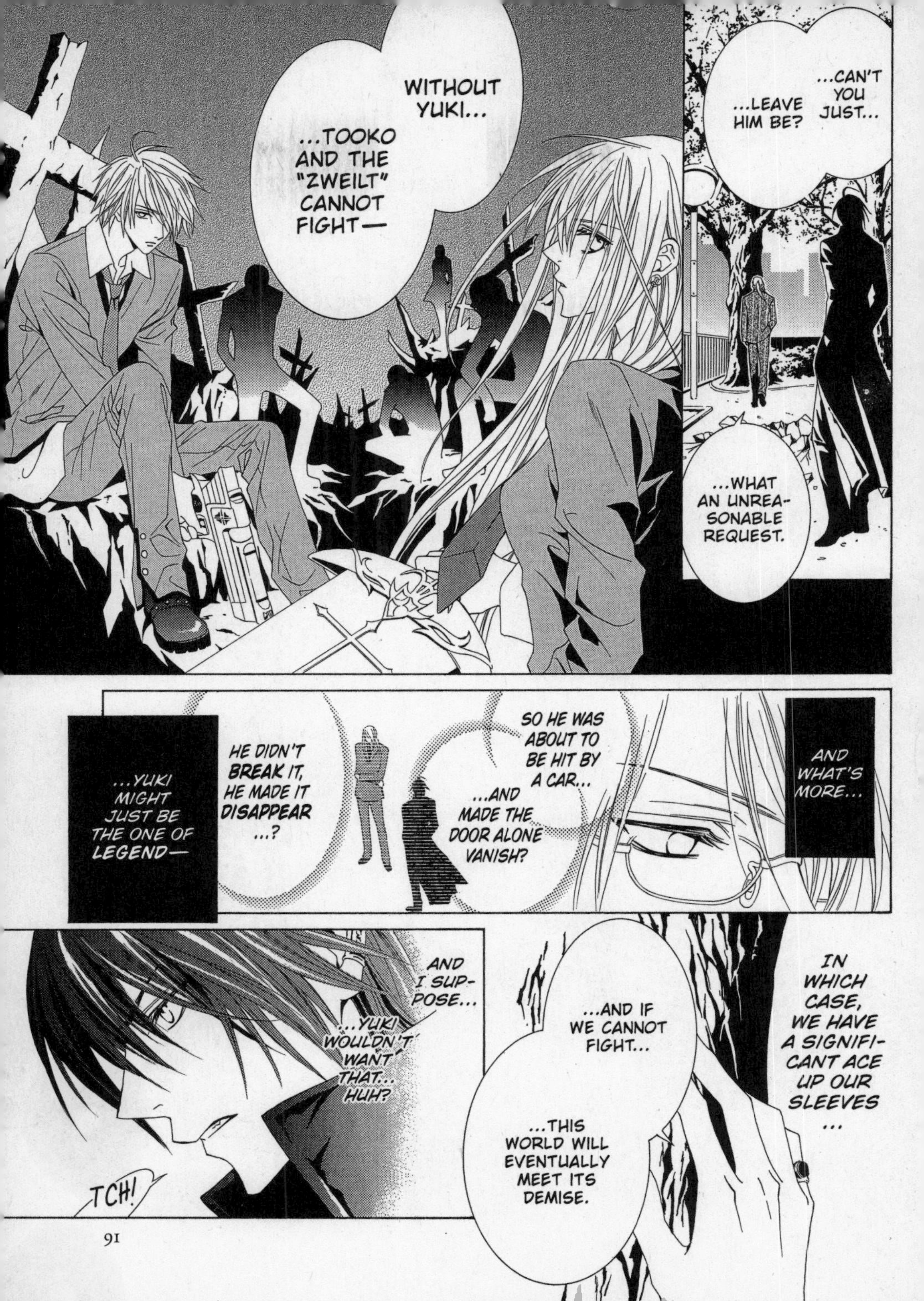
...CAN'T YOU JUST...
...LEAVE HIM BE?
WITHOUT YUKI...
...TOOKO AND THE "ZWEILT" CANNOT FIGHT—
...WHAT AN UNREA-SONABLE REQUEST.
AND WHAT'S MORE...
SO HE WAS ABOUT TO BE HIT BY A CAR...
...AND MADE THE DOOR ALONE VANISH?
HE DIDN'T BREAK IT, HE MADE IT DISAPPEAR ...?
...YUKI MIGHT JUST BE THE ONE OF LEGEND—
IN WHICH CASE, WE HAVE A SIGNIFI-CANT ACE UP OUR SLEEVES ...
...AND IF WE CANNOT FIGHT...
...THIS WORLD WILL EVENTUALLY MEET ITS DEMISE.
AND I SUP-POSE...
...YUKI WOULDN'T WANT THAT... HUH?
TCH!

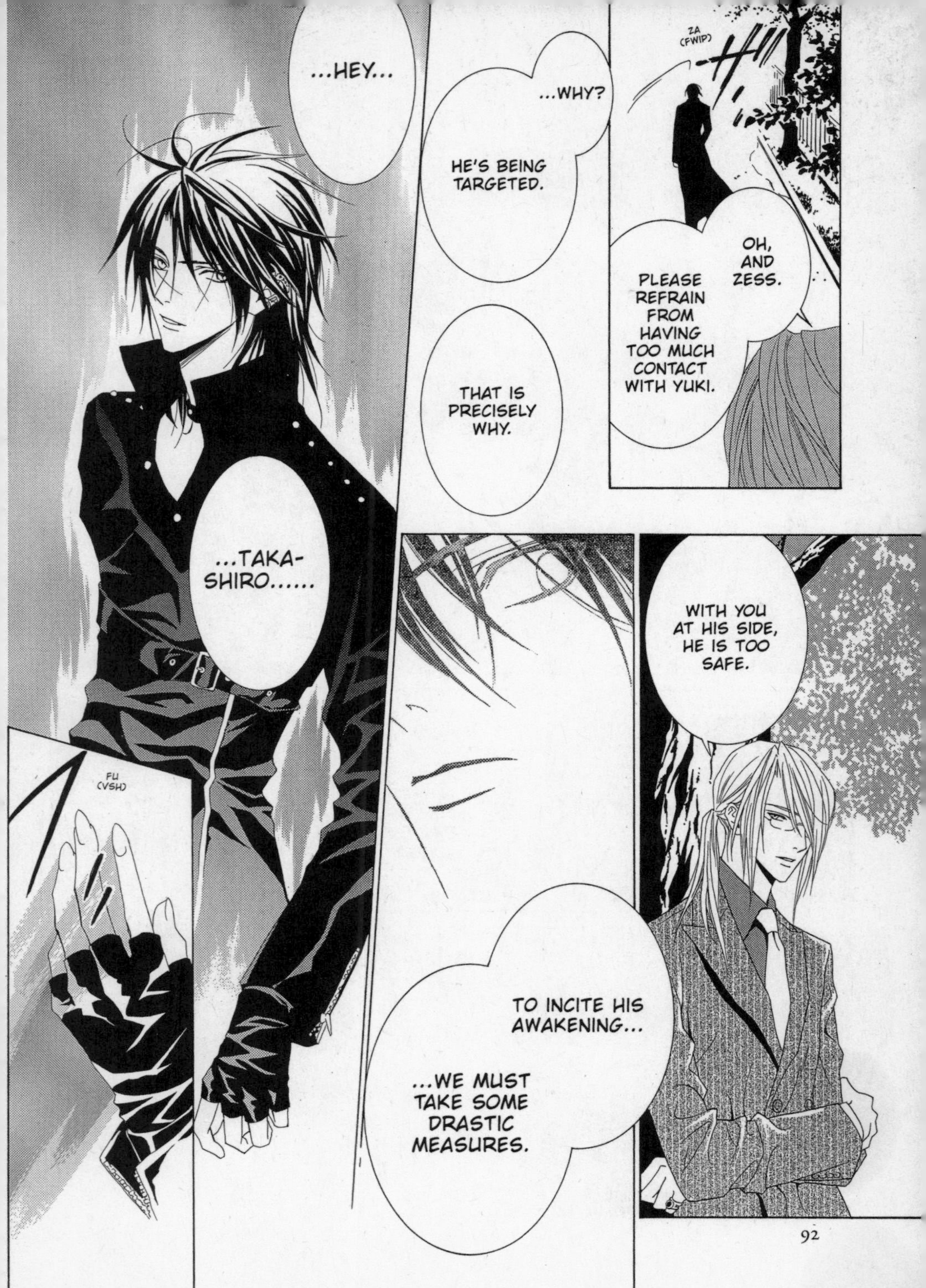
ZA (FWIP)
OH, AND ZESS.
PLEASE REFRAIN FROM HAVING TOO MUCH CONTACT WITH YUKI.
...WHY?
HE'S BEING TARGETED.
THAT IS PRECISELY WHY.
...HEY...
...TAKA-SHIRO......
WITH YOU AT HIS SIDE, HE IS TOO SAFE.
TO INCITE HIS AWAKENING...
...WE MUST TAKE SOME DRASTIC MEASURES.
FU (VSH)

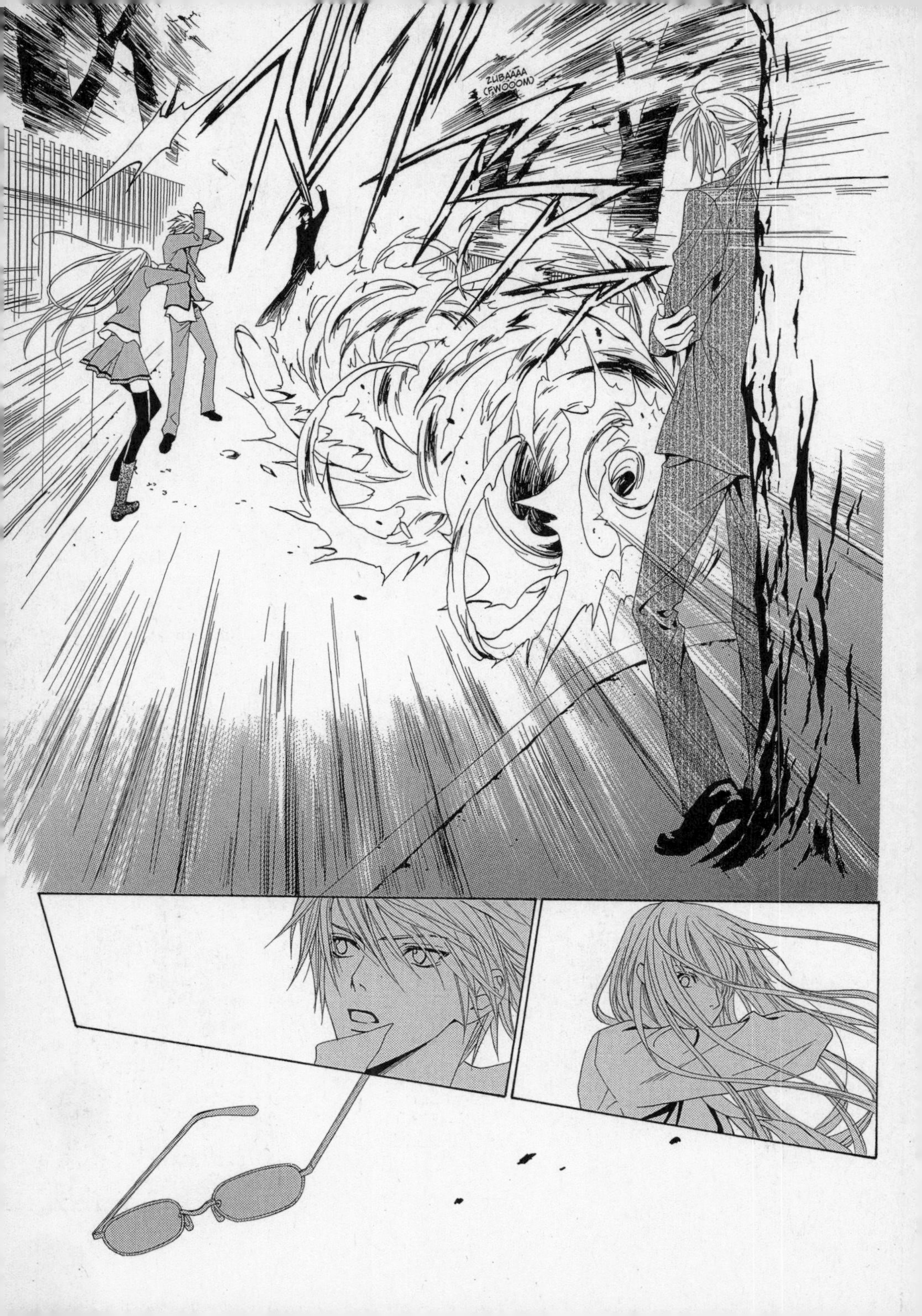
ZUBAAAA
(FWOOOM)

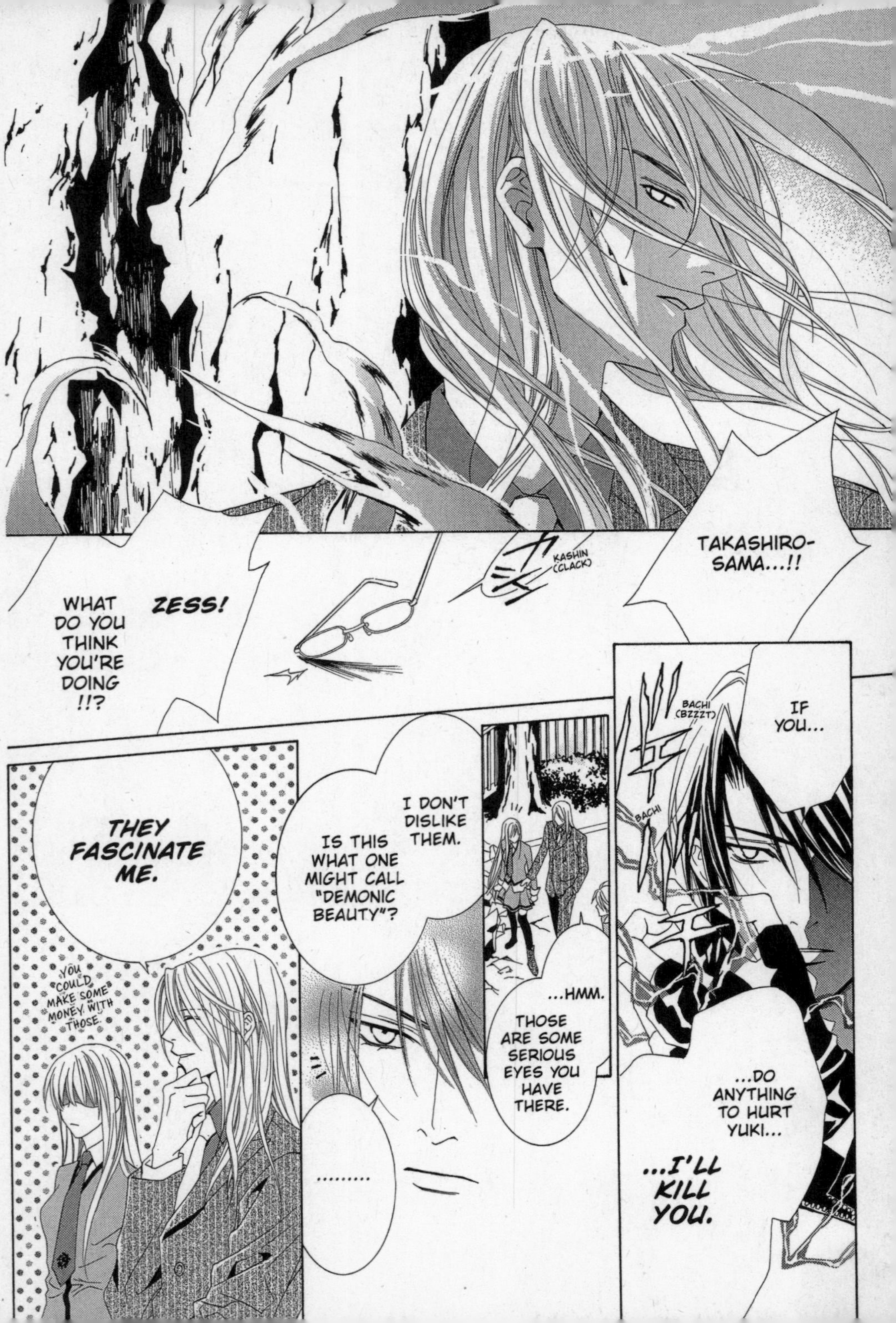
TAKASHIRO-SAMA...!!
KASHIN (CLACK)
ZESS!
WHAT DO YOU THINK YOU'RE DOING!!?
BACHI (BZZZT)
BACHI
IF YOU...
...DO ANYTHING TO HURT YUKI...
...I'LL KILL YOU.
...HMM.
THOSE ARE SOME SERIOUS EYES YOU HAVE THERE.
....
I DON'T DISLIKE THEM.
IS THIS WHAT ONE MIGHT CALL "DEMONIC BEAUTY"?
THEY FASCINATE ME.
YOU COULD MAKE SOME MONEY WITH THOSE.

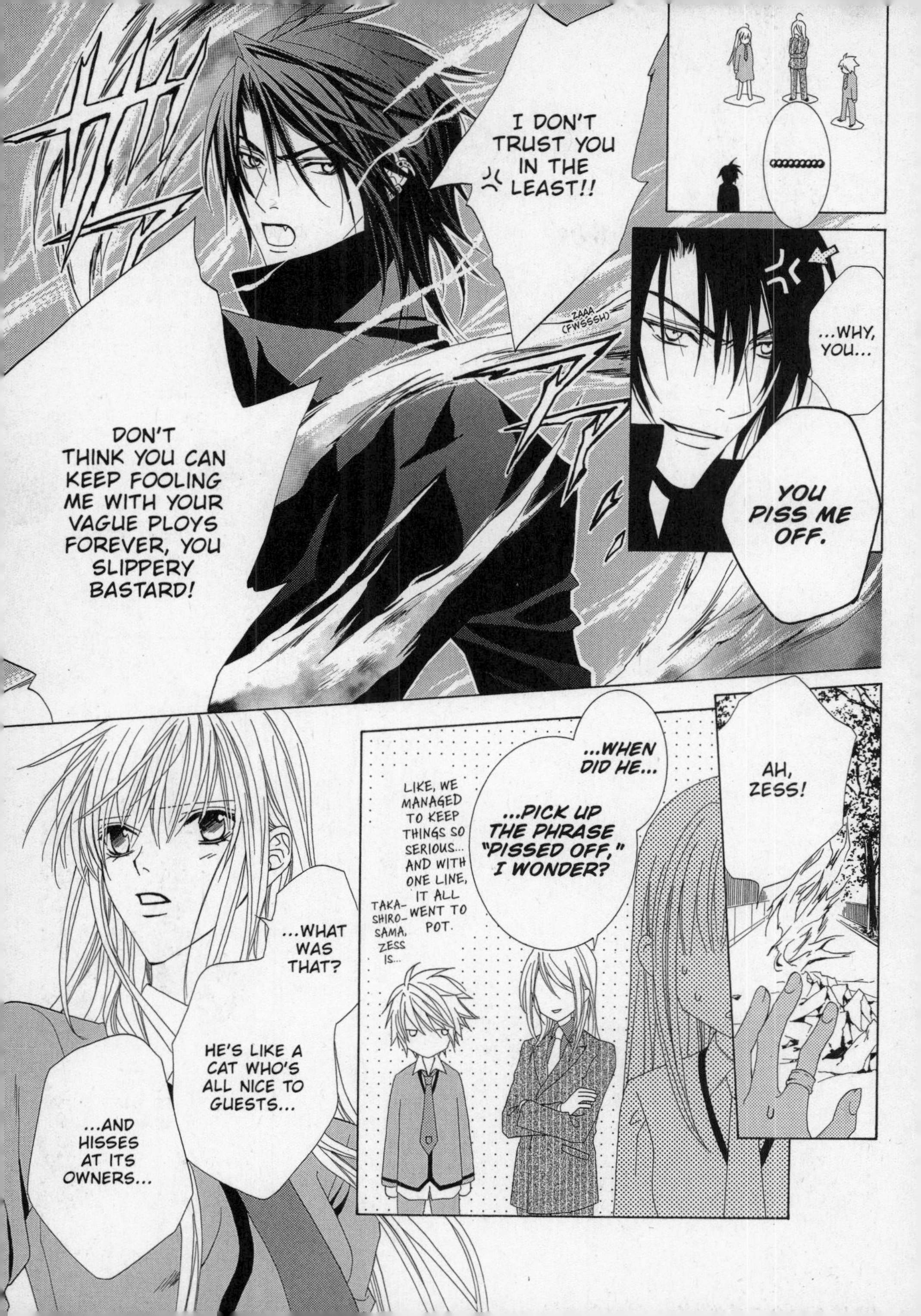
I DON'T TRUST YOU IN THE LEAST!!
DON'T THINK YOU CAN KEEP FOOLING ME WITH YOUR VAGUE PLOYS FOREVER, YOU SLIPPERY BASTARD!
ZAAA (FWSSSH)
...WHY, YOU...
YOU PISS ME OFF.
AH, ZESS!
...WHEN DID HE...
...PICK UP THE PHRASE "PISSED OFF," I WONDER?
LIKE, WE MANAGED TO KEEP THINGS SO SERIOUS... AND WITH ONE LINE, IT ALL WENT TO POT.
TAKA-SHIRO-SAMA, ZESS IS...
...WHAT WAS THAT?
HE'S LIKE A CAT WHO'S ALL NICE TO GUESTS...
...AND HISSES AT ITS OWNERS...

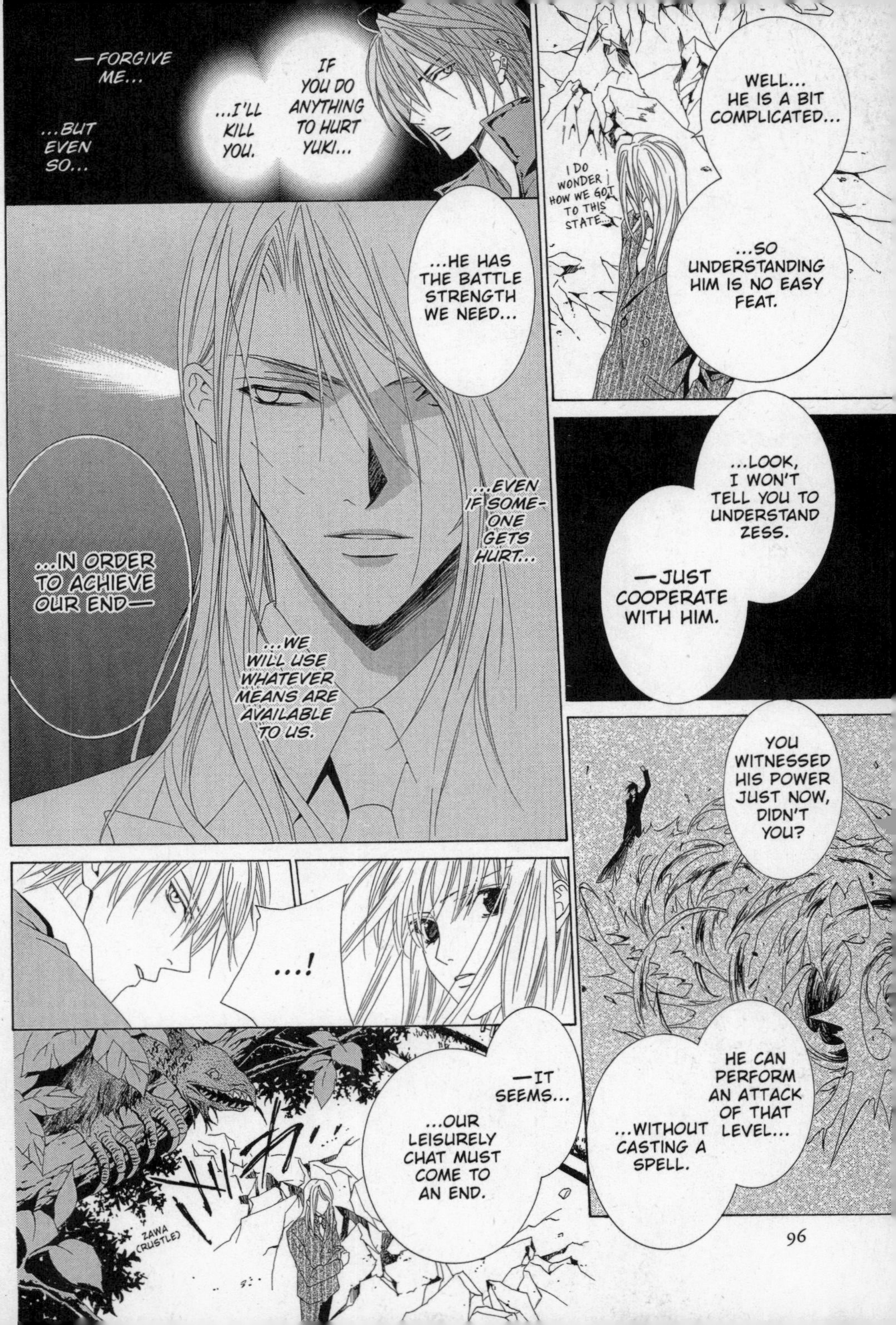
WELL... HE IS A BIT COMPLICATED...
I DO WONDER HOW WE GOT TO THIS STATE...
...SO UNDERSTANDING HIM IS NO EASY FEAT.
IF YOU DO ANYTHING TO HURT YUKI...
...I'LL KILL YOU.
—FORGIVE ME...
...BUT EVEN SO...
...HE HAS THE BATTLE STRENGTH WE NEED...
...EVEN IF SOMEONE GETS HURT...
...IN ORDER TO ACHIEVE OUR END—
...WE WILL USE WHATEVER MEANS ARE AVAILABLE TO US.
...LOOK, I WON'T TELL YOU TO UNDERSTAND ZESS.
—JUST COOPERATE WITH HIM.
YOU WITNESSED HIS POWER JUST NOW, DIDN'T YOU?
HE CAN PERFORM AN ATTACK OF THAT LEVEL...
...WITHOUT CASTING A SPELL.
...!
—IT SEEMS...
...OUR LEISURELY CHAT MUST COME TO AN END.
ZAWA (RUSTLE)

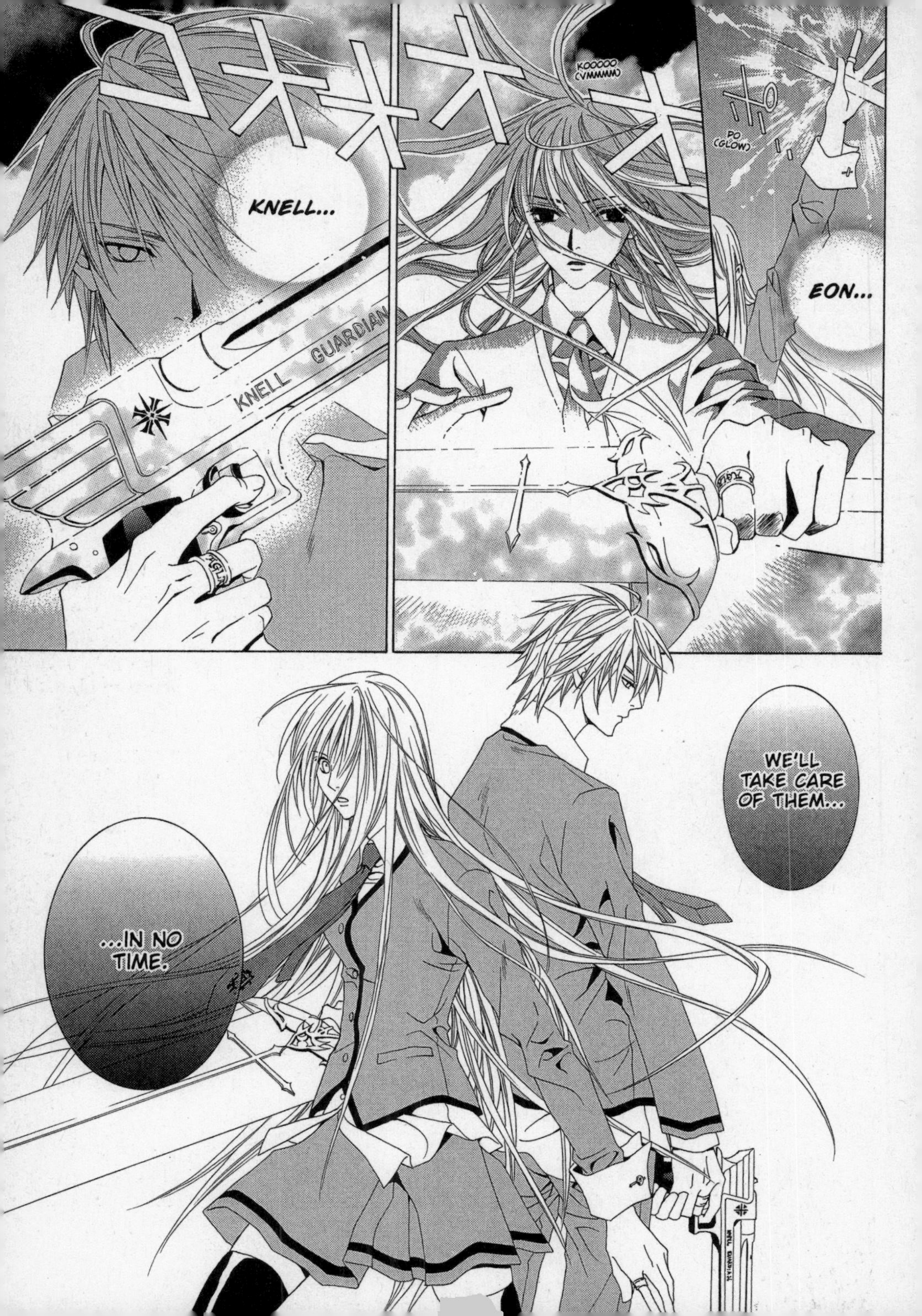
KOOOOO (VMMMM)
PO (GLOW)
EON...
KNELL...
KNELL GUARDIAN
WE'LL TAKE CARE OF THEM...
...IN NO TIME.

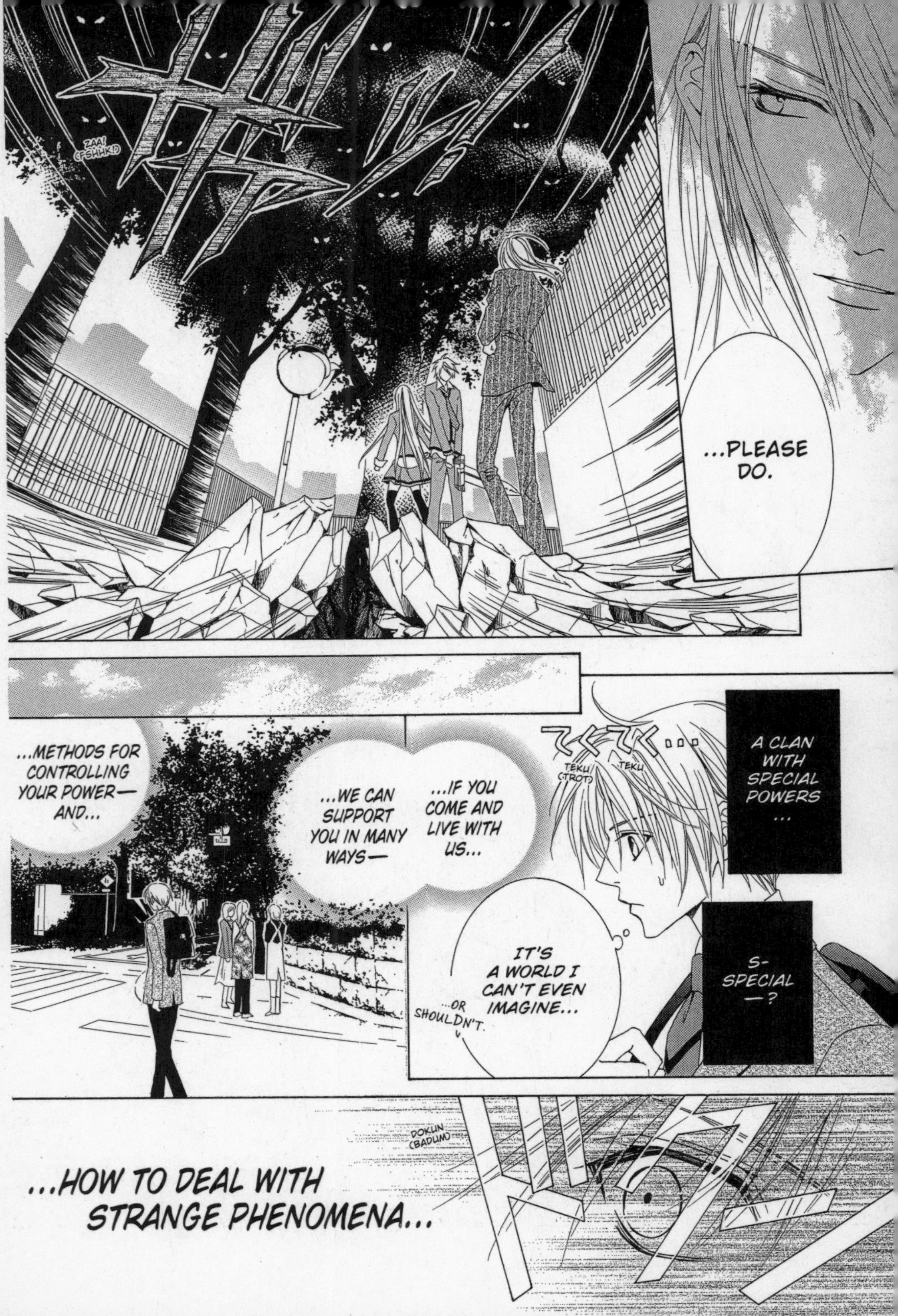
...PLEASE DO.
ZAA! (PSHHK!)
A CLAN WITH SPECIAL POWERS...
TEKU (TROT) TEKU
S-SPECIAL—?
IT'S A WORLD I CAN'T EVEN IMAGINE...
...OR SHOULDN'T.
...IF YOU COME AND LIVE WITH US...
...WE CAN SUPPORT YOU IN MANY WAYS—
...METHODS FOR CONTROLLING YOUR POWER—AND...
DOKUN (BADUMP)
...HOW TO DEAL WITH STRANGE PHENOMENA...

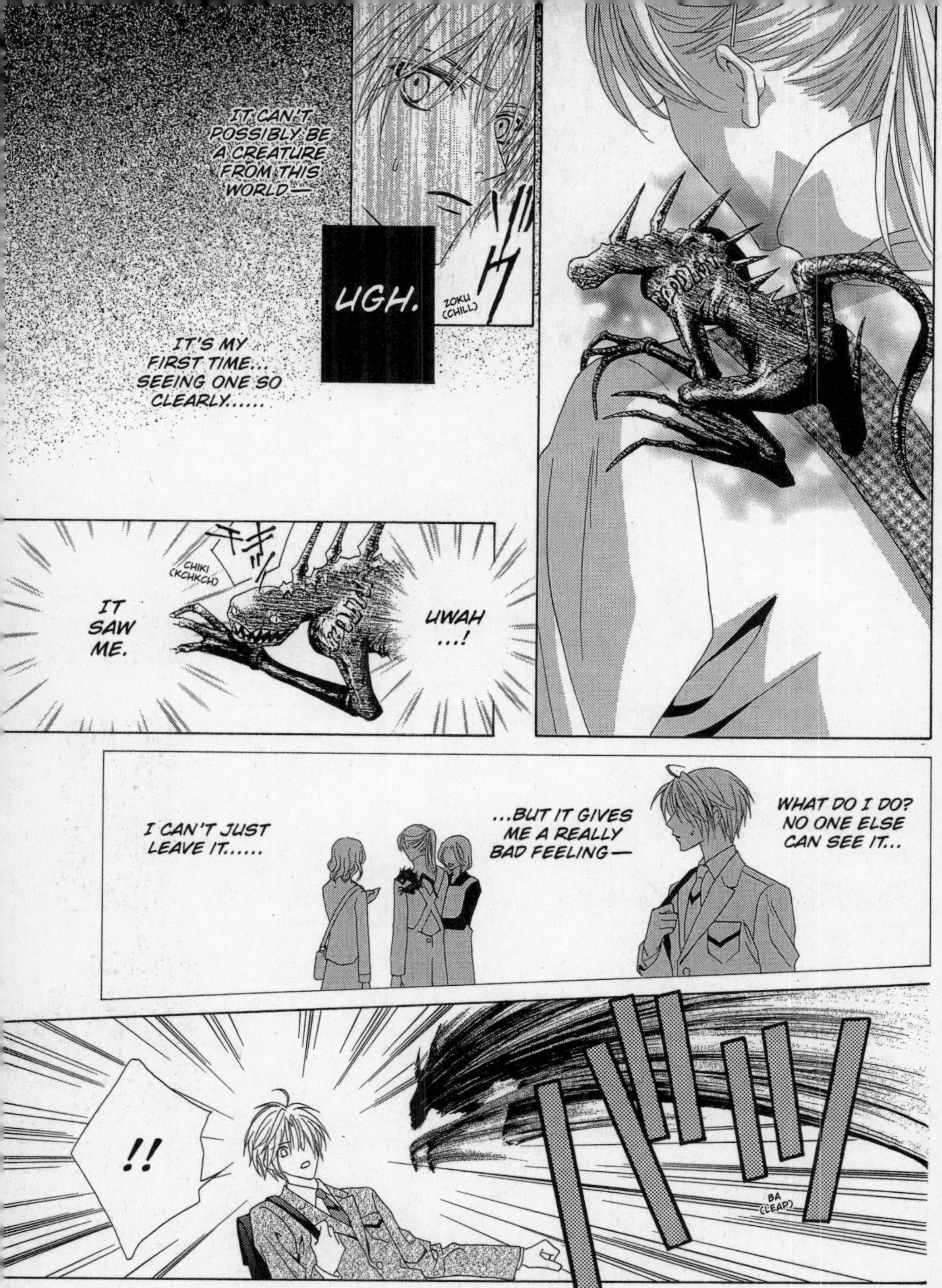
IT CAN'T POSSIBLY BE A CREATURE FROM THIS WORLD—
ZOKU (CHILL)
UGH.
IT'S MY FIRST TIME... SEEING ONE SO CLEARLY......
UWAH ...!
CHIKI (KCHKCH)
IT SAW ME.
WHAT DO I DO? NO ONE ELSE CAN SEE IT...
...BUT IT GIVES ME A REALLY BAD FEELING—
I CAN'T JUST LEAVE IT......
BA (LEAP)
!!

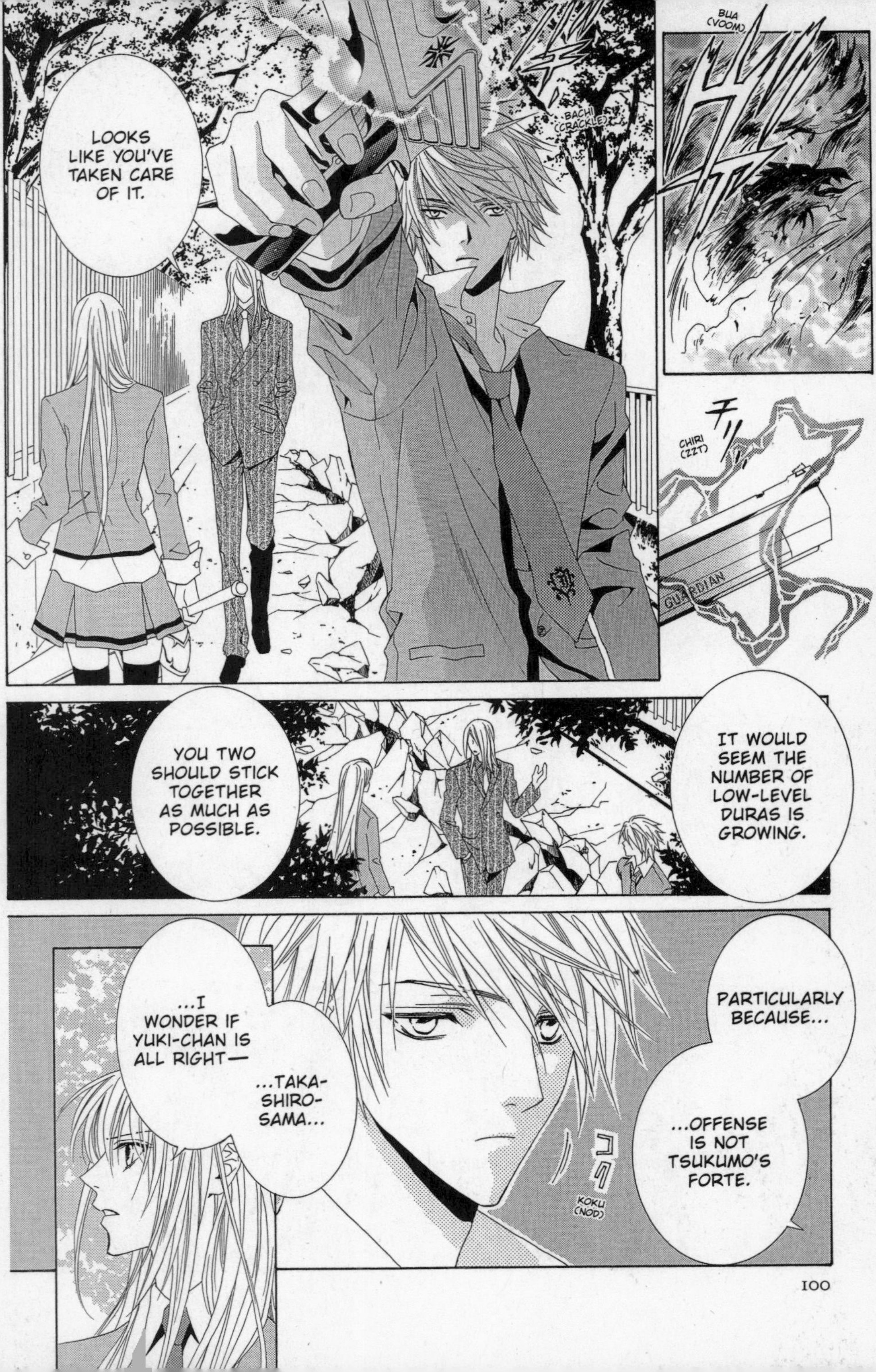
BUA (VOOM)
BACHI (CRACKLE)
LOOKS LIKE YOU'VE TAKEN CARE OF IT.
CHIRI (ZZT)
GUARDIAN
IT WOULD SEEM THE NUMBER OF LOW-LEVEL DURAS IS GROWING.
YOU TWO SHOULD STICK TOGETHER AS MUCH AS POSSIBLE.
PARTICULARLY BECAUSE...
...OFFENSE IS NOT TSUKUMO'S FORTE.
KOKU (NOD)
...I WONDER IF YUKI-CHAN IS ALL RIGHT—
...TAKA-SHIRO-SAMA...

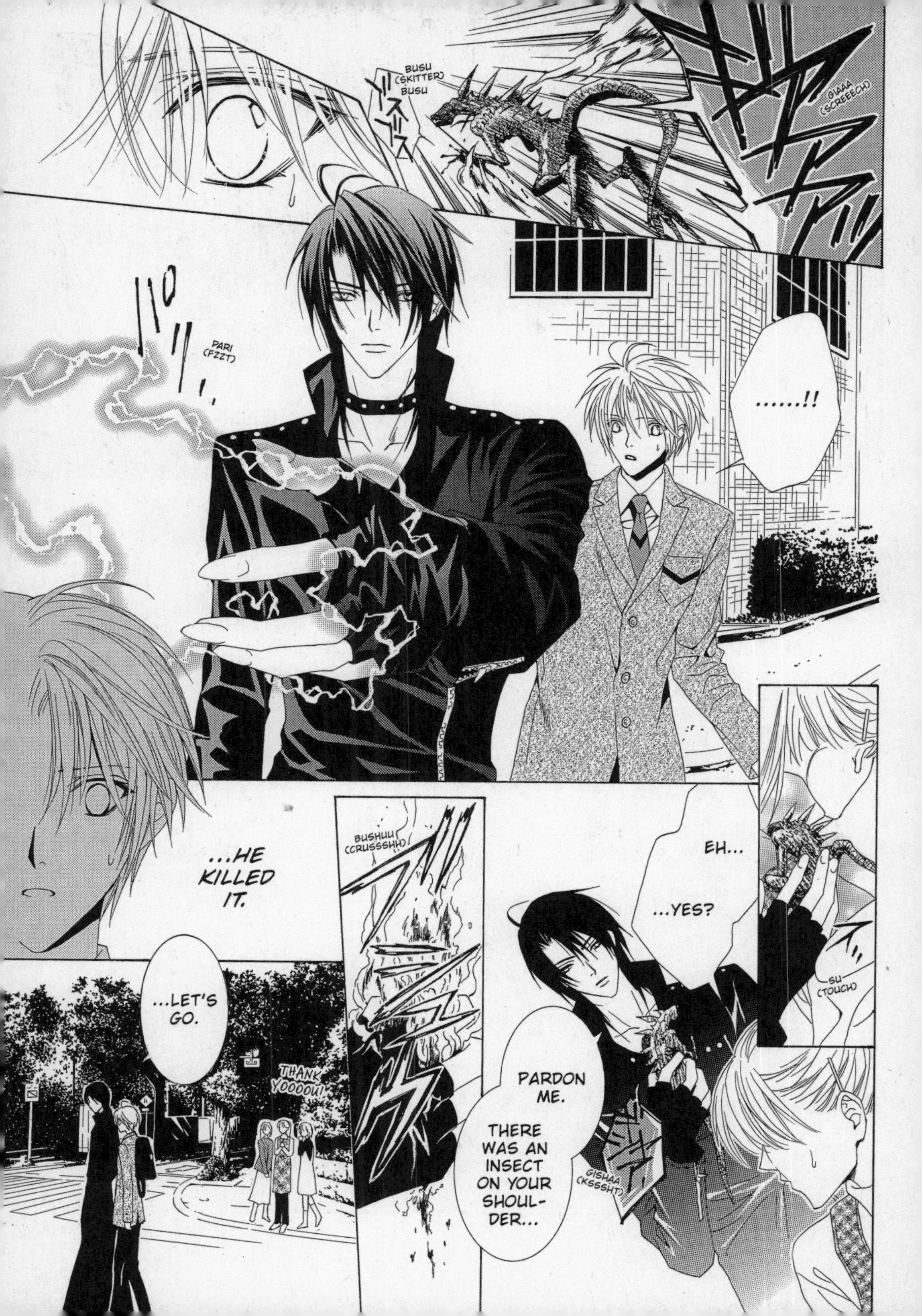
GIAAA (SCREEECH)
BUSU (SKITTER) BUSU
......!!
PARI (FZZT)
...HE KILLED IT.
SU (TOUCH)
EH...
...YES?
PARDON ME.
THERE WAS AN INSECT ON YOUR SHOULDER...
GISHAA (KSSSHT)
BUSHUU (CRUSSSHH)
...LET'S GO.
THANK YOOOOU!

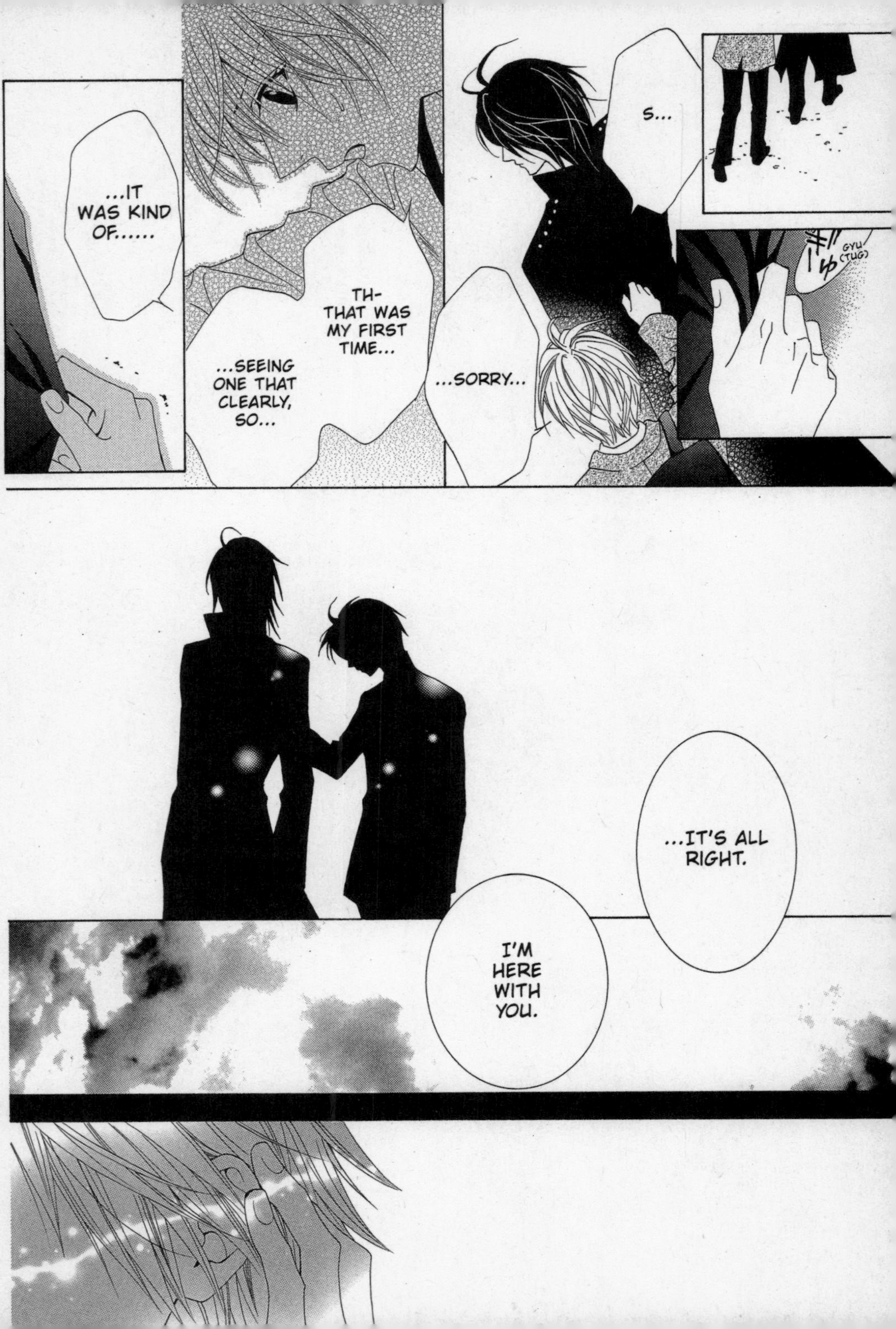
GYU (TUG)
S...
...SORRY...
TH- THAT WAS MY FIRST TIME...
...SEEING ONE THAT CLEARLY, SO...
...IT WAS KIND OF......
...IT'S ALL RIGHT.
I'M HERE WITH YOU.

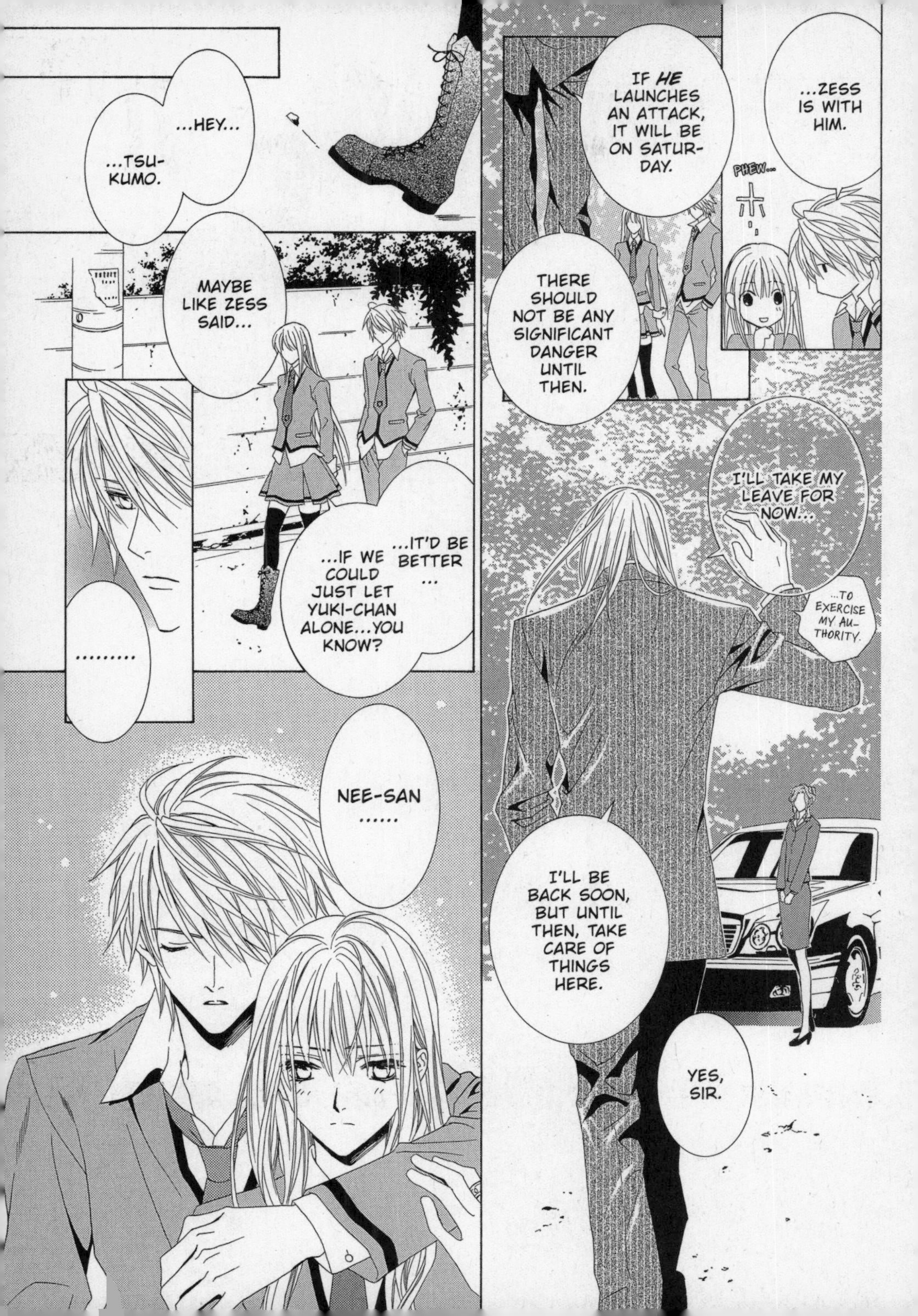
...ZESS IS WITH HIM.
PHEW...
IF HE LAUNCHES AN ATTACK, IT WILL BE ON SATURDAY.
THERE SHOULD NOT BE ANY SIGNIFICANT DANGER UNTIL THEN.
I'LL TAKE MY LEAVE FOR NOW...
...TO EXERCISE MY AUTHORITY.
I'LL BE BACK SOON, BUT UNTIL THEN, TAKE CARE OF THINGS HERE.
YES, SIR.
...HEY...
...TSUKUMO.
MAYBE LIKE ZESS SAID...
...IT'D BE BETTER...
...IF WE COULD JUST LET YUKI-CHAN ALONE...YOU KNOW?
....
NEE-SAN ......

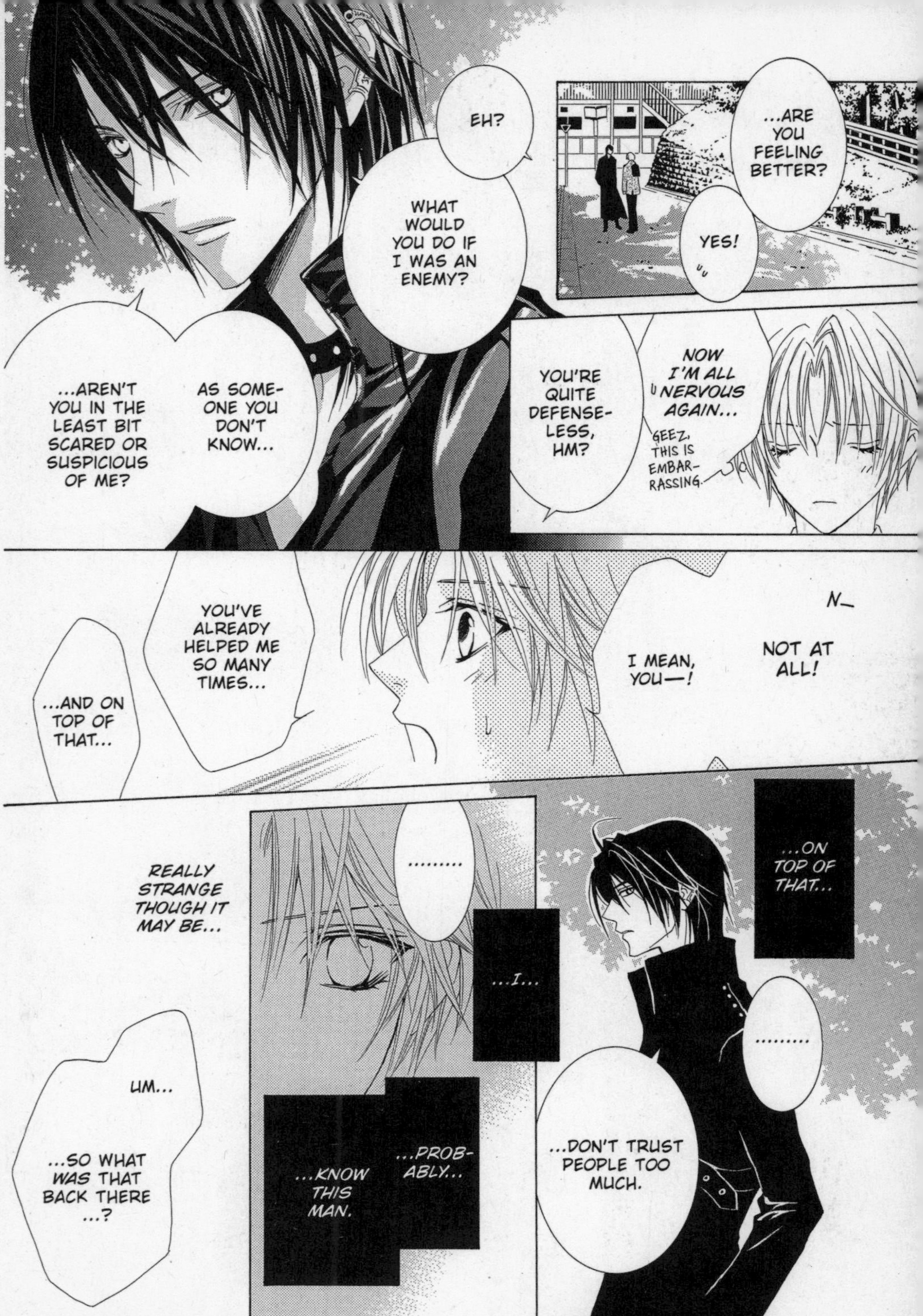
...ARE YOU FEELING BETTER?
YES!
NOW I'M ALL NERVOUS AGAIN...
GEEZ, THIS IS EMBARRASSING.
YOU'RE QUITE DEFENSELESS, HM?
EH?
WHAT WOULD YOU DO IF I WAS AN ENEMY?
AS SOMEONE YOU DON'T KNOW...
...AREN'T YOU IN THE LEAST BIT SCARED OR SUSPICIOUS OF ME?
N—
NOT AT ALL!
I MEAN, YOU—!
YOU'VE ALREADY HELPED ME SO MANY TIMES...
...AND ON TOP OF THAT...
...ON TOP OF THAT...
....
...DON'T TRUST PEOPLE TOO MUCH.
....
...I...
REALLY STRANGE THOUGH IT MAY BE...
...PROBABLY...
...KNOW THIS MAN.
UM...
...SO WHAT WAS THAT BACK THERE ...?

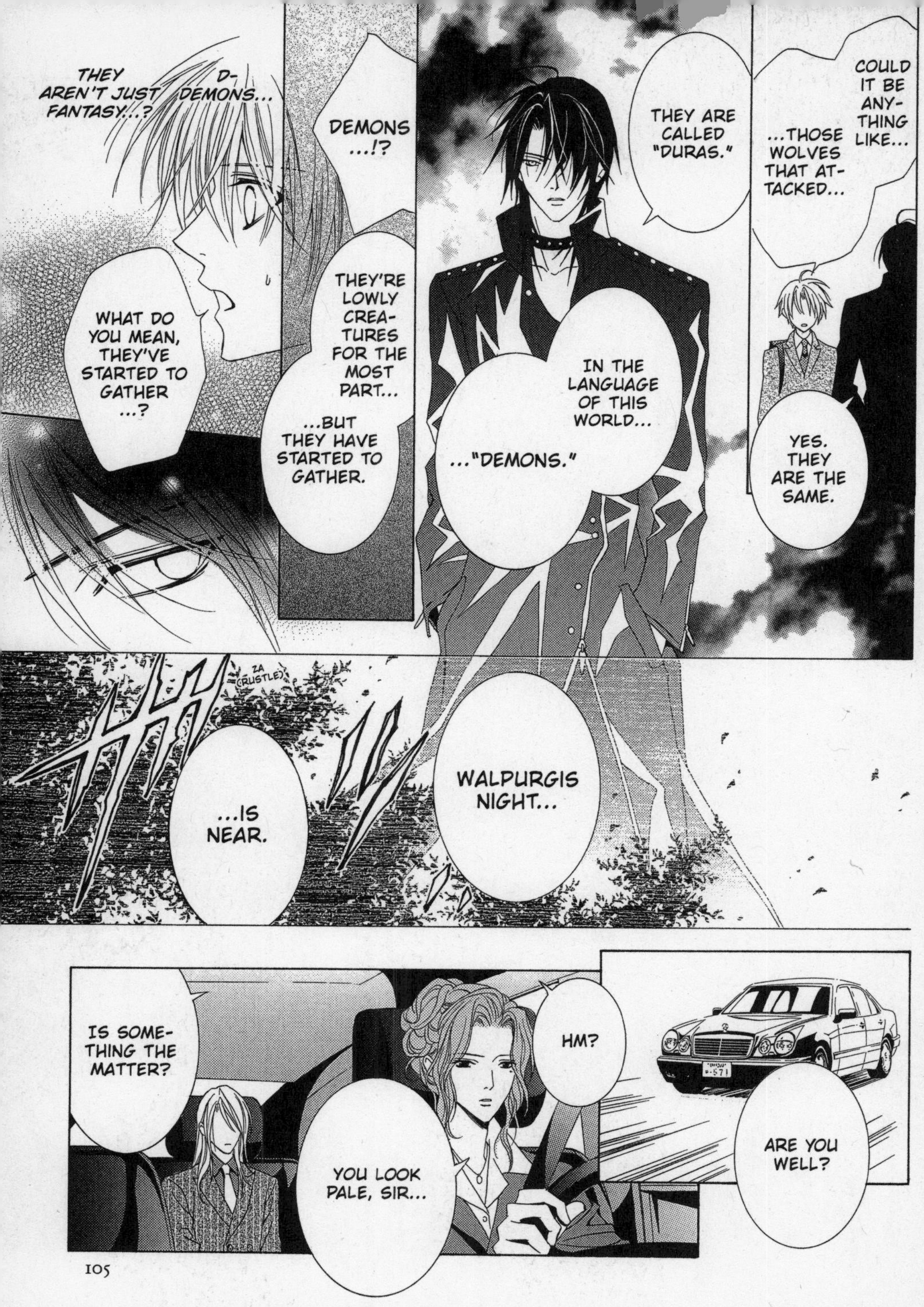
COULD IT BE ANYTHING LIKE...
...THOSE WOLVES THAT ATTACKED...
YES. THEY ARE THE SAME.
THEY ARE CALLED "DURAS."
IN THE LANGUAGE OF THIS WORLD...
..."DEMONS."
DEMONS...!?
THEY'RE LOWLY CREATURES FOR THE MOST PART...
...BUT THEY HAVE STARTED TO GATHER.
D-DEMONS...
THEY AREN'T JUST FANTASY...?
WHAT DO YOU MEAN, THEY'VE STARTED TO GATHER...?
ZA (RUSTLE)
WALPURGIS NIGHT...
...IS NEAR.
HM?
ARE YOU WELL?
YOU LOOK PALE, SIR...
IS SOMETHING THE MATTER?

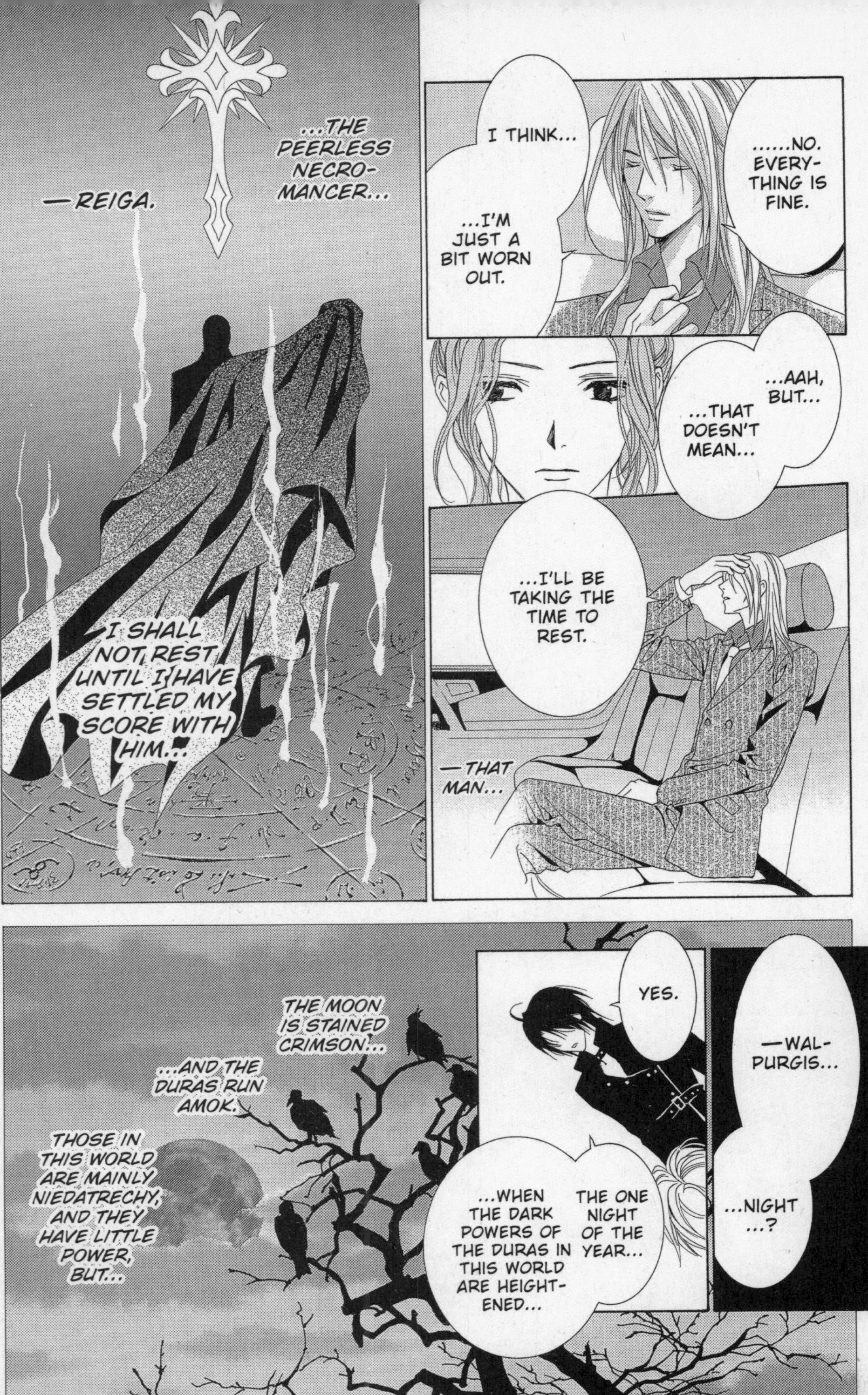
......NO. EVERYTHING IS FINE.
I THINK...
...I'M JUST A BIT WORN OUT.
...AAH, BUT...
...THAT DOESN'T MEAN...
...I'LL BE TAKING THE TIME TO REST.
—THAT MAN...
...THE PEERLESS NECROMANCER...
—REIGA.
I SHALL NOT REST UNTIL I HAVE SETTLED MY SCORE WITH HIM...
—WALPURGIS...
...NIGHT...?
YES.
THE ONE NIGHT OF THE YEAR...
...WHEN THE DARK POWERS OF THE DURAS IN THIS WORLD ARE HEIGHTENED...
THE MOON IS STAINED CRIMSON...
...AND THE DURAS RUN AMOK.
THOSE IN THIS WORLD ARE MAINLY NIEDATRECHY, AND THEY HAVE LITTLE POWER, BUT...

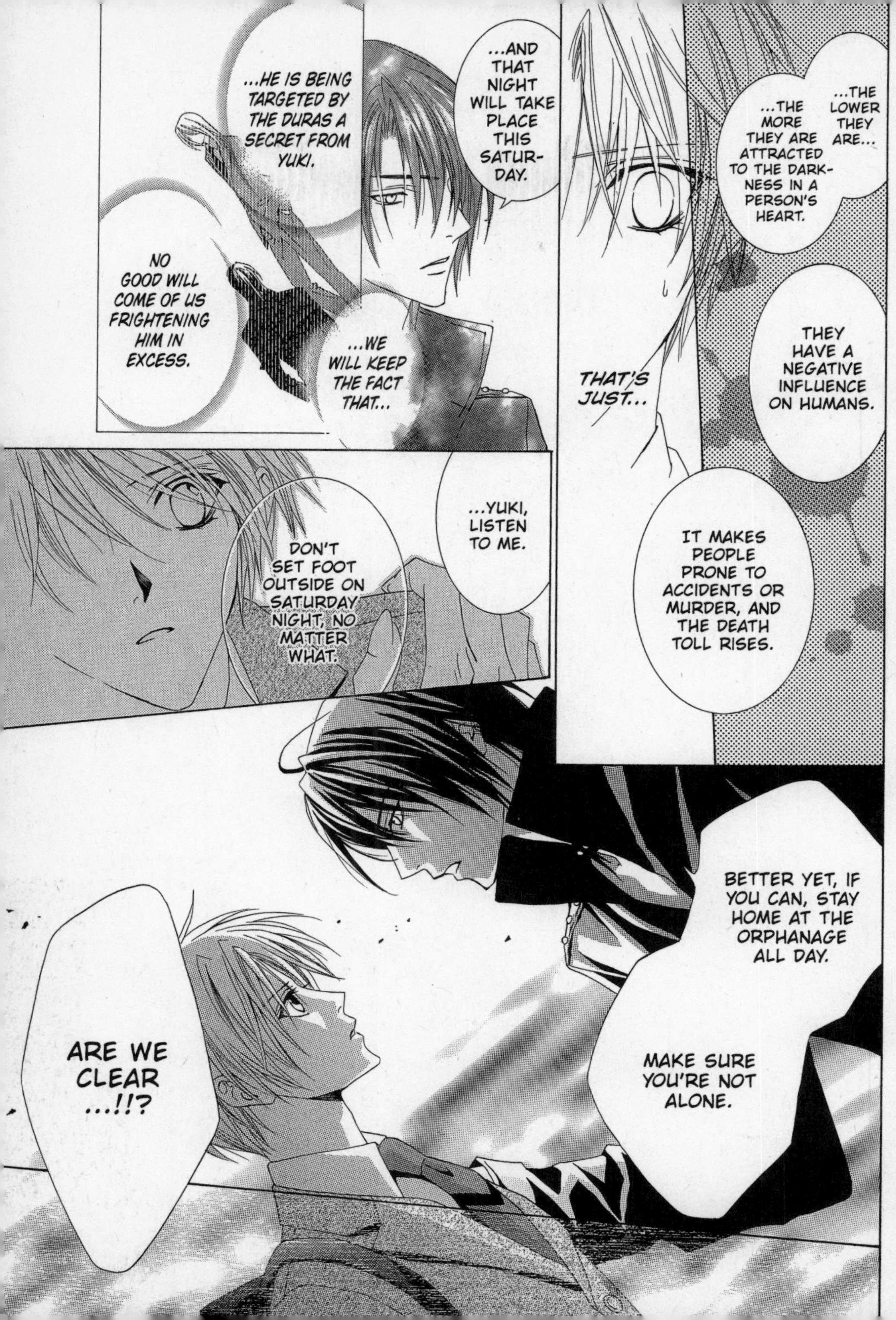

...THE LOWER THEY ARE...
...THE MORE THEY ARE ATTRACTED TO THE DARKNESS IN A PERSON'S HEART.
THEY HAVE A NEGATIVE INFLUENCE ON HUMANS.
IT MAKES PEOPLE PRONE TO ACCIDENTS OR MURDER, AND THE DEATH TOLL RISES.
THAT'S JUST...
...AND THAT NIGHT WILL TAKE PLACE THIS SATURDAY.
...WE WILL KEEP THE FACT THAT...
...HE IS BEING TARGETED BY THE DURAS A SECRET FROM YUKI.
NO GOOD WILL COME OF US FRIGHTENING HIM IN EXCESS.
...YUKI, LISTEN TO ME.
DON'T SET FOOT OUTSIDE ON SATURDAY NIGHT, NO MATTER WHAT.
BETTER YET, IF YOU CAN, STAY HOME AT THE ORPHANAGE ALL DAY.
MAKE SURE YOU'RE NOT ALONE.
ARE WE CLEAR ...!!?

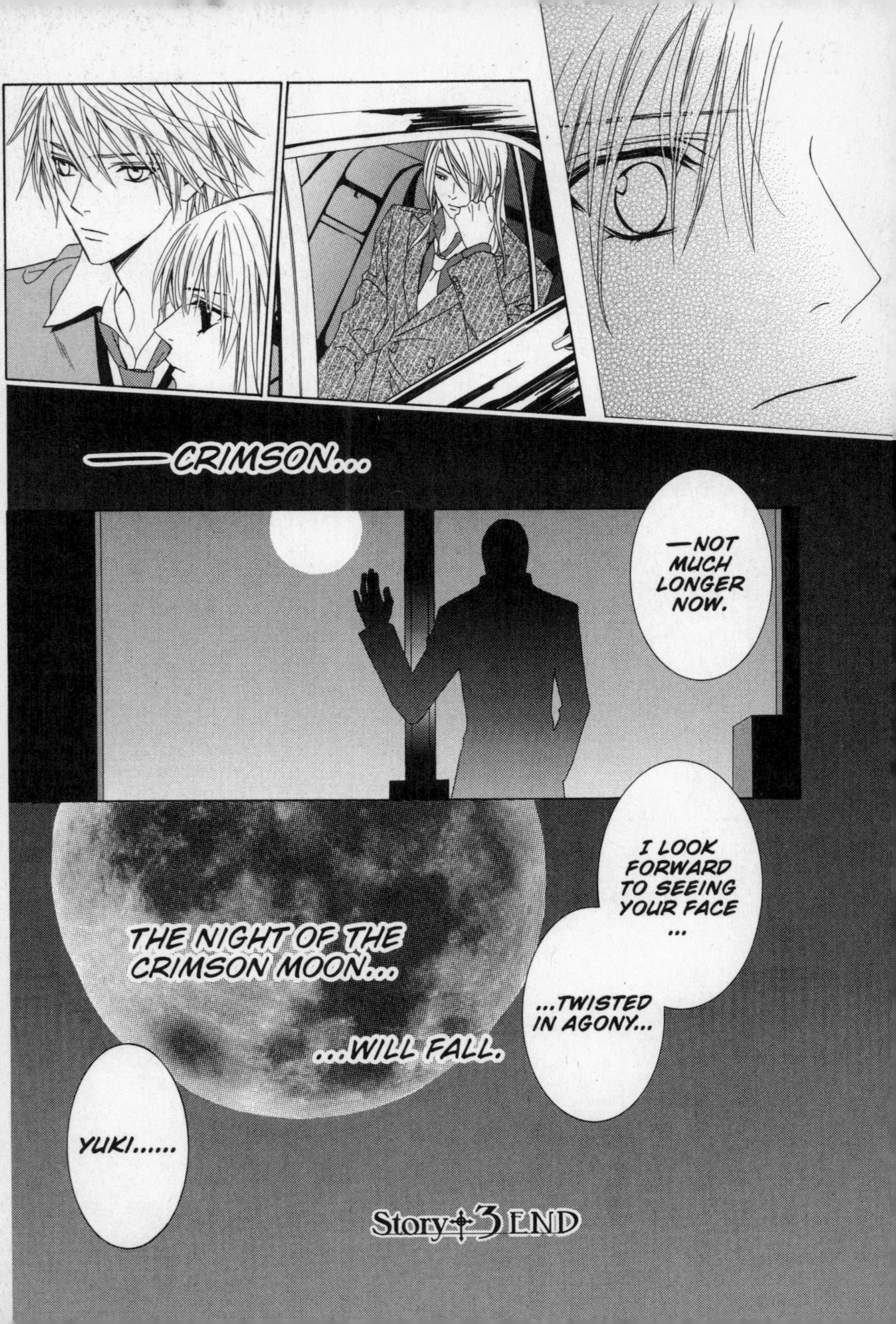
—CRIMSON...
—NOT MUCH LONGER NOW.
THE NIGHT OF THE CRIMSON MOON...
...WILL FALL.
I LOOK FORWARD TO SEEING YOUR FACE ...
...TWISTED IN AGONY...
YUKI......
Story 3 END

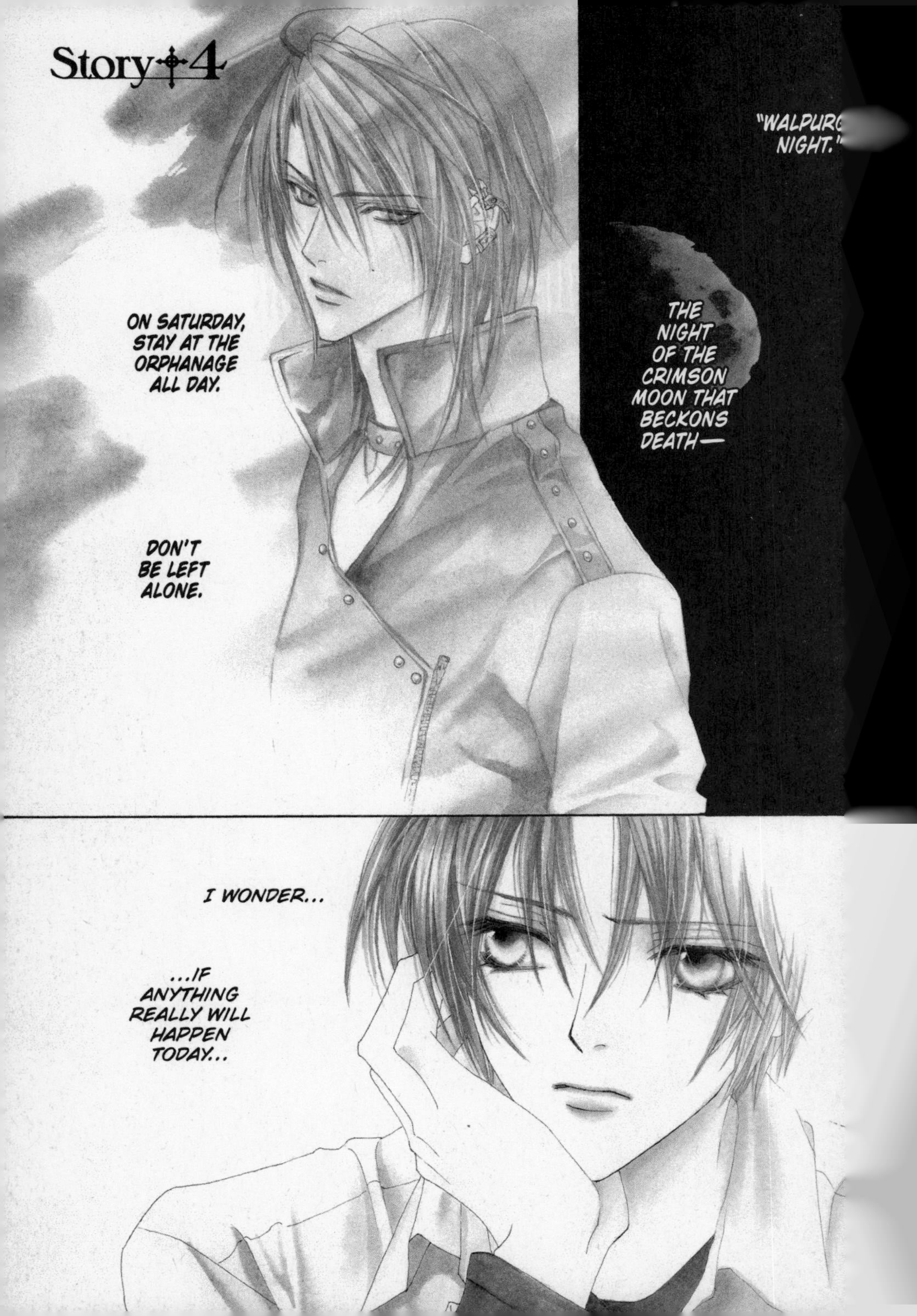
Story 4
"WALPURG
NIGHT."
THE NIGHT OF THE CRIMSON MOON THAT BECKONS DEATH—
ON SATURDAY, STAY AT THE ORPHANAGE ALL DAY.
DON'T BE LEFT ALONE.
I WONDER...
...IF ANYTHING REALLY WILL HAPPEN TODAY...

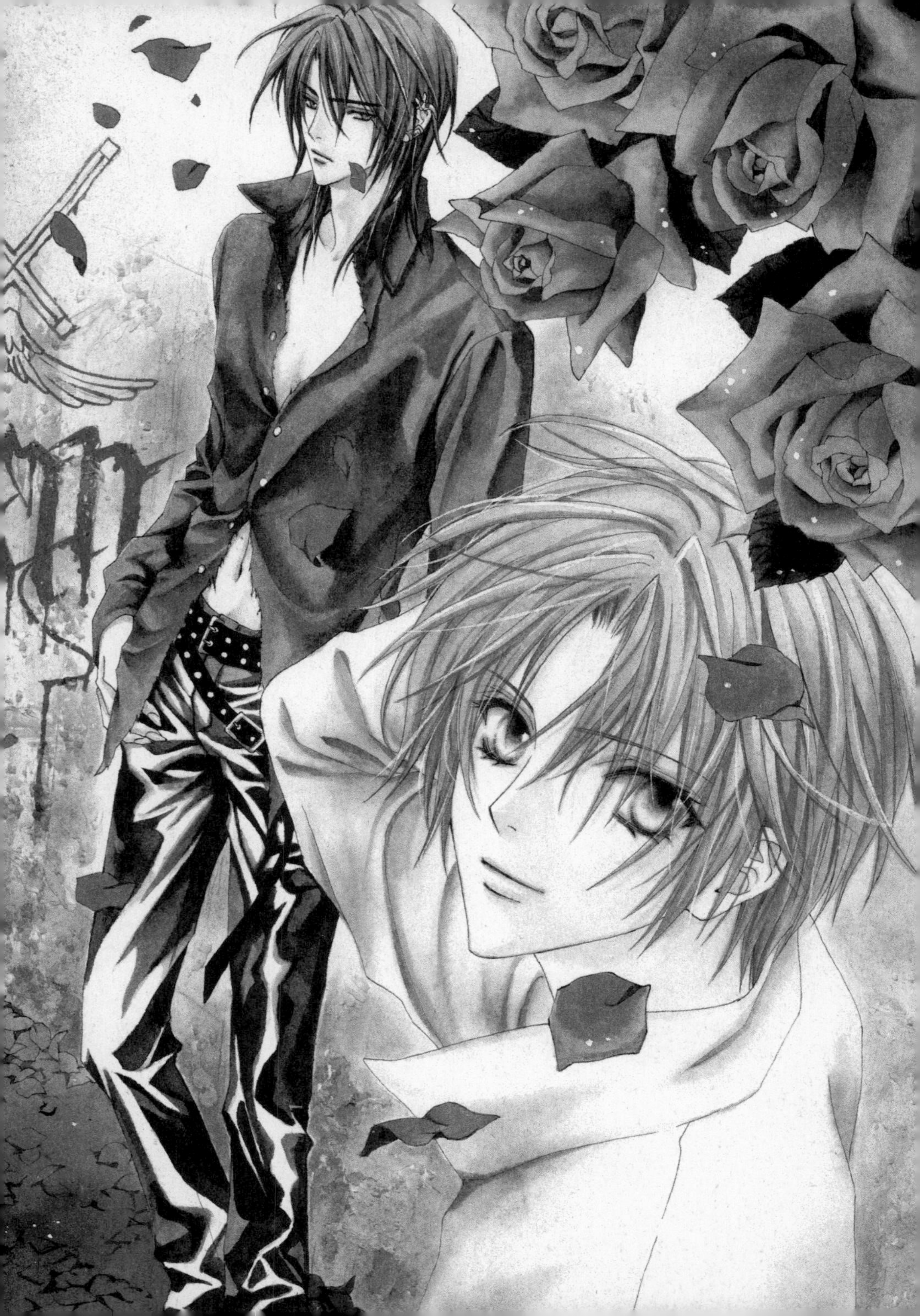

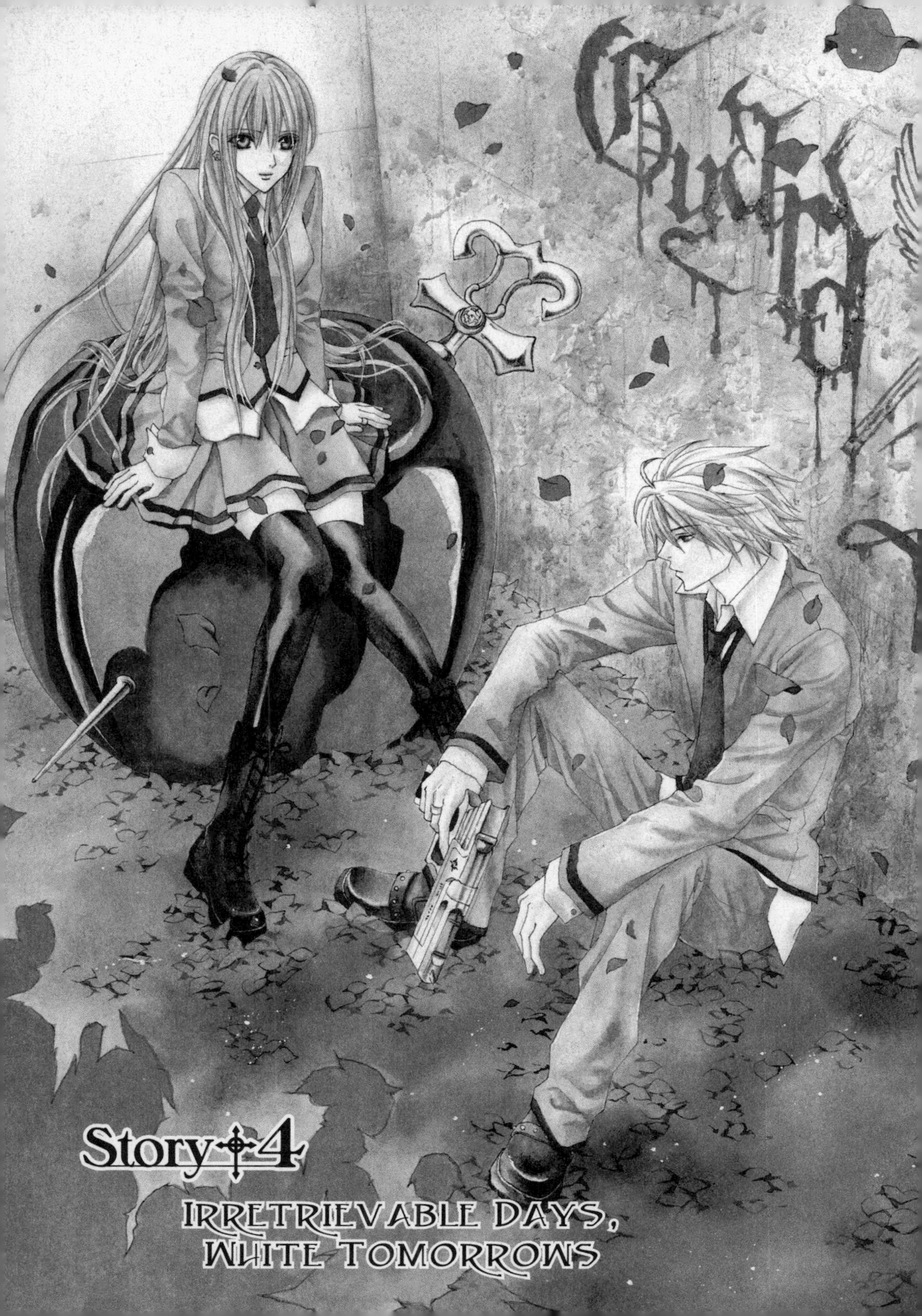
Crack'd
Story 4
IRRETRIEVABLE DAYS, WHITE TOMORROWS

The Betrayal Knows My Name

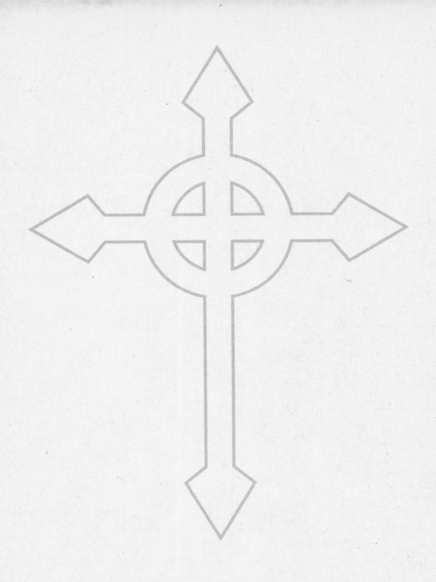

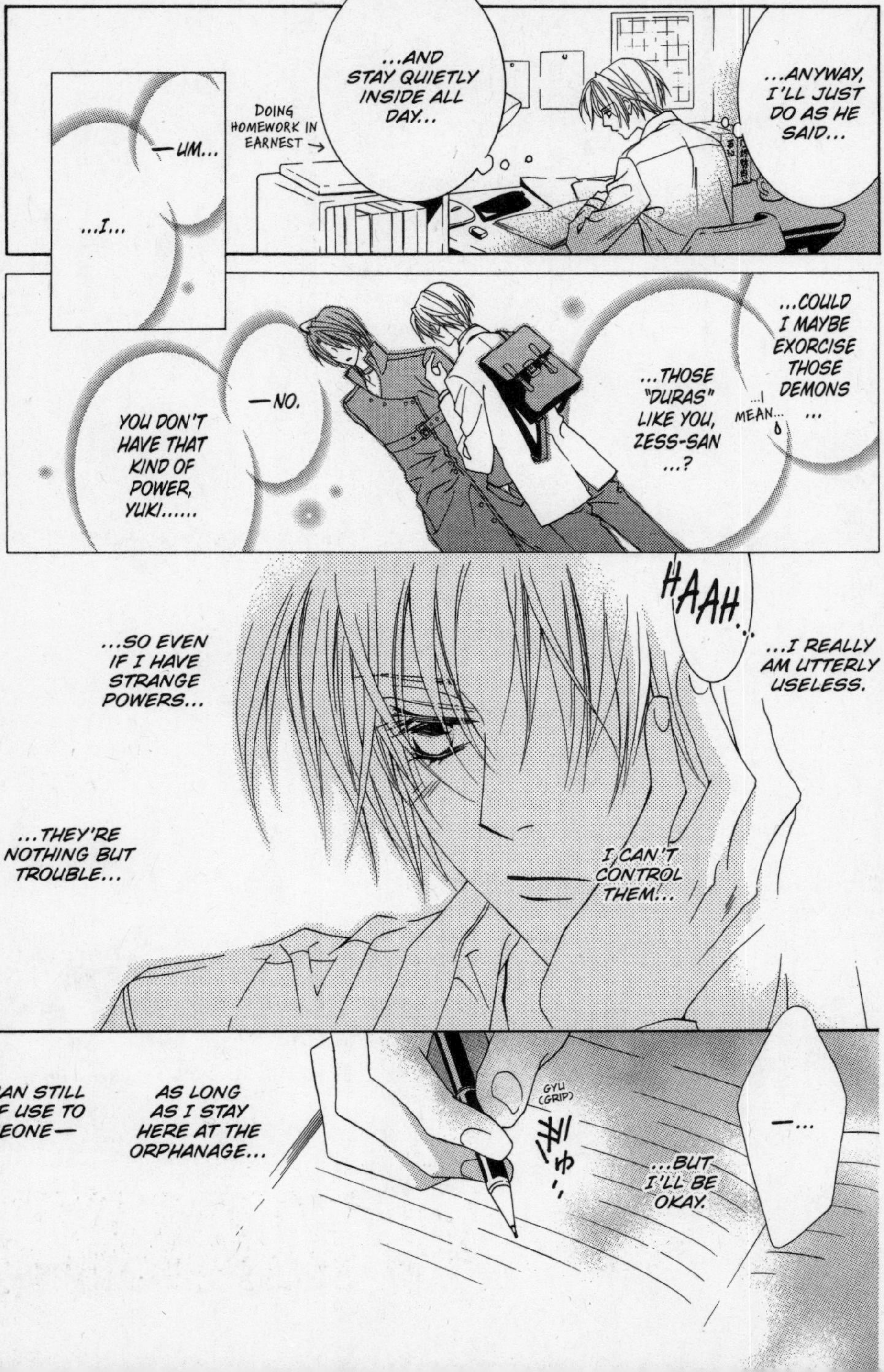

...ANYWAY, I'LL JUST DO AS HE SAID...
...AND STAY QUIETLY INSIDE ALL DAY...
DOING HOMEWORK IN EARNEST
—UM...
...I...
...COULD I MAYBE EXORCISE THOSE DEMONS ...
...I MEAN...
...THOSE "DURAS" LIKE YOU, ZESS-SAN ...?
—NO.
YOU DON'T HAVE THAT KIND OF POWER, YUKI......
HAAAH...
...I REALLY AM UTTERLY USELESS.
I CAN'T CONTROL THEM!...
...SO EVEN IF I HAVE STRANGE POWERS...
...THEY'RE NOTHING BUT TROUBLE...
—...
...BUT I'LL BE OKAY.
GYU (GRIP)
AS LONG AS I STAY HERE AT THE ORPHANAGE...
...I CAN STILL BE OF USE TO SOMEONE—

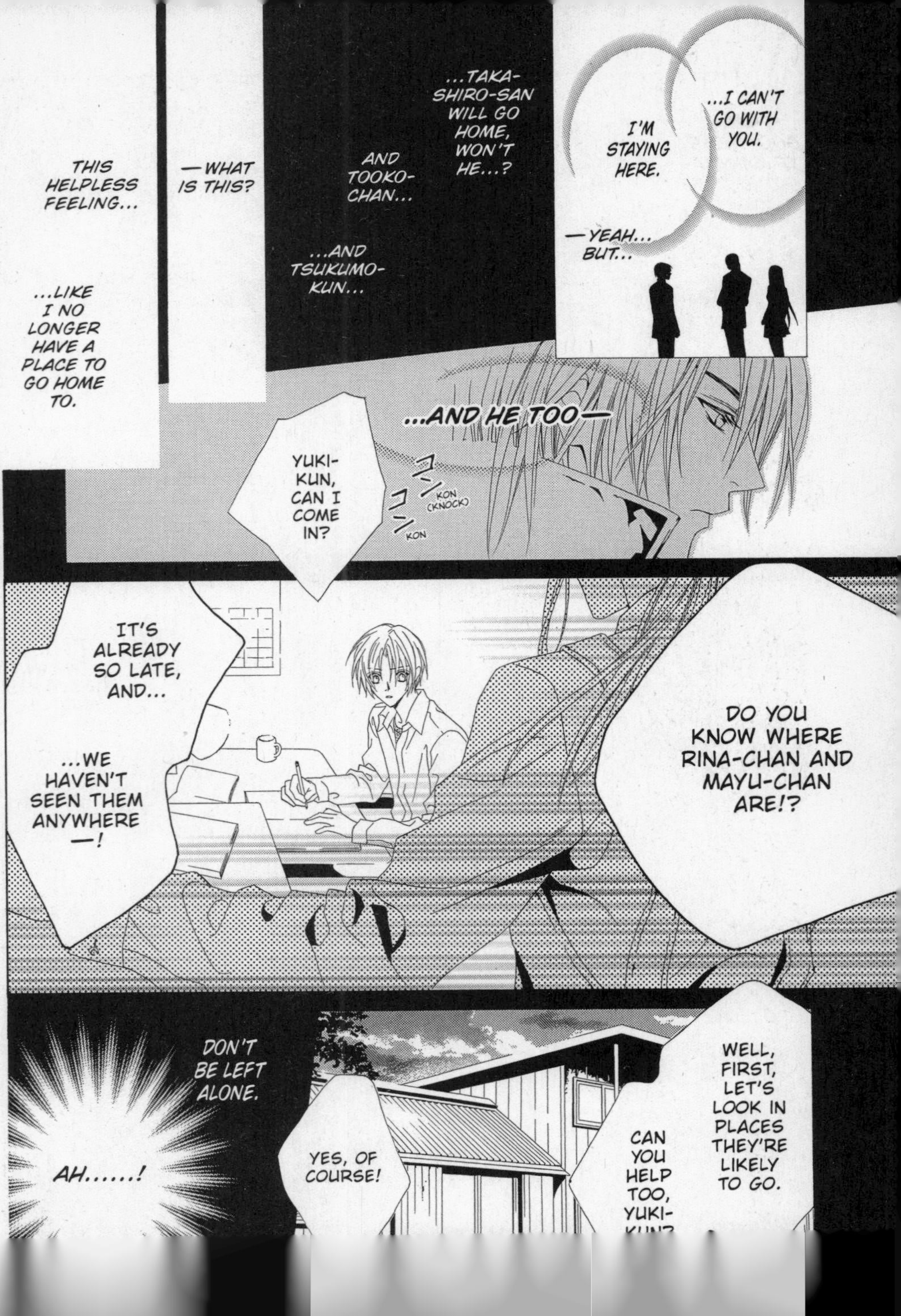
...I CAN'T GO WITH YOU.
I'M STAYING HERE.
—YEAH... BUT...
...TAKA-SHIRO-SAN WILL GO HOME, WON'T HE...?
AND TOOKO-CHAN...
...AND TSUKUMO-KUN...
—WHAT IS THIS?
THIS HELPLESS FEELING...
...LIKE I NO LONGER HAVE A PLACE TO GO HOME TO.
...AND HE TOO—
KON (KNOCK)
KON
YUKI-KUN, CAN I COME IN?
DO YOU KNOW WHERE RINA-CHAN AND MAYU-CHAN ARE!?
IT'S ALREADY SO LATE, AND...
...WE HAVEN'T SEEN THEM ANYWHERE—!
WELL, FIRST, LET'S LOOK IN PLACES THEY'RE LIKELY TO GO.
CAN YOU HELP TOO, YUKI-
YES, OF COURSE!
DON'T BE LEFT ALONE.
AH......!

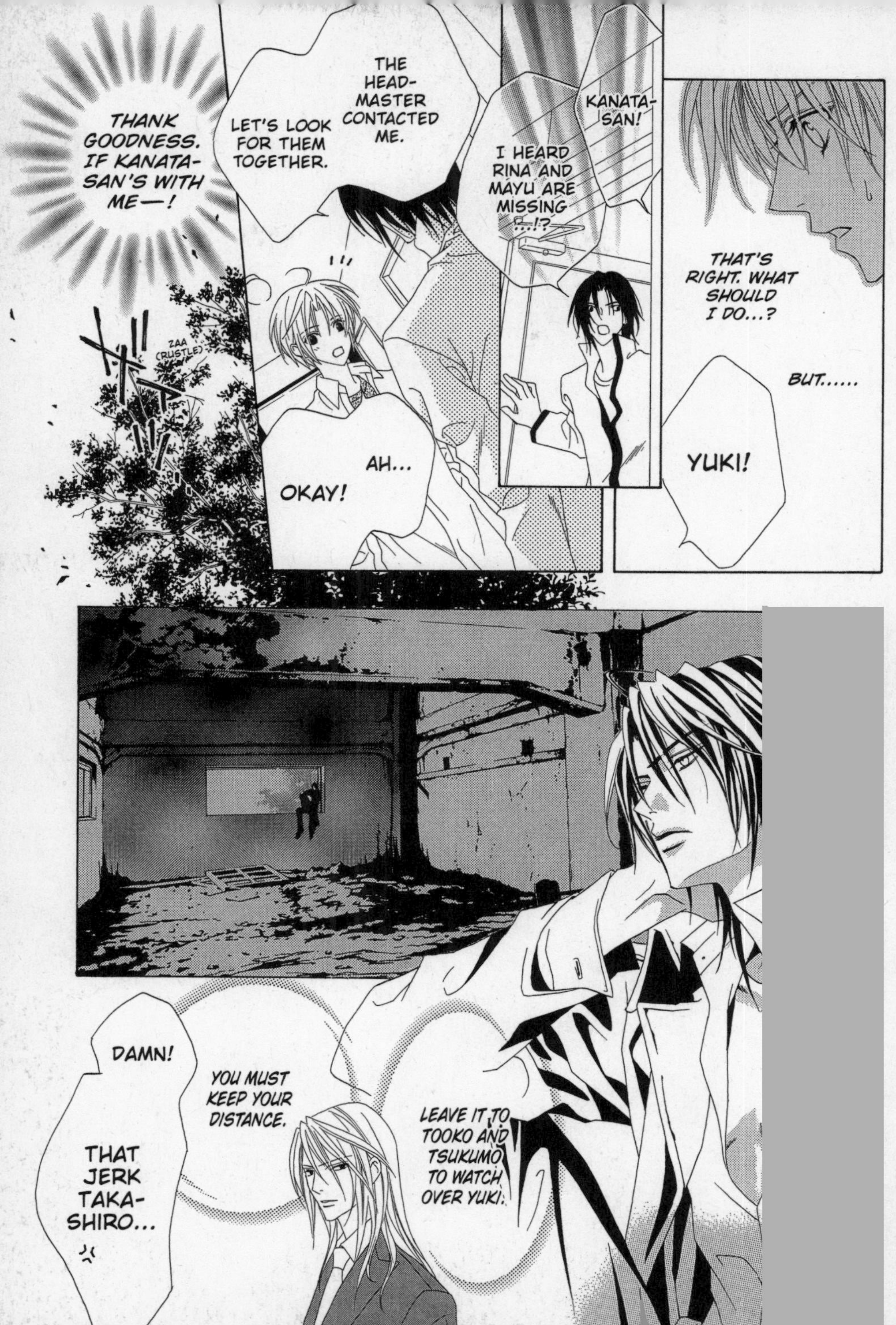
THAT'S RIGHT. WHAT SHOULD I DO...?
BUT......
YUKI!
KANATA-SAN!
I HEARD RINA AND MAYU ARE MISSING ...!?
THE HEAD-MASTER CONTACTED ME.
LET'S LOOK FOR THEM TOGETHER.
AH...
OKAY!
THANK GOODNESS. IF KANATA-SAN'S WITH ME—!
ZAA (RUSTLE)
LEAVE IT TO TOOKO AND TSUKUMO TO WATCH OVER YUKI.
YOU MUST KEEP YOUR DISTANCE.
DAMN!
THAT JERK TAKA-SHIRO...

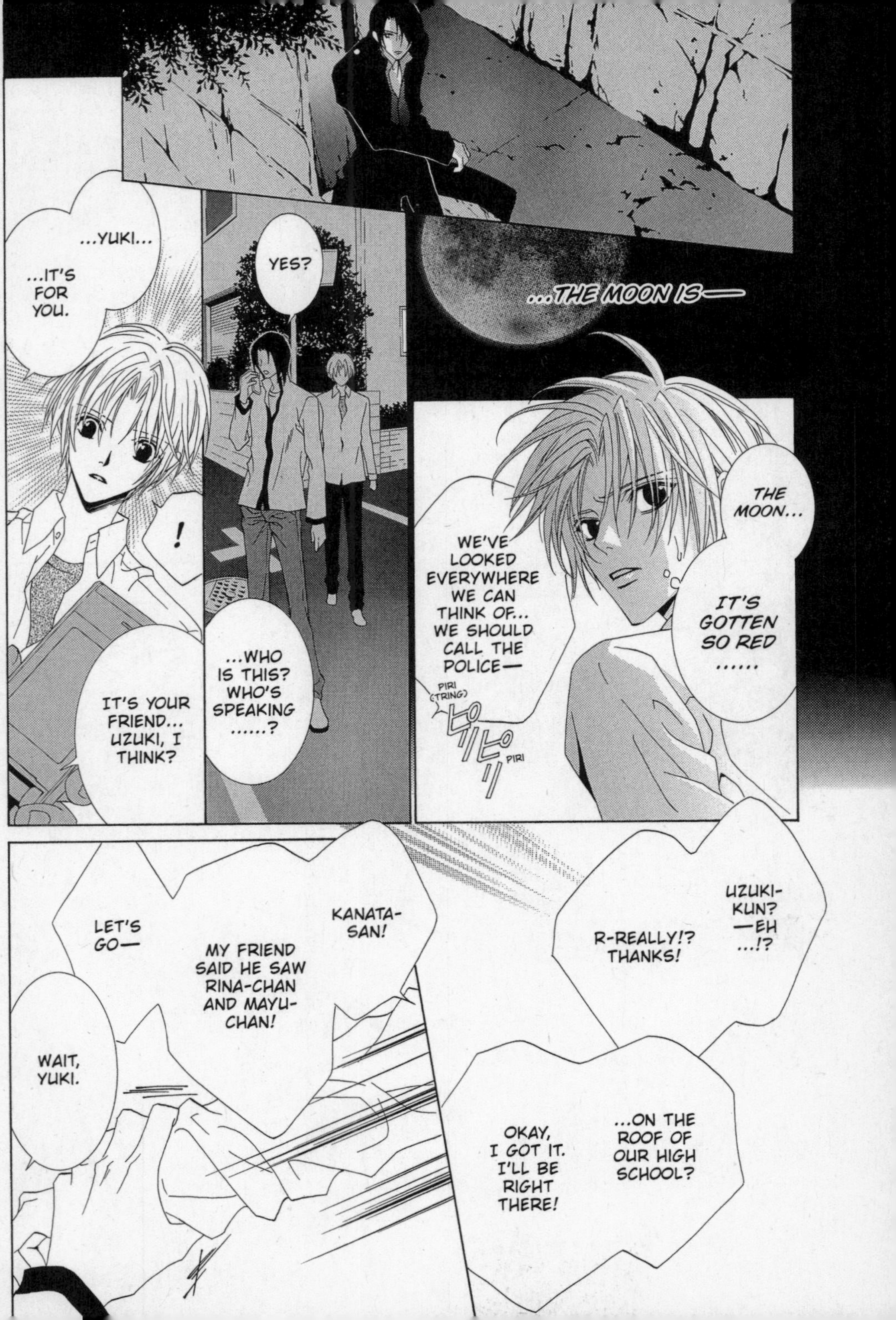

...THE MOON IS—
THE MOON...
IT'S GOTTEN SO RED ......
WE'VE LOOKED EVERYWHERE WE CAN THINK OF... WE SHOULD CALL THE POLICE—
PIRI (TRING)
ピリピリ
PIRI
YES?
...WHO IS THIS? WHO'S SPEAKING ......?
...YUKI...
...IT'S FOR YOU.
!
IT'S YOUR FRIEND... UZUKI, I THINK?
UZUKI-KUN? —EH ...!?
R-REALLY!? THANKS!
...ON THE ROOF OF OUR HIGH SCHOOL?
OKAY, I GOT IT. I'LL BE RIGHT THERE!
KANATA-SAN!
MY FRIEND SAID HE SAW RINA-CHAN AND MAYU-CHAN!
LET'S GO—
WAIT, YUKI.

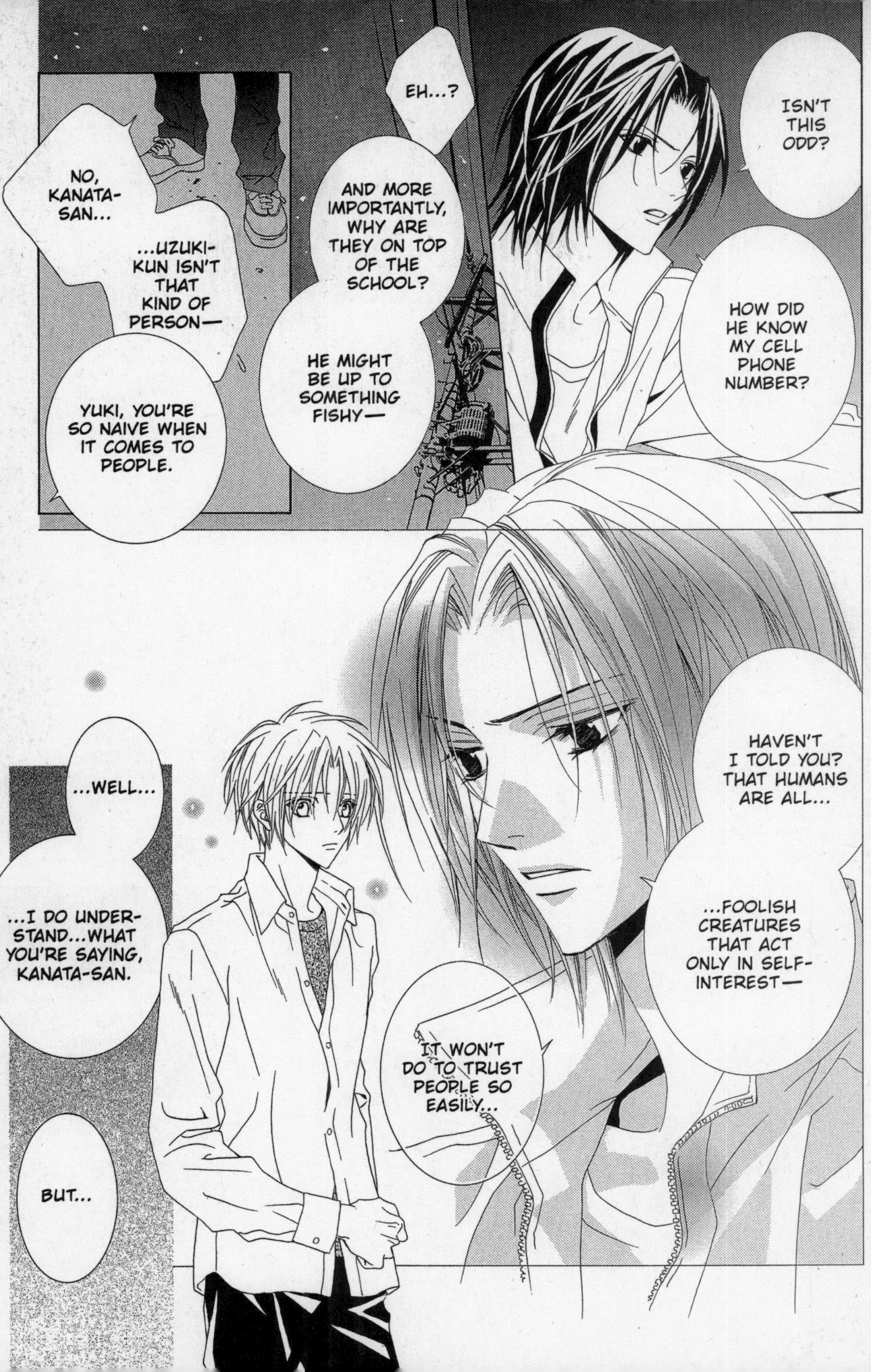
ISN'T THIS ODD?
HOW DID HE KNOW MY CELL PHONE NUMBER?
EH...?
AND MORE IMPORTANTLY, WHY ARE THEY ON TOP OF THE SCHOOL?
HE MIGHT BE UP TO SOMETHING FISHY—
NO, KANATA-SAN...
...UZUKI-KUN ISN'T THAT KIND OF PERSON—
YUKI, YOU'RE SO NAIVE WHEN IT COMES TO PEOPLE.
HAVEN'T I TOLD YOU? THAT HUMANS ARE ALL...
...FOOLISH CREATURES THAT ACT ONLY IN SELF-INTEREST—
IT WON'T DO TO TRUST PEOPLE SO EASILY...
...WELL...
...I DO UNDERSTAND...WHAT YOU'RE SAYING, KANATA-SAN.
BUT...

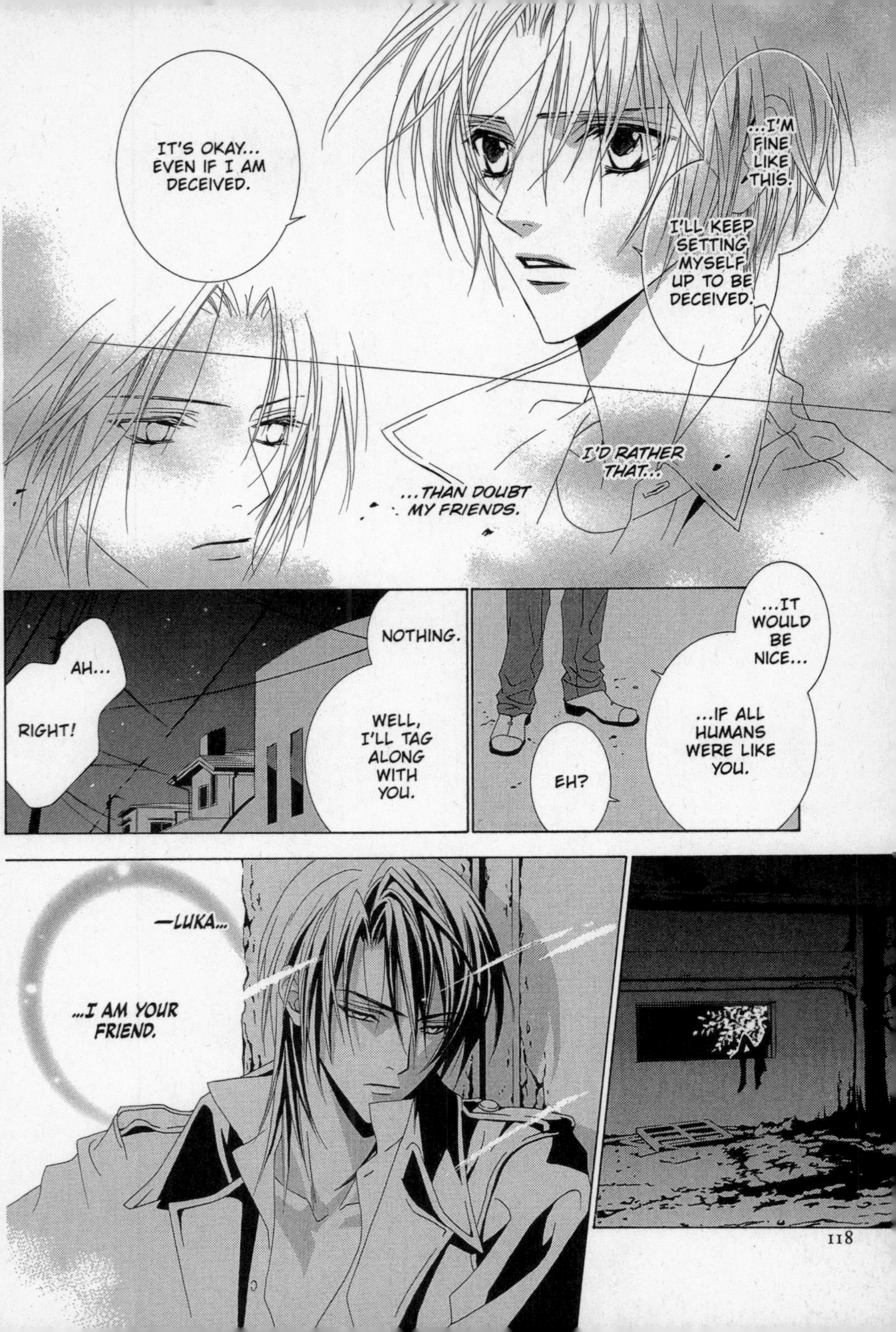
...I'M FINE LIKE THIS.
I'LL KEEP SETTING MYSELF UP TO BE DECEIVED.
IT'S OKAY... EVEN IF I AM DECEIVED.
I'D RATHER THAT...
...THAN DOUBT MY FRIENDS.
...IT WOULD BE NICE...
...IF ALL HUMANS WERE LIKE YOU.
EH?
NOTHING.
WELL, I'LL TAG ALONG WITH YOU.
AH...
RIGHT!
—LUKA...
...I AM YOUR FRIEND.

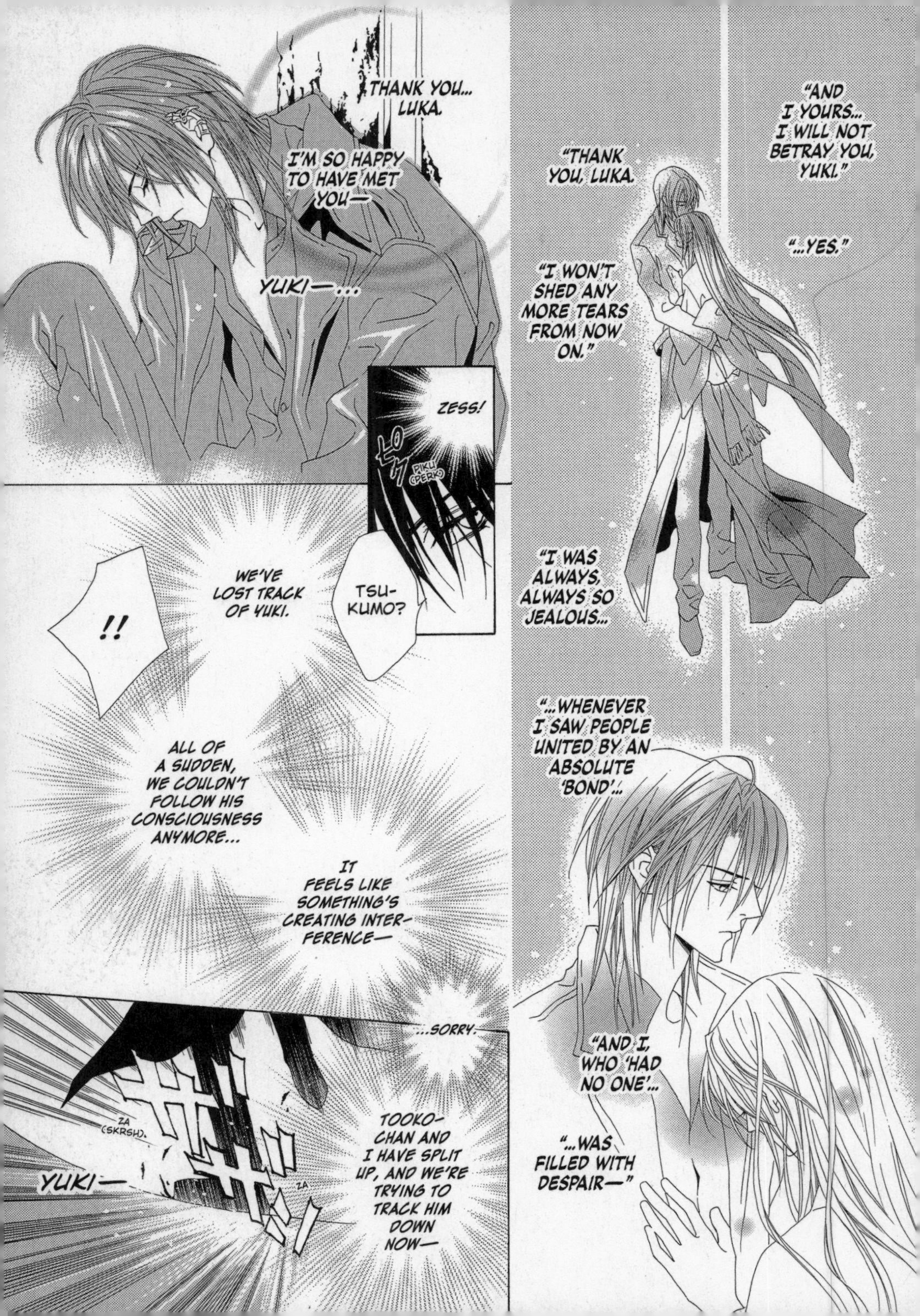
THANK YOU... LUKA.
I'M SO HAPPY TO HAVE MET YOU—
YUKI—...
ZESS!
PIKU (PERK)
TSU-KUMO?
WE'VE LOST TRACK OF YUKI.
!!
ALL OF A SUDDEN, WE COULDN'T FOLLOW HIS CONSCIOUSNESS ANYMORE...
IT FEELS LIKE SOMETHING'S CREATING INTER-FERENCE—
...SORRY.
TOOKO-CHAN AND I HAVE SPLIT UP, AND WE'RE TRYING TO TRACK HIM DOWN NOW—
ZA (SKRSH)
YUKI—
ZA
"AND I YOURS... I WILL NOT BETRAY YOU, YUKI."
"...YES."
"THANK YOU, LUKA.
"I WON'T SHED ANY MORE TEARS FROM NOW ON."
"I WAS ALWAYS, ALWAYS SO JEALOUS...
"...WHENEVER I SAW PEOPLE UNITED BY AN ABSOLUTE 'BOND'...
"AND I, WHO 'HAD NO ONE'...
"...WAS FILLED WITH DESPAIR—"

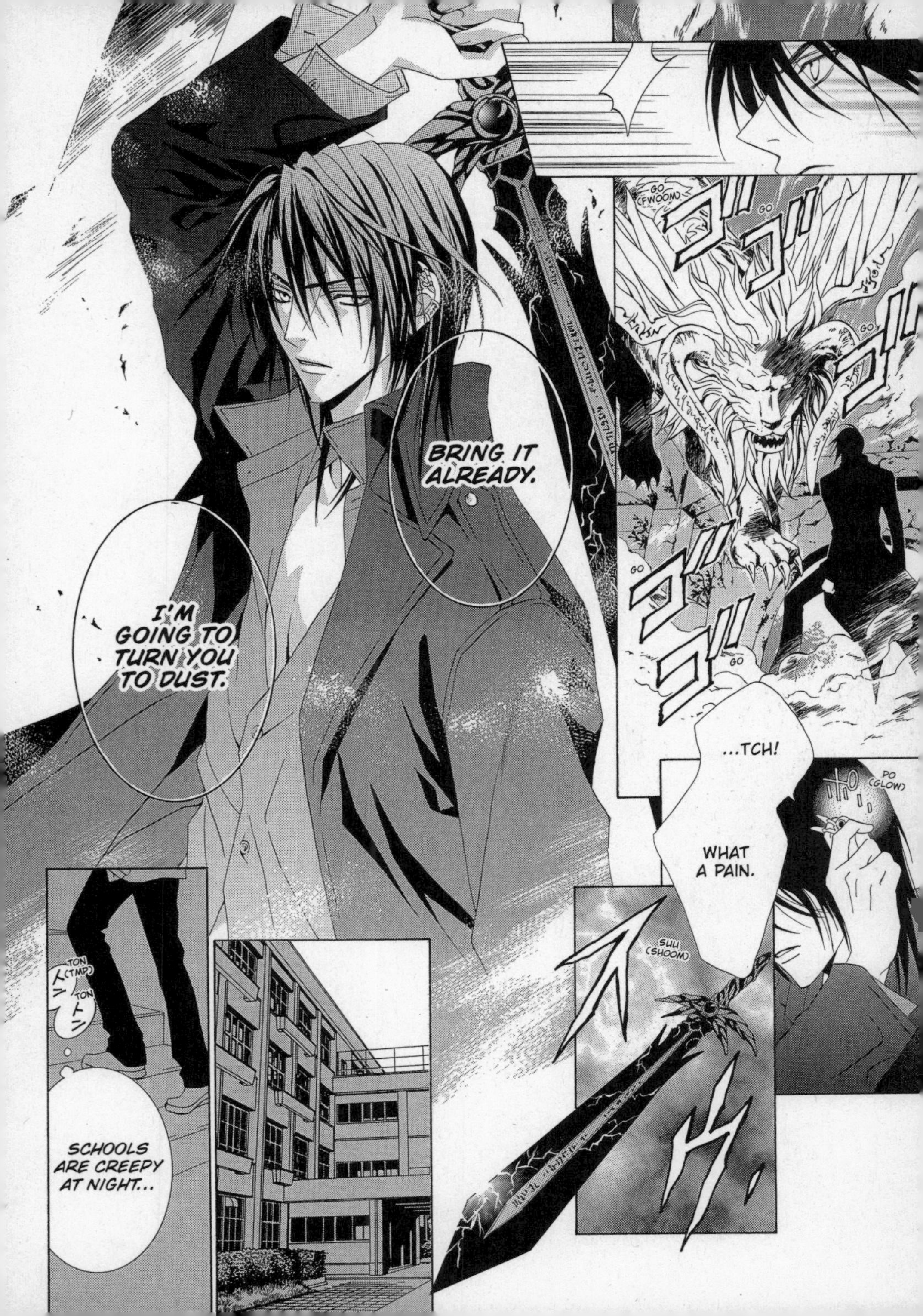
GO (FWOOM)
GO
GO
GO
GO
BRING IT ALREADY.
I'M GOING TO TURN YOU TO DUST.
...TCH!
WHAT A PAIN.
PO (GLOW)
SUU (SHOOM)
TON (TMP) TON
SCHOOLS ARE CREEPY AT NIGHT...

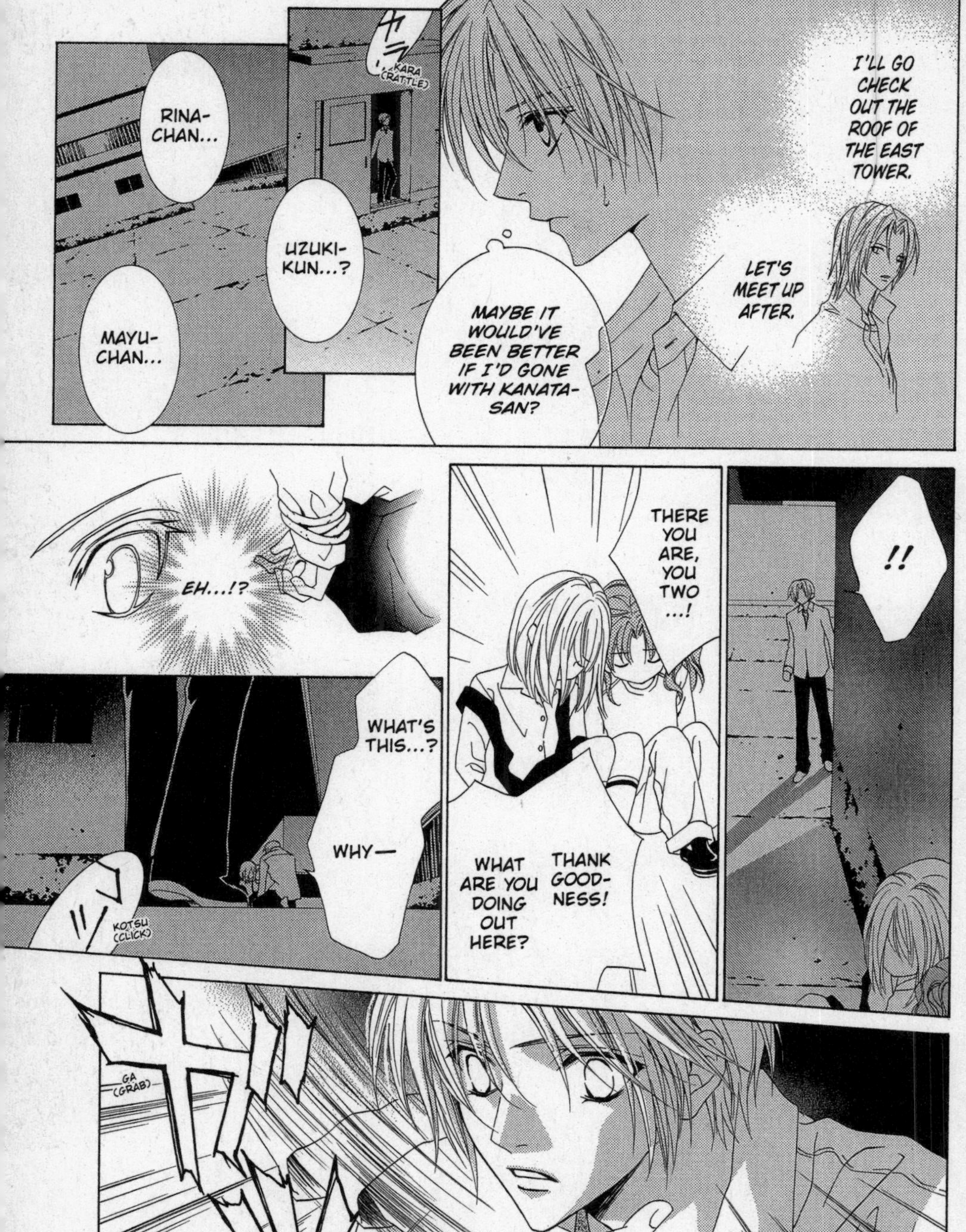
I'LL GO CHECK OUT THE ROOF OF THE EAST TOWER.
LET'S MEET UP AFTER.
MAYBE IT WOULD'VE BEEN BETTER IF I'D GONE WITH KANATA-SAN?
KARA (RATTLE)
UZUKI-KUN...?
RINA-CHAN...
MAYU-CHAN...
!!
THERE YOU ARE, YOU TWO...!
THANK GOODNESS!
WHAT ARE YOU DOING OUT HERE?
EH...!?
WHAT'S THIS...?
WHY—
KOTSU (CLICK)
GA (GRAB)

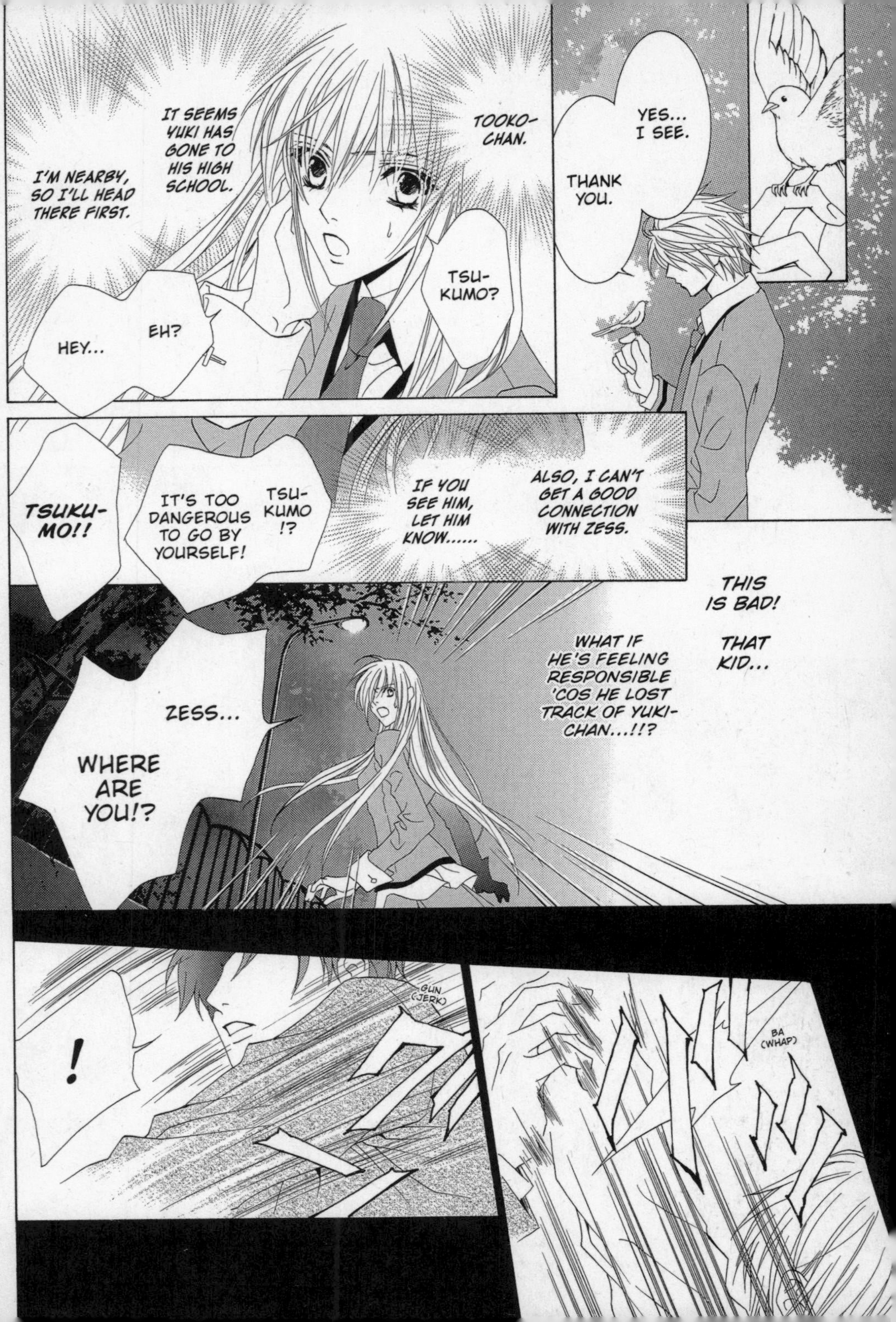
YES... I SEE.
THANK YOU.
TOOKO-CHAN.
IT SEEMS YUKI HAS GONE TO HIS HIGH SCHOOL.
I'M NEARBY, SO I'LL HEAD THERE FIRST.
TSU-KUMO?
EH?
HEY...
ALSO, I CAN'T GET A GOOD CONNECTION WITH ZESS.
IF YOU SEE HIM, LET HIM KNOW......
TSU-KUMO!?
IT'S TOO DANGEROUS TO GO BY YOURSELF!
TSUKU-MO!!
THIS IS BAD!
THAT KID...
WHAT IF HE'S FEELING RESPONSIBLE 'COS HE LOST TRACK OF YUKI-CHAN...!!?
ZESS...
WHERE ARE YOU!?
BA (WHAP)
GUN (JERK)
!

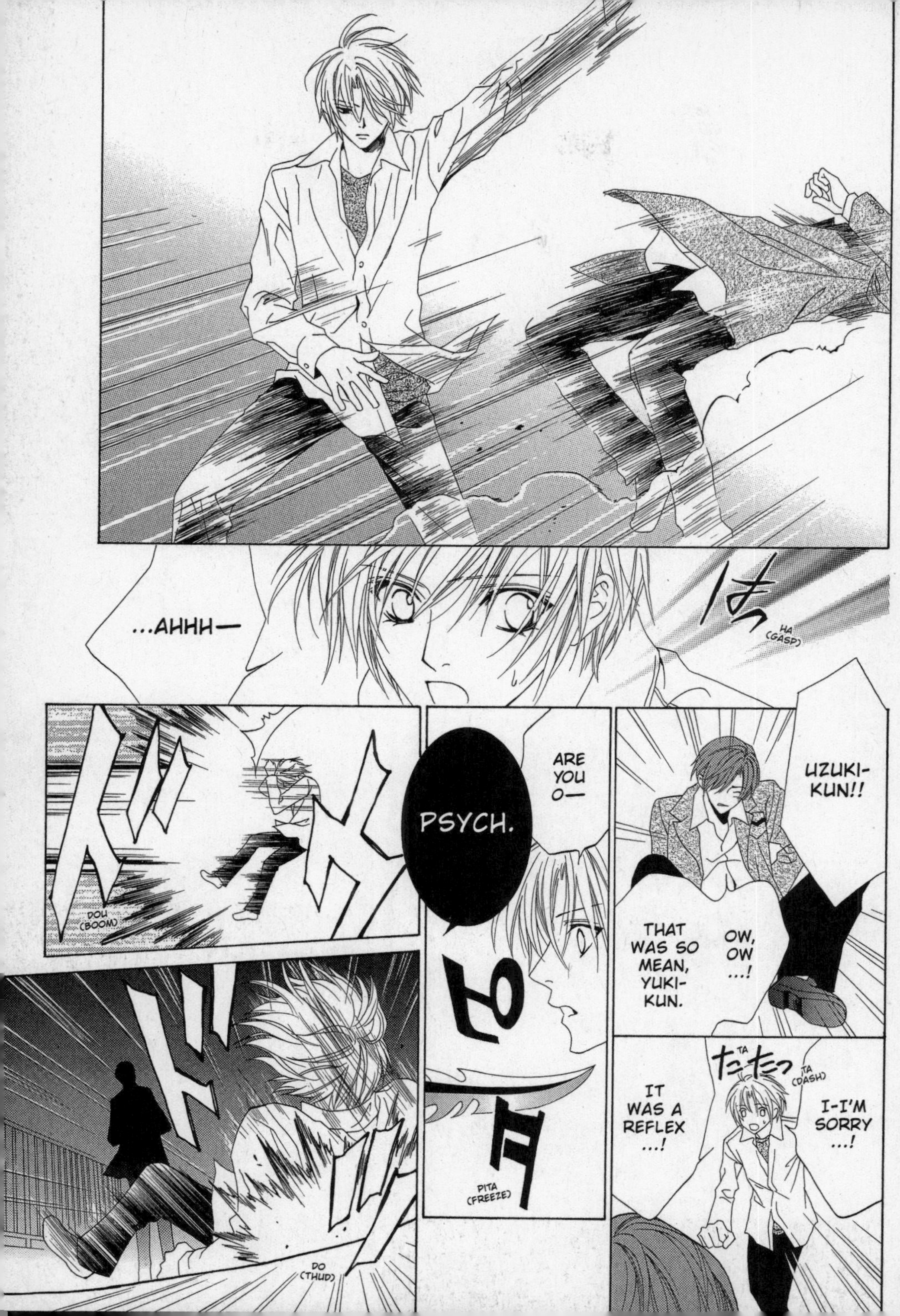
HA
(GASP)
...AHHH—
UZUKI-KUN!!
OW, OW ...!
THAT WAS SO MEAN, YUKI-KUN.
ARE YOU O—
PSYCH.
PITA
(FREEZE)
DOU
(BOOM)
TA
TA
(DASH)
I-I'M SORRY ...!
IT WAS A REFLEX ...!
DO
(THUD)

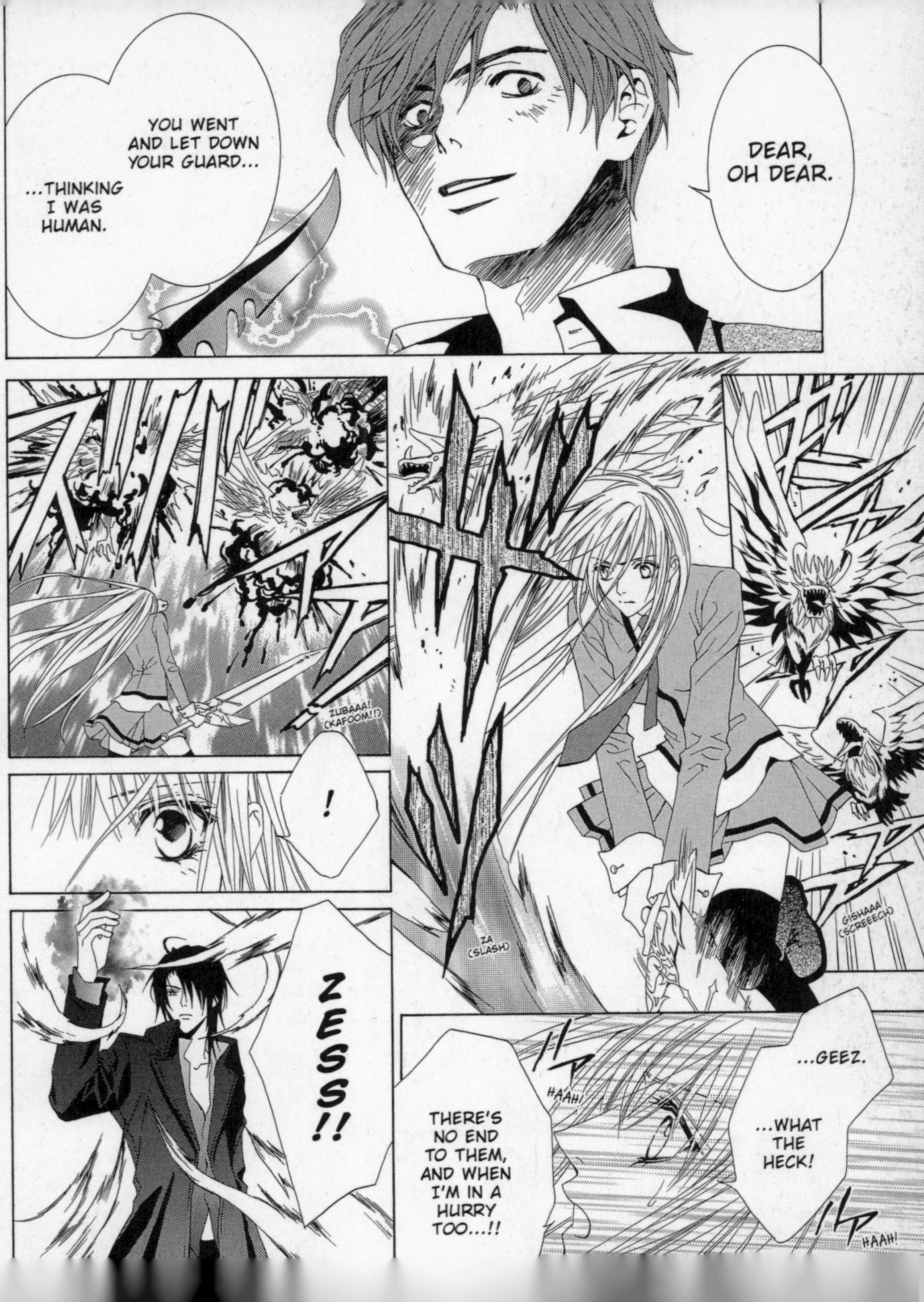
DEAR, OH DEAR.
YOU WENT AND LET DOWN YOUR GUARD...
...THINKING I WAS HUMAN.
GISHAAA (SCREEECH)
ZA (SLASH)
ZUBAAA! (KAFOOM!)
!
ZESS!!
...GEEZ.
...WHAT THE HECK!
HAAH!
THERE'S NO END TO THEM, AND WHEN I'M IN A HURRY TOO...!!
HAAH!

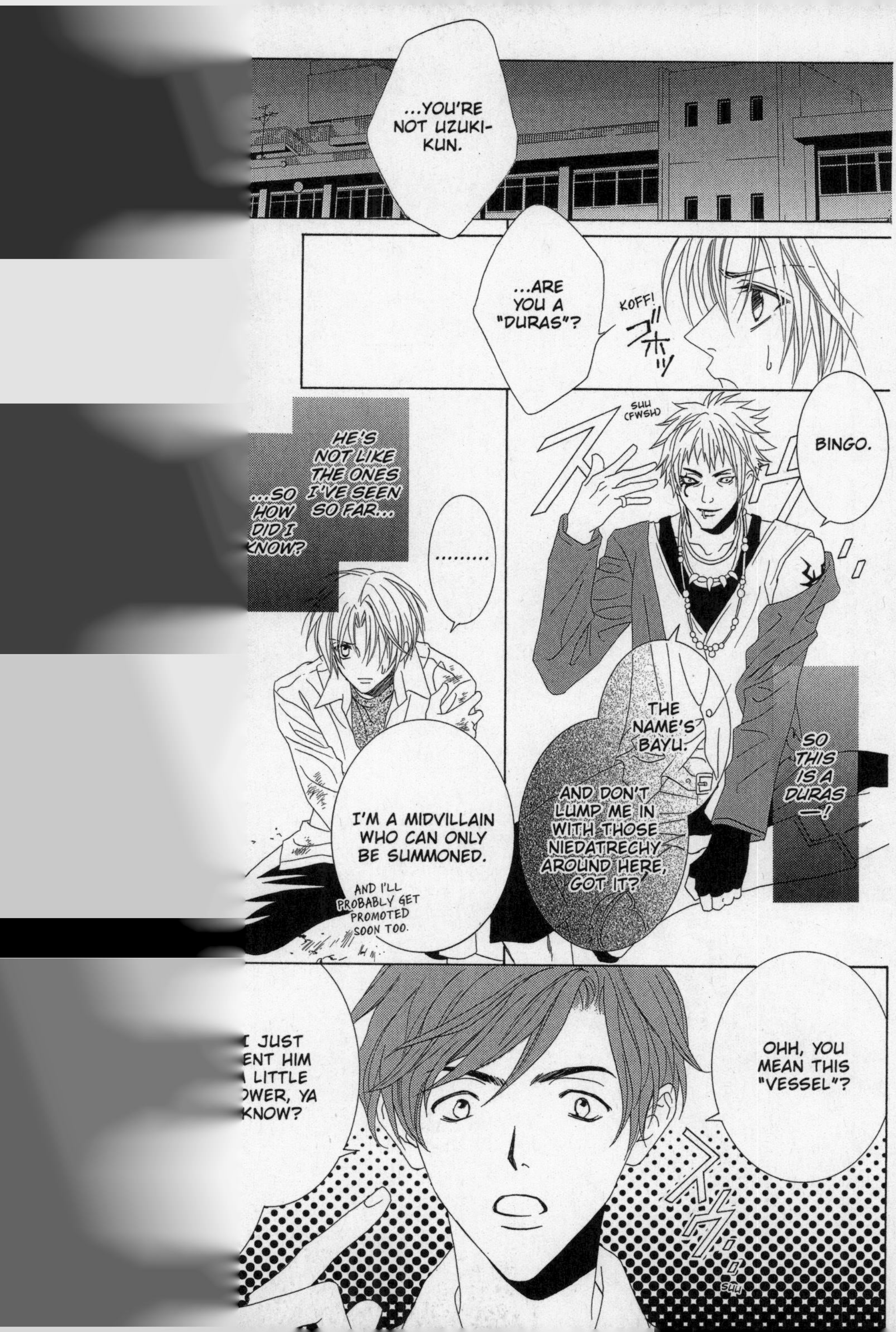

...YOU'RE NOT UZUKI-KUN.
...ARE YOU A "DURAS"?
KOFF!
ゴホッ
SUU (FWSH)
BINGO.
HE'S NOT LIKE THE ONES I'VE SEEN SO FAR...
...SO HOW DID I
KNOW?
....
SO THIS IS A DURAS—!
THE NAME'S BAYU.
AND DON'T LUMP ME IN WITH THOSE NIEDATRECHY AROUND HERE, GOT IT?
I'M A MIDVILLAIN WHO CAN ONLY BE SUMMONED.
AND I'LL PROBABLY GET PROMOTED SOON TOO.
OHH, YOU MEAN THIS "VESSEL"?
SUU
I JUST
ENT HIM
LITTLE
OWER, YA
KNOW?

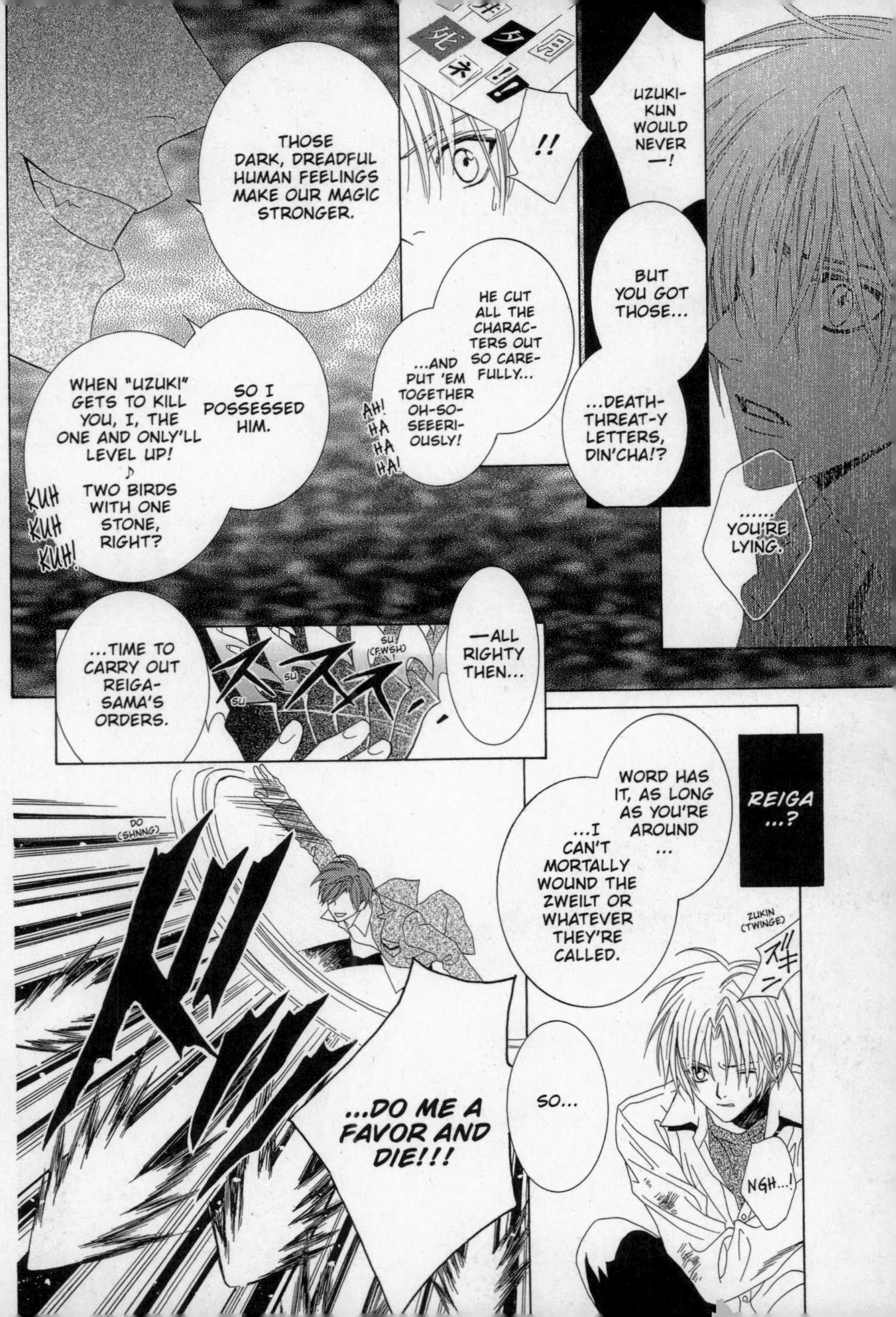
UZUKI-KUN WOULD NEVER—!
BUT YOU GOT THOSE...
...DEATH-THREAT-Y LETTERS, DIN'CHA!?
......YOU'RE LYING.
!!
HE CUT ALL THE CHARACTERS OUT SO CAREFULLY...
...AND PUT 'EM TOGETHER OH-SO-SEEERIOUSLY!
AH! HA HA HA!
THOSE DARK, DREADFUL HUMAN FEELINGS MAKE OUR MAGIC STRONGER.
SO I POSSESSED HIM.
WHEN "UZUKI" GETS TO KILL YOU, I, THE ONE AND ONLY'LL LEVEL UP! ♪ TWO BIRDS WITH ONE STONE, RIGHT?
KUH KUH KUH!
—ALL RIGHTY THEN...
SU (CFWSH)
SU
SU
...TIME TO CARRY OUT REIGA-SAMA'S ORDERS.
REIGA ...?
WORD HAS IT, AS LONG AS YOU'RE AROUND ...
...I CAN'T MORTALLY WOUND THE ZWEILT OR WHATEVER THEY'RE CALLED.
ZUKIN (TWINGE)
SO...
NGH...!
DO (SHNNG)
...DO ME A FAVOR AND DIE!!!

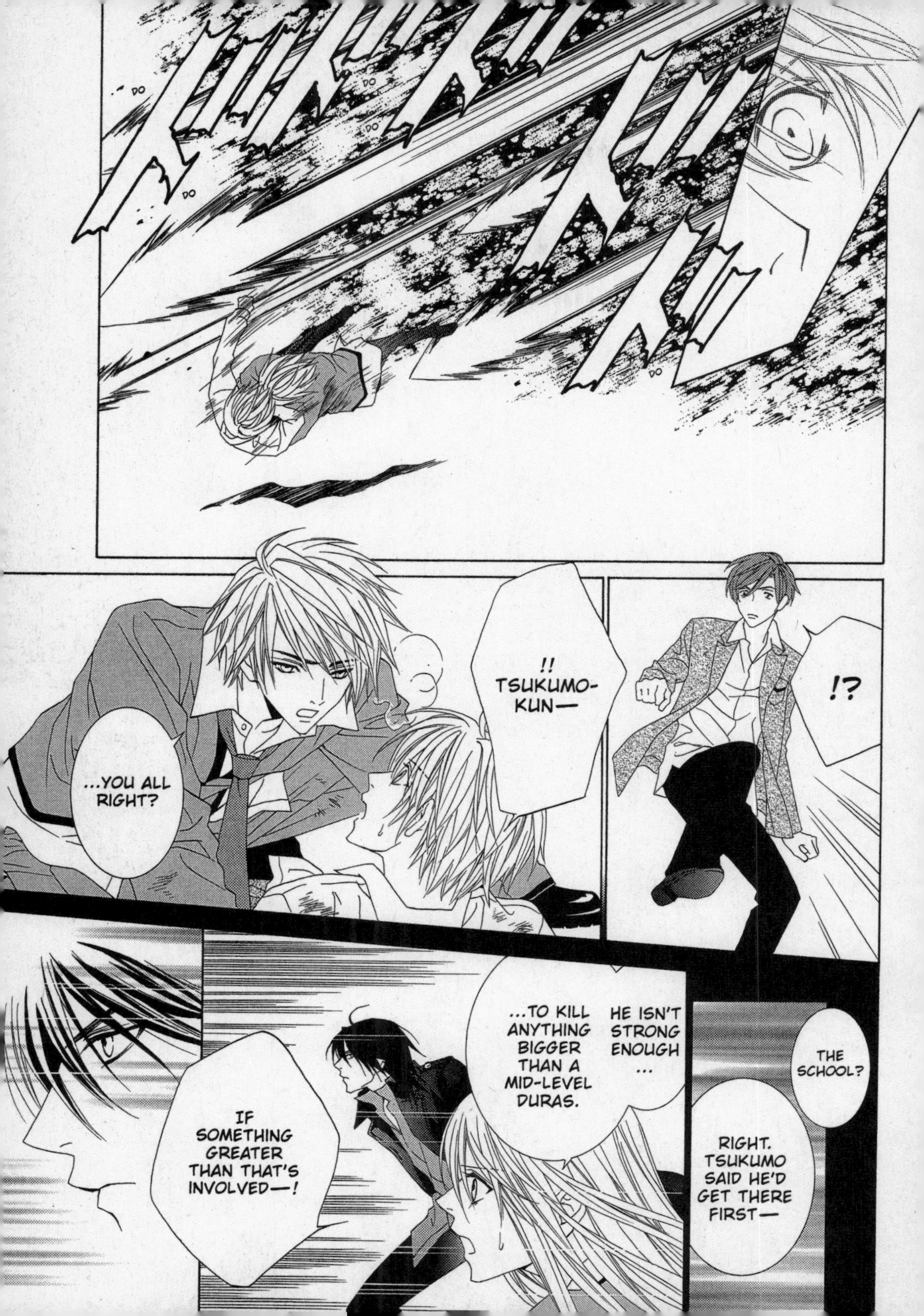
DO
DO
DO
DO
DO
DO
!?
!! TSUKUMO-KUN—
...YOU ALL RIGHT?
THE SCHOOL?
RIGHT. TSUKUMO SAID HE'D GET THERE FIRST—
HE ISN'T STRONG ENOUGH ...
...TO KILL ANYTHING BIGGER THAN A MID-LEVEL DURAS.
IF SOMETHING GREATER THAN THAT'S INVOLVED—!

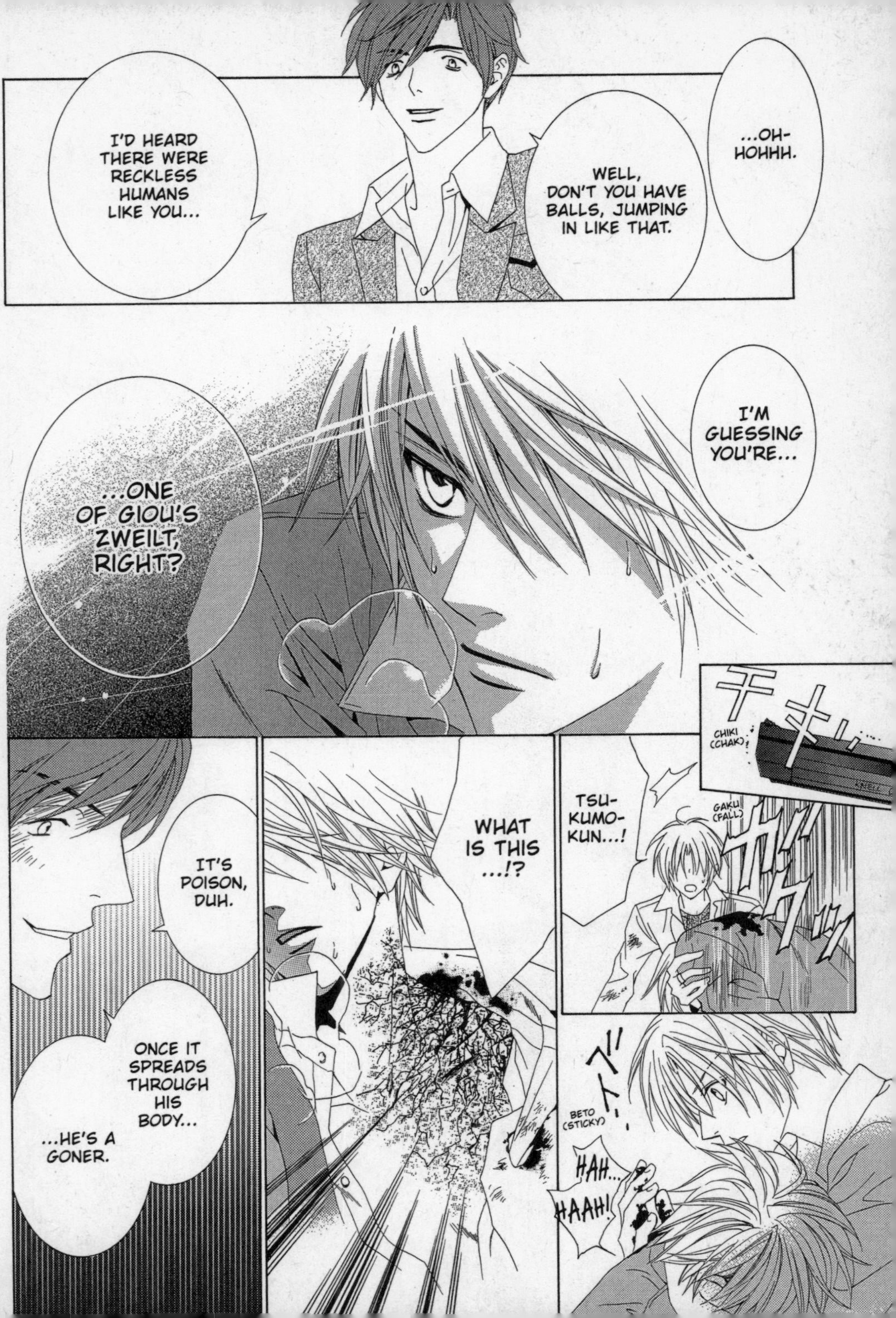
...OH-
HOHHH.
WELL, DON'T YOU HAVE BALLS, JUMPING IN LIKE THAT.
I'D HEARD THERE WERE RECKLESS HUMANS LIKE YOU...
I'M GUESSING YOU'RE...
...ONE OF GIOU'S ZWEILT, RIGHT?
CHIKI (CHAK)
GAKU (FALL)
TSU-KUMO-KUN...!
WHAT IS THIS ...!?
IT'S POISON, DUH.
BETO (STICKY)
HAH...
HAAH!
ONCE IT SPREADS THROUGH HIS BODY...
...HE'S A GONER.

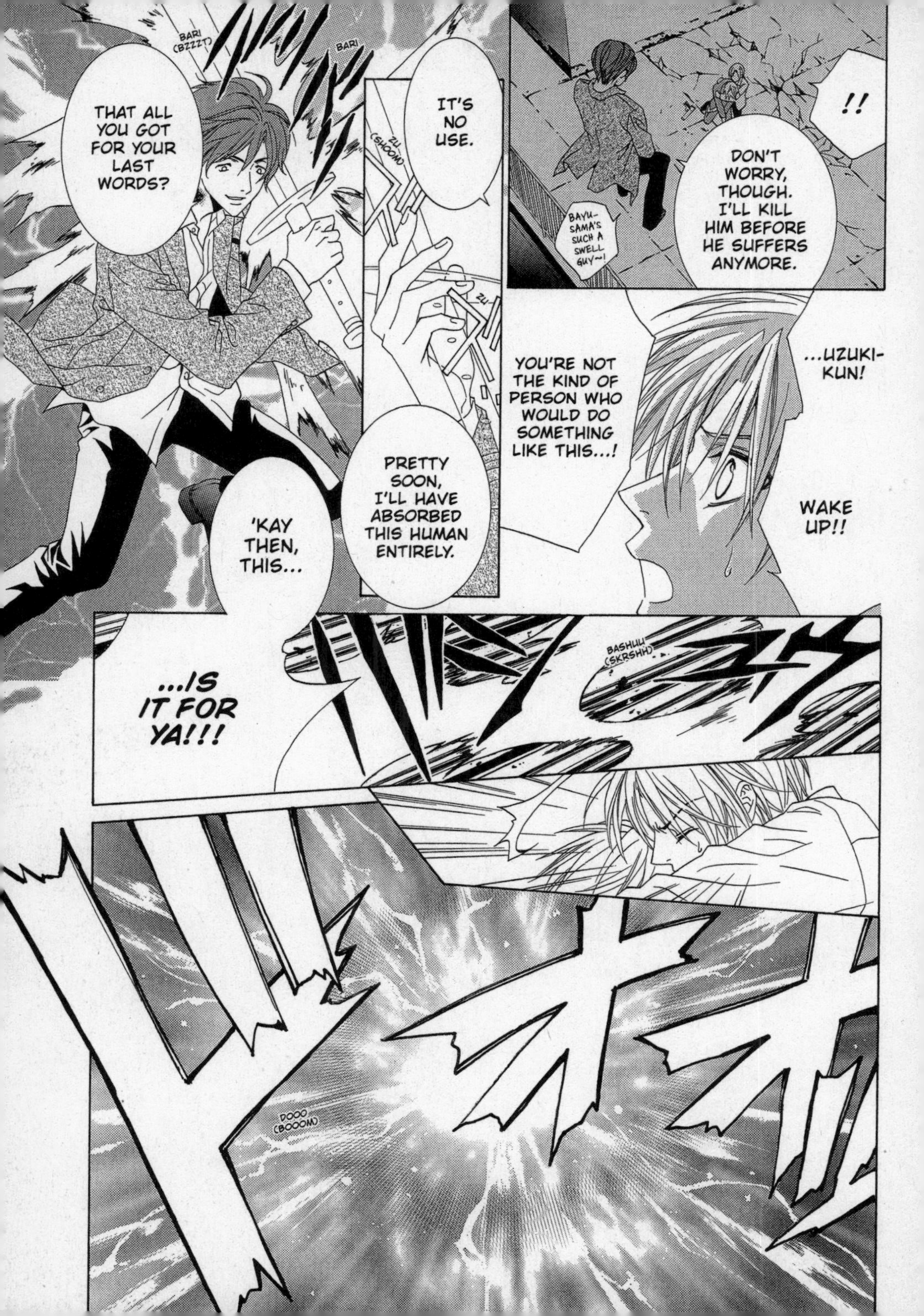
!!
DON'T WORRY, THOUGH. I'LL KILL HIM BEFORE HE SUFFERS ANYMORE.
BAYU-SAMA'S SUCH A SWELL GUY~!
IT'S NO USE.
ZU (SHOOM)
ZU
BARI
BARI (BZZZT)
THAT ALL YOU GOT FOR YOUR LAST WORDS?
...UZUKI-KUN!
YOU'RE NOT THE KIND OF PERSON WHO WOULD DO SOMETHING LIKE THIS...!
WAKE UP!!
PRETTY SOON, I'LL HAVE ABSORBED THIS HUMAN ENTIRELY.
'KAY THEN, THIS...
BASHUU (SKRSHH)
...IS IT FOR YA!!!
DOOO (BOOOM)

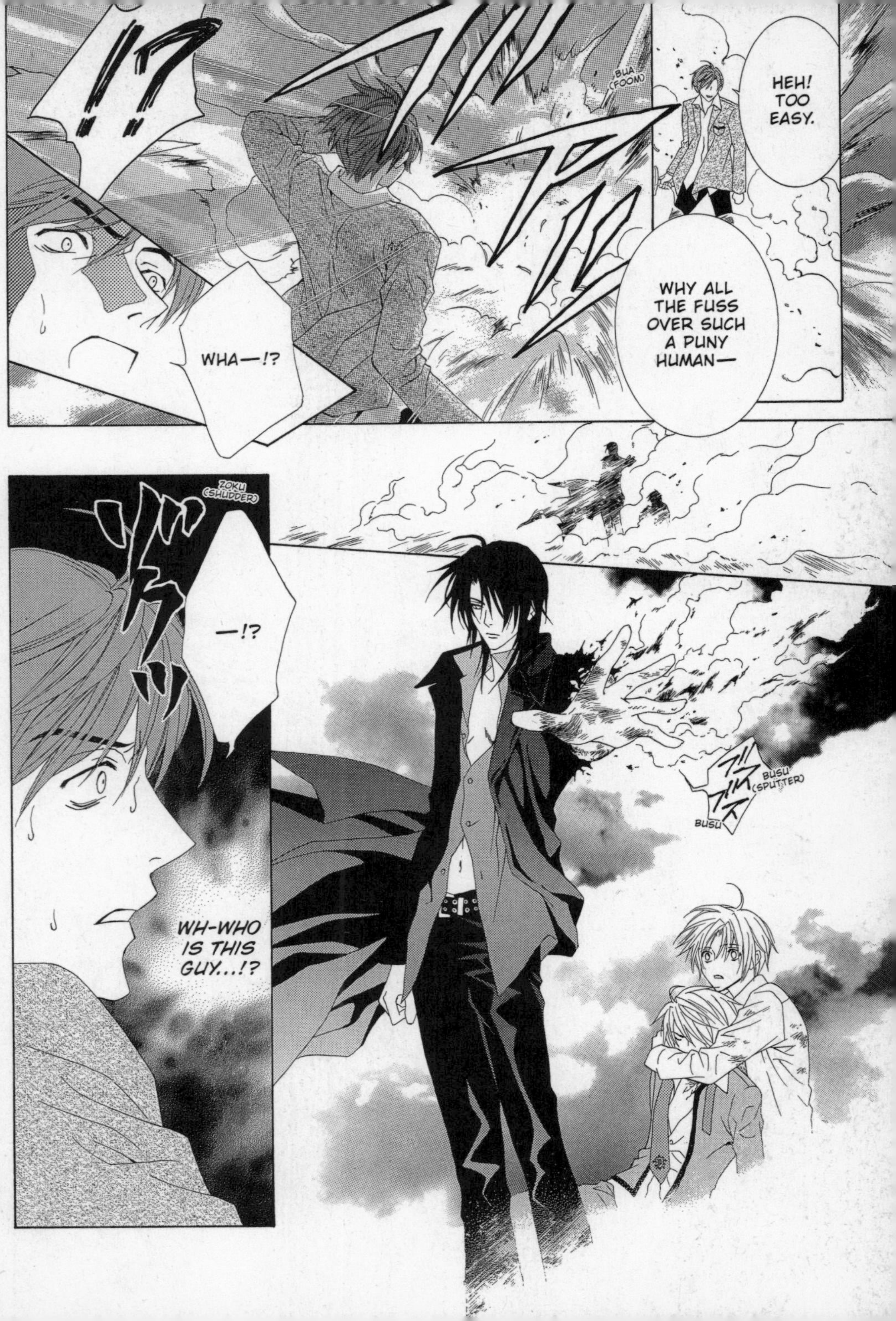

HEH! TOO EASY.
BUA (FOOM)
WHY ALL THE FUSS OVER SUCH A PUNY HUMAN—
!?
WHA—!?
BUSU (SPUTTER)
BUSU
ZOKU (SHUDDER)
—!?
WH-WHO IS THIS GUY...!?

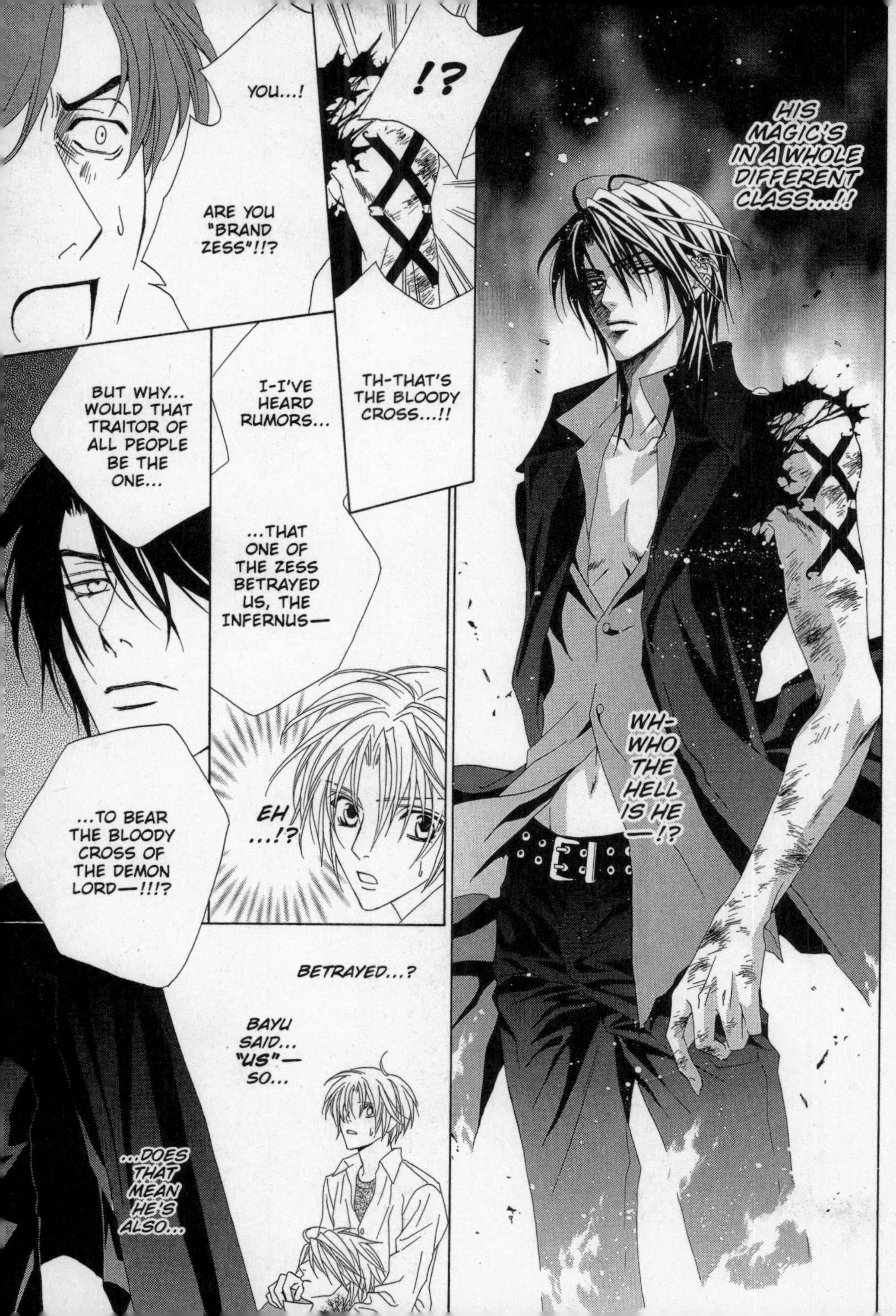
HIS MAGIC'S IN A WHOLE DIFFERENT CLASS...!!
!?
YOU...!
ARE YOU "BRAND ZESS"!!?
TH-THAT'S THE BLOODY CROSS...!!
I-I'VE HEARD RUMORS...
...THAT ONE OF THE ZESS BETRAYED US, THE INFERNUS—
BUT WHY... WOULD THAT TRAITOR OF ALL PEOPLE BE THE ONE...
...TO BEAR THE BLOODY CROSS OF THE DEMON LORD—!!!?
EH ...!?
WH-WHO THE HELL IS HE—!?
BETRAYED...?
BAYU SAID... "US"— SO...
...DOES THAT MEAN HE'S ALSO...

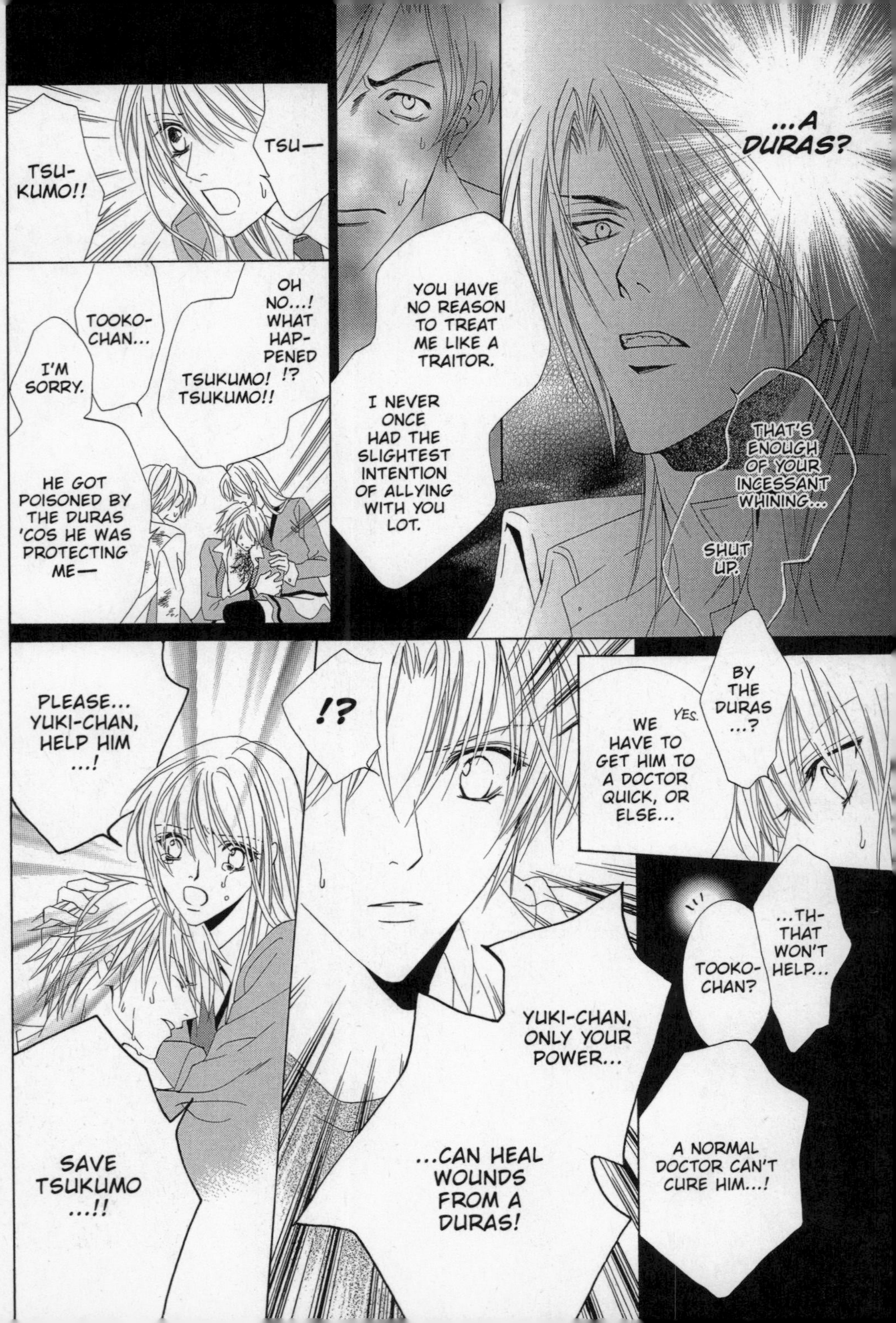
...A DURAS?
THAT'S ENOUGH OF YOUR INCESSANT WHINING...
SHUT UP.
YOU HAVE NO REASON TO TREAT ME LIKE A TRAITOR.
I NEVER ONCE HAD THE SLIGHTEST INTENTION OF ALLYING WITH YOU LOT.
TSU—
TSU-KUMO!!
OH NO...! WHAT HAP-PENED !?
TSUKUMO! TSUKUMO!!
TOOKO-CHAN...
I'M SORRY.
HE GOT POISONED BY THE DURAS 'COS HE WAS PROTECTING ME—
BY THE DURAS ...?
YES.
WE HAVE TO GET HIM TO A DOCTOR QUICK, OR ELSE...
...TH-THAT WON'T HELP...
TOOKO-CHAN?
A NORMAL DOCTOR CAN'T CURE HIM...!
!?
YUKI-CHAN, ONLY YOUR POWER...
...CAN HEAL WOUNDS FROM A DURAS!
PLEASE... YUKI-CHAN, HELP HIM ...!
SAVE TSUKUMO ...!!

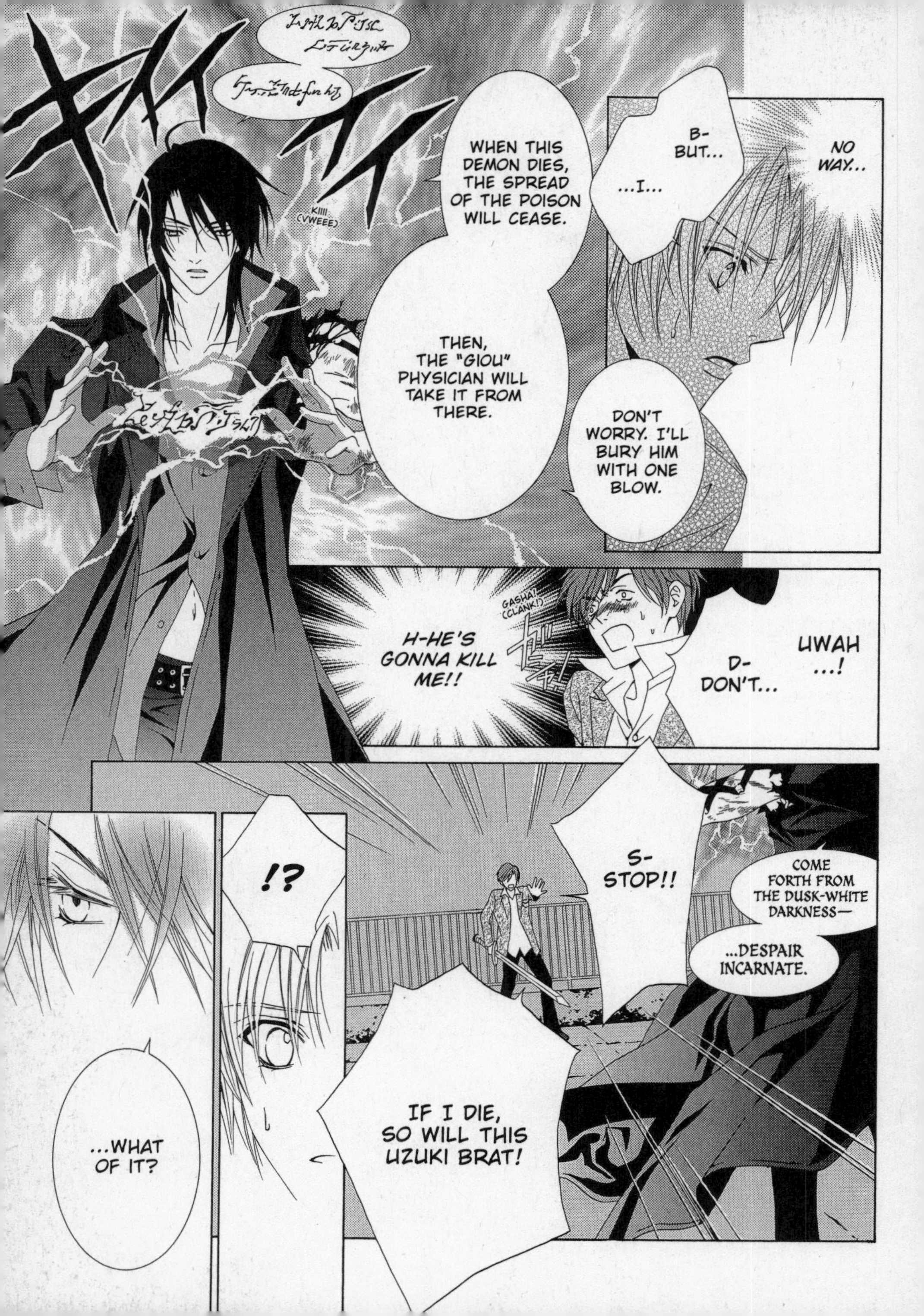
NO WAY...
B- BUT...
...I...
WHEN THIS DEMON DIES, THE SPREAD OF THE POISON WILL CEASE.
KIII (VWEEE)
THEN, THE "GIOU" PHYSICIAN WILL TAKE IT FROM THERE.
DON'T WORRY. I'LL BURY HIM WITH ONE BLOW.
UWAH ...!
D- DON'T...
GASHA! (CLANK!)
H-HE'S GONNA KILL ME!!
COME FORTH FROM THE DUSK-WHITE DARKNESS—
...DESPAIR INCARNATE.
S- STOP!!
IF I DIE, SO WILL THIS UZUKI BRAT!
!?
...WHAT OF IT?

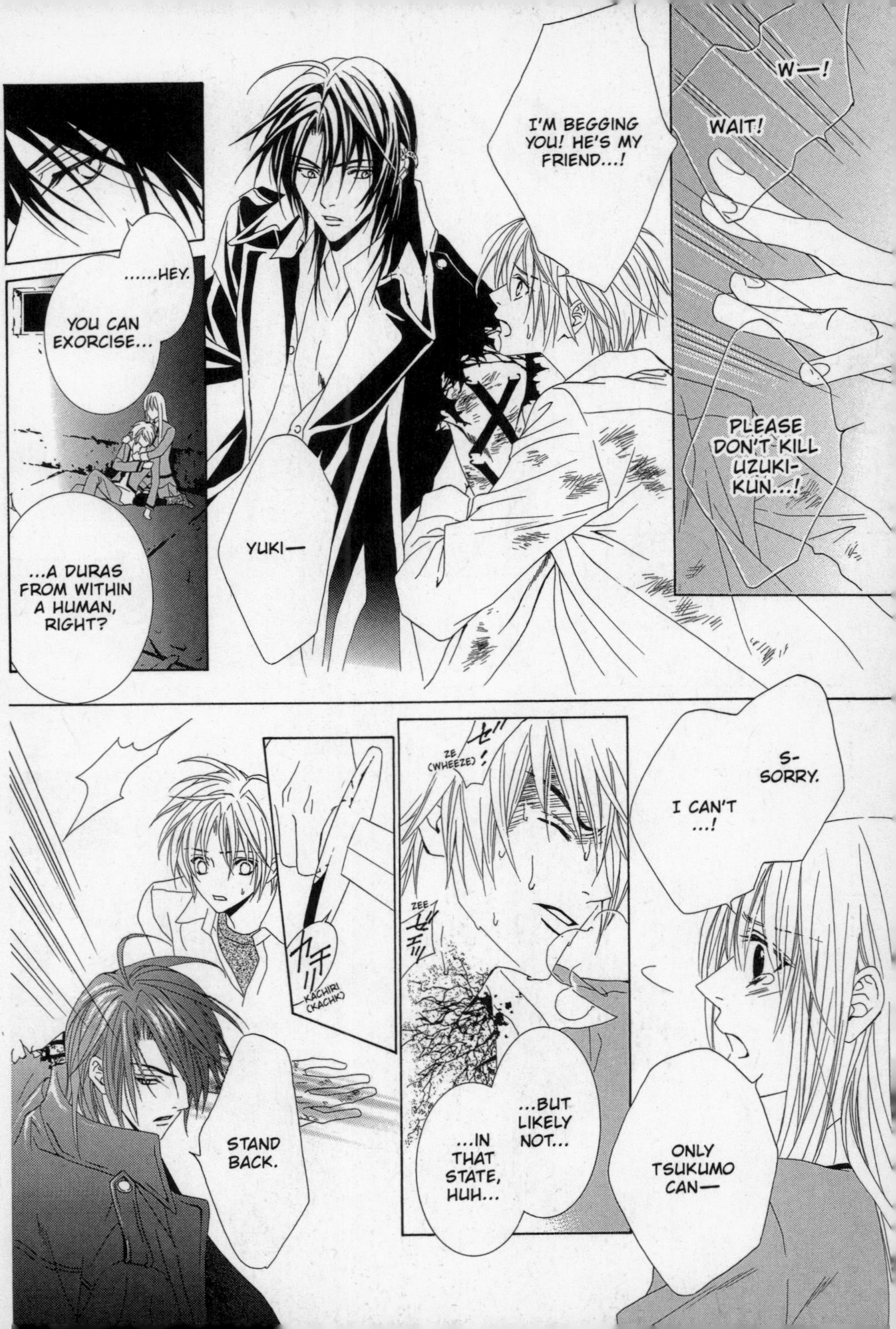
W—!
WAIT!
PLEASE DON'T KILL UZUKI-KUN...!
I'M BEGGING YOU! HE'S MY FRIEND...!
YUKI—
......HEY.
YOU CAN EXORCISE...
...A DURAS FROM WITHIN A HUMAN, RIGHT?
S-SORRY.
I CAN'T ...!
ONLY TSUKUMO CAN—
ZE (WHEEZE)
ZEE
...BUT LIKELY NOT...
...IN THAT STATE, HUH...
KACHIRI (KACHK)
STAND BACK.

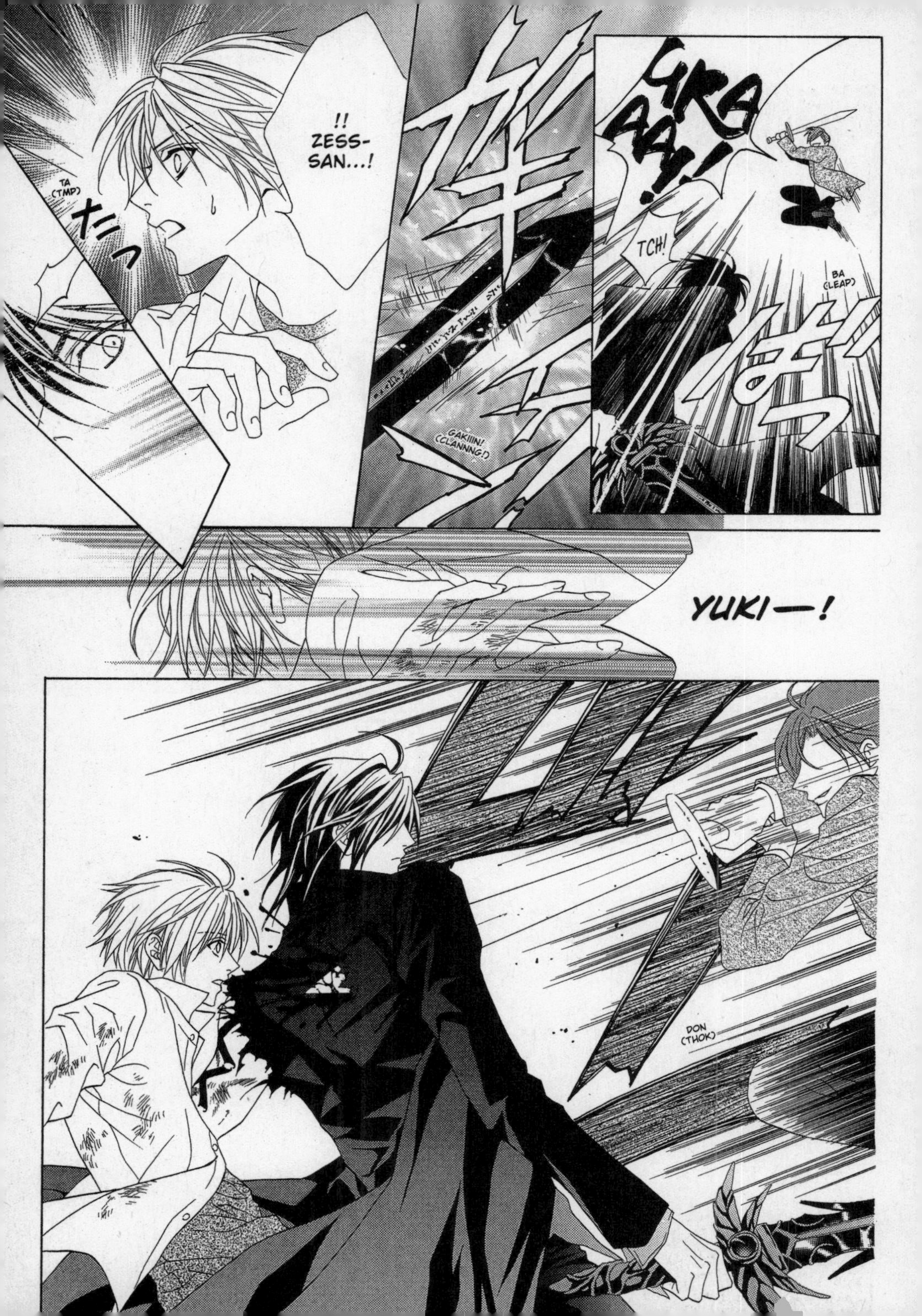
GRAAA!!
TCH!
BA
(LEAP)
ばっ
GAKIIN!
(CLANNNG!)
!!
ZESS-SAN...!
TA
(TMP)
たっ
YUKI—!
DON
(THOK)

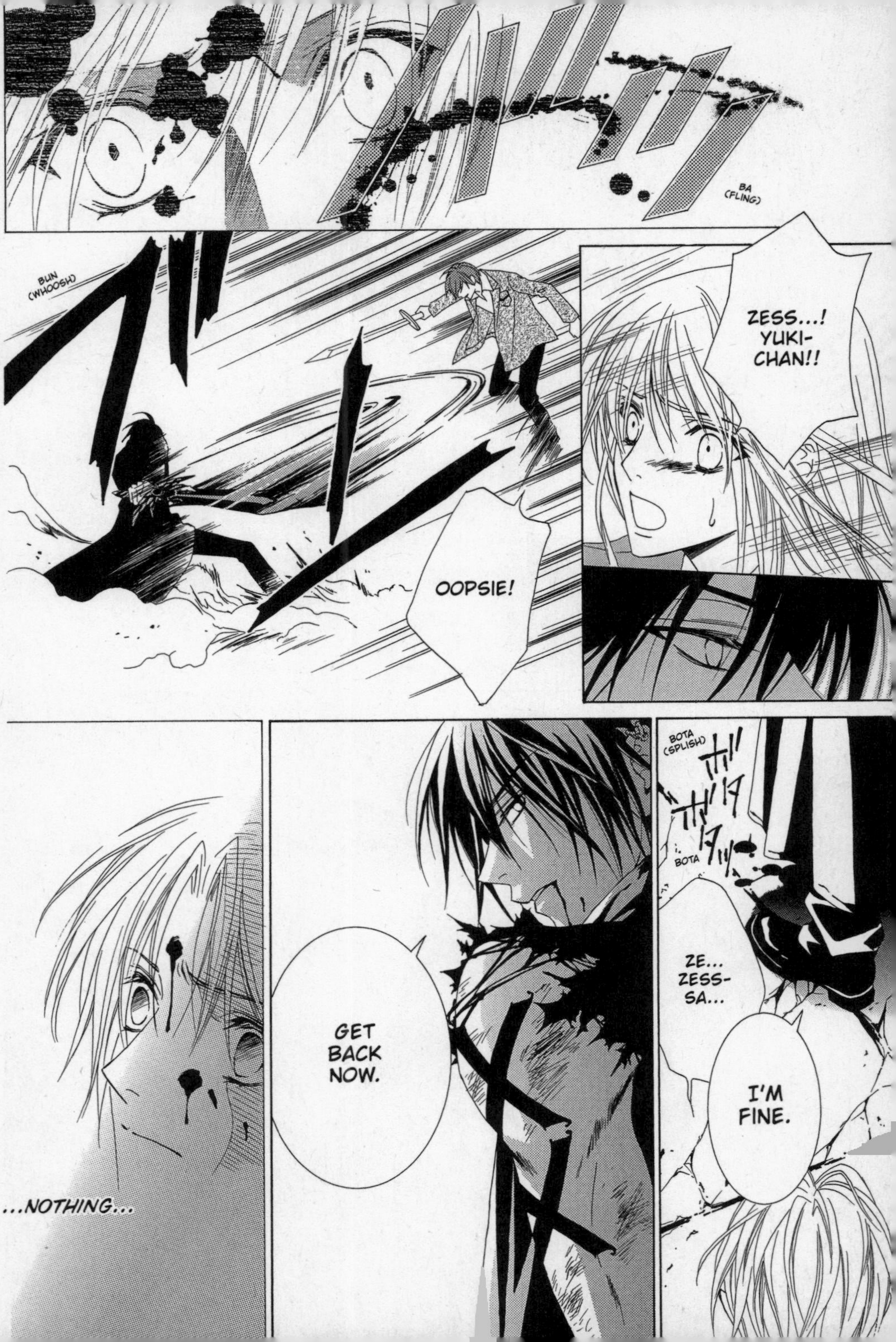
BA (FLING)
ZESS...! YUKI-CHAN!!
BUN (WHOOSH)
OOPSIE!
BOTA (SPLISH)
BOTA
ZE... ZESS-SA...
I'M FINE.
GET BACK NOW.
...NOTHING...

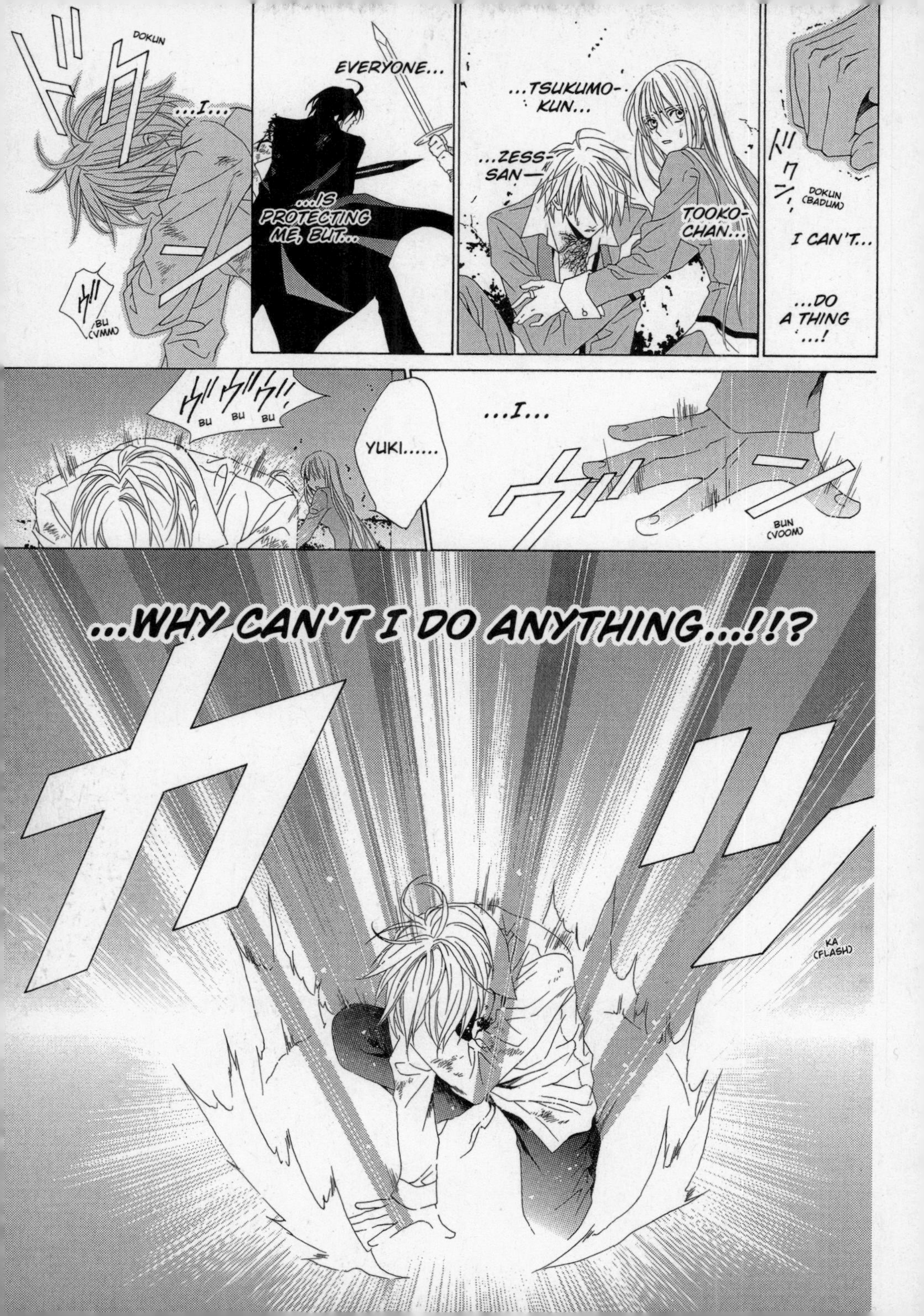
DOKUN (BADUM)
I CAN'T...
...DO A THING ...!
...TSUKUMO-KUN...
...ZESS-SAN—
TOOKO-CHAN...
EVERYONE...
...IS PROTECTING ME, BUT...
DOKUN
...I...
BU (VMM)
...I...
BUN (VOOM)
BU BU BU
YUKI......
...WHY CAN'T I DO ANYTHING...!!?
KA (FLASH)

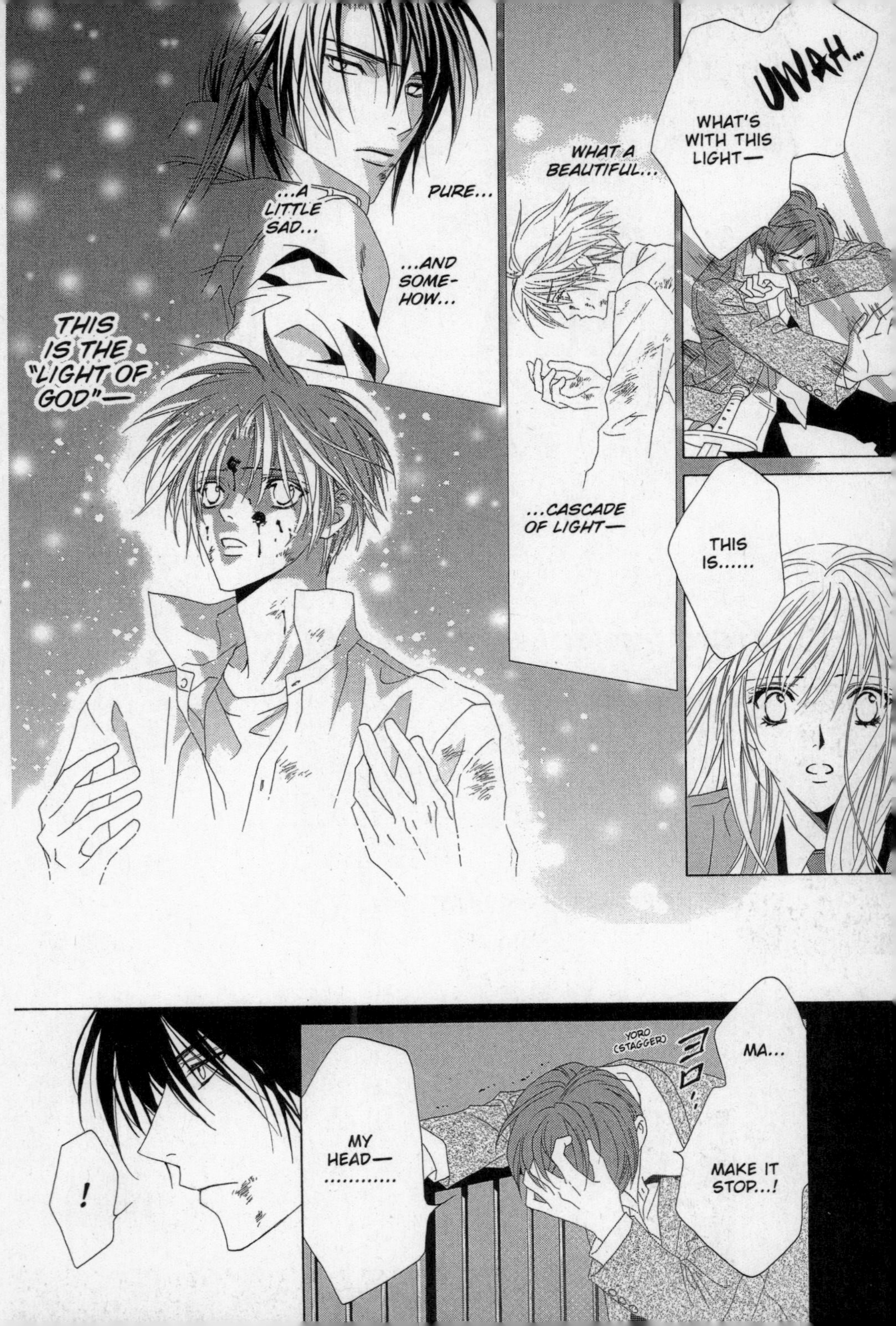
UWAH...
WHAT'S WITH THIS LIGHT—
WHAT A BEAUTIFUL...
PURE...
...A LITTLE SAD...
...AND SOMEHOW...
...CASCADE OF LIGHT—
THIS IS THE "LIGHT OF GOD"—
THIS IS......
MA...
MAKE IT STOP...!
YORO (STAGGER)
MY HEAD— ....
!

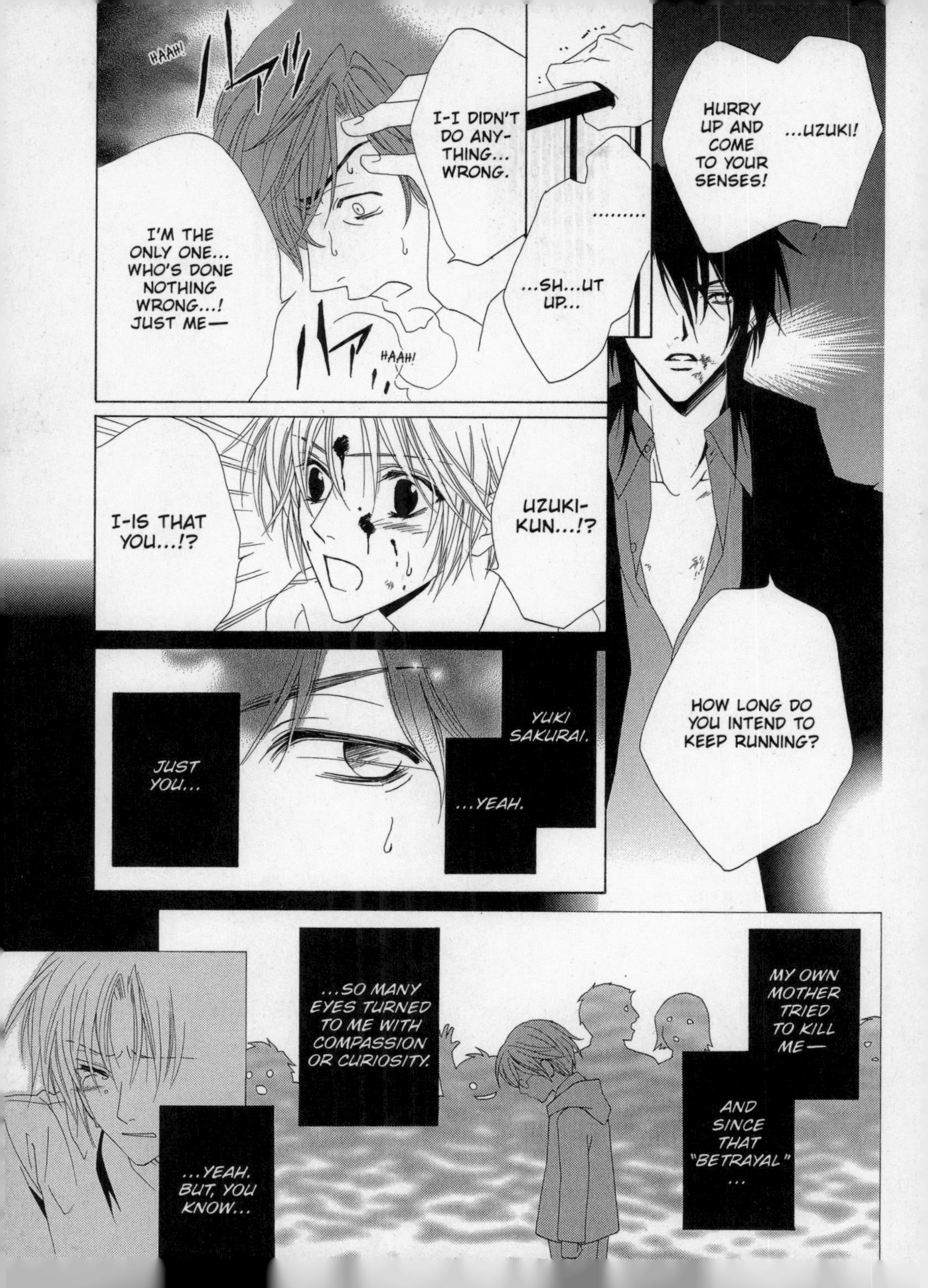

HURRY UP AND COME TO YOUR SENSES!
...UZUKI!
I-I DIDN'T DO ANY-THING... WRONG.
....
...SH...UT UP...
HAAH!
I'M THE ONLY ONE... WHO'S DONE NOTHING WRONG...! JUST ME—
HAAH!
UZUKI-KUN...!?
I-IS THAT YOU...!?
HOW LONG DO YOU INTEND TO KEEP RUNNING?
YUKI SAKURAI.
...YEAH.
JUST YOU...
MY OWN MOTHER TRIED TO KILL ME—
AND SINCE THAT "BETRAYAL" ...
...SO MANY EYES TURNED TO ME WITH COMPASSION OR CURIOSITY.
...YEAH. BUT, YOU KNOW...

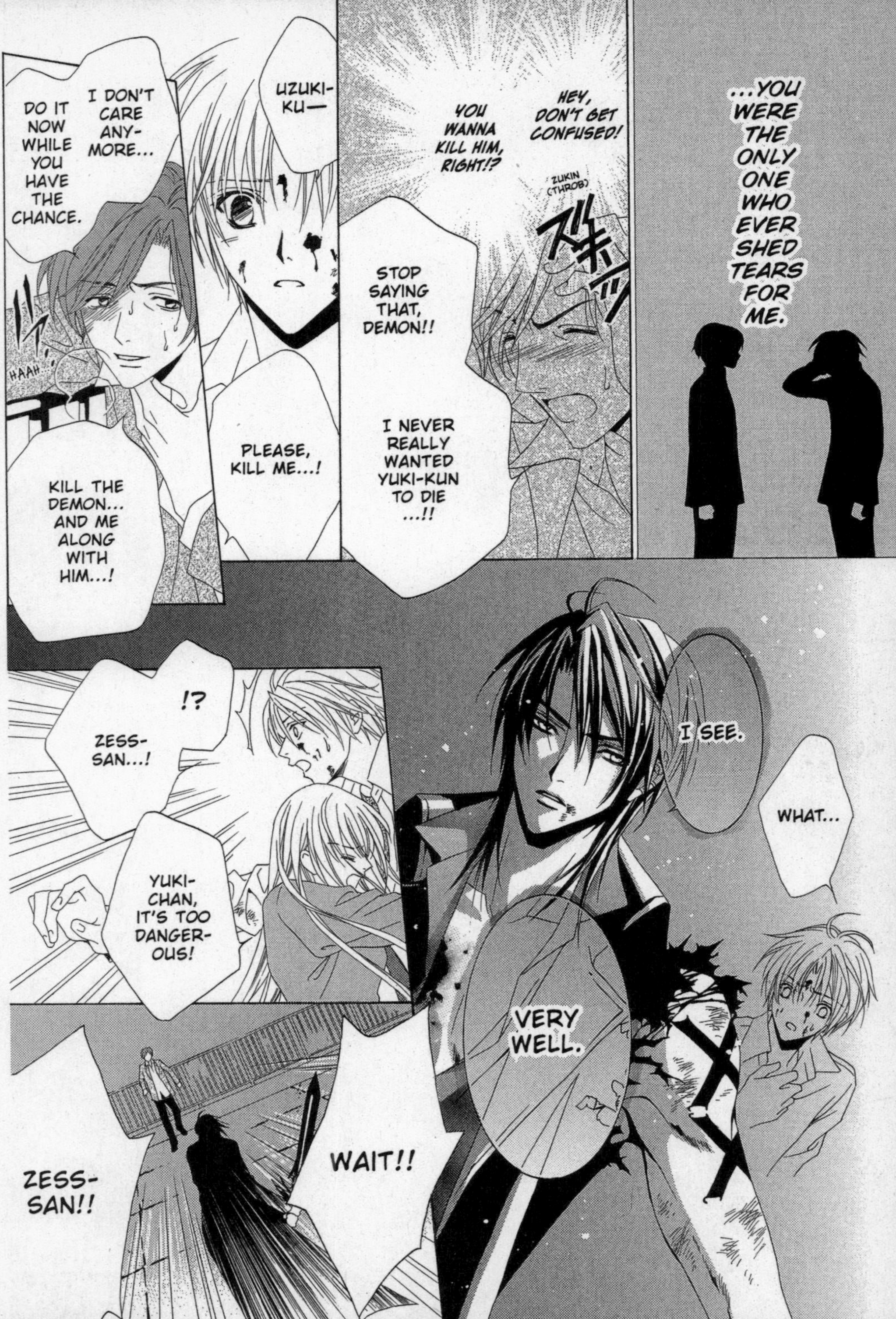
...YOU WERE THE ONLY ONE WHO EVER SHED TEARS FOR ME.
HEY, DON'T GET CONFUSED!
YOU WANNA KILL HIM, RIGHT!?
ZUKIN (THROB)
STOP SAYING THAT, DEMON!!
I NEVER REALLY WANTED YUKI-KUN TO DIE ...!!
UZUKI-KU—
I DON'T CARE ANYMORE...
DO IT NOW WHILE YOU HAVE THE CHANCE.
HAAH
PLEASE, KILL ME...!
KILL THE DEMON... AND ME ALONG WITH HIM...!
I SEE.
WHAT...
VERY WELL.
!?
ZESS-SAN...!
YUKI-CHAN, IT'S TOO DANGEROUS!
WAIT!!
ZESS-SAN!!

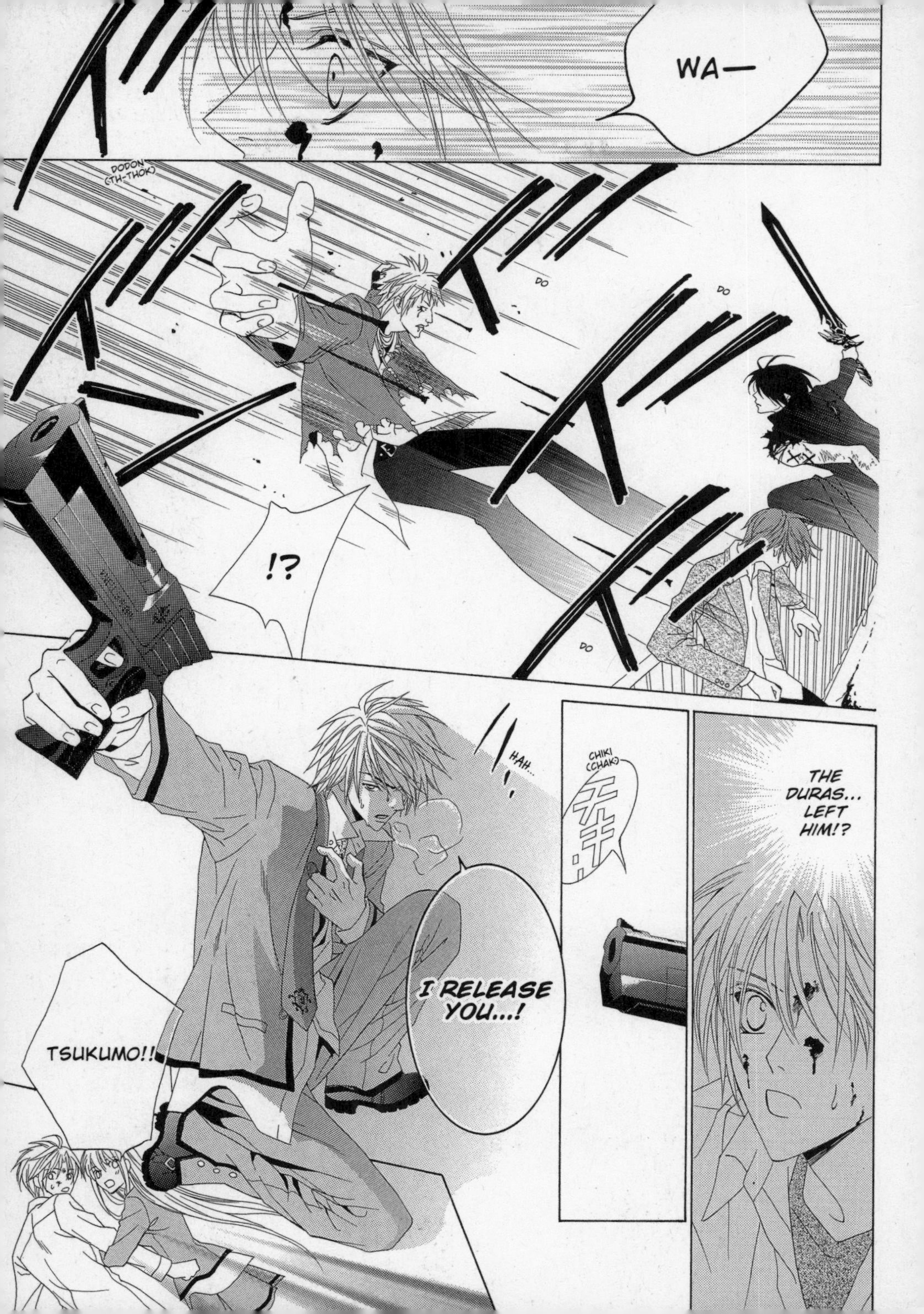

WA—
DODON (TH-THOK)
DO
DO
DO
!?
THE DURAS... LEFT HIM!?
CHIKI (CHAK)
HAH...
I RELEASE YOU...!
TSUKUMO!!

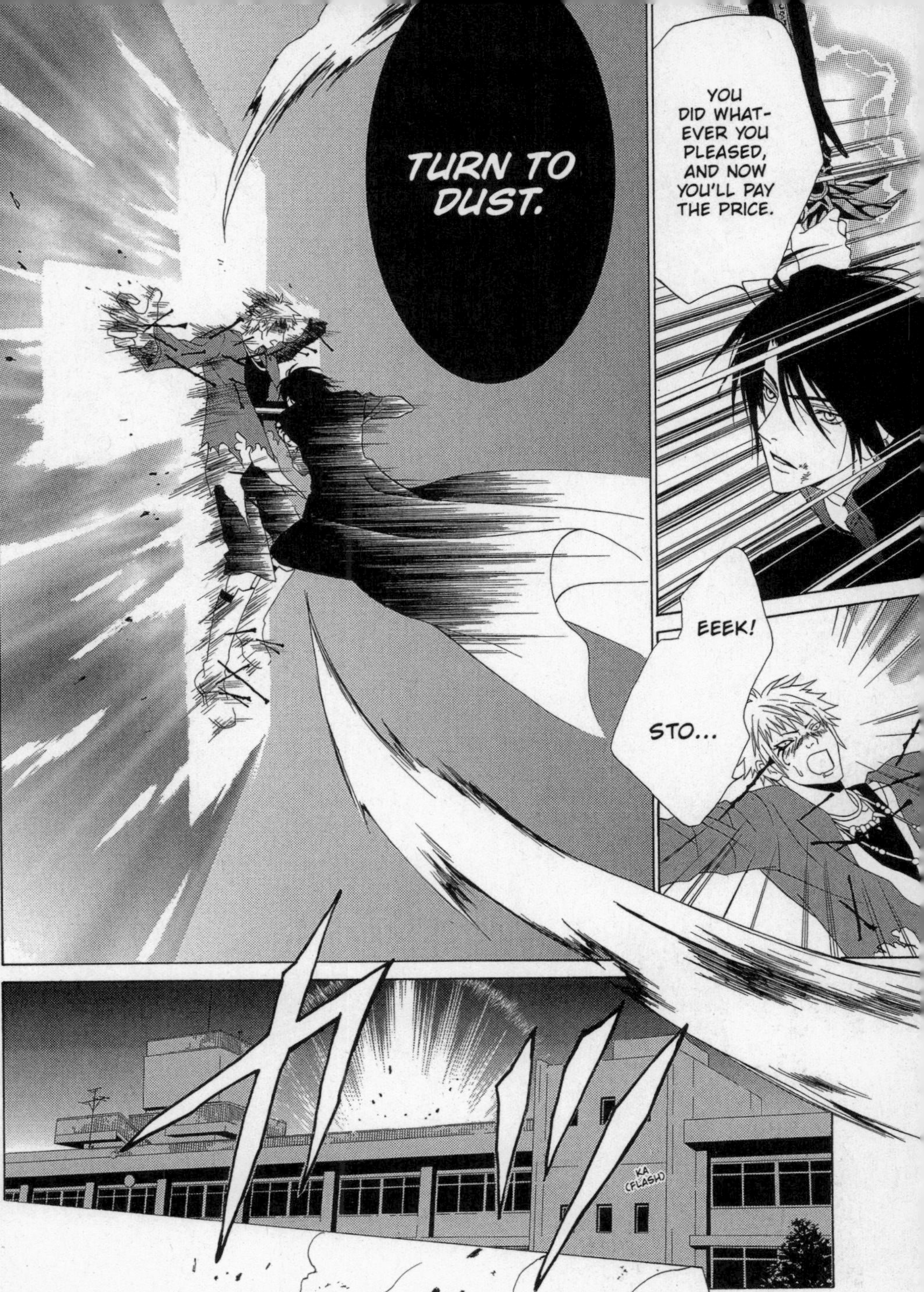

YOU DID WHATEVER YOU PLEASED, AND NOW YOU'LL PAY THE PRICE.
EEEK!
STO...
TURN TO DUST.
KA (FLASH)

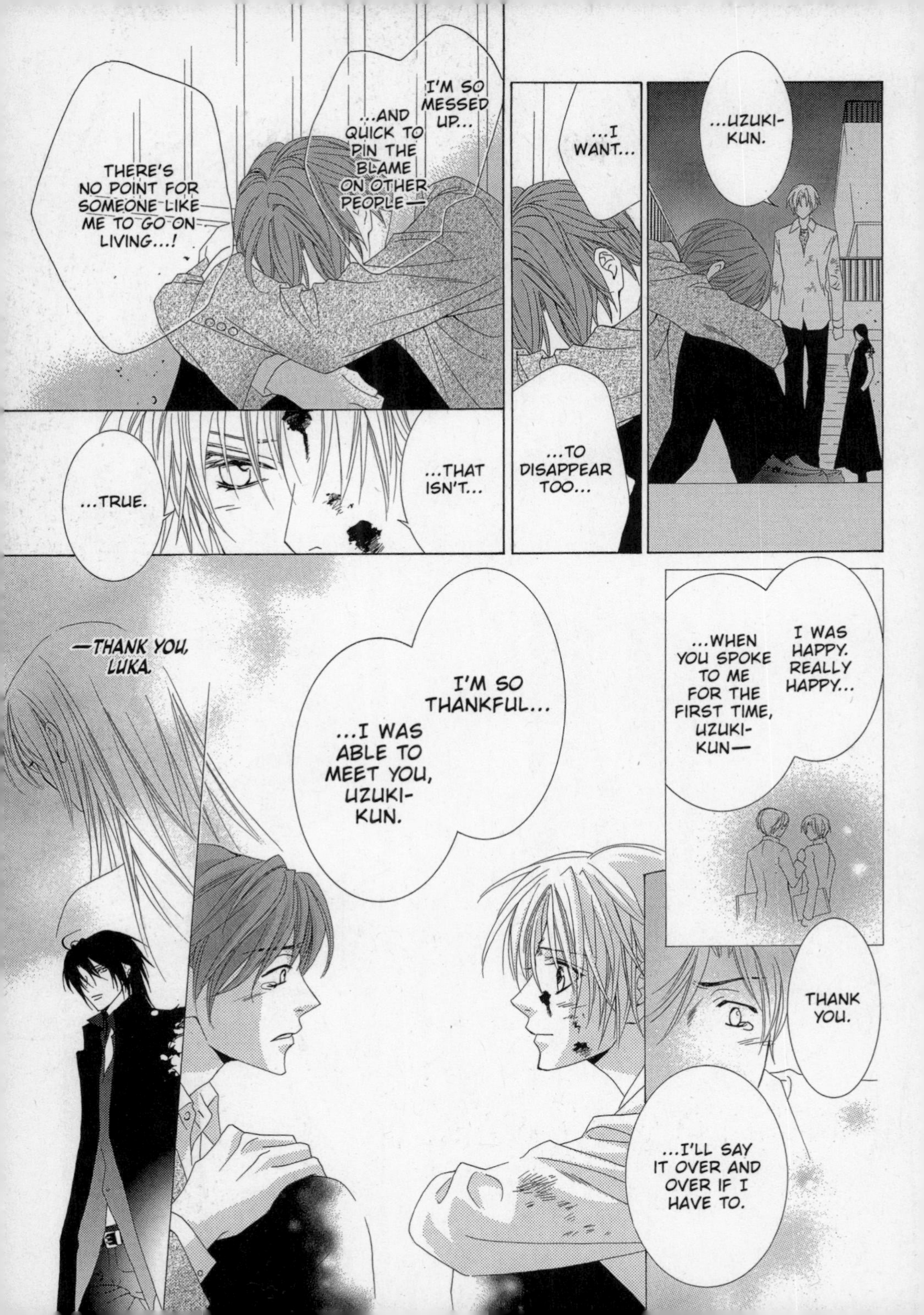
...UZUKI-KUN.
...I WANT...
...TO DISAPPEAR TOO...
I'M SO MESSED UP...
...AND QUICK TO PIN THE BLAME ON OTHER PEOPLE—
THERE'S NO POINT FOR SOMEONE LIKE ME TO GO ON LIVING...!
...THAT ISN'T...
...TRUE.
I WAS HAPPY. REALLY HAPPY...
...WHEN YOU SPOKE TO ME FOR THE FIRST TIME, UZUKI-KUN—
I'M SO THANKFUL...
...I WAS ABLE TO MEET YOU, UZUKI-KUN.
THANK YOU.
...I'LL SAY IT OVER AND OVER IF I HAVE TO.
—THANK YOU, LUKA.

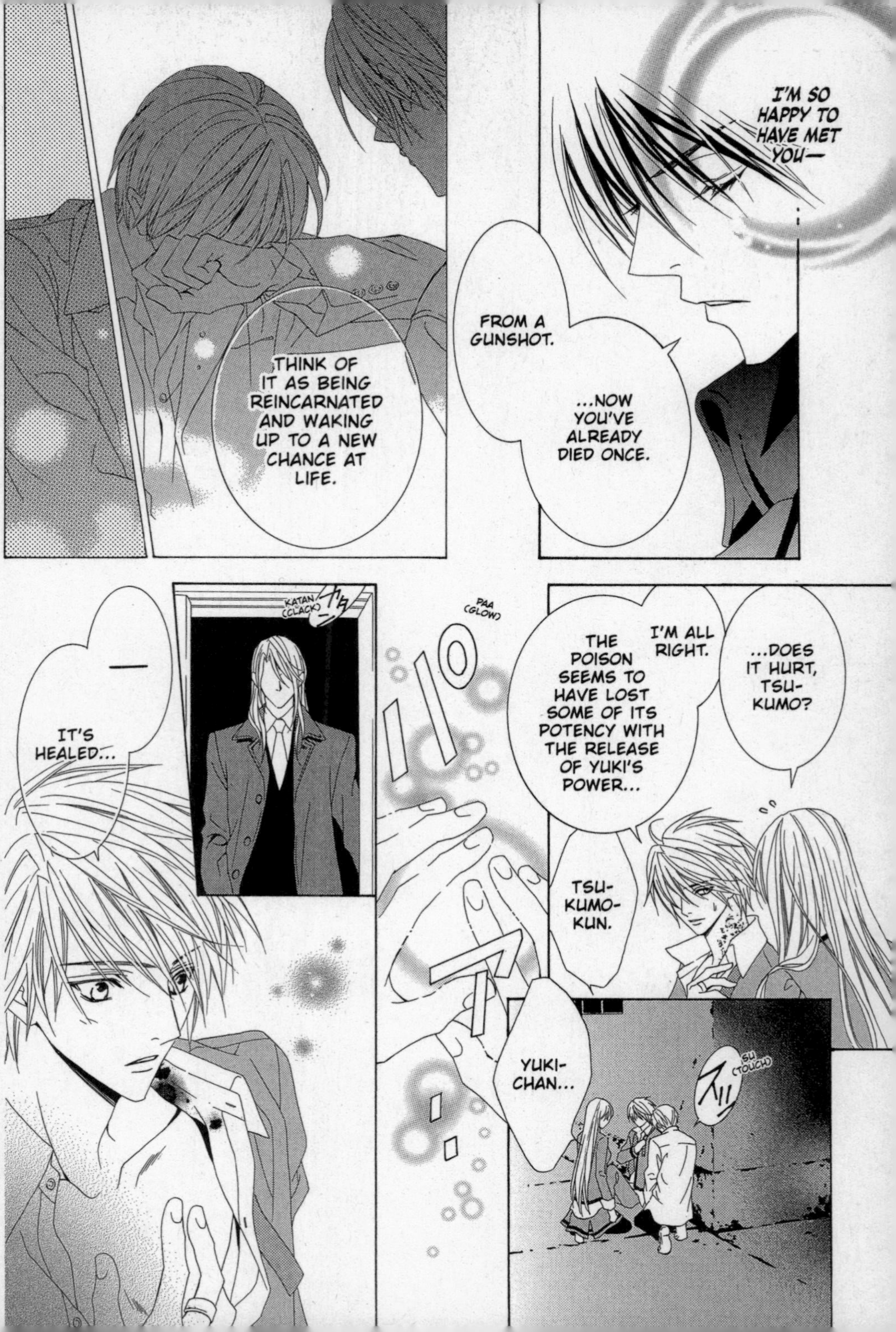
I'M SO HAPPY TO HAVE MET YOU—
FROM A GUNSHOT. ...NOW YOU'VE ALREADY DIED ONCE.
THINK OF IT AS BEING REINCARNATED AND WAKING UP TO A NEW CHANCE AT LIFE.
...DOES IT HURT, TSU-KUMO?
I'M ALL RIGHT.
THE POISON SEEMS TO HAVE LOST SOME OF ITS POTENCY WITH THE RELEASE OF YUKI'S POWER...
TSU-KUMO-KUN.
SU (TOUCH)
YUKI-CHAN...
PAA (GLOW)
KATAN (CLACK)
—
IT'S HEALED...

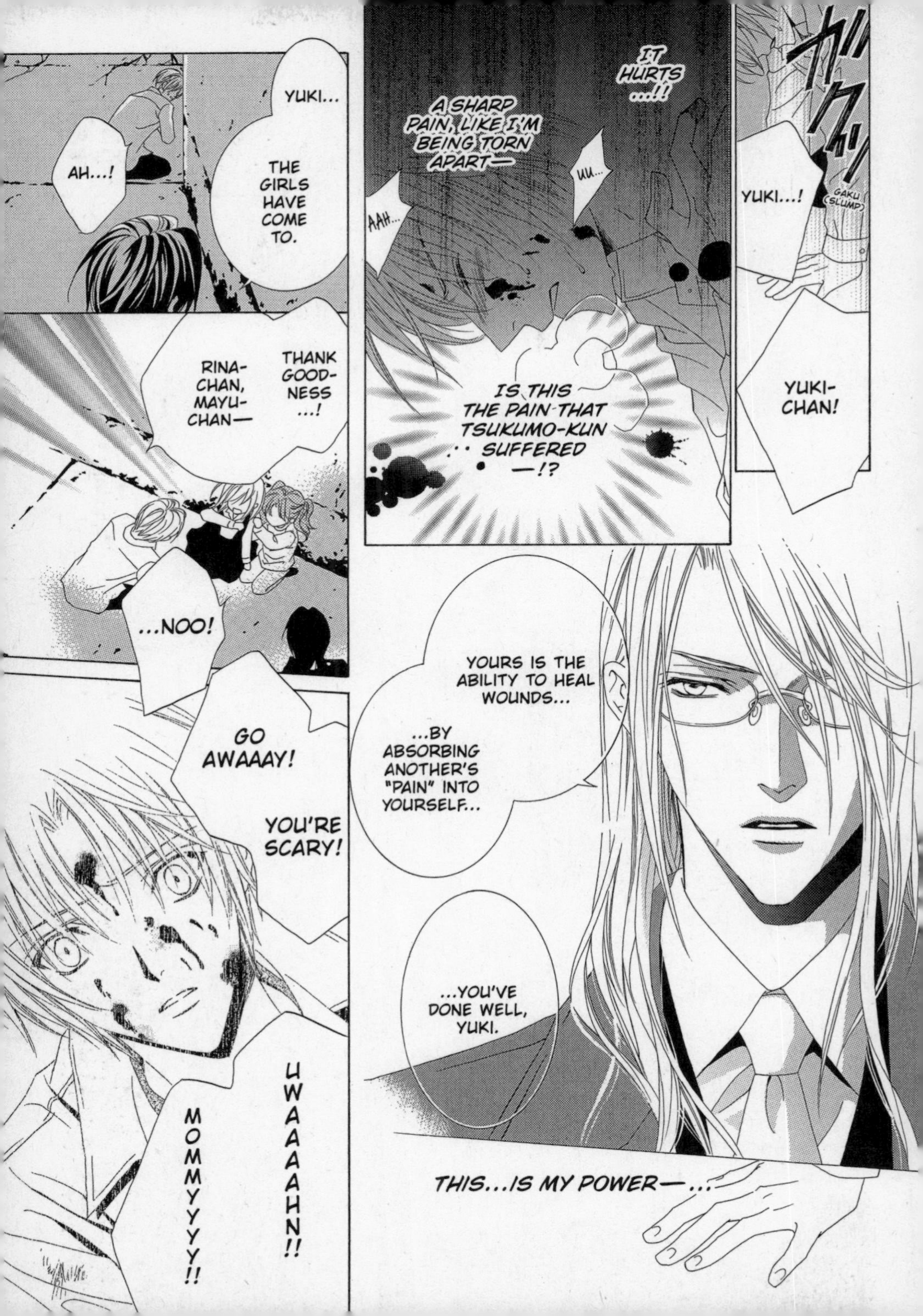
YUKI...!
GAKU (SLUMP)
YUKI-CHAN!
IT HURTS...!!
A SHARP PAIN, LIKE I'M BEING TORN APART—
UU...
AAH...
IS THIS THE PAIN THAT TSUKUMO-KUN SUFFERED—!?
YUKI...
THE GIRLS HAVE COME TO.
AH...!
THANK GOODNESS...!
RINA-CHAN, MAYU-CHAN—
...NOO!
GO AWAAAY!
YOU'RE SCARY!
UWAAAAAHN!!
MOMMYYYY!!
YOURS IS THE ABILITY TO HEAL WOUNDS...
...BY ABSORBING ANOTHER'S "PAIN" INTO YOURSELF...
...YOU'VE DONE WELL, YUKI.
THIS...IS MY POWER—...

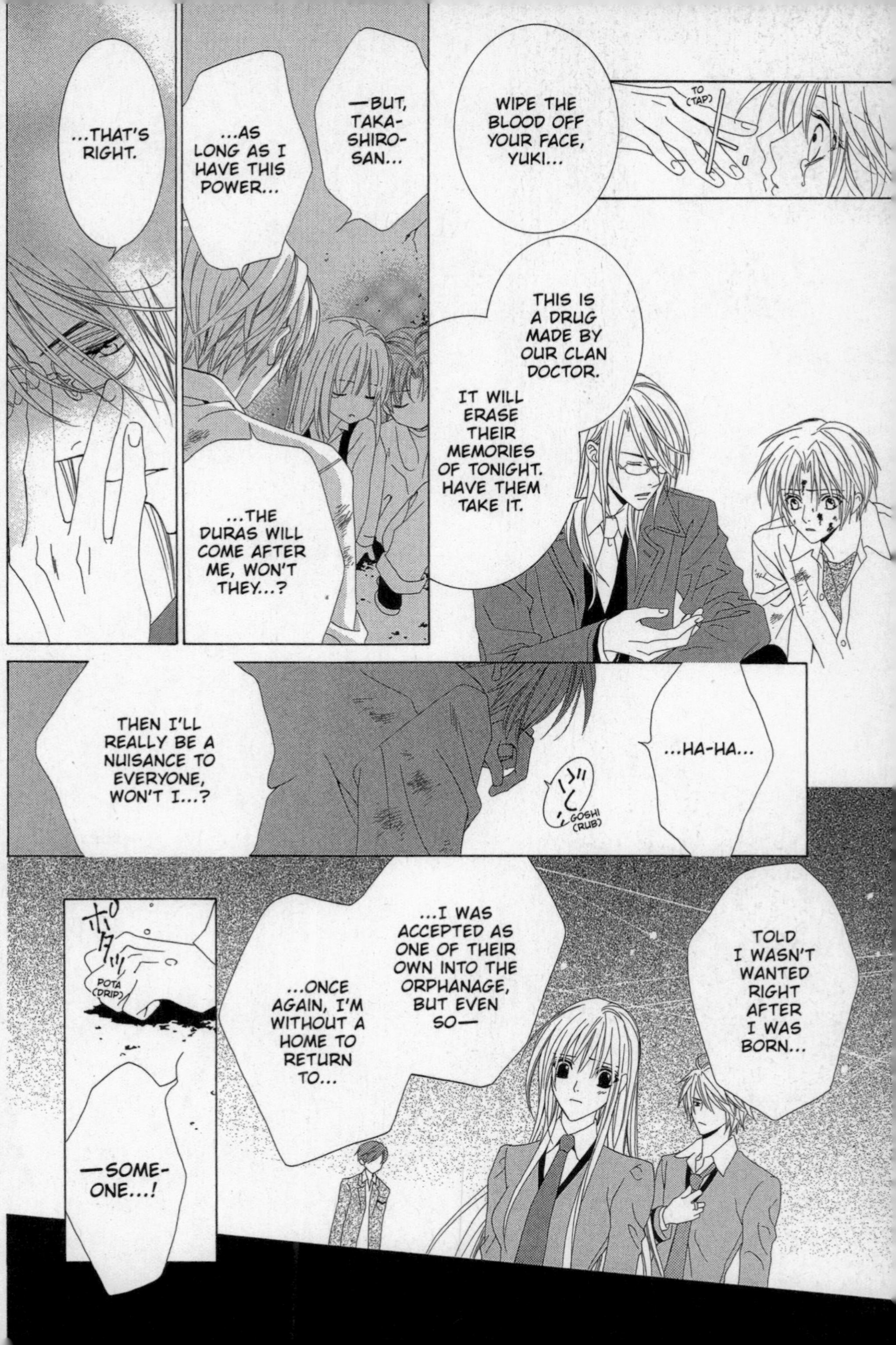
TO (TAP)
WIPE THE BLOOD OFF YOUR FACE, YUKI...
THIS IS A DRUG MADE BY OUR CLAN DOCTOR.
IT WILL ERASE THEIR MEMORIES OF TONIGHT. HAVE THEM TAKE IT.
—BUT, TAKA-SHIRO-SAN...
...AS LONG AS I HAVE THIS POWER...
...THE DURAS WILL COME AFTER ME, WON'T THEY...?
...THAT'S RIGHT.
...HA-HA...
GOSHI (RUB)
THEN I'LL REALLY BE A NUISANCE TO EVERYONE, WON'T I...?
TOLD I WASN'T WANTED RIGHT AFTER I WAS BORN...
...I WAS ACCEPTED AS ONE OF THEIR OWN INTO THE ORPHANAGE, BUT EVEN SO—
...ONCE AGAIN, I'M WITHOUT A HOME TO RETURN TO...
POTA (DRIP)
—SOME-ONE...!

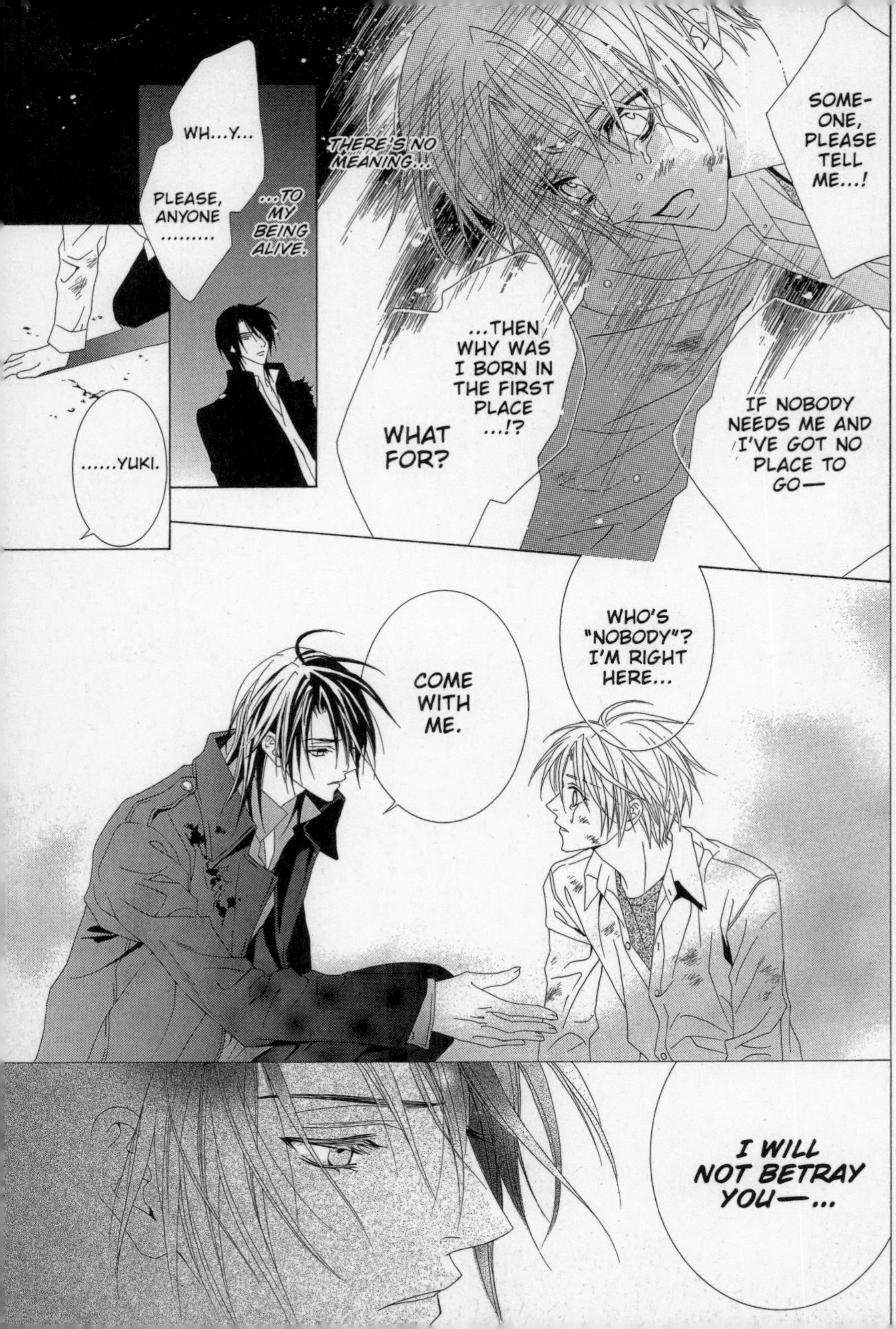

SOME-ONE, PLEASE TELL ME...!
IF NOBODY NEEDS ME AND I'VE GOT NO PLACE TO GO—
...THEN WHY WAS I BORN IN THE FIRST PLACE ...!?
WHAT FOR?
THERE'S NO MEANING...
...TO MY BEING ALIVE.
WH...Y...
PLEASE, ANYONE ....
......YUKI.
WHO'S "NOBODY"? I'M RIGHT HERE...
COME WITH ME.
I WILL NOT BETRAY YOU—...

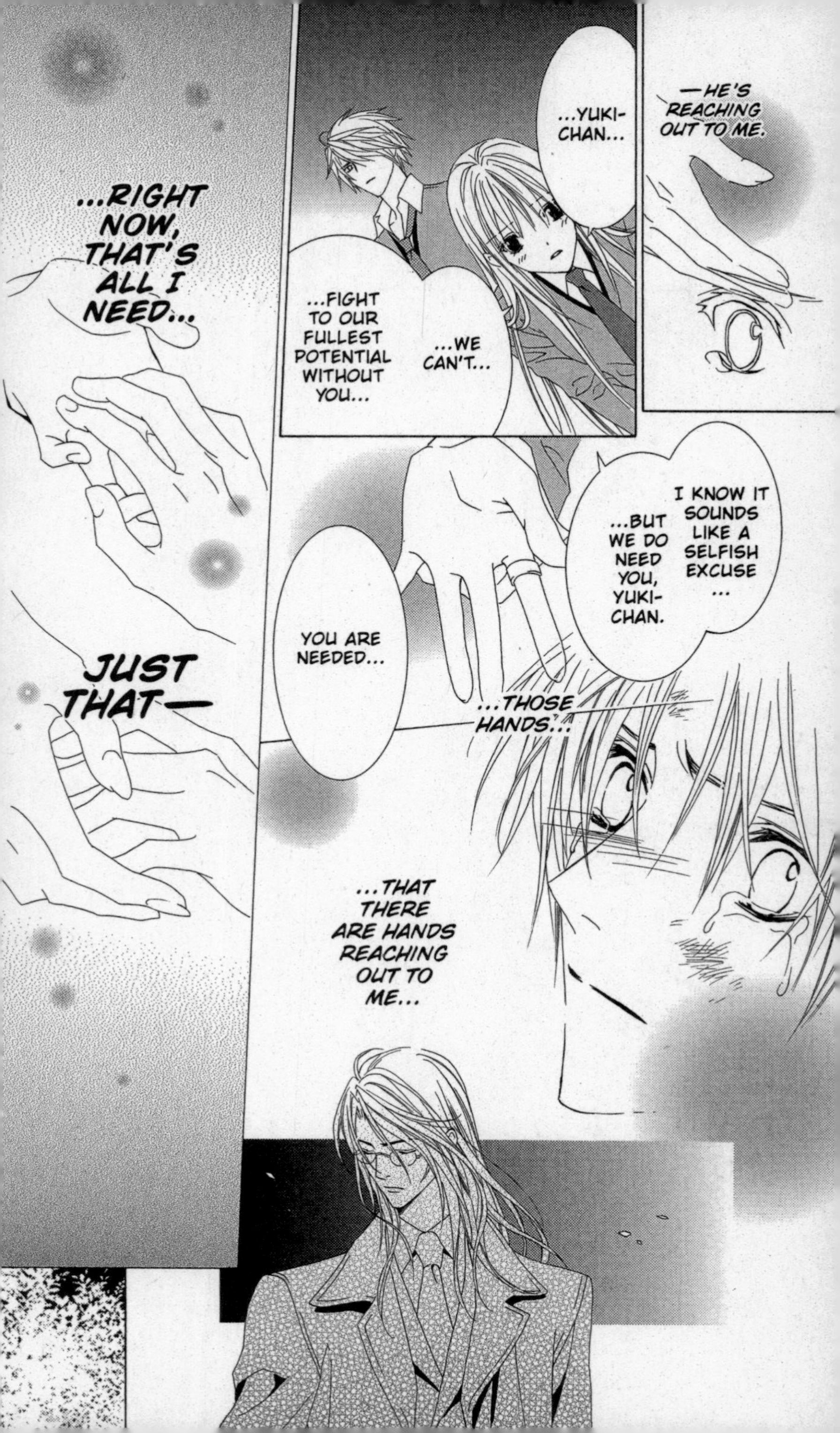
—HE'S REACHING OUT TO ME.
...YUKI-CHAN...
...WE CAN'T...
...FIGHT TO OUR FULLEST POTENTIAL WITHOUT YOU...
I KNOW IT SOUNDS LIKE A SELFISH EXCUSE...
...BUT WE DO NEED YOU, YUKI-CHAN.
YOU ARE NEEDED...
...THOSE HANDS...
...THAT THERE ARE HANDS REACHING OUT TO ME...
...RIGHT NOW, THAT'S ALL I NEED...
JUST THAT—

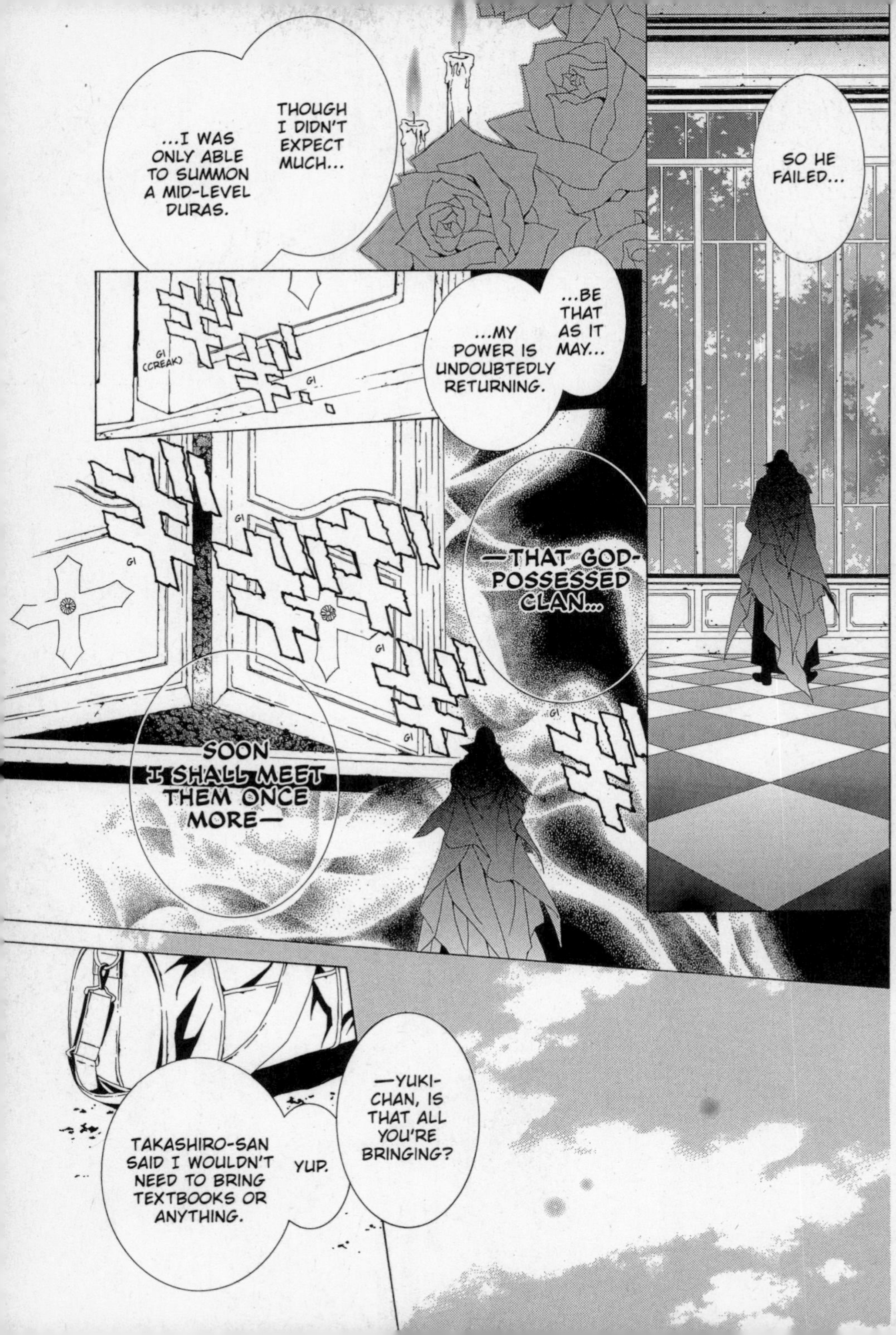
SO HE FAILED...
THOUGH I DIDN'T EXPECT MUCH...
...I WAS ONLY ABLE TO SUMMON A MID-LEVEL DURAS.
...BE THAT AS IT MAY...
...MY POWER IS UNDOUBTEDLY RETURNING.
GI (CREAK)
GI
—THAT GOD-POSSESSED CLAN...
GI
SOON I SHALL MEET THEM ONCE MORE—
—YUKI-CHAN, IS THAT ALL YOU'RE BRINGING?
YUP.
TAKASHIRO-SAN SAID I WOULDN'T NEED TO BRING TEXTBOOKS OR ANYTHING.

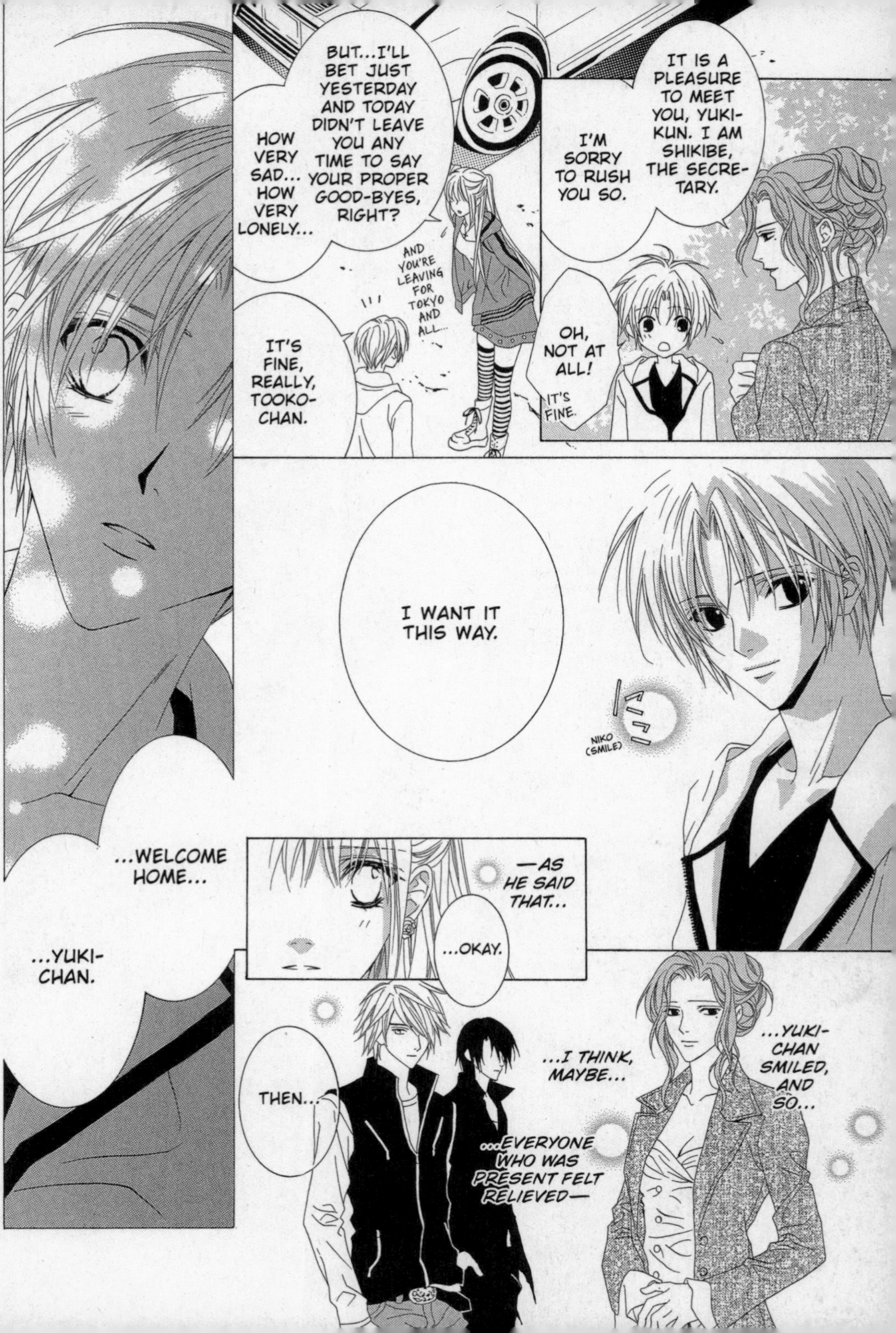
IT IS A PLEASURE TO MEET YOU, YUKI-KUN. I AM SHIKIBE, THE SECRETARY.
I'M SORRY TO RUSH YOU SO.
OH, NOT AT ALL!
IT'S FINE.
BUT...I'LL BET JUST YESTERDAY AND TODAY DIDN'T LEAVE YOU ANY TIME TO SAY YOUR PROPER GOOD-BYES, RIGHT?
HOW VERY SAD... HOW VERY LONELY...
AND YOU'RE LEAVING FOR TOKYO AND ALL...
IT'S FINE, REALLY, TOOKO-CHAN.
I WANT IT THIS WAY.
NIKO (SMILE)
—AS HE SAID THAT...
...OKAY.
...YUKI-CHAN SMILED, AND SO...
...I THINK, MAYBE...
...EVERYONE WHO WAS PRESENT FELT RELIEVED—
THEN...
...WELCOME HOME...
...YUKI-CHAN.

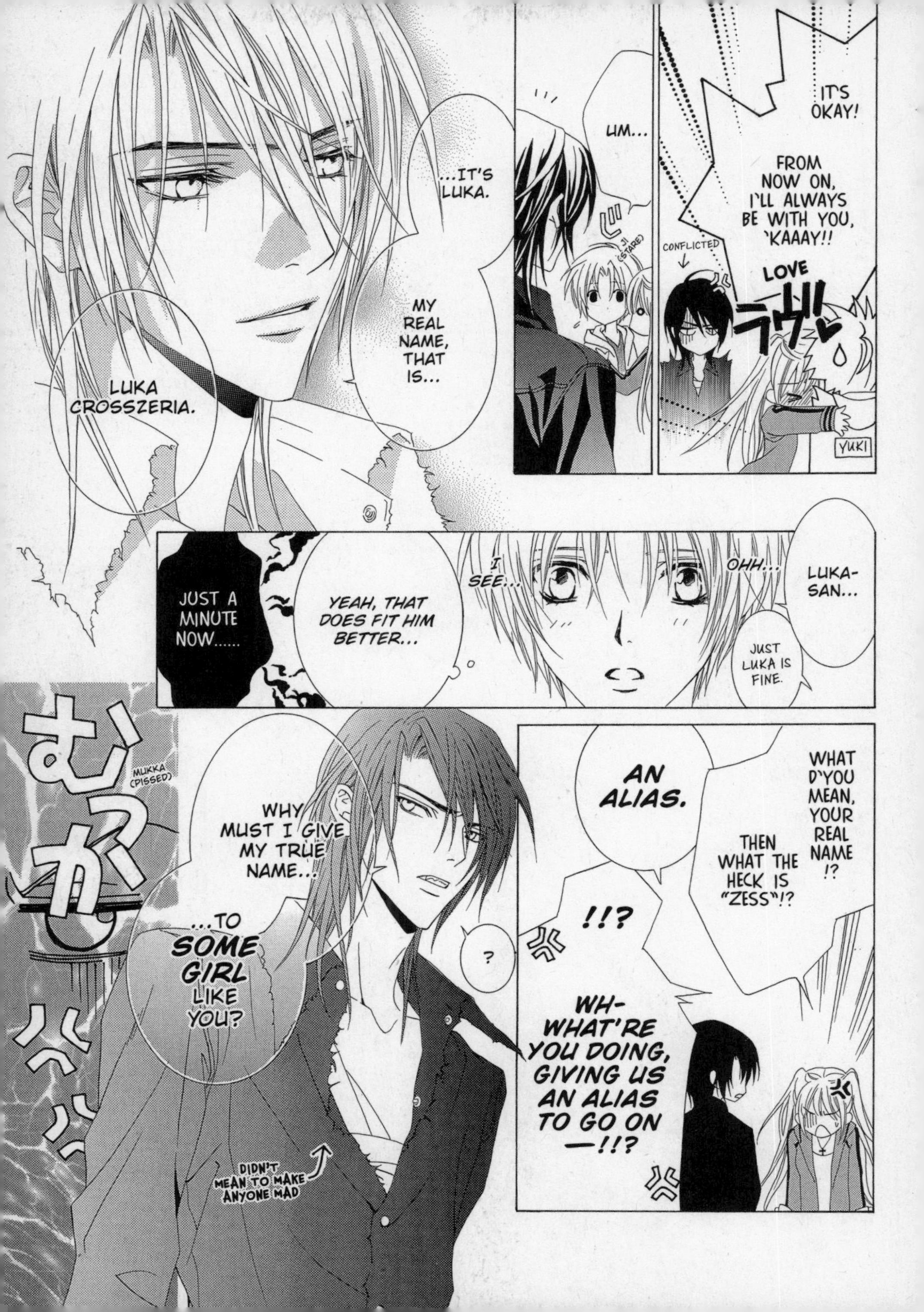
IT'S OKAY!
FROM NOW ON, I'LL ALWAYS BE WITH YOU, 'KAAAY!!
LOVE
CONFLICTED
YUKI
UM...
JI (STARE)
...IT'S LUKA.
MY REAL NAME, THAT IS...
LUKA CROSSZERIA.
LUKA-SAN...
OHH...
JUST LUKA IS FINE.
I SEE...
YEAH, THAT DOES FIT HIM BETTER...
JUST A MINUTE NOW......
WHAT D'YOU MEAN, YOUR REAL NAME !?
THEN WHAT THE HECK IS "ZESS"!?
AN ALIAS.
!!?
?
WH-WHAT'RE YOU DOING, GIVING US AN ALIAS TO GO ON—!!?
MUKKA (PISSED)
WHY MUST I GIVE MY TRUE NAME...
...TO SOME GIRL LIKE YOU?
DIDN'T MEAN TO MAKE ANYONE MAD

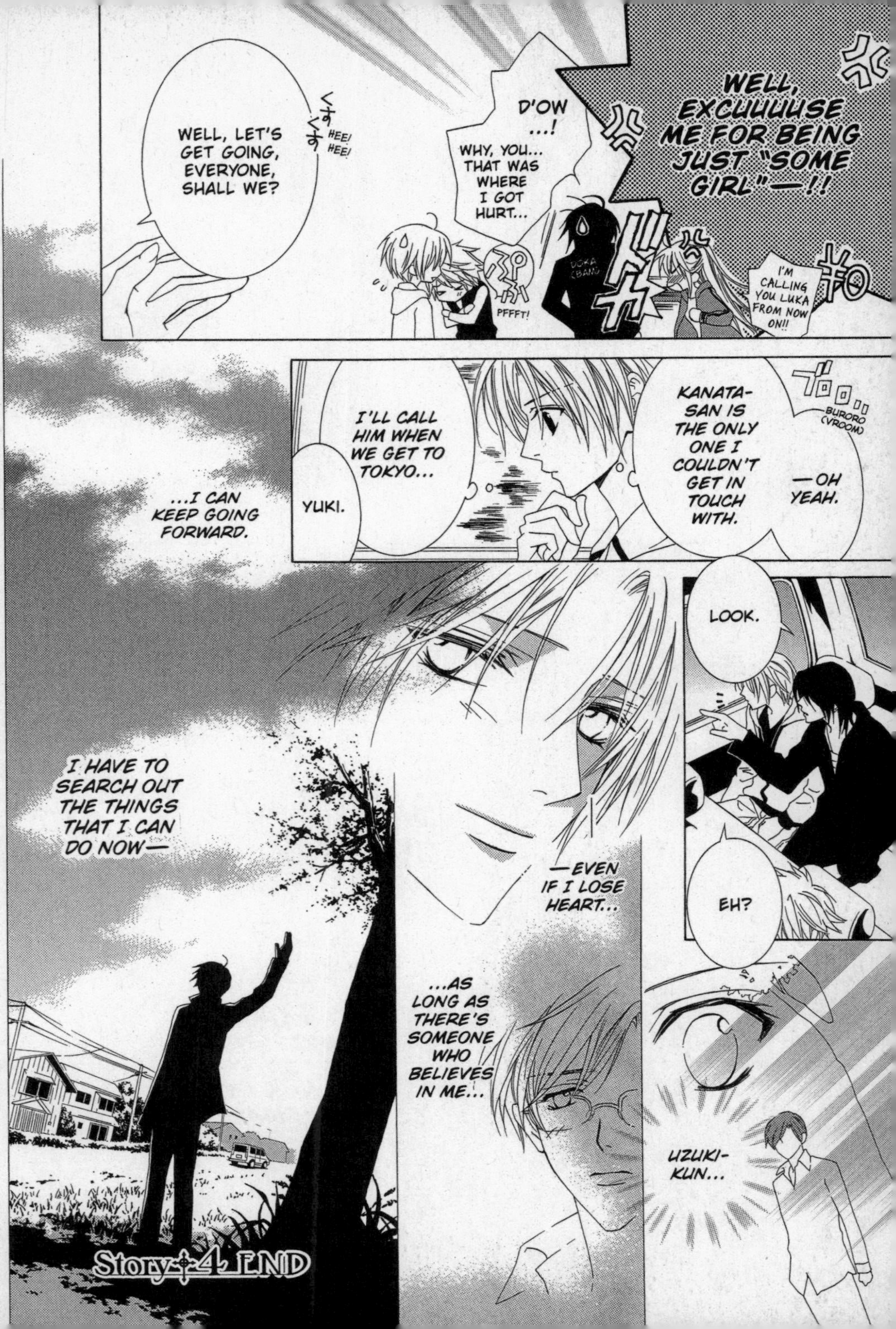
WELL, EXCUUUUSE ME FOR BEING JUST "SOME GIRL"—!!
I'M CALLING YOU LUKA FROM NOW ON!!
D'OW ...!
WHY, YOU... THAT WAS WHERE I GOT HURT...
DOKA (BAM)
PFFFT!
くすくす HEE! HEE!
WELL, LET'S GET GOING, EVERYONE, SHALL WE?
BURORO (VROOM)
—OH YEAH.
KANATA-SAN IS THE ONLY ONE I COULDN'T GET IN TOUCH WITH.
I'LL CALL HIM WHEN WE GET TO TOKYO...
YUKI.
...I CAN KEEP GOING FORWARD.
LOOK.
EH?
—EVEN IF I LOSE HEART...
I HAVE TO SEARCH OUT THE THINGS THAT I CAN DO NOW—
UZUKI-KUN...
...AS LONG AS THERE'S SOMEONE WHO BELIEVES IN ME...
Story 4 END

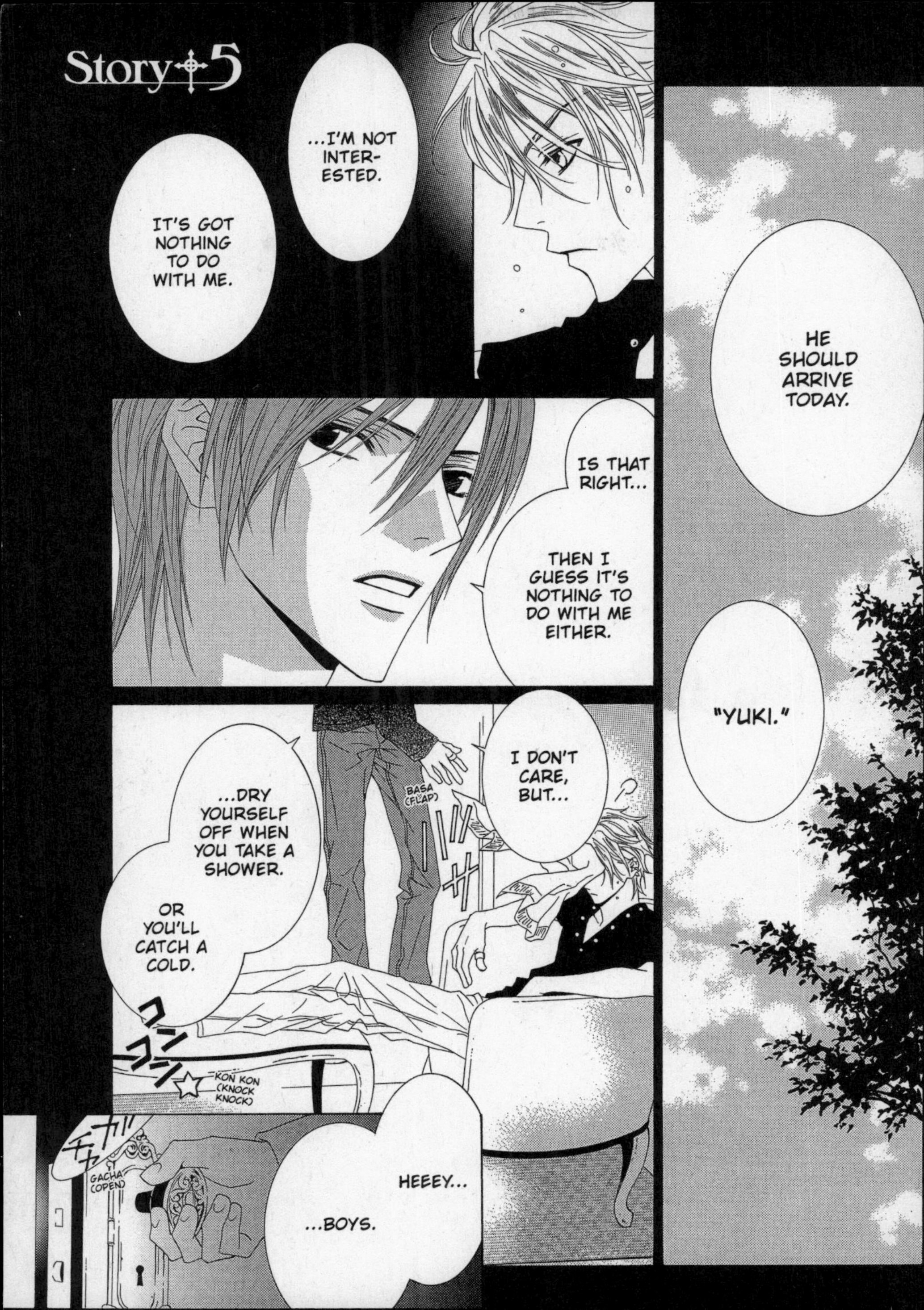
Story 5
HE SHOULD ARRIVE TODAY.
"YUKI."
...I'M NOT INTER-ESTED.
IT'S GOT NOTHING TO DO WITH ME.
IS THAT RIGHT...
THEN I GUESS IT'S NOTHING TO DO WITH ME EITHER.
I DON'T CARE, BUT...
BASA (FLAP)
...DRY YOURSELF OFF WHEN YOU TAKE A SHOWER.
OR YOU'LL CATCH A COLD.
KON KON (KNOCK KNOCK)
GACHA (OPEN)
HEEEY...
...BOYS.

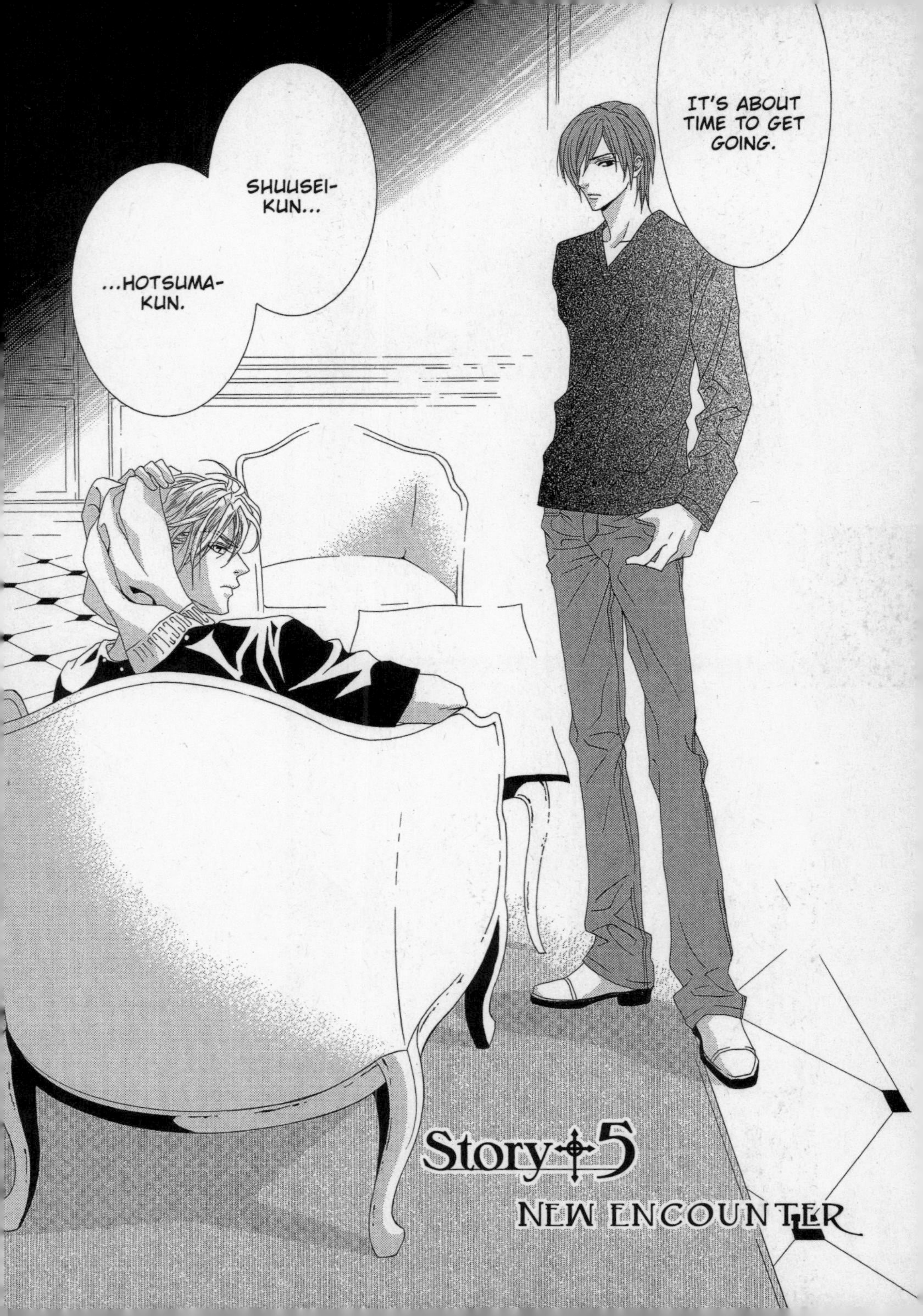
IT'S ABOUT TIME TO GET GOING.
SHUUSEI-KUN...
...HOTSUMA-KUN.
Story 5
NEW ENCOUNTER

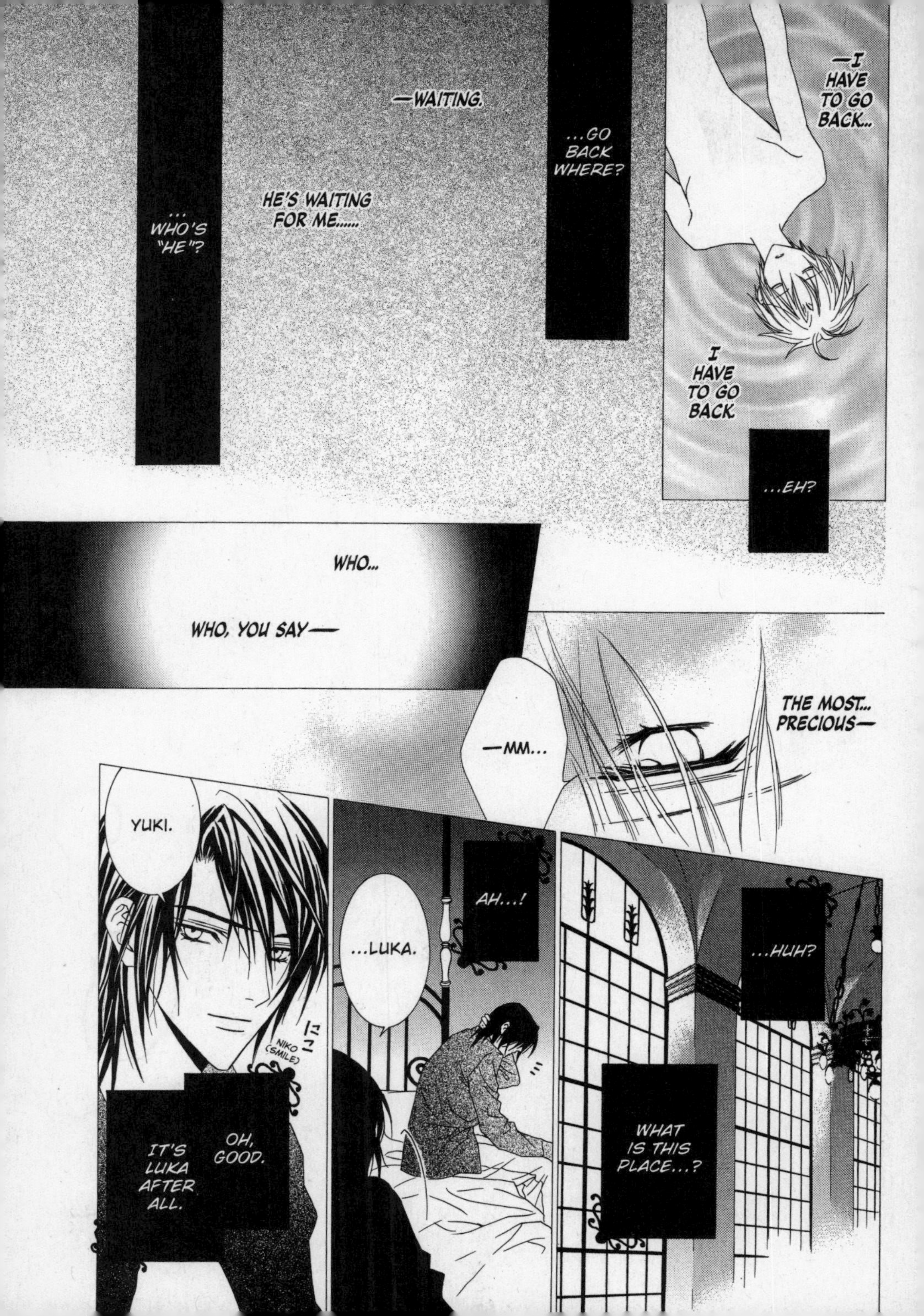
—I HAVE TO GO BACK...
I HAVE TO GO BACK.
...EH?
...GO BACK WHERE?
—WAITING.
HE'S WAITING FOR ME......
... WHO'S "HE"?
WHO...
WHO, YOU SAY—
THE MOST... PRECIOUS—
—MM...
...HUH?
WHAT IS THIS PLACE...?
AH...!
...LUKA.
YUKI.
NIKO (SMILE)
OH, GOOD.
IT'S LUKA AFTER ALL.

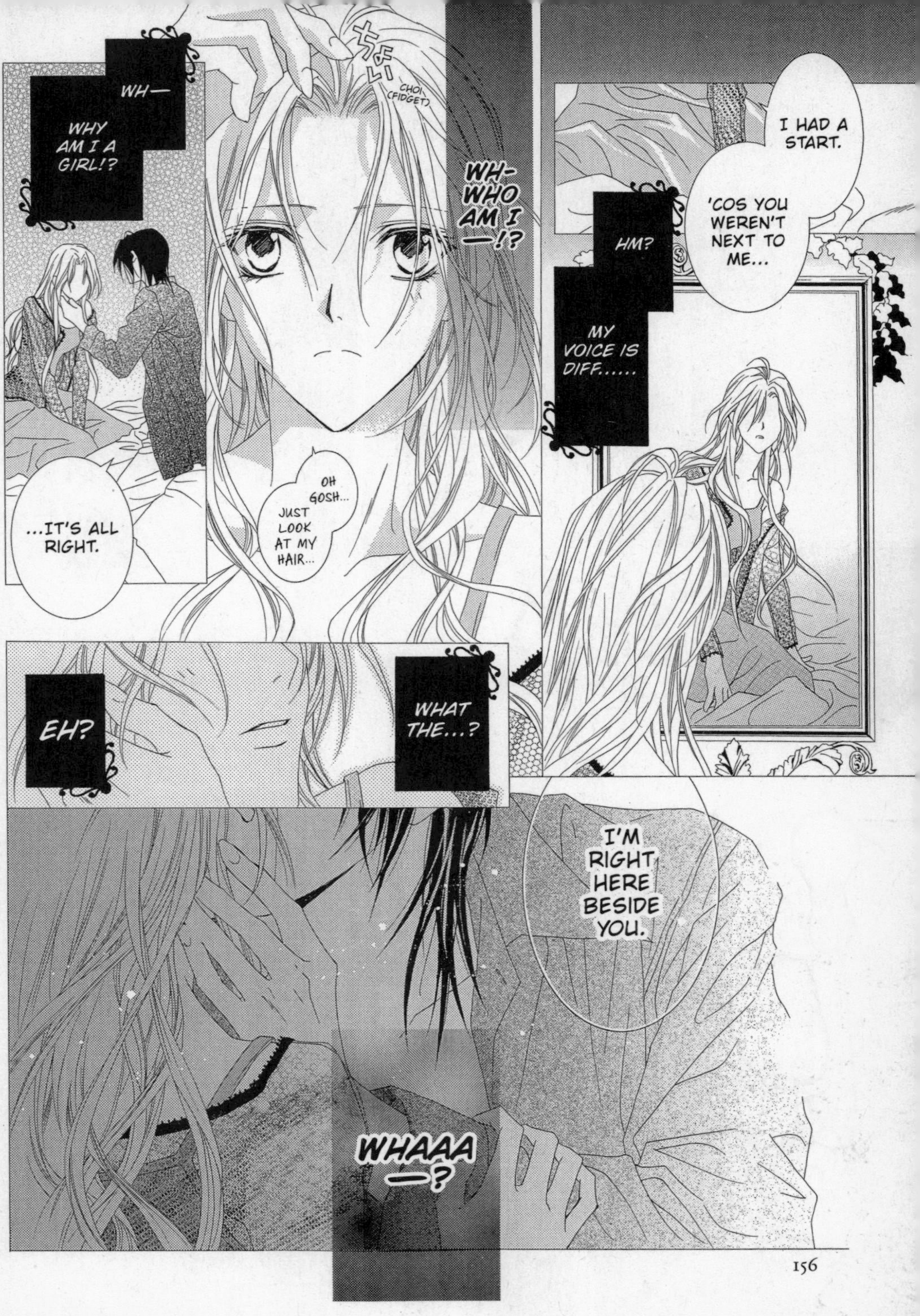
I HAD A START.
'COS YOU WEREN'T NEXT TO ME...
HM?
MY VOICE IS DIFF......
ちょい
CHOI (FIDGET)
WH-WHO AM I—!?
OH GOSH... JUST LOOK AT MY HAIR...
WH—
WHY AM I A GIRL!?
...IT'S ALL RIGHT.
WHAT THE...?
EH?
I'M RIGHT HERE BESIDE YOU.
WHAAA—?

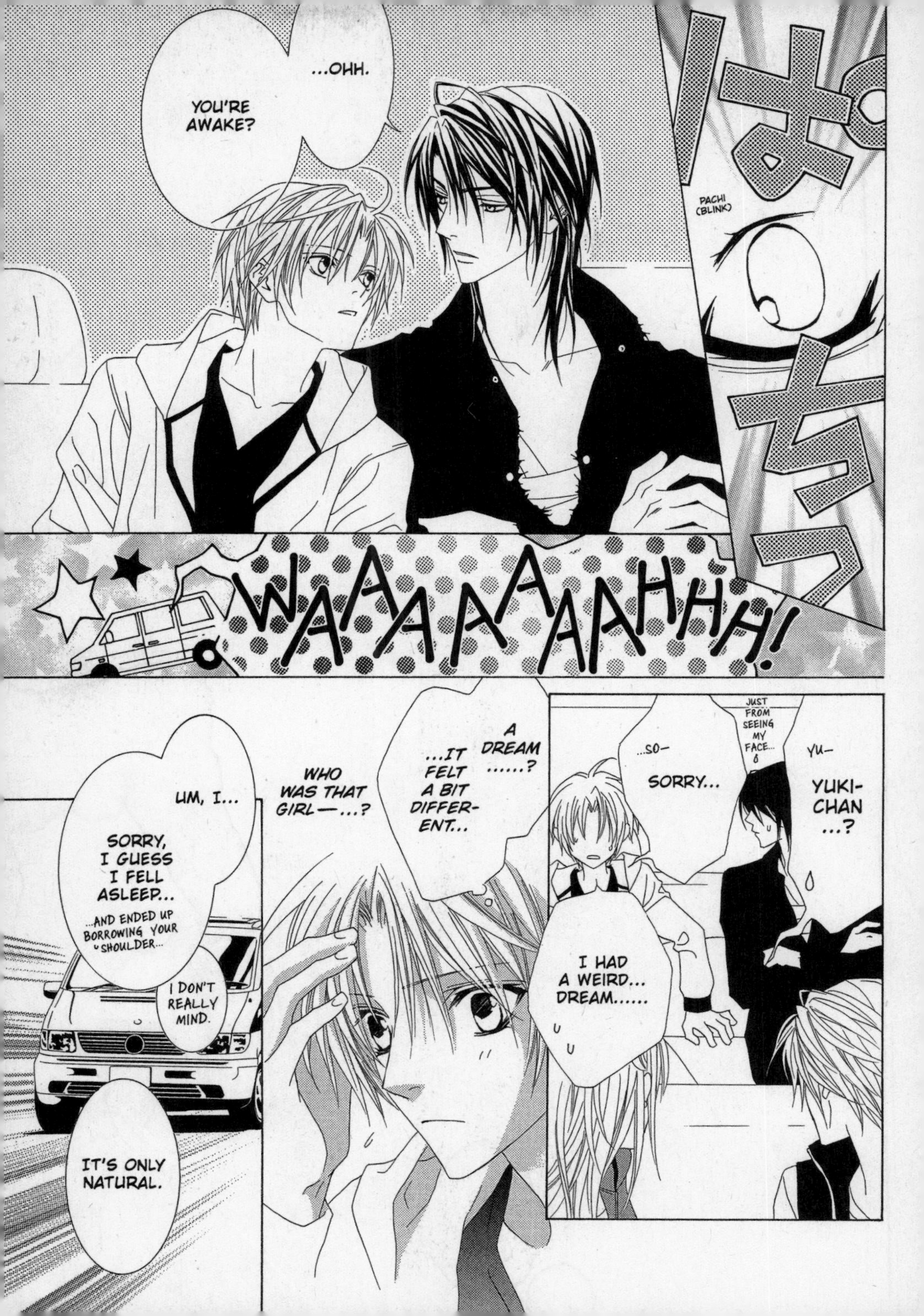
ぱちっ
PACHI (BLINK)
...OHH.
YOU'RE AWAKE?
WAAAAAAAHHH!
YU—
YUKI-CHAN ...?
JUST FROM SEEING MY FACE...
...SO—
SORRY...
I HAD A WEIRD... DREAM......
A DREAM ......?
...IT FELT A BIT DIFFERENT...
WHO WAS THAT GIRL—...?
UM, I...
SORRY, I GUESS I FELL ASLEEP...
...AND ENDED UP BORROWING YOUR SHOULDER...
I DON'T REALLY MIND.
IT'S ONLY NATURAL.

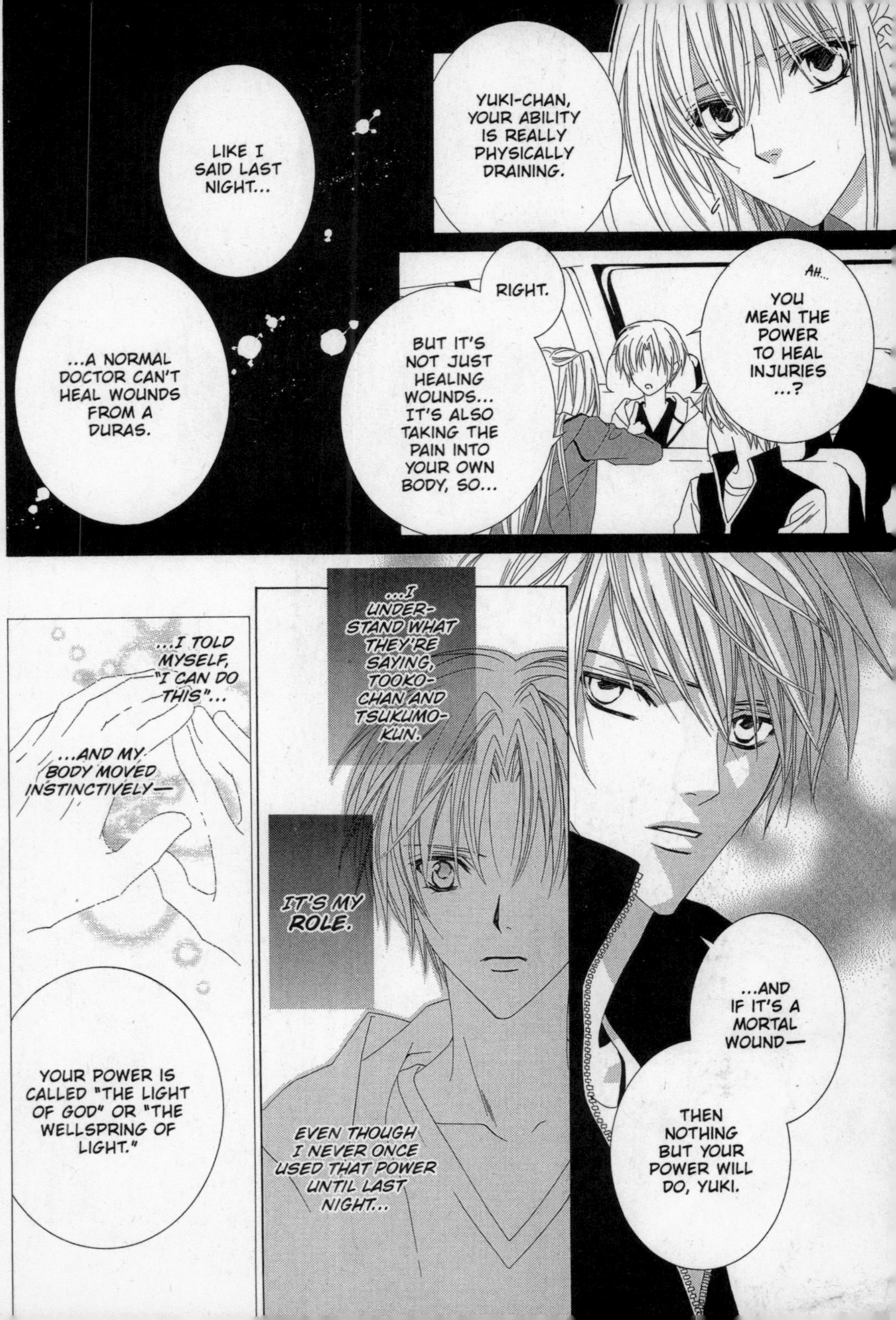
YUKI-CHAN, YOUR ABILITY IS REALLY PHYSICALLY DRAINING.
LIKE I SAID LAST NIGHT...
...A NORMAL DOCTOR CAN'T HEAL WOUNDS FROM A DURAS.
AH... YOU MEAN THE POWER TO HEAL INJURIES ...?
RIGHT.
BUT IT'S NOT JUST HEALING WOUNDS... IT'S ALSO TAKING THE PAIN INTO YOUR OWN BODY, SO...
...AND IF IT'S A MORTAL WOUND—
THEN NOTHING BUT YOUR POWER WILL DO, YUKI.
...I UNDER-STAND WHAT THEY'RE SAYING, TOOKO-CHAN AND TSUKUMO-KUN.
IT'S MY ROLE.
...I TOLD MYSELF, "I CAN DO THIS"...
...AND MY BODY MOVED INSTINCTIVELY—
YOUR POWER IS CALLED "THE LIGHT OF GOD" OR "THE WELLSPRING OF LIGHT."
EVEN THOUGH I NEVER ONCE USED THAT POWER UNTIL LAST NIGHT...

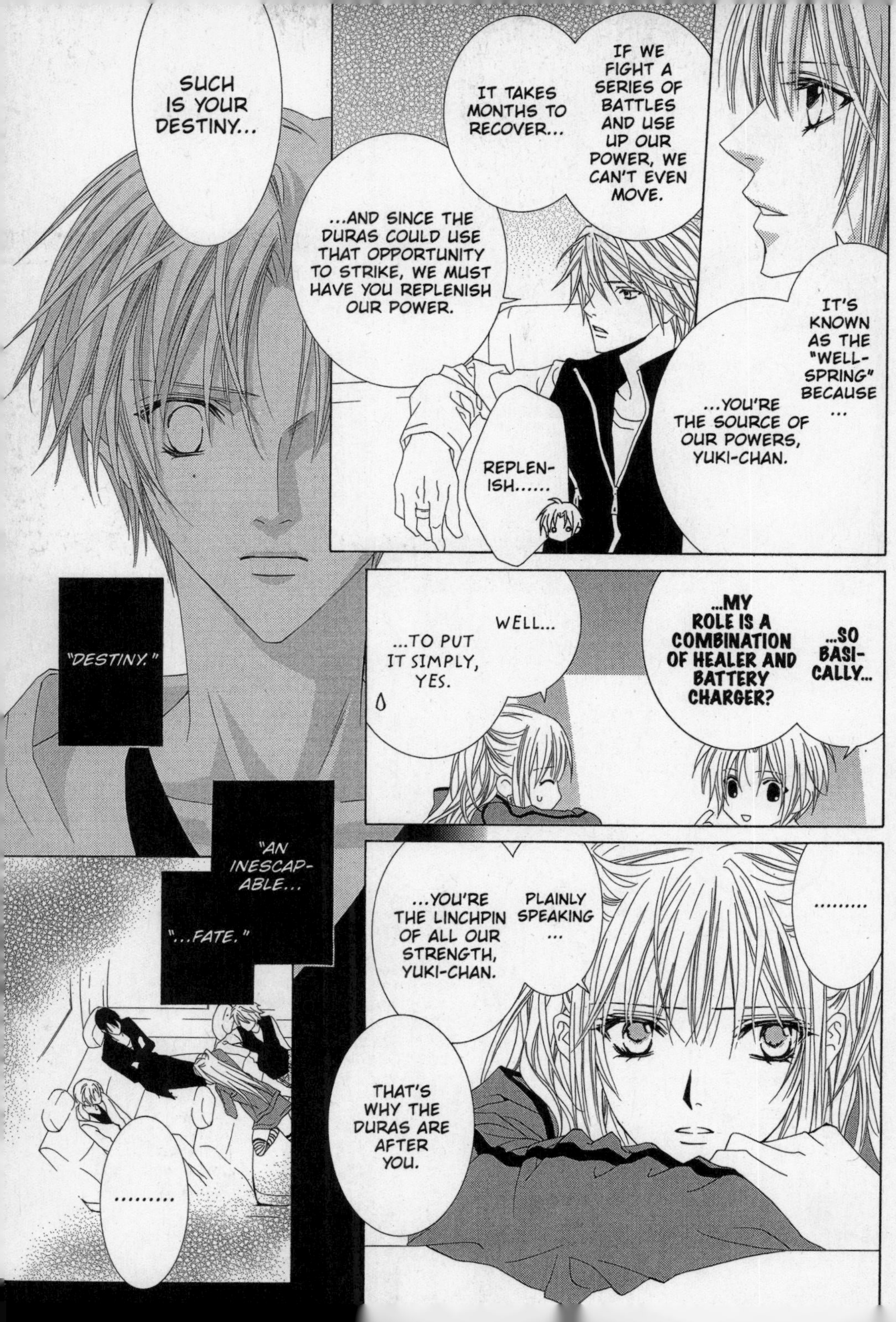
IF WE FIGHT A SERIES OF BATTLES AND USE UP OUR POWER, WE CAN'T EVEN MOVE.
IT TAKES MONTHS TO RECOVER...
...AND SINCE THE DURAS COULD USE THAT OPPORTUNITY TO STRIKE, WE MUST HAVE YOU REPLENISH OUR POWER.
IT'S KNOWN AS THE "WELL-SPRING" BECAUSE ...
...YOU'RE THE SOURCE OF OUR POWERS, YUKI-CHAN.
REPLEN-ISH......
SUCH IS YOUR DESTINY...
"DESTINY."
...SO BASI-CALLY...
...MY ROLE IS A COMBINATION OF HEALER AND BATTERY CHARGER?
WELL...
...TO PUT IT SIMPLY, YES.
....
PLAINLY SPEAKING ...
...YOU'RE THE LINCHPIN OF ALL OUR STRENGTH, YUKI-CHAN.
THAT'S WHY THE DURAS ARE AFTER YOU.
"AN INESCAP-ABLE...
"...FATE."
....

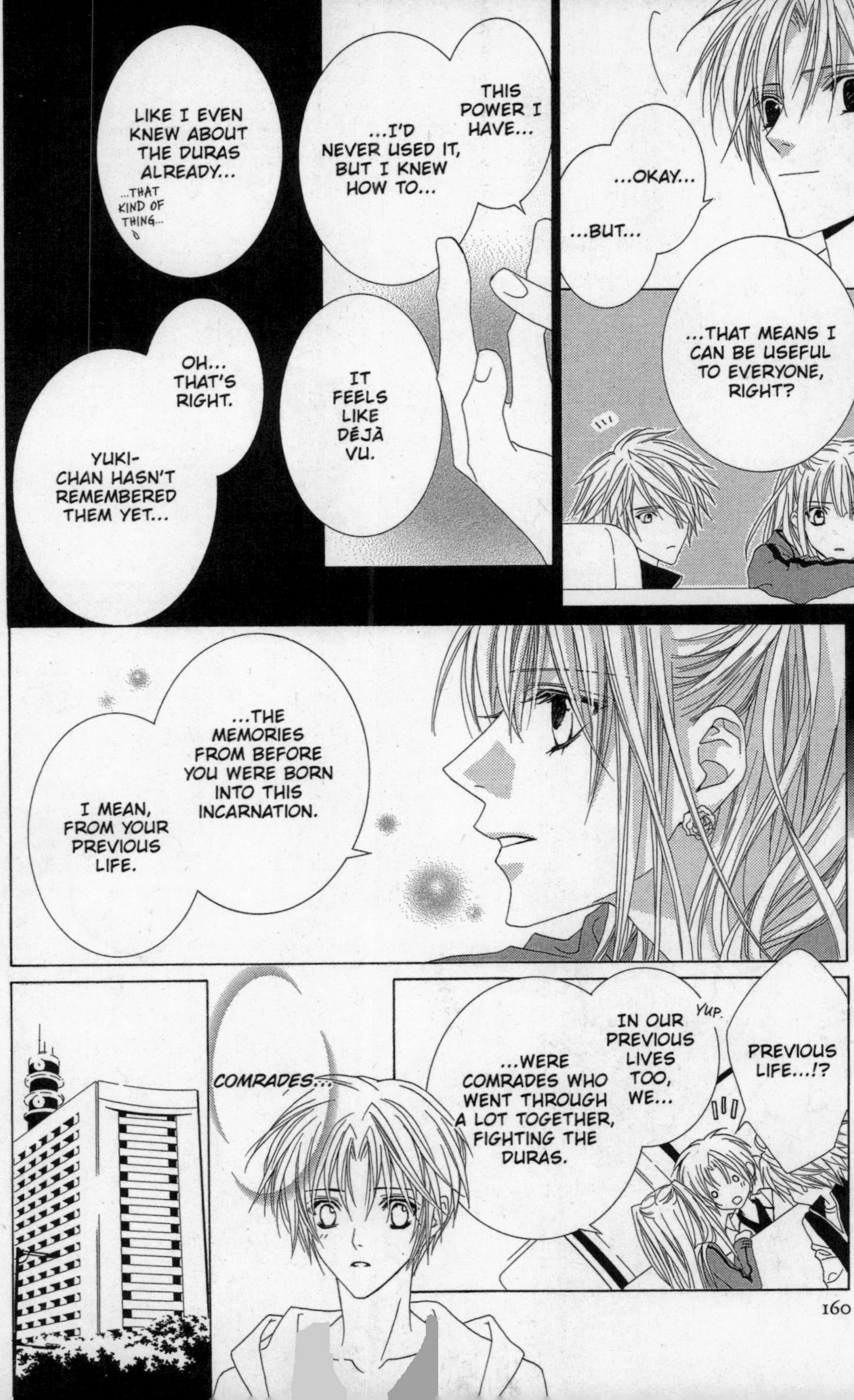
...OKAY...
...BUT...
...THAT MEANS I CAN BE USEFUL TO EVERYONE, RIGHT?
THIS POWER I HAVE...
...I'D NEVER USED IT, BUT I KNEW HOW TO...
IT FEELS LIKE DÉJÀ VU.
LIKE I EVEN KNEW ABOUT THE DURAS ALREADY...
...THAT KIND OF THING...
OH... THAT'S RIGHT.
YUKI-CHAN HASN'T REMEMBERED THEM YET...
...THE MEMORIES FROM BEFORE YOU WERE BORN INTO THIS INCARNATION.
I MEAN, FROM YOUR PREVIOUS LIFE.
PREVIOUS LIFE...!?
YUP.
IN OUR PREVIOUS LIVES TOO, WE...
...WERE COMRADES WHO WENT THROUGH A LOT TOGETHER, FIGHTING THE DURAS.
COMRADES...

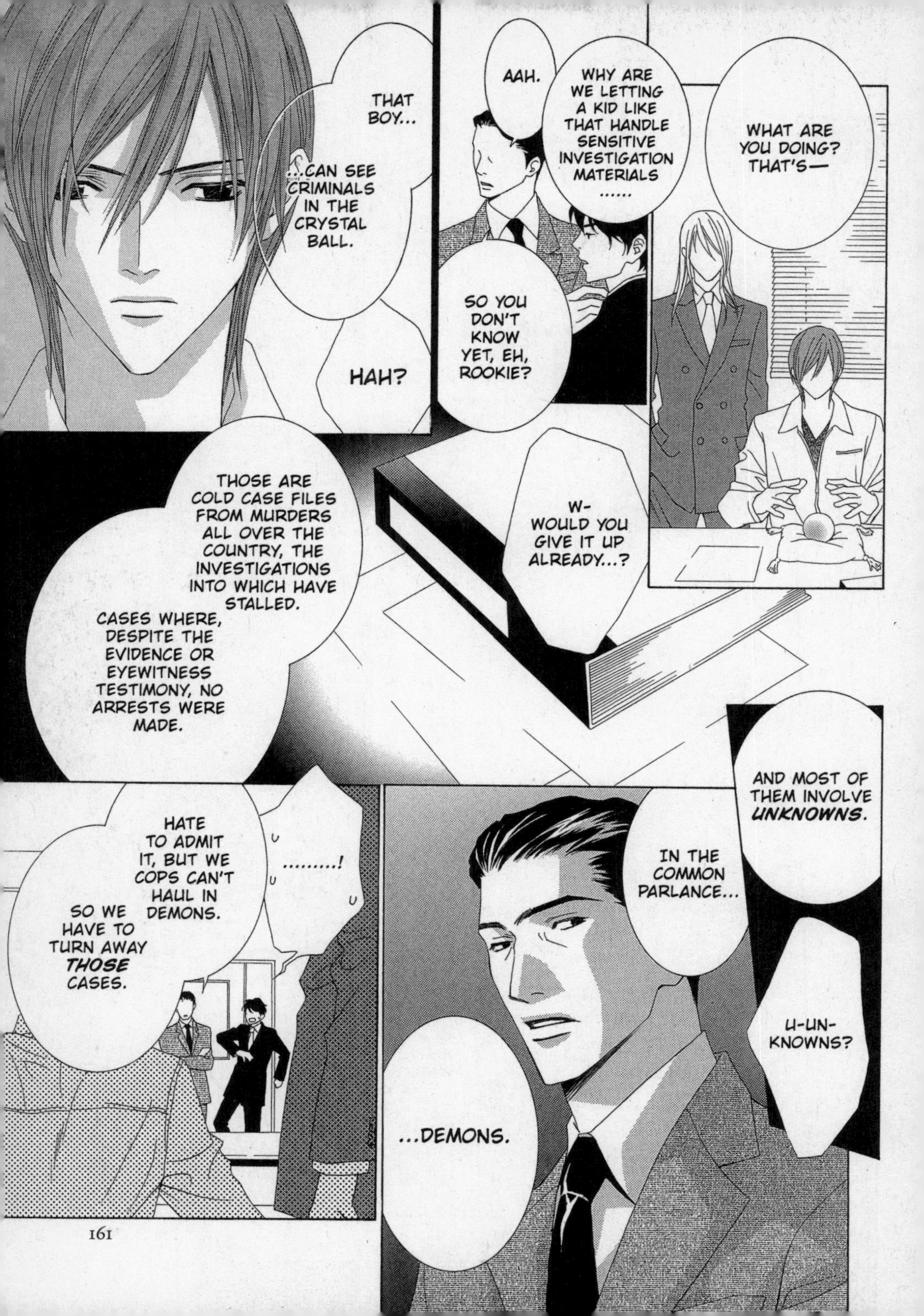
WHAT ARE YOU DOING? THAT'S—
WHY ARE WE LETTING A KID LIKE THAT HANDLE SENSITIVE INVESTIGATION MATERIALS ......
AAH.
SO YOU DON'T KNOW YET, EH, ROOKIE?
HAH?
THAT BOY...
...CAN SEE CRIMINALS IN THE CRYSTAL BALL.
W-WOULD YOU GIVE IT UP ALREADY...?
THOSE ARE COLD CASE FILES FROM MURDERS ALL OVER THE COUNTRY, THE INVESTIGATIONS INTO WHICH HAVE STALLED.
CASES WHERE, DESPITE THE EVIDENCE OR EYEWITNESS TESTIMONY, NO ARRESTS WERE MADE.
AND MOST OF THEM INVOLVE *UNKNOWNS*.
IN THE COMMON PARLANCE...
U-UNKNOWNS?
...DEMONS.
HATE TO ADMIT IT, BUT WE COPS CAN'T HAUL IN DEMONS.
SO WE HAVE TO TURN AWAY *THOSE* CASES.
.........!

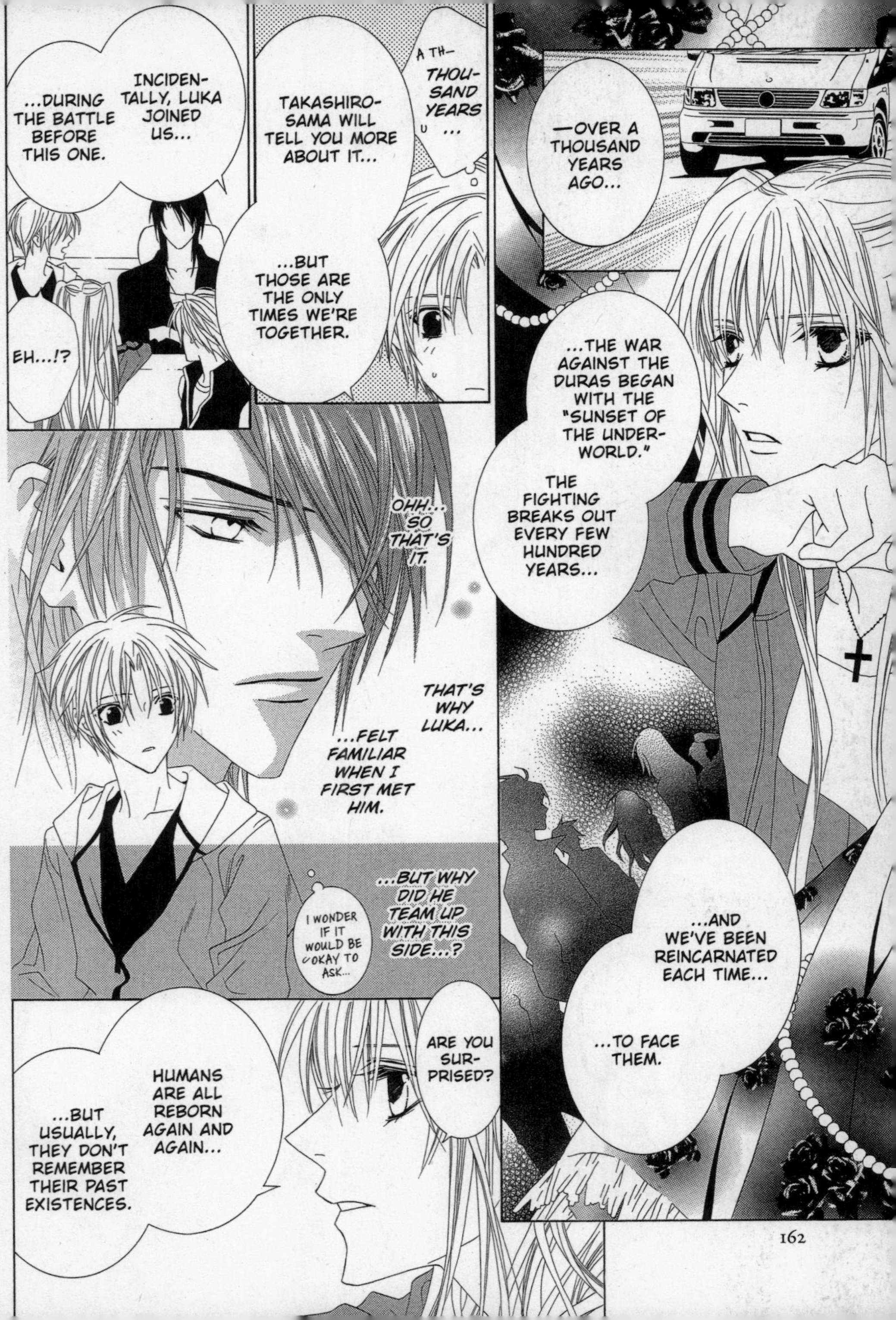
—OVER A THOUSAND YEARS AGO...
...THE WAR AGAINST THE DURAS BEGAN WITH THE "SUNSET OF THE UNDER-WORLD."
THE FIGHTING BREAKS OUT EVERY FEW HUNDRED YEARS...
...AND WE'VE BEEN REINCARNATED EACH TIME...
...TO FACE THEM.
A TH— THOUSAND YEARS...
TAKASHIRO-SAMA WILL TELL YOU MORE ABOUT IT...
...BUT THOSE ARE THE ONLY TIMES WE'RE TOGETHER.
INCIDEN-TALLY, LUKA JOINED US...
...DURING THE BATTLE BEFORE THIS ONE.
EH...!?
OHH... SO THAT'S IT.
THAT'S WHY LUKA...
...FELT FAMILIAR WHEN I FIRST MET HIM.
...BUT WHY DID HE TEAM UP WITH THIS SIDE...?
I WONDER IF IT WOULD BE OKAY TO ASK...
ARE YOU SURPRISED?
HUMANS ARE ALL REBORN AGAIN AND AGAIN...
...BUT USUALLY, THEY DON'T REMEMBER THEIR PAST EXISTENCES.

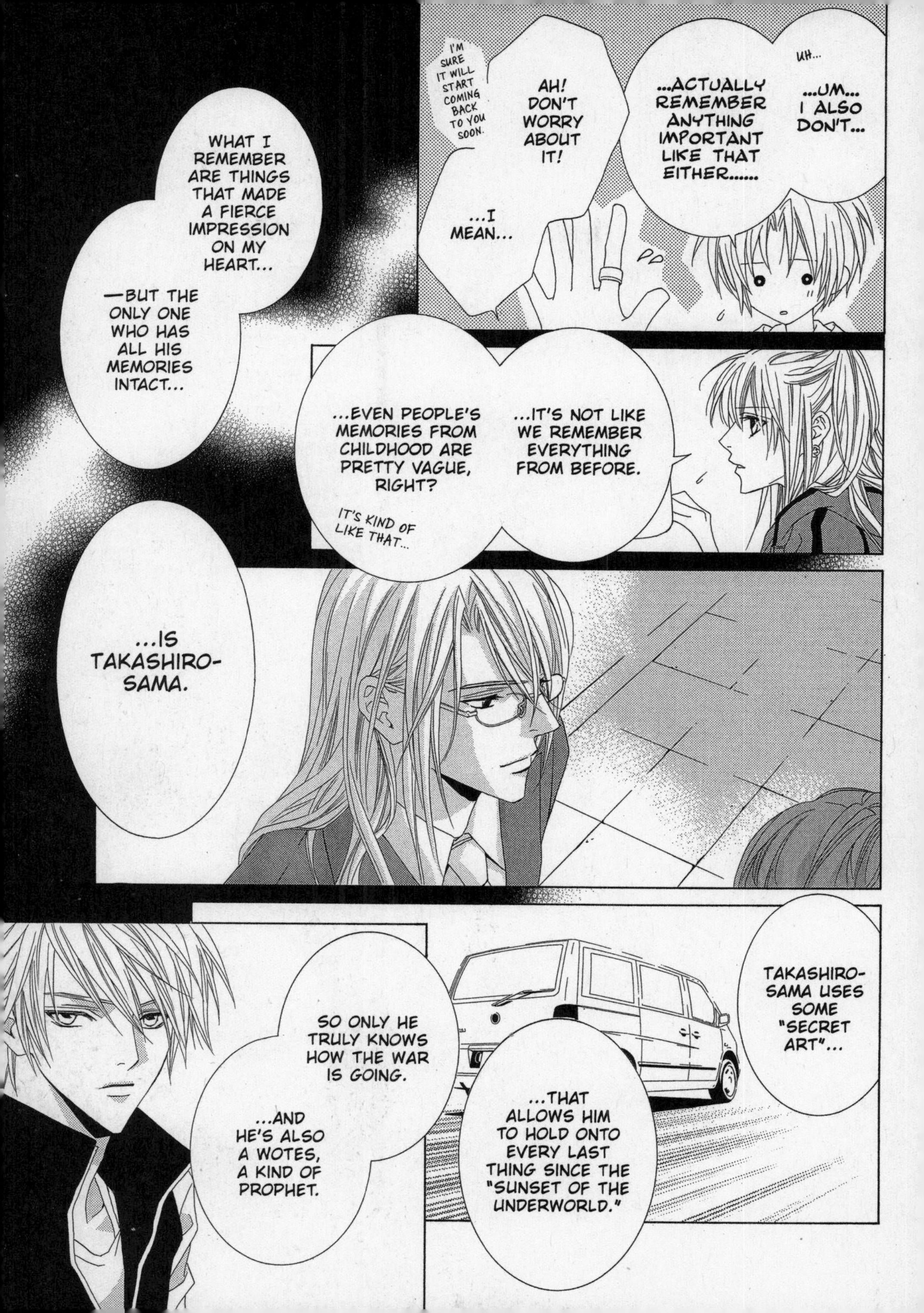
UH...
...UM... I ALSO DON'T...
...ACTUALLY REMEMBER ANYTHING IMPORTANT LIKE THAT EITHER......
AH! DON'T WORRY ABOUT IT!
I'M SURE IT WILL START COMING BACK TO YOU SOON.
...I MEAN...
...IT'S NOT LIKE WE REMEMBER EVERYTHING FROM BEFORE.
...EVEN PEOPLE'S MEMORIES FROM CHILDHOOD ARE PRETTY VAGUE, RIGHT?
IT'S KIND OF LIKE THAT...
WHAT I REMEMBER ARE THINGS THAT MADE A FIERCE IMPRESSION ON MY HEART...
—BUT THE ONLY ONE WHO HAS ALL HIS MEMORIES INTACT...
...IS TAKASHIRO-SAMA.
TAKASHIRO-SAMA USES SOME "SECRET ART"...
...THAT ALLOWS HIM TO HOLD ONTO EVERY LAST THING SINCE THE "SUNSET OF THE UNDERWORLD."
SO ONLY HE TRULY KNOWS HOW THE WAR IS GOING.
...AND HE'S ALSO A WOTES, A KIND OF PROPHET.

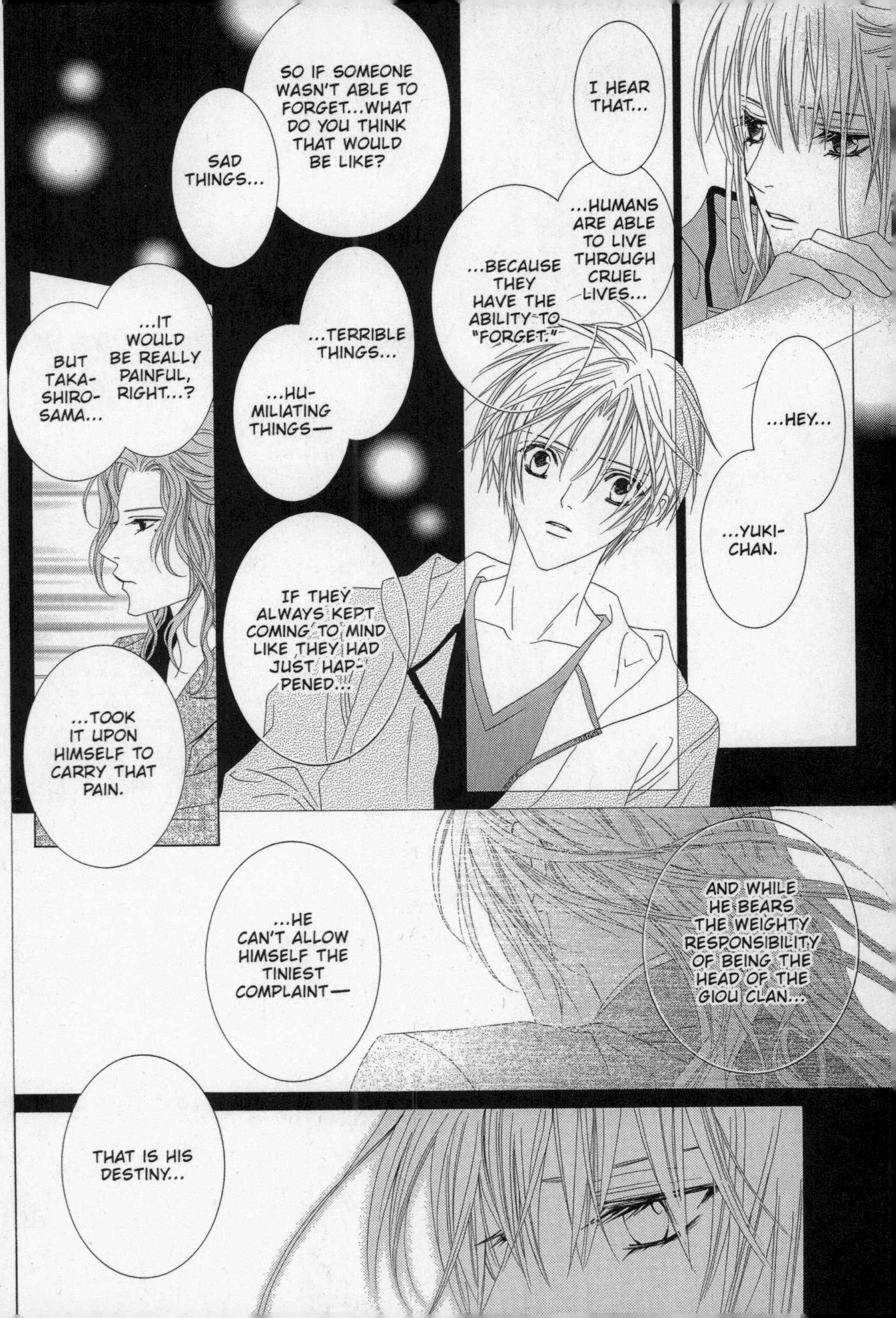
I HEAR THAT...
...HUMANS ARE ABLE TO LIVE THROUGH CRUEL LIVES...
...BECAUSE THEY HAVE THE ABILITY TO "FORGET."
SO IF SOMEONE WASN'T ABLE TO FORGET...WHAT DO YOU THINK THAT WOULD BE LIKE?
SAD THINGS...
...TERRIBLE THINGS...
...HU-MILIATING THINGS—
IF THEY ALWAYS KEPT COMING TO MIND LIKE THEY HAD JUST HAP-PENED...
...IT WOULD BE REALLY PAINFUL, RIGHT...?
...HEY...
...YUKI-CHAN.
BUT TAKA-SHIRO-SAMA...
...TOOK IT UPON HIMSELF TO CARRY THAT PAIN.
AND WHILE HE BEARS THE WEIGHTY RESPONSIBILITY OF BEING THE HEAD OF THE GIOU CLAN...
...HE CAN'T ALLOW HIMSELF THE TINIEST COMPLAINT—
THAT IS HIS DESTINY...

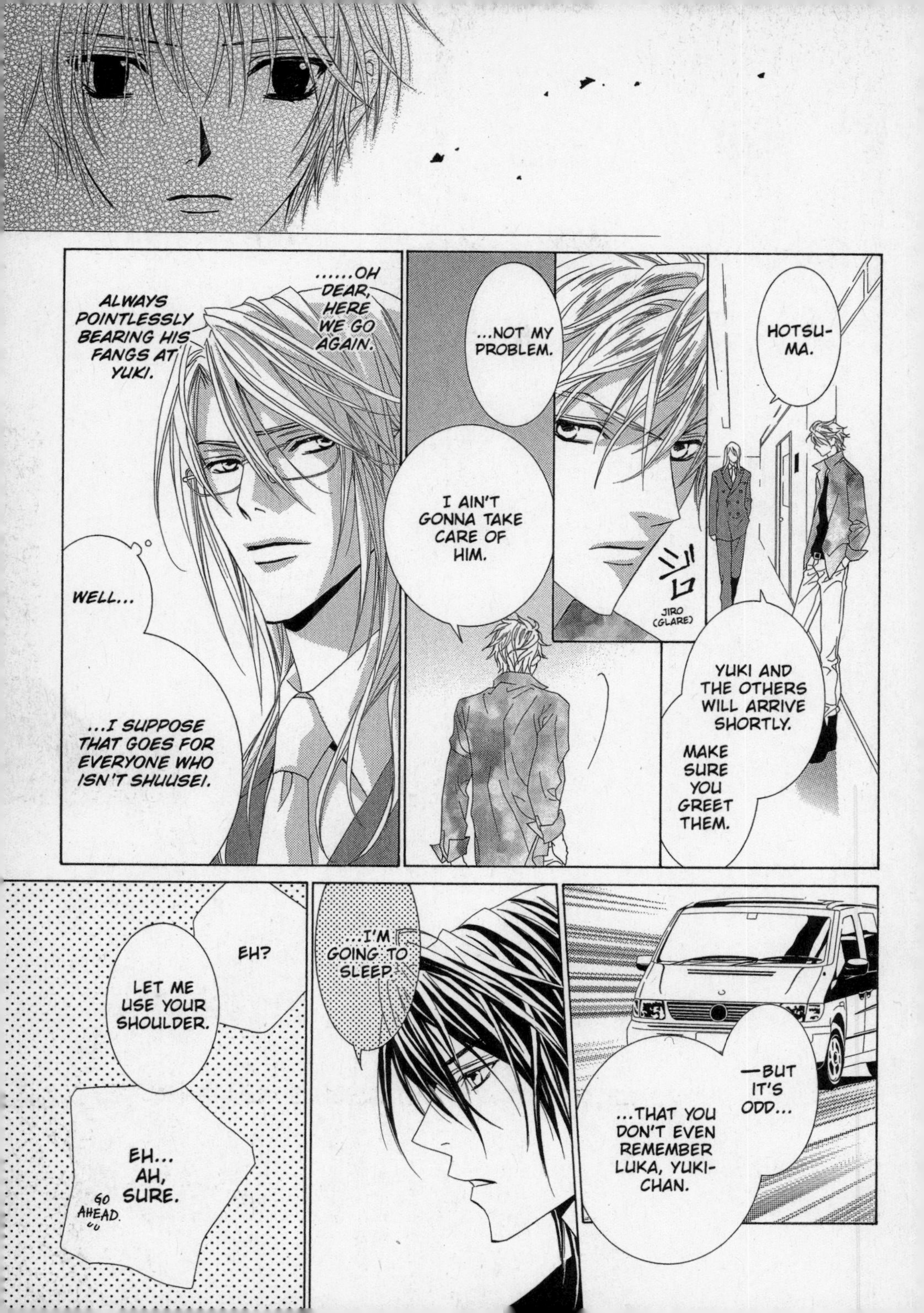
HOTSU-MA.
YUKI AND THE OTHERS WILL ARRIVE SHORTLY.
MAKE SURE YOU GREET THEM.
...NOT MY PROBLEM.
JIRO (GLARE)
I AIN'T GONNA TAKE CARE OF HIM.
......OH DEAR, HERE WE GO AGAIN.
ALWAYS POINTLESSLY BEARING HIS FANGS AT YUKI.
WELL...
...I SUPPOSE THAT GOES FOR EVERYONE WHO ISN'T SHUUSEI.
—BUT IT'S ODD...
...THAT YOU DON'T EVEN REMEMBER LUKA, YUKI-CHAN.
...I'M GOING TO SLEEP.
EH?
LET ME USE YOUR SHOULDER.
EH... AH, SURE.
GO AHEAD.

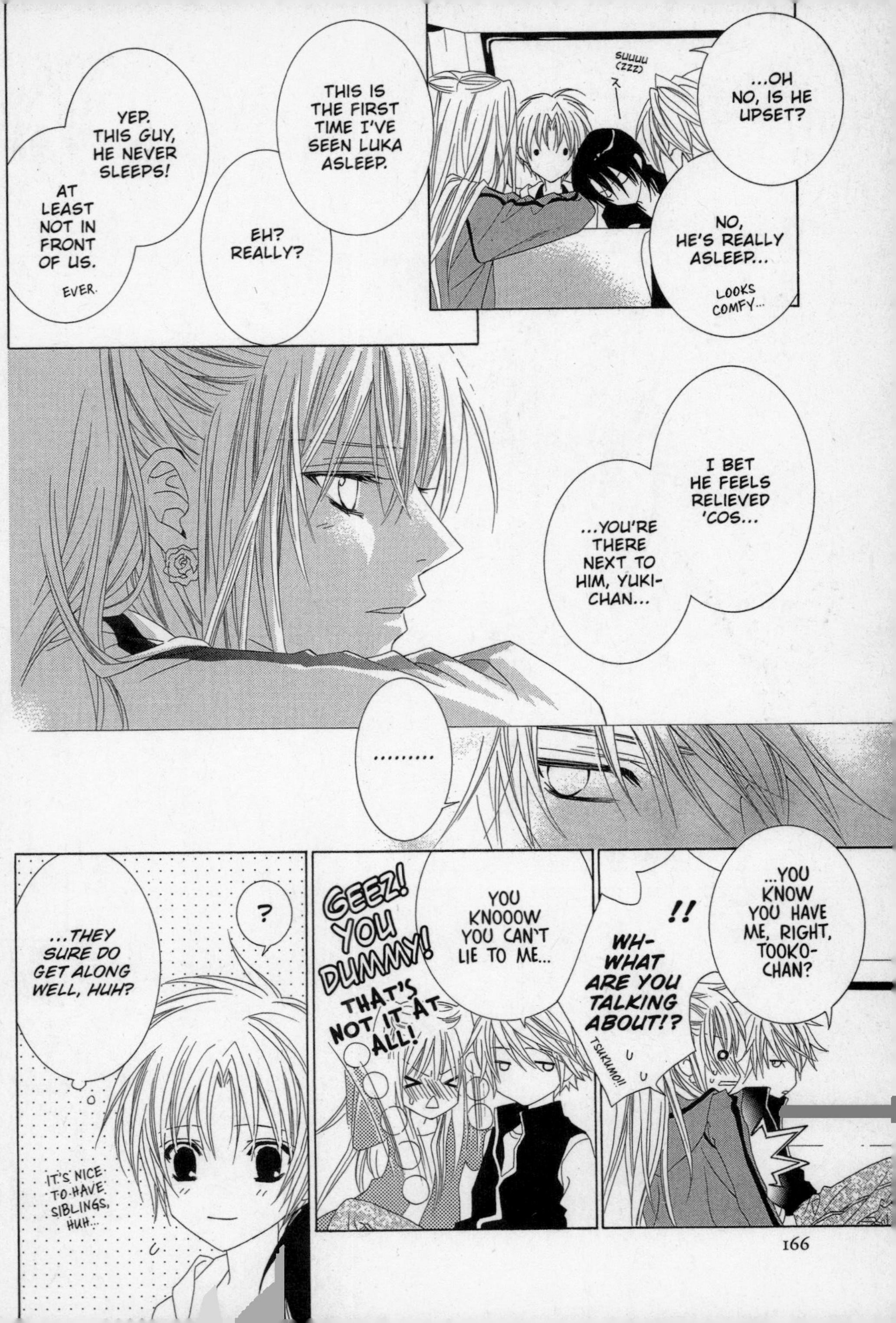
SUUUU (ZZZ)
ス
...OH NO, IS HE UPSET?
NO, HE'S REALLY ASLEEP...
LOOKS COMFY...
THIS IS THE FIRST TIME I'VE SEEN LUKA ASLEEP.
EH? REALLY?
YEP. THIS GUY, HE NEVER SLEEPS!
AT LEAST NOT IN FRONT OF US.
EVER.
I BET HE FEELS RELIEVED 'COS...
...YOU'RE THERE NEXT TO HIM, YUKI-CHAN...
....
...YOU KNOW YOU HAVE ME, RIGHT, TOOKO-CHAN?
!!
WH-WHAT ARE YOU TALKING ABOUT!?
TSUKUMO!!
YOU KNOOOW YOU CAN'T LIE TO ME...
GEEZ! YOU DUMMY!
THAT'S NOT IT AT ALL!
?
...THEY SURE DO GET ALONG WELL, HUH?
IT'S NICE TO HAVE SIBLINGS, HUH...

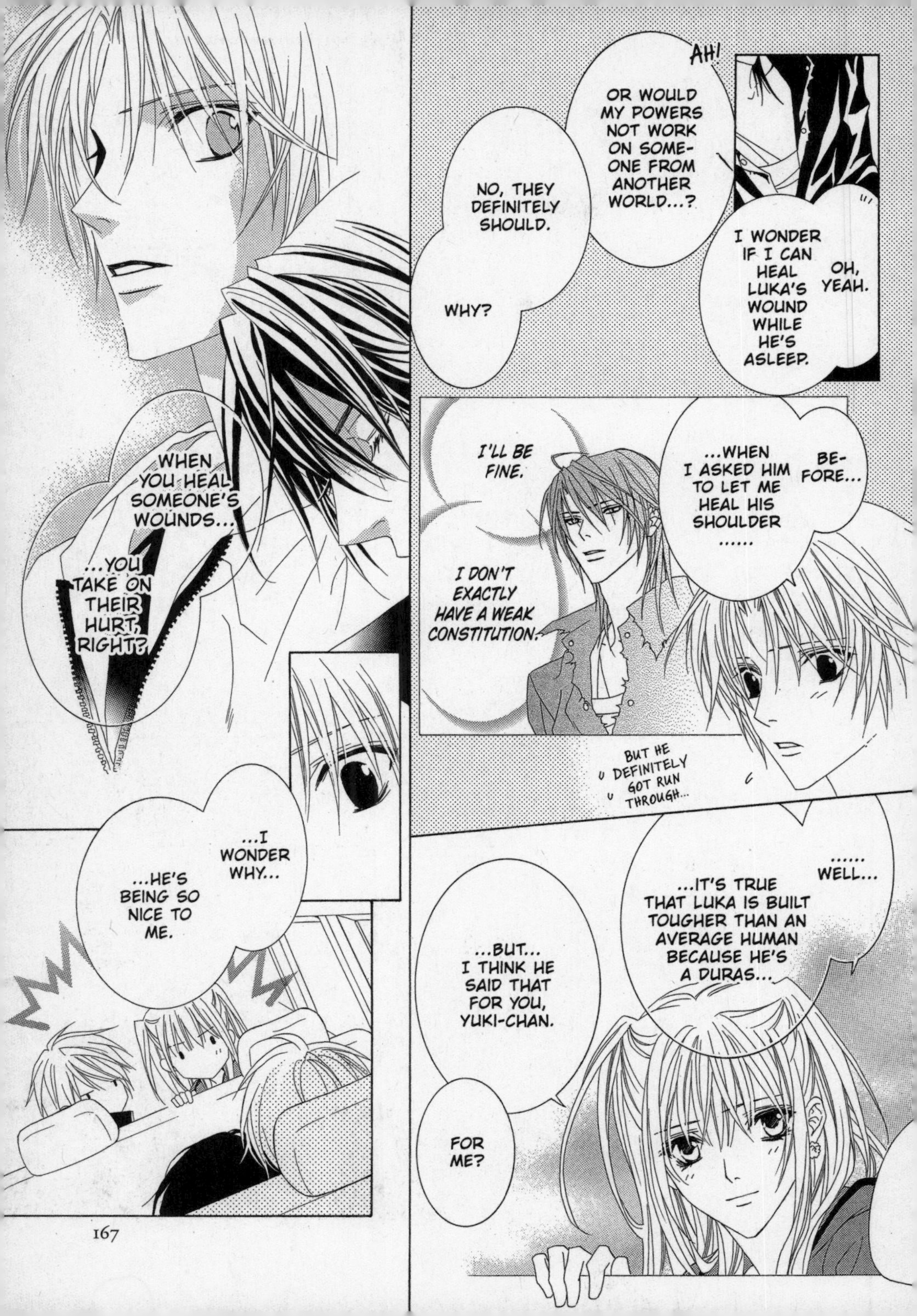
AH!
OH, YEAH.
I WONDER IF I CAN HEAL LUKA'S WOUND WHILE HE'S ASLEEP.
OR WOULD MY POWERS NOT WORK ON SOMEONE FROM ANOTHER WORLD...?
NO, THEY DEFINITELY SHOULD.
WHY?
BE-FORE...
...WHEN I ASKED HIM TO LET ME HEAL HIS SHOULDER ......
I'LL BE FINE.
I DON'T EXACTLY HAVE A WEAK CONSTITUTION.
BUT HE DEFINITELY GOT RUN THROUGH...
...... WELL...
...IT'S TRUE THAT LUKA IS BUILT TOUGHER THAN AN AVERAGE HUMAN BECAUSE HE'S A DURAS...
...BUT... I THINK HE SAID THAT FOR YOU, YUKI-CHAN.
FOR ME?
WHEN YOU HEAL SOMEONE'S WOUNDS...
...YOU TAKE ON THEIR HURT, RIGHT?
...I WONDER WHY...
...HE'S BEING SO NICE TO ME.

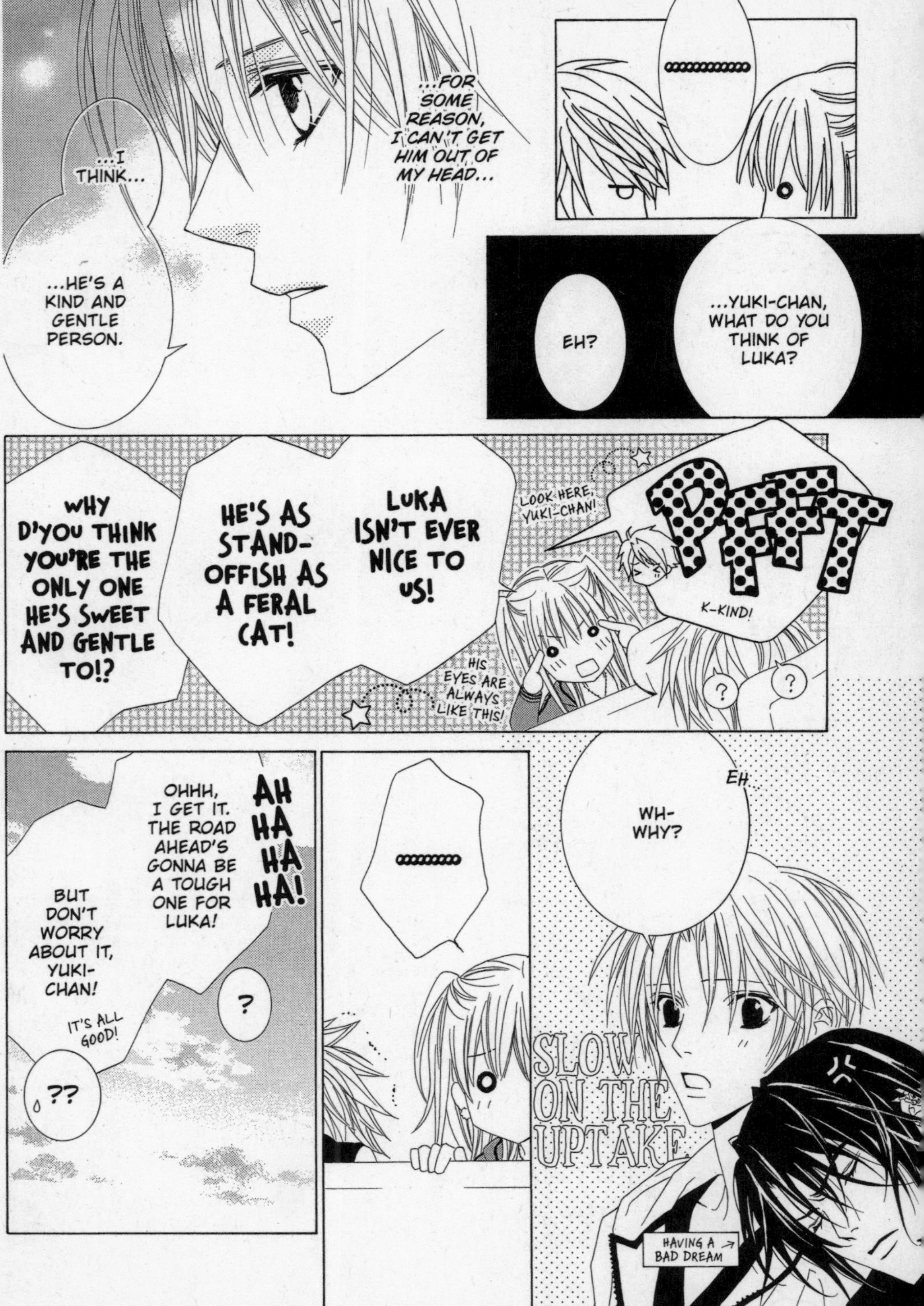
....
...YUKI-CHAN, WHAT DO YOU THINK OF LUKA?
EH?
...FOR SOME REASON, I CAN'T GET HIM OUT OF MY HEAD...
...I THINK...
...HE'S A KIND AND GENTLE PERSON.
PFFFT
K-KIND!
LOOK HERE, YUKI-CHAN!
HIS EYES ARE ALWAYS LIKE THIS!
?
?
LUKA ISN'T EVER NICE TO US!
HE'S AS STAND-OFFISH AS A FERAL CAT!
WHY D'YOU THINK YOU'RE THE ONLY ONE HE'S SWEET AND GENTLE TO!?
EH...
WH-WHY?
SLOW ON THE UPTAKE
HAVING A BAD DREAM
....
AH HA HA HA HA!
OHHH, I GET IT. THE ROAD AHEAD'S GONNA BE A TOUGH ONE FOR LUKA!
BUT DON'T WORRY ABOUT IT, YUKI-CHAN!
IT'S ALL GOOD!
?
??

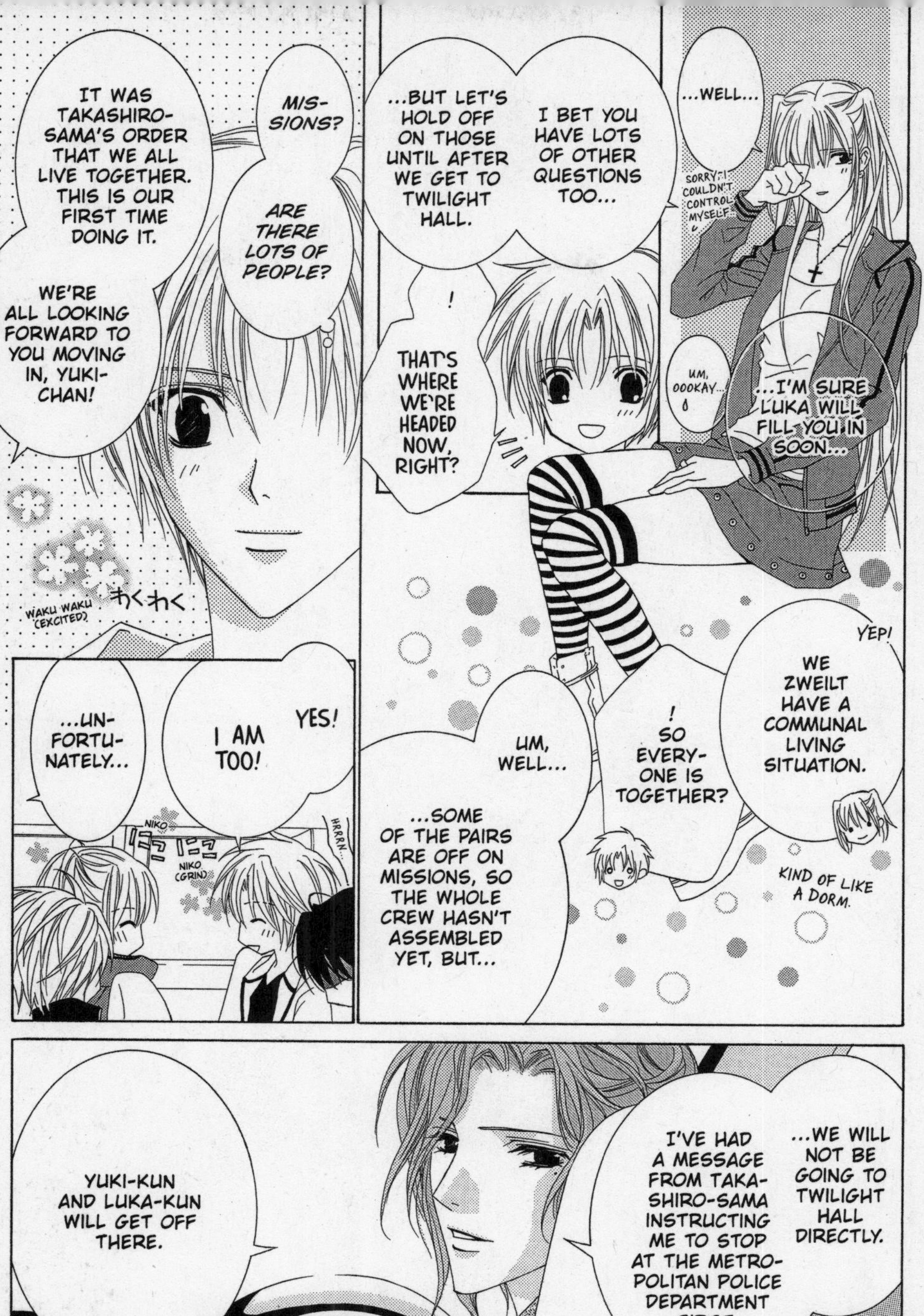
...WELL...
SORRY, I COULDN'T CONTROL MYSELF.
I BET YOU HAVE LOTS OF OTHER QUESTIONS TOO...
...BUT LET'S HOLD OFF ON THOSE UNTIL AFTER WE GET TO TWILIGHT HALL.
!
THAT'S WHERE WE'RE HEADED NOW, RIGHT?
UM, OOOKAY...
...I'M SURE LUKA WILL FILL YOU IN SOON...
YEP!
WE ZWEILT HAVE A COMMUNAL LIVING SITUATION.
KIND OF LIKE A DORM.
! SO EVERY-ONE IS TOGETHER?
UM, WELL...
...SOME OF THE PAIRS ARE OFF ON MISSIONS, SO THE WHOLE CREW HASN'T ASSEMBLED YET, BUT...
MIS-SIONS?
ARE THERE LOTS OF PEOPLE?
IT WAS TAKASHIRO-SAMA'S ORDER THAT WE ALL LIVE TOGETHER. THIS IS OUR FIRST TIME DOING IT.
WE'RE ALL LOOKING FORWARD TO YOU MOVING IN, YUKI-CHAN!
わくわく
WAKU WAKU (EXCITED)
YES!
I AM TOO!
...UN-FORTU-NATELY...
NIKO NIKO (GRIN)
HRRRN...
...WE WILL NOT BE GOING TO TWILIGHT HALL DIRECTLY.
I'VE HAD A MESSAGE FROM TAKA-SHIRO-SAMA INSTRUCTING ME TO STOP AT THE METRO-POLITAN POLICE DEPARTMENT FIRST.
YUKI-KUN AND LUKA-KUN WILL GET OFF THERE.

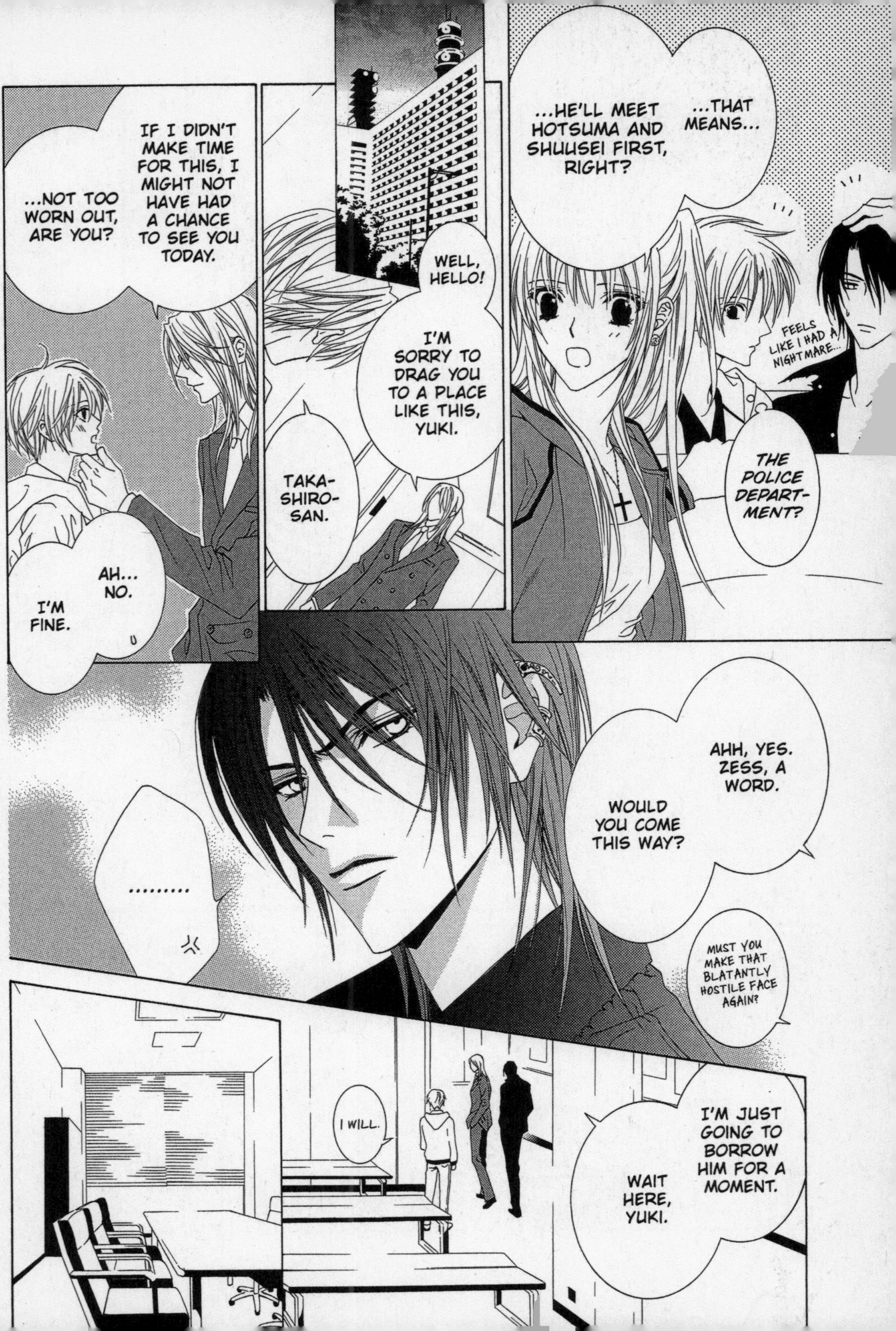
...THAT MEANS...
...HE'LL MEET HOTSUMA AND SHUUSEI FIRST, RIGHT?
FEELS LIKE I HAD A NIGHTMARE...
THE POLICE DEPARTMENT?
WELL, HELLO!
I'M SORRY TO DRAG YOU TO A PLACE LIKE THIS, YUKI.
TAKA-SHIRO-SAN.
IF I DIDN'T MAKE TIME FOR THIS, I MIGHT NOT HAVE HAD A CHANCE TO SEE YOU TODAY.
...NOT TOO WORN OUT, ARE YOU?
AH... NO.
I'M FINE.
AHH, YES. ZESS, A WORD.
WOULD YOU COME THIS WAY?
MUST YOU MAKE THAT BLATANTLY HOSTILE FACE AGAIN?
....
I'M JUST GOING TO BORROW HIM FOR A MOMENT.
WAIT HERE, YUKI.
I WILL.

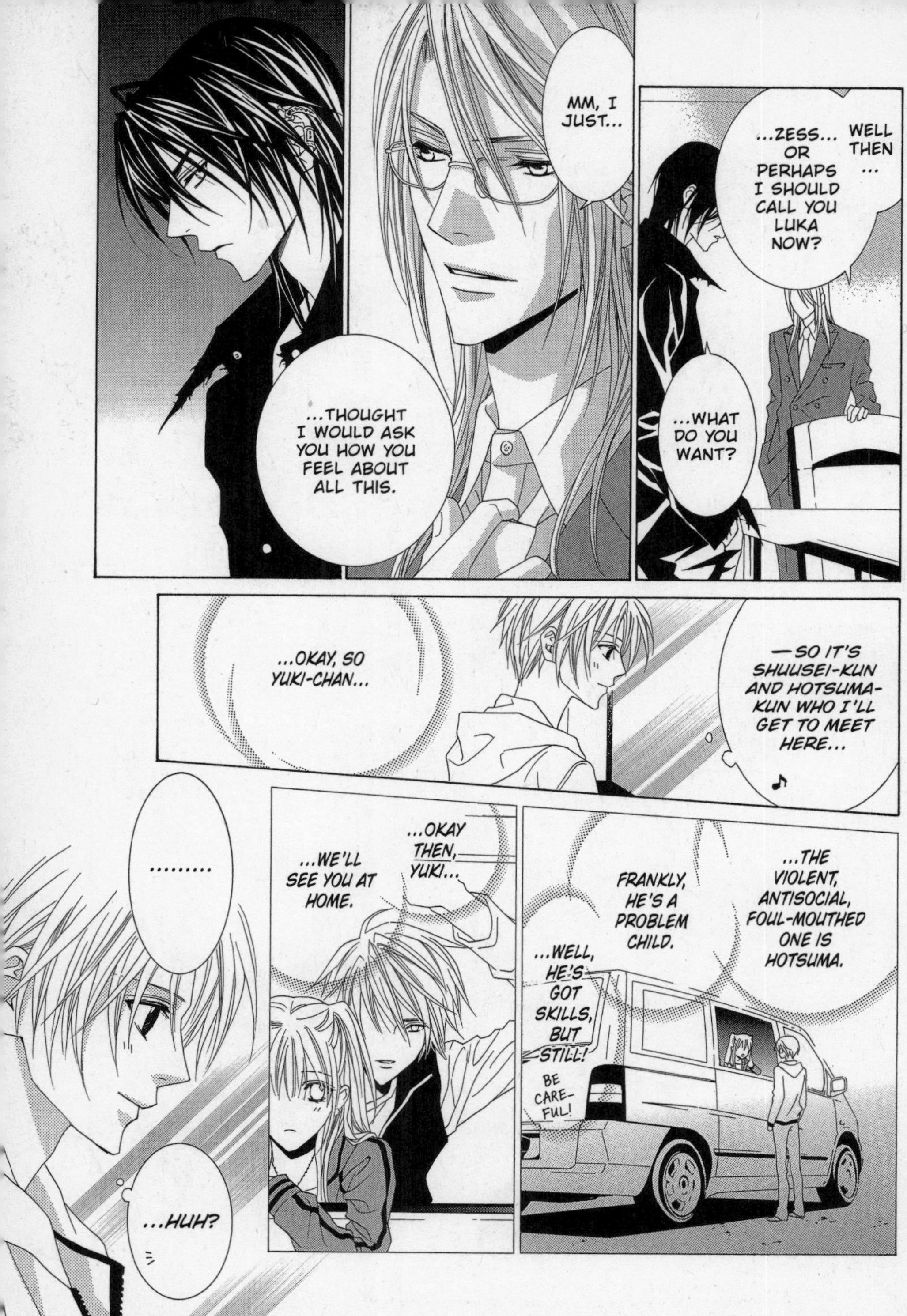
WELL THEN ...
...ZESS... OR PERHAPS I SHOULD CALL YOU LUKA NOW?
...WHAT DO YOU WANT?
MM, I JUST...
...THOUGHT I WOULD ASK YOU HOW YOU FEEL ABOUT ALL THIS.
—SO IT'S SHUUSEI-KUN AND HOTSUMA-KUN WHO I'LL GET TO MEET HERE... ♪
...OKAY, SO YUKI-CHAN...
...THE VIOLENT, ANTISOCIAL, FOUL-MOUTHED ONE IS HOTSUMA.
FRANKLY, HE'S A PROBLEM CHILD.
...WELL, HE'S GOT SKILLS, BUT STILL!
BE CARE-FUL!
...OKAY THEN, YUKI...
...WE'LL SEE YOU AT HOME.
....
...HUH?

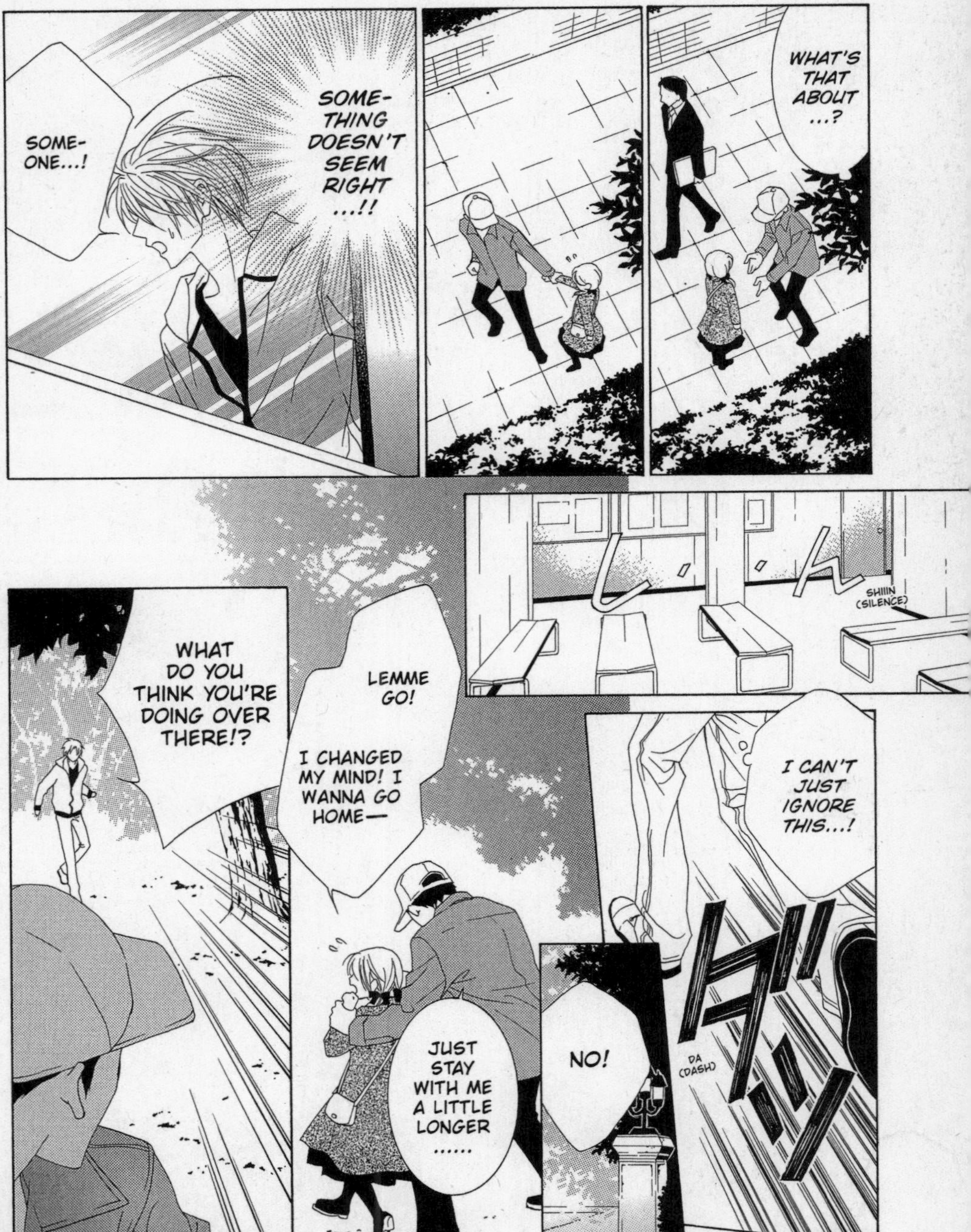
WHAT'S THAT ABOUT ...?
SOME-THING DOESN'T SEEM RIGHT ...!!
SOME-ONE...!
SHIIIN (SILENCE)
I CAN'T JUST IGNORE THIS...!
DA (DASH)
LEMME GO!
I CHANGED MY MIND! I WANNA GO HOME—
WHAT DO YOU THINK YOU'RE DOING OVER THERE!?
NO!
JUST STAY WITH ME A LITTLE LONGER ......

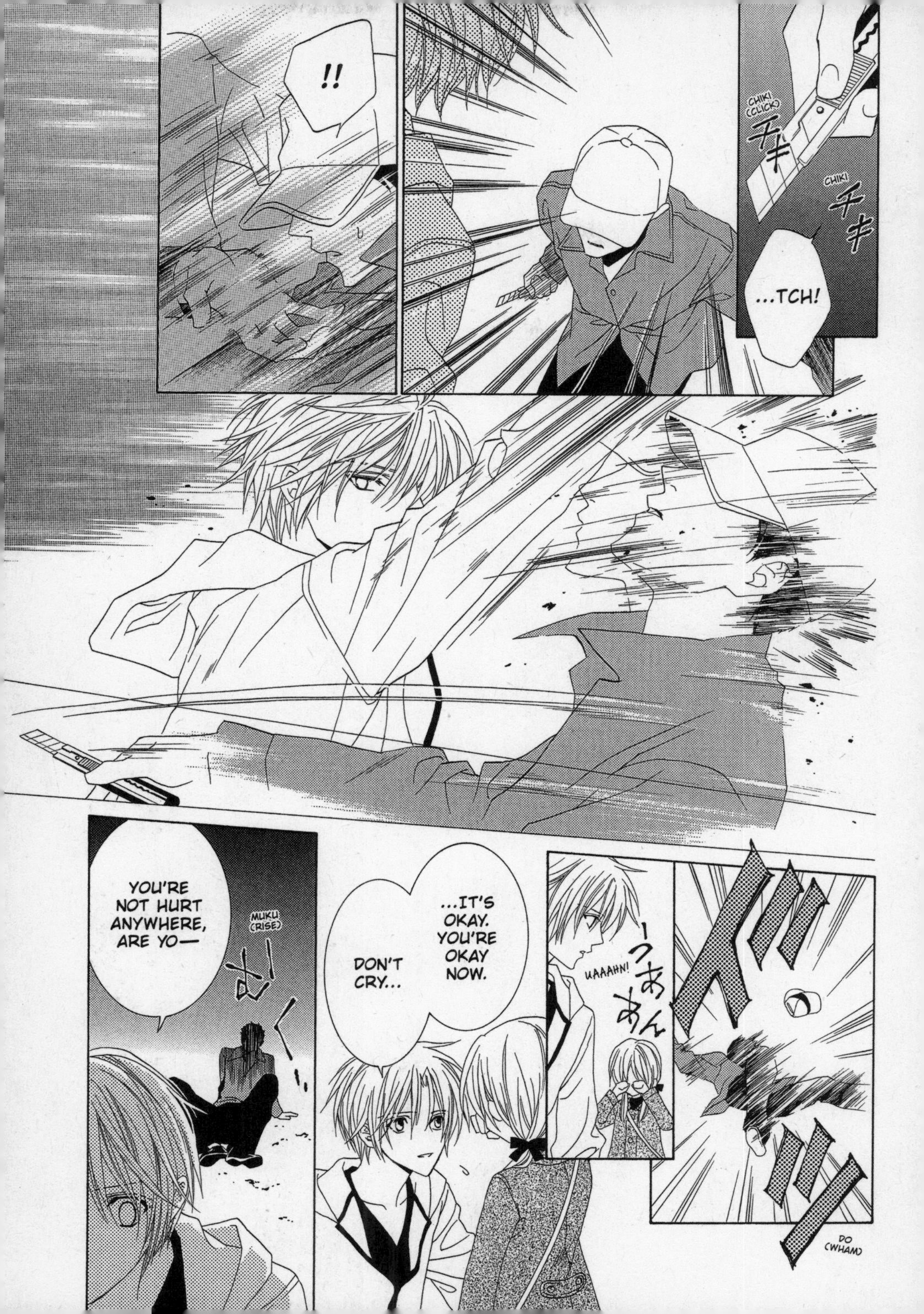
CHIKI (CLICK)
チキ
CHIKI
チキ
...TCH!
!!
DO (WHAM)
UAAAHN!
うあんあん
...IT'S OKAY. YOU'RE OKAY NOW.
DON'T CRY...
YOU'RE NOT HURT ANYWHERE, ARE YO—
MUKU (RISE)
むく

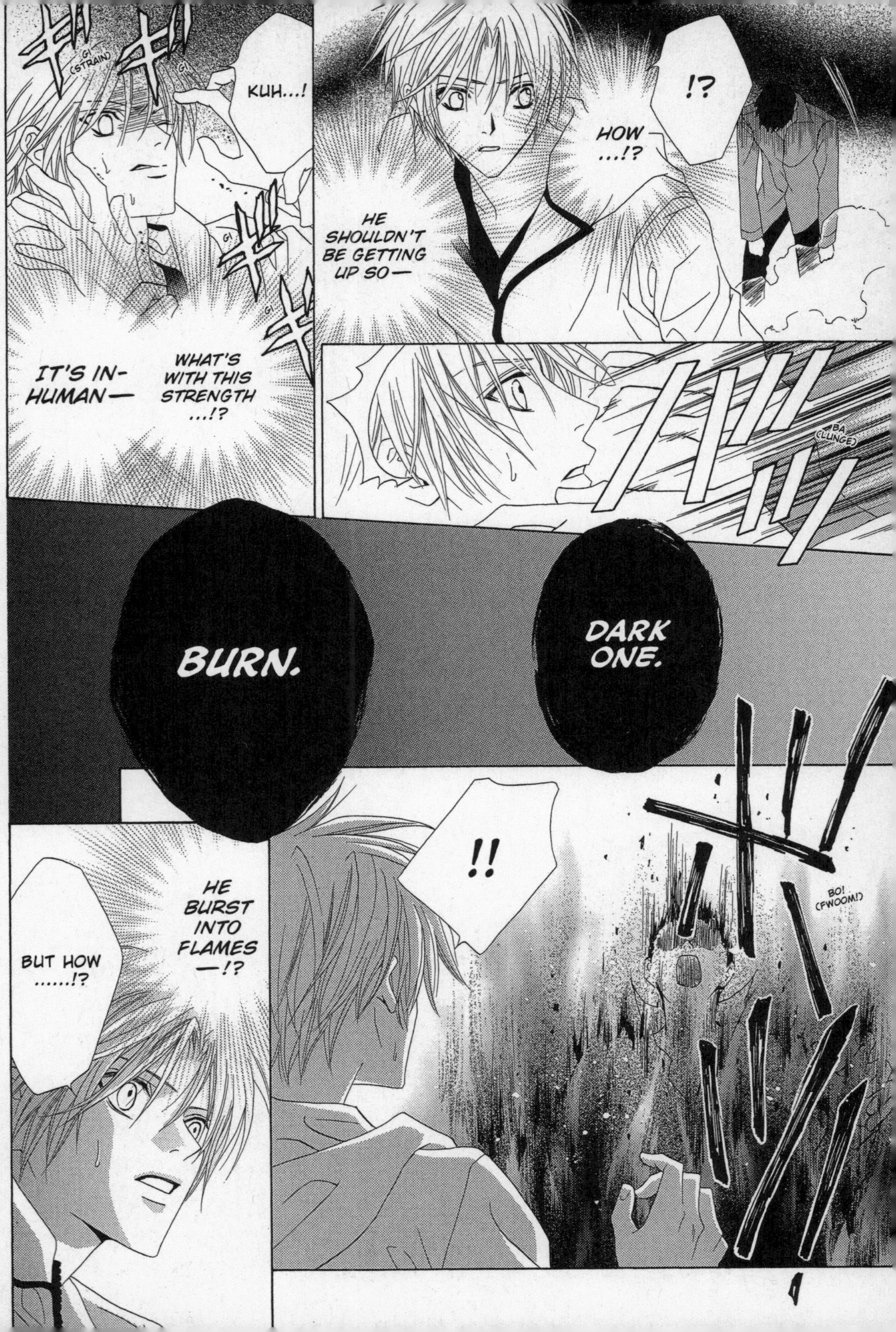
!?
HOW—
...!?
HE SHOULDN'T BE GETTING UP SO—
GI (STRAIN)
GI
KUH...!
GI
GI
WHAT'S WITH THIS STRENGTH ...!?
IT'S IN-HUMAN—
BA (LUNGE)
DARK ONE.
BURN.
BO! (FWOOM!)
!!
HE BURST INTO FLAMES—!?
BUT HOW ......!?

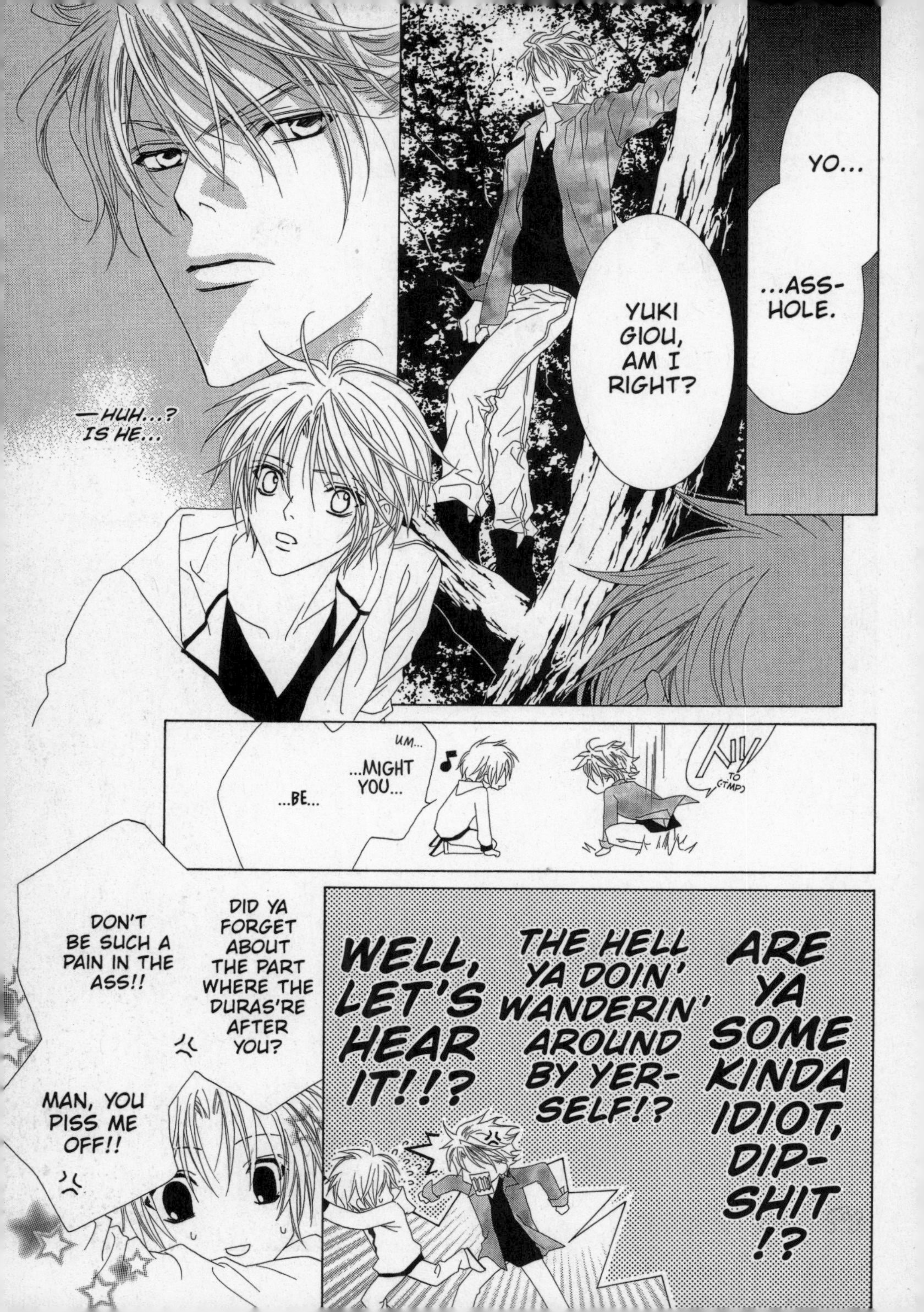
YO...
...ASS-HOLE.
YUKI GIOU, AM I RIGHT?
—HUH...? IS HE...
TO (TMP)
UM...
...MIGHT YOU...
...BE...
ARE YA SOME KINDA IDIOT, DIP-SHIT!?
THE HELL YA DOIN' WANDERIN' AROUND BY YER-SELF!?
WELL, LET'S HEAR IT!!?
DID YA FORGET ABOUT THE PART WHERE THE DURAS'RE AFTER YOU?
DON'T BE SUCH A PAIN IN THE ASS!!
MAN, YOU PISS ME OFF!!

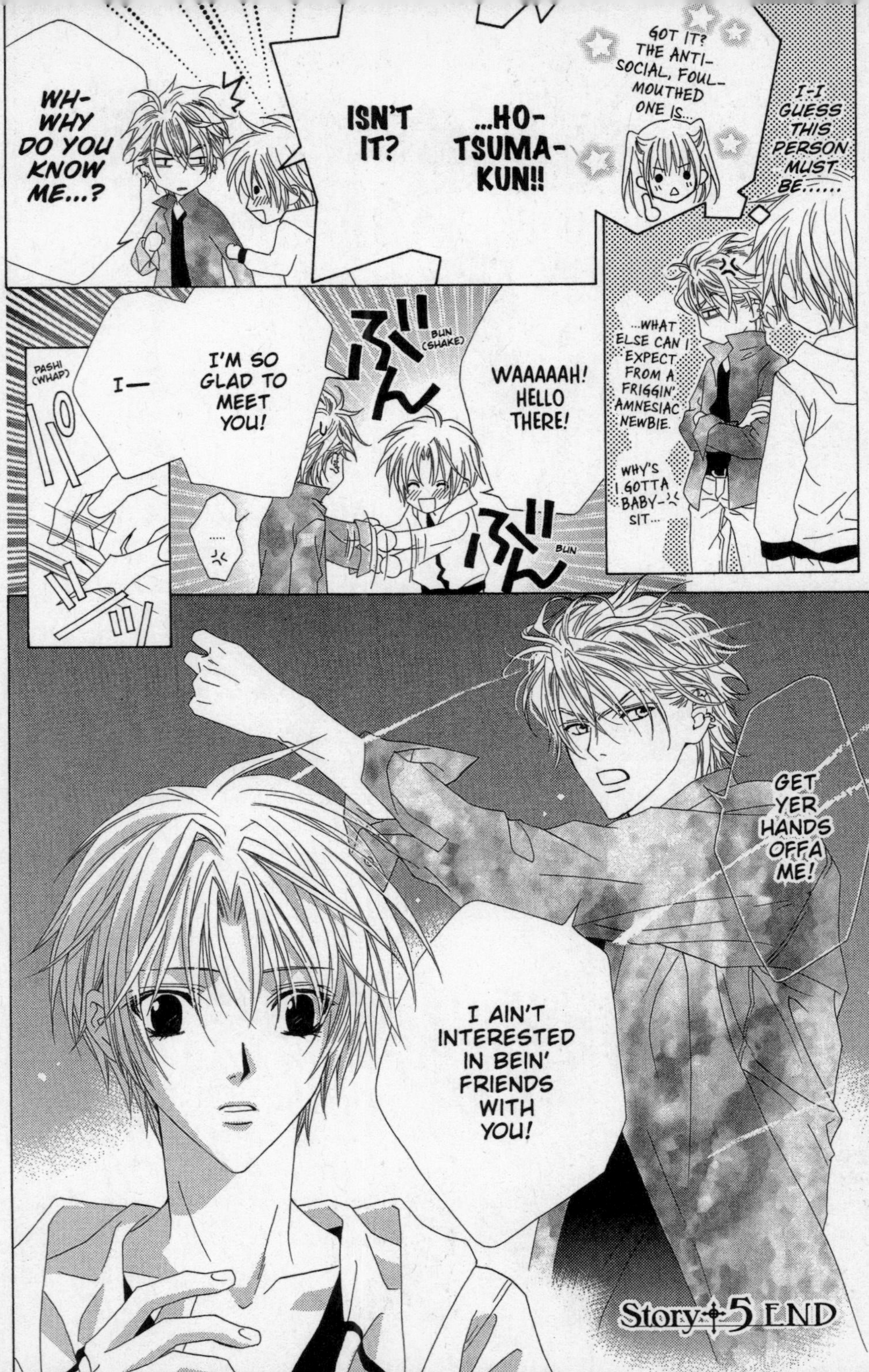
GOT IT? THE ANTI-SOCIAL, FOUL-MOUTHED ONE IS...
I-I GUESS THIS PERSON MUST BE......
...HO-TSUMA-KUN!!
ISN'T IT?
WH-WHY DO YOU KNOW ME...?
...WHAT ELSE CAN I EXPECT FROM A FRIGGIN' AMNESIAC NEWBIE.
WHY'S I GOTTA BABY-SIT...
WAAAAAH! HELLO THERE!
ぶん
BUN (SHAKE)
ぶん
BUN
I'M SO GLAD TO MEET YOU!
.....
PASHI (WHAP)
I—
GET YER HANDS OFFA ME!
I AIN'T INTERESTED IN BEIN' FRIENDS WITH YOU!
Story 5 END

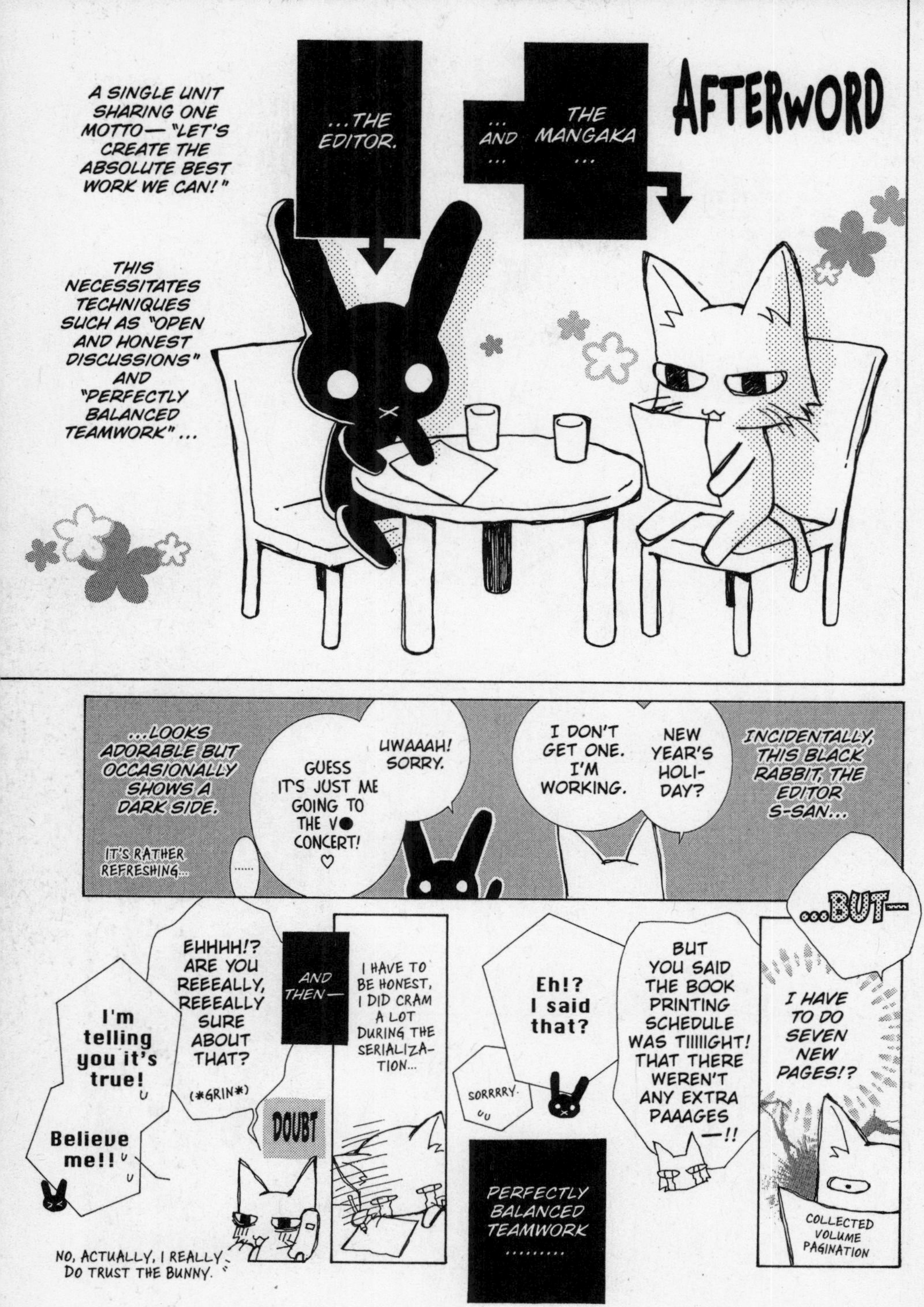
AFTERWORD
THE MANGAKA ...
... AND ...
...THE EDITOR.
A SINGLE UNIT SHARING ONE MOTTO— "LET'S CREATE THE ABSOLUTE BEST WORK WE CAN!"
THIS NECESSITATES TECHNIQUES SUCH AS "OPEN AND HONEST DISCUSSIONS" AND "PERFECTLY BALANCED TEAMWORK"...
INCIDENTALLY, THIS BLACK RABBIT, THE EDITOR S-SAN...
NEW YEAR'S HOLI-DAY?
I DON'T GET ONE. I'M WORKING.
UWAAAH! SORRY.
GUESS IT'S JUST ME GOING TO THE V● CONCERT! ♡
......
...LOOKS ADORABLE BUT OCCASIONALLY SHOWS A DARK SIDE.
IT'S RATHER REFRESHING...
...BUT—
I HAVE TO DO SEVEN NEW PAGES!?
COLLECTED VOLUME PAGINATION
BUT YOU SAID THE BOOK PRINTING SCHEDULE WAS TIIIIIGHT! THAT THERE WEREN'T ANY EXTRA PAAAGES—!!
Eh!? I said that?
SORRRRY.
PERFECTLY BALANCED TEAMWORK.........
I HAVE TO BE HONEST, I DID CRAM A LOT DURING THE SERIALIZA-TION...
AND THEN—
EHHHH!? ARE YOU REEEALLY, REEEALLY SURE ABOUT THAT?
(*GRIN*)
DOUBT
I'm telling you it's true!
Believe me!!
NO, ACTUALLY, I REALLY DO TRUST THE BUNNY.

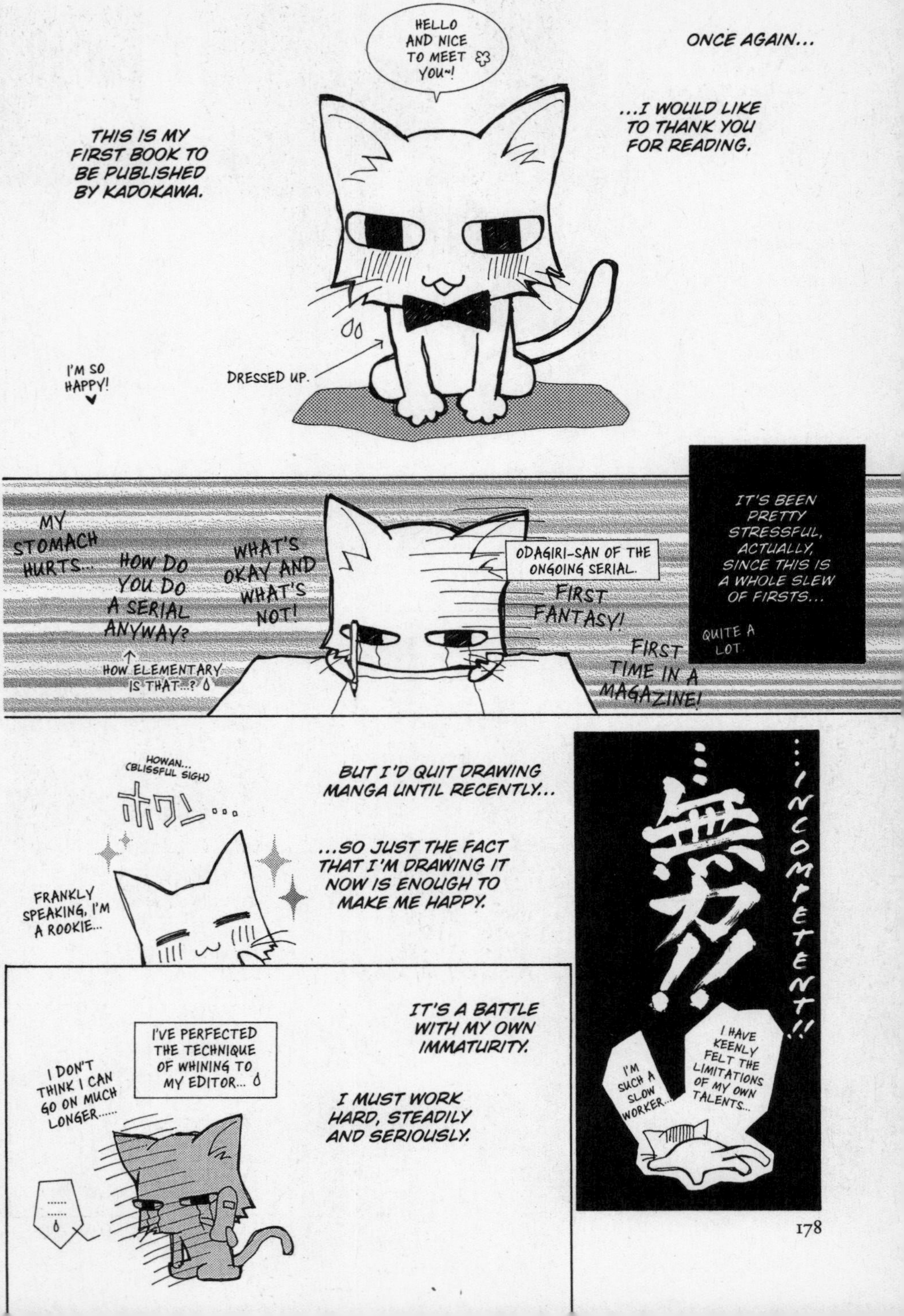

ONCE AGAIN...
...I WOULD LIKE TO THANK YOU FOR READING.
HELLO AND NICE TO MEET YOU~!
THIS IS MY FIRST BOOK TO BE PUBLISHED BY KADOKAWA.
DRESSED UP.
I'M SO HAPPY!
IT'S BEEN PRETTY STRESSFUL, ACTUALLY, SINCE THIS IS A WHOLE SLEW OF FIRSTS...
QUITE A LOT.
ODAGIRI-SAN OF THE ONGOING SERIAL.
FIRST FANTASY!
FIRST TIME IN A MAGAZINE!
WHAT'S OKAY AND WHAT'S NOT!
HOW DO YOU DO A SERIAL ANYWAY?
HOW ELEMENTARY IS THAT...?
MY STOMACH HURTS...
無力!!
...INCOMPETENT!!
I HAVE KEENLY FELT THE LIMITATIONS OF MY OWN TALENTS...
I'M SUCH A SLOW WORKER...
BUT I'D QUIT DRAWING MANGA UNTIL RECENTLY...
...SO JUST THE FACT THAT I'M DRAWING IT NOW IS ENOUGH TO MAKE ME HAPPY.
ホワン…
HOWAN... (BLISSFUL SIGH)
FRANKLY SPEAKING, I'M A ROOKIE...
IT'S A BATTLE WITH MY OWN IMMATURITY.
I MUST WORK HARD, STEADILY AND SERIOUSLY.
I'VE PERFECTED THE TECHNIQUE OF WHINING TO MY EDITOR...
I DON'T THINK I CAN GO ON MUCH LONGER......
......
......

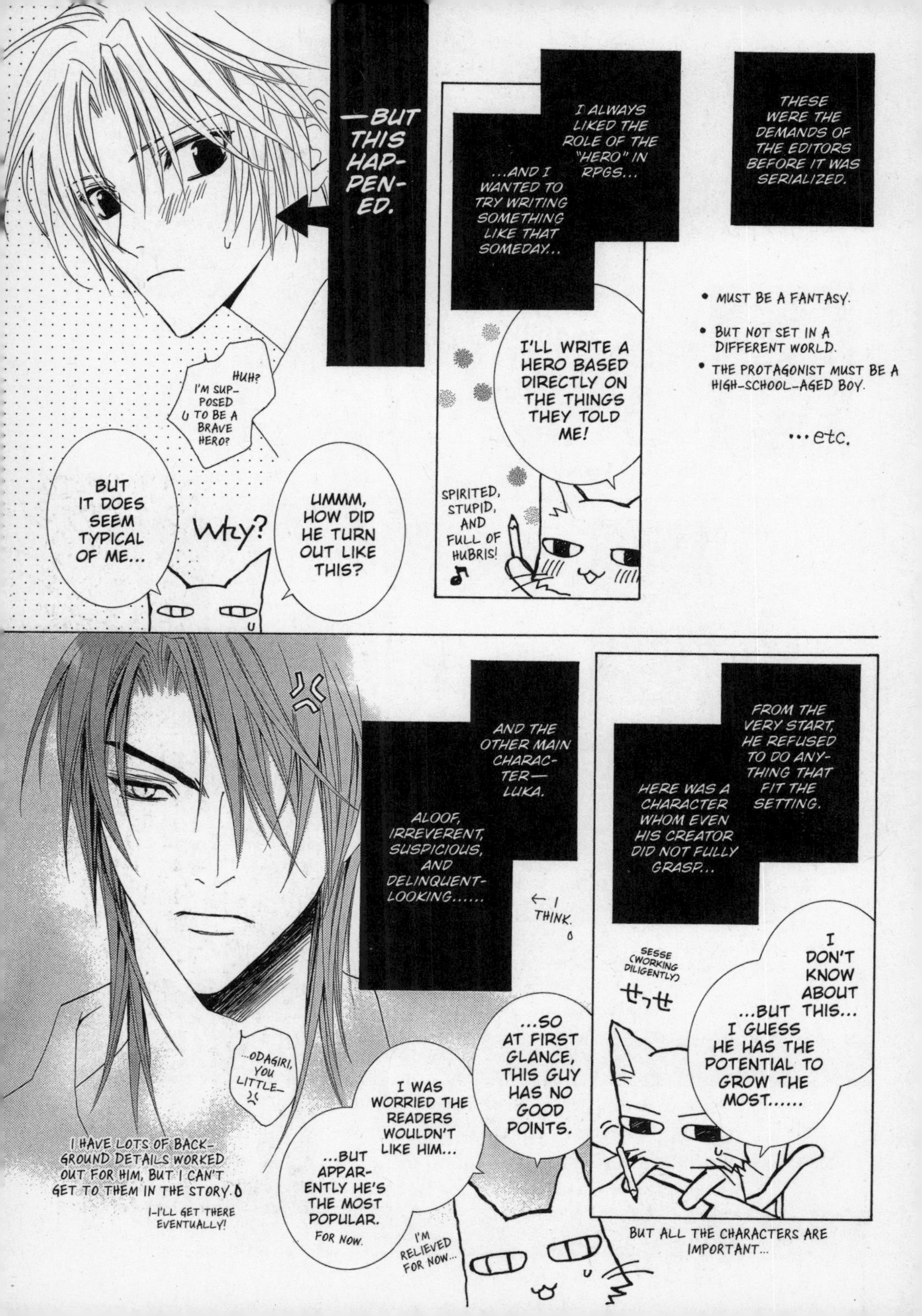
THESE WERE THE DEMANDS OF THE EDITORS BEFORE IT WAS SERIALIZED.
• MUST BE A FANTASY.
• BUT NOT SET IN A DIFFERENT WORLD.
• THE PROTAGONIST MUST BE A HIGH-SCHOOL-AGED BOY.
...etc.
I ALWAYS LIKED THE ROLE OF THE "HERO" IN RPGS...
...AND I WANTED TO TRY WRITING SOMETHING LIKE THAT SOMEDAY...
I'LL WRITE A HERO BASED DIRECTLY ON THE THINGS THEY TOLD ME!
SPIRITED, STUPID, AND FULL OF HUBRIS!
—BUT THIS HAPPENED.
HUH? I'M SUPPOSED TO BE A BRAVE HERO?
UMMM, HOW DID HE TURN OUT LIKE THIS?
Why?
BUT IT DOES SEEM TYPICAL OF ME...
FROM THE VERY START, HE REFUSED TO DO ANYTHING THAT FIT THE SETTING.
HERE WAS A CHARACTER WHOM EVEN HIS CREATOR DID NOT FULLY GRASP...
I DON'T KNOW ABOUT THIS...
...BUT I GUESS HE HAS THE POTENTIAL TO GROW THE MOST......
SESSE (WORKING DILIGENTLY)
せっせ
BUT ALL THE CHARACTERS ARE IMPORTANT...
AND THE OTHER MAIN CHARACTER—LUKA.
ALOOF, IRREVERENT, SUSPICIOUS, AND DELINQUENT-LOOKING......
← I THINK.
...SO AT FIRST GLANCE, THIS GUY HAS NO GOOD POINTS.
I WAS WORRIED THE READERS WOULDN'T LIKE HIM...
...BUT APPARENTLY HE'S THE MOST POPULAR.
FOR NOW.
I'M RELIEVED FOR NOW...
...ODAGIRI, YOU LITTLE—
I HAVE LOTS OF BACKGROUND DETAILS WORKED OUT FOR HIM, BUT I CAN'T GET TO THEM IN THE STORY.
I-I'LL GET THERE EVENTUALLY!

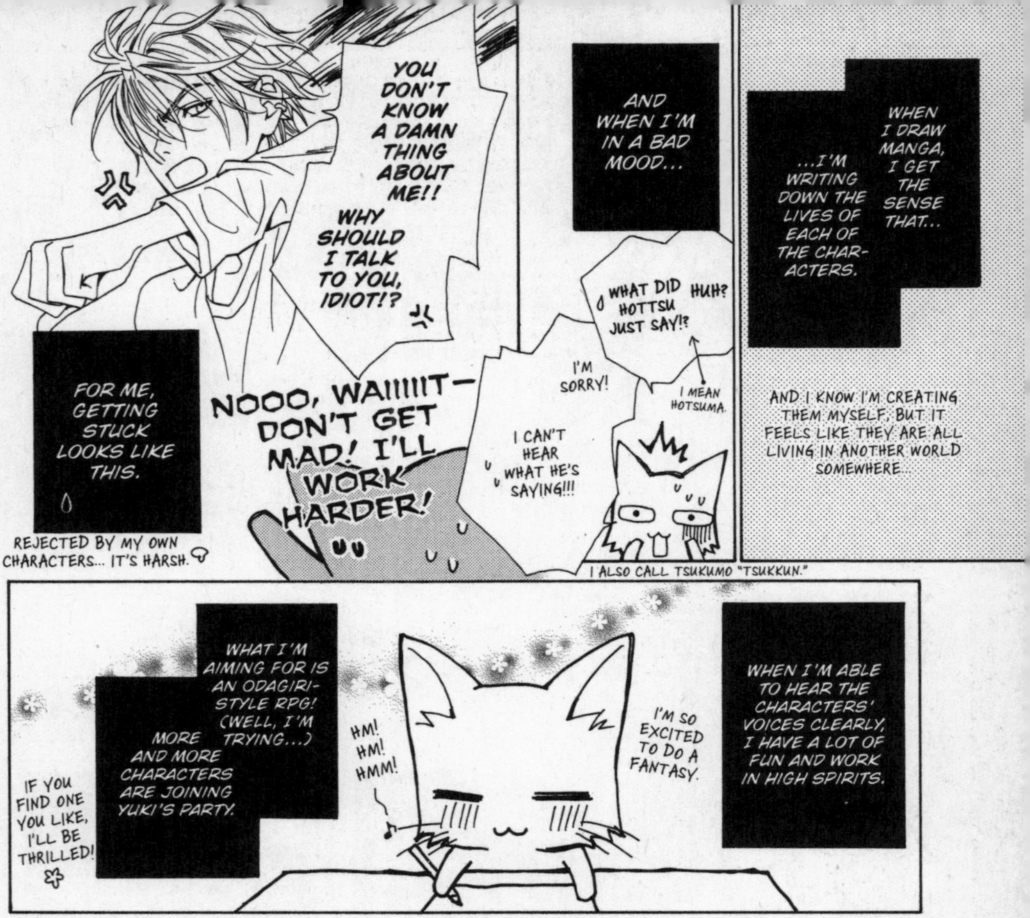
WHEN I DRAW MANGA, I GET THE SENSE THAT...
...I'M WRITING DOWN THE LIVES OF EACH OF THE CHARACTERS.
AND I KNOW I'M CREATING THEM MYSELF, BUT IT FEELS LIKE THEY ARE ALL LIVING IN ANOTHER WORLD SOMEWHERE...
AND WHEN I'M IN A BAD MOOD...
HUH?
WHAT DID HOTTSU JUST SAY!?
I MEAN HOTSUMA.
I'M SORRY!
I CAN'T HEAR WHAT HE'S SAYING!!!
I ALSO CALL TSUKUMO "TSUKKUN."
YOU DON'T KNOW A DAMN THING ABOUT ME!!
WHY SHOULD I TALK TO YOU, IDIOT!?
FOR ME, GETTING STUCK LOOKS LIKE THIS.
NOOO, WAIIIIIT— DON'T GET MAD! I'LL WORK HARDER!
REJECTED BY MY OWN CHARACTERS... IT'S HARSH.
WHEN I'M ABLE TO HEAR THE CHARACTERS' VOICES CLEARLY, I HAVE A LOT OF FUN AND WORK IN HIGH SPIRITS.
I'M SO EXCITED TO DO A FANTASY.
HM! HM! HMM!
WHAT I'M AIMING FOR IS AN ODAGIRI-STYLE RPG! (WELL, I'M TRYING...)
MORE AND MORE CHARACTERS ARE JOINING YUKI'S PARTY.
IF YOU FIND ONE YOU LIKE, I'LL BE THRILLED!

AS FOR HOW THINGS WILL DEVELOP FROM HERE ON OUT...EVEN THE AUTHOR DOESN'T KNOW. BUT SECRETLY, I'M THINKING, IF IT CAN SOMEHOW BENEFIT EVERYONE WHO READS IT...WELL, THAT'S THE KIND OF MANGA I'M HOPING TO WRITE. IF YOU HAVE ANY THOUGHTS OR OPINIONS, I WOULD LOVE TO RECEIVE A LETTER.

ALTHOUGH IT'LL BE HARD TO REPLY.

I KNOW THERE ARE A LOT OF POINTS THAT STILL NEED WORK, BUT I HOPE EVERYONE WILL KEEP FOLLOWING THE JOURNEY OF YUKI AND HIS PARTY!

OH! AND TAKE A PEEK AT ASUKA. (IT HAS *URABOKU** PAGES!) ➡ TO BE CONTINUED.

THOUGH I MADE SOME MINOR CHANGES FOR THE BOOKS, LIKE IN THE TONES AND THE DIALOGUE.

Special Thanks ➡ Y. Suzuki (EDITOR) / K-san / A.F. / H.M. / K.O. / E.Y. / K.T.

EVERYONE IN EDITING • EVERYONE INVOLVED WITH THIS WORK ...AND MY LOVELY READERS

HP ➡ http://www17a.biglobe.ne.jp/~ethereal-code/ (MOBILE-COMPATIBLE; JAPANESE-ONLY)

IT'S JUST DRY INFORMATION... BUT I'VE SET UP A BLOG! (YOU CAN'T READ IT FROM A PHONE, THOUGH.)

**URABOKU* IS A CONTRACTION OF THE JAPANESE TITLE, *URAGIRI WA BOKU NO NAMAE WO SHITTEIRU*, AND IS OFTEN USED TO REFER TO THE SERIES BOTH IN JAPAN AND AROUND THE WORLD.

Official Fan Corner

UraBoku FC☆

Vol. I

THE FIRST VOLUME OF THE BETRAYAL KNOWS MY NAME WILL BE IN STORES SOON. TO MEET POPULAR DEMAND, THIS MONTH WE'LL START A SEGMENT TO FOCUS ON THE MAIN CHARACTERS— "WE WANT TO KNOW EVERYTHING! BECAUSE WE'RE FANCY CHILDREN"— ABBREVIATED "URABOKU FC"!

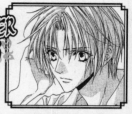

CHARACTER FOCUS

YUKI GIOU (YUKI SAKURAI) 15, HIGH SCHOOL FIRST-YEAR

URABOKU'S MAIN CHARACTER, A HEALER. ALTHOUGH HE HASN'T HAD AN EASY LIFE, BY NATURE HE IS PURE, TRUSTING AND NAIVE, WITH A POSITIVE OUTLOOK AND A HARDWORKING ETHIC. BUT THE "YUKI" OF HIS PREVIOUS LIFE IS INTRIGUING AS WELL......

—HELLO! THANKS FOR COMING TODAY!

YUKI: "TH-THANKS FOR HAVING ME." (÷NERVOUS UNDER THE SUDDEN SPOTLIGHT÷)

—YUKI-CHAN, YOU'RE STRONGER THAN YOU LOOK. WERE YOU TRAINING IN MARTIAL ARTS AT THE ORPHANAGE?

YUKI: "YES, THAT'S RIGHT. THE HEADMASTER BEGAN TEACHING ME AS A HOBBY AT FIRST, AND I'VE BEEN LEARNING FOR MORE THAN TEN YEARS."

—TEN YEARS!? THEN NO WONDER YOU CAN KICK SOME BUTT. SO IS IT JUDO OR......?

YUKI: "NO. IT'S A COMBINATION OF A FEW DIFFERENT MARTIAL ARTS, SO IT DOESN'T HAVE A REAL NAME, BUT IF I HAD TO CALL IT SOMETHING, IT WOULD BE HEADMASTER-STYLE MARTIAL ARTS."

—I SEE. (HOW...DESCRIPTIVE.) BY THE WAY, WITH YOUR COOL BIG BROTHER TAKASHIRO-SAN AND ALL YOUR GIOU RELATIVES, YOU'VE MET A LOT OF CHARACTERS—DO YOU HAVE ANY THOUGHTS ABOUT THAT?

YUKI: "IT WAS STARTLING. I ALWAYS THOUGHT I WAS TOTALLY ALONE IN THE WORLD...SO I'M HAPPY TOO. EVERYONE IS SO COOL AND BEAUTIFUL, IT JUST MAKES MY HEART POUND."

—NEXT TIME, WE'D LIKE TO HAVE LUKA MAKE AN APPEARANCE HERE. DO YOU HAVE A MESSAGE OR ANYTHING FOR HIM?

YUKI: "LUKA, I KNOW YOU DON'T REALLY TAKE TO PEOPLE RIGHT AWAY, SO I'M WORRIED ABOUT WHETHER YOU'LL ANSWER THE QUESTIONS WELL. PLEASE DO SPEAK PROPERLY AND DON'T JUST ANSWER WITH GRUNTS."

—THAT'S ALL, THEN! THANK YOU, YUKI-CHAN.

...AND NEXT TIME (IF OUR NEGOTIATIONS GO WELL), WE'LL HAVE LUKA-SAN WITH US! ☆

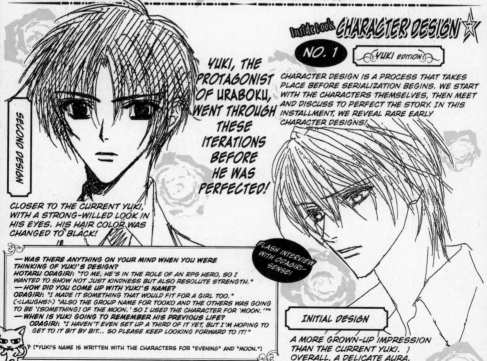

Inside Look CHARACTER DESIGN☆

NO. 1 YUKI EDITION

CHARACTER DESIGN IS A PROCESS THAT TAKES PLACE BEFORE SERIALIZATION BEGINS. WE START WITH THE CHARACTERS THEMSELVES, THEN MEET AND DISCUSS TO PERFECT THE STORY. IN THIS INSTALLMENT, WE REVEAL RARE EARLY CHARACTER DESIGNS!

YUKI, THE PROTAGONIST OF URABOKU, WENT THROUGH THESE ITERATIONS BEFORE HE WAS PERFECTED!

SECOND DESIGN

CLOSER TO THE CURRENT YUKI, WITH A STRONG-WILLED LOOK IN HIS EYES. HIS HAIR COLOR WAS CHANGED TO BLACK!

INITIAL DESIGN

A MORE GROWN-UP IMPRESSION THAN THE CURRENT YUKI. OVERALL, A DELICATE AURA.

FLASH INTERVIEW WITH ODAGIRI-SENSEI

—WAS THERE ANYTHING ON YOUR MIND WHEN YOU WERE THINKING OF YUKI'S DESIGN?

HOTARU ODAGIRI: "TO ME, HE'S IN THE ROLE OF AN RPG HERO, SO I WANTED TO SHOW NOT JUST KINDNESS BUT ALSO RESOLUTE STRENGTH."

—HOW DID YOU COME UP WITH YUKI'S NAME?

ODAGIRI: "I MADE IT SOMETHING THAT WOULD FIT FOR A GIRL TOO." (÷LAUGHS÷) "ALSO THE GROUP NAME FOR TOOKO AND THE OTHERS WAS GOING TO BE '[SOMETHING] OF THE MOON.' SO I USED THE CHARACTER FOR 'MOON.'"*

—WHEN IS YUKI GOING TO REMEMBER HIS PREVIOUS LIFE?

ODAGIRI: "I HAVEN'T EVEN SET UP A THIRD OF IT YET, BUT I'M HOPING TO GET TO IT BIT BY BIT... SO PLEASE KEEP LOOKING FORWARD TO IT!"

[*YUKI'S NAME IS WRITTEN WITH THE CHARACTERS FOR "EVENING" AND "MOON."]

NOTE: THIS PAGE APPEARED IN THE JULY 2006 ISSUE OF ASUKA MONTHLY. SOME PARTS HAVE BEEN SLIGHTLY MODIFIED FROM THEIR ORIGINAL FORM.

Uraboku Term & Character Lexicon
Supervised by Hotaru Odagiri

Bayu
The Midvillain that possessed Uzuki. It seems he was ordered to kill Yuki by someone called "Reiga," but Luka and Tsukumo worked together to destroy him.

The Bloody Cross
The double X-shaped mark on Luka's left arm. Seeing this mark, Bayu calls Luka "Brand Zess" and trembles with fear, but what exactly this means is uncertain. This is written with characters that read "cross of the Demon Lord's blood" in Japanese.

Luka Crosszeria
For the fifteen years since Yuki was born, this handsome young man with black hair and silver eyes has been watching over him from the shadows. Although he is actually a Duras, he is currently cooperating with the Giou clan. His age is unclear, but in human terms appears to be about that of a university student. Quiet and expressionless by nature, he does show a softer side around Yuki. In the last war he sided with the humans, and apparently he has a deep connection with Yuki's previous incarnation, but the details of that past and his motivations are still shrouded in mystery.

Demonbane weapons
Embodiments of the abilities of the Zweilt. They take on various shapes depending on the user's preference, such as a sword or a gun, but all have in common the power to bring Duras to their knees.

Duras
The Infernus word for "demons," which actually means "prideful ones." Duras are classified into levels based on the strength of their abilities. Because those abilities grow by taking in the negative emotions of humans, Duras who come to the human world often possess humans who hold darkness in their hearts. This is written as "demons" in Japanese.

Eon
The spell cast by Tooko when summoning her Demonbane weapon. Spells such as this are a word decided long ago by the person in a far-off previous life, and also serve as the name of the weapon.

The Giou clan
A lineage possessing special abilities through the generations. They also sometimes exert influence in political and financial spheres. Currently, Takashiro is the leader and is organizing the clan. Yuki and the members of the Zweilt are also of the Giou clan.

Takashiro Giou
The head of the Giou clan. He has all his memories intact since the "Sunset of the Underworld" over a millennium ago, and has the most powerful abilities in the clan.

Infernus
A general term for the demon world. Details are uncertain. The beings called Duras come from here, either spontaneously or by being summoned, to the human world.

The Key of Raziel
A book that Kanata had when he came to Morning Sun House. It is uncertain what language the book is written in, but according to Kanata it contains "things that will help the world." More light should be shed on this mystery in time.

Knell
The spell recited by Tsukumo to summon his Demonbane weapon. Tsukumo's ability is to "release" the Duras possessing a human and "bind" it so that it cannot move. He is nearly powerless to kill Duras. Like Tooko's, this spell was a word decided upon by Tsukumo in a previous life.

The Light of God
Also called "The Wellspring of Light," this refers to Yuki's ability. By taking another's pain into himself, he heals that person's wounds. As a general rule, wounds made by Duras can only be healed by this ability of Yuki's. He also makes the Zweilt stronger.

Midvillain
While Niedatrechy can spontaneously appear in the human world under certain conditions, Duras ranked Midvillain and higher can only be called forth by summoning. Like Niedatrechy, Midvillains possess and cause harm to humans who have darkness in their hearts, and seek to level up their magic powers. Compared to Niedatrechy, Midvillains have much greater intelligence and sentience. When a Midvillain possesses a human, a mark indicating that possession appears somewhere on the human's body. This is written as "mid-level demon" in Japanese.

Morning Sun House
The orphanage where Yuki has lived since he was a baby. The headmaster's hobby is martial arts, in which he has instructed Yuki from childhood.

Tooko Murasame
A second-year high school student. Paired with her younger brother Tsukumo, she is a Zweilt specializing in offense. She summons her greatsword, Eon, to battle Duras. She has some memories from her previous lives. Her epithet is "The One Who Inquires," but her ability corresponding to this name is not as strong as Tsukumo's.

Tsukumo Murasame
Paired with his elder sister Tooko, he is a member of Zweilt specializing in defense, using his gun, Knell, to "release" Duras. The same as Tooko, his epithet is also "The One Who Inquires." It seems he can speak with animals such as birds (but beyond this, it is still uncertain what abilities he has). A first-year high school student, he cares deeply about his sister. It seems he is also fond of sweets...

Necromancer
This refers to one who has the ability to summon and use Duras to their ends. Originally, they would summon Duras in order to find answers to difficult problems that could not solved by other means, or to gain information. This is written as "demon summoner" in Japanese.

Niedatrechy
The name for low-level Duras. They frequently take the forms of beasts or reptiles. Most of the Duras in the human world fall into this category (some have always existed in the human world). When possessed by one, a person becomes controlled by negative emotions and does terrible things. This is written "low-level demon" in Japanese.

Reiga
A peerless necromancer. Apparently it was he who summoned Bayu, who came to kill Yuki. At the moment, he only appears in Takashiro's recollections and nothing is known about him but that he is targeting Yuki. It seems Takashiro might also be after him...?

Yuki Sakurai
The main character, a first-year high school student. Abandoned in front of Morning Sun House soon after his birth, he has spent the first fifteen years of his life there. On occasion, he can read the emotions of someone he touches, and although this has caused him a good deal of pain, he has managed to grow up without being ruined by it. He remembers nothing from his previous lives, but he feels Luka is familiar and has opened up to him. After Takashiro finds him, he goes by Yuki Giou.

Spells
This refers to the words recited when those with the ability summon their weapons or use their powers.

Sunset of the Underworld
Refers to the war between the Giou clan and the Duras over a millennium ago. Takashiro's memory-holding and the reincarnations of the Zweilt began at that time, but further details are still unclear. It seems only Takashiro knows the whole story. Since then, the thousand-year war against the Duras has flared up again every few hundred years.

Twilight Hall
The mansion in Tokyo where the Zweilt live together. Apparently, a doctor and a cook are also on staff there.

Unknown
Used by the police force, this refers to the Duras. (The word "Duras" is not in common usage.) Crimes with physical evidence but no suspects are often connected to the Duras, and those cases are all handed over to the Giou clan.

Uzuki
Yuki's classmate. After Yuki sees the trauma of his complicated past, Uzuki starts to hate Yuki, and then he gets possessed by the Duras Bayu. But thanks to Yuki's words he is able to recover.

Kanata Wakamiya
A young man who is like a big brother to Yuki. He lived at Morning Sun House until his second year of high school, and currently lives on his own.

Walpurgis Night
The one night of the year when the powers of the Duras in the human world are at their strongest. The Duras go wild and crime rates spike. It is also called "the night of the crimson moon that beckons death." To seize the opportunity while his powers were heightened, Bayu chose this night to attack Yuki.

Wotes
One who reads the future. Takashiro is currently the only one possessing this ability. This is written as "soothsayer" in Japanese.

Zess
Luka's code name. In the language of Infernus, "Zess" means "sinful one," but it is uncertain exactly why Luka is called this. Based on what Bayu said, it would seem there is more than one "Zess"...

Zweilt
Those among the Giou clan gifted with especially strong abilities. They have been tasked with watching over Yuki and hunting down Duras. As a rule, they act in pairs. Each one wears a ring infused with spells, in which his or her Demonbane weapon is sealed. Compared to normal people, they also are much more athletic and heal much faster. To preserve their abilities they are reincarnated over and over. Zweilt is written as "hand of admonition" in Japanese.

The Betrayal Knows My Name

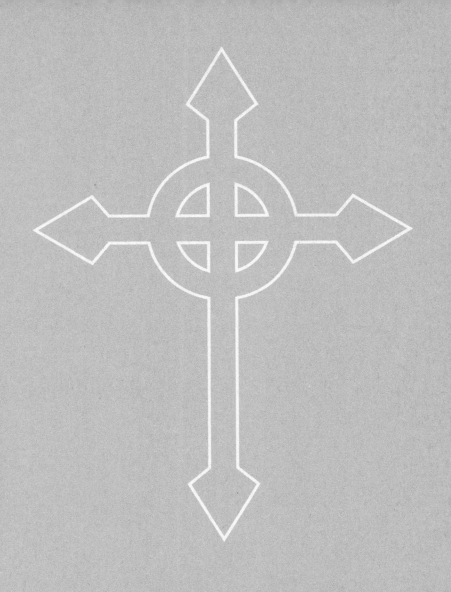

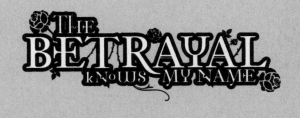

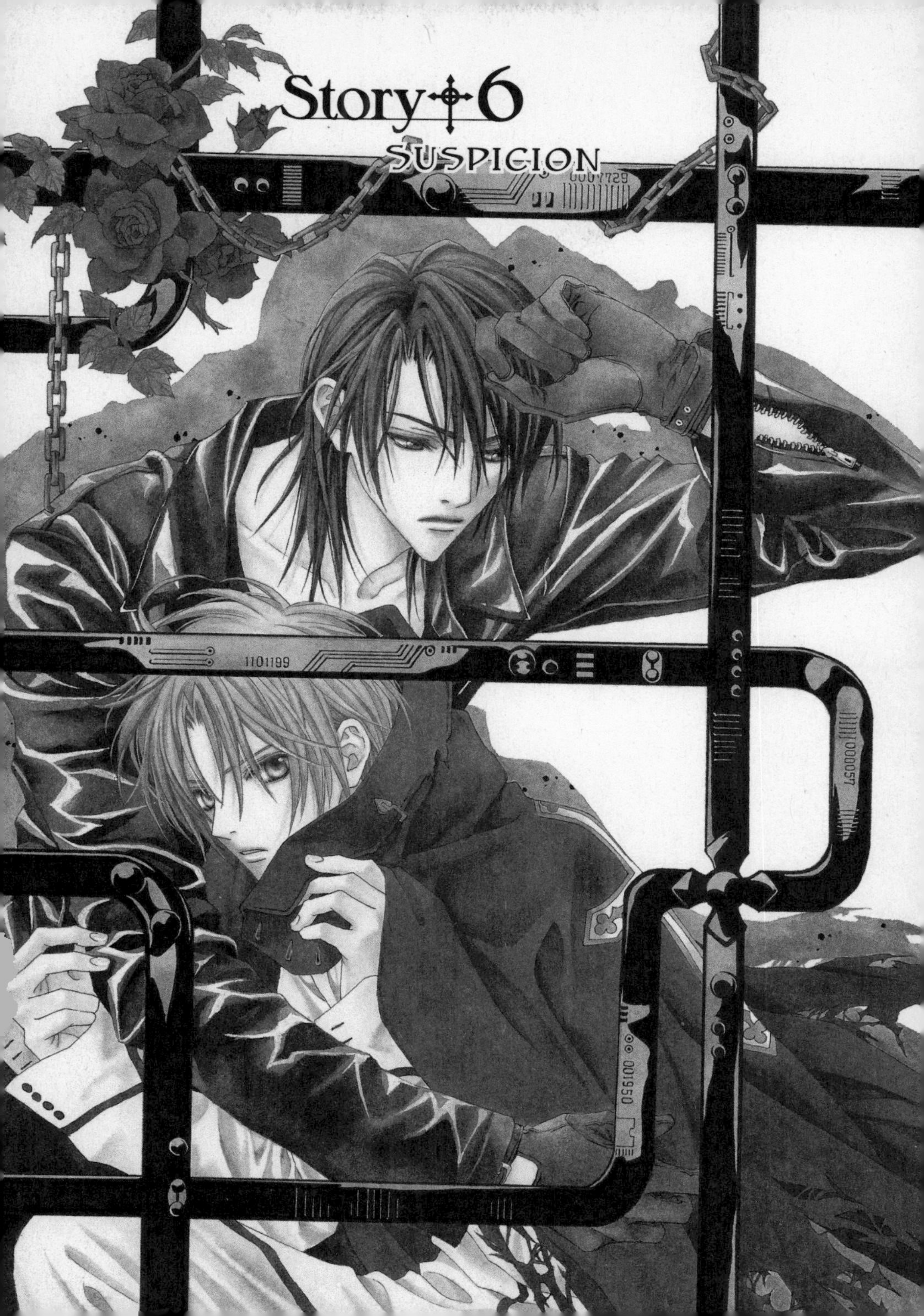
Story 6
SUSPICION

The Betrayal Knows My Name

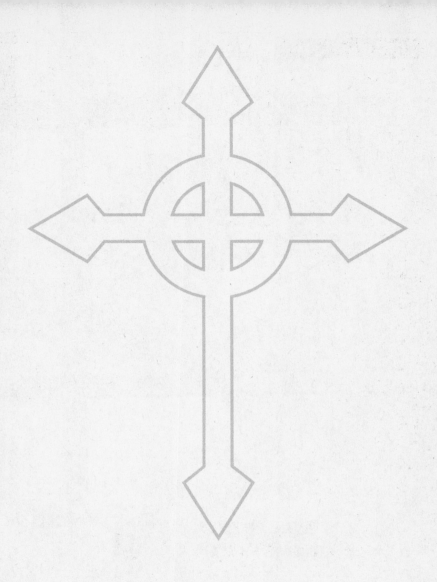

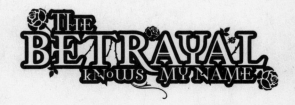

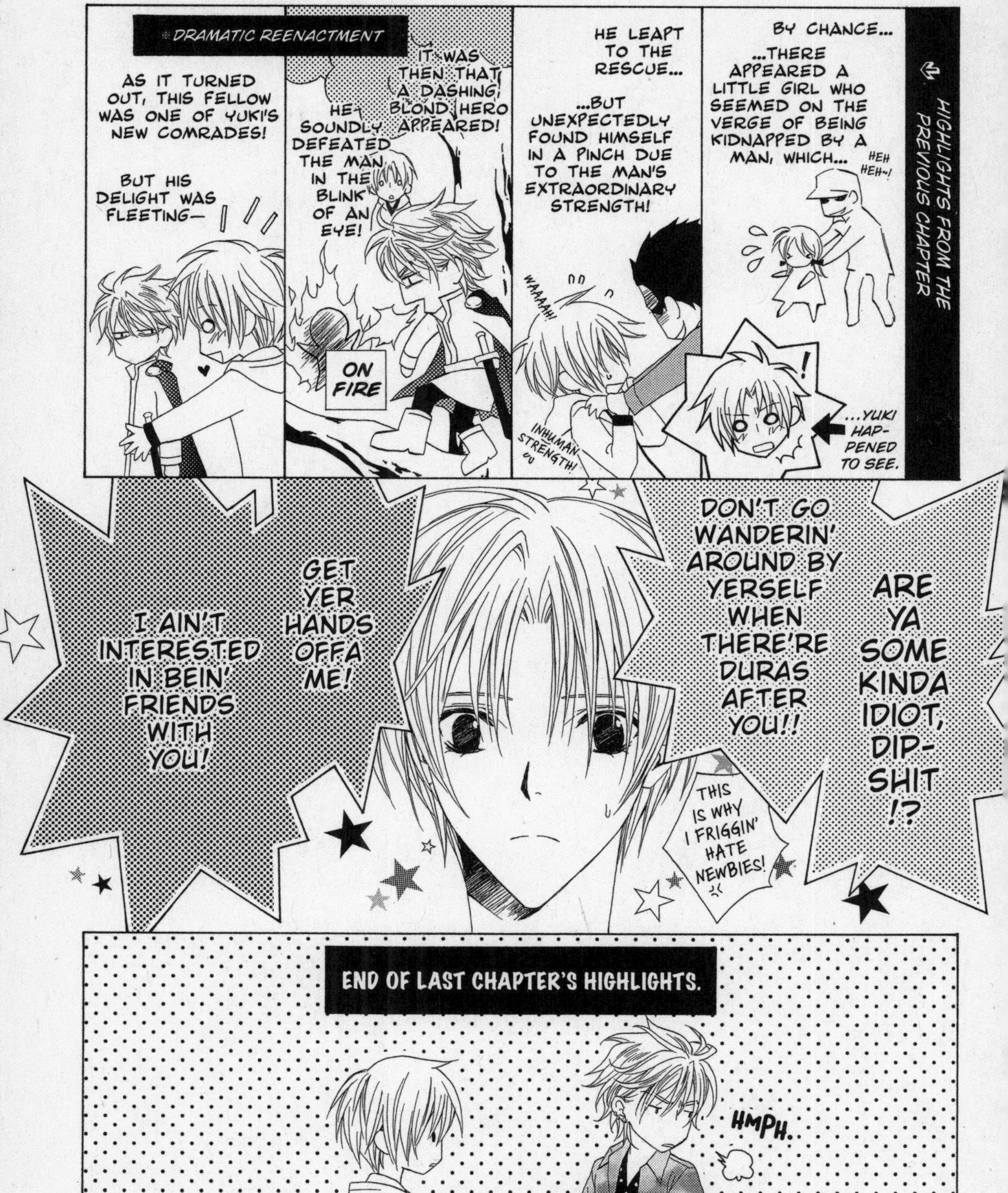
HIGHLIGHTS FROM THE PREVIOUS CHAPTER
BY CHANCE...
...THERE APPEARED A LITTLE GIRL WHO SEEMED ON THE VERGE OF BEING KIDNAPPED BY A MAN, WHICH...
HEH HEH~!
!
...YUKI HAPPENED TO SEE.
HE LEAPT TO THE RESCUE...
...BUT UNEXPECTEDLY FOUND HIMSELF IN A PINCH DUE TO THE MAN'S EXTRAORDINARY STRENGTH!
WAAAAH!
INHUMAN STRENGTH!
IT WAS THEN THAT A DASHING, BLOND HERO APPEARED!
HE SOUNDLY DEFEATED THE MAN IN THE BLINK OF AN EYE!
ON FIRE
※DRAMATIC REENACTMENT
AS IT TURNED OUT, THIS FELLOW WAS ONE OF YUKI'S NEW COMRADES!
BUT HIS DELIGHT WAS FLEETING—
ARE YA SOME KINDA IDIOT, DIP-SHIT!?
DON'T GO WANDERIN' AROUND BY YERSELF WHEN THERE'RE DURAS AFTER YOU!!
THIS IS WHY I FRIGGIN' HATE NEWBIES!
GET YER HANDS OFFA ME!
I AIN'T INTERESTED IN BEIN' FRIENDS WITH YOU!
END OF LAST CHAPTER'S HIGHLIGHTS.
HMPH.

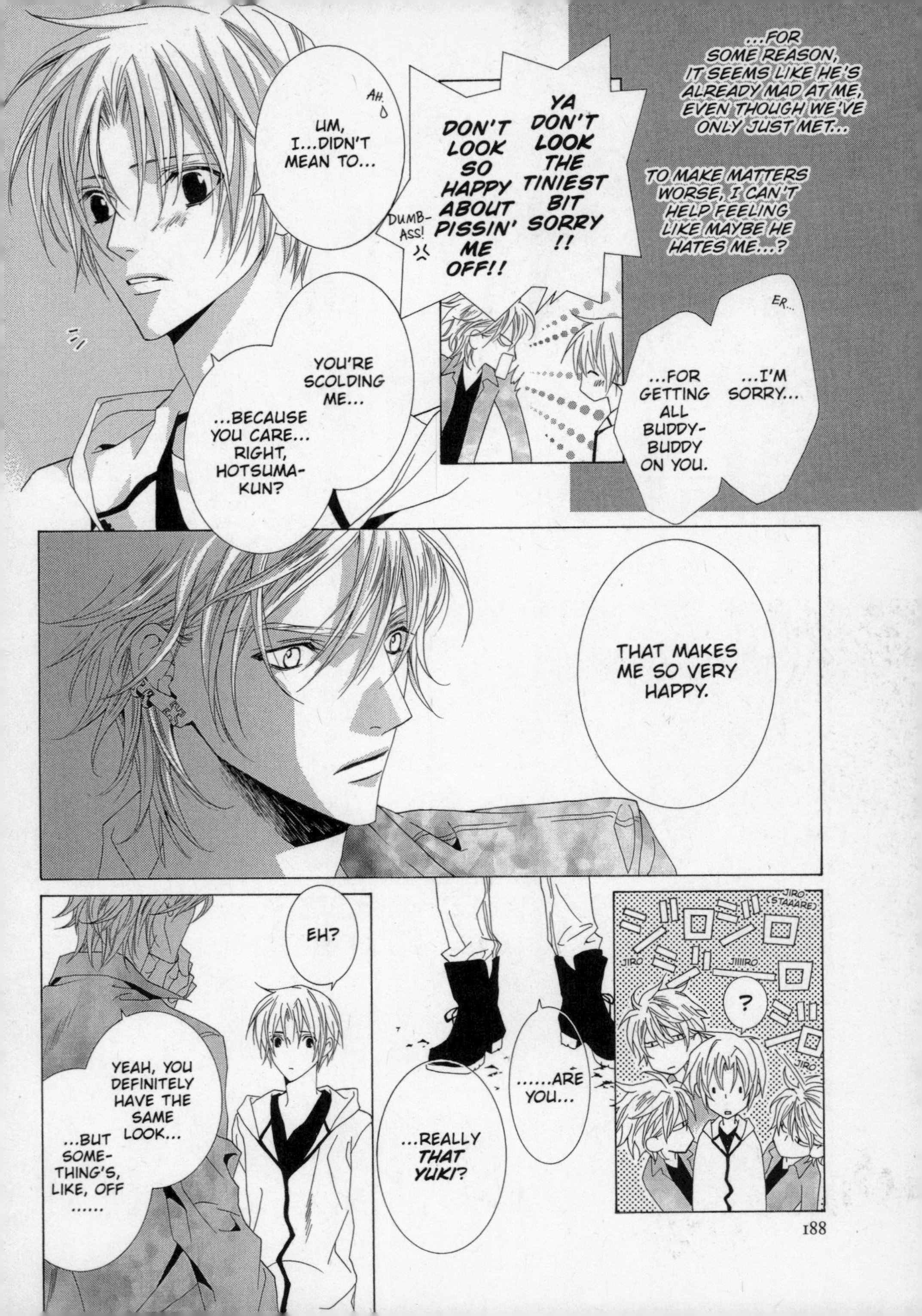
...FOR SOME REASON, IT SEEMS LIKE HE'S ALREADY MAD AT ME, EVEN THOUGH WE'VE ONLY JUST MET...
TO MAKE MATTERS WORSE, I CAN'T HELP FEELING LIKE MAYBE HE HATES ME...?
ER...
...I'M SORRY...
...FOR GETTING ALL BUDDY-BUDDY ON YOU.
YA DON'T LOOK THE TINIEST BIT SORRY!!
DON'T LOOK SO HAPPY ABOUT PISSIN' ME OFF!!
DUMB-ASS!
AH.
UM, I...DIDN'T MEAN TO...
YOU'RE SCOLDING ME...
...BECAUSE YOU CARE... RIGHT, HOTSUMA-KUN?
THAT MAKES ME SO VERY HAPPY.
JIRO (STAAARE)
JIRO
JIIIRO
JIRO
?
......ARE YOU...
...REALLY *THAT* YUKI?
EH?
YEAH, YOU DEFINITELY HAVE THE SAME LOOK...
...BUT SOMETHING'S, LIKE, OFF ......

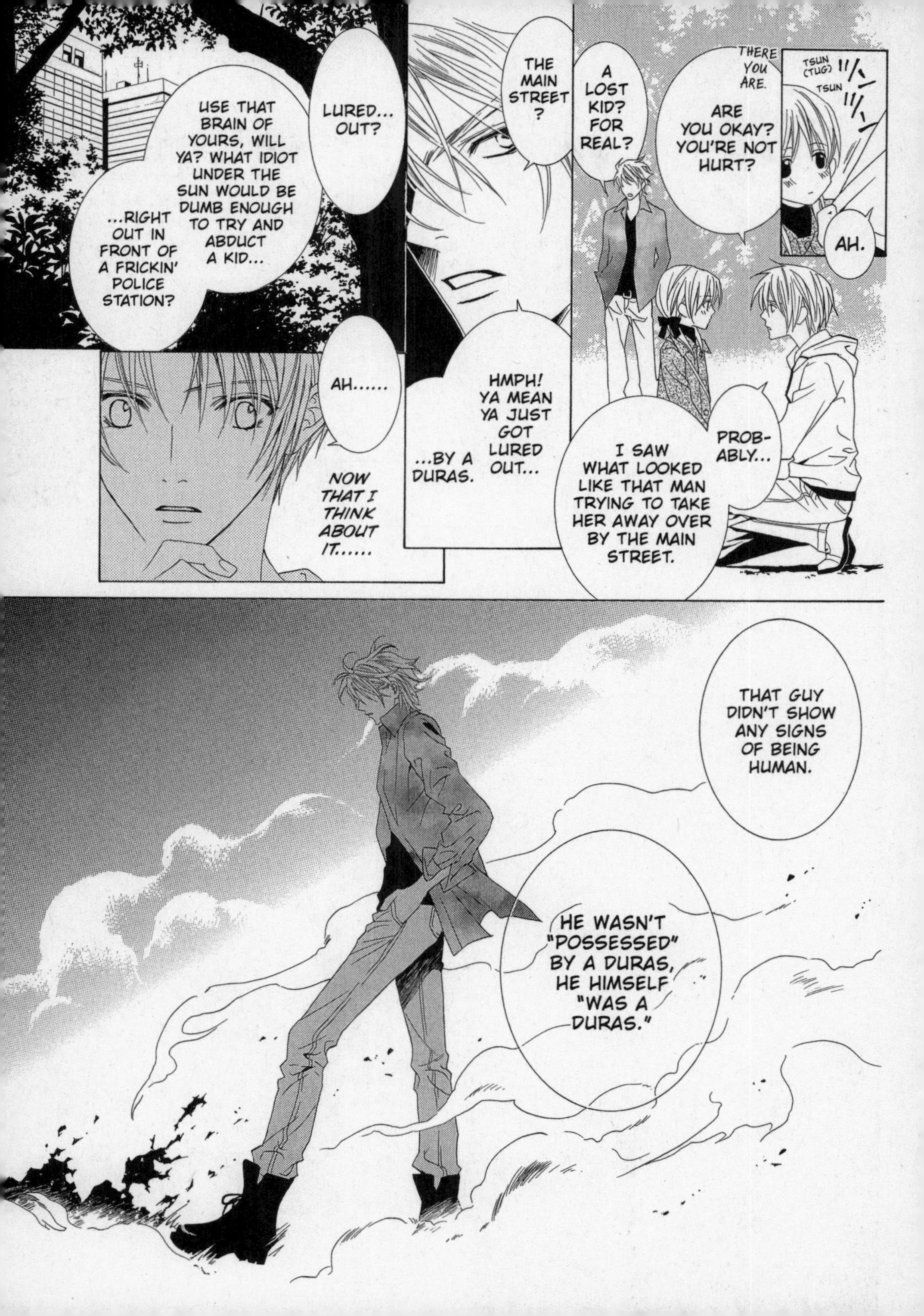
TSUN (TUG)
TSUN
THERE YOU ARE.
ARE YOU OKAY? YOU'RE NOT HURT?
AH.
A LOST KID? FOR REAL?
THE MAIN STREET?
PROB-ABLY...
I SAW WHAT LOOKED LIKE THAT MAN TRYING TO TAKE HER AWAY OVER BY THE MAIN STREET.
LURED... OUT?
USE THAT BRAIN OF YOURS, WILL YA? WHAT IDIOT UNDER THE SUN WOULD BE DUMB ENOUGH TO TRY AND ABDUCT A KID...
...RIGHT OUT IN FRONT OF A FRICKIN' POLICE STATION?
HMPH! YA MEAN YA JUST GOT LURED OUT...
...BY A DURAS.
AH......
NOW THAT I THINK ABOUT IT......
THAT GUY DIDN'T SHOW ANY SIGNS OF BEING HUMAN.
HE WASN'T "POSSESSED" BY A DURAS, HE HIMSELF "WAS A DURAS."

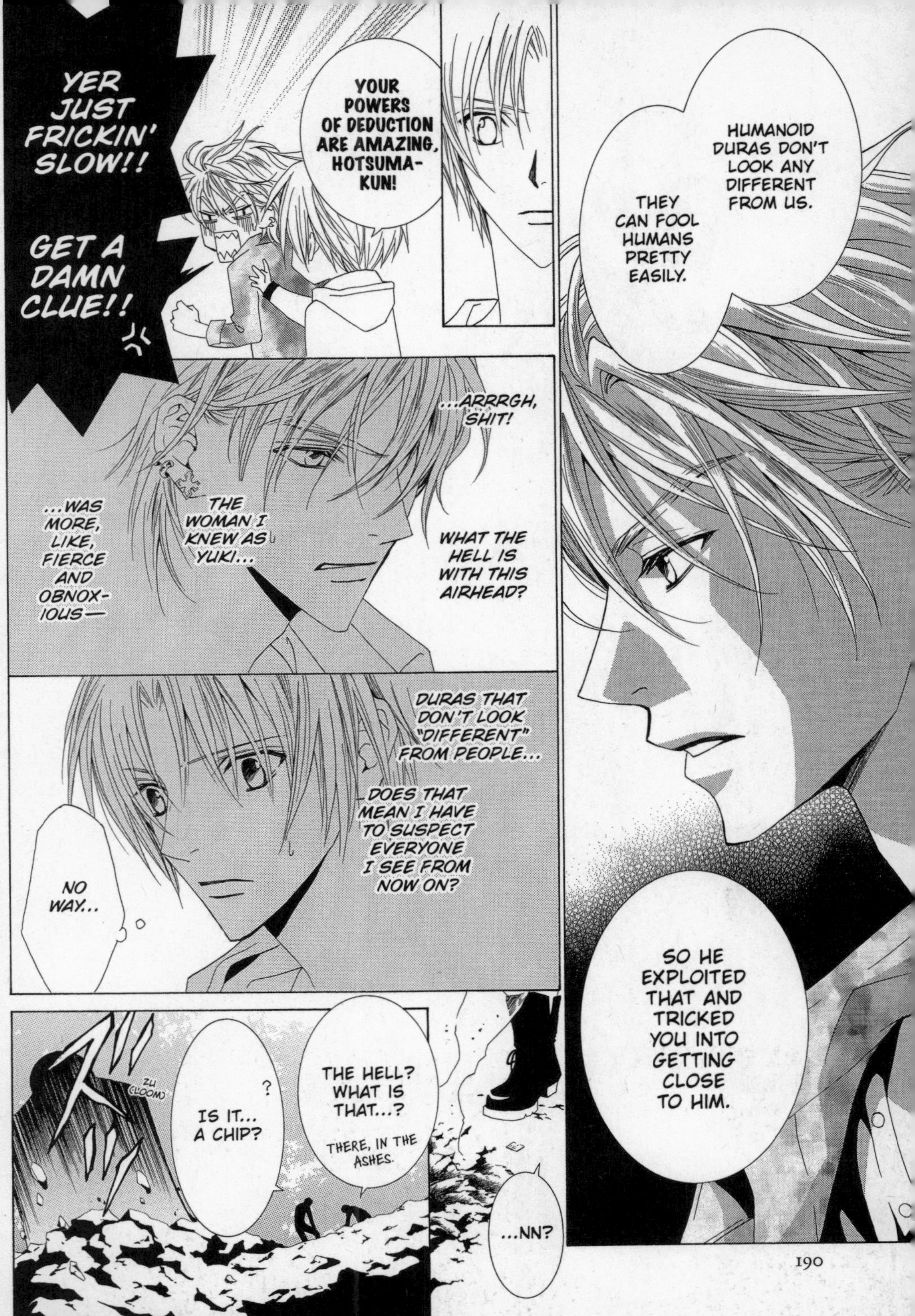

HUMANOID DURAS DON'T LOOK ANY DIFFERENT FROM US.
THEY CAN FOOL HUMANS PRETTY EASILY.
YOUR POWERS OF DEDUCTION ARE AMAZING, HOTSUMA-KUN!
YER JUST FRICKIN' SLOW!!
GET A DAMN CLUE!!
...ARRRGH, SHIT!
WHAT THE HELL IS WITH THIS AIRHEAD?
THE WOMAN I KNEW AS YUKI...
...WAS MORE, LIKE, FIERCE AND OBNOXIOUS—
SO HE EXPLOITED THAT AND TRICKED YOU INTO GETTING CLOSE TO HIM.
DURAS THAT DON'T LOOK "DIFFERENT" FROM PEOPLE...
DOES THAT MEAN I HAVE TO SUSPECT EVERYONE I SEE FROM NOW ON?
NO WAY...
...NN?
THE HELL? WHAT IS THAT...?
THERE, IN THE ASHES.
IS IT... A CHIP?
?
ZU (CLOOM)

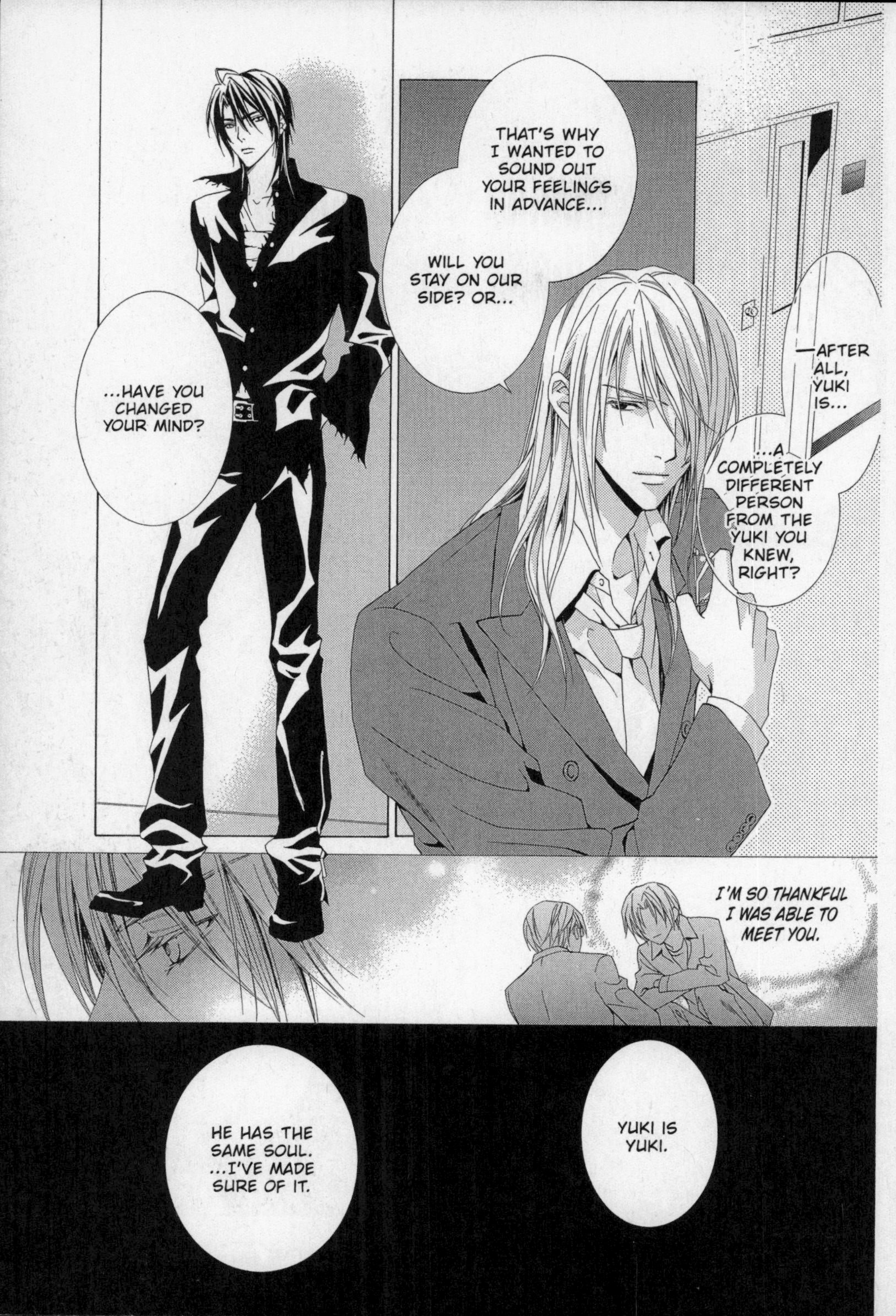
—AFTER ALL, YUKI IS...
...A COMPLETELY DIFFERENT PERSON FROM THE YUKI YOU KNEW, RIGHT?
THAT'S WHY I WANTED TO SOUND OUT YOUR FEELINGS IN ADVANCE...
WILL YOU STAY ON OUR SIDE? OR...
...HAVE YOU CHANGED YOUR MIND?
I'M SO THANKFUL I WAS ABLE TO MEET YOU.
YUKI IS YUKI.
HE HAS THE SAME SOUL. ...I'VE MADE SURE OF IT.

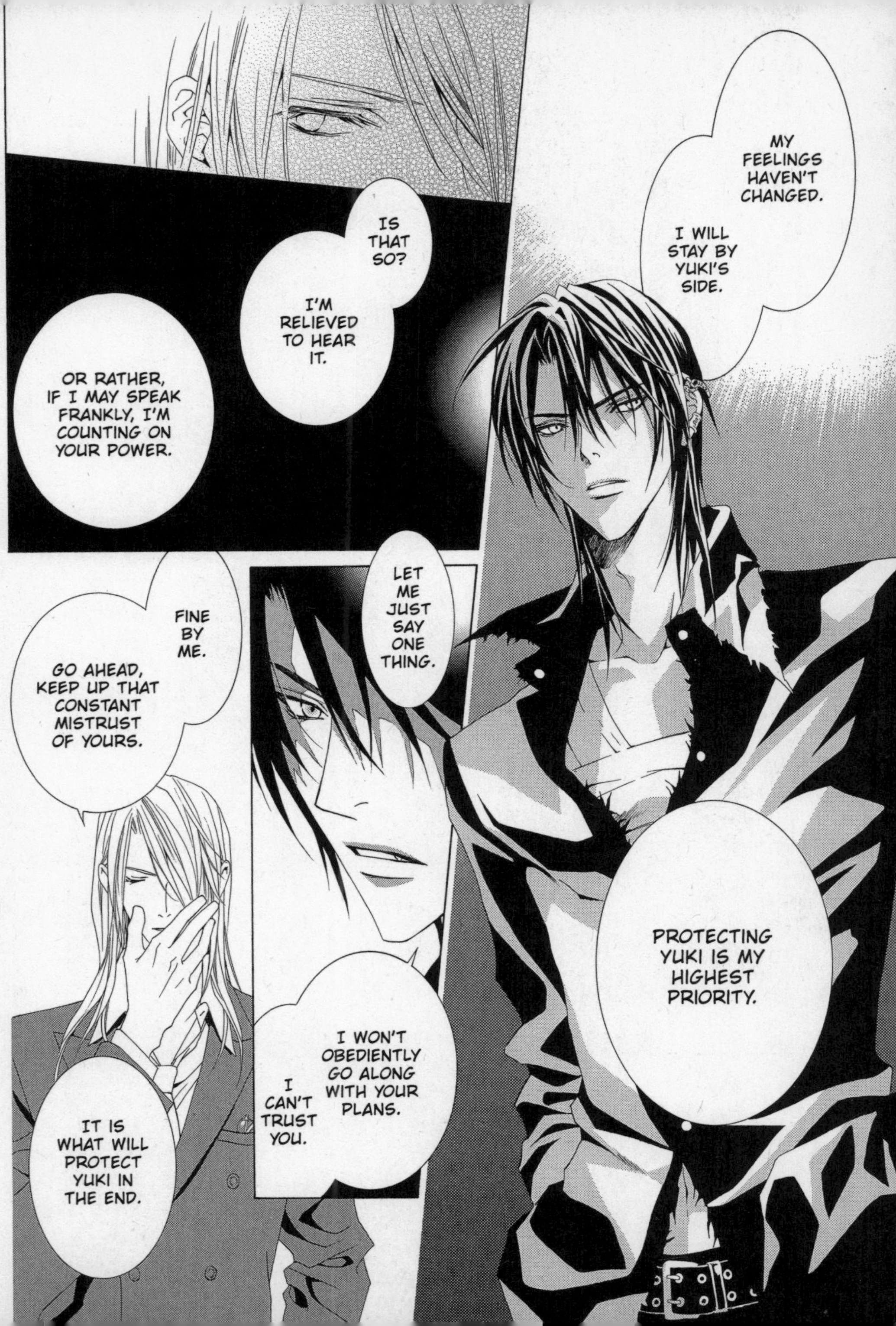
MY FEELINGS HAVEN'T CHANGED.
I WILL STAY BY YUKI'S SIDE.
IS THAT SO?
I'M RELIEVED TO HEAR IT.
OR RATHER, IF I MAY SPEAK FRANKLY, I'M COUNTING ON YOUR POWER.
LET ME JUST SAY ONE THING.
I WON'T OBEDIENTLY GO ALONG WITH YOUR PLANS.
I CAN'T TRUST YOU.
PROTECTING YUKI IS MY HIGHEST PRIORITY.
FINE BY ME.
GO AHEAD, KEEP UP THAT CONSTANT MISTRUST OF YOURS.
IT IS WHAT WILL PROTECT YUKI IN THE END.

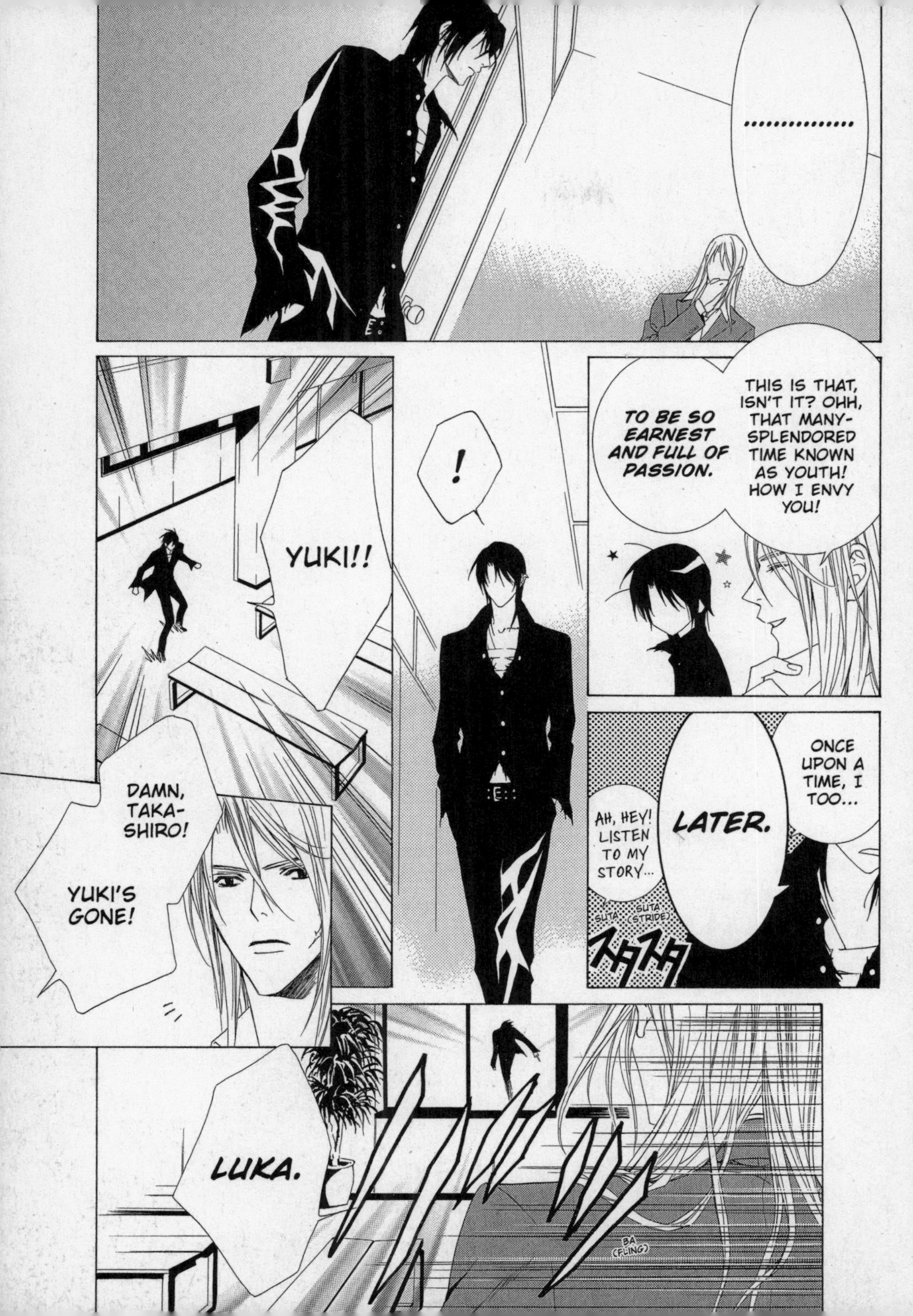
....
THIS IS THAT, ISN'T IT? OHH, THAT MANY-SPLENDORED TIME KNOWN AS YOUTH! HOW I ENVY YOU!
TO BE SO EARNEST AND FULL OF PASSION.
!
ONCE UPON A TIME, I TOO...
LATER.
AH, HEY! LISTEN TO MY STORY...
SUTA SUTA (STRIDE)
YUKI!!
DAMN, TAKA-SHIRO!
YUKI'S GONE!
LUKA.
BA (FLING)

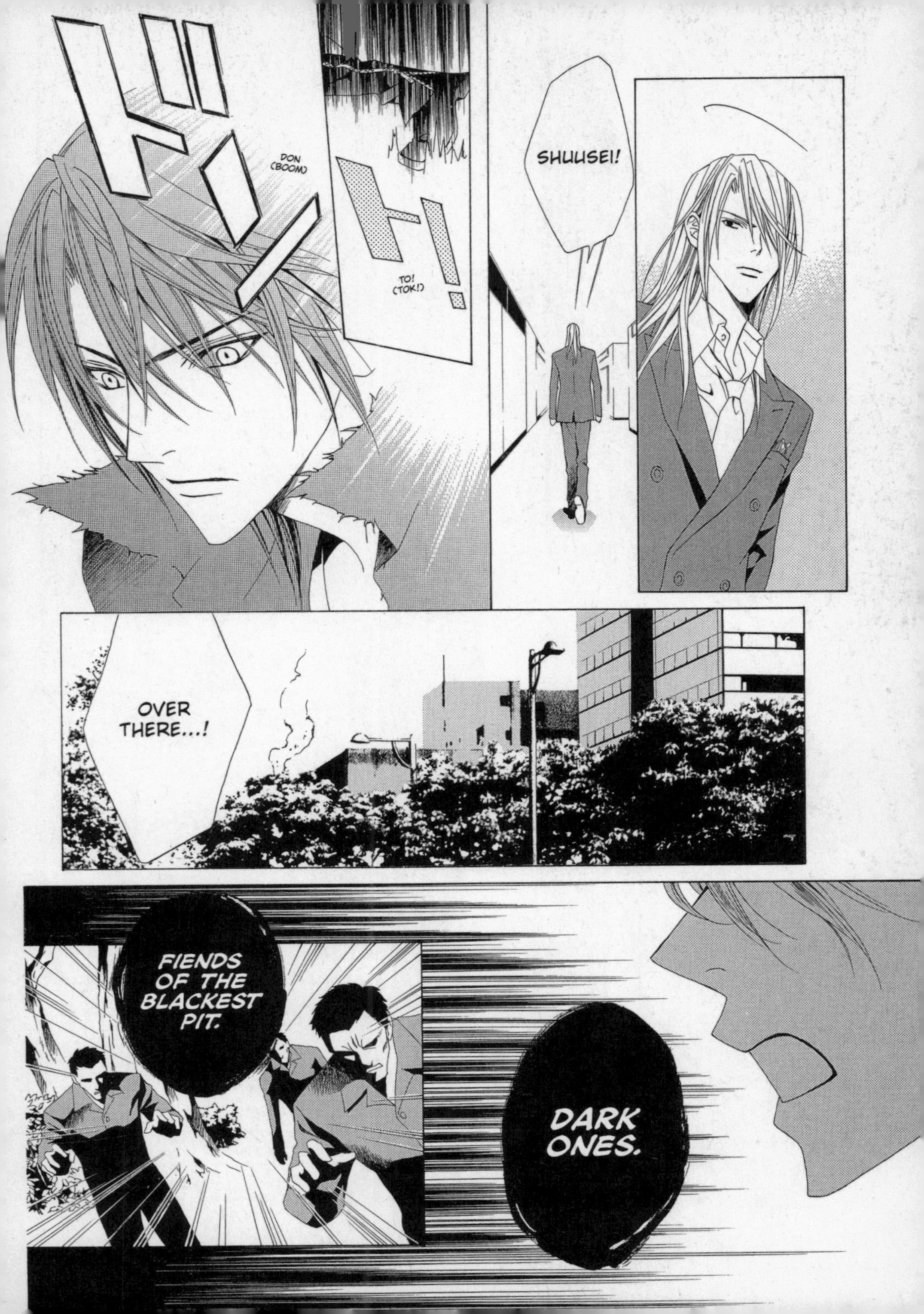
SHUUSEI!
TO! (TOK!)
DON (BOOM)
OVER THERE...!
DARK ONES.
FIENDS OF THE BLACKEST PIT.

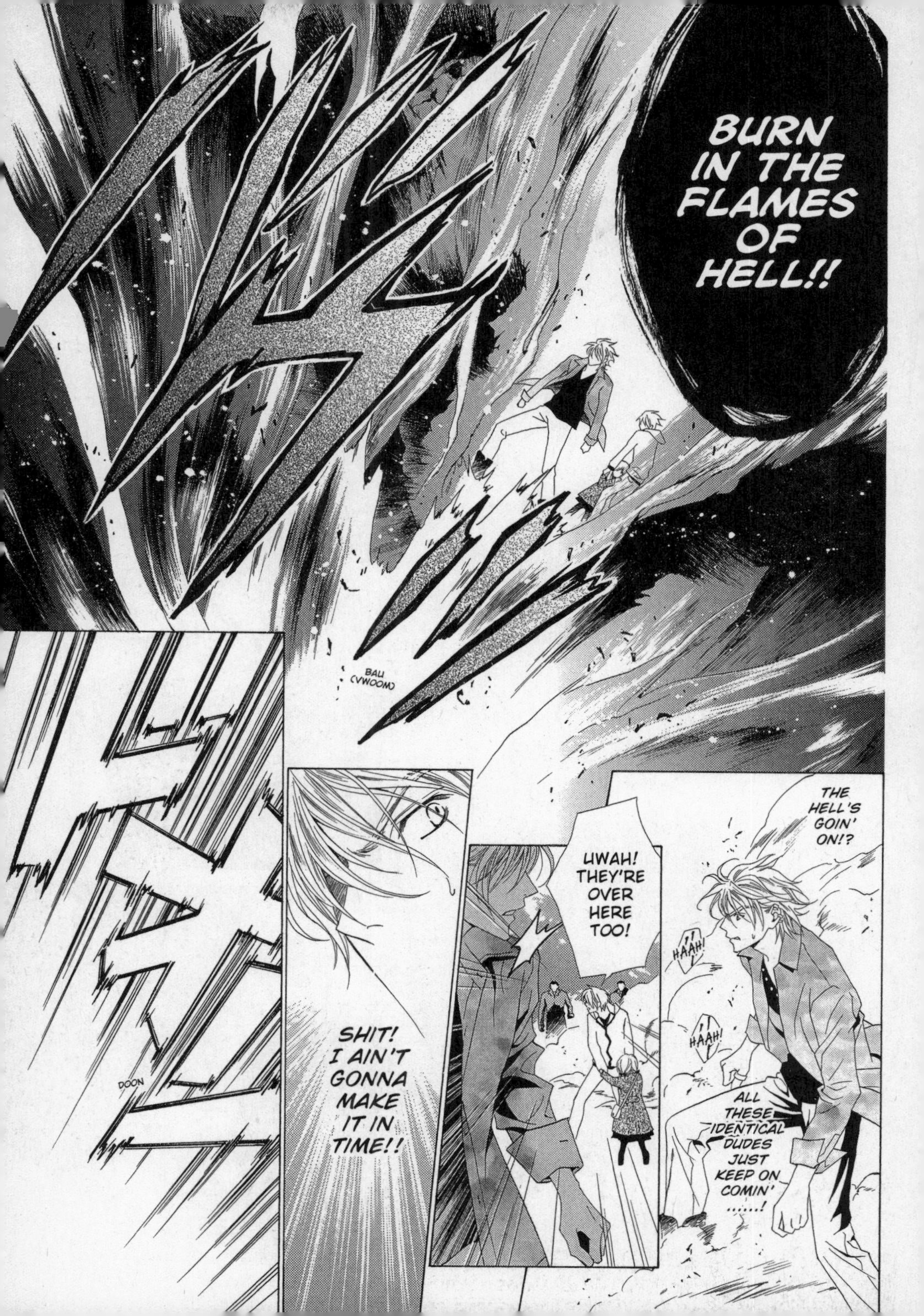

BURN IN THE FLAMES OF HELL!!
BAU (VWOOM)
THE HELL'S GOIN' ON!?
UWAH! THEY'RE OVER HERE TOO!
HAAH!
HAAH!
ALL THESE IDENTICAL DUDES JUST KEEP ON COMIN' ......!
SHIT! I AIN'T GONNA MAKE IT IN TIME!!
DOON

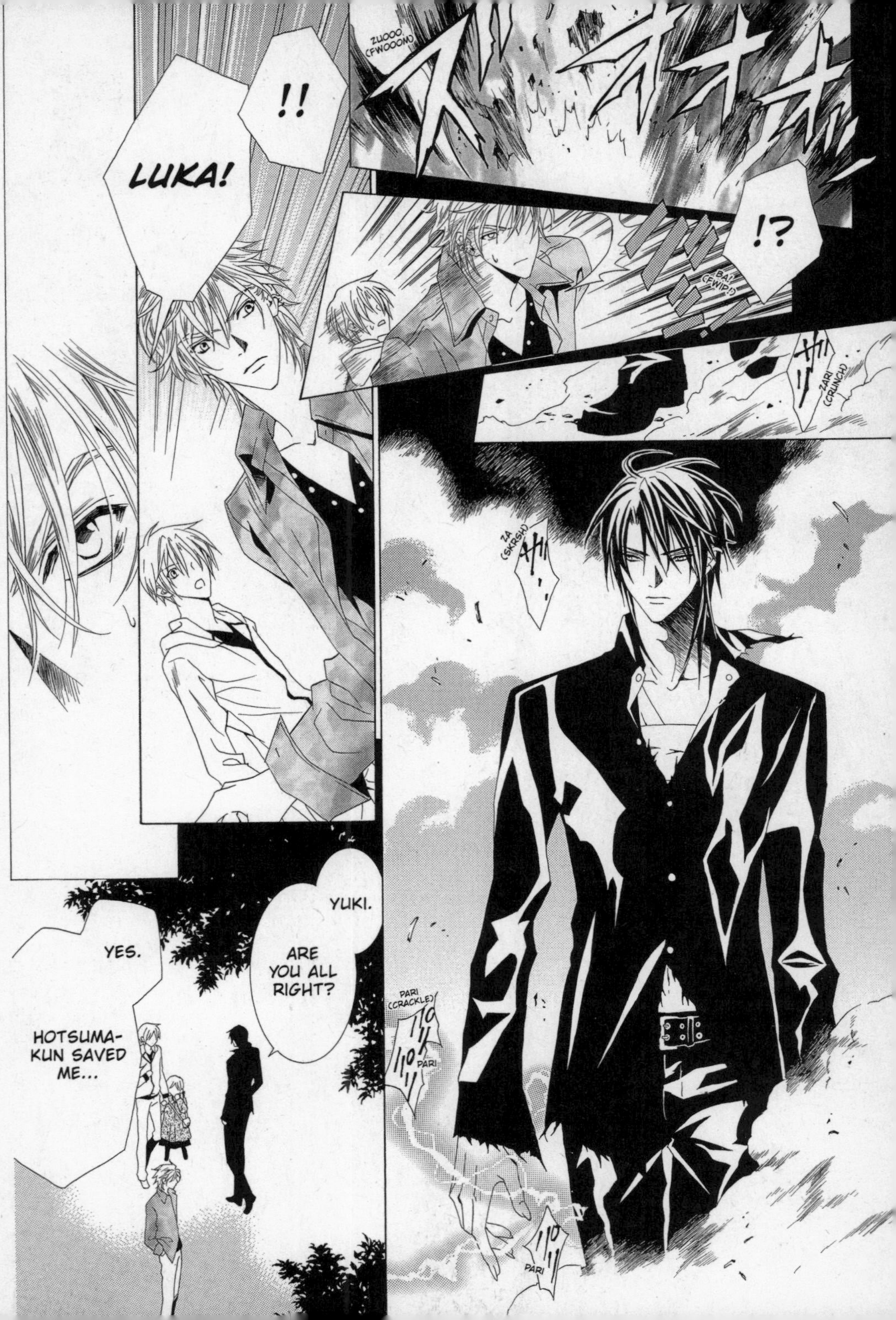
ZUOOO (FWOOOM)
!!
LUKA!
BA! (FWIP!)
!?
ZARI (CRUNCH)
ZA (SKRSH)
PARI (CRACKLE)
PARI
PARI
YUKI.
ARE YOU ALL RIGHT?
YES.
HOTSUMA-KUN SAVED ME...

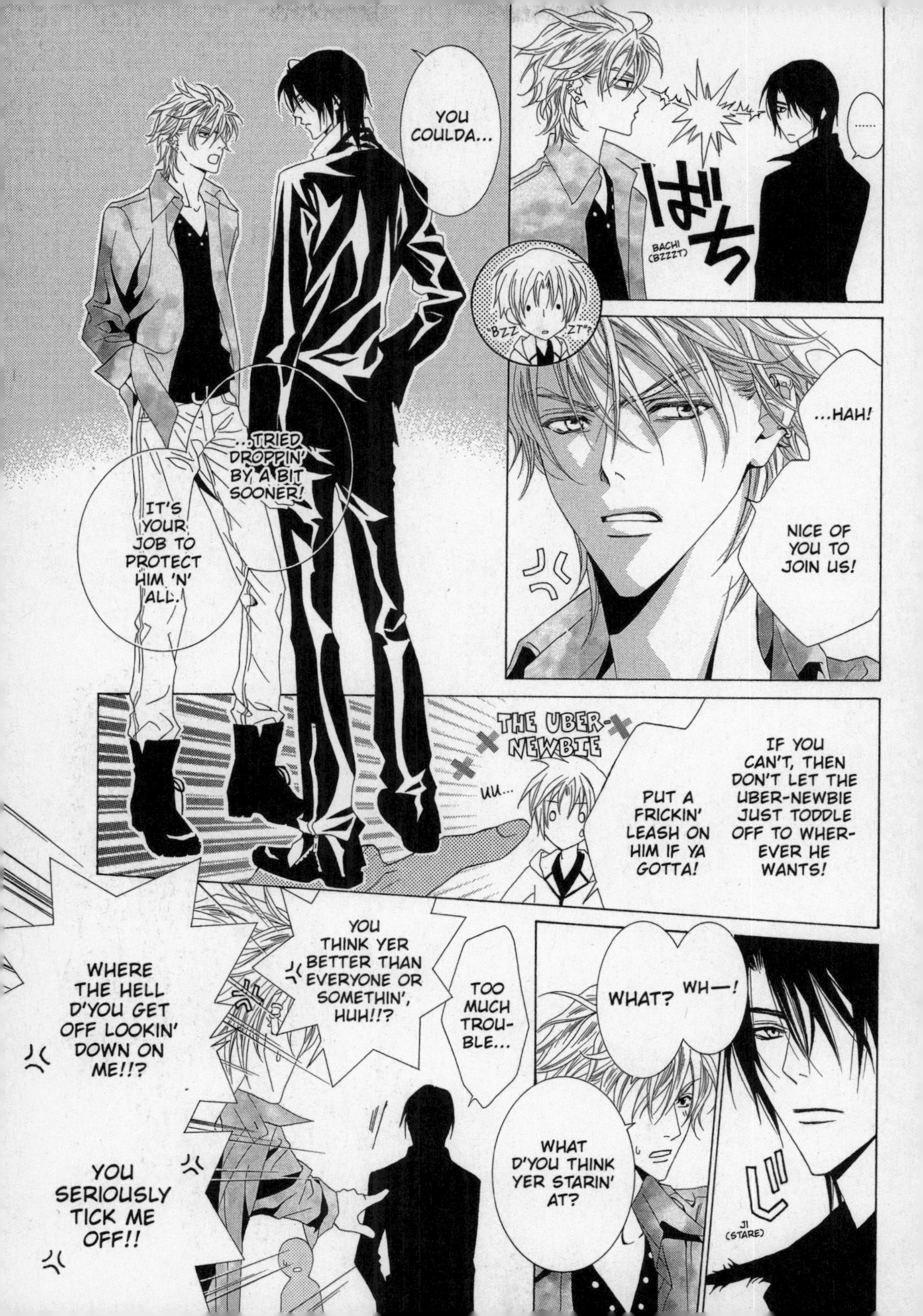

YOU COULDA...
...TRIED DROPPIN' BY A BIT SOONER!
IT'S YOUR JOB TO PROTECT HIM 'N' ALL.
......
ばち
BACHI (BZZZT)
BZZ ZT"?
...HAH!
NICE OF YOU TO JOIN US!
IF YOU CAN'T, THEN DON'T LET THE UBER-NEWBIE JUST TODDLE OFF TO WHER-EVER HE WANTS!
PUT A FRICKIN' LEASH ON HIM IF YA GOTTA!
THE UBER-NEWBIE
UU...
WH—!
WHAT?
WHAT D'YOU THINK YER STARIN' AT?
じ
JI (STARE)
TOO MUCH TROUBLE...
YOU THINK YER BETTER THAN EVERYONE OR SOMETHIN', HUH!!?
WHERE THE HELL D'YOU GET OFF LOOKIN' DOWN ON ME!!?
YOU SERIOUSLY TICK ME OFF!!

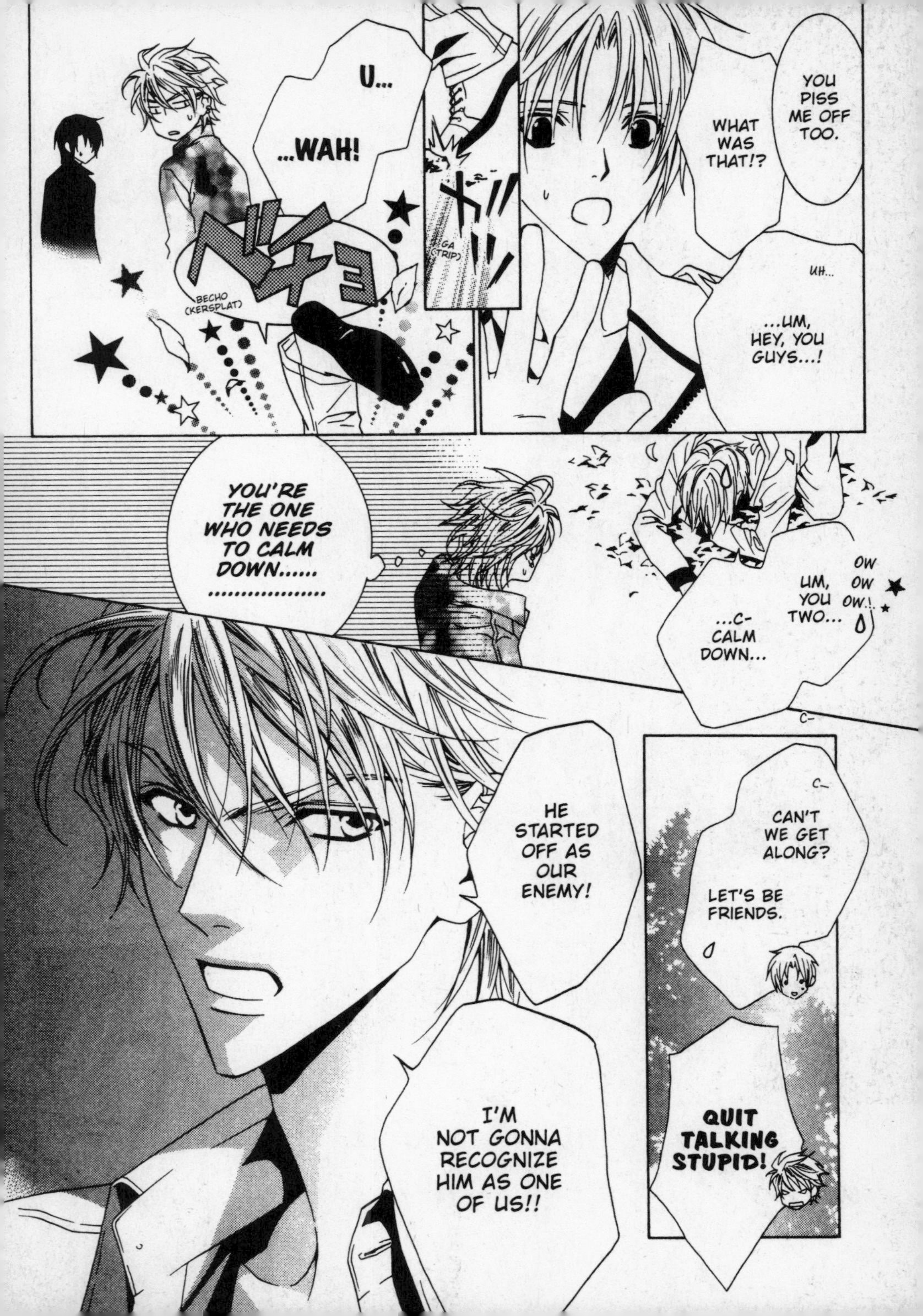
YOU PISS ME OFF TOO.
WHAT WAS THAT!?
UH...
...UM, HEY, YOU GUYS...!
GA (TRIP)
U...
...WAH!
BECHO (KERSPLAT)
OW OW OW!
UM, YOU TWO...
...C-CALM DOWN...
YOU'RE THE ONE WHO NEEDS TO CALM DOWN......
C-
C-
CAN'T WE GET ALONG?
LET'S BE FRIENDS.
QUIT TALKING STUPID!
HE STARTED OFF AS OUR ENEMY!
I'M NOT GONNA RECOGNIZE HIM AS ONE OF US!!

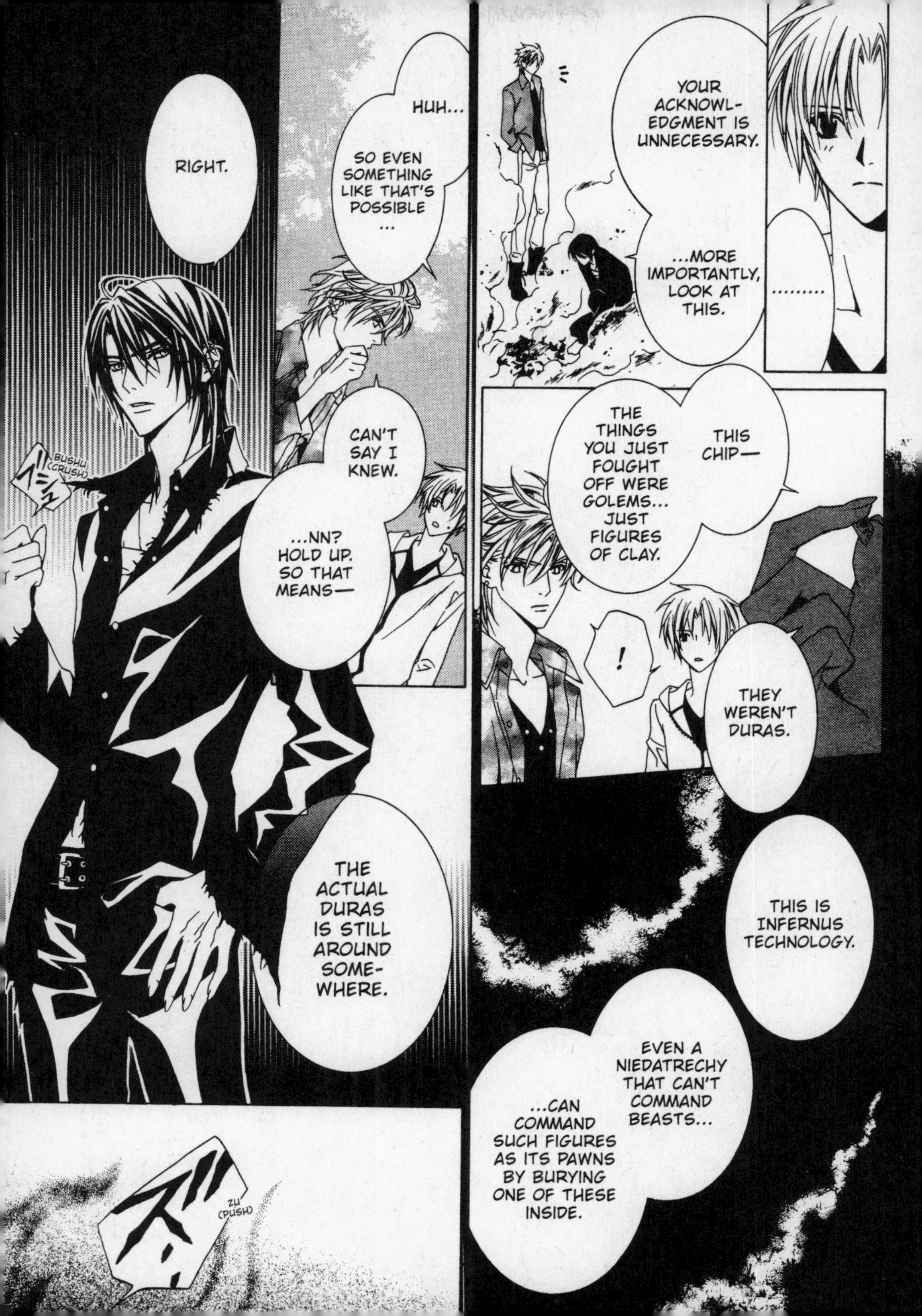
YOUR ACKNOWLEDGMENT IS UNNECESSARY.
...MORE IMPORTANTLY, LOOK AT THIS.
....
THIS CHIP—
THE THINGS YOU JUST FOUGHT OFF WERE GOLEMS... JUST FIGURES OF CLAY.
!
THEY WEREN'T DURAS.
THIS IS INFERNUS TECHNOLOGY.
EVEN A NIEDATRECHY THAT CAN'T COMMAND BEASTS...
...CAN COMMAND SUCH FIGURES AS ITS PAWNS BY BURYING ONE OF THESE INSIDE.
HUH...
SO EVEN SOMETHING LIKE THAT'S POSSIBLE...
CAN'T SAY I KNEW.
...NN? HOLD UP. SO THAT MEANS—
RIGHT.
BUSHU (CRUSH)
THE ACTUAL DURAS IS STILL AROUND SOMEWHERE.
ZU' (PUSH)

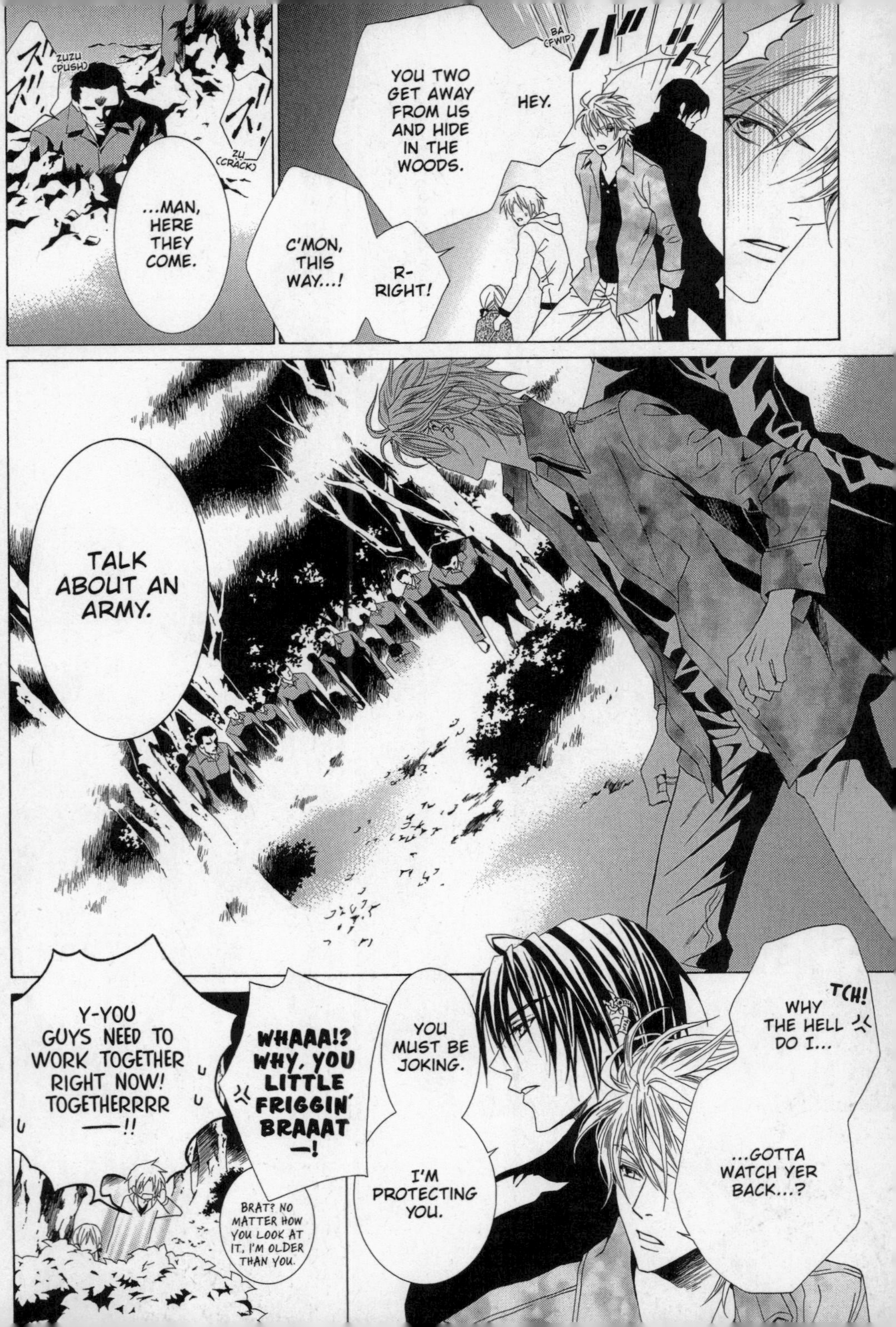
BA (FWIP)
HEY.
YOU TWO GET AWAY FROM US AND HIDE IN THE WOODS.
R-RIGHT!
C'MON, THIS WAY...!
ZUZU (PUSH)
ZU (CRACK)
...MAN, HERE THEY COME.
TALK ABOUT AN ARMY.
TCH! WHY THE HELL DO I...
...GOTTA WATCH YER BACK...?
YOU MUST BE JOKING.
I'M PROTECTING YOU.
WHAAA!? WHY, YOU LITTLE FRIGGIN' BRAAAT—!
BRAT? NO MATTER HOW YOU LOOK AT IT, I'M OLDER THAN YOU.
Y-YOU GUYS NEED TO WORK TOGETHER RIGHT NOW! TOGETHERRRR—!!

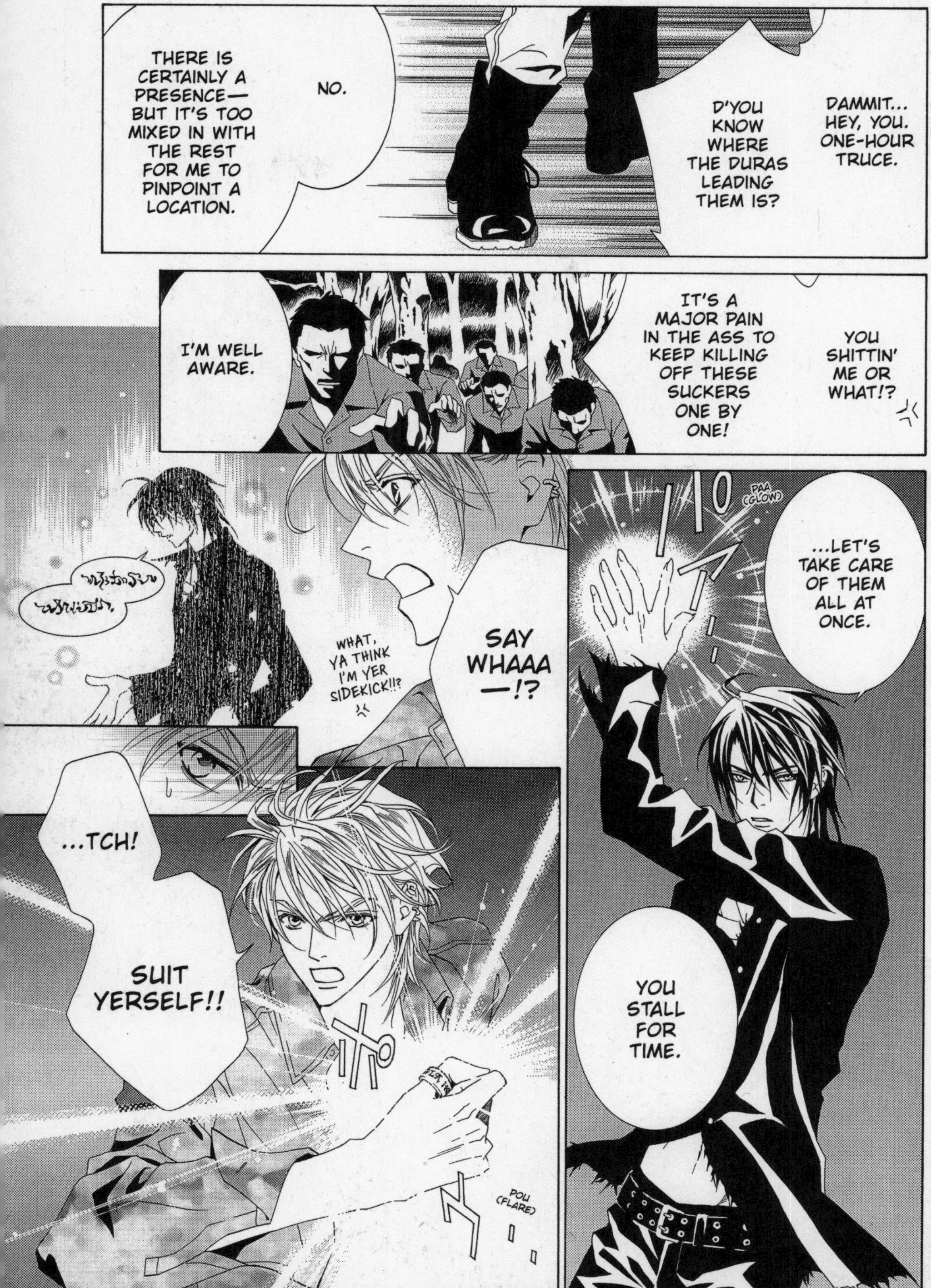
DAMMIT... HEY, YOU. ONE-HOUR TRUCE.
D'YOU KNOW WHERE THE DURAS LEADING THEM IS?
NO.
THERE IS CERTAINLY A PRESENCE— BUT IT'S TOO MIXED IN WITH THE REST FOR ME TO PINPOINT A LOCATION.
YOU SHITTIN' ME OR WHAT!?
IT'S A MAJOR PAIN IN THE ASS TO KEEP KILLING OFF THESE SUCKERS ONE BY ONE!
I'M WELL AWARE.
PAA (GLOW)
...LET'S TAKE CARE OF THEM ALL AT ONCE.
SAY WHAAA—!?
WHAT, YA THINK I'M YER SIDEKICK!!?
YOU STALL FOR TIME.
...TCH!
SUIT YERSELF!!
POU (FLARE)

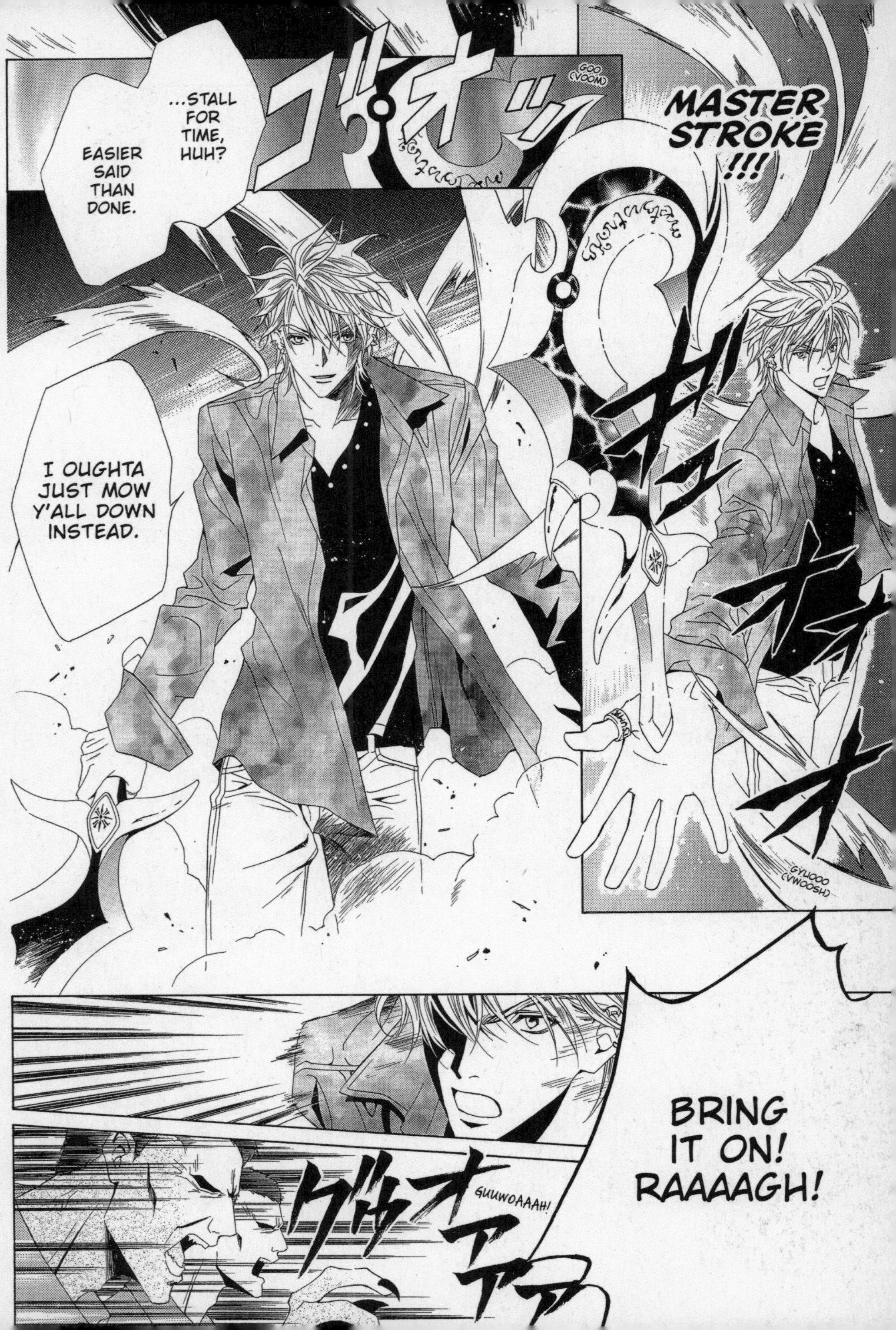
GOO (VOOM)
MASTER STROKE!!!
...STALL FOR TIME, HUH?
EASIER SAID THAN DONE.
I OUGHTA JUST MOW Y'ALL DOWN INSTEAD.
GYUOOO (VWOOSH)
BRING IT ON! RAAAAGH!
GUUWOAAAH!

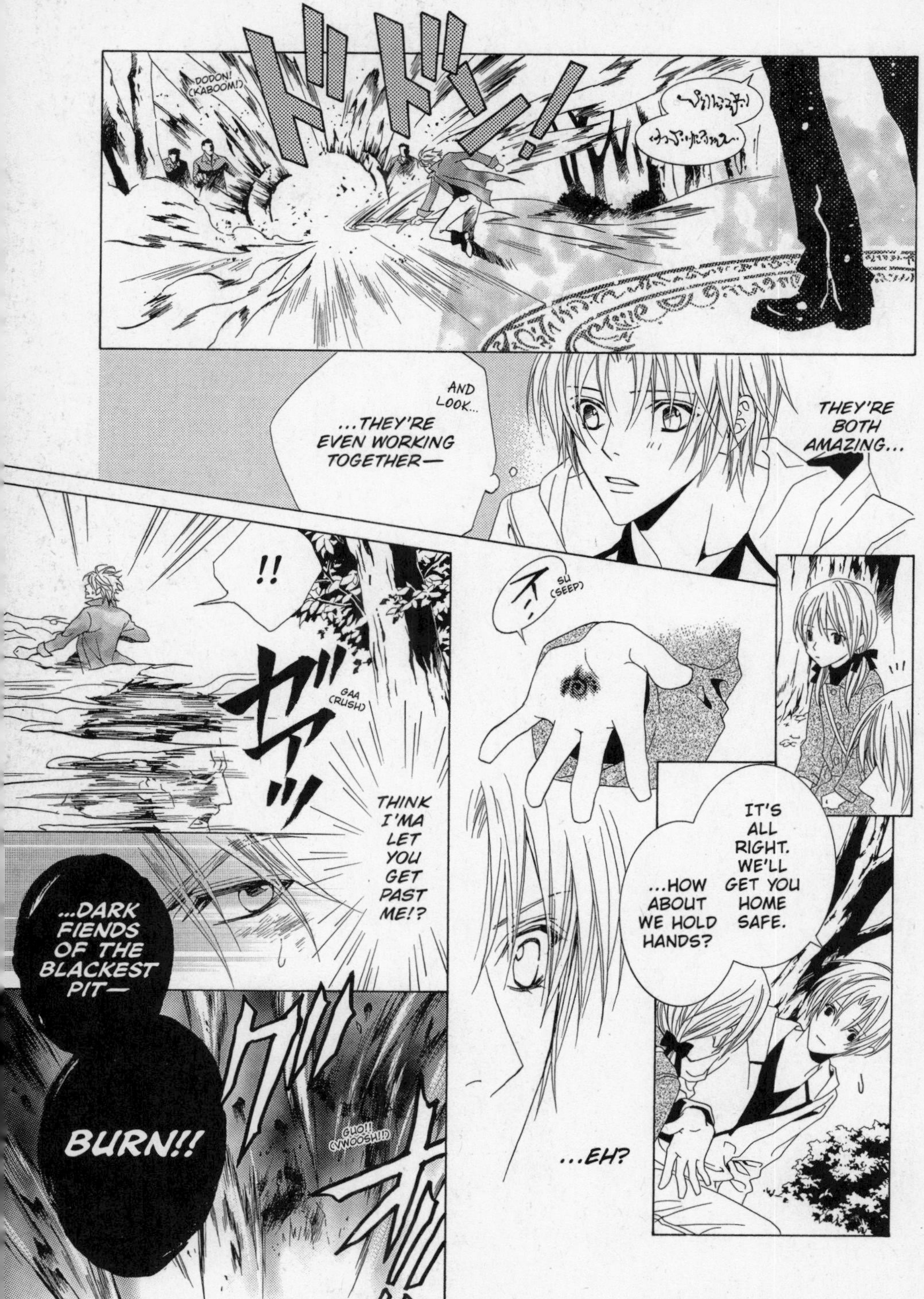
DODON! (KABOOM!)
AND LOOK...
...THEY'RE EVEN WORKING TOGETHER—
THEY'RE BOTH AMAZING...
SU (SEEP)
!!
GAA (RUSH)
THINK I'MA LET YOU GET PAST ME!?
IT'S ALL RIGHT. WE'LL GET YOU HOME SAFE.
...HOW ABOUT WE HOLD HANDS?
...EH?
...DARK FIENDS OF THE BLACKEST PIT—
BURN!!
GUO!! (WHOOSH!!)

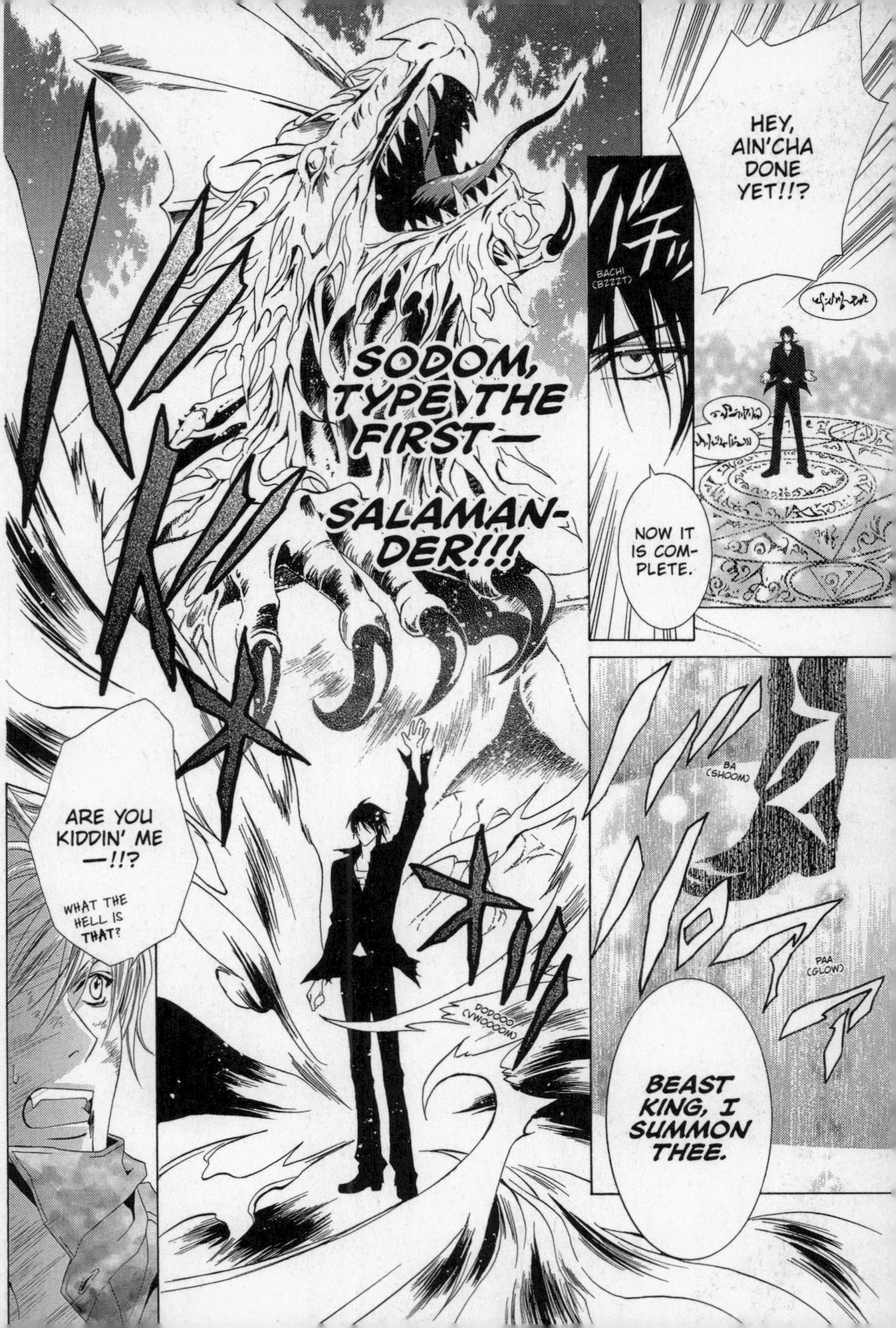
HEY, AIN'CHA DONE YET!!?
BACHI (BZZZT)
NOW IT IS COMPLETE.
BA (SHOOM)
PAA (GLOW)
BEAST KING, I SUMMON THEE.
SODOM, TYPE THE FIRST—
SALAMANDER!!!
DODOOO (VWOOOOM)
ARE YOU KIDDIN' ME—!!?
WHAT THE HELL IS THAT?

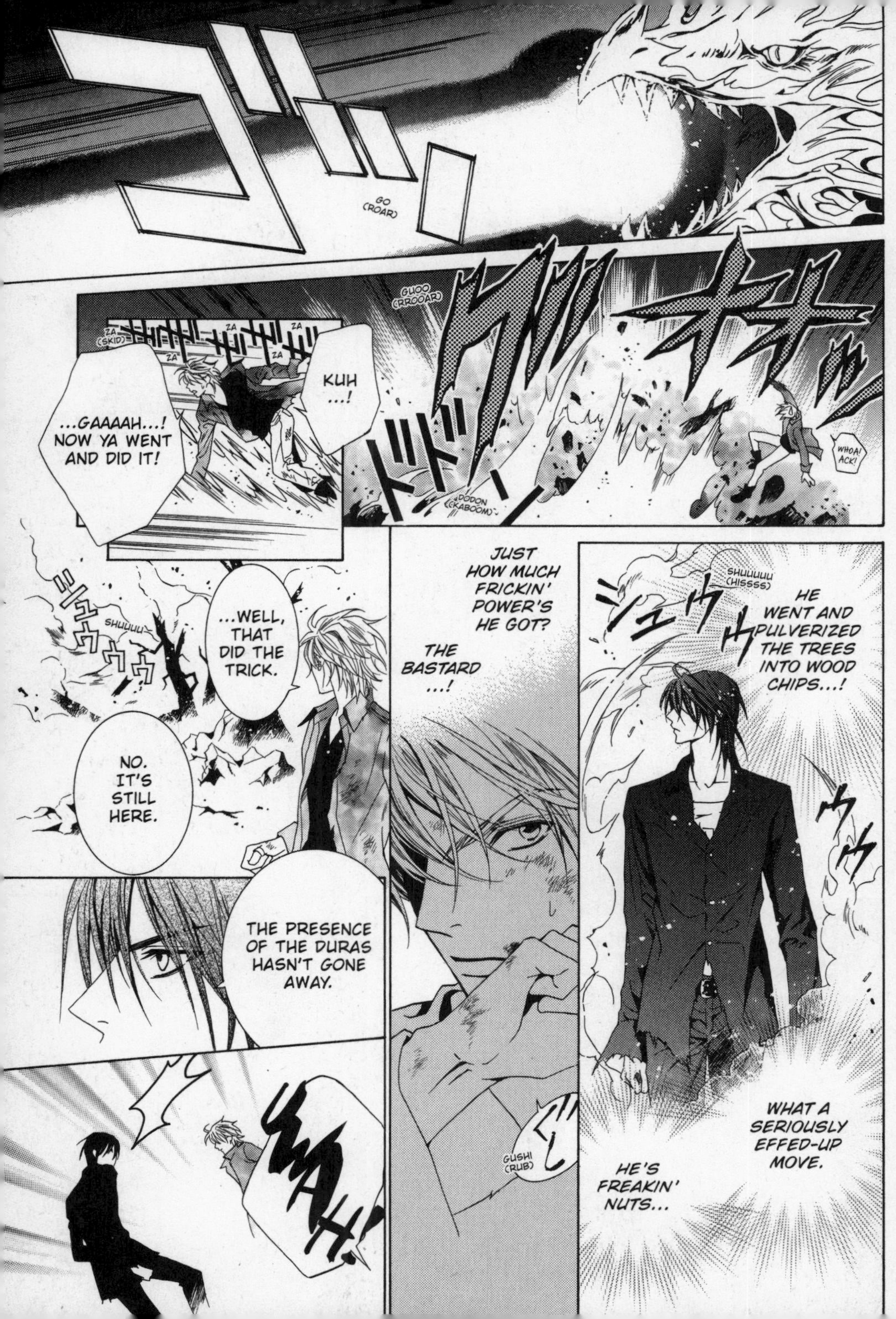

GO (ROAR)
GUOO (RROOAR)
WHOA! ACK!
DODON (KABOOM)
KUH ...!
ZA (SKID) ZA ZA ZA ZA
...GAAAAH...! NOW YA WENT AND DID IT!
SHUUUUU (HISSSS)
HE WENT AND PULVERIZED THE TREES INTO WOOD CHIPS...!
JUST HOW MUCH FRICKIN' POWER'S HE GOT?
THE BASTARD ...!
SHUUUU
...WELL, THAT DID THE TRICK.
NO. IT'S STILL HERE.
THE PRESENCE OF THE DURAS HASN'T GONE AWAY.
WHAT A SERIOUSLY EFFED-UP MOVE.
HE'S FREAKIN' NUTS...
GUSHI (RUB)

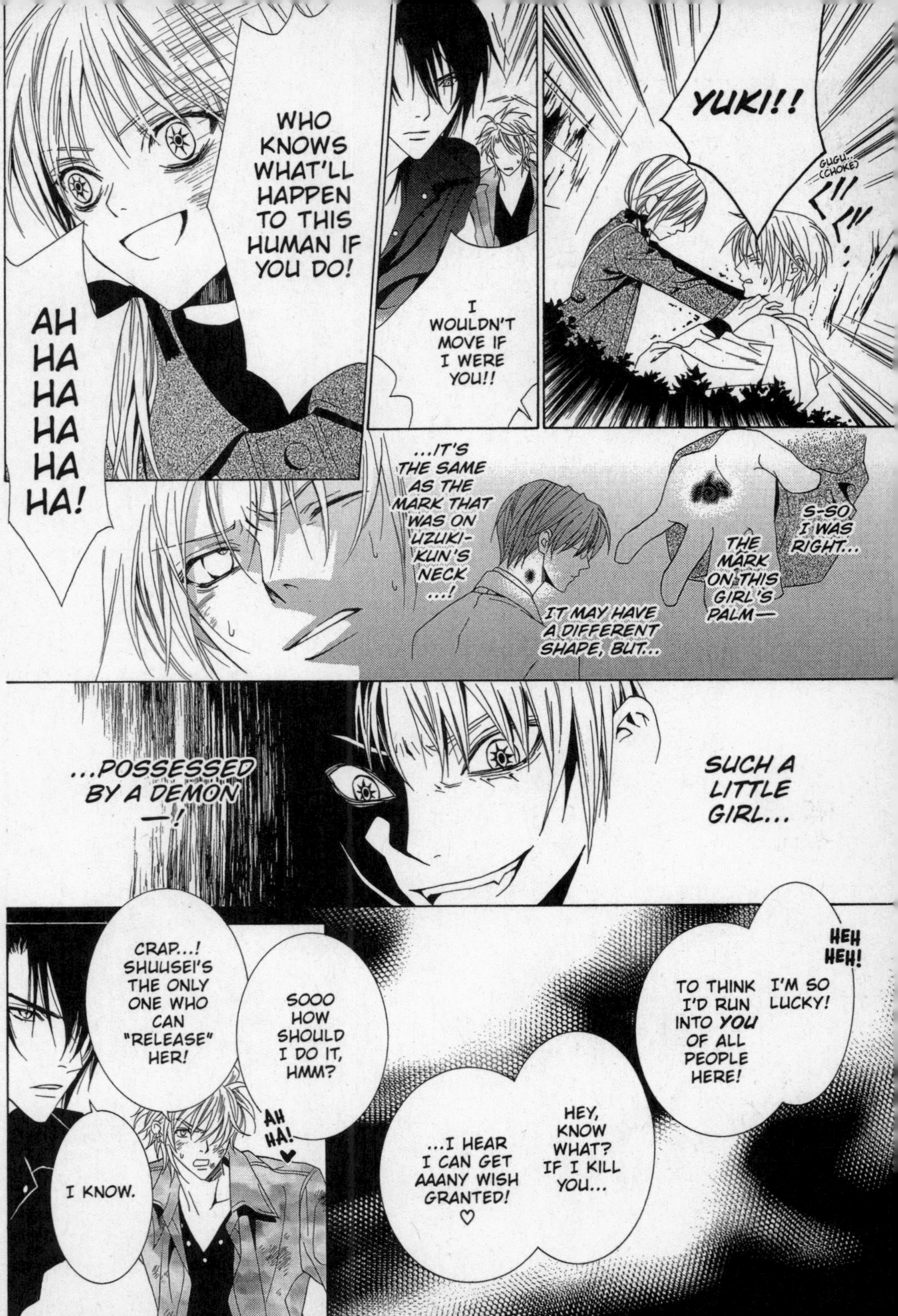
YUKI!!
GUGU.. (CHOKE)
I WOULDN'T MOVE IF I WERE YOU!!
WHO KNOWS WHAT'LL HAPPEN TO THIS HUMAN IF YOU DO!
AH HA HA HA HA HA HA!
S-SO I WAS RIGHT...
THE MARK ON THIS GIRL'S PALM—
IT MAY HAVE A DIFFERENT SHAPE, BUT...
...IT'S THE SAME AS THE MARK THAT WAS ON UZUKI-KUN'S NECK...!
SUCH A LITTLE GIRL...
...POSSESSED BY A DEMON—!
HEH HEH!
I'M SO LUCKY!
TO THINK I'D RUN INTO *YOU* OF ALL PEOPLE HERE!
HEY, KNOW WHAT? IF I KILL YOU...
...I HEAR I CAN GET AAANY WISH GRANTED! ♡
AH HA! ♥
SOOO HOW SHOULD I DO IT, HMM?
CRAP...! SHUUSEI'S THE ONLY ONE WHO CAN "RELEASE" HER!
I KNOW.

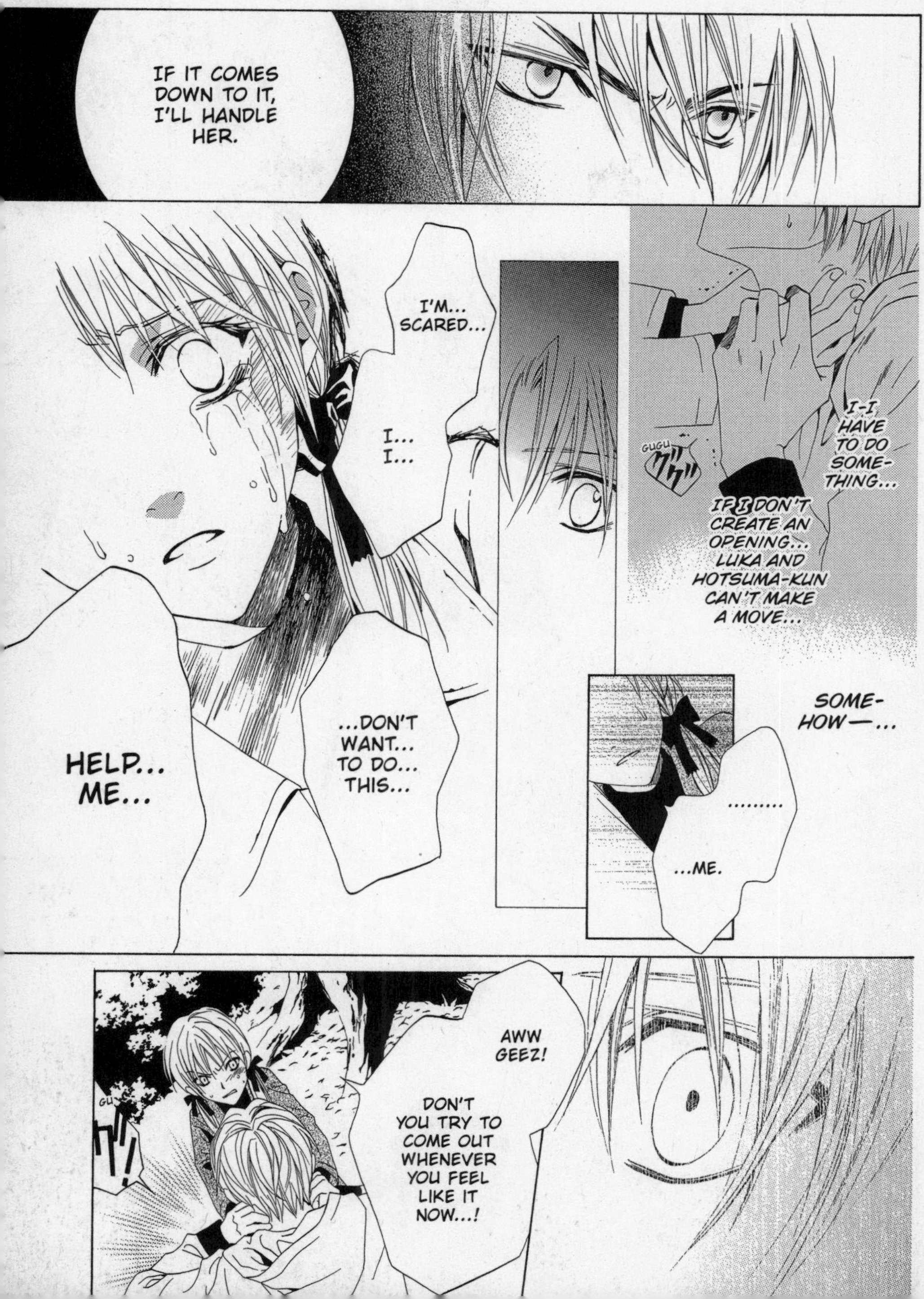
IF IT COMES DOWN TO IT, I'LL HANDLE HER.
I-I HAVE TO DO SOME-THING...
GUGU
IF I DON'T CREATE AN OPENING... LUKA AND HOTSUMA-KUN CAN'T MAKE A MOVE...
SOME-HOW—...
....
...ME.
I'M... SCARED...
I... I...
...DON'T WANT... TO DO... THIS...
HELP... ME...
AWW GEEZ!
DON'T YOU TRY TO COME OUT WHENEVER YOU FEEL LIKE IT NOW...!
GU

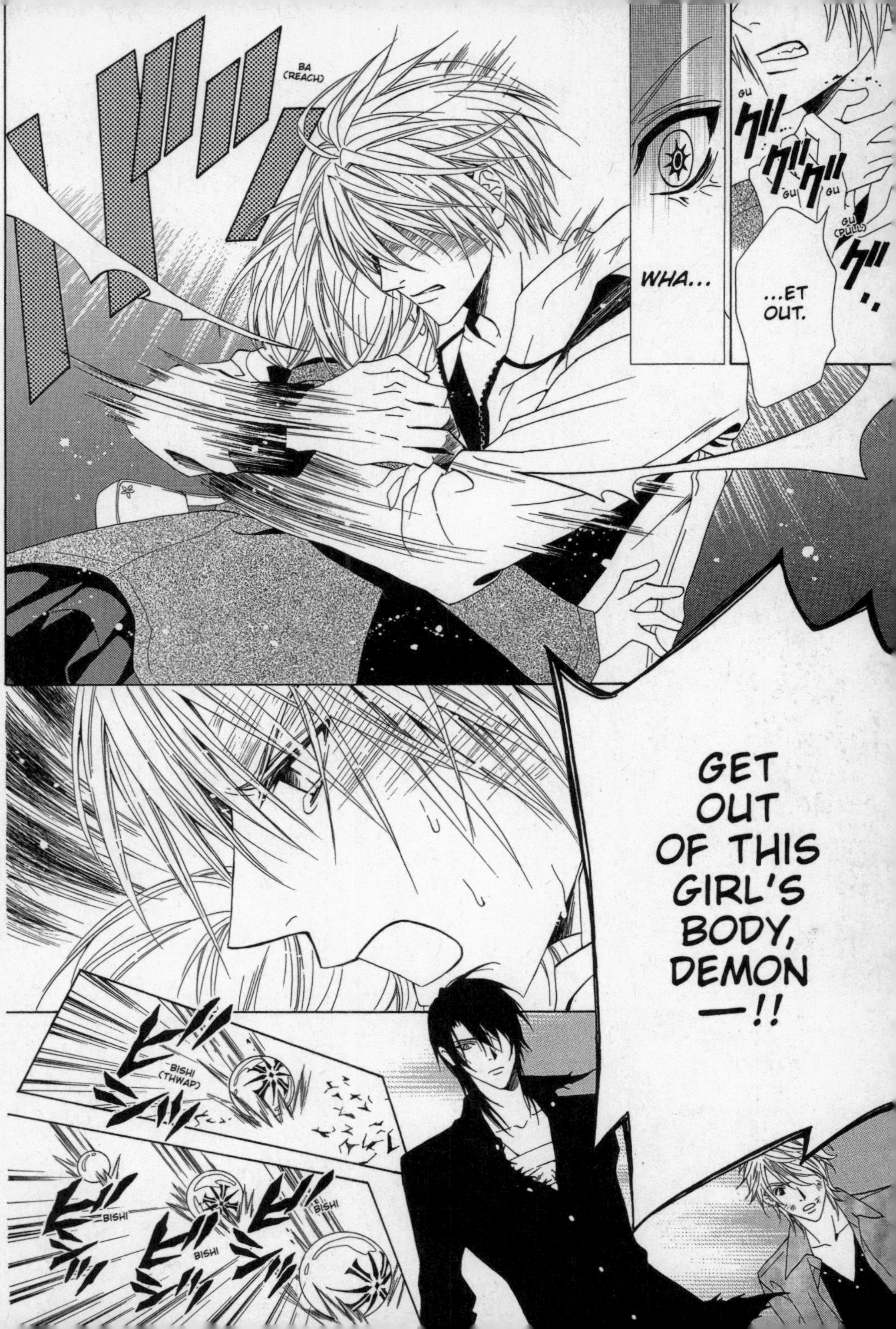
GU
GU
GU
GU (PULL)
WHA...
...ET OUT.
BA (REACH)
GET OUT OF THIS GIRL'S BODY, DEMON—!!
BISHI (THWAP)
BISHI
BISHI
BISHI

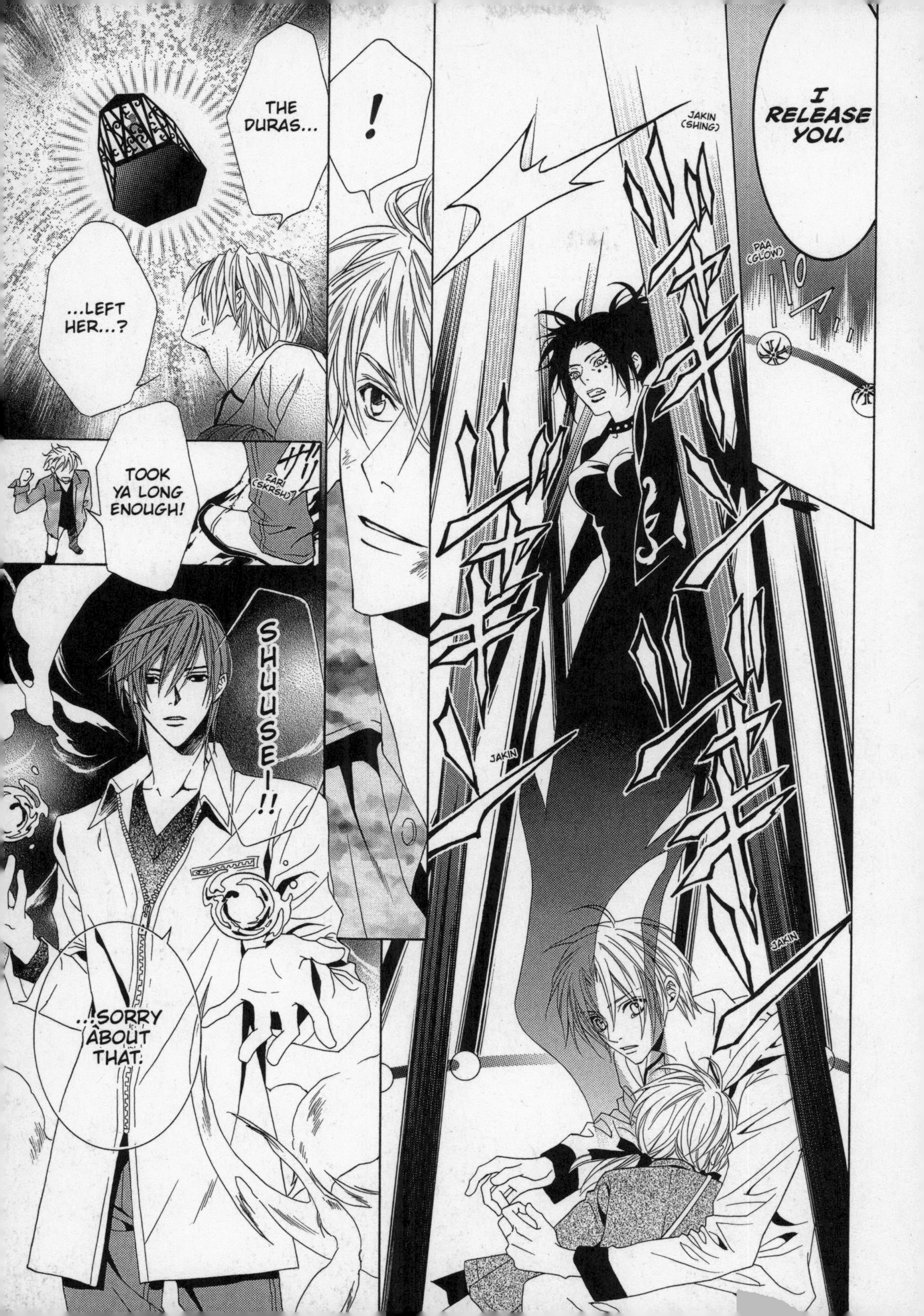
I RELEASE YOU.
PAA (GLOW)
JAKIN (SHING)
JAKIN
JAKIN
!
THE DURAS...
...LEFT HER...?
TOOK YA LONG ENOUGH!
ZARI (SKRSH)
SHUUSE-I!!
...SORRY ABOUT THAT.

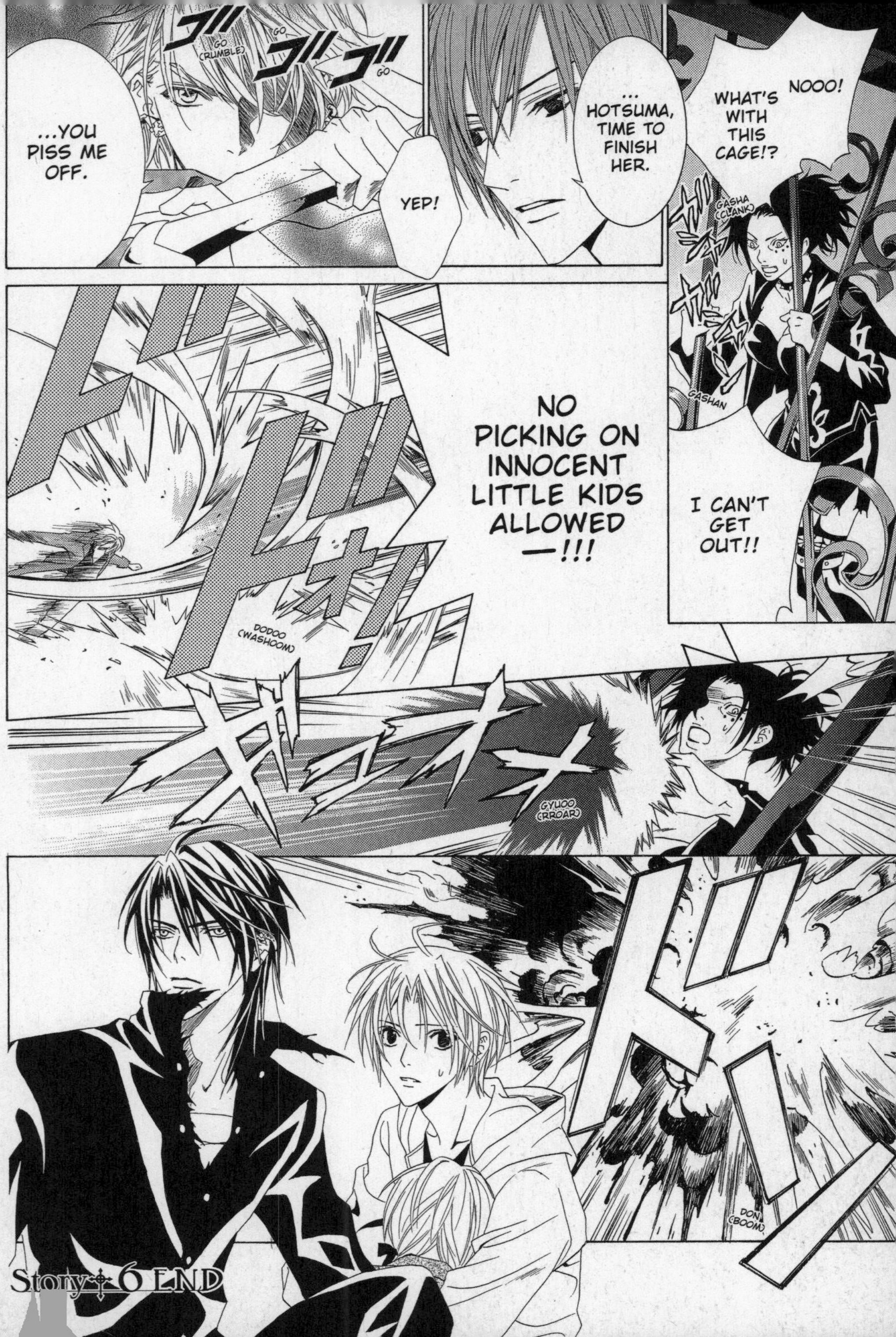

NOOO!
WHAT'S WITH THIS CAGE!?
GASHA (CLANK)
GASHAN
... HOTSUMA, TIME TO FINISH HER.
YEP!
GO (RUMBLE)
GO
...YOU PISS ME OFF.
I CAN'T GET OUT!!
NO PICKING ON INNOCENT LITTLE KIDS ALLOWED—!!!
DODOO (WASHOOM)
GYUOO (RROAR)
DON (BOOM)
Story 6 END

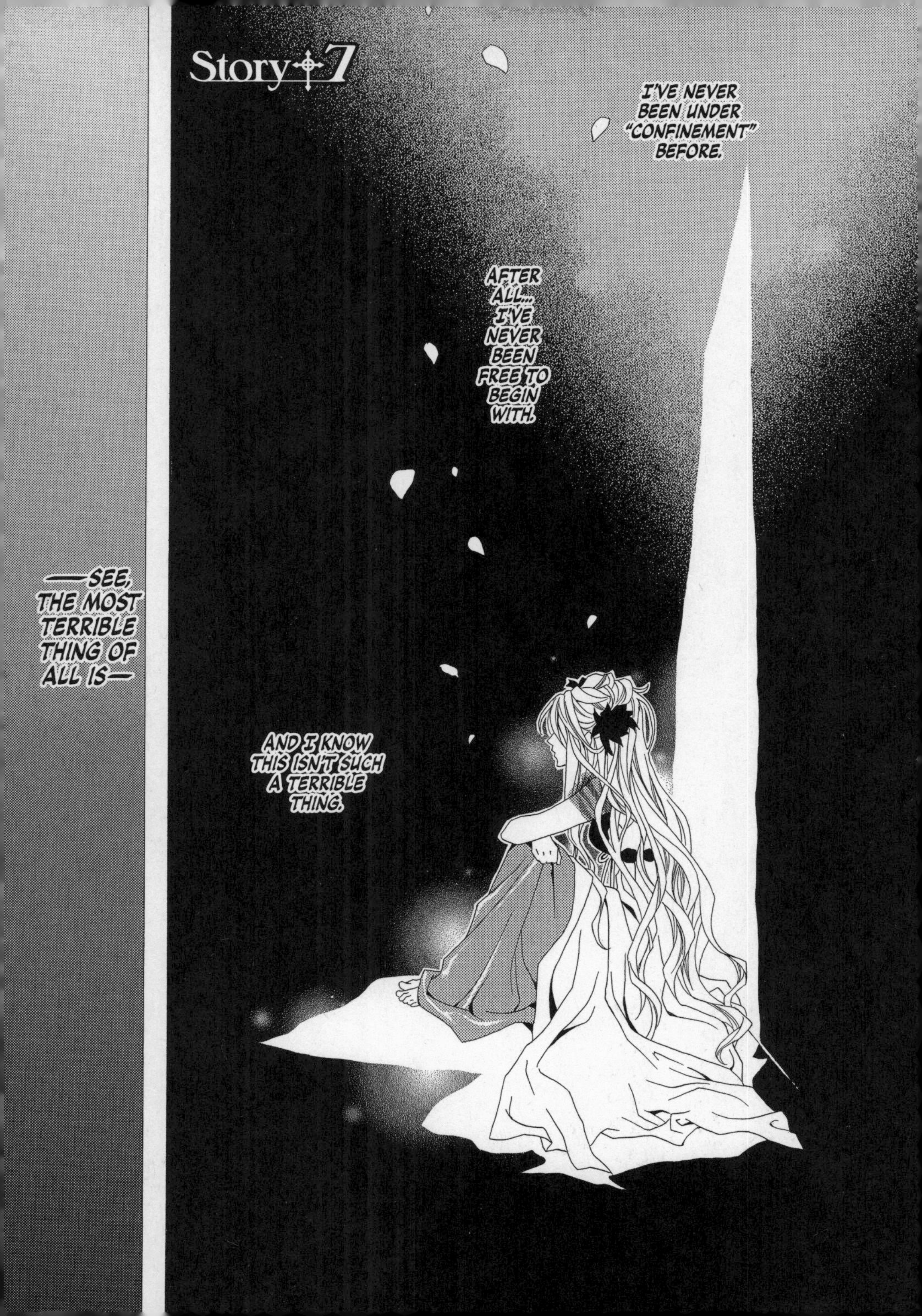
Story 7
I'VE NEVER BEEN UNDER "CONFINEMENT" BEFORE.
AFTER ALL... I'VE NEVER BEEN FREE TO BEGIN WITH.
AND I KNOW THIS ISN'T SUCH A TERRIBLE THING.
—SEE, THE MOST TERRIBLE THING OF ALL IS—

Story 7
THE LINE BETWEEN LIGHT AND DESPAIR

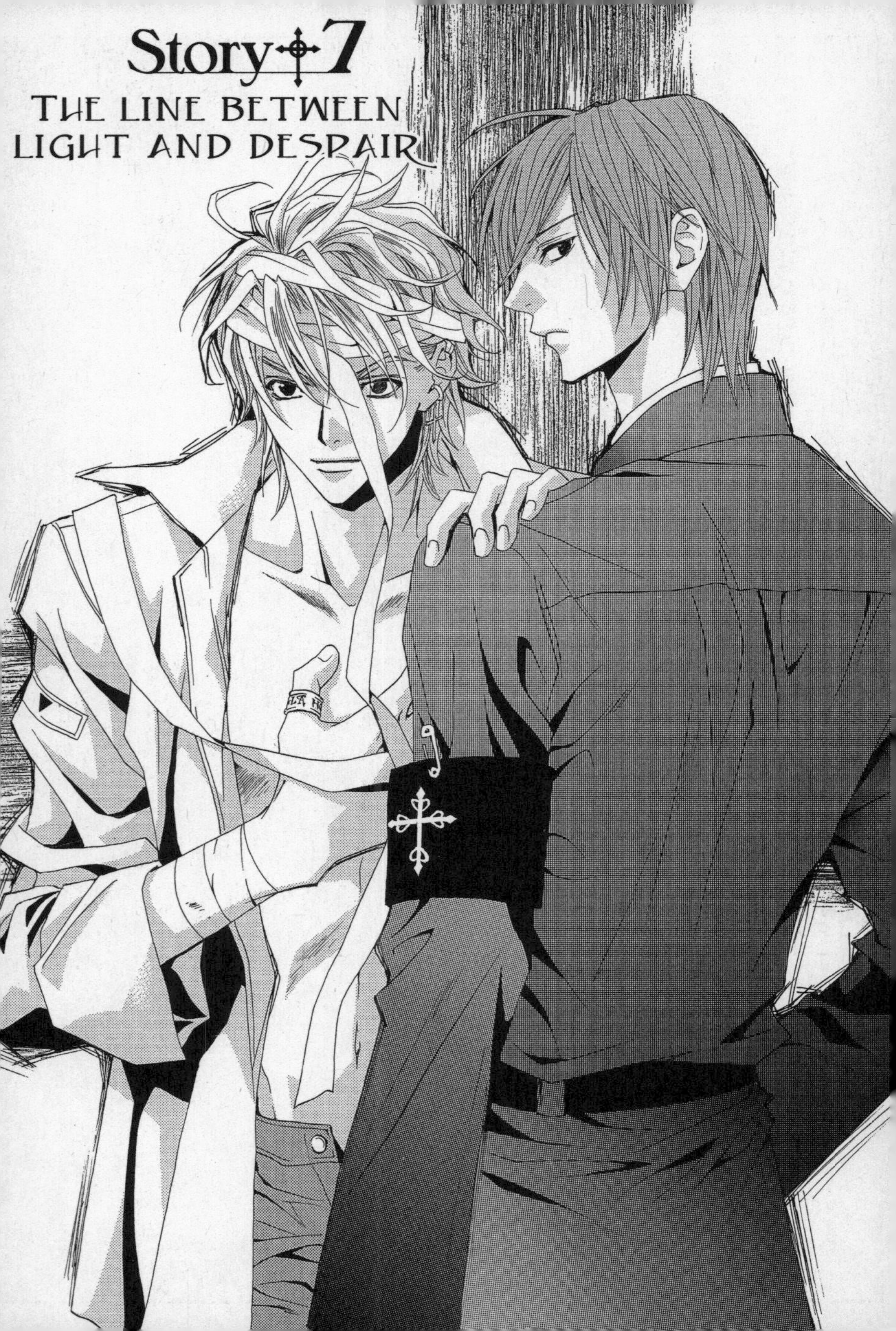

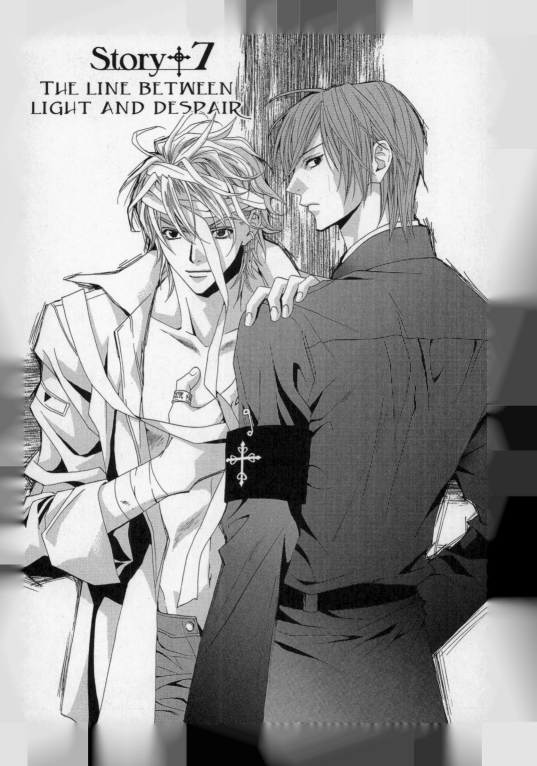

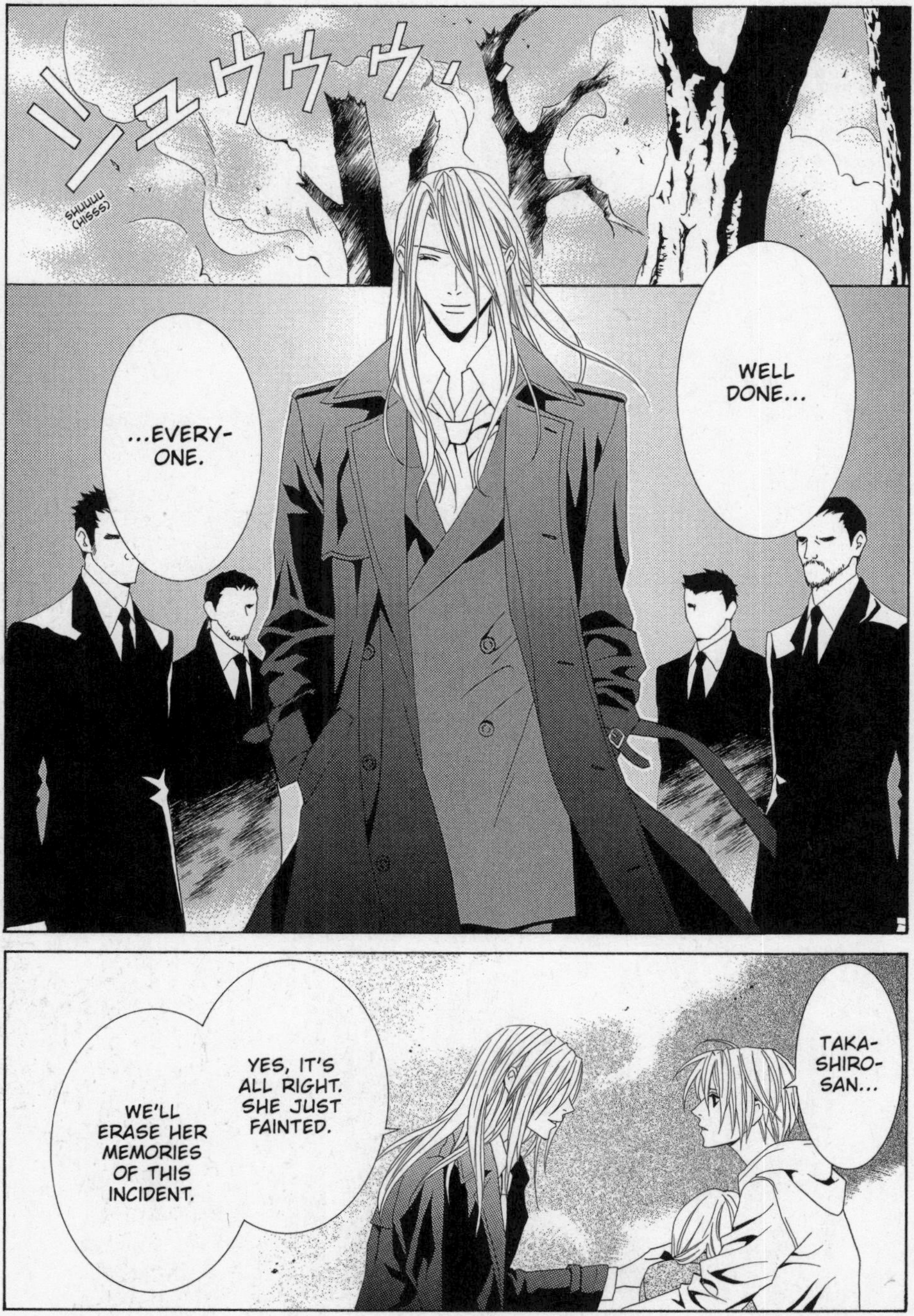
シュウウウ
SHUUUU (HISSS)
WELL DONE...
...EVERY-ONE.
TAKA-SHIRO-SAN...
YES, IT'S ALL RIGHT. SHE JUST FAINTED.
WE'LL ERASE HER MEMORIES OF THIS INCIDENT.

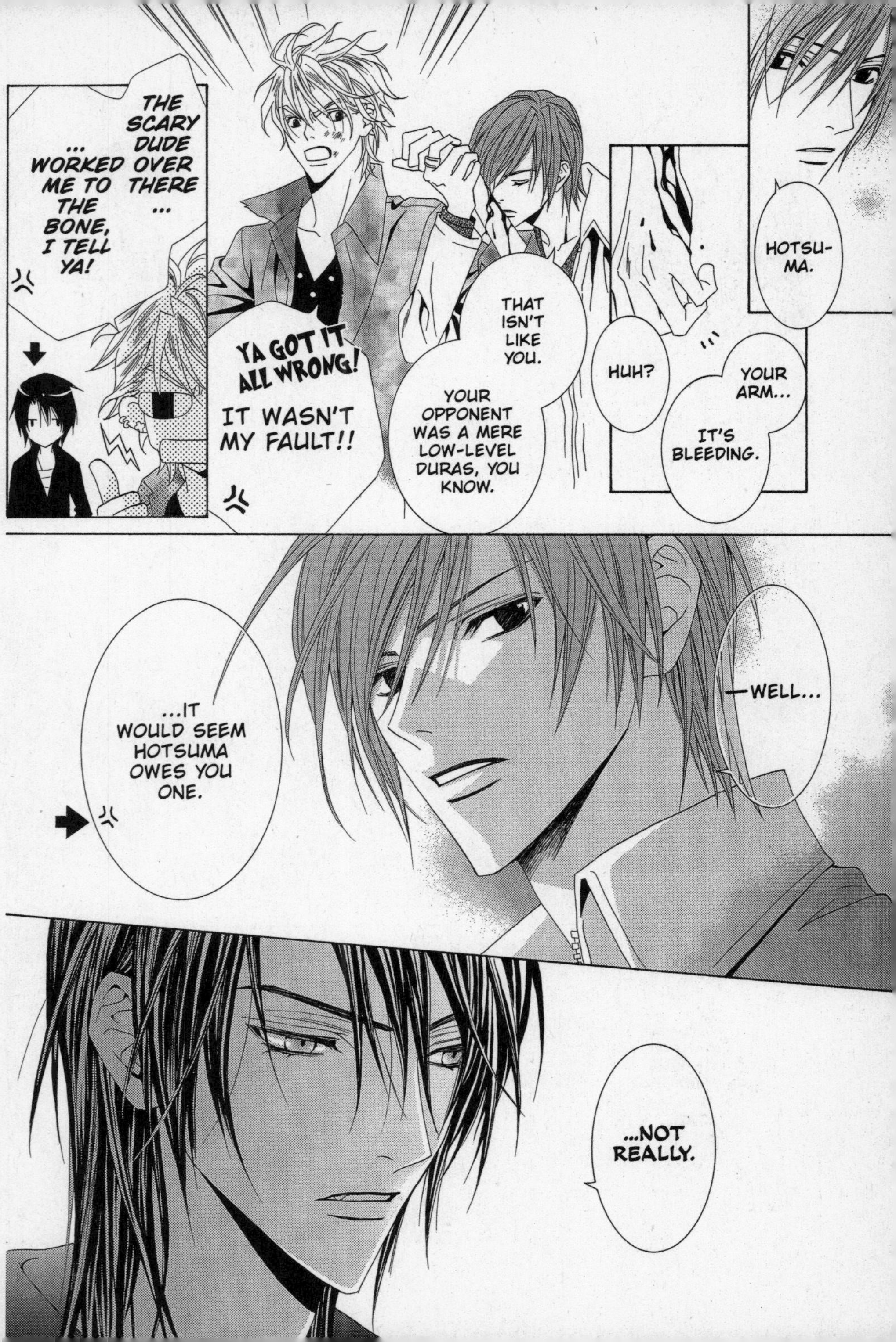
HOTSU-MA.
YOUR ARM...
IT'S BLEEDING.
HUH?
THAT ISN'T LIKE YOU.
YOUR OPPONENT WAS A MERE LOW-LEVEL DURAS, YOU KNOW.
YA GOT IT ALL WRONG!
IT WASN'T MY FAULT!!
THE SCARY DUDE OVER THERE...
...WORKED ME TO THE BONE, I TELL YA!
—WELL...
...IT WOULD SEEM HOTSUMA OWES YOU ONE.
...NOT REALLY.

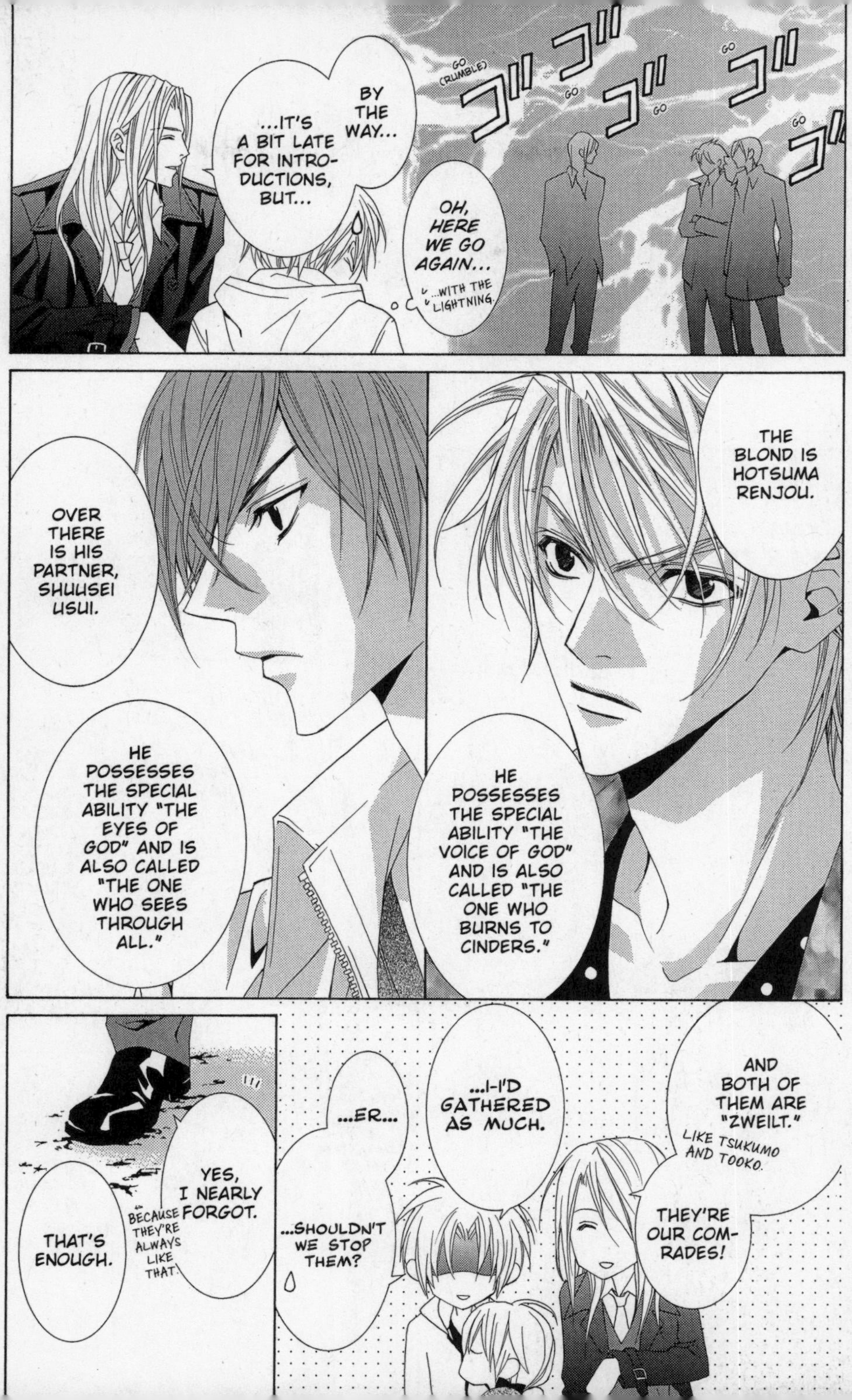
GO GO GO GO GO (RUMBLE)
BY THE WAY...
...IT'S A BIT LATE FOR INTRODUCTIONS, BUT...
OH, HERE WE GO AGAIN...
...WITH THE LIGHTNING.
THE BLOND IS HOTSUMA RENJOU.
HE POSSESSES THE SPECIAL ABILITY "THE VOICE OF GOD" AND IS ALSO CALLED "THE ONE WHO BURNS TO CINDERS."
OVER THERE IS HIS PARTNER, SHUUSEI USUI.
HE POSSESSES THE SPECIAL ABILITY "THE EYES OF GOD" AND IS ALSO CALLED "THE ONE WHO SEES THROUGH ALL."
AND BOTH OF THEM ARE "ZWEILT."
LIKE TSUKUMO AND TOOKO.
THEY'RE OUR COMRADES!
...I-I'D GATHERED AS MUCH.
...ER...
...SHOULDN'T WE STOP THEM?
YES, I NEARLY FORGOT.
BECAUSE THEY'RE ALWAYS LIKE THAT.
THAT'S ENOUGH.

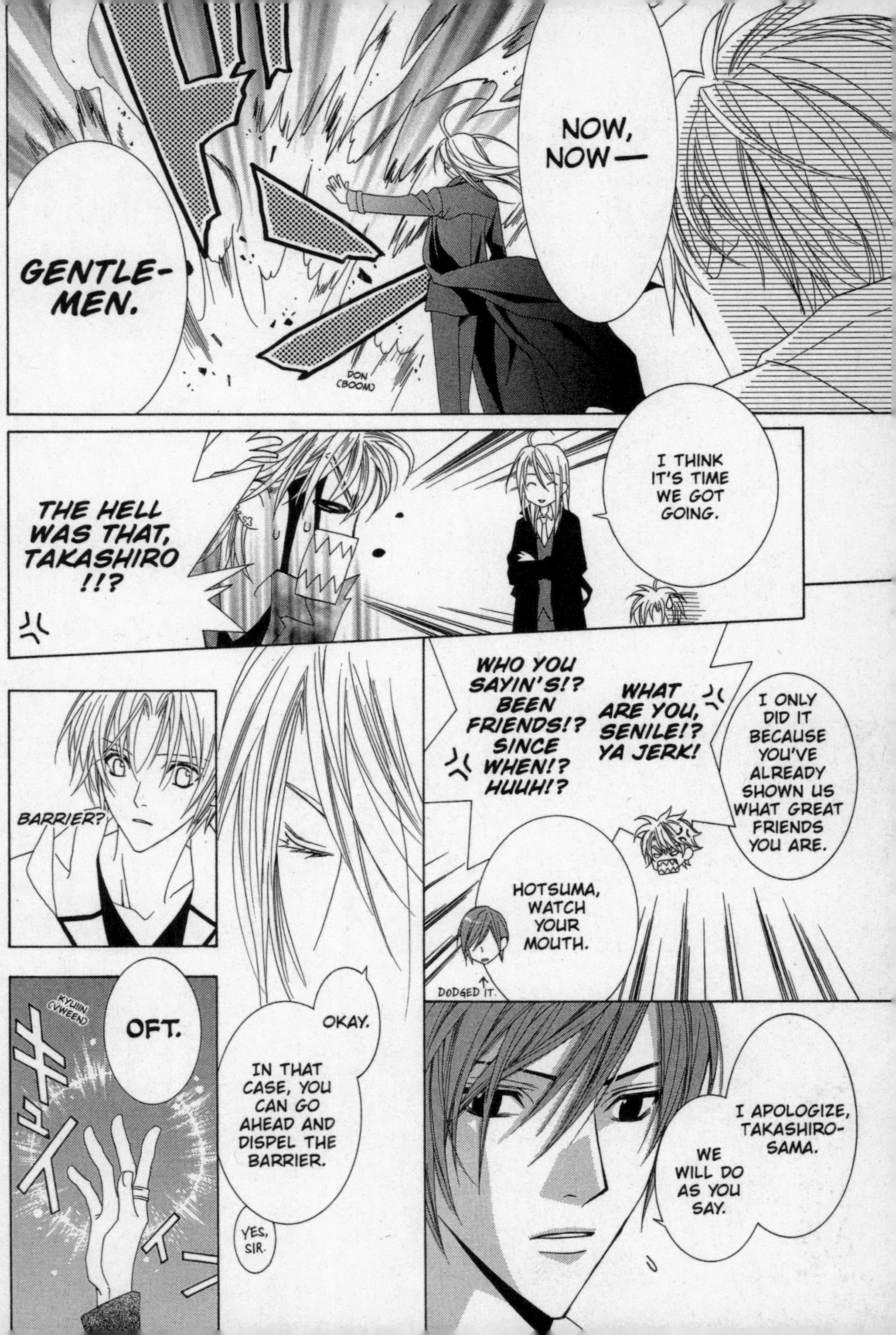
NOW, NOW—
GENTLE-MEN.
DON (BOOM)
I THINK IT'S TIME WE GOT GOING.
THE HELL WAS THAT, TAKASHIRO!!?
I ONLY DID IT BECAUSE YOU'VE ALREADY SHOWN US WHAT GREAT FRIENDS YOU ARE.
WHAT ARE YOU, SENILE!? YA JERK!
WHO YOU SAYIN'S!? BEEN FRIENDS!? SINCE WHEN!? HUUH!?
HOTSUMA, WATCH YOUR MOUTH.
DODGED IT.
BARRIER?
I APOLOGIZE, TAKASHIRO-SAMA.
WE WILL DO AS YOU SAY.
OKAY.
IN THAT CASE, YOU CAN GO AHEAD AND DISPEL THE BARRIER.
YES, SIR.
OFT.
KYUIIN (VWEEN)

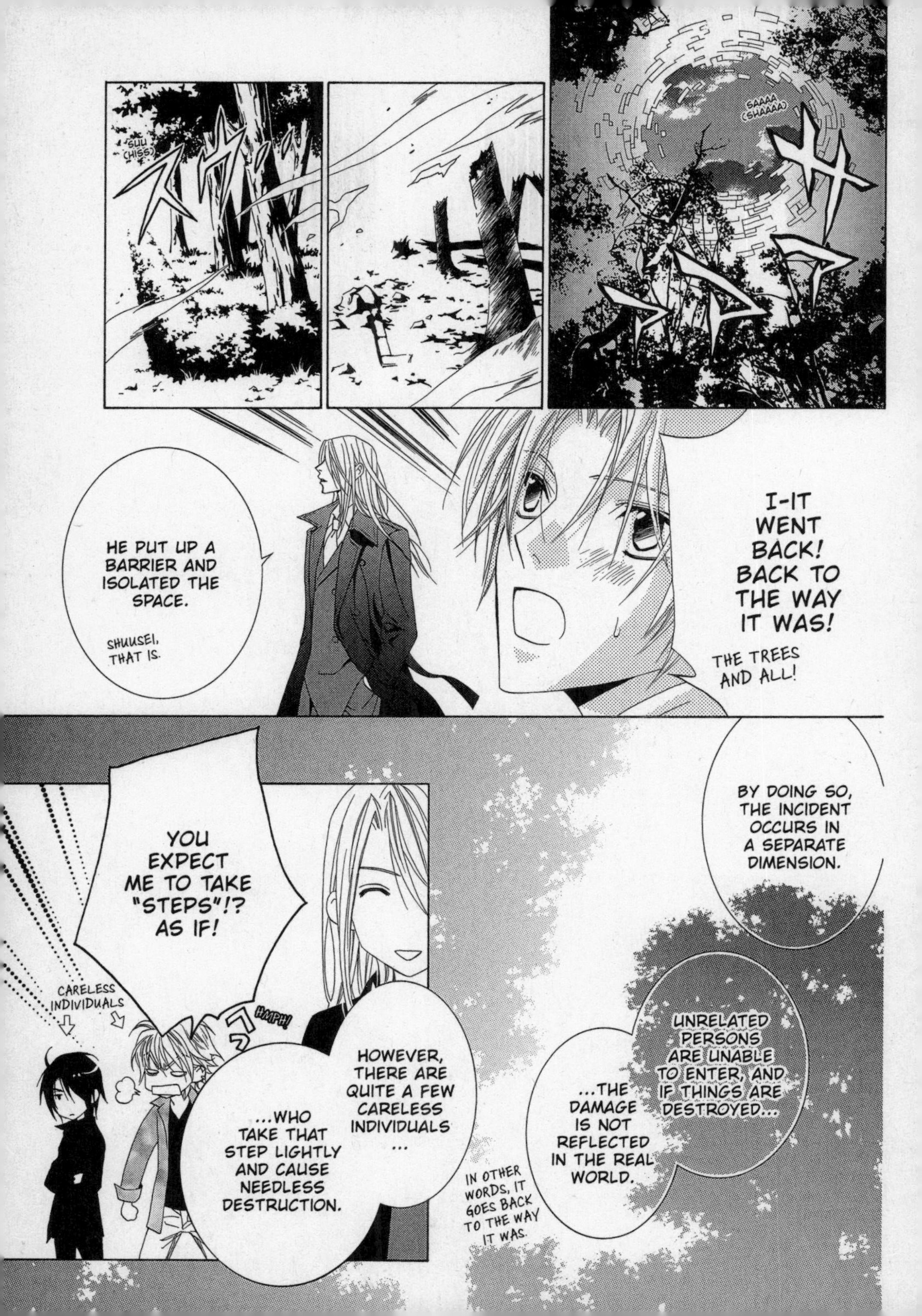
SAAAA (SHAAAA)
SUU (CHISS)
I-IT WENT BACK! BACK TO THE WAY IT WAS!
THE TREES AND ALL!
HE PUT UP A BARRIER AND ISOLATED THE SPACE.
SHUUSEI, THAT IS.
BY DOING SO, THE INCIDENT OCCURS IN A SEPARATE DIMENSION.
UNRELATED PERSONS ARE UNABLE TO ENTER, AND IF THINGS ARE DESTROYED...
...THE DAMAGE IS NOT REFLECTED IN THE REAL WORLD.
IN OTHER WORDS, IT GOES BACK TO THE WAY IT WAS.
HOWEVER, THERE ARE QUITE A FEW CARELESS INDIVIDUALS ...
...WHO TAKE THAT STEP LIGHTLY AND CAUSE NEEDLESS DESTRUCTION.
HMPH!
YOU EXPECT ME TO TAKE "STEPS"!? AS IF!
CARELESS INDIVIDUALS

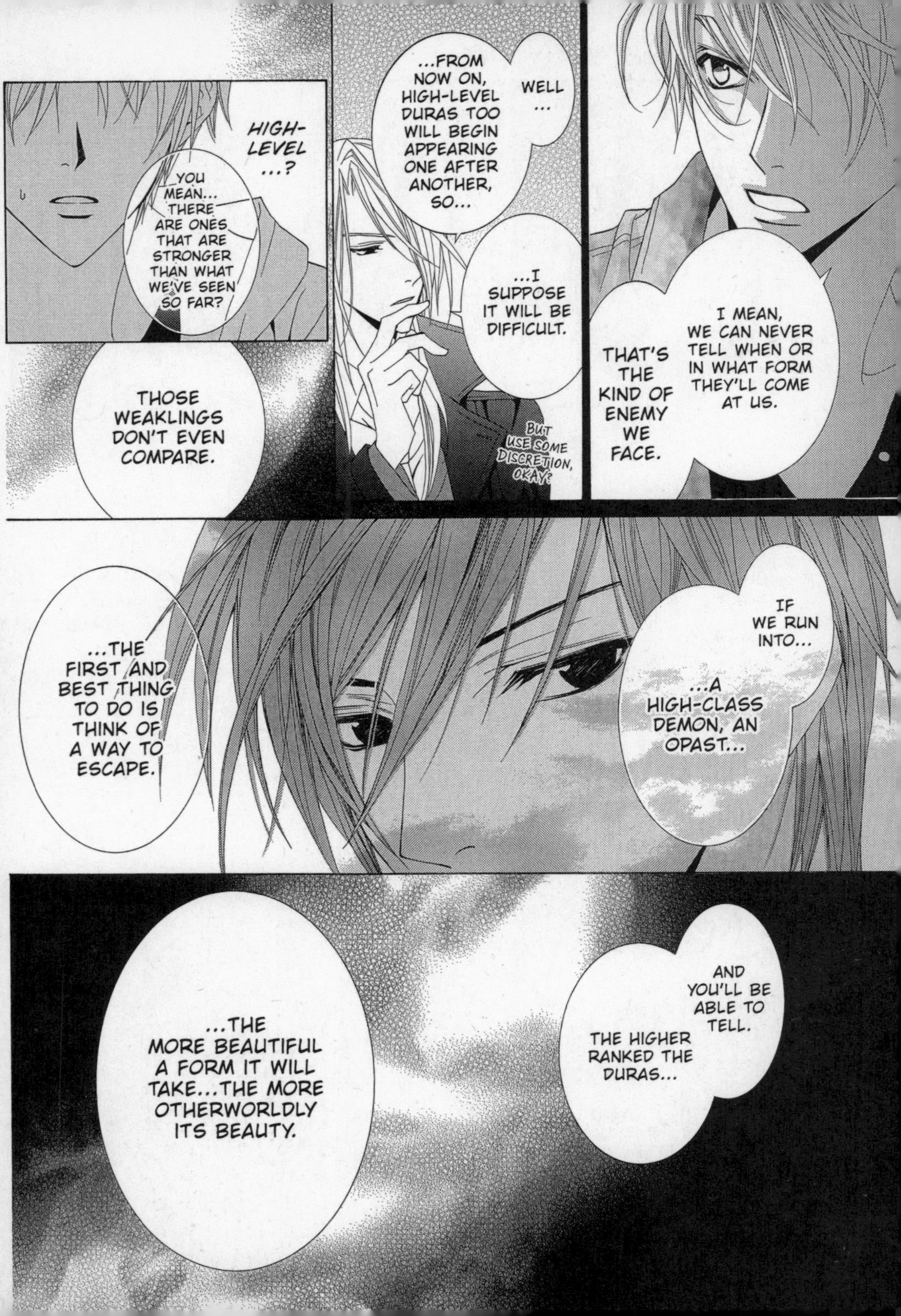
I MEAN, WE CAN NEVER TELL WHEN OR IN WHAT FORM THEY'LL COME AT US.
THAT'S THE KIND OF ENEMY WE FACE.
WELL ...
...FROM NOW ON, HIGH-LEVEL DURAS TOO WILL BEGIN APPEARING ONE AFTER ANOTHER, SO...
...I SUPPOSE IT WILL BE DIFFICULT.
BUT USE SOME DISCRETION, OKAY?
HIGH-LEVEL ...?
YOU MEAN... THERE ARE ONES THAT ARE STRONGER THAN WHAT WE'VE SEEN SO FAR?
THOSE WEAKLINGS DON'T EVEN COMPARE.
IF WE RUN INTO...
...A HIGH-CLASS DEMON, AN OPAST...
...THE FIRST AND BEST THING TO DO IS THINK OF A WAY TO ESCAPE.
AND YOU'LL BE ABLE TO TELL.
THE HIGHER RANKED THE DURAS...
...THE MORE BEAUTIFUL A FORM IT WILL TAKE...THE MORE OTHERWORLDLY ITS BEAUTY.

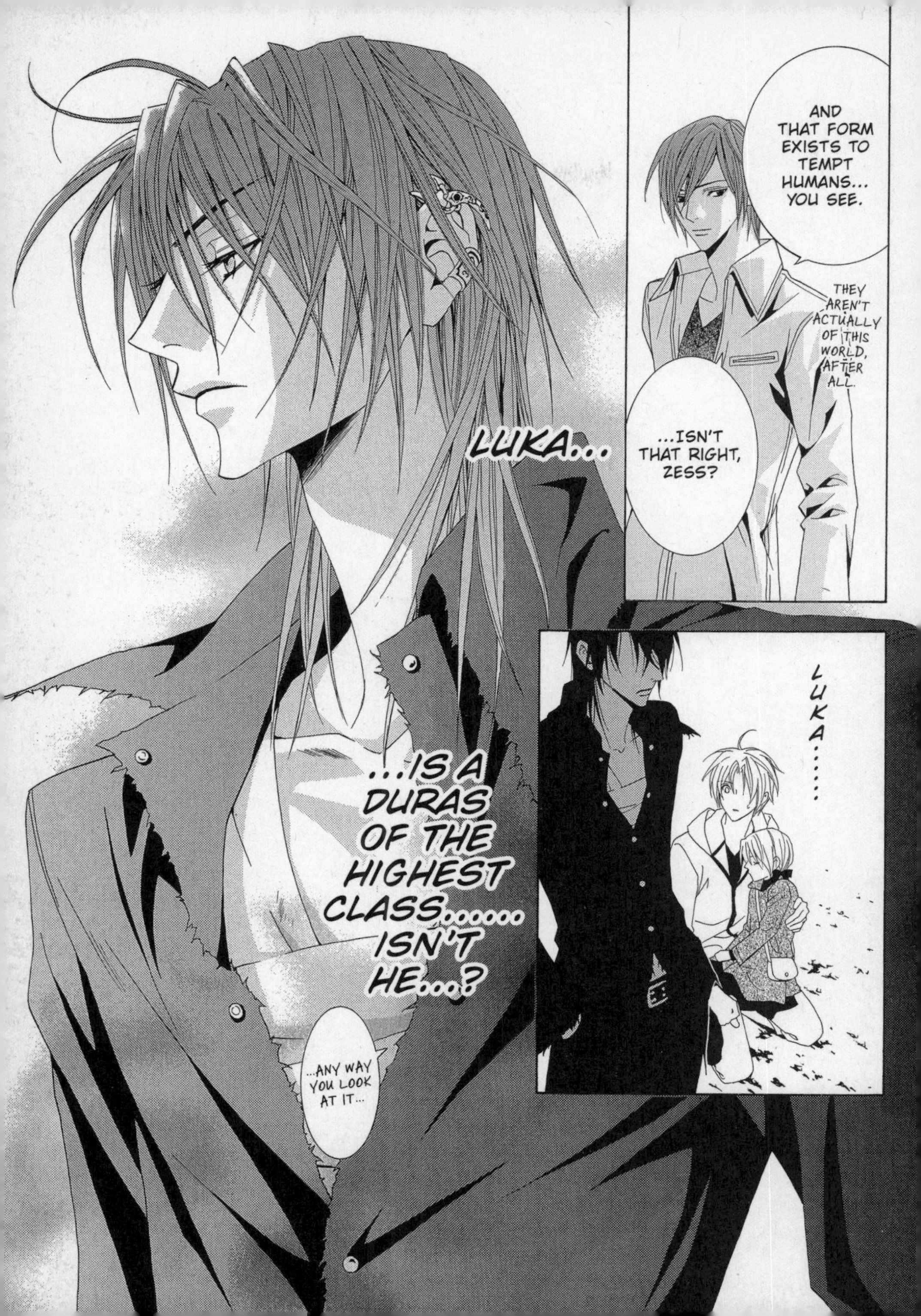
AND THAT FORM EXISTS TO TEMPT HUMANS... YOU SEE.
THEY AREN'T ACTUALLY OF THIS WORLD, AFTER ALL.
...ISN'T THAT RIGHT, ZESS?
LUKA...
LUKA......
...IS A DURAS OF THE HIGHEST CLASS....... ISN'T HE...?
...ANY WAY YOU LOOK AT IT...

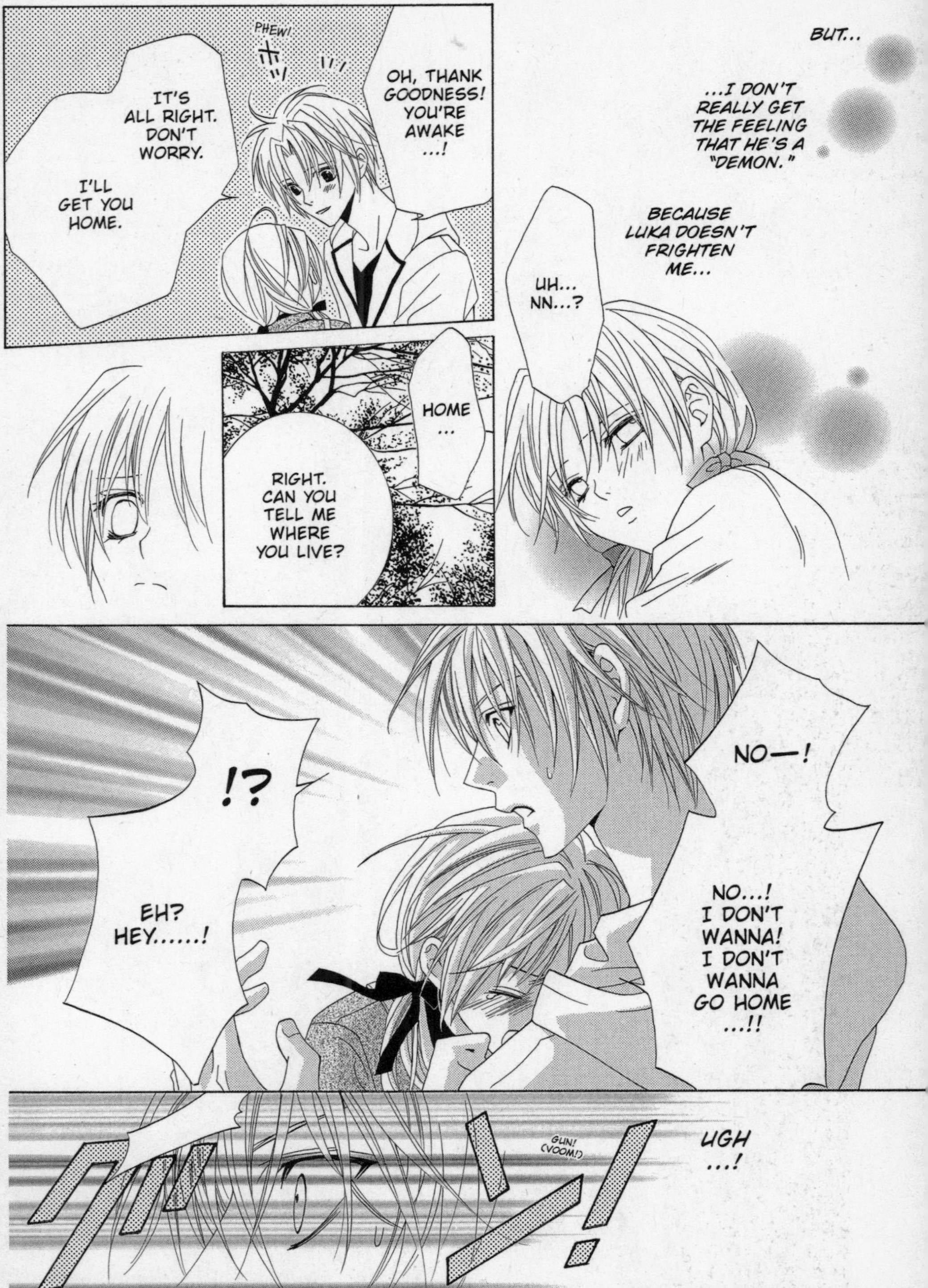
BUT...
...I DON'T REALLY GET THE FEELING THAT HE'S A "DEMON."
BECAUSE LUKA DOESN'T FRIGHTEN ME...
PHEW!
OH, THANK GOODNESS! YOU'RE AWAKE ...!
IT'S ALL RIGHT. DON'T WORRY.
I'LL GET YOU HOME.
UH... NN...?
HOME ...
RIGHT. CAN YOU TELL ME WHERE YOU LIVE?
NO—!
NO...! I DON'T WANNA! I DON'T WANNA GO HOME ...!!
!?
EH? HEY......!
UGH ...!
GUN! (VOOM!)

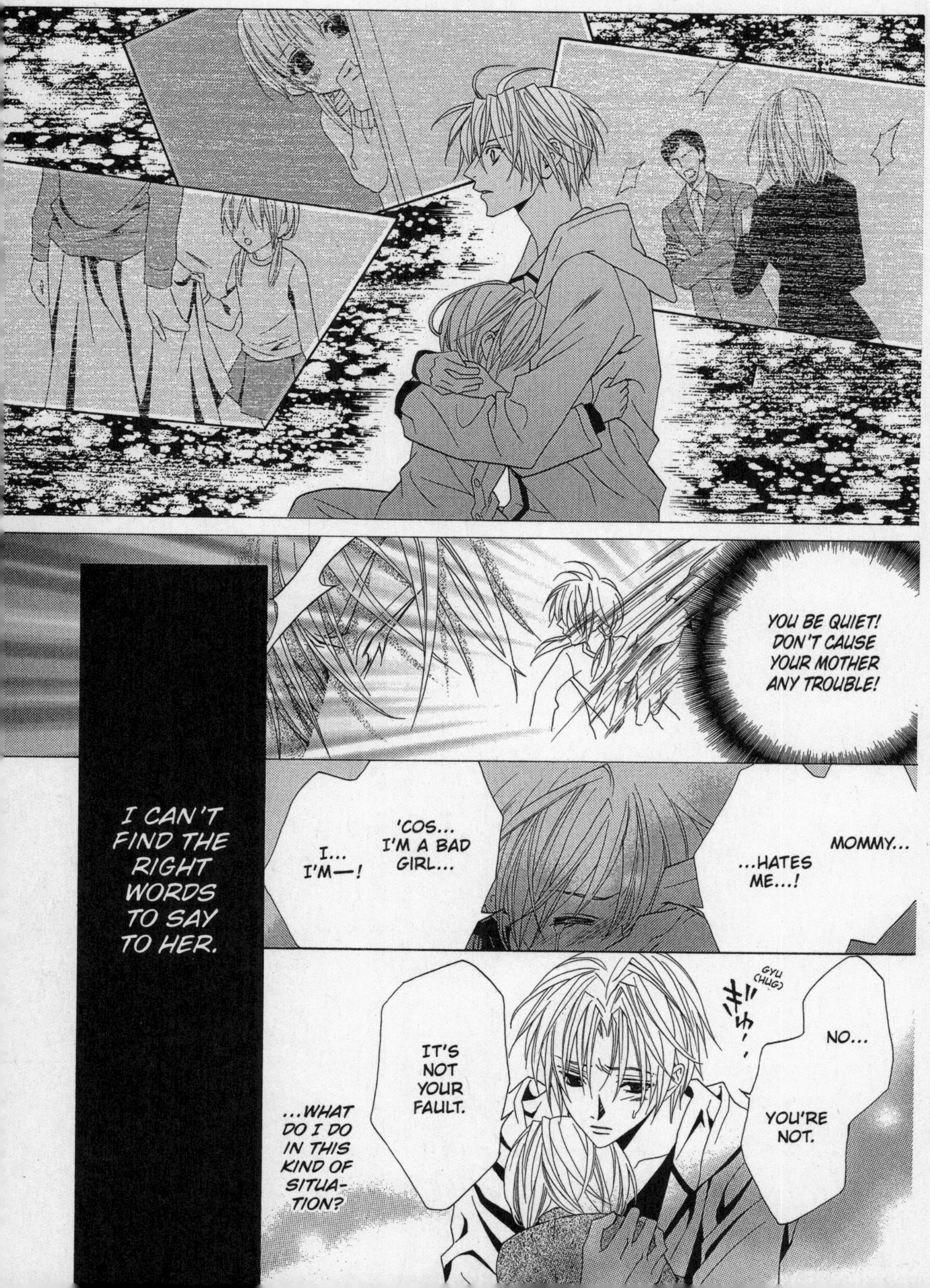
YOU BE QUIET! DON'T CAUSE YOUR MOTHER ANY TROUBLE!
MOMMY...
...HATES ME...!
'COS... I'M A BAD GIRL...
I... I'M—!
I CAN'T FIND THE RIGHT WORDS TO SAY TO HER.
NO...
YOU'RE NOT.
GYU (HUG)
IT'S NOT YOUR FAULT.
...WHAT DO I DO IN THIS KIND OF SITUATION?

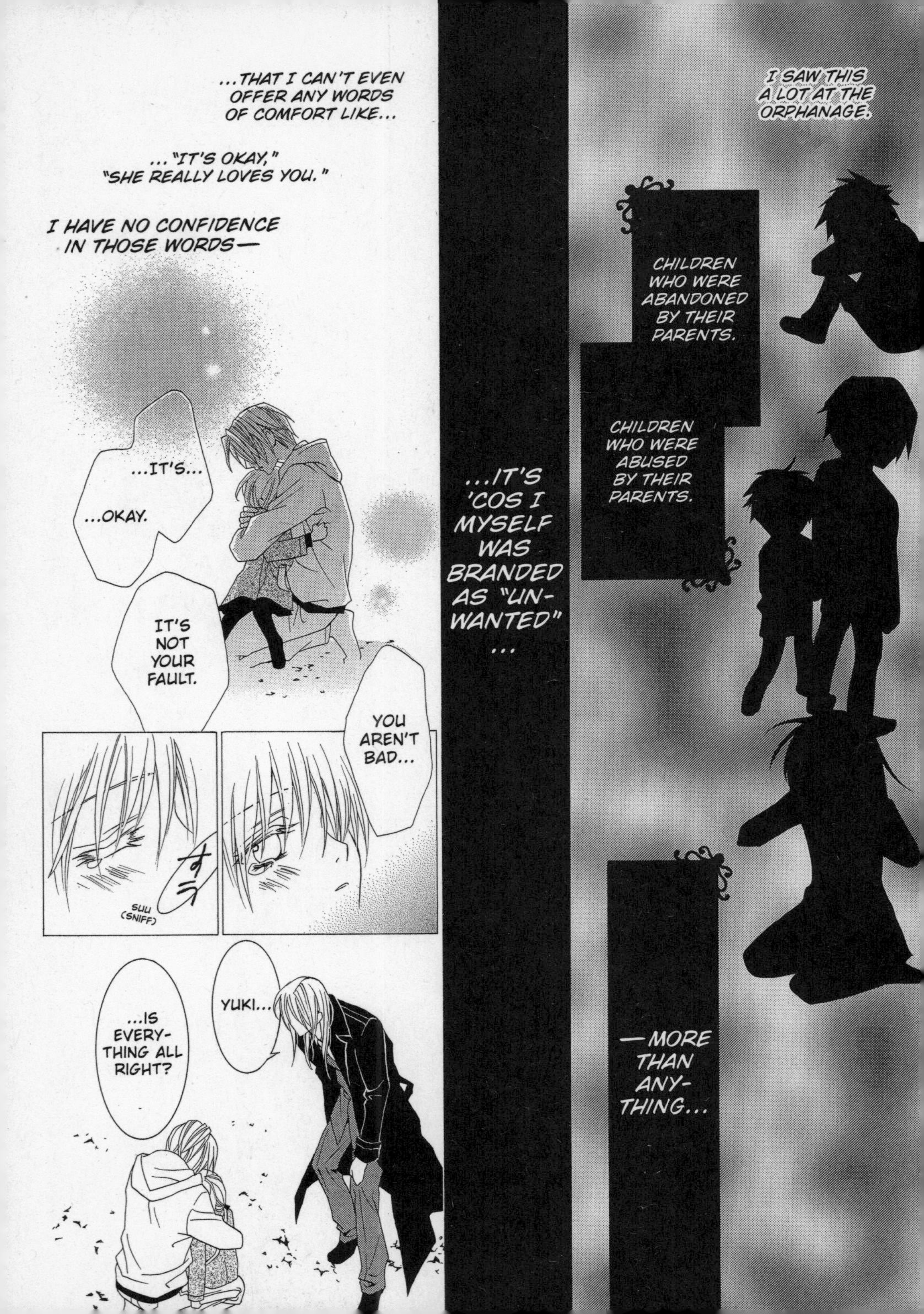
I SAW THIS A LOT AT THE ORPHANAGE.
CHILDREN WHO WERE ABANDONED BY THEIR PARENTS.
CHILDREN WHO WERE ABUSED BY THEIR PARENTS.
—MORE THAN ANYTHING...
...IT'S 'COS I MYSELF WAS BRANDED AS "UN-WANTED"...
...THAT I CAN'T EVEN OFFER ANY WORDS OF COMFORT LIKE...
..."IT'S OKAY," "SHE REALLY LOVES YOU."
I HAVE NO CONFIDENCE IN THOSE WORDS—
...IT'S...
...OKAY.
IT'S NOT YOUR FAULT.
YOU AREN'T BAD...
SUU (SNIFF)
YUKI...
...IS EVERYTHING ALL RIGHT?

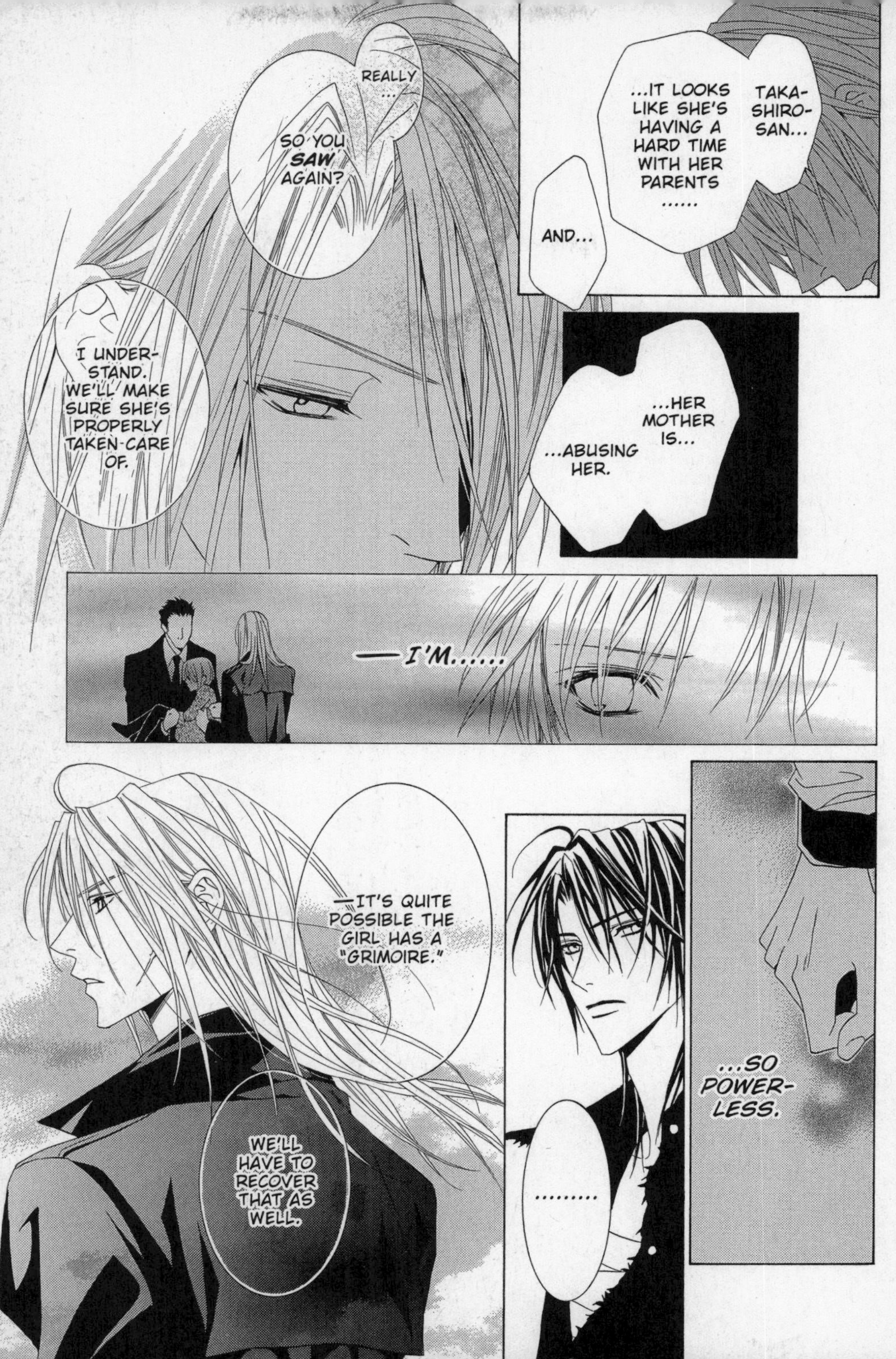
TAKA-SHIRO-SAN...
...IT LOOKS LIKE SHE'S HAVING A HARD TIME WITH HER PARENTS ......
AND...
REALLY ...
SO YOU SAW AGAIN?
...HER MOTHER IS...
...ABUSING HER.
I UNDER-STAND. WE'LL MAKE SURE SHE'S PROPERLY TAKEN-CARE OF.
—I'M......
...SO POWER-LESS.
....
—IT'S QUITE POSSIBLE THE GIRL HAS A "GRIMOIRE."
WE'LL HAVE TO RECOVER THAT AS WELL.

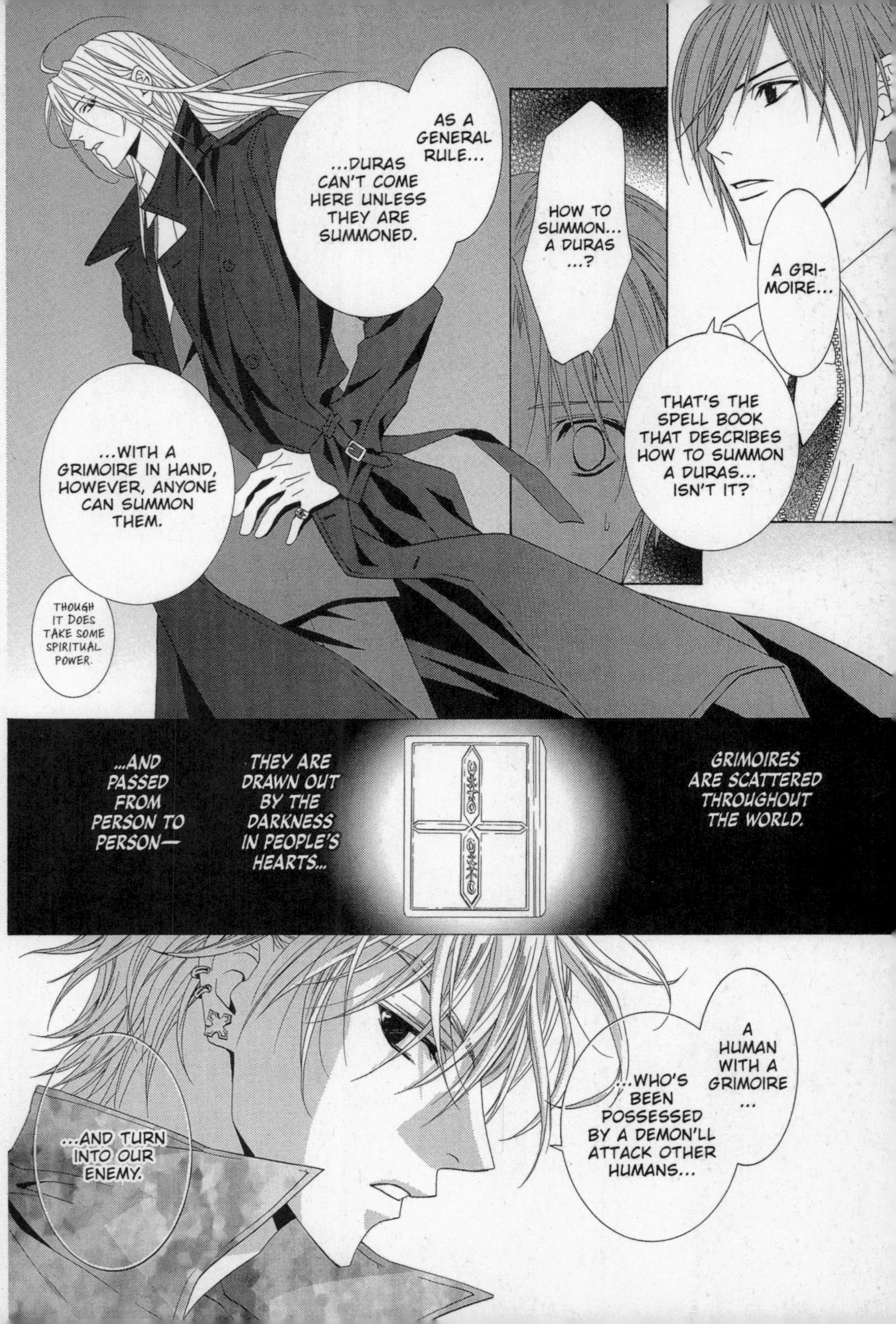
A GRI-MOIRE...
THAT'S THE SPELL BOOK THAT DESCRIBES HOW TO SUMMON A DURAS... ISN'T IT?
HOW TO SUMMON... A DURAS ...?
AS A GENERAL RULE...
...DURAS CAN'T COME HERE UNLESS THEY ARE SUMMONED.
...WITH A GRIMOIRE IN HAND, HOWEVER, ANYONE CAN SUMMON THEM.
THOUGH IT DOES TAKE SOME SPIRITUAL POWER.
GRIMOIRES ARE SCATTERED THROUGHOUT THE WORLD.
THEY ARE DRAWN OUT BY THE DARKNESS IN PEOPLE'S HEARTS...
...AND PASSED FROM PERSON TO PERSON—
A HUMAN WITH A GRIMOIRE ...
...WHO'S BEEN POSSESSED BY A DEMON'LL ATTACK OTHER HUMANS...
...AND TURN INTO OUR ENEMY.

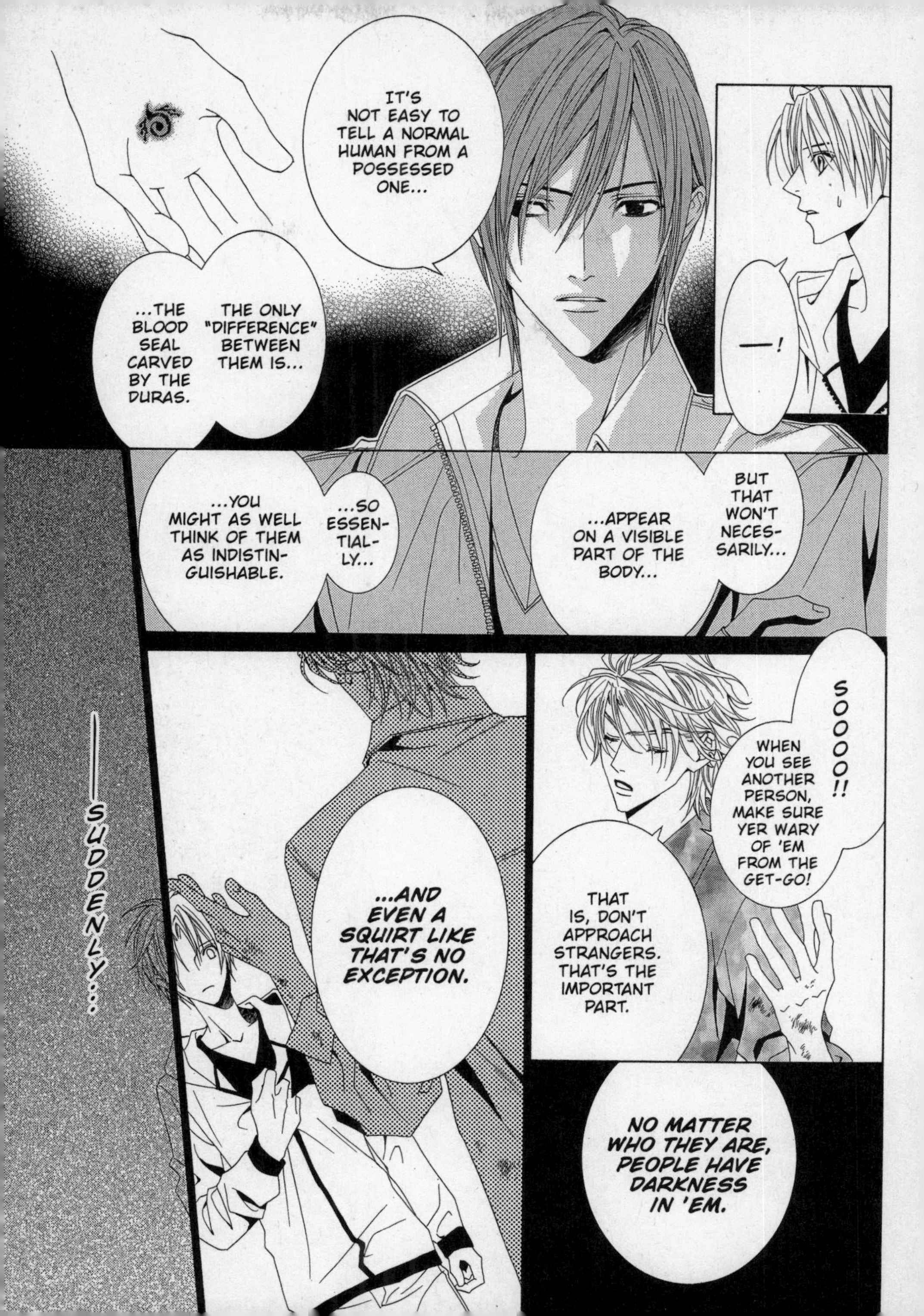
IT'S NOT EASY TO TELL A NORMAL HUMAN FROM A POSSESSED ONE...
—!
THE ONLY "DIFFERENCE" BETWEEN THEM IS...
...THE BLOOD SEAL CARVED BY THE DURAS.
BUT THAT WON'T NECES-SARILY...
...APPEAR ON A VISIBLE PART OF THE BODY...
...SO ESSEN-TIAL-LY...
...YOU MIGHT AS WELL THINK OF THEM AS INDISTIN-GUISHABLE.
SOOOOO!!
WHEN YOU SEE ANOTHER PERSON, MAKE SURE YER WARY OF 'EM FROM THE GET-GO!
THAT IS, DON'T APPROACH STRANGERS. THAT'S THE IMPORTANT PART.
NO MATTER WHO THEY ARE, PEOPLE HAVE DARKNESS IN 'EM.
...AND EVEN A SQUIRT LIKE THAT'S NO EXCEPTION.
—SUDDENLY...

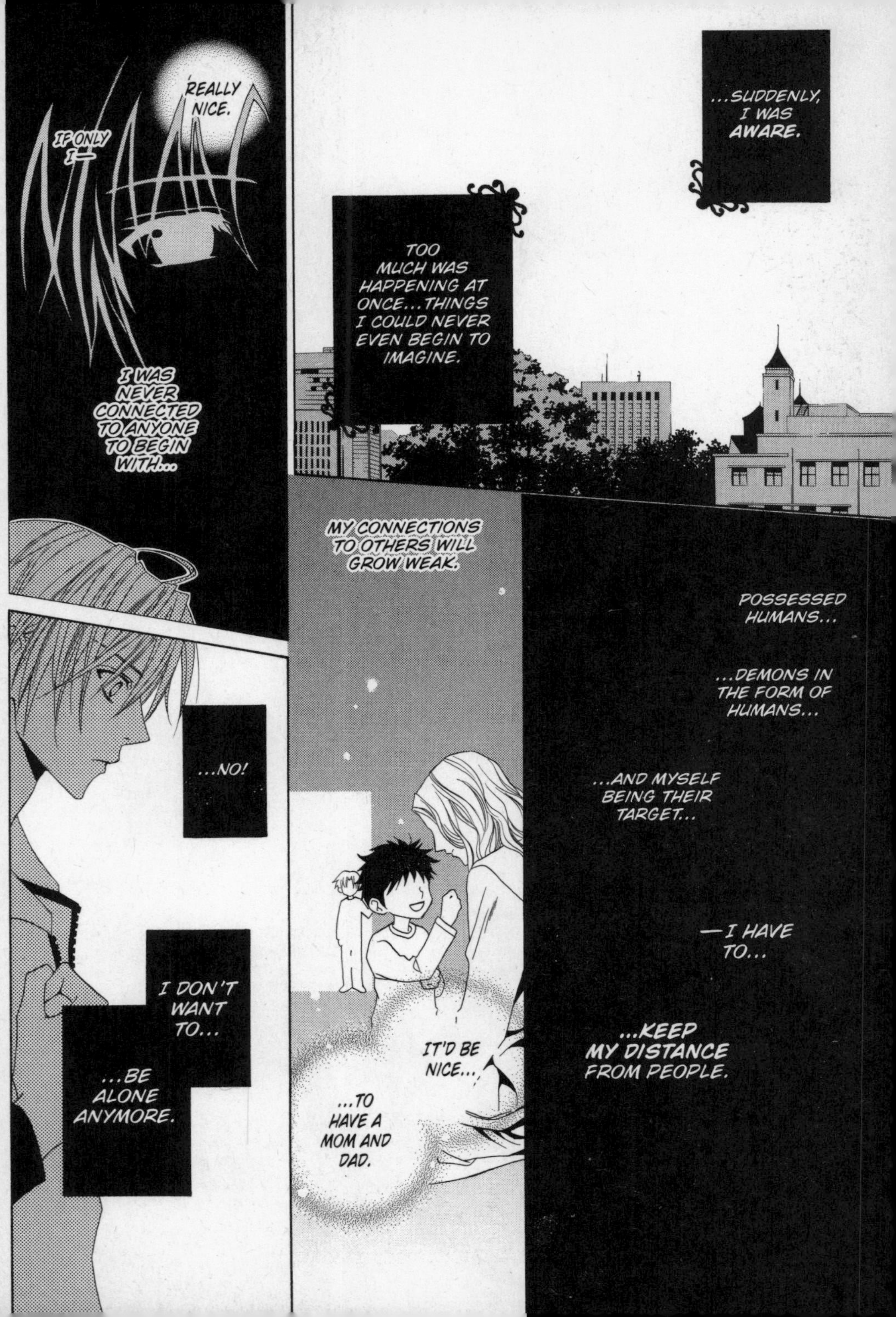

...SUDDENLY, I WAS AWARE.
TOO MUCH WAS HAPPENING AT ONCE...THINGS I COULD NEVER EVEN BEGIN TO IMAGINE.
POSSESSED HUMANS...
...DEMONS IN THE FORM OF HUMANS...
...AND MYSELF BEING THEIR TARGET...
—I HAVE TO...
...KEEP MY DISTANCE FROM PEOPLE.
MY CONNECTIONS TO OTHERS WILL GROW WEAK.
IT'D BE NICE...
...TO HAVE A MOM AND DAD.
REALLY NICE.
IF ONLY I—
I WAS NEVER CONNECTED TO ANYONE TO BEGIN WITH...
...NO!
I DON'T WANT TO...
...BE ALONE ANYMORE.

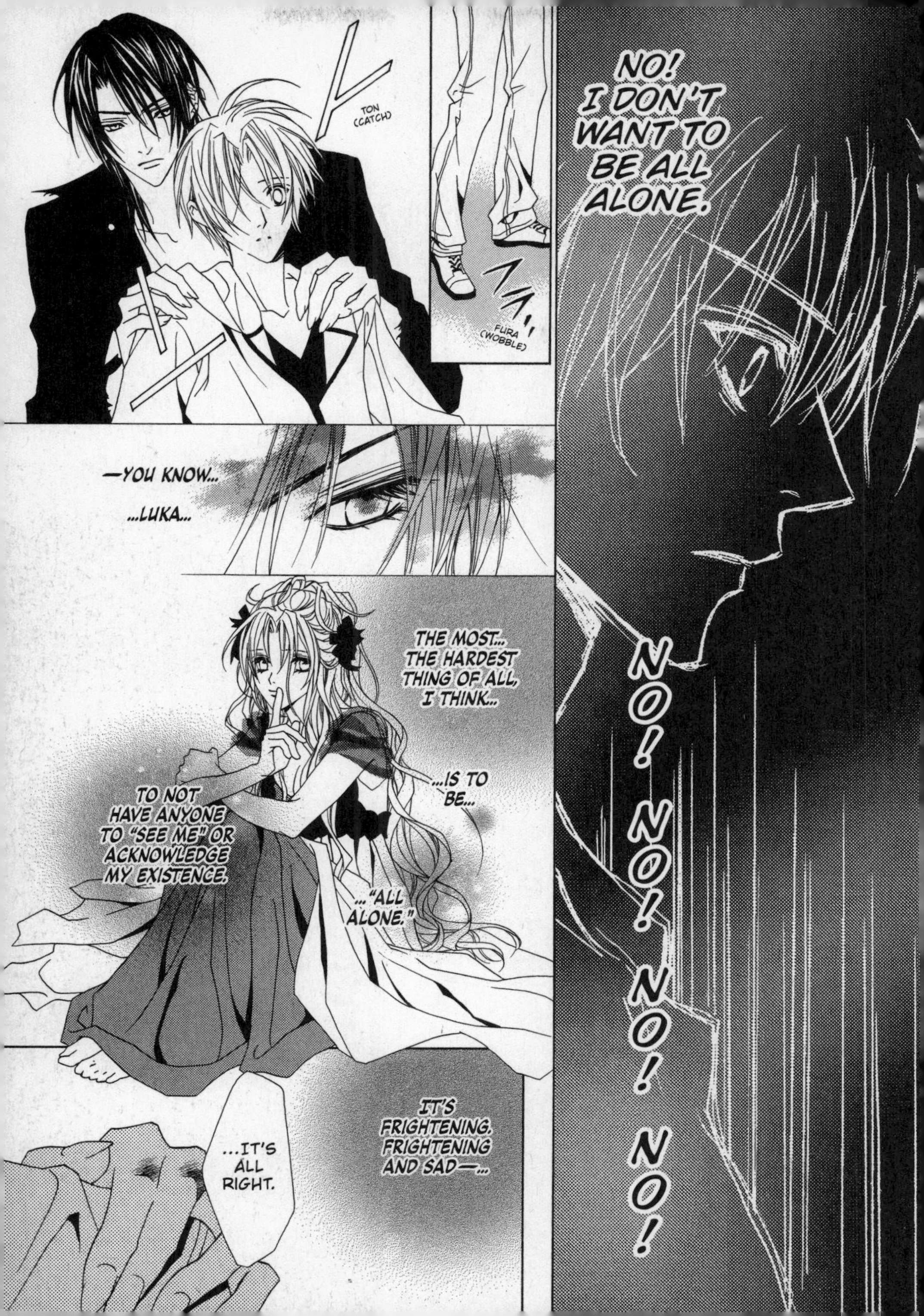
FURA (WOBBLE)
TON (CATCH)
—YOU KNOW...
...LUKA...
THE MOST... THE HARDEST THING OF ALL, I THINK...
...IS TO BE...
..."ALL ALONE."
TO NOT HAVE ANYONE TO "SEE ME" OR ACKNOWLEDGE MY EXISTENCE.
IT'S FRIGHTENING. FRIGHTENING AND SAD—...
...IT'S ALL RIGHT.
NO! I DON'T WANT TO BE ALL ALONE.
NO! NO! NO! NO! NO! NO!

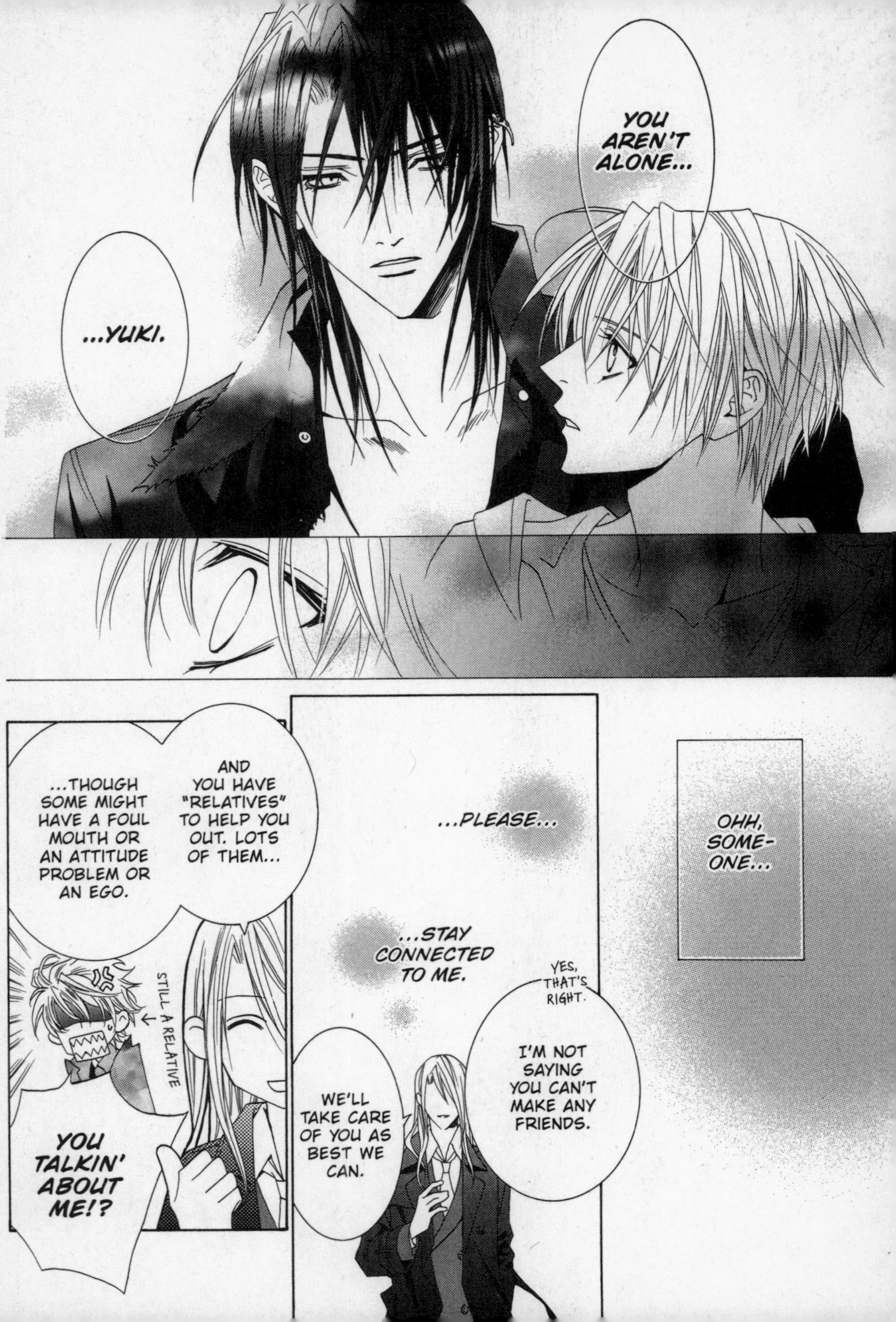
YOU AREN'T ALONE...
...YUKI.
OHH, SOME-ONE...
...PLEASE...
...STAY CONNECTED TO ME.
AND YOU HAVE "RELATIVES" TO HELP YOU OUT. LOTS OF THEM...
...THOUGH SOME MIGHT HAVE A FOUL MOUTH OR AN ATTITUDE PROBLEM OR AN EGO.
STILL A RELATIVE
YOU TALKIN' ABOUT ME!?
YES, THAT'S RIGHT.
I'M NOT SAYING YOU CAN'T MAKE ANY FRIENDS.
WE'LL TAKE CARE OF YOU AS BEST WE CAN.

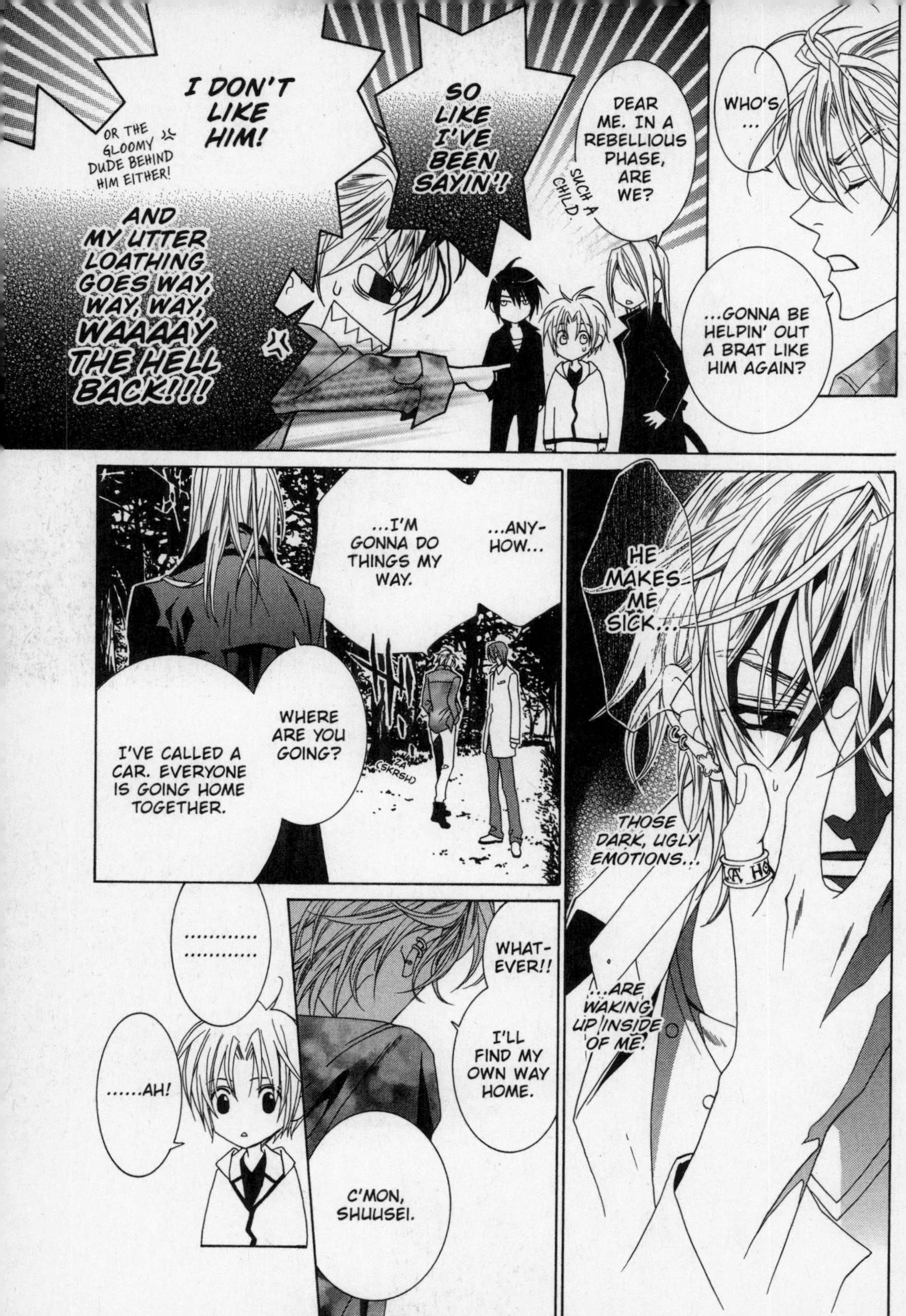
WHO'S...
...GONNA BE HELPIN' OUT A BRAT LIKE HIM AGAIN?
DEAR ME. IN A REBELLIOUS PHASE, ARE WE?
SUCH A CHILD.
SO LIKE I'VE BEEN SAYIN'!
I DON'T LIKE HIM!
OR THE GLOOMY DUDE BEHIND HIM EITHER!
AND MY UTTER LOATHING GOES WAY, WAY, WAY, WAAAAY THE HELL BACK!!!
HE MAKES ME SICK...
THOSE DARK, UGLY EMOTIONS...
...ARE WAKING UP INSIDE OF ME.
...ANY-HOW...
...I'M GONNA DO THINGS MY WAY.
WHERE ARE YOU GOING?
I'VE CALLED A CAR. EVERYONE IS GOING HOME TOGETHER.
ZA (SKRSH)
WHAT-EVER!!
I'LL FIND MY OWN WAY HOME.
C'MON, SHUUSEI.
....
....
......AH!

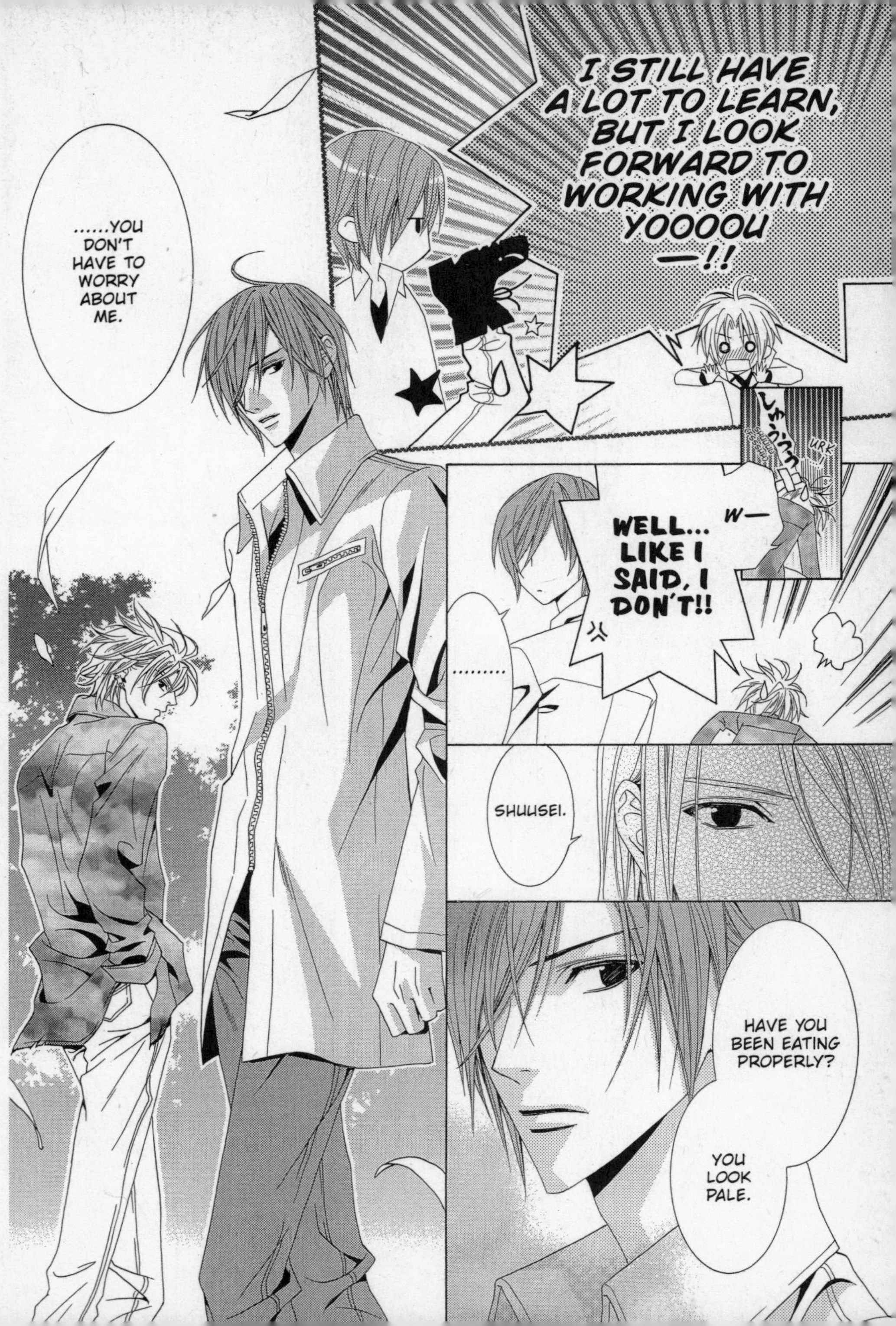

I STILL HAVE A LOT TO LEARN, BUT I LOOK FORWARD TO WORKING WITH YOOOOU—!!
URK
W—
WELL... LIKE I SAID, I DON'T!!
....
SHUUSEI.
HAVE YOU BEEN EATING PROPERLY?
YOU LOOK PALE.
......YOU DON'T HAVE TO WORRY ABOUT ME.

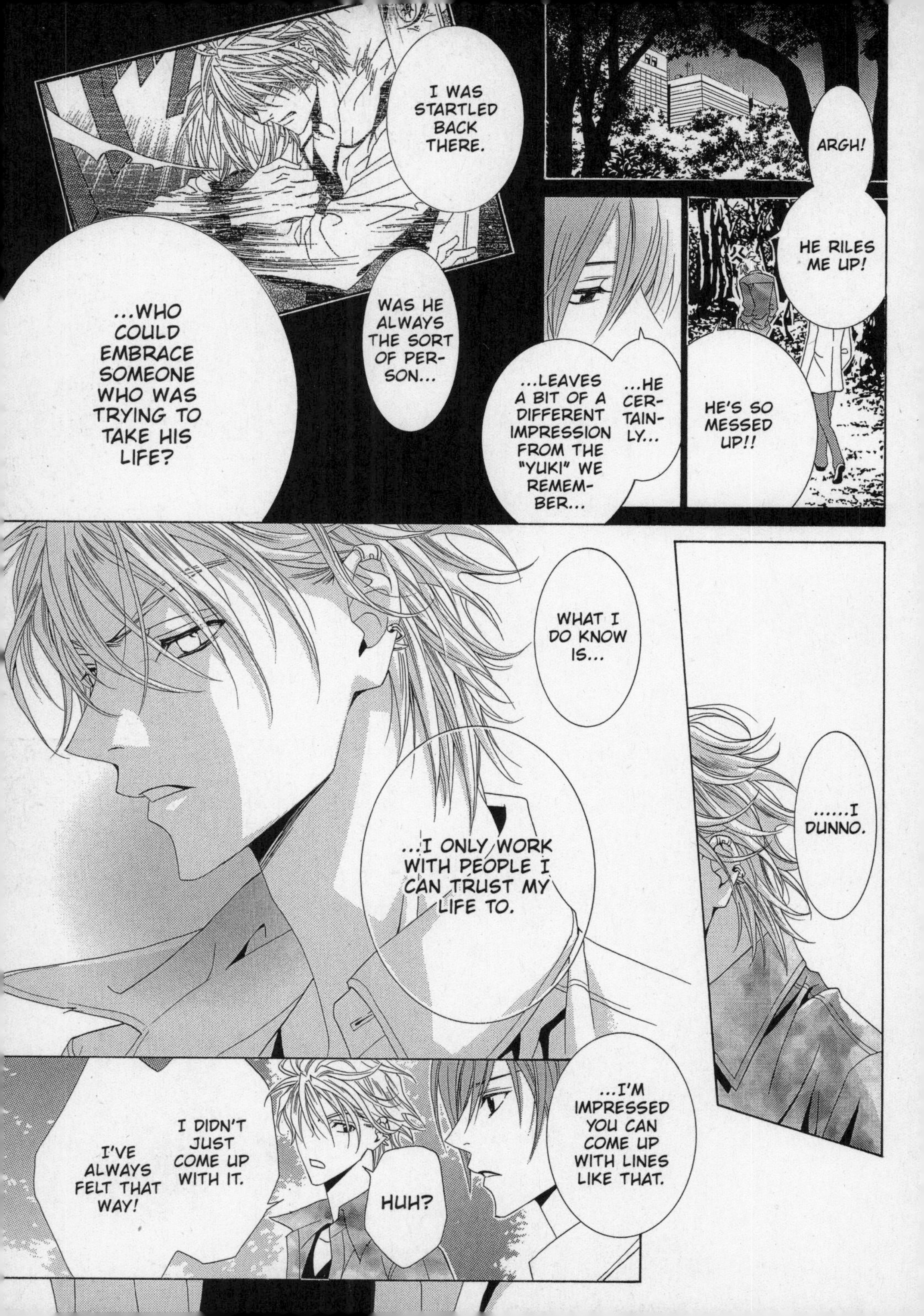
ARGH!
HE RILES ME UP!
HE'S SO MESSED UP!!
...HE CERTAINLY...
...LEAVES A BIT OF A DIFFERENT IMPRESSION FROM THE "YUKI" WE REMEMBER...
I WAS STARTLED BACK THERE.
WAS HE ALWAYS THE SORT OF PERSON...
...WHO COULD EMBRACE SOMEONE WHO WAS TRYING TO TAKE HIS LIFE?
......I DUNNO.
WHAT I DO KNOW IS...
...I ONLY WORK WITH PEOPLE I CAN TRUST MY LIFE TO.
...I'M IMPRESSED YOU CAN COME UP WITH LINES LIKE THAT.
HUH?
I DIDN'T JUST COME UP WITH IT.
I'VE ALWAYS FELT THAT WAY!

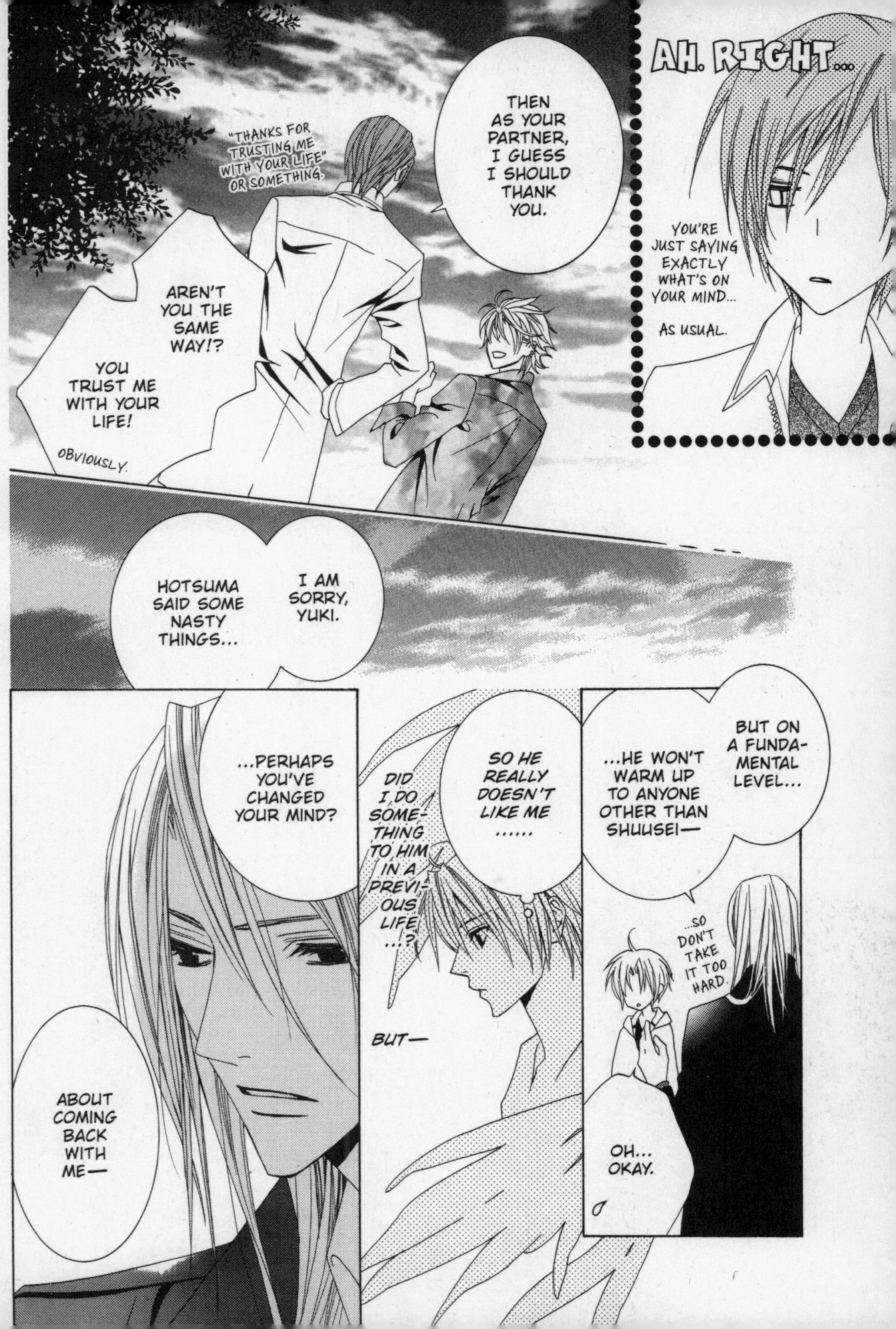
AH. RIGHT...
YOU'RE JUST SAYING EXACTLY WHAT'S ON YOUR MIND...
AS USUAL.
THEN AS YOUR PARTNER, I GUESS I SHOULD THANK YOU.
"THANKS FOR TRUSTING ME WITH YOUR LIFE" OR SOMETHING.
AREN'T YOU THE SAME WAY!?
YOU TRUST ME WITH YOUR LIFE!
OBVIOUSLY.
I AM SORRY, YUKI.
HOTSUMA SAID SOME NASTY THINGS...
BUT ON A FUNDA-MENTAL LEVEL...
...HE WON'T WARM UP TO ANYONE OTHER THAN SHUUSEI—
...SO DON'T TAKE IT TOO HARD.
OH... OKAY.
SO HE REALLY DOESN'T LIKE ME ......
DID I DO SOME-THING TO HIM IN A PREVI-OUS LIFE ...?
BUT—
...PERHAPS YOU'VE CHANGED YOUR MIND?
ABOUT COMING BACK WITH ME—

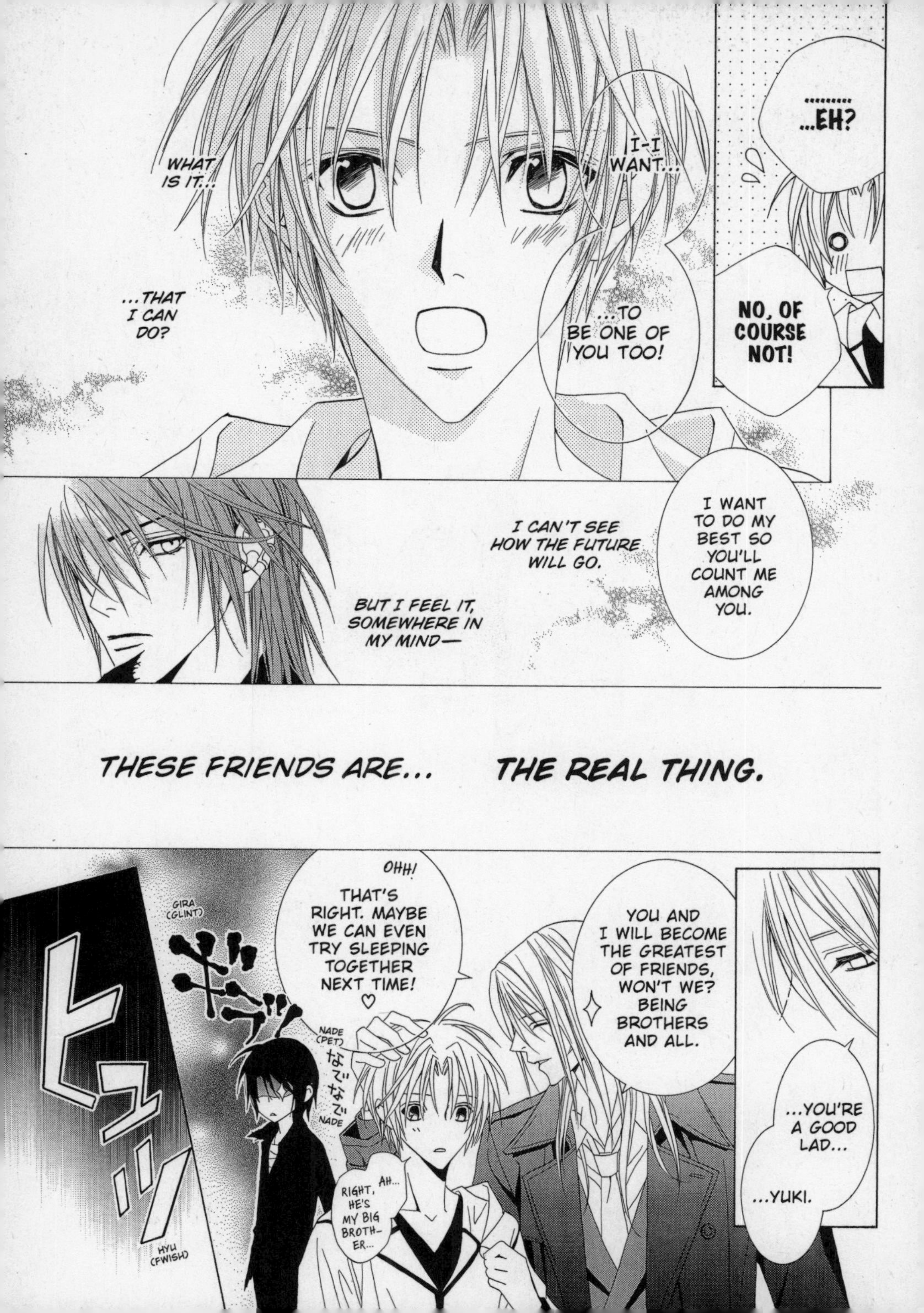

....
...EH?
NO, OF COURSE NOT!
I-I WANT...
...TO BE ONE OF YOU TOO!
WHAT IS IT...
...THAT I CAN DO?
I WANT TO DO MY BEST SO YOU'LL COUNT ME AMONG YOU.
I CAN'T SEE HOW THE FUTURE WILL GO.
BUT I FEEL IT, SOMEWHERE IN MY MIND—
THESE FRIENDS ARE...
THE REAL THING.
...YOU'RE A GOOD LAD...
...YUKI.
YOU AND I WILL BECOME THE GREATEST OF FRIENDS, WON'T WE? BEING BROTHERS AND ALL.
OHH!
THAT'S RIGHT. MAYBE WE CAN EVEN TRY SLEEPING TOGETHER NEXT TIME! ♡
AH...
RIGHT, HE'S MY BIG BROTH-ER...
NADE (PET)
なでなで
NADE
GIRA (GLINT)
ギラッ
ヒュッ
HYU (FWISH)

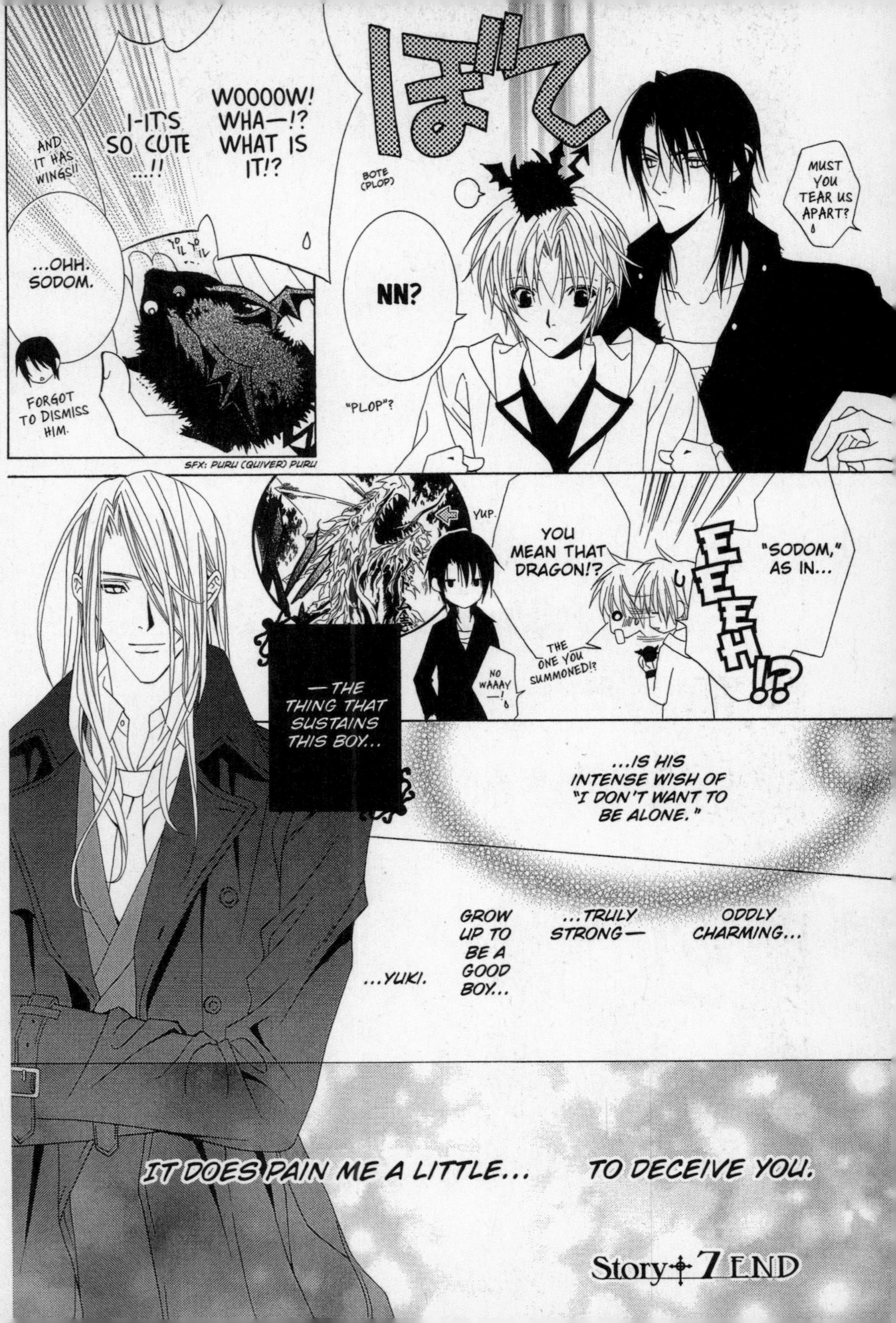
MUST YOU TEAR US APART?
ぼて
BOTE (PLOP)
NN?
"PLOP"?
WOOOOW! WHA—!? WHAT IS IT!?
I-IT'S SO CUTE ...!!
AND IT HAS WINGS!!
...OHH. SODOM.
FORGOT TO DISMISS HIM.
SFX: PURU (QUIVER) PURU
"SODOM," AS IN...
EEEEH!?
THE ONE YOU SUMMONED!?
YOU MEAN THAT DRAGON!?
YUP.
NO WAAAY—!
—THE THING THAT SUSTAINS THIS BOY...
...IS HIS INTENSE WISH OF "I DON'T WANT TO BE ALONE."
ODDLY CHARMING...
...TRULY STRONG—
GROW UP TO BE A GOOD BOY...
...YUKI.
IT DOES PAIN ME A LITTLE...
TO DECEIVE YOU.
Story 7 END

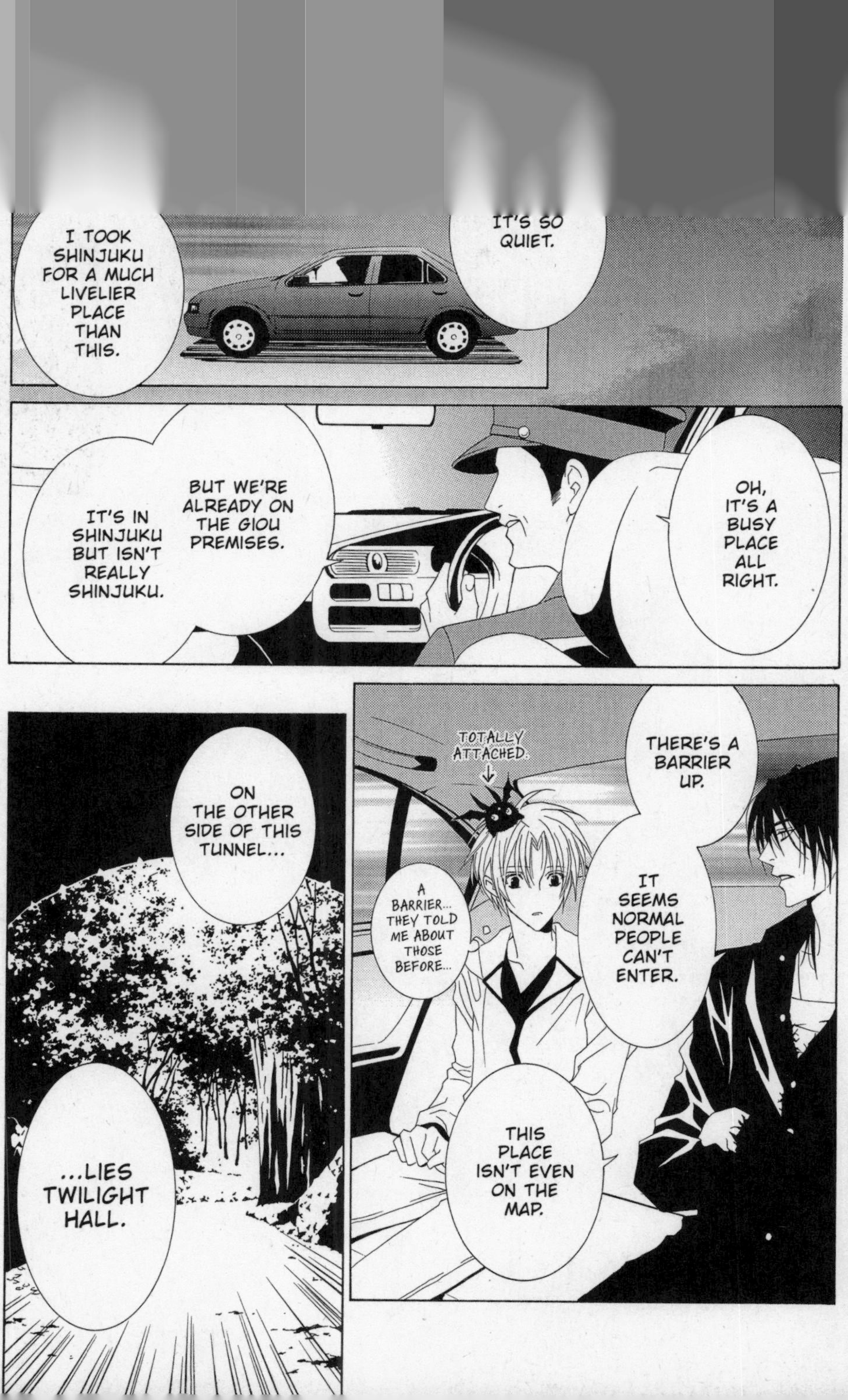
IT'S SO QUIET.
I TOOK SHINJUKU FOR A MUCH LIVELIER PLACE THAN THIS.
OH, IT'S A BUSY PLACE ALL RIGHT.
BUT WE'RE ALREADY ON THE GIOU PREMISES.
IT'S IN SHINJUKU BUT ISN'T REALLY SHINJUKU.
THERE'S A BARRIER UP.
IT SEEMS NORMAL PEOPLE CAN'T ENTER.
TOTALLY ATTACHED.
A BARRIER... THEY TOLD ME ABOUT THOSE BEFORE...
THIS PLACE ISN'T EVEN ON THE MAP.
ON THE OTHER SIDE OF THIS TUNNEL...
...LIES TWILIGHT HALL.

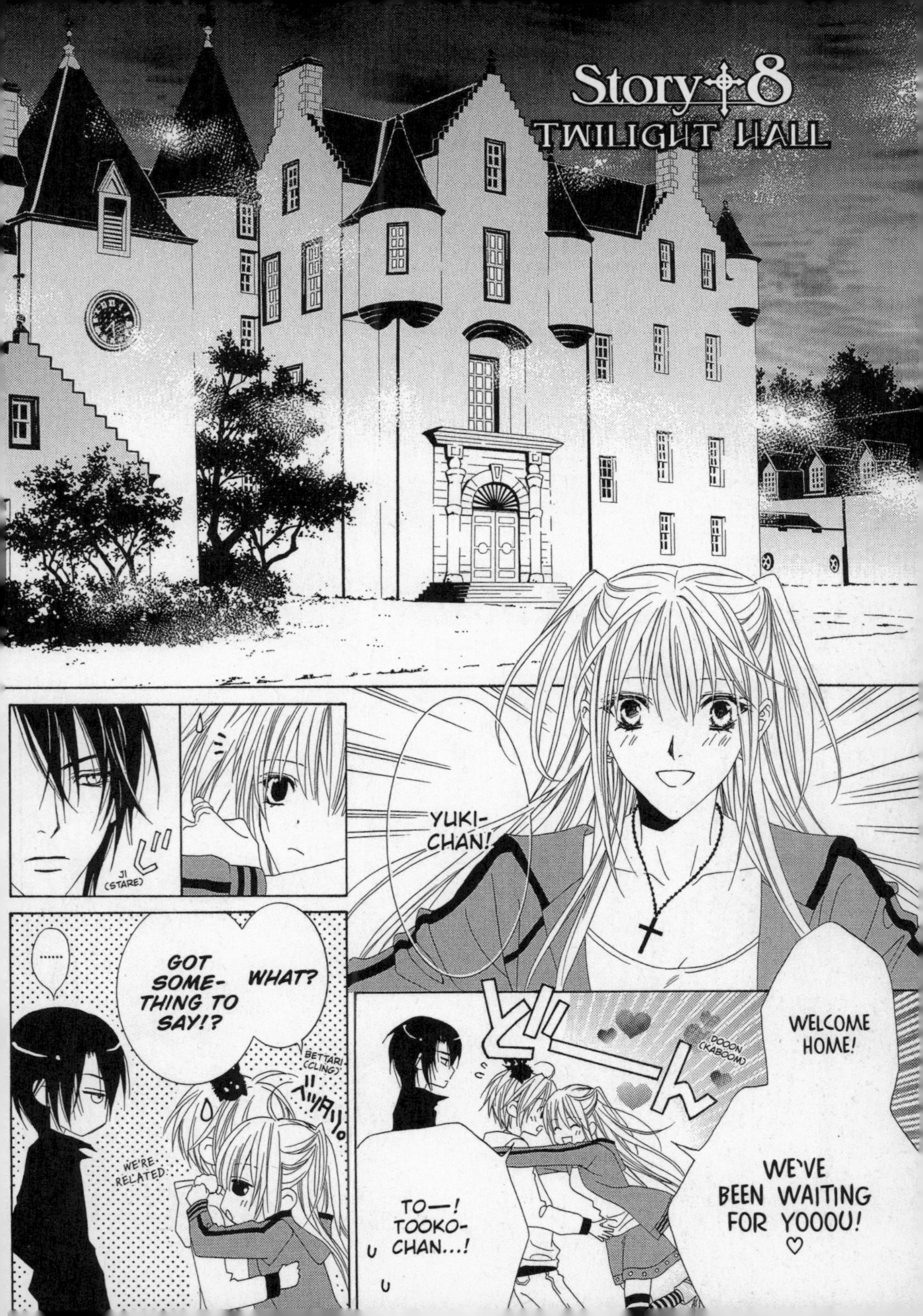
Story 8
TWILIGHT HALL
YUKI-CHAN!
JI (STARE)
WELCOME HOME!
DOOON (KABOOM)
WE'VE BEEN WAITING FOR YOOOU! ♡
TO—! TOOKO-CHAN...!
WHAT?
GOT SOME-THING TO SAY!?
......
BETTARI (CLING)
WE'RE RELATED

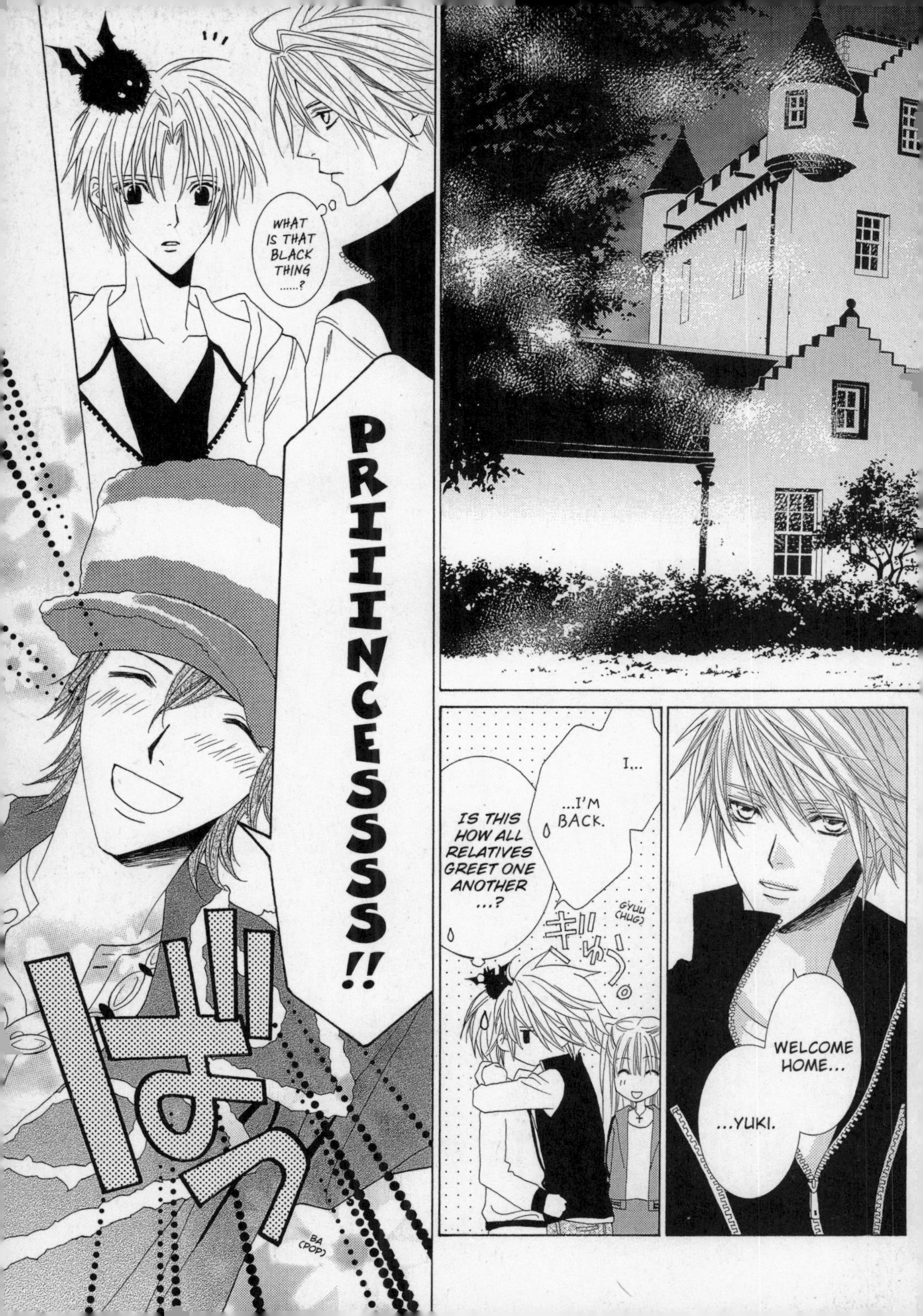
I...
...I'M BACK.
WELCOME HOME...
...YUKI.
IS THIS HOW ALL RELATIVES GREET ONE ANOTHER ...?
GYUU (HUG)
WHAT IS THAT BLACK THING ......?
PRIIINCESSSS!!
BA (POP)

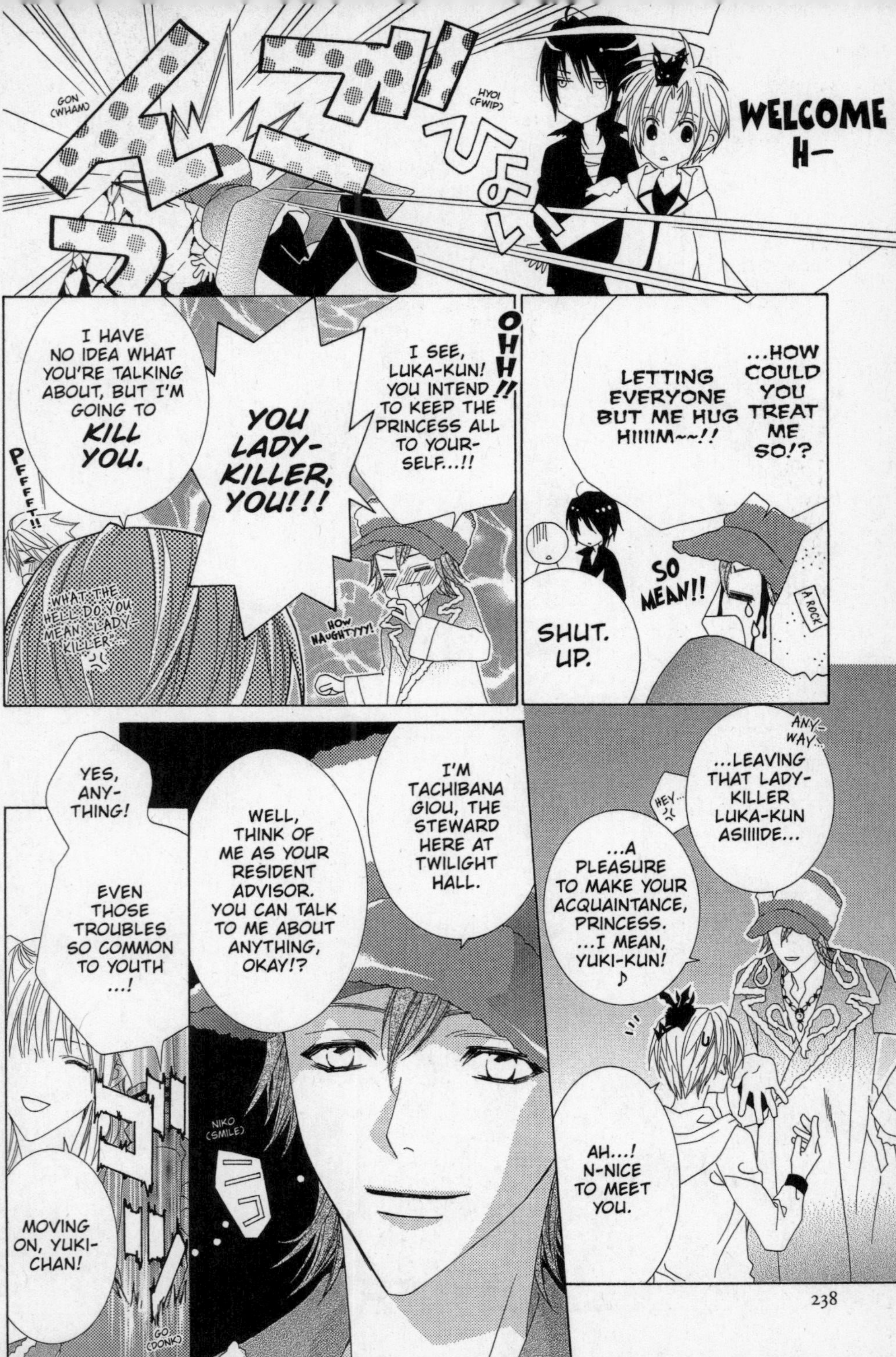
WELCOME H—
HYOI (FWIP)
GON (WHAM)
...HOW COULD YOU TREAT ME SO!?
LETTING EVERYONE BUT ME HUG HIIIIM~~!!
SO MEAN!!
A ROCK
SHUT. UP.
I SEE, LUKA-KUN! YOU INTEND TO KEEP THE PRINCESS ALL TO YOURSELF...!!
OHH!!
YOU LADY-KILLER, YOU!!!
HOW NAUGHTYYY!
I HAVE NO IDEA WHAT YOU'RE TALKING ABOUT, BUT I'M GOING TO KILL YOU.
PFFFFT!!
WHAT THE HELL DO YOU MEAN "LADY-KILLER"...
ANY-WAY...
...LEAVING THAT LADY-KILLER LUKA-KUN ASIIIIDE...
HEY...
...A PLEASURE TO MAKE YOUR ACQUAINTANCE, PRINCESS. ...I MEAN, YUKI-KUN! ♪
AH...! N-NICE TO MEET YOU.
I'M TACHIBANA GIOU, THE STEWARD HERE AT TWILIGHT HALL.
WELL, THINK OF ME AS YOUR RESIDENT ADVISOR. YOU CAN TALK TO ME ABOUT ANYTHING, OKAY!?
NIKO (SMILE)
YES, ANYTHING!
EVEN THOSE TROUBLES SO COMMON TO YOUTH ...!
MOVING ON, YUKI-CHAN!
GO (DONK)

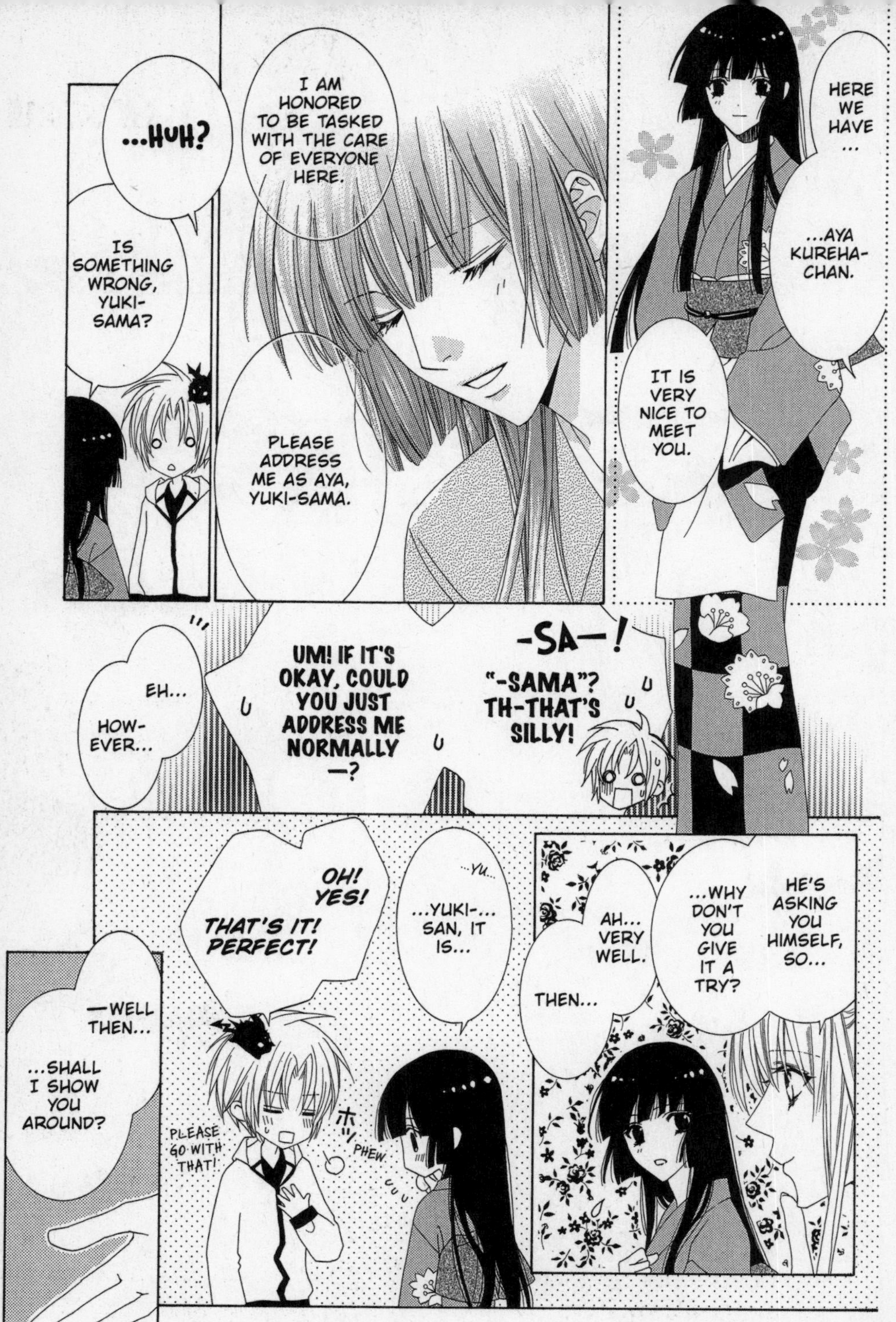
HERE WE HAVE...
...AYA KUREHA-CHAN.
IT IS VERY NICE TO MEET YOU.
I AM HONORED TO BE TASKED WITH THE CARE OF EVERYONE HERE.
PLEASE ADDRESS ME AS AYA, YUKI-SAMA.
...HUH?
IS SOMETHING WRONG, YUKI-SAMA?
-SA—!
"-SAMA"? TH-THAT'S SILLY!
UM! IF IT'S OKAY, COULD YOU JUST ADDRESS ME NORMALLY—?
EH... HOW-EVER...
HE'S ASKING YOU HIMSELF, SO...
...WHY DON'T YOU GIVE IT A TRY?
AH... VERY WELL.
THEN...
...YU...
...YUKI-... SAN, IT IS...
OH! YES! THAT'S IT! PERFECT!
PLEASE GO WITH THAT!
PHEW
—WELL THEN...
...SHALL I SHOW YOU AROUND?

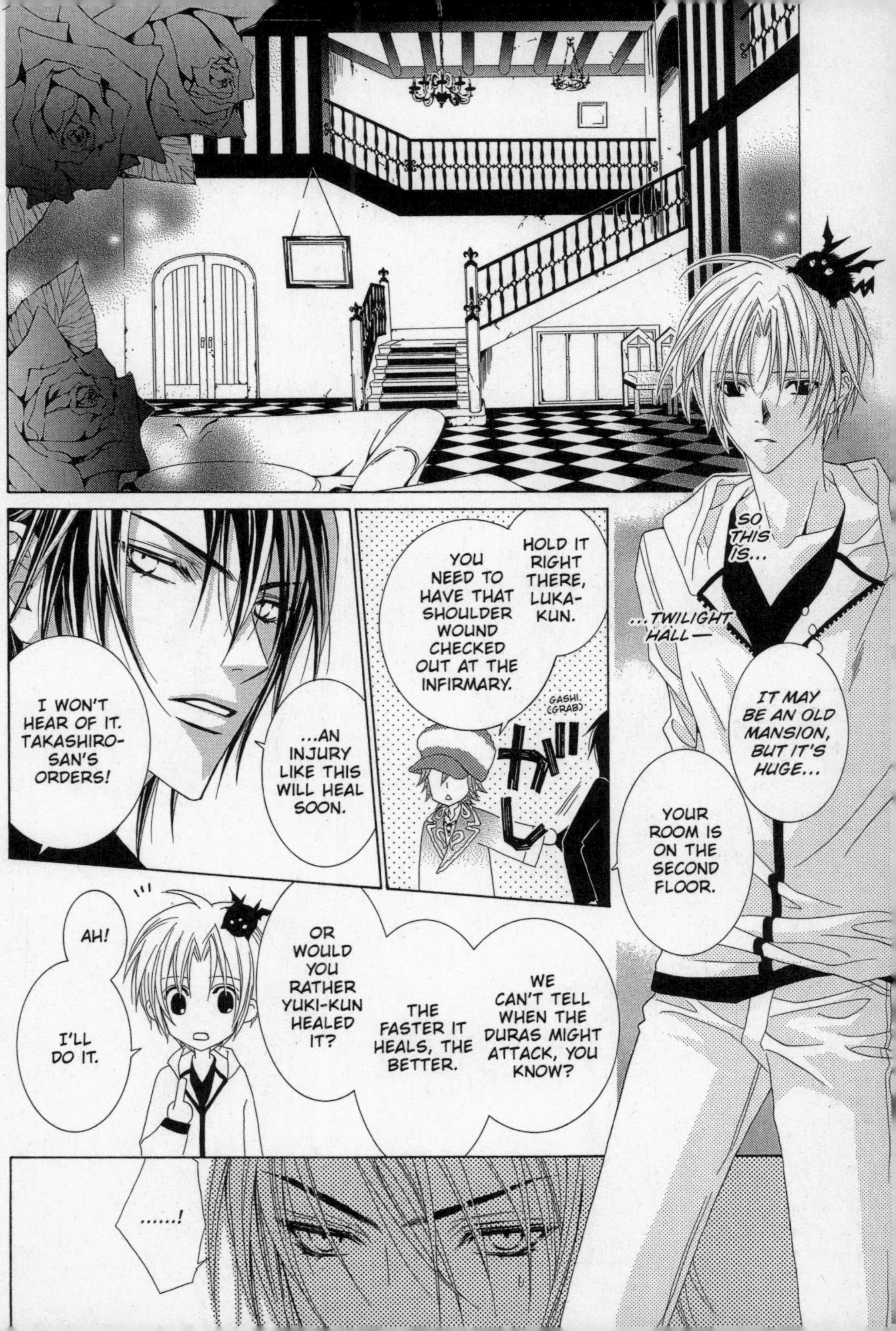

SO THIS IS...
...TWILIGHT HALL—
IT MAY BE AN OLD MANSION, BUT IT'S HUGE...
YOUR ROOM IS ON THE SECOND FLOOR.
HOLD IT RIGHT THERE, LUKA-KUN.
YOU NEED TO HAVE THAT SHOULDER WOUND CHECKED OUT AT THE INFIRMARY.
GASHI (GRAB)
...AN INJURY LIKE THIS WILL HEAL SOON.
I WON'T HEAR OF IT. TAKASHIRO-SAN'S ORDERS!
WE CAN'T TELL WHEN THE DURAS MIGHT ATTACK, YOU KNOW?
THE FASTER IT HEALS, THE BETTER.
OR WOULD YOU RATHER YUKI-KUN HEALED IT?
AH!
I'LL DO IT.
......!

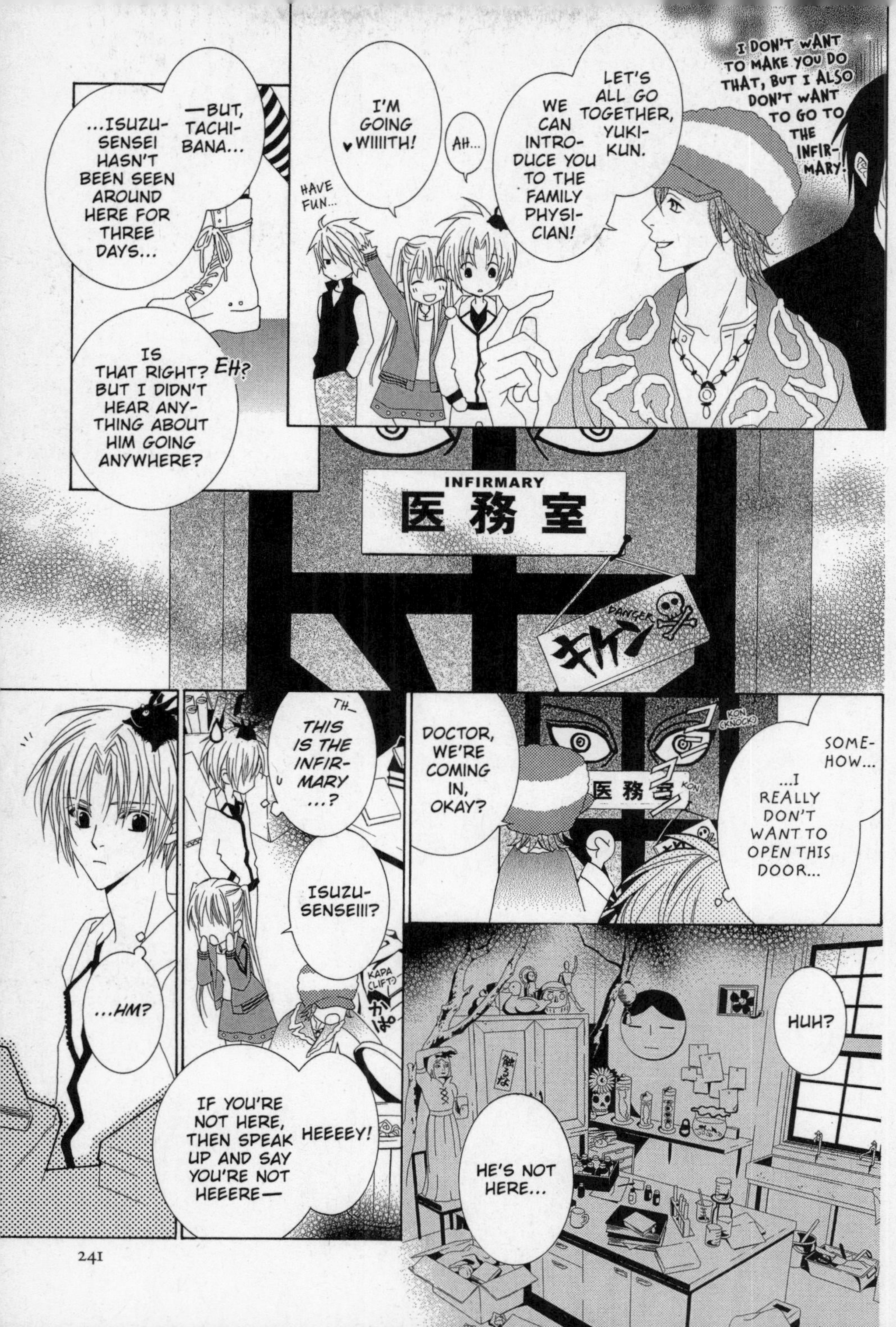
I DON'T WANT TO MAKE YOU DO THAT, BUT I ALSO DON'T WANT TO GO TO THE INFIRMARY!
LET'S ALL GO TOGETHER, YUKI-KUN.
WE CAN INTRODUCE YOU TO THE FAMILY PHYSICIAN!
AH...
I'M GOING WIIIITH!
HAVE FUN...
—BUT, TACHIBANA...
...ISUZU-SENSEI HASN'T BEEN SEEN AROUND HERE FOR THREE DAYS...
EH?
IS THAT RIGHT? BUT I DIDN'T HEAR ANYTHING ABOUT HIM GOING ANYWHERE?
INFIRMARY
医務室
DANGER
キケン
SOMEHOW...
...I REALLY DON'T WANT TO OPEN THIS DOOR...
KON (KNOCK)
KON
DOCTOR, WE'RE COMING IN, OKAY?
TH—
THIS IS THE INFIRMARY...?
ISUZU-SENSEIII?
KAPA (LIFT)
かぱ
HUH?
HE'S NOT HERE...
HEEEEY!
IF YOU'RE NOT HERE, THEN SPEAK UP AND SAY YOU'RE NOT HEEERE—
...HM?

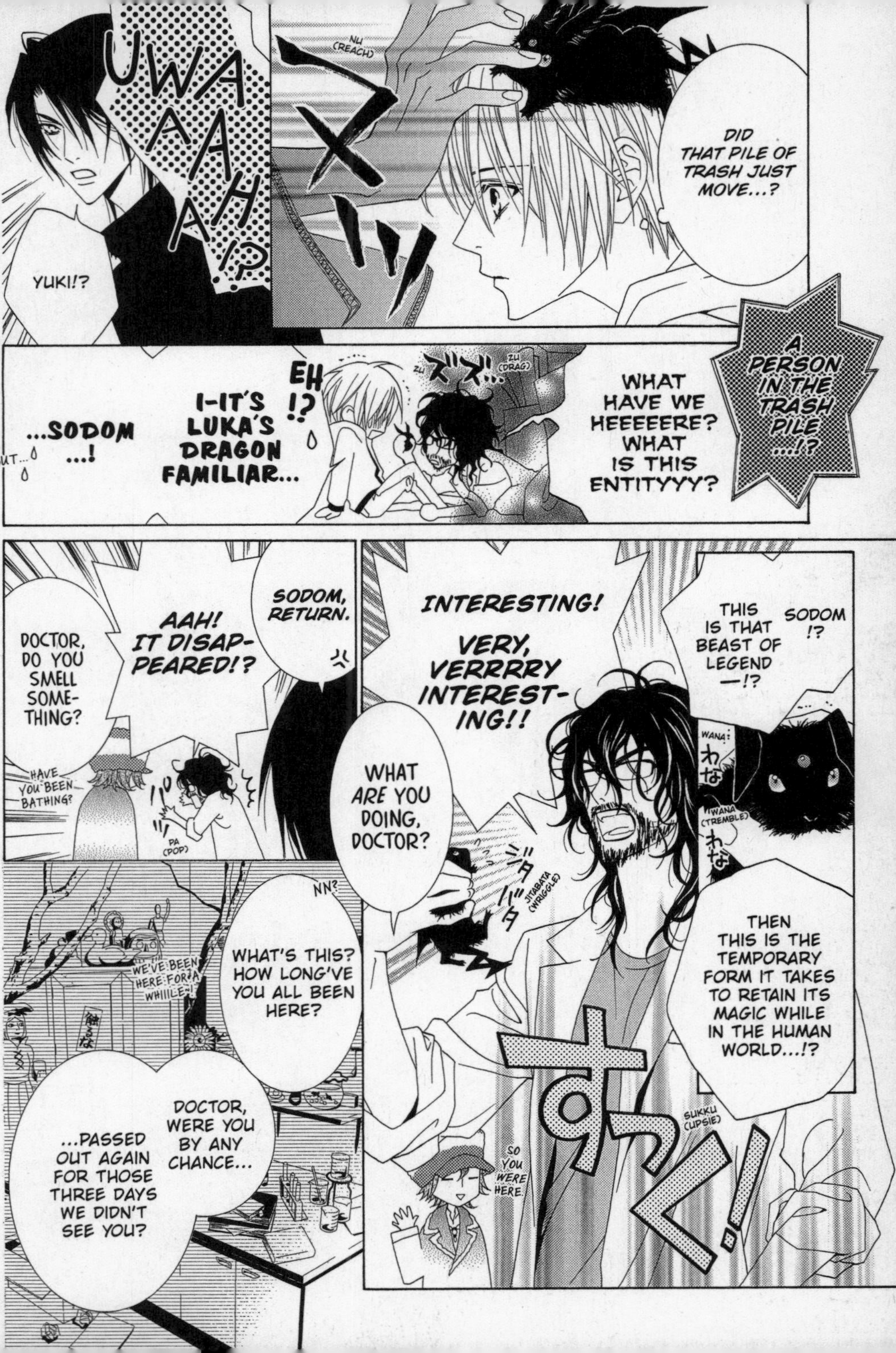
DID THAT PILE OF TRASH JUST MOVE...?
NU (REACH)
UWAAAHA!?
YUKI!?
A PERSON IN THE TRASH PILE...!?
WHAT HAVE WE HEEEEERE? WHAT IS THIS ENTITYYY?
ZU ZU (DRAG)
EH !?
I-IT'S LUKA'S DRAGON FAMILIAR...
...SODOM ...!
BUT...
SODOM !?
THIS IS THAT BEAST OF LEGEND—!?
...
WANA WANA (TREMBLE)
INTERESTING!
VERY, VERRRRY INTERESTING!!
THEN THIS IS THE TEMPORARY FORM IT TAKES TO RETAIN ITS MAGIC WHILE IN THE HUMAN WORLD...!?
JITABATA (WRIGGLE)
WHAT ARE YOU DOING, DOCTOR?
SUKKU (UPSIE)
SO YOU WERE HERE.
SODOM, RETURN.
AAH! IT DISAPPEARED!?
DOCTOR, DO YOU SMELL SOMETHING?
HAVE YOU BEEN BATHING?
PA (POP)
NN?
WHAT'S THIS? HOW LONG'VE YOU ALL BEEN HERE?
WE'VE BEEN HERE FOR A WHIIILE!
DOCTOR, WERE YOU BY ANY CHANCE...
...PASSED OUT AGAIN FOR THOSE THREE DAYS WE DIDN'T SEE YOU?

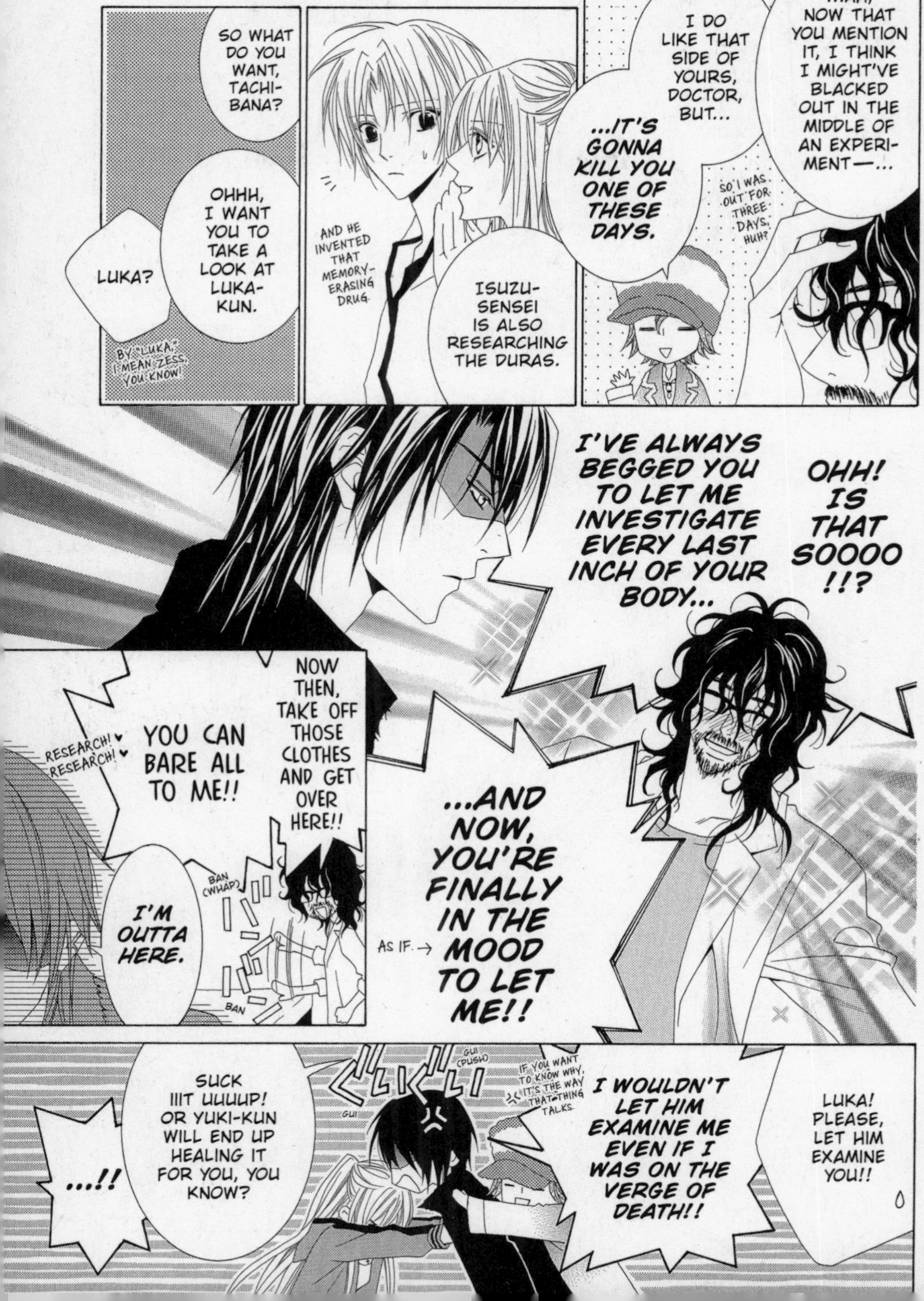
...AH, NOW THAT YOU MENTION IT, I THINK I MIGHT'VE BLACKED OUT IN THE MIDDLE OF AN EXPERIMENT—...
SO I WAS OUT FOR THREE DAYS, HUH?
I DO LIKE THAT SIDE OF YOURS, DOCTOR, BUT...
...IT'S GONNA KILL YOU ONE OF THESE DAYS.
ISUZU-SENSEI IS ALSO RESEARCHING THE DURAS.
AND HE INVENTED THAT MEMORY-ERASING DRUG.
SO WHAT DO YOU WANT, TACHIBANA?
OHHH, I WANT YOU TO TAKE A LOOK AT LUKA-KUN.
LUKA?
BY "LUKA," I MEAN ZESS, YOU KNOW!
OHH! IS THAT SOOOO!!?
I'VE ALWAYS BEGGED YOU TO LET ME INVESTIGATE EVERY LAST INCH OF YOUR BODY...
...AND NOW, YOU'RE FINALLY IN THE MOOD TO LET ME!!
AS IF. →
NOW THEN, TAKE OFF THOSE CLOTHES AND GET OVER HERE!!
YOU CAN BARE ALL TO ME!!
RESEARCH! RESEARCH!
I'M OUTTA HERE.
BAN (WHAP)
BAN
LUKA! PLEASE, LET HIM EXAMINE YOU!!
I WOULDN'T LET HIM EXAMINE ME EVEN IF I WAS ON THE VERGE OF DEATH!!
IF YOU WANT TO KNOW WHY, IT'S THE WAY THAT THING TALKS.
GUI (PUSH)
GUI
SUCK IIIT UUUUP! OR YUKI-KUN WILL END UP HEALING IT FOR YOU, YOU KNOW?
...!!

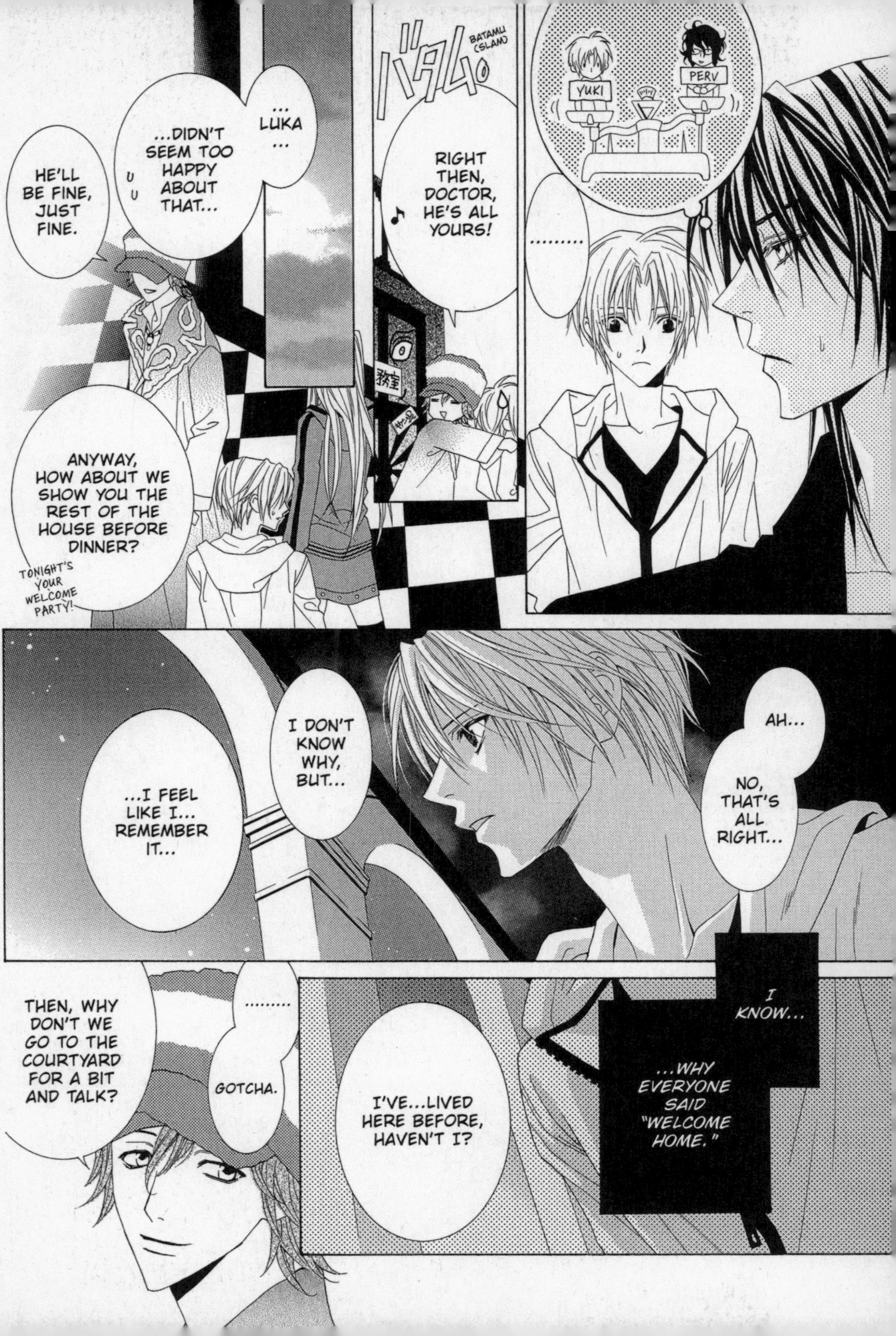

PERV
YUKI
....
バタム。
BATAMU (SLAM)
RIGHT THEN, DOCTOR, HE'S ALL YOURS!
... LUKA ...
...DIDN'T SEEM TOO HAPPY ABOUT THAT...
HE'LL BE FINE, JUST FINE.
ANYWAY, HOW ABOUT WE SHOW YOU THE REST OF THE HOUSE BEFORE DINNER?
TONIGHT'S YOUR WELCOME PARTY!
AH...
NO, THAT'S ALL RIGHT...
I DON'T KNOW WHY, BUT...
...I FEEL LIKE I... REMEMBER IT...
I KNOW...
...WHY EVERYONE SAID "WELCOME HOME."
I'VE...LIVED HERE BEFORE, HAVEN'T I?
....
GOTCHA.
THEN, WHY DON'T WE GO TO THE COURTYARD FOR A BIT AND TALK?

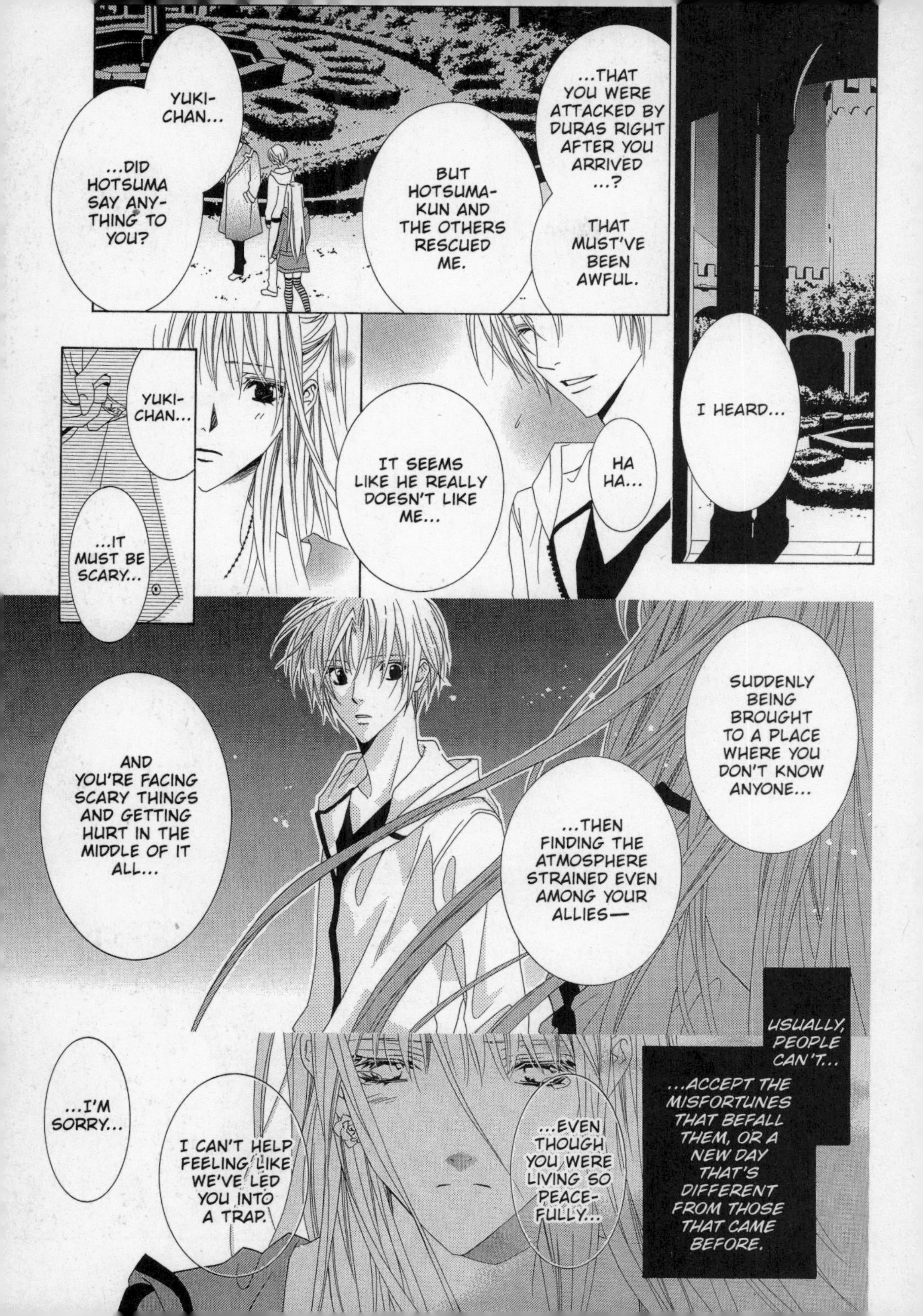
I HEARD...
...THAT YOU WERE ATTACKED BY DURAS RIGHT AFTER YOU ARRIVED ...?
THAT MUST'VE BEEN AWFUL.
BUT HOTSUMA-KUN AND THE OTHERS RESCUED ME.
YUKI-CHAN...
...DID HOTSUMA SAY ANY-THING TO YOU?
HA HA...
IT SEEMS LIKE HE REALLY DOESN'T LIKE ME...
YUKI-CHAN...
...IT MUST BE SCARY...
SUDDENLY BEING BROUGHT TO A PLACE WHERE YOU DON'T KNOW ANYONE...
...THEN FINDING THE ATMOSPHERE STRAINED EVEN AMONG YOUR ALLIES—
AND YOU'RE FACING SCARY THINGS AND GETTING HURT IN THE MIDDLE OF IT ALL...
USUALLY, PEOPLE CAN'T...
...ACCEPT THE MISFORTUNES THAT BEFALL THEM, OR A NEW DAY THAT'S DIFFERENT FROM THOSE THAT CAME BEFORE.
...EVEN THOUGH YOU WERE LIVING SO PEACE-FULLY...
I CAN'T HELP FEELING LIKE WE'VE LED YOU INTO A TRAP.
...I'M SORRY...

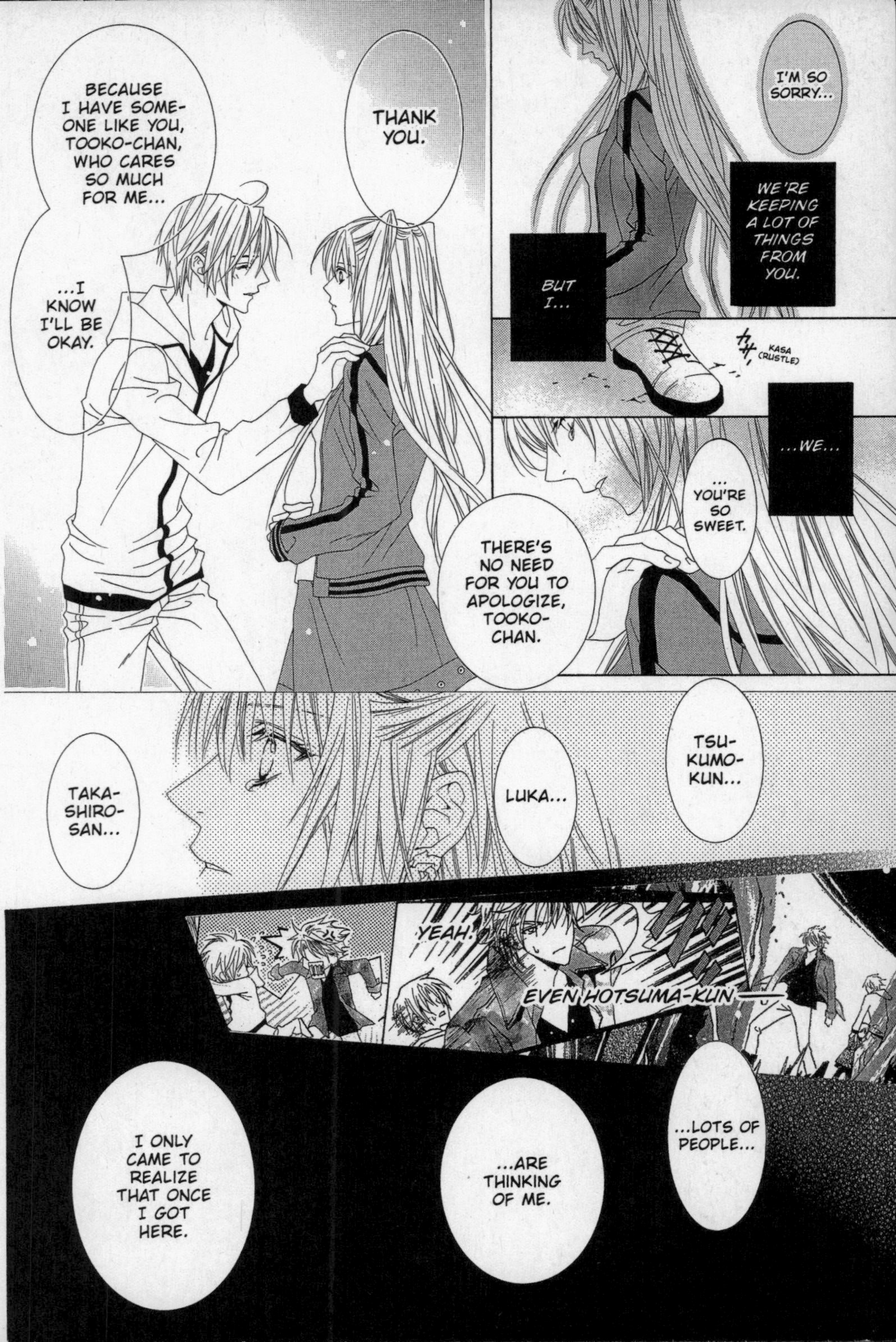

I'M SO SORRY...
WE'RE KEEPING A LOT OF THINGS FROM YOU.
BUT I...
KASA (RUSTLE)
...WE...
...YOU'RE SO SWEET.
THERE'S NO NEED FOR YOU TO APOLOGIZE, TOOKO-CHAN.
THANK YOU.
BECAUSE I HAVE SOME-ONE LIKE YOU, TOOKO-CHAN, WHO CARES SO MUCH FOR ME...
...I KNOW I'LL BE OKAY.
TSU-KUMO-KUN...
LUKA...
TAKA-SHIRO-SAN...
YEAH!
EVEN HOTSUMA-KUN—
...LOTS OF PEOPLE...
...ARE THINKING OF ME.
I ONLY CAME TO REALIZE THAT ONCE I GOT HERE.

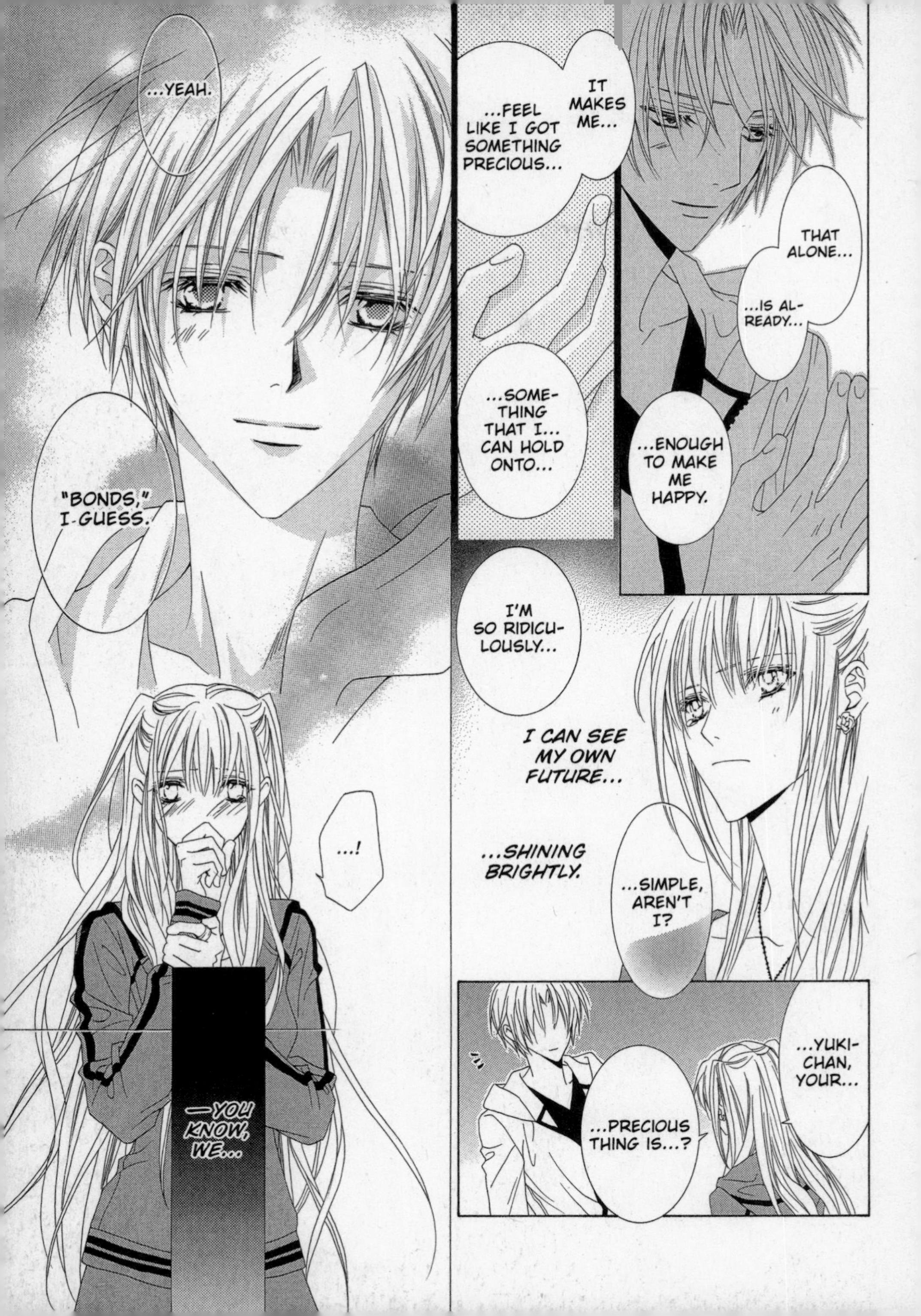
IT MAKES ME...
...FEEL LIKE I GOT SOMETHING PRECIOUS...
THAT ALONE...
...IS AL-READY...
...SOME-THING THAT I... CAN HOLD ONTO...
...ENOUGH TO MAKE ME HAPPY.
I'M SO RIDICU-LOUSLY...
I CAN SEE MY OWN FUTURE...
...SHINING BRIGHTLY.
...SIMPLE, AREN'T I?
...YUKI-CHAN, YOUR...
...PRECIOUS THING IS...?
...YEAH.
"BONDS," I GUESS.
...!
—YOU KNOW, WE...

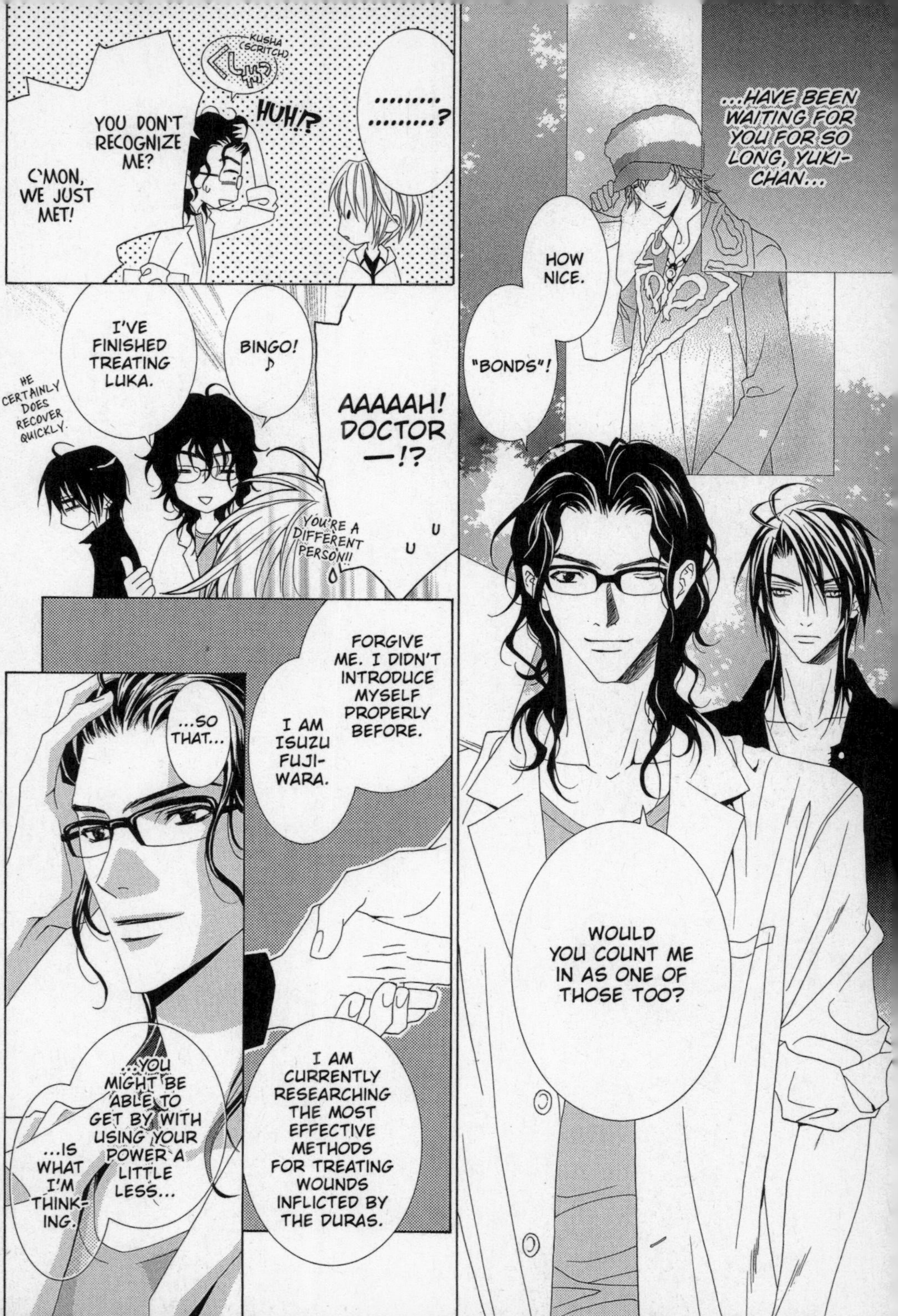

....
.........?
KUSHA (SCRITCH)
HUH!?
YOU DON'T RECOGNIZE ME?
C'MON, WE JUST MET!
AAAAAH! DOCTOR—!?
BINGO! ♪
I'VE FINISHED TREATING LUKA.
HE CERTAINLY DOES RECOVER QUICKLY.
YOU'RE A DIFFERENT PERSON!!
FORGIVE ME. I DIDN'T INTRODUCE MYSELF PROPERLY BEFORE.
I AM ISUZU FUJIWARA.
I AM CURRENTLY RESEARCHING THE MOST EFFECTIVE METHODS FOR TREATING WOUNDS INFLICTED BY THE DURAS.
...SO THAT...
...YOU MIGHT BE ABLE TO GET BY WITH USING YOUR POWER A LITTLE LESS...
...IS WHAT I'M THINKING.
...HAVE BEEN WAITING FOR YOU FOR SO LONG, YUKI-CHAN...
HOW NICE.
"BONDS"!
WOULD YOU COUNT ME IN AS ONE OF THOSE TOO?

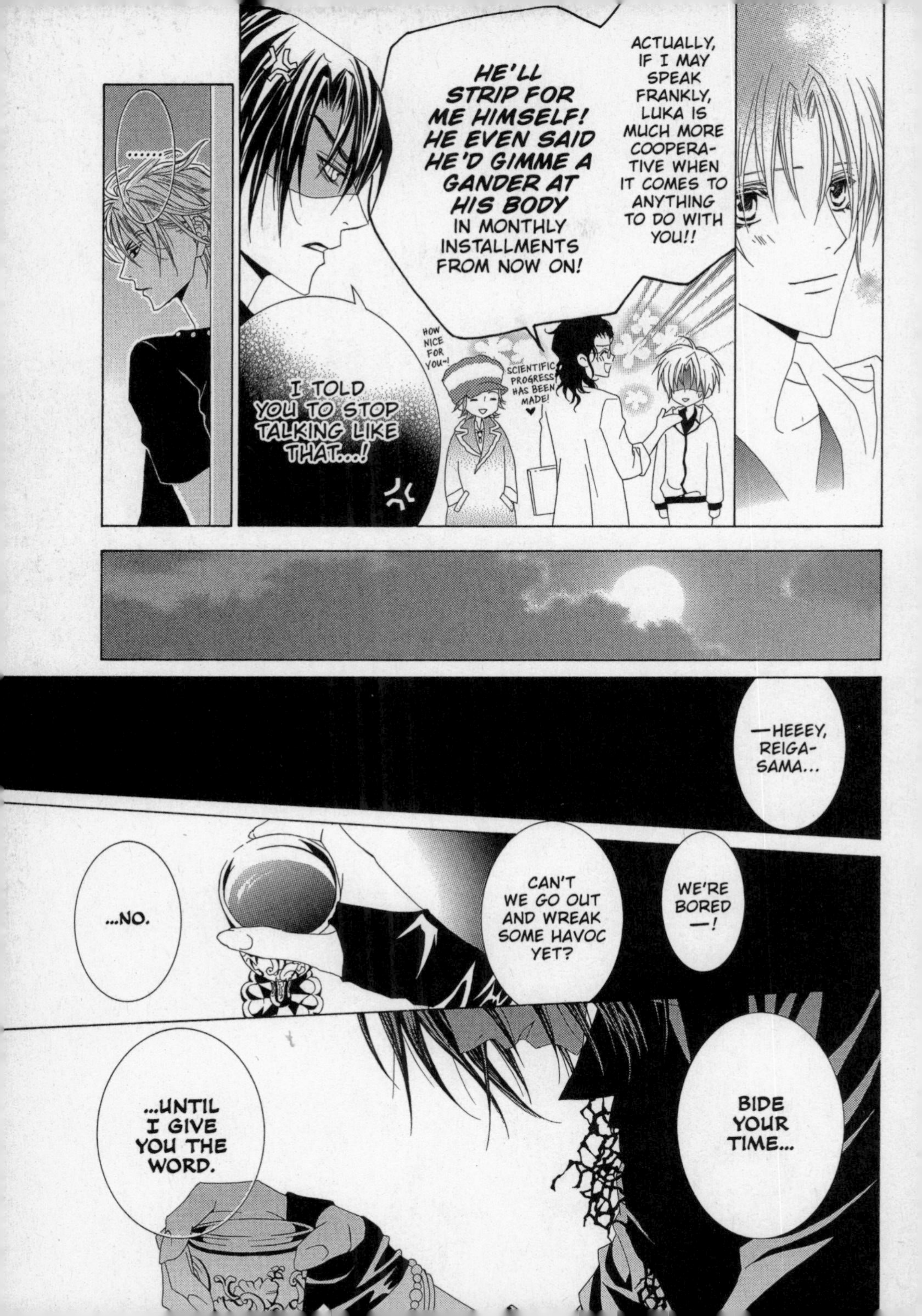
ACTUALLY, IF I MAY SPEAK FRANKLY, LUKA IS MUCH MORE COOPERA-TIVE WHEN IT COMES TO ANYTHING TO DO WITH YOU!!
HE'LL STRIP FOR ME HIMSELF! HE EVEN SAID HE'D GIMME A GANDER AT HIS BODY IN MONTHLY INSTALLMENTS FROM NOW ON!
SCIENTIFIC PROGRESS HAS BEEN MADE! ♥
HOW NICE FOR YOU~!
I TOLD YOU TO STOP TALKING LIKE THAT...!
......
—HEEEY, REIGA-SAMA...
WE'RE BORED—!
CAN'T WE GO OUT AND WREAK SOME HAVOC YET?
...NO.
BIDE YOUR TIME...
...UNTIL I GIVE YOU THE WORD.

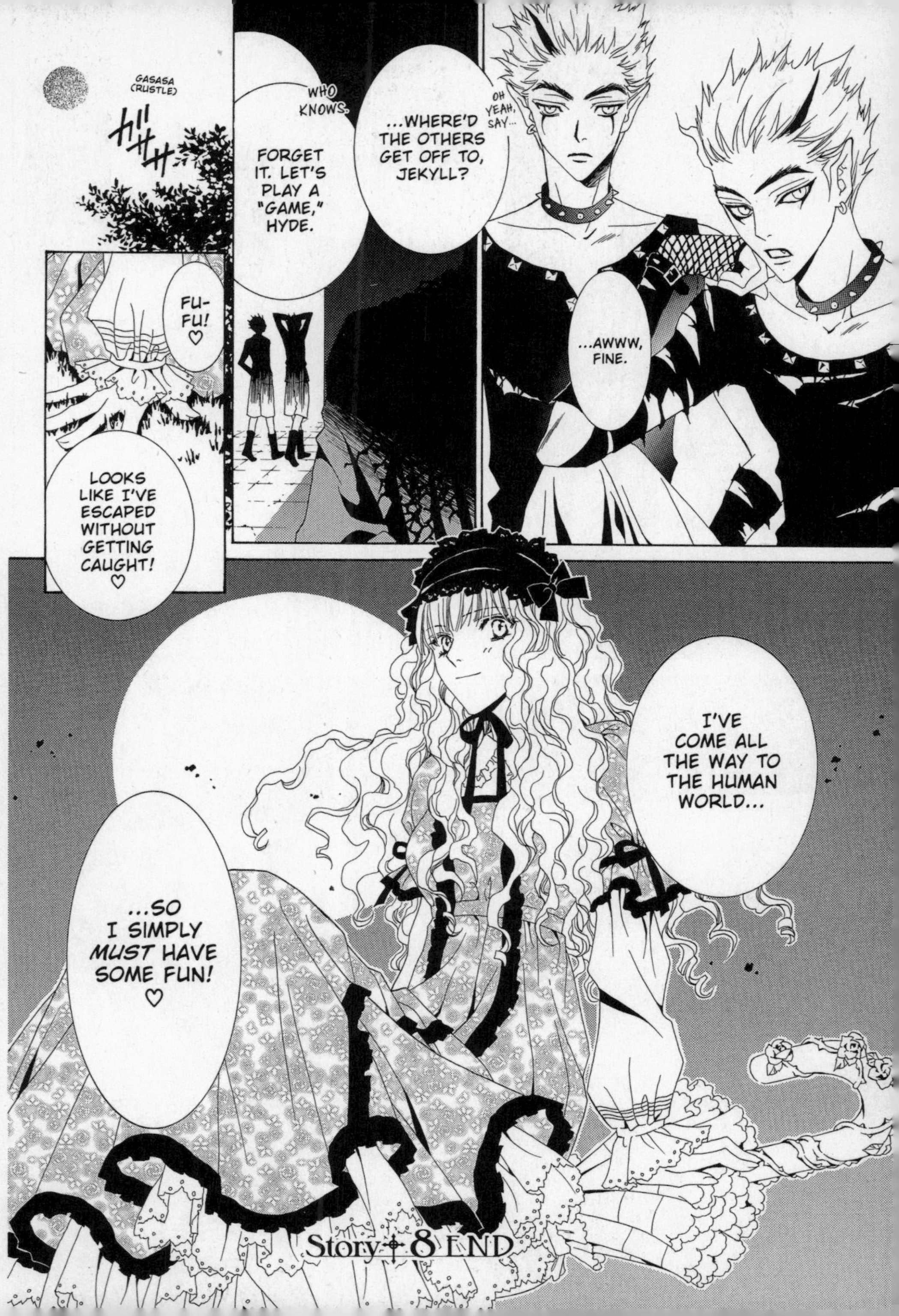

OH YEAH, SAY...
...WHERE'D THE OTHERS GET OFF TO, JEKYLL?
WHO KNOWS.
FORGET IT. LET'S PLAY A "GAME," HYDE.
...AWWW, FINE.
GASASA (RUSTLE)
FU-FU! ♡
LOOKS LIKE I'VE ESCAPED WITHOUT GETTING CAUGHT! ♡
I'VE COME ALL THE WAY TO THE HUMAN WORLD...
...SO I SIMPLY *MUST* HAVE SOME FUN! ♡
Story 8 END

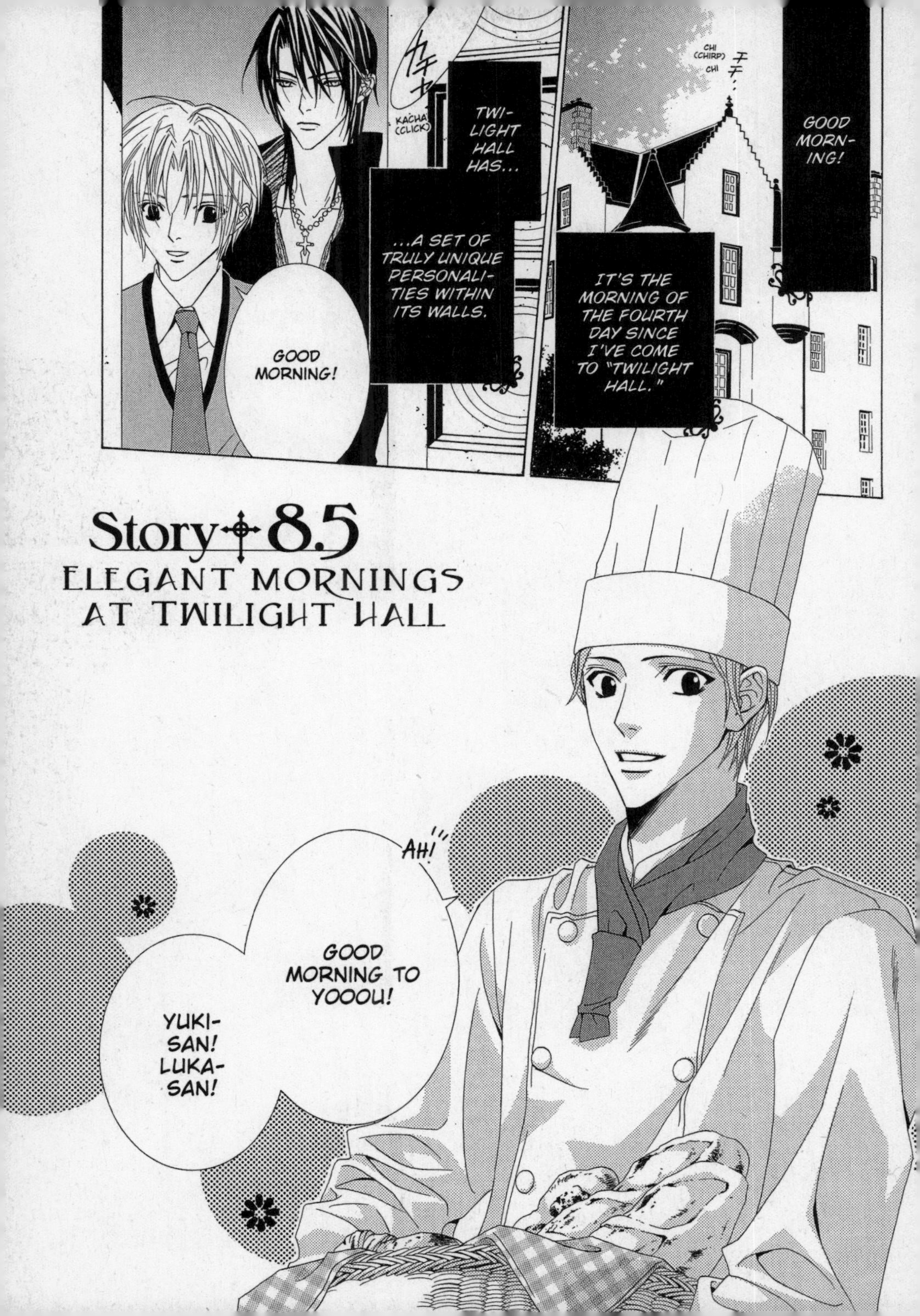
CHI (CHIRP) CHI
GOOD MORNING!
IT'S THE MORNING OF THE FOURTH DAY SINCE I'VE COME TO "TWILIGHT HALL."
KACHA (CLICK)
TWILIGHT HALL HAS...
...A SET OF TRULY UNIQUE PERSONALITIES WITHIN ITS WALLS.
GOOD MORNING!
Story 8.5
ELEGANT MORNINGS AT TWILIGHT HALL
AH!
GOOD MORNING TO YOOOU!
YUKI-SAN! LUKA-SAN!

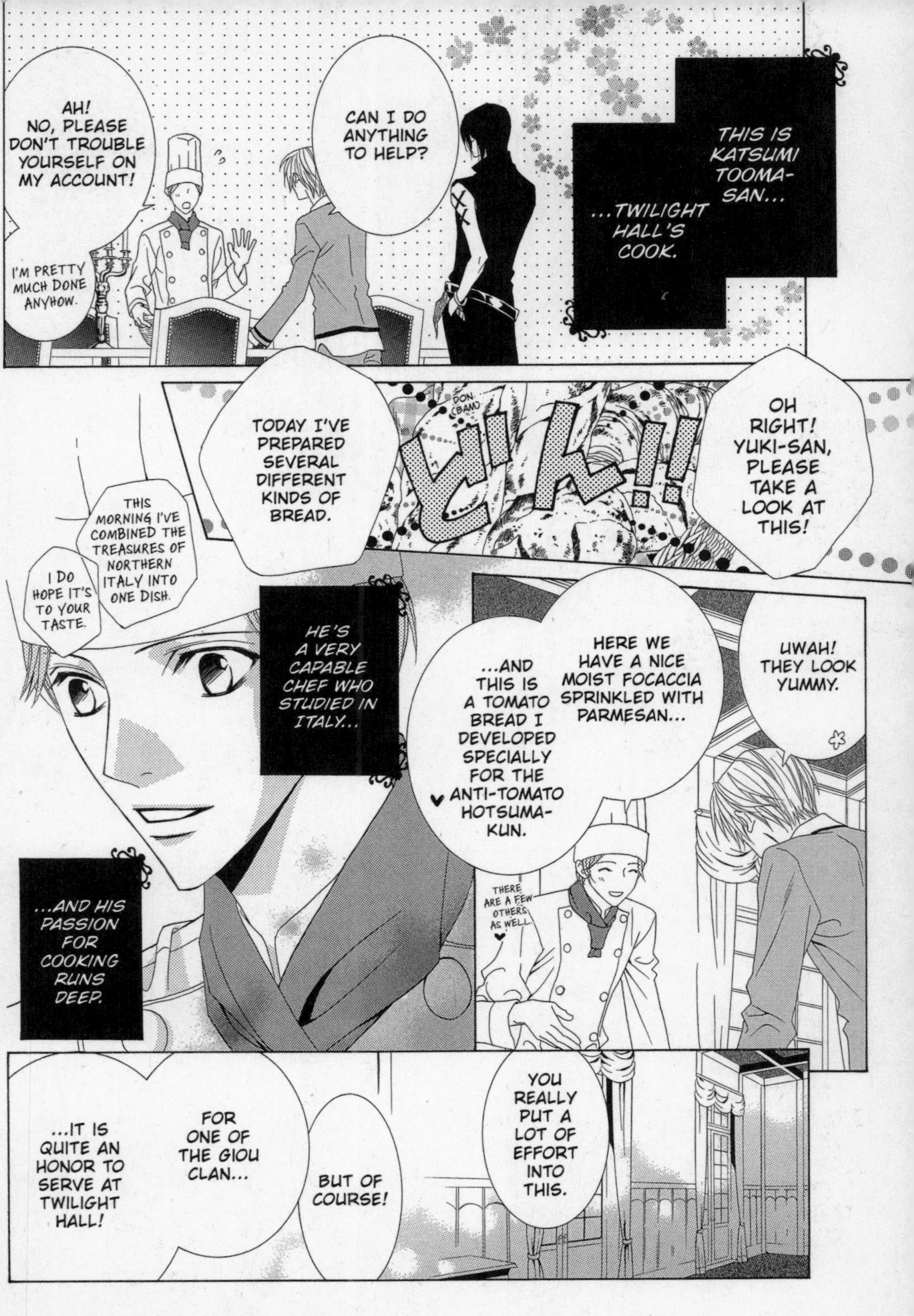
THIS IS KATSUMI TOOMA-SAN...
...TWILIGHT HALL'S COOK.
CAN I DO ANYTHING TO HELP?
AH! NO, PLEASE DON'T TROUBLE YOURSELF ON MY ACCOUNT!
I'M PRETTY MUCH DONE ANYHOW.
OH RIGHT! YUKI-SAN, PLEASE TAKE A LOOK AT THIS!
DON (BAM)
TODAY I'VE PREPARED SEVERAL DIFFERENT KINDS OF BREAD.
UWAH! THEY LOOK YUMMY.
HERE WE HAVE A NICE MOIST FOCACCIA SPRINKLED WITH PARMESAN...
...AND THIS IS A TOMATO BREAD I DEVELOPED SPECIALLY FOR THE ANTI-TOMATO HOTSUMA-KUN.
THERE ARE A FEW OTHERS AS WELL.
HE'S A VERY CAPABLE CHEF WHO STUDIED IN ITALY...
THIS MORNING I'VE COMBINED THE TREASURES OF NORTHERN ITALY INTO ONE DISH.
I DO HOPE IT'S TO YOUR TASTE.
...AND HIS PASSION FOR COOKING RUNS DEEP.
YOU REALLY PUT A LOT OF EFFORT INTO THIS.
BUT OF COURSE!
FOR ONE OF THE GIOU CLAN...
...IT IS QUITE AN HONOR TO SERVE AT TWILIGHT HALL!

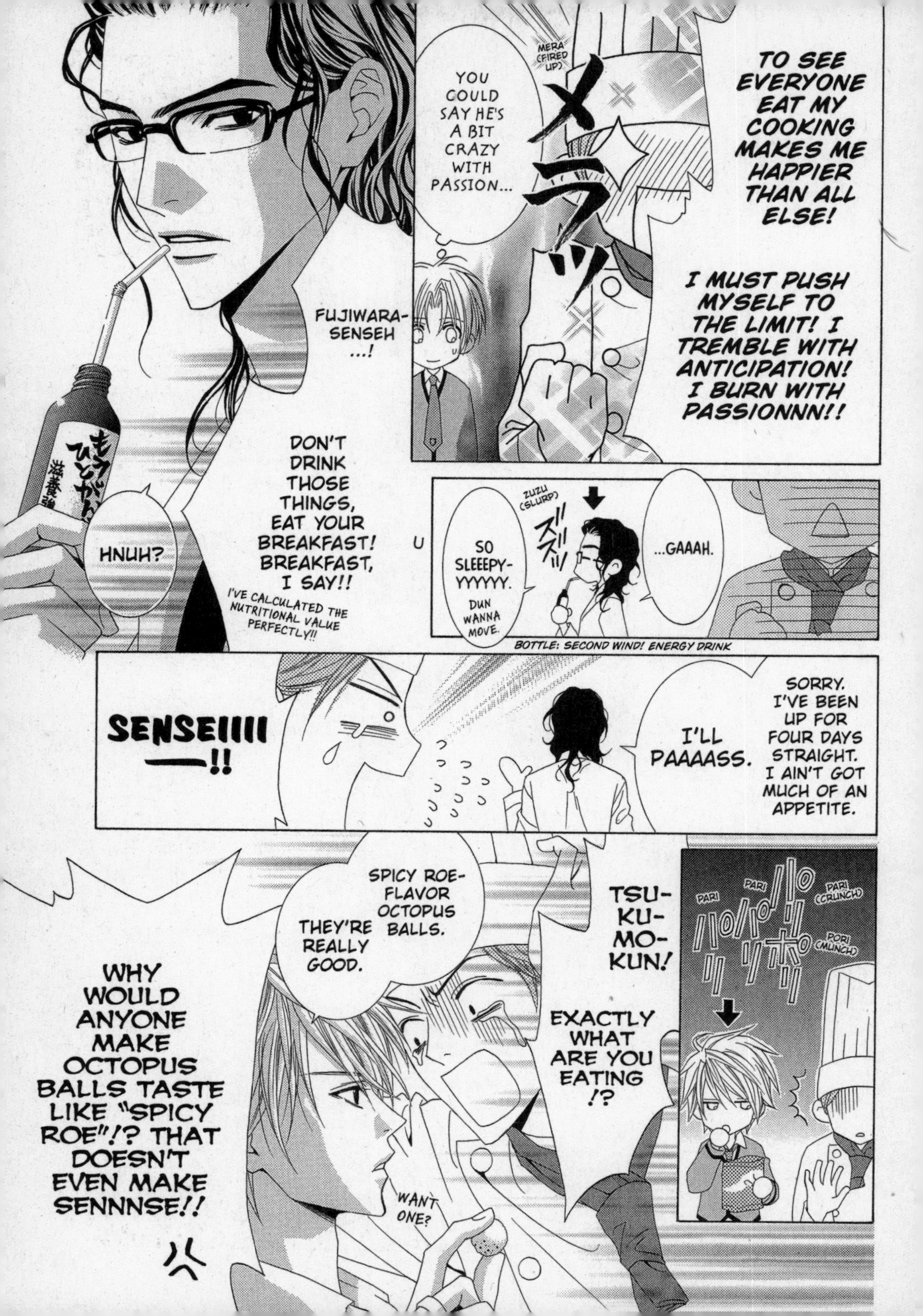

TO SEE EVERYONE EAT MY COOKING MAKES ME HAPPIER THAN ALL ELSE!
I MUST PUSH MYSELF TO THE LIMIT! I TREMBLE WITH ANTICIPATION! I BURN WITH PASSIONNN!!
MERA (FIRED UP)
YOU COULD SAY HE'S A BIT CRAZY WITH PASSION...
FUJIWARA-SENSEH...!
DON'T DRINK THOSE THINGS, EAT YOUR BREAKFAST! BREAKFAST, I SAY!!
I'VE CALCULATED THE NUTRITIONAL VALUE PERFECTLY!!
HNUH?
...GAAAH.
ZUZU (SLURP)
SO SLEEEPY-YYYYYY.
DUN WANNA MOVE.
BOTTLE: SECOND WIND! ENERGY DRINK
SORRY. I'VE BEEN UP FOR FOUR DAYS STRAIGHT. I AIN'T GOT MUCH OF AN APPETITE.
I'LL PAAAASS.
SENSEIIIII—!!
PARI PARI PARI (CRUNCH)
PORI (MUNCH)
TSU-KU-MO-KUN!
EXACTLY WHAT ARE YOU EATING!?
SPICY ROE-FLAVOR OCTOPUS BALLS.
THEY'RE REALLY GOOD.
WANT ONE?
WHY WOULD ANYONE MAKE OCTOPUS BALLS TASTE LIKE "SPICY ROE"!? THAT DOESN'T EVEN MAKE SENNNSE!!

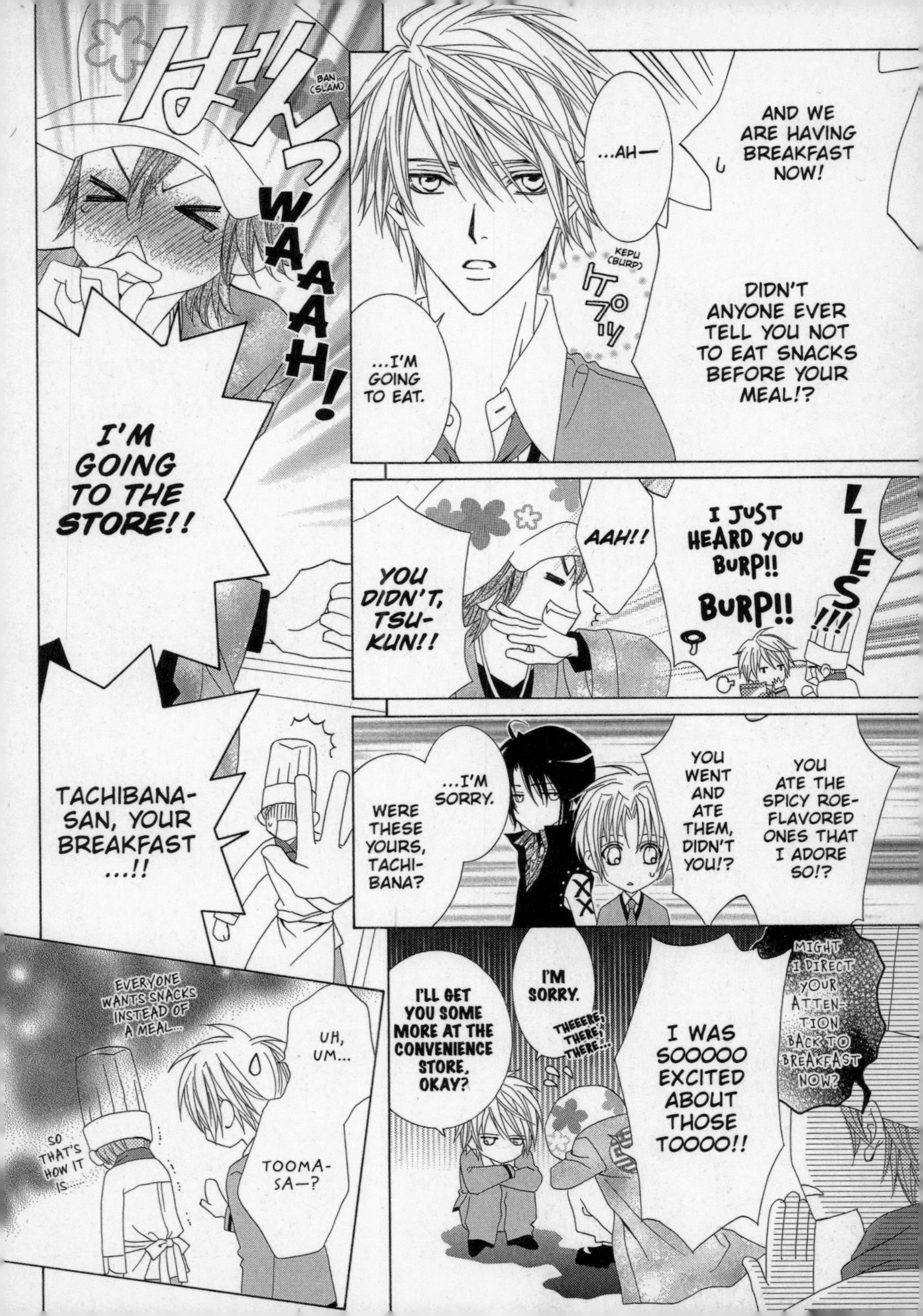
AND WE ARE HAVING BREAKFAST NOW!
...AH—
KEPU (BURP)
ケプッ
DIDN'T ANYONE EVER TELL YOU NOT TO EAT SNACKS BEFORE YOUR MEAL!?
...I'M GOING TO EAT.
LIES!!!
I JUST HEARD YOU BURP!!
BURP!!
AAH!!
YOU DIDN'T, TSU-KUN!!
YOU ATE THE SPICY ROE-FLAVORED ONES THAT I ADORE SO!?
YOU WENT AND ATE THEM, DIDN'T YOU!?
...I'M SORRY.
WERE THESE YOURS, TACHIBANA?
はんっ
BAN (SLAM)
WAAAAH!
I'M GOING TO THE STORE!!
TACHIBANA-SAN, YOUR BREAKFAST ...!!
MIGHT I DIRECT YOUR ATTENTION BACK TO BREAKFAST NOW?
I WAS SOOOOO EXCITED ABOUT THOSE TOOOO!!
I'M SORRY.
THEEERE, THERE, THERE...
I'LL GET YOU SOME MORE AT THE CONVENIENCE STORE, OKAY?
UH, UM...
TOOMA-SA—?
EVERYONE WANTS SNACKS INSTEAD OF A MEAL...
SO THAT'S HOW IT IS......

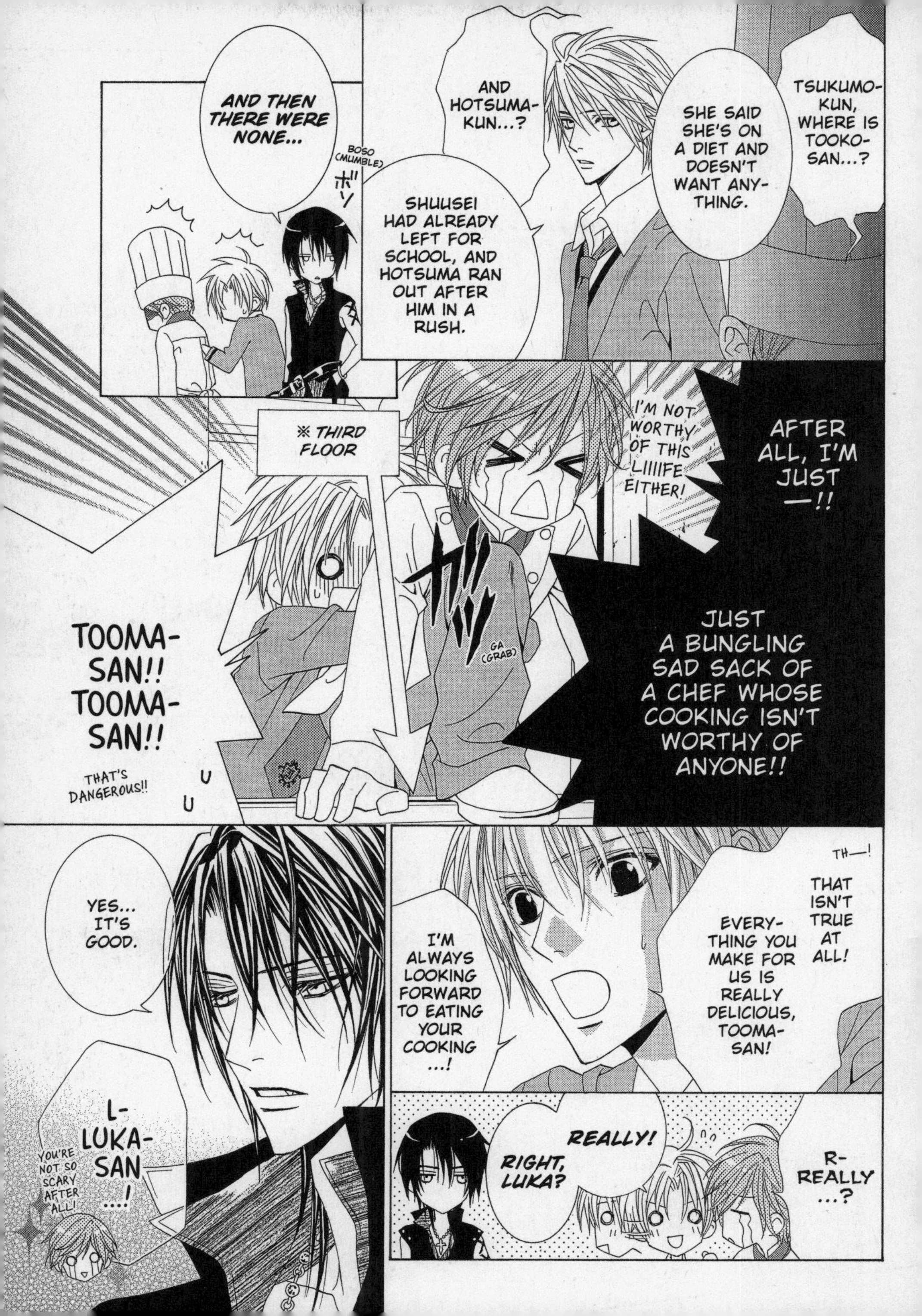

TSUKUMO-KUN, WHERE IS TOOKO-SAN...?
SHE SAID SHE'S ON A DIET AND DOESN'T WANT ANYTHING.
AND HOTSUMA-KUN...?
SHUUSEI HAD ALREADY LEFT FOR SCHOOL, AND HOTSUMA RAN OUT AFTER HIM IN A RUSH.
BOSO (MUMBLE)
AND THEN THERE WERE NONE...
AFTER ALL, I'M JUST—!!
I'M NOT WORTHY OF THIS LIIIIFE EITHER!
JUST A BUNGLING SAD SACK OF A CHEF WHOSE COOKING ISN'T WORTHY OF ANYONE!!
GA (GRAB)
※ THIRD FLOOR
TOOMA-SAN!! TOOMA-SAN!!
THAT'S DANGEROUS!!
U
U
TH—!
THAT ISN'T TRUE AT ALL!
EVERYTHING YOU MAKE FOR US IS REALLY DELICIOUS, TOOMA-SAN!
I'M ALWAYS LOOKING FORWARD TO EATING YOUR COOKING...!
YES... IT'S GOOD.
R-REALLY...?
REALLY!
RIGHT, LUKA?
L-LUKA-SAN...!
YOU'RE NOT SO SCARY AFTER ALL!

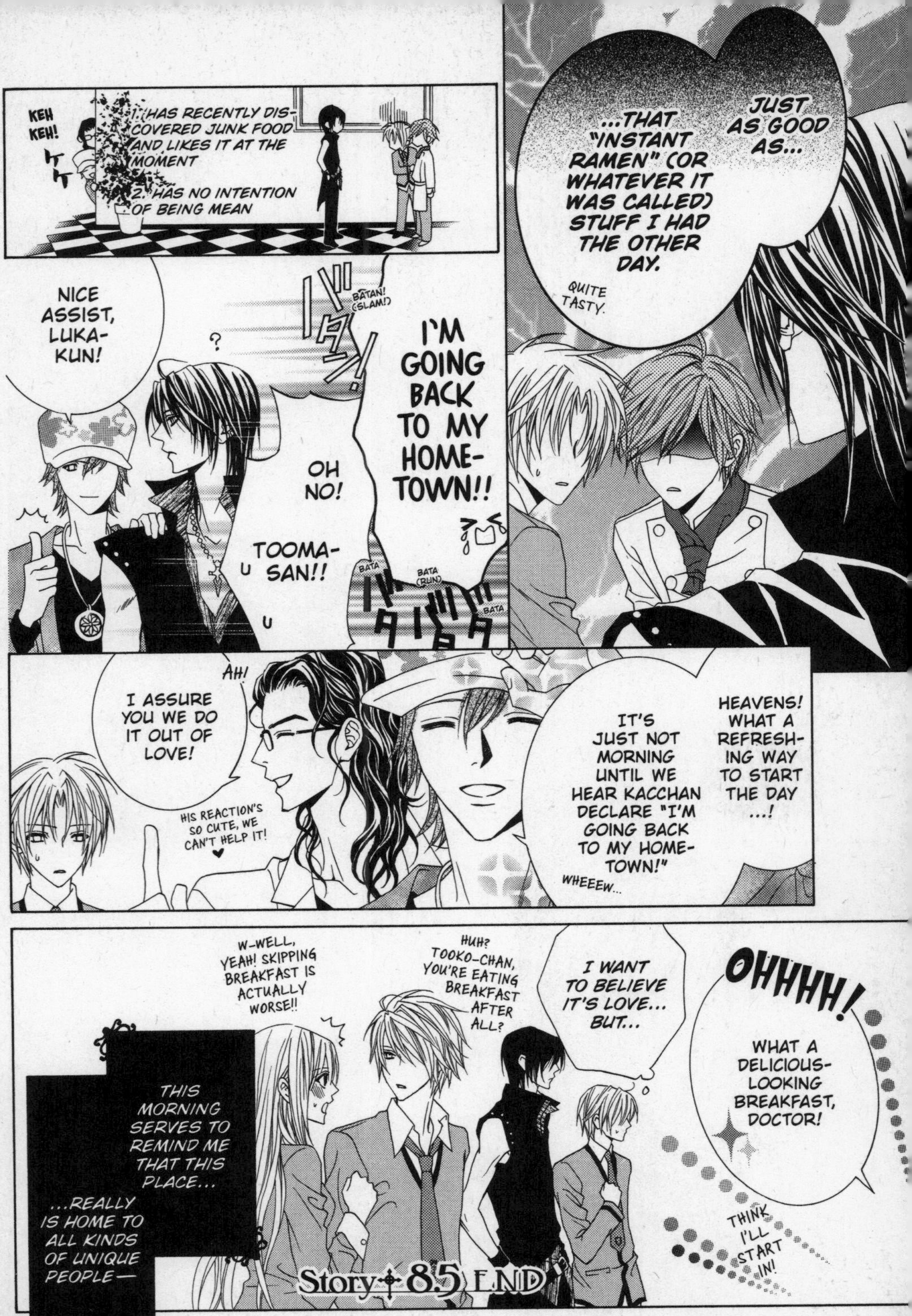

JUST AS GOOD AS...
...THAT "INSTANT RAMEN" (OR WHATEVER IT WAS CALLED) STUFF I HAD THE OTHER DAY.
QUITE TASTY.
KEH KEH!
1. HAS RECENTLY DISCOVERED JUNK FOOD AND LIKES IT AT THE MOMENT
2. HAS NO INTENTION OF BEING MEAN
BATAN! (SLAM!)
I'M GOING BACK TO MY HOMETOWN!!
BATA BATA (RUN) BATA
OH NO!
TOOMA-SAN!!
?
NICE ASSIST, LUKA-KUN!
HEAVENS! WHAT A REFRESHING WAY TO START THE DAY...!
IT'S JUST NOT MORNING UNTIL WE HEAR KACCHAN DECLARE "I'M GOING BACK TO MY HOMETOWN!"
WHEEEW...
AH!
I ASSURE YOU WE DO IT OUT OF LOVE!
HIS REACTION'S SO CUTE, WE CAN'T HELP IT! ♥
OHHHH!
WHAT A DELICIOUS-LOOKING BREAKFAST, DOCTOR!
THINK I'LL START IN!
I WANT TO BELIEVE IT'S LOVE... BUT...
HUH? TOOKO-CHAN, YOU'RE EATING BREAKFAST AFTER ALL?
W-WELL, YEAH! SKIPPING BREAKFAST IS ACTUALLY WORSE!!
THIS MORNING SERVES TO REMIND ME THAT THIS PLACE...
...REALLY IS HOME TO ALL KINDS OF UNIQUE PEOPLE—
Story 8.5 END

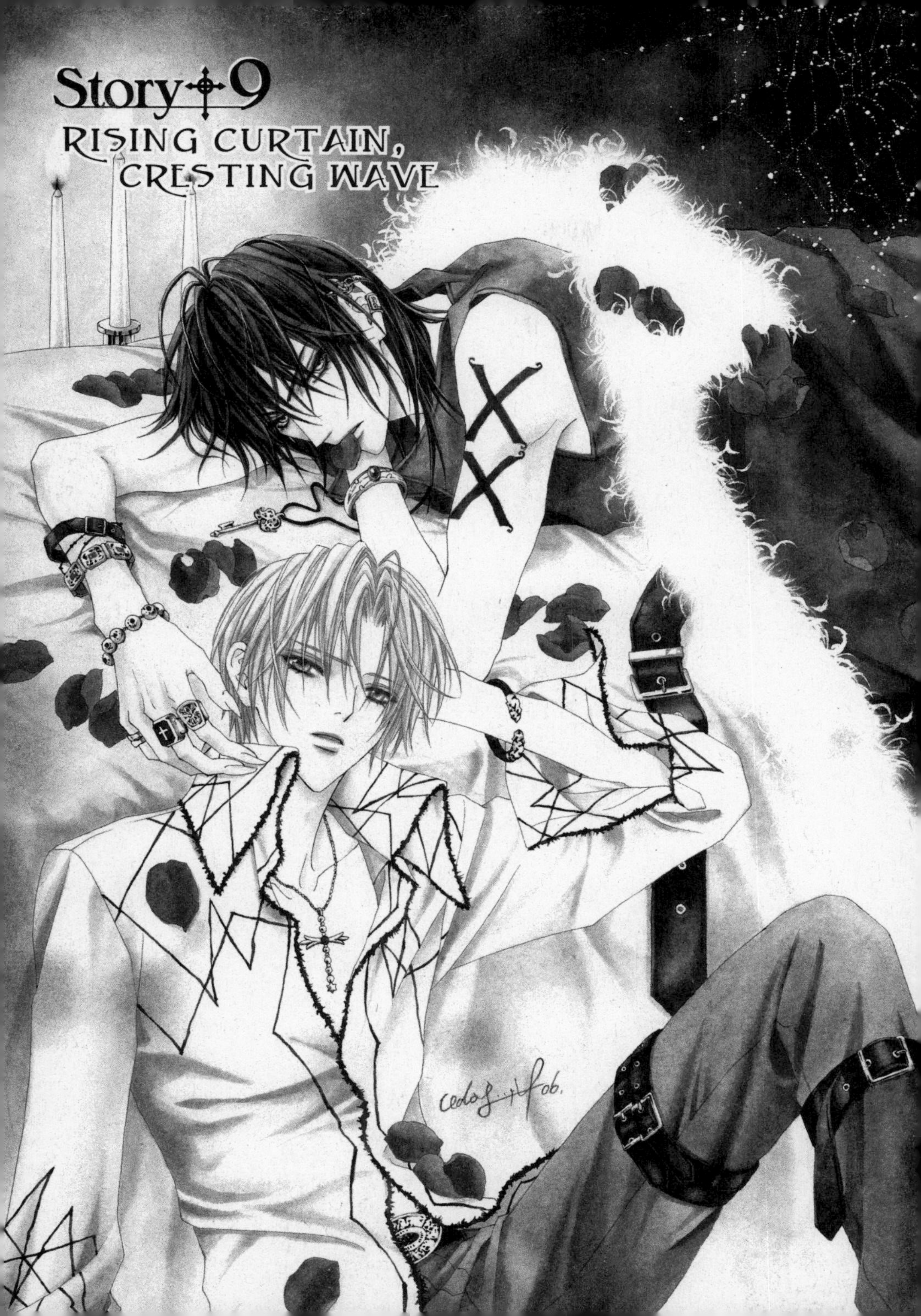
Story 9
RISING CURTAIN,
CRESTING WAVE

The Betrayal Knows My Name

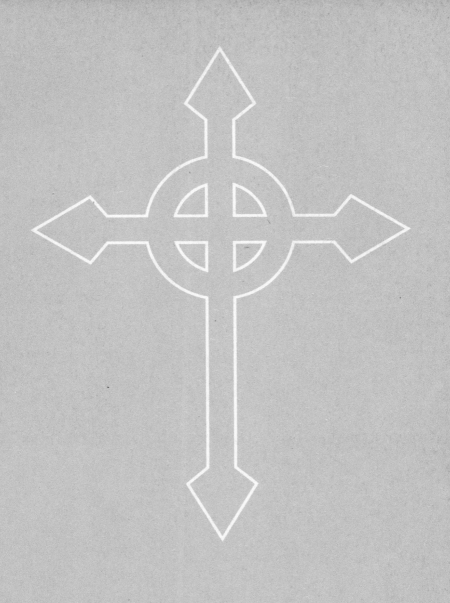

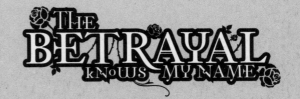

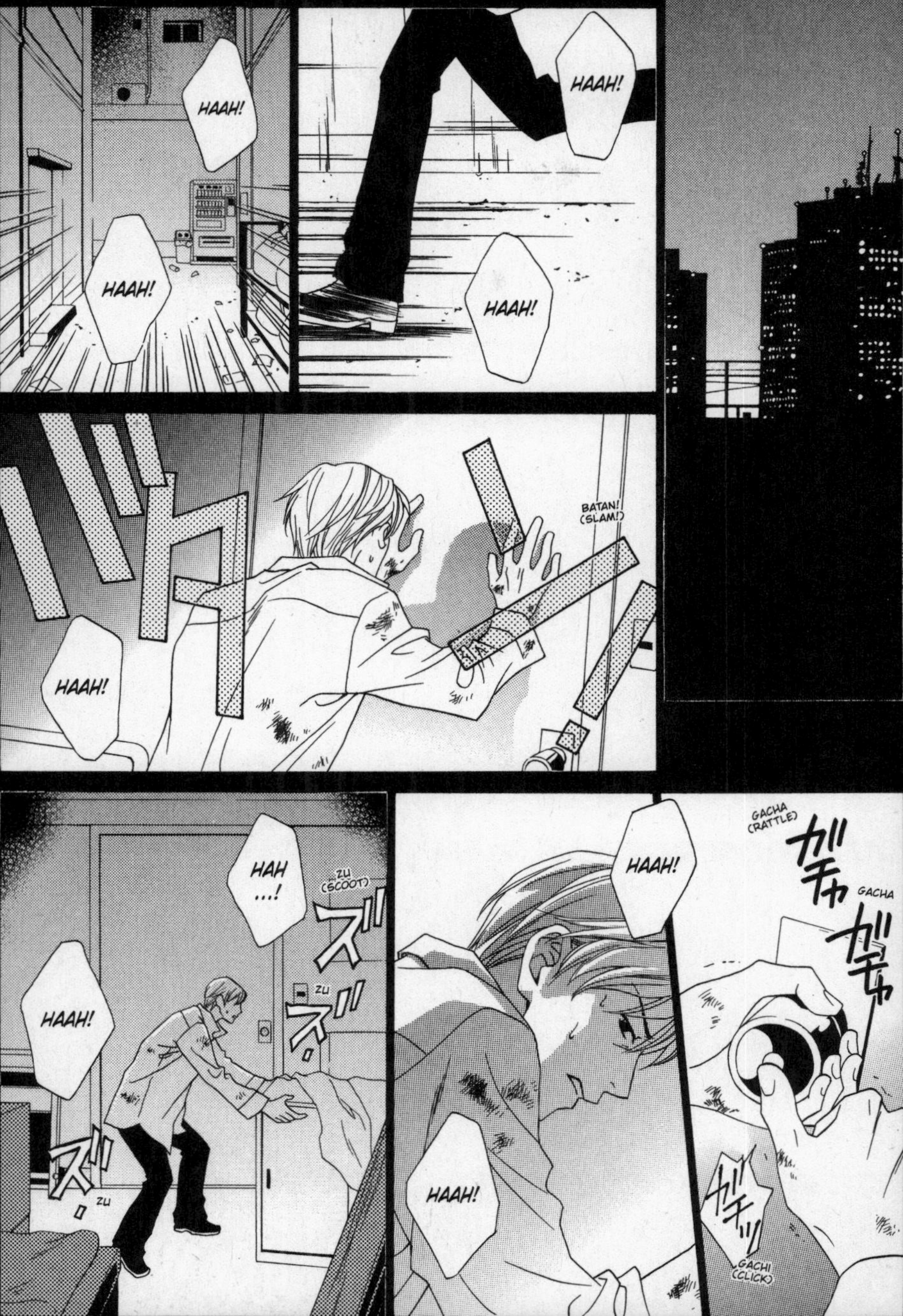
HAAH!
HAAH!
HAAH!
HAAH!
BATAN! (SLAM!)
HAAH!
GACHA (RATTLE)
GACHA
HAAH!
HAAH!
GACHI (CLICK)
HAH ...!
ZU (SCOOT)
ZU
HAAH!
ZU

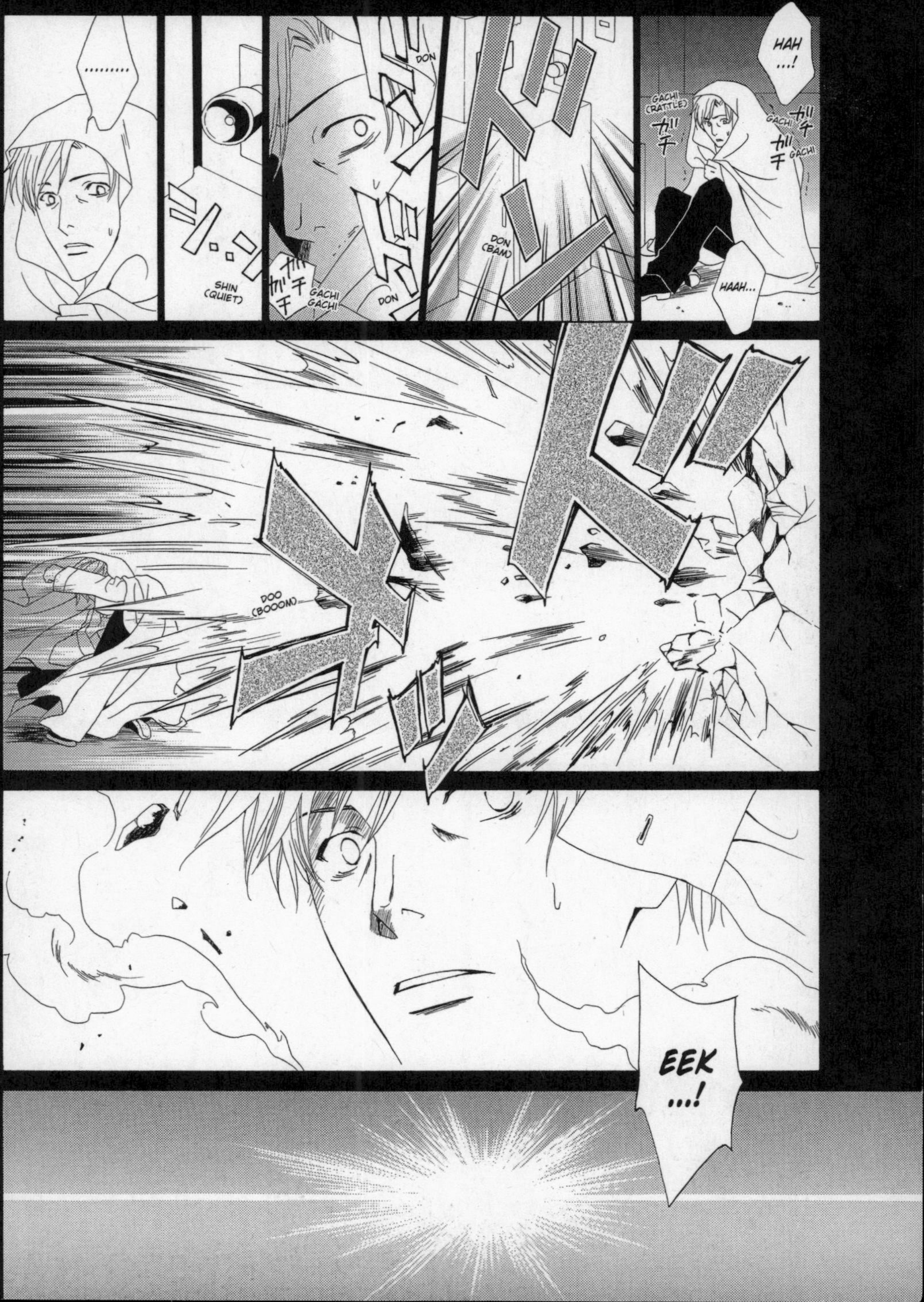

HAH ...!
GACHI (RATTLE)
GACHI
GACHI
HAAH...
DON
DON (BAM)
DON
GACHI GACHI
SHIN (QUIET)
....
DOO (BOOOM)
EEK ...!

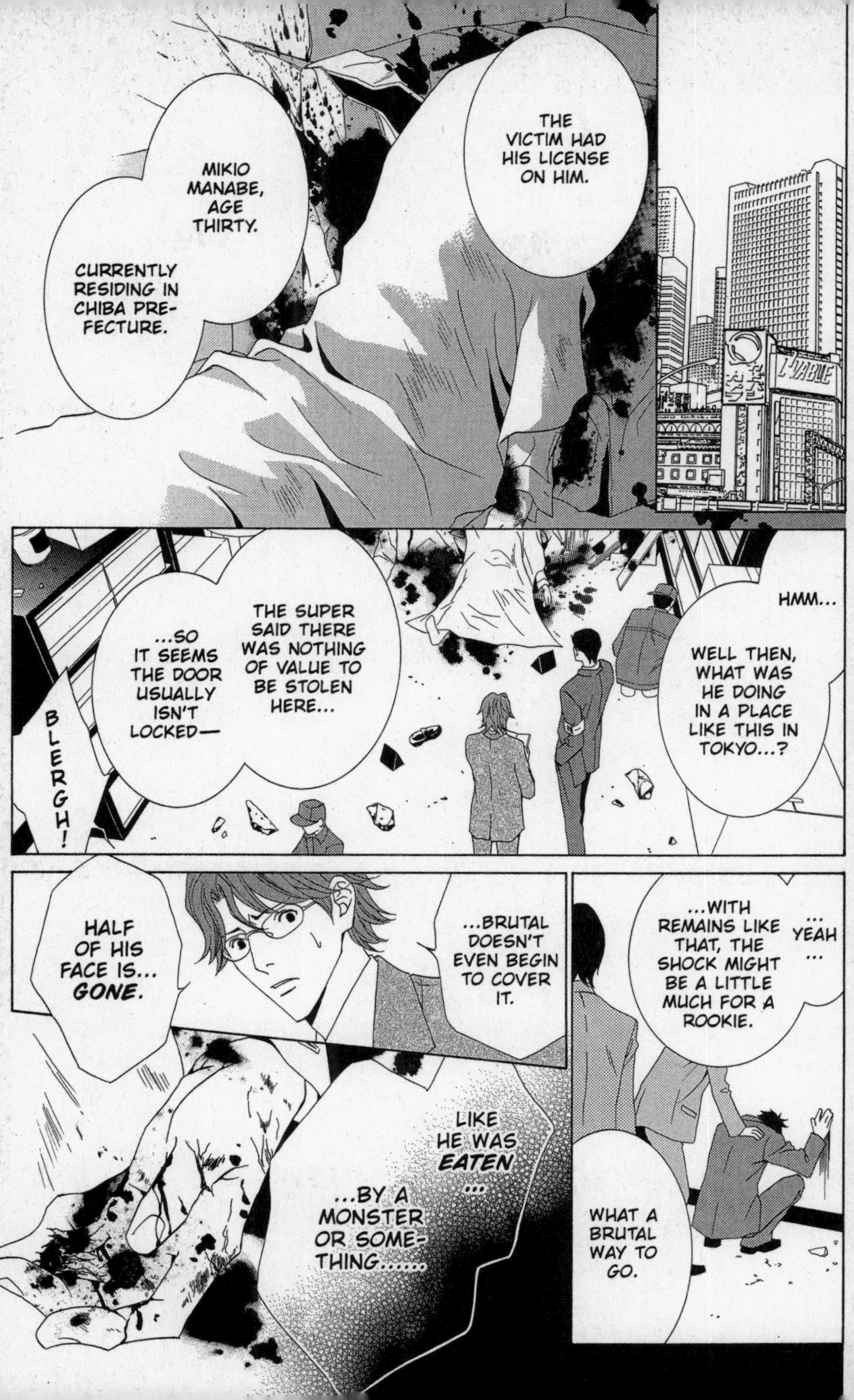
THE VICTIM HAD HIS LICENSE ON HIM.
MIKIO MANABE, AGE THIRTY.
CURRENTLY RESIDING IN CHIBA PREFECTURE.
HMM...
WELL THEN, WHAT WAS HE DOING IN A PLACE LIKE THIS IN TOKYO...?
THE SUPER SAID THERE WAS NOTHING OF VALUE TO BE STOLEN HERE...
...SO IT SEEMS THE DOOR USUALLY ISN'T LOCKED—
BLERGH!
...WITH REMAINS LIKE THAT, THE SHOCK MIGHT BE A LITTLE MUCH FOR A ROOKIE.
...YEAH...
WHAT A BRUTAL WAY TO GO.
...BRUTAL DOESN'T EVEN BEGIN TO COVER IT.
HALF OF HIS FACE IS... GONE.
LIKE HE WAS EATEN...
...BY A MONSTER OR SOMETHING......

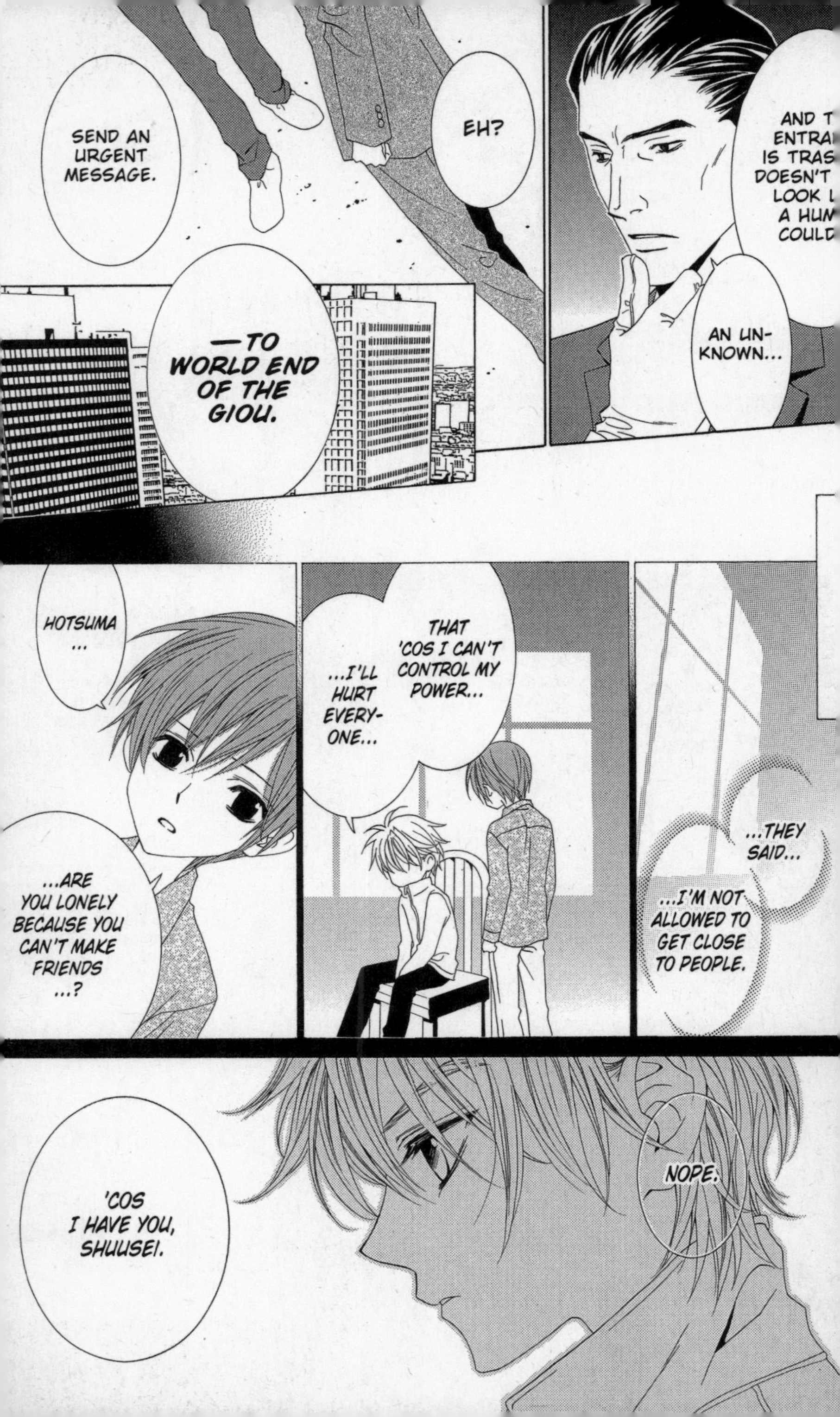
AND T ENTRA IS TRAS DOESN'T LOOK L A HUM COULD
AN UN-KNOWN...
EH?
SEND AN URGENT MESSAGE.
—TO WORLD END OF THE GIOU.
...THEY SAID...
...I'M NOT ALLOWED TO GET CLOSE TO PEOPLE.
THAT 'COS I CAN'T CONTROL MY POWER...
...I'LL HURT EVERY-ONE...
HOTSUMA...
...ARE YOU LONELY BECAUSE YOU CAN'T MAKE FRIENDS...?
NOPE.
'COS I HAVE YOU, SHUUSEI.

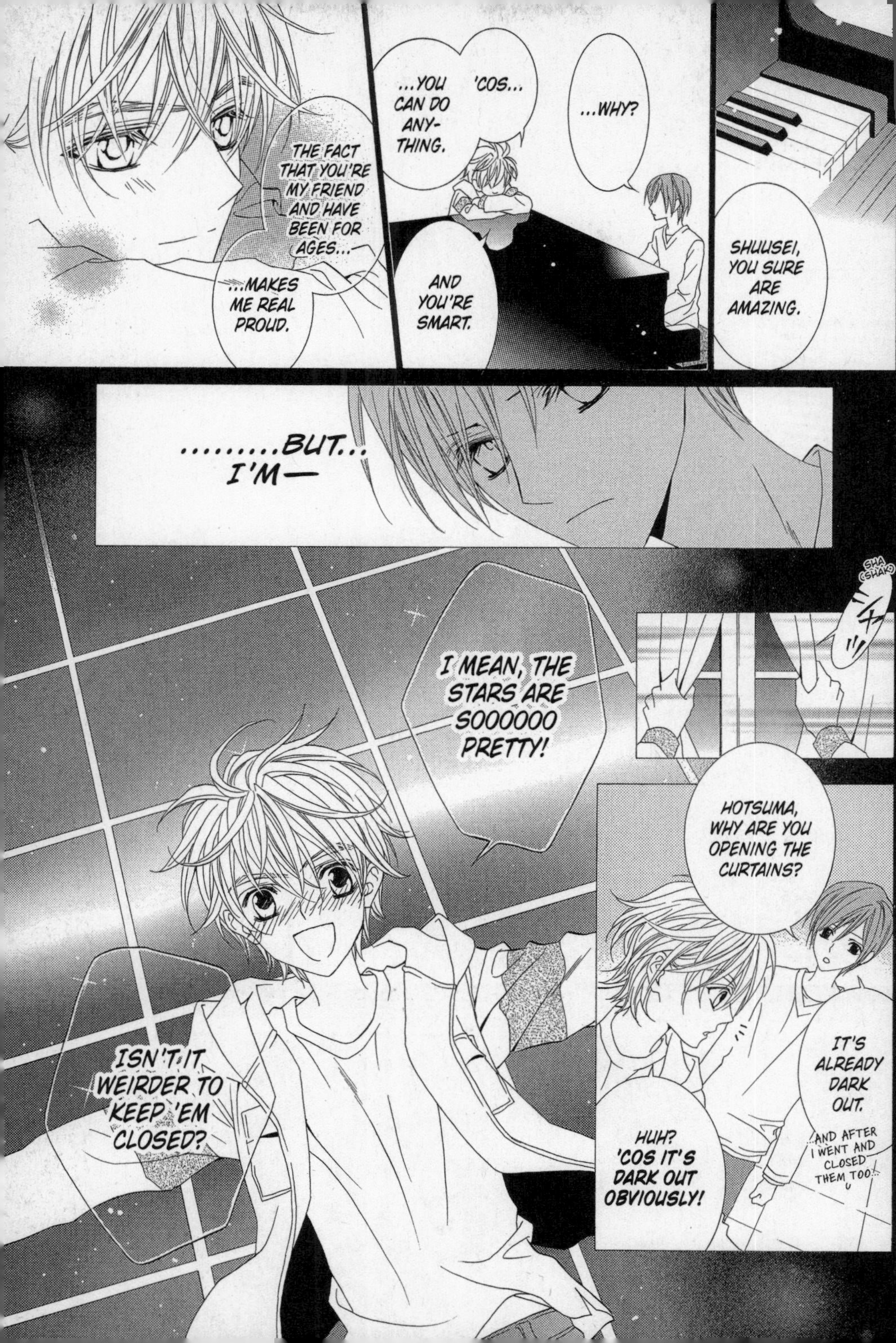
SHUUSEI, YOU SURE ARE AMAZING.
...WHY?
'COS...
...YOU CAN DO ANY-THING.
AND YOU'RE SMART.
THE FACT THAT YOU'RE MY FRIEND AND HAVE BEEN FOR AGES...
...MAKES ME REAL PROUD.
.........BUT... I'M—
SHA (SHAK)
HOTSUMA, WHY ARE YOU OPENING THE CURTAINS?
IT'S ALREADY DARK OUT.
...AND AFTER I WENT AND CLOSED THEM TOO...
HUH? 'COS IT'S DARK OUT OBVIOUSLY!
I MEAN, THE STARS ARE SOOOOOO PRETTY!
ISN'T IT WEIRDER TO KEEP 'EM CLOSED?

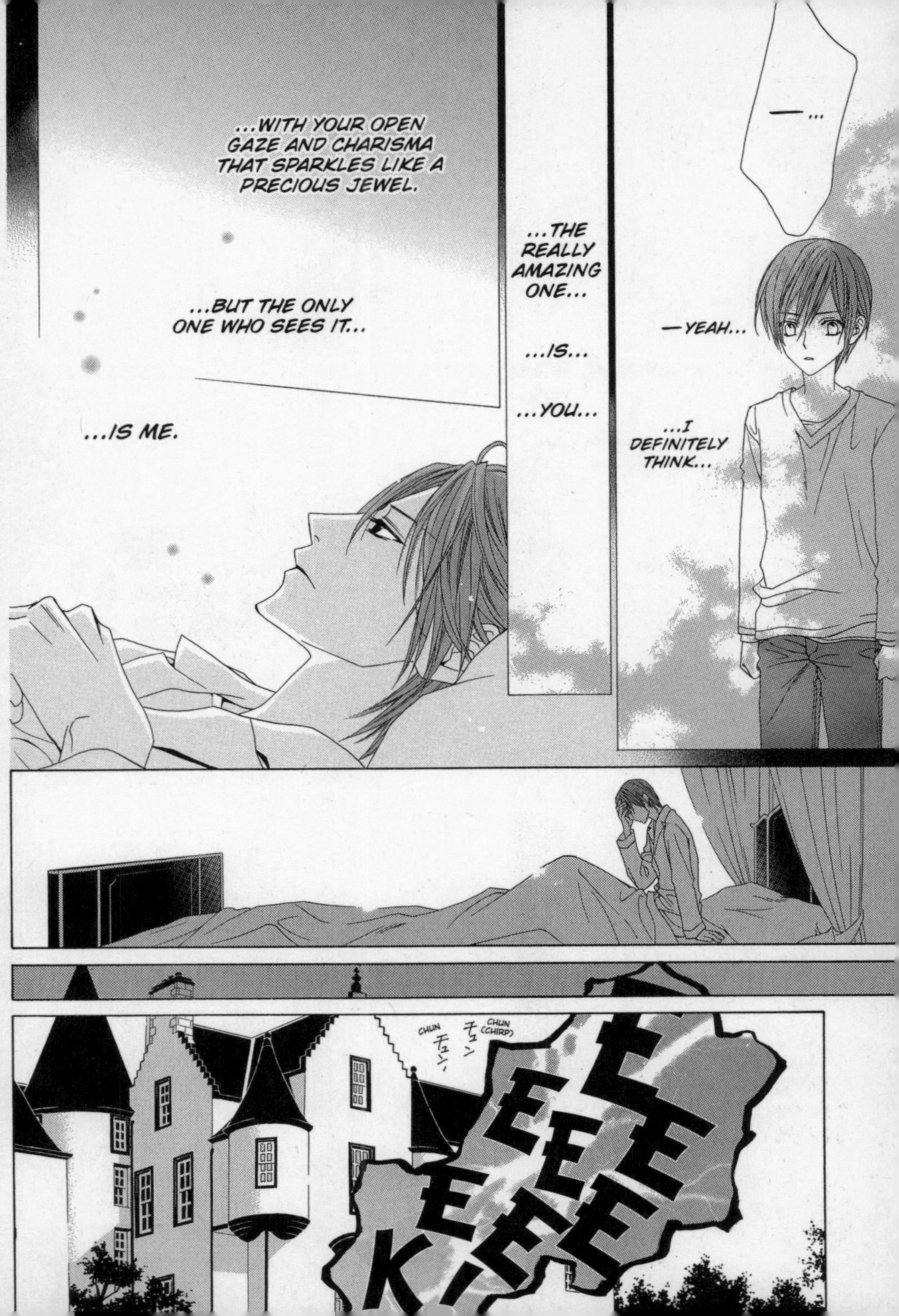
—...
—YEAH...
...I DEFINITELY THINK...
...THE REALLY AMAZING ONE...
...IS...
...YOU...
...WITH YOUR OPEN GAZE AND CHARISMA THAT SPARKLES LIKE A PRECIOUS JEWEL.
...BUT THE ONLY ONE WHO SEES IT...
...IS ME.
チュン CHUN (CHIRP)
チュン CHUN
KIEEEEEEEEEE

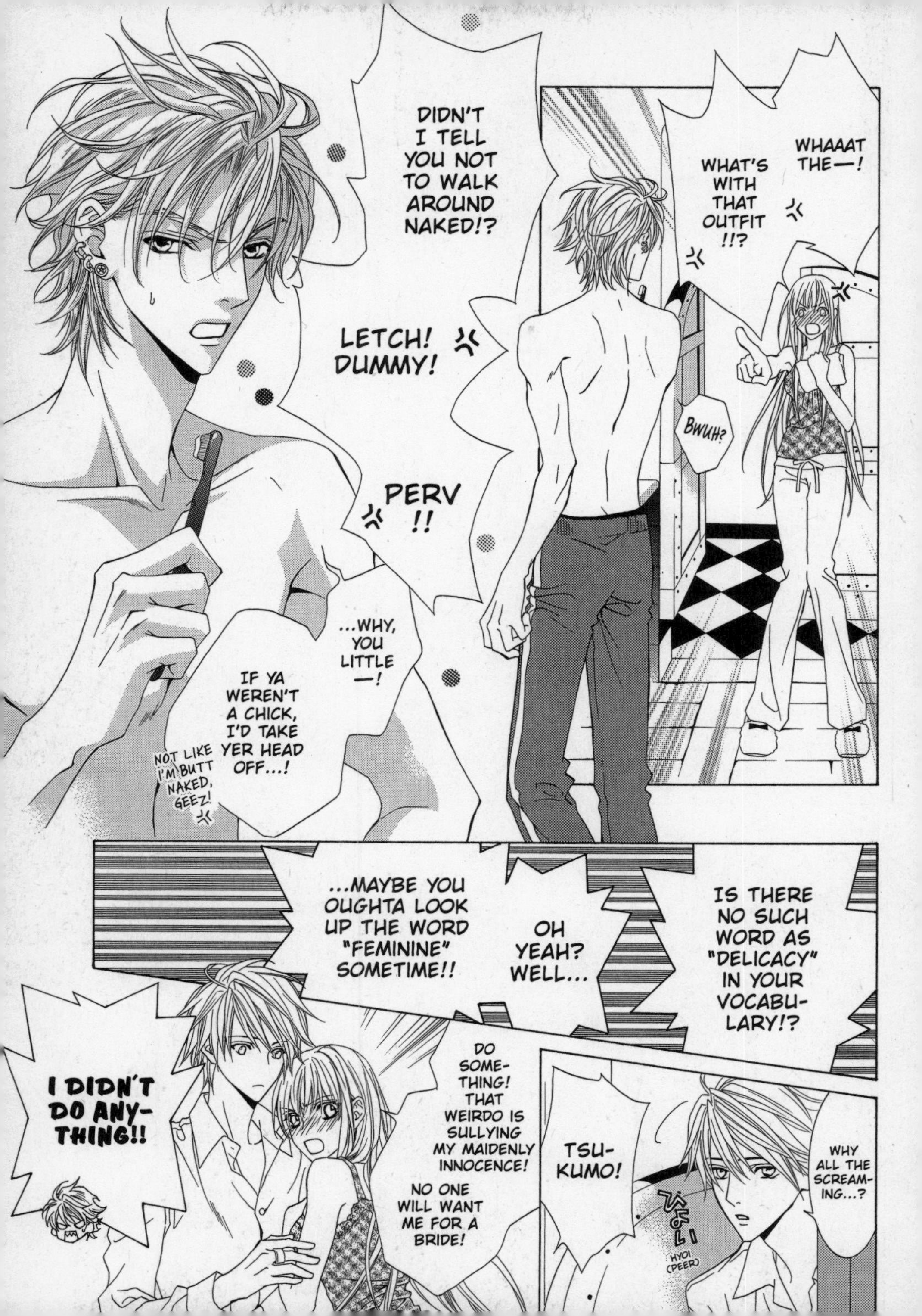
WHAAAT THE—!
WHAT'S WITH THAT OUTFIT !!?
BWUH?
DIDN'T I TELL YOU NOT TO WALK AROUND NAKED!?
LETCH! DUMMY!
PERV !!
...WHY, YOU LITTLE —!
IF YA WEREN'T A CHICK, I'D TAKE YER HEAD OFF...!
NOT LIKE I'M BUTT NAKED, GEEZ!
IS THERE NO SUCH WORD AS "DELICACY" IN YOUR VOCABULARY!?
OH YEAH? WELL...
...MAYBE YOU OUGHTA LOOK UP THE WORD "FEMININE" SOMETIME!!
WHY ALL THE SCREAMING...?
HYOI (PEER)
TSU-KUMO!
DO SOMETHING! THAT WEIRDO IS SULLYING MY MAIDENLY INNOCENCE!
NO ONE WILL WANT ME FOR A BRIDE!
I DIDN'T DO ANY-THING!!

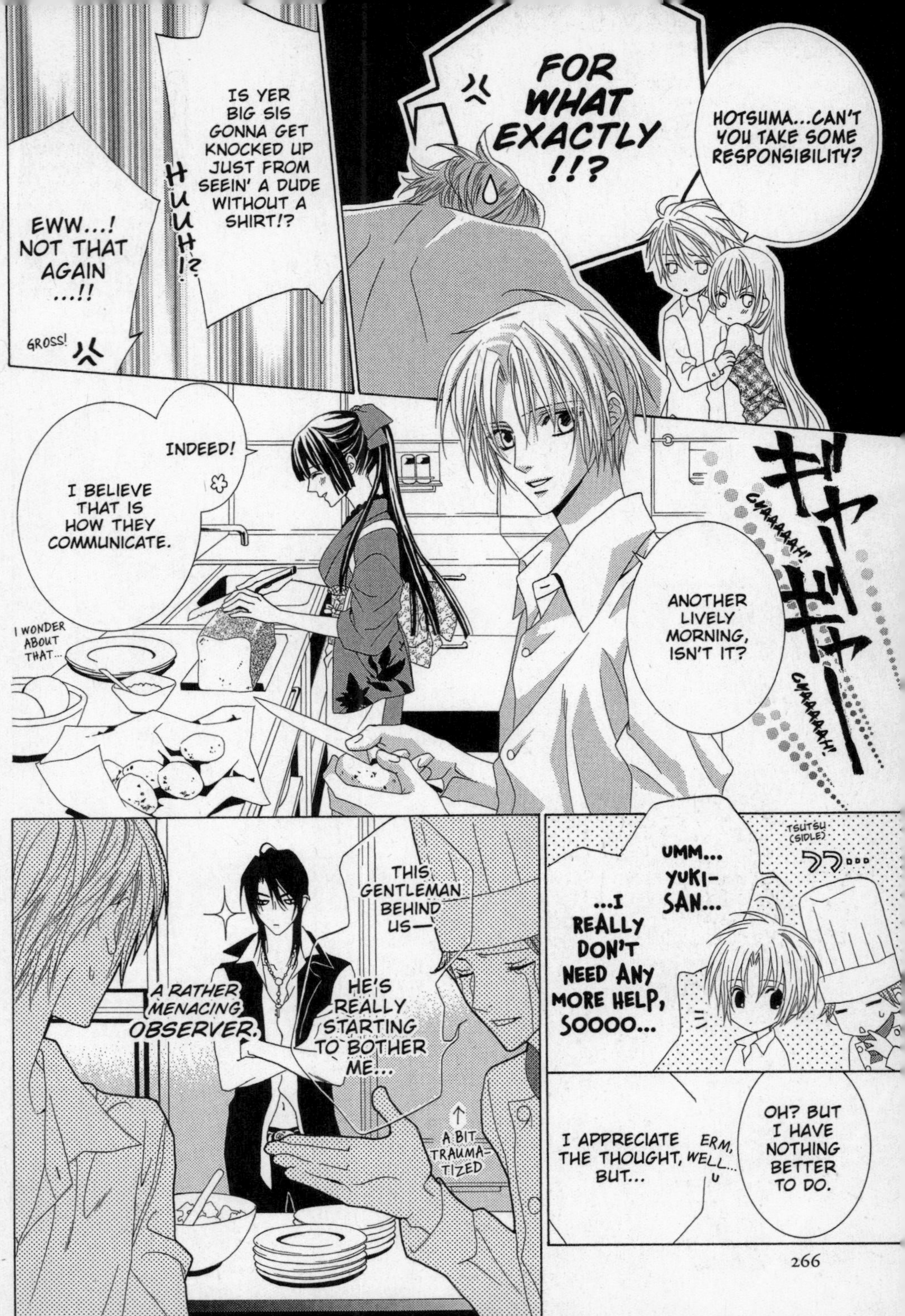
HOTSUMA...CAN'T YOU TAKE SOME RESPONSIBILITY?
FOR WHAT EXACTLY!!?
IS YER BIG SIS GONNA GET KNOCKED UP JUST FROM SEEIN' A DUDE WITHOUT A SHIRT!?
HUUUH!?
EWW...! NOT THAT AGAIN...!!
GROSS!
ギャーギャー
GYAAAAAH!
GYAAAAAH!
ANOTHER LIVELY MORNING, ISN'T IT?
INDEED!
I BELIEVE THAT IS HOW THEY COMMUNICATE.
I WONDER ABOUT THAT...
TSUTSU (SIDLE)
つつ...
UMM... YUKI-SAN...
...I REALLY DON'T NEED ANY MORE HELP, SOOOO...
OH? BUT I HAVE NOTHING BETTER TO DO.
ERM, WELL...
I APPRECIATE THE THOUGHT, BUT...
THIS GENTLEMAN BEHIND US—
HE'S REALLY STARTING TO BOTHER ME...
A RATHER MENACING OBSERVER.
A BIT TRAUMATIZED

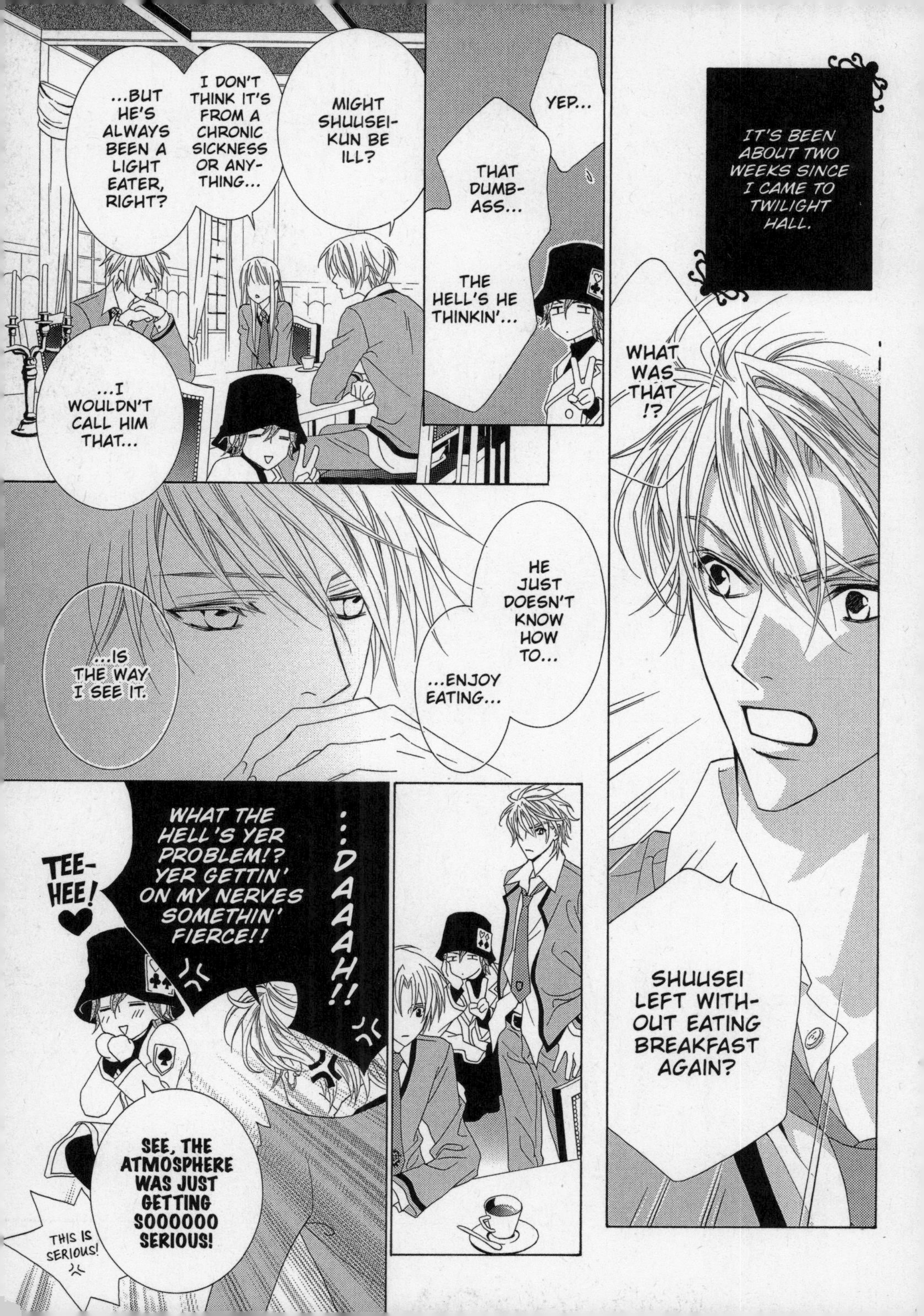

IT'S BEEN ABOUT TWO WEEKS SINCE I CAME TO TWILIGHT HALL.
WHAT WAS THAT !?
SHUUSEI LEFT WITH-OUT EATING BREAKFAST AGAIN?
YEP...
THAT DUMB-ASS...
THE HELL'S HE THINKIN'...
MIGHT SHUUSEI-KUN BE ILL?
I DON'T THINK IT'S FROM A CHRONIC SICKNESS OR ANY-THING...
...BUT HE'S ALWAYS BEEN A LIGHT EATER, RIGHT?
...I WOULDN'T CALL HIM THAT...
HE JUST DOESN'T KNOW HOW TO...
...ENJOY EATING...
...IS THE WAY I SEE IT.
...DAAAAH!!
WHAT THE HELL'S YER PROBLEM!? YER GETTIN' ON MY NERVES SOMETHIN' FIERCE!!
TEE-HEE!
SEE, THE ATMOSPHERE WAS JUST GETTING SOOOOOO SERIOUS!
THIS IS SERIOUS!

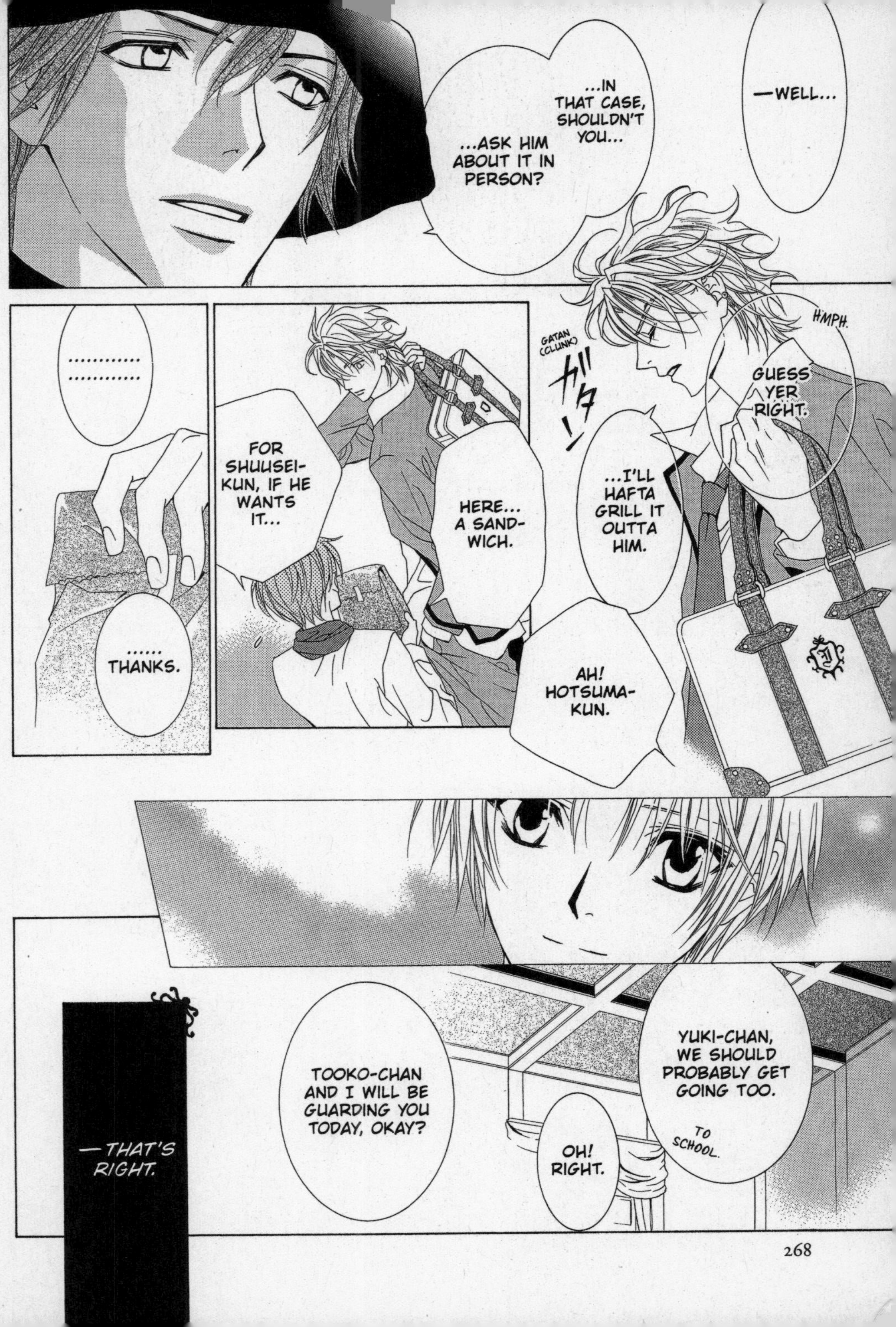
—WELL...
...IN THAT CASE, SHOULDN'T YOU...
...ASK HIM ABOUT IT IN PERSON?
HMPH.
GUESS YER RIGHT.
GATAN (CLUNK)
...I'LL HAFTA GRILL IT OUTTA HIM.
AH! HOTSUMA-KUN.
HERE... A SAND-WICH.
FOR SHUUSEI-KUN, IF HE WANTS IT...
....
....
...... THANKS.
YUKI-CHAN, WE SHOULD PROBABLY GET GOING TOO.
TO SCHOOL.
OH! RIGHT.
TOOKO-CHAN AND I WILL BE GUARDING YOU TODAY, OKAY?
—THAT'S RIGHT.

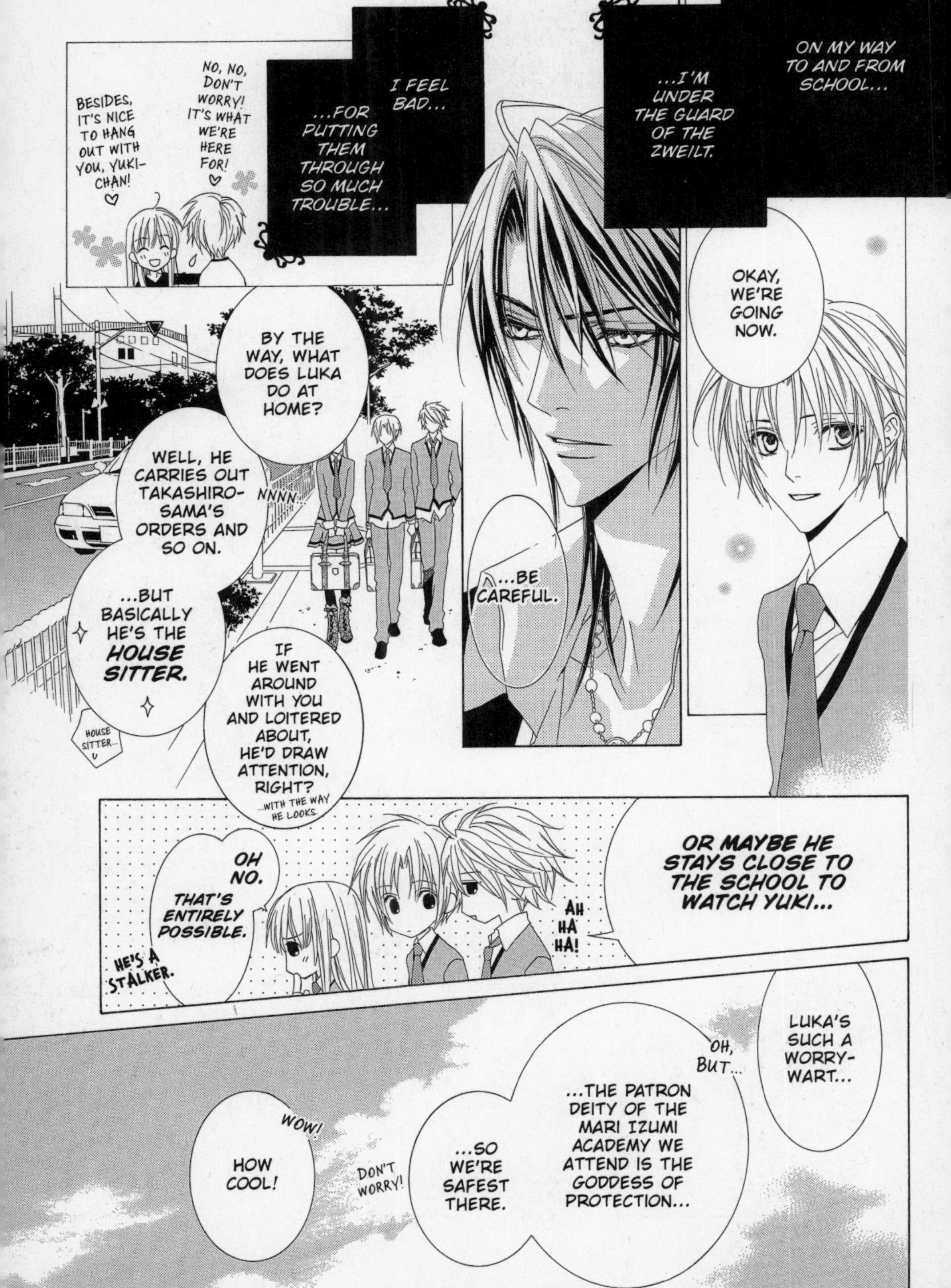
ON MY WAY TO AND FROM SCHOOL...
...I'M UNDER THE GUARD OF THE ZWEILT.
I FEEL BAD...
...FOR PUTTING THEM THROUGH SO MUCH TROUBLE...
NO, NO, DON'T WORRY! IT'S WHAT WE'RE HERE FOR!
BESIDES, IT'S NICE TO HANG OUT WITH YOU, YUKI-CHAN!
OKAY, WE'RE GOING NOW.
...BE CAREFUL.
BY THE WAY, WHAT DOES LUKA DO AT HOME?
WELL, HE CARRIES OUT TAKASHIRO-SAMA'S ORDERS AND SO ON.
NNNN.
...BUT BASICALLY HE'S THE HOUSE SITTER.
HOUSE SITTER...
IF HE WENT AROUND WITH YOU AND LOITERED ABOUT, HE'D DRAW ATTENTION, RIGHT?
...WITH THE WAY HE LOOKS.
OR MAYBE HE STAYS CLOSE TO THE SCHOOL TO WATCH YUKI...
AH HA HA!
OH NO. THAT'S ENTIRELY POSSIBLE.
HE'S A STALKER.
LUKA'S SUCH A WORRY-WART...
OH, BUT...
...THE PATRON DEITY OF THE MARI IZUMI ACADEMY WE ATTEND IS THE GODDESS OF PROTECTION...
...SO WE'RE SAFEST THERE.
DON'T WORRY!
HOW COOL!
WOW!

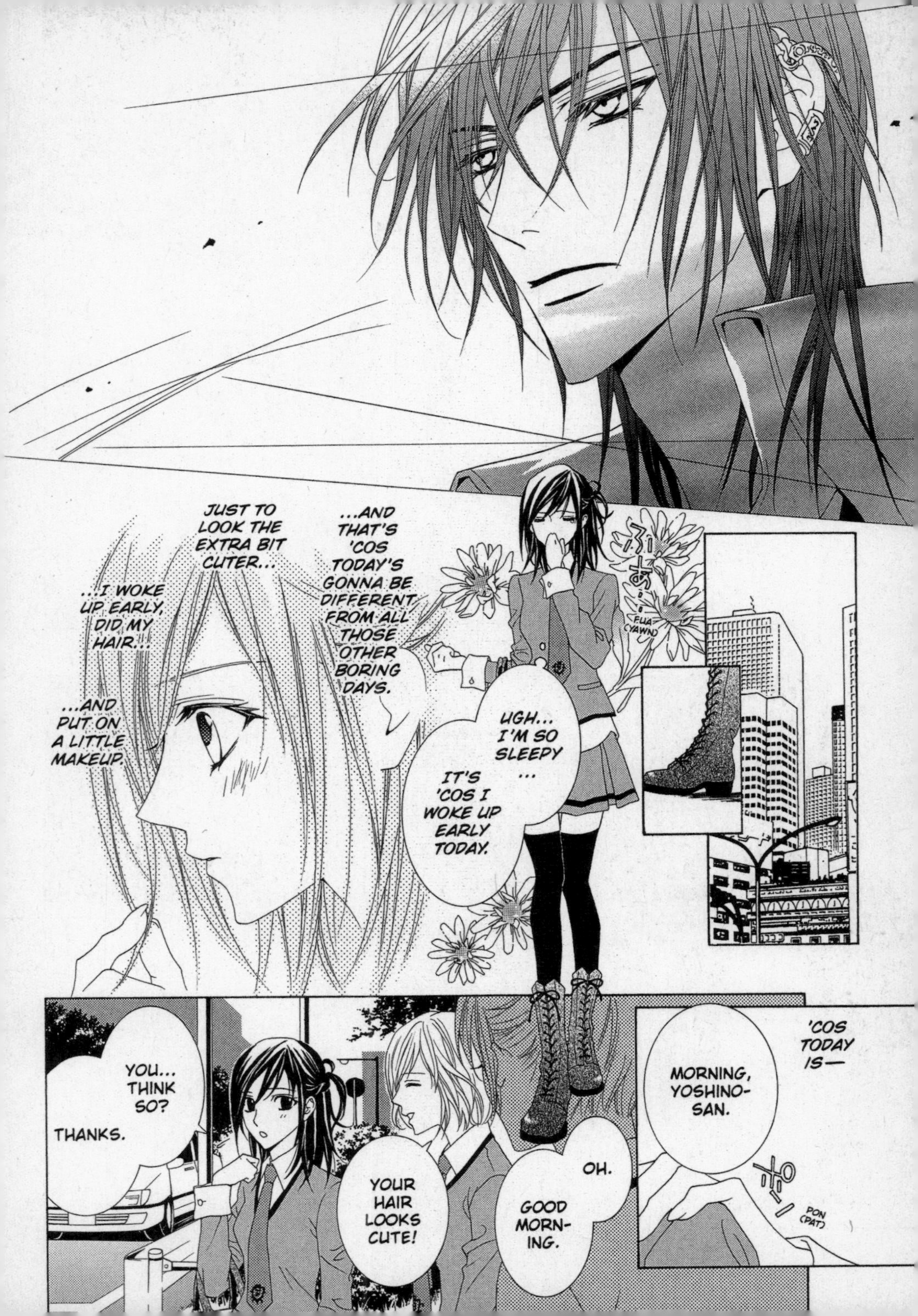
ふぁ…
FUA (YAWN)
UGH... I'M SO SLEEPY...
IT'S 'COS I WOKE UP EARLY TODAY.
...AND THAT'S 'COS TODAY'S GONNA BE DIFFERENT FROM ALL THOSE OTHER BORING DAYS.
JUST TO LOOK THE EXTRA BIT CUTER...
...I WOKE UP EARLY, DID MY HAIR...
...AND PUT ON A LITTLE MAKEUP.
'COS TODAY IS—
MORNING, YOSHINO-SAN.
ぽん
PON (PAT)
OH.
GOOD MORN-ING.
YOUR HAIR LOOKS CUTE!
YOU... THINK SO?
THANKS.

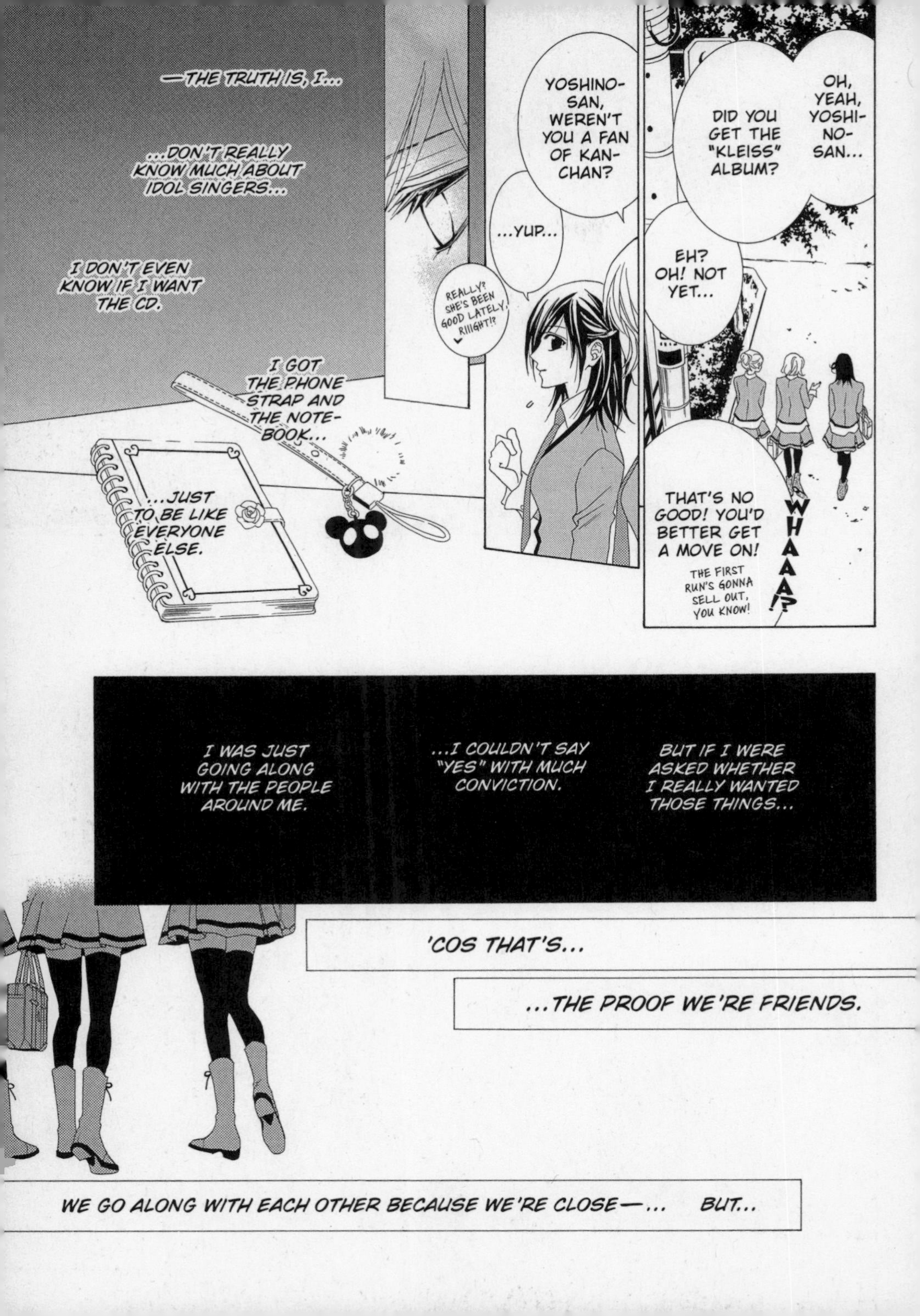
OH, YEAH, YOSHINO-SAN...
DID YOU GET THE "KLEISS" ALBUM?
EH? OH! NOT YET...
THAT'S NO GOOD! YOU'D BETTER GET A MOVE ON!
THE FIRST RUN'S GONNA SELL OUT, YOU KNOW!
WHAAA!?
YOSHINO-SAN, WEREN'T YOU A FAN OF KAN-CHAN?
...YUP...
REALLY? SHE'S BEEN GOOD LATELY, RIIIGHT!?
—THE TRUTH IS, I...
...DON'T REALLY KNOW MUCH ABOUT IDOL SINGERS...
I DON'T EVEN KNOW IF I WANT THE CD.
I GOT THE PHONE STRAP AND THE NOTE-BOOK...
...JUST TO BE LIKE EVERYONE ELSE.
BUT IF I WERE ASKED WHETHER I REALLY WANTED THOSE THINGS...
...I COULDN'T SAY "YES" WITH MUCH CONVICTION.
I WAS JUST GOING ALONG WITH THE PEOPLE AROUND ME.
'COS THAT'S...
...THE PROOF WE'RE FRIENDS.
WE GO ALONG WITH EACH OTHER BECAUSE WE'RE CLOSE—... BUT...

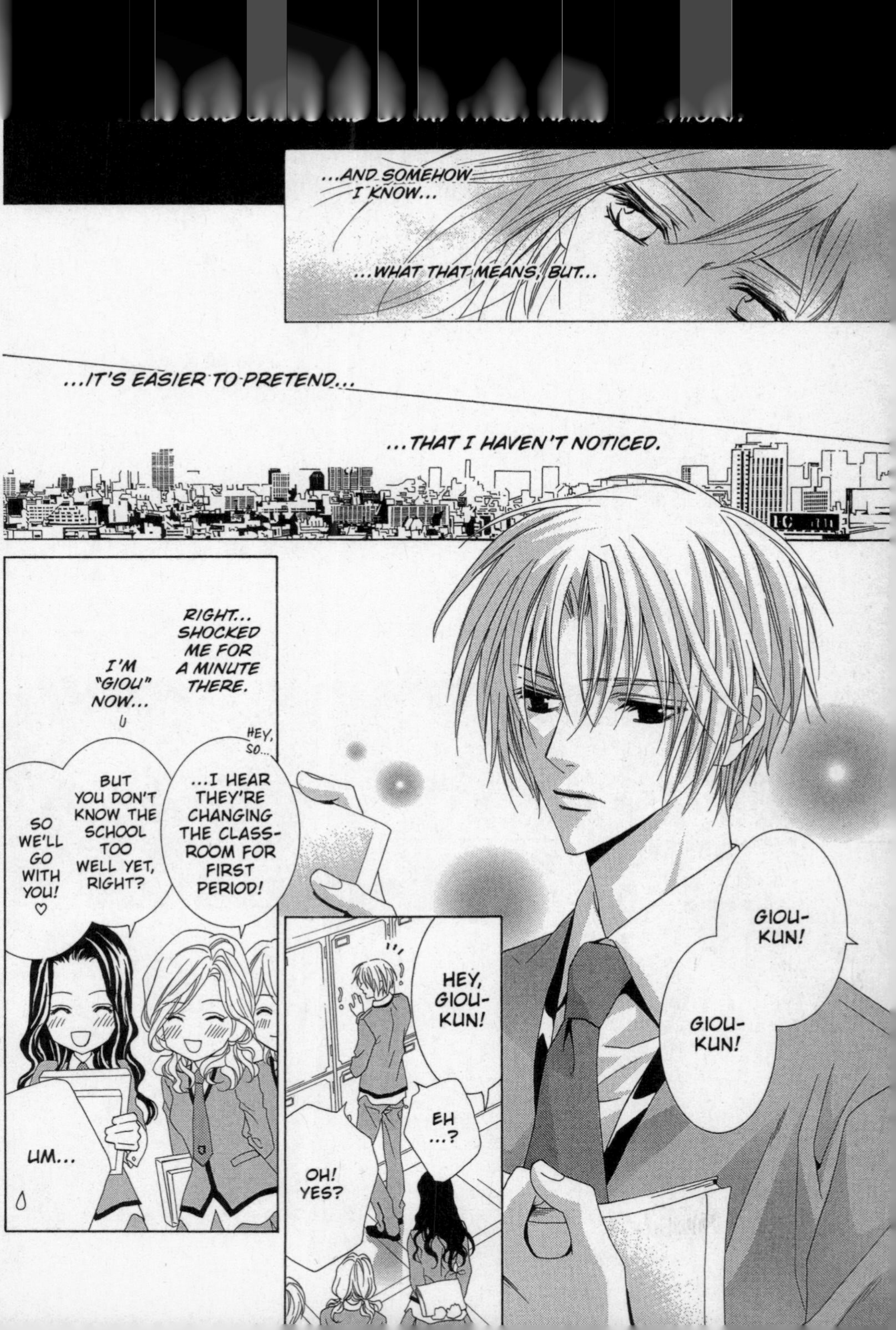
...AND SOMEHOW I KNOW...
...WHAT THAT MEANS, BUT...
...IT'S EASIER TO PRETEND...
...THAT I HAVEN'T NOTICED.
GIOU-KUN!
GIOU-KUN!
HEY, GIOU-KUN!
EH ...?
OH! YES?
RIGHT... SHOCKED ME FOR A MINUTE THERE.
I'M "GIOU" NOW...
HEY, SO...
...I HEAR THEY'RE CHANGING THE CLASS-ROOM FOR FIRST PERIOD!
BUT YOU DON'T KNOW THE SCHOOL TOO WELL YET, RIGHT?
SO WE'LL GO WITH YOU! ♡
UM...

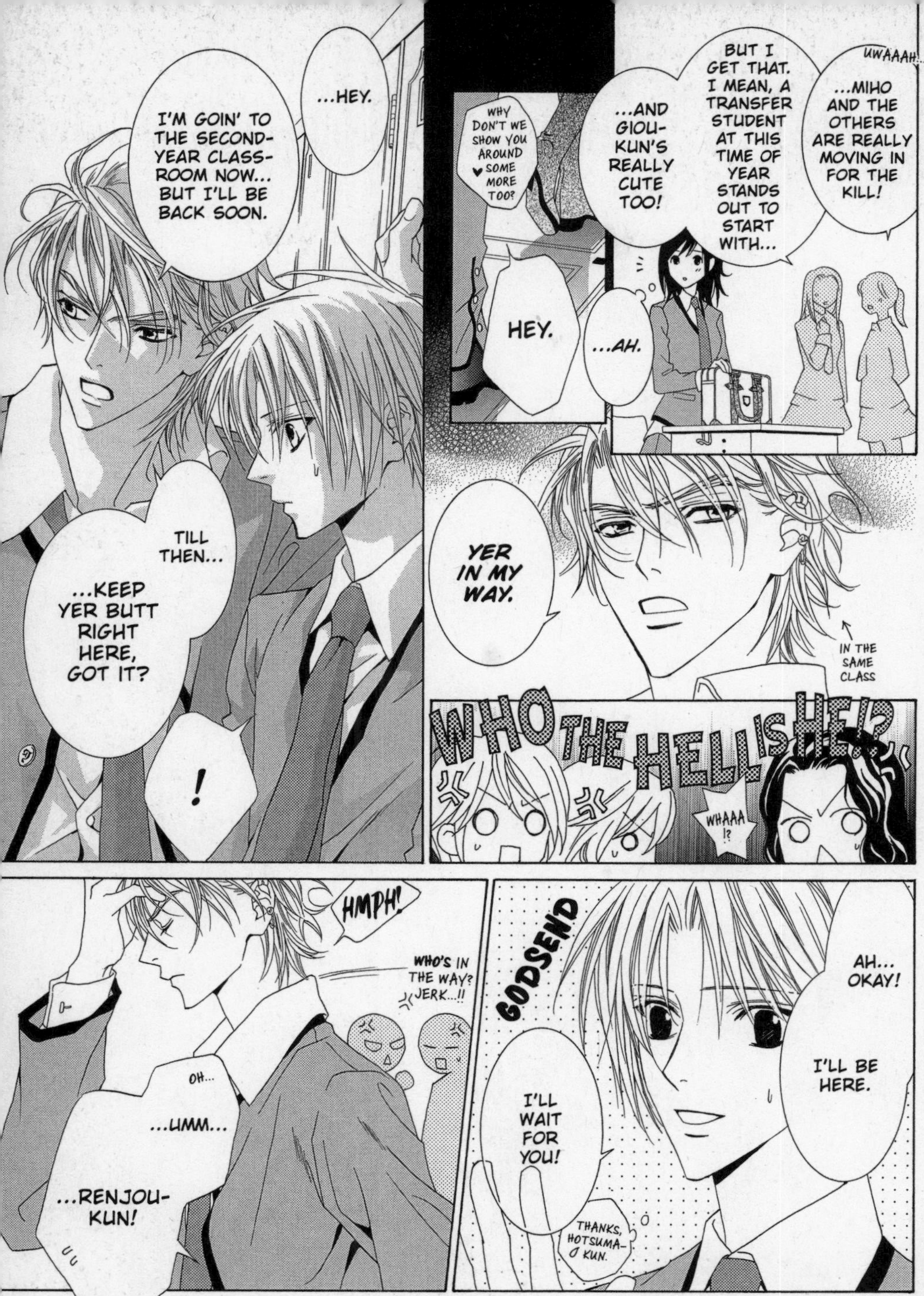
UWAAAH...
...MIHO AND THE OTHERS ARE REALLY MOVING IN FOR THE KILL!
BUT I GET THAT. I MEAN, A TRANSFER STUDENT AT THIS TIME OF YEAR STANDS OUT TO START WITH...
...AND GIOU-KUN'S REALLY CUTE TOO!
...AH.
WHY DON'T WE SHOW YOU AROUND SOME MORE TOO?
HEY.
YER IN MY WAY.
IN THE SAME CLASS
WHO THE HELL IS HE!?
WHAAA!?
...HEY.
I'M GOIN' TO THE SECOND-YEAR CLASSROOM NOW... BUT I'LL BE BACK SOON.
TILL THEN...
...KEEP YER BUTT RIGHT HERE, GOT IT?
!
AH... OKAY!
I'LL BE HERE.
GODSEND
I'LL WAIT FOR YOU!
THANKS, HOTSUMA-KUN.
HMPH!
WHO'S IN THE WAY? JERK...!!
OH...
...UMM...
...RENJOU-KUN!

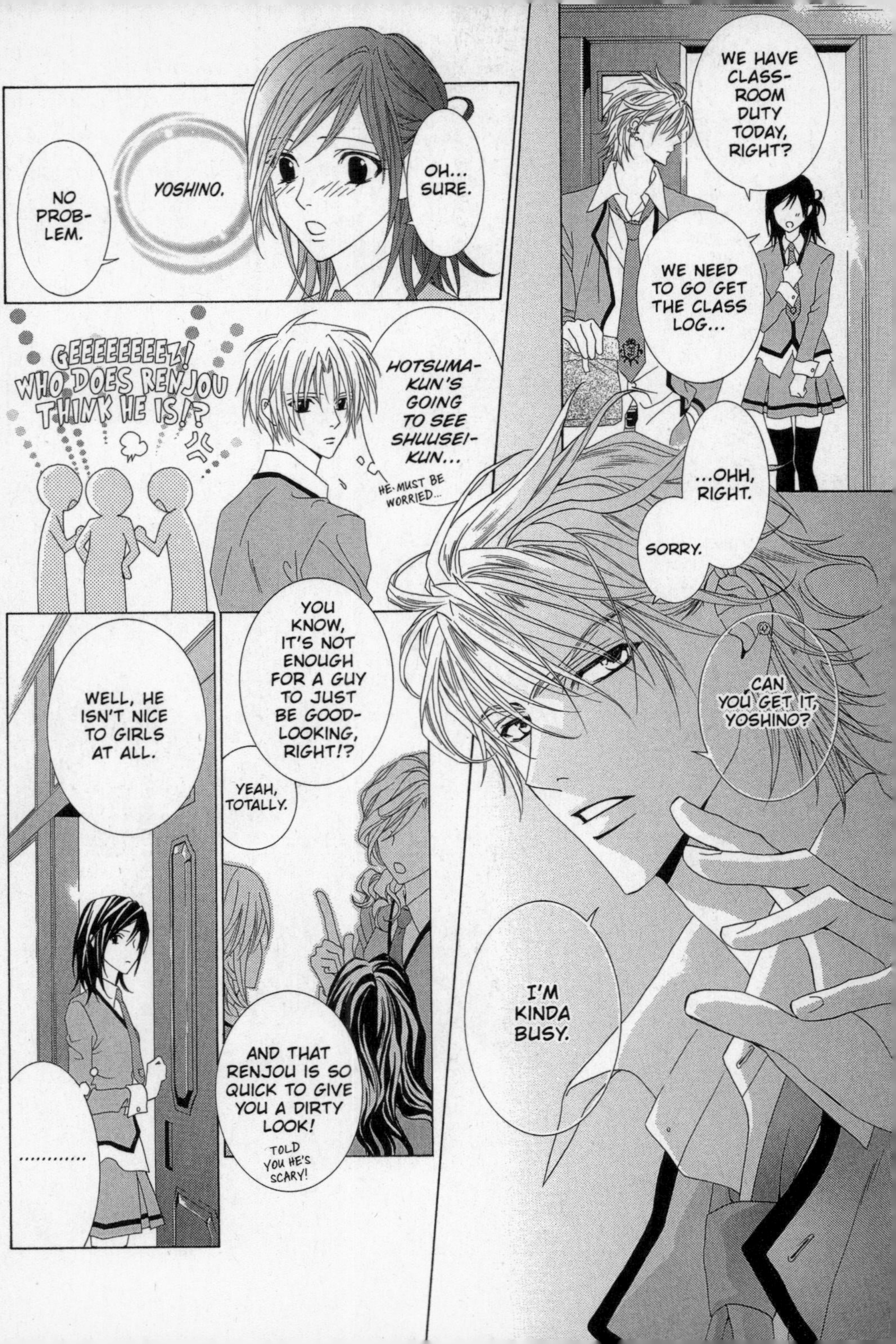
WE HAVE CLASS-ROOM DUTY TODAY, RIGHT?
WE NEED TO GO GET THE CLASS LOG...
...OHH, RIGHT.
SORRY.
CAN YOU GET IT, YOSHINO?
I'M KINDA BUSY.
OH... SURE.
YOSHINO.
NO PROB-LEM.
HOTSUMA-KUN'S GOING TO SEE SHUUSEI-KUN...
HE MUST BE WORRIED...
GEEEEEEEEZ! WHO DOES RENJOU THINK HE IS!?
YOU KNOW, IT'S NOT ENOUGH FOR A GUY TO JUST BE GOOD-LOOKING, RIGHT!?
YEAH, TOTALLY.
AND THAT RENJOU IS SO QUICK TO GIVE YOU A DIRTY LOOK!
TOLD YOU HE'S SCARY!
WELL, HE ISN'T NICE TO GIRLS AT ALL.
....

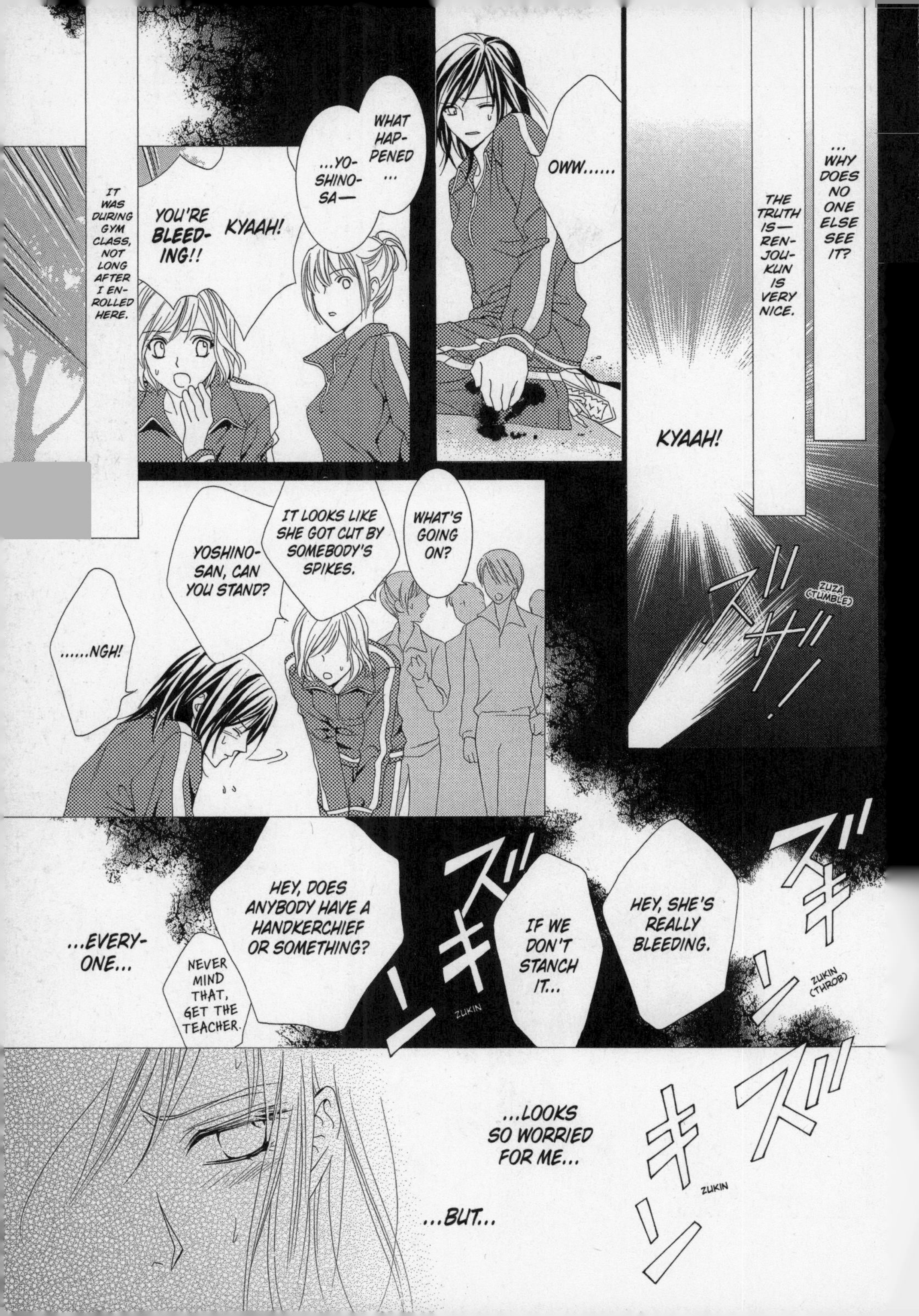
...WHY DOES NO ONE ELSE SEE IT?
THE TRUTH IS— RENJOU-KUN IS VERY NICE.
OWW......
WHAT HAPPENED...
...YOSHINO-SA—
KYAAH!
YOU'RE BLEEDING!!
IT WAS DURING GYM CLASS, NOT LONG AFTER I ENROLLED HERE.
KYAAH!
ZUZA (TUMBLE)
WHAT'S GOING ON?
IT LOOKS LIKE SHE GOT CUT BY SOMEBODY'S SPIKES.
YOSHINO-SAN, CAN YOU STAND?
......NGH!
ZUKIN (THROB)
HEY, SHE'S REALLY BLEEDING.
IF WE DON'T STANCH IT...
ZUKIN
HEY, DOES ANYBODY HAVE A HANDKERCHIEF OR SOMETHING?
NEVER MIND THAT, GET THE TEACHER.
...EVERYONE...
ZUKIN
...LOOKS SO WORRIED FOR ME...
...BUT...

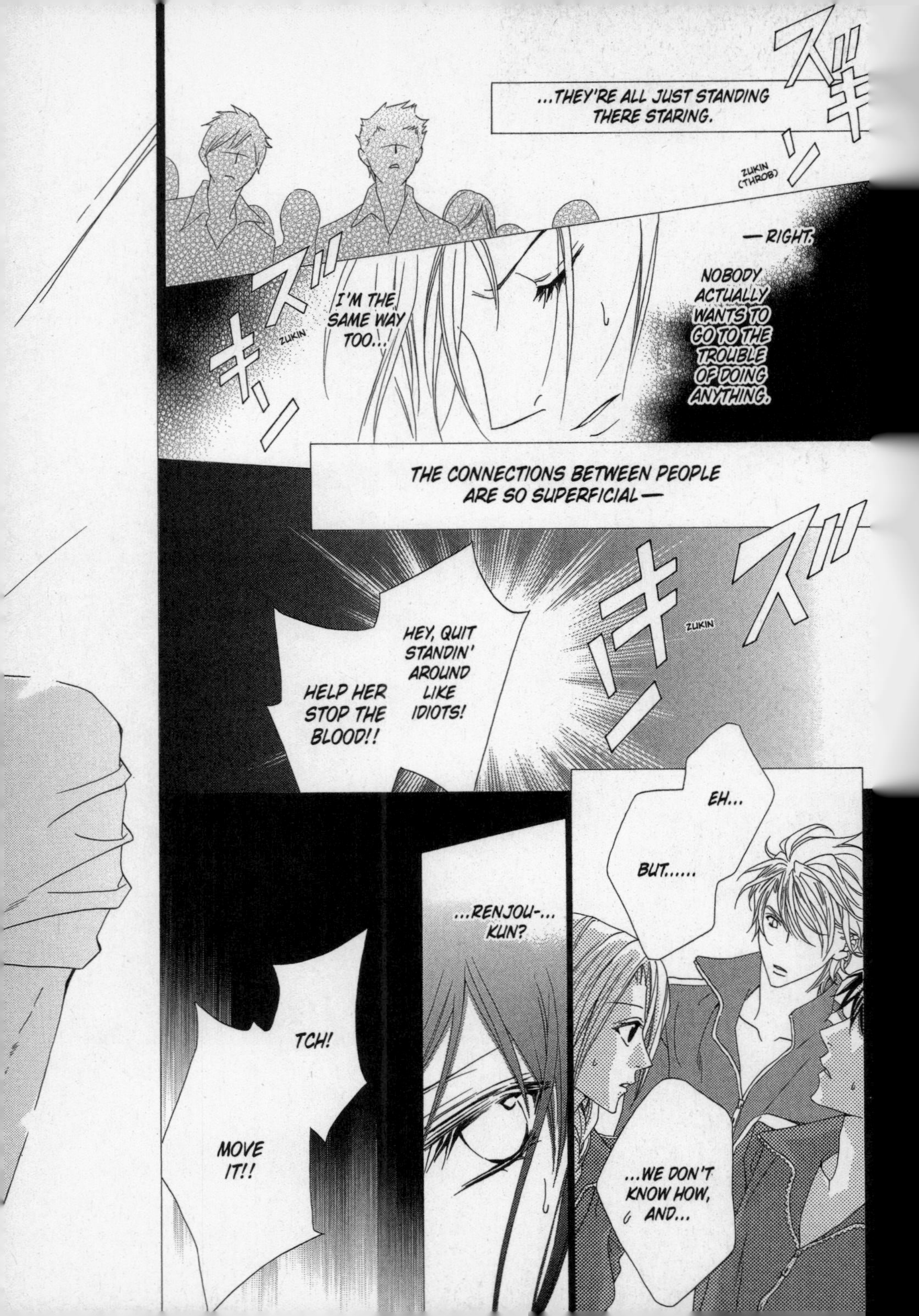

...THEY'RE ALL JUST STANDING THERE STARING.
ZUKIN (THROB)
—RIGHT.
NOBODY ACTUALLY WANTS TO GO TO THE TROUBLE OF DOING ANYTHING.
I'M THE SAME WAY TOO...
ZUKIN
THE CONNECTIONS BETWEEN PEOPLE ARE SO SUPERFICIAL—
ZUKIN
HEY, QUIT STANDIN' AROUND LIKE IDIOTS!
HELP HER STOP THE BLOOD!!
EH...
BUT......
...RENJOU-... KUN?
...WE DON'T KNOW HOW, AND...
TCH!
MOVE IT!!

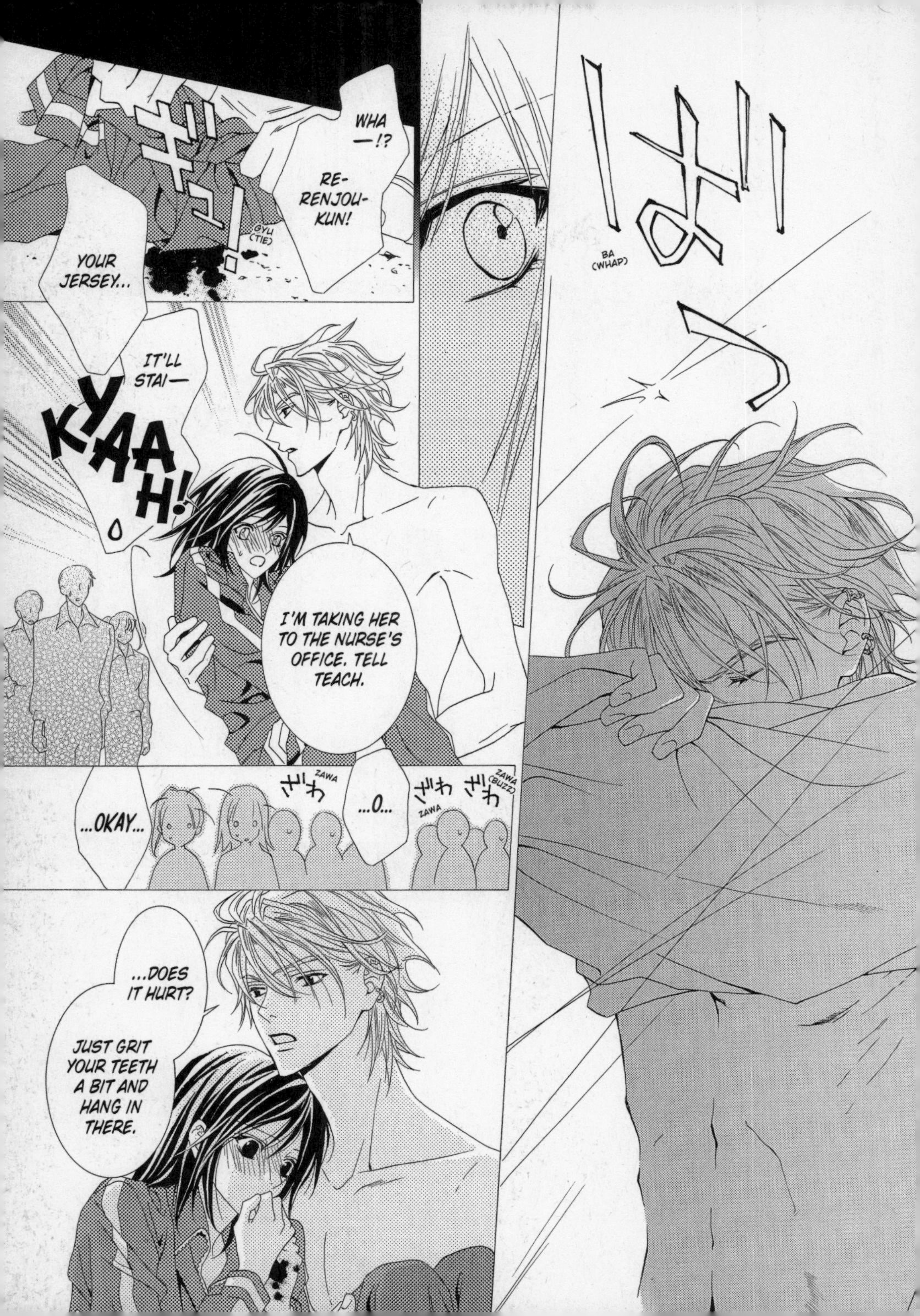

ばっ
BA (WHAP)
WHA—!?
RE-RENJOU-KUN!
ギュ!
GYU (TIE)
YOUR JERSEY...
IT'LL STAI—
KYAAH!
I'M TAKING HER TO THE NURSE'S OFFICE. TELL TEACH.
ざわ ざわ
ZAWA ZAWA (BUZZ)
...O...
ざわ
ZAWA
...OKAY...
...DOES IT HURT?
JUST GRIT YOUR TEETH A BIT AND HANG IN THERE.

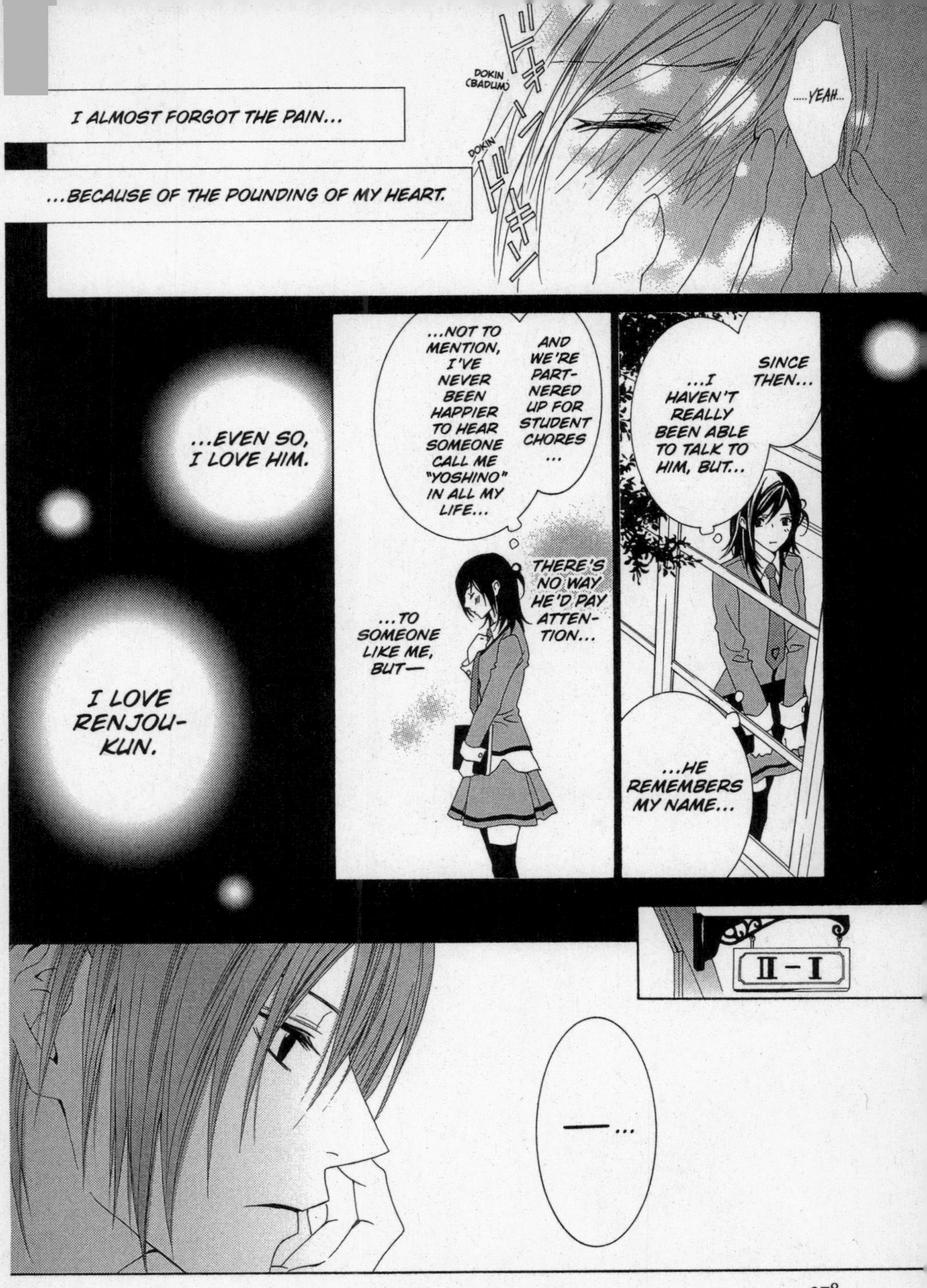

....YEAH...
DOKIN (BADUM)
DOKIN
I ALMOST FORGOT THE PAIN...
...BECAUSE OF THE POUNDING OF MY HEART.
SINCE THEN...
...I HAVEN'T REALLY BEEN ABLE TO TALK TO HIM, BUT...
...HE REMEMBERS MY NAME...
AND WE'RE PARTNERED UP FOR STUDENT CHORES...
...NOT TO MENTION, I'VE NEVER BEEN HAPPIER TO HEAR SOMEONE CALL ME "YOSHINO" IN ALL MY LIFE...
THERE'S NO WAY HE'D PAY ATTENTION...
...TO SOMEONE LIKE ME, BUT—
...EVEN SO, I LOVE HIM.
I LOVE RENJOU-KUN.
II - I
—...

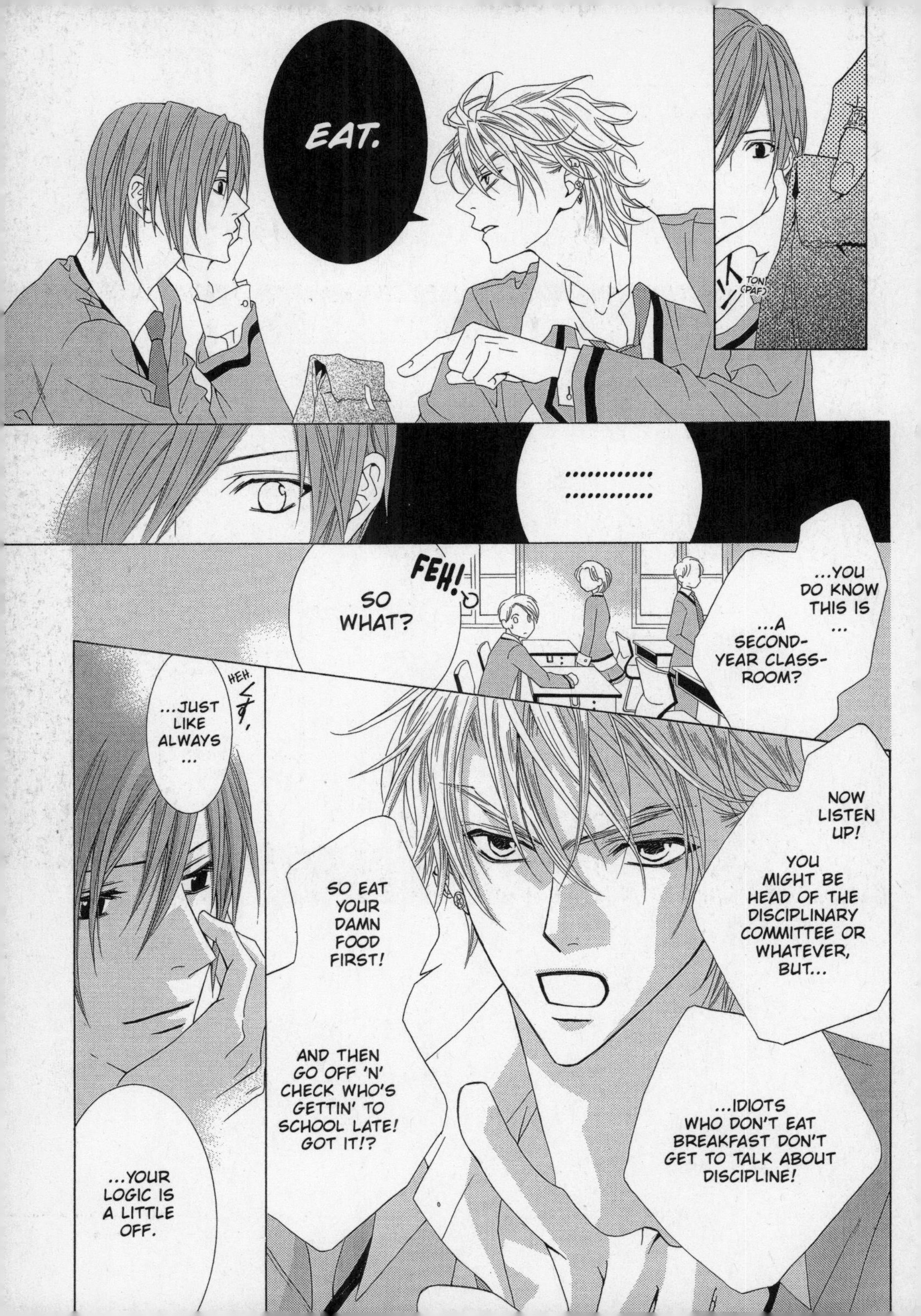
TON (PAF)
EAT.
....
....
...YOU DO KNOW THIS IS ...
...A SECOND-YEAR CLASS-ROOM?
FEH!
SO WHAT?
NOW LISTEN UP!
YOU MIGHT BE HEAD OF THE DISCIPLINARY COMMITTEE OR WHATEVER, BUT...
...IDIOTS WHO DON'T EAT BREAKFAST DON'T GET TO TALK ABOUT DISCIPLINE!
SO EAT YOUR DAMN FOOD FIRST!
AND THEN GO OFF 'N' CHECK WHO'S GETTIN' TO SCHOOL LATE! GOT IT!?
HEH.
...JUST LIKE ALWAYS ...
...YOUR LOGIC IS A LITTLE OFF.

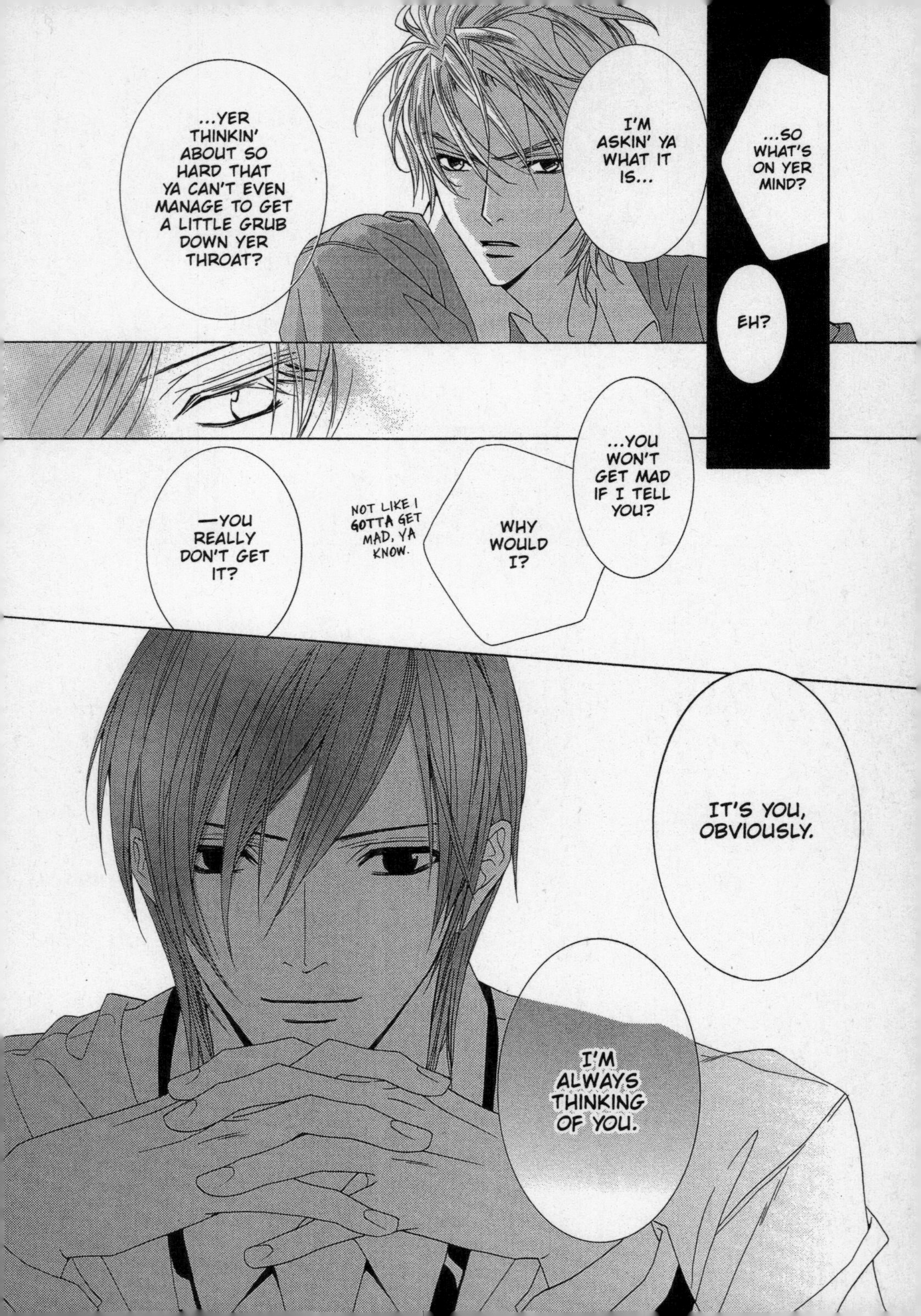
...SO WHAT'S ON YER MIND?
EH?
I'M ASKIN' YA WHAT IT IS...
...YER THINKIN' ABOUT SO HARD THAT YA CAN'T EVEN MANAGE TO GET A LITTLE GRUB DOWN YER THROAT?
...YOU WON'T GET MAD IF I TELL YOU?
WHY WOULD I?
NOT LIKE I GOTTA GET MAD, YA KNOW.
—YOU REALLY DON'T GET IT?
IT'S YOU, OBVIOUSLY.
I'M ALWAYS THINKING OF YOU.

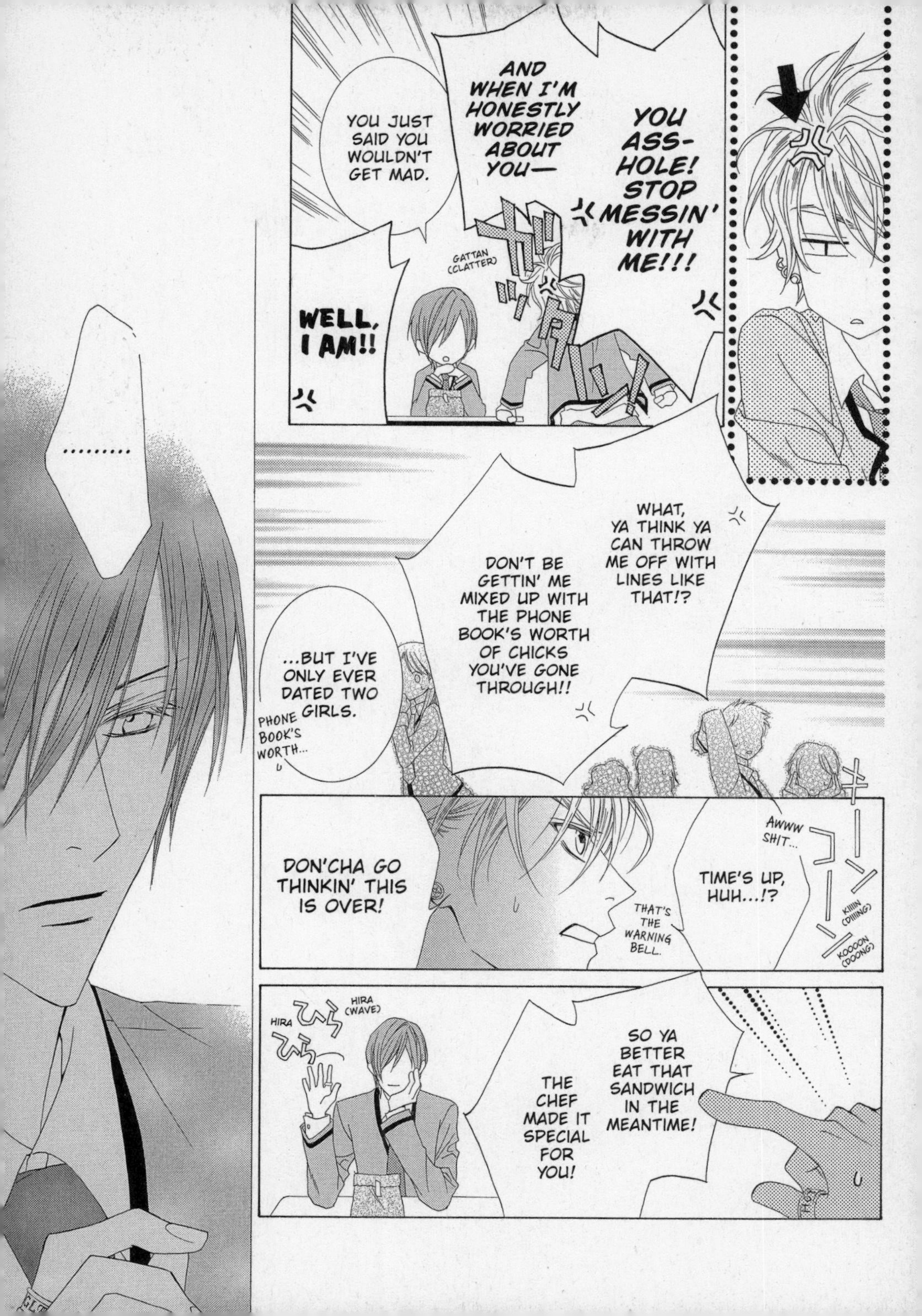

AND WHEN I'M HONESTLY WORRIED ABOUT YOU—
YOU ASS-HOLE! STOP MESSIN' WITH ME!!!
YOU JUST SAID YOU WOULDN'T GET MAD.
GATTAN (CLATTER)
WELL, I AM!!
WHAT, YA THINK YA CAN THROW ME OFF WITH LINES LIKE THAT!?
DON'T BE GETTIN' ME MIXED UP WITH THE PHONE BOOK'S WORTH OF CHICKS YOU'VE GONE THROUGH!!
...BUT I'VE ONLY EVER DATED TWO GIRLS.
PHONE BOOK'S WORTH...
KIIIN (DIIIING)
KOOOON (DOONG)
AWWW SHIT...
TIME'S UP, HUH...!?
THAT'S THE WARNING BELL.
DON'CHA GO THINKIN' THIS IS OVER!
SO YA BETTER EAT THAT SANDWICH IN THE MEANTIME!
THE CHEF MADE IT SPECIAL FOR YOU!
HIRA (WAVE)
HIRA
....

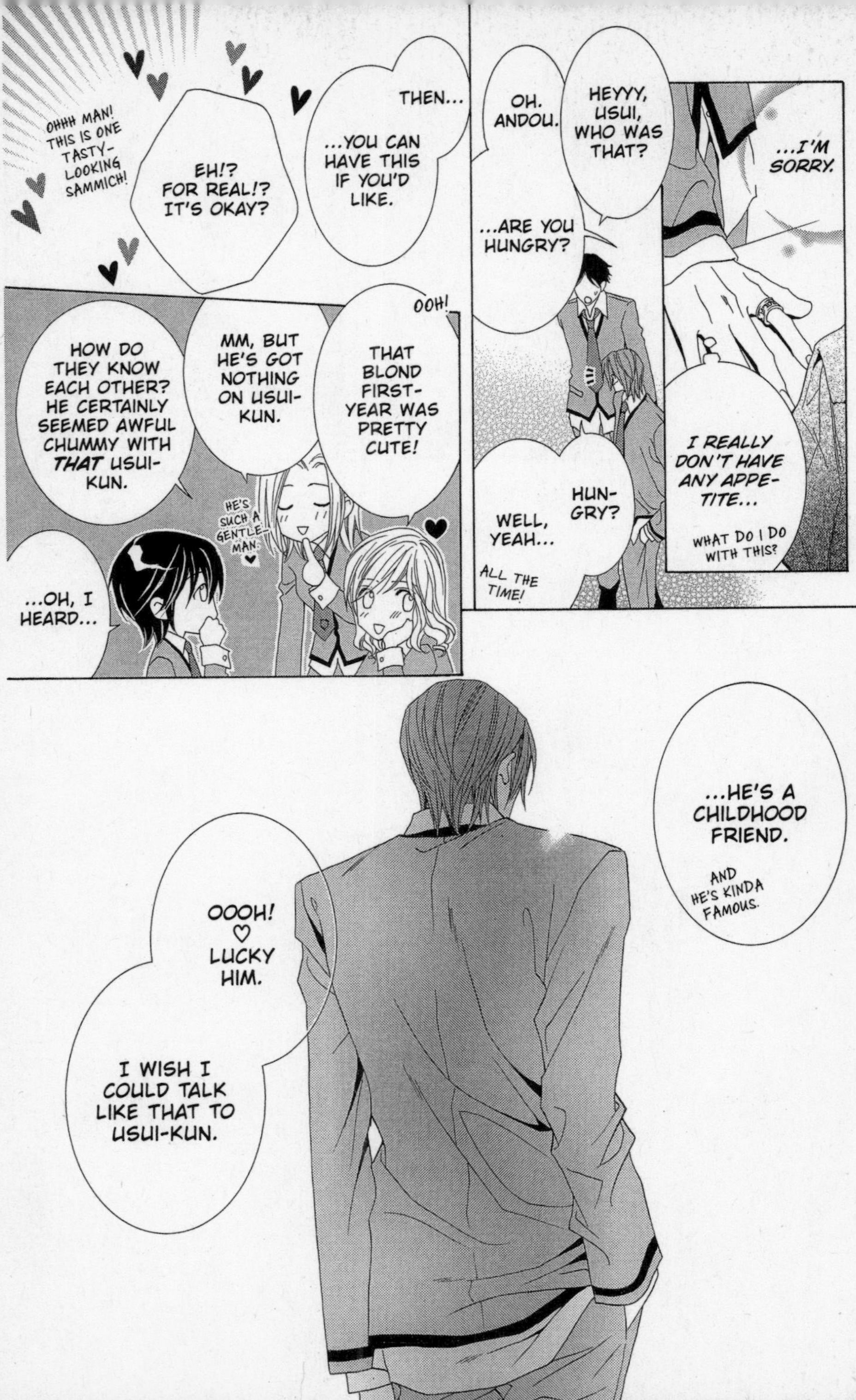
...I'M SORRY.
I REALLY DON'T HAVE ANY APPETITE...
WHAT DO I DO WITH THIS?
HEYYY, USUI, WHO WAS THAT?
OH. ANDOU.
...ARE YOU HUNGRY?
HUNGRY?
WELL, YEAH...
ALL THE TIME!
THEN...
...YOU CAN HAVE THIS IF YOU'D LIKE.
EH!? FOR REAL!? IT'S OKAY?
OHHH MAN! THIS IS ONE TASTY-LOOKING SAMMICH!
OOH!
THAT BLOND FIRST-YEAR WAS PRETTY CUTE!
MM, BUT HE'S GOT NOTHING ON USUI-KUN.
HE'S SUCH A GENTLEMAN.
HOW DO THEY KNOW EACH OTHER? HE CERTAINLY SEEMED AWFUL CHUMMY WITH THAT USUI-KUN.
...OH, I HEARD...
...HE'S A CHILDHOOD FRIEND.
AND HE'S KINDA FAMOUS.
OOOH! ♡ LUCKY HIM.
I WISH I COULD TALK LIKE THAT TO USUI-KUN.

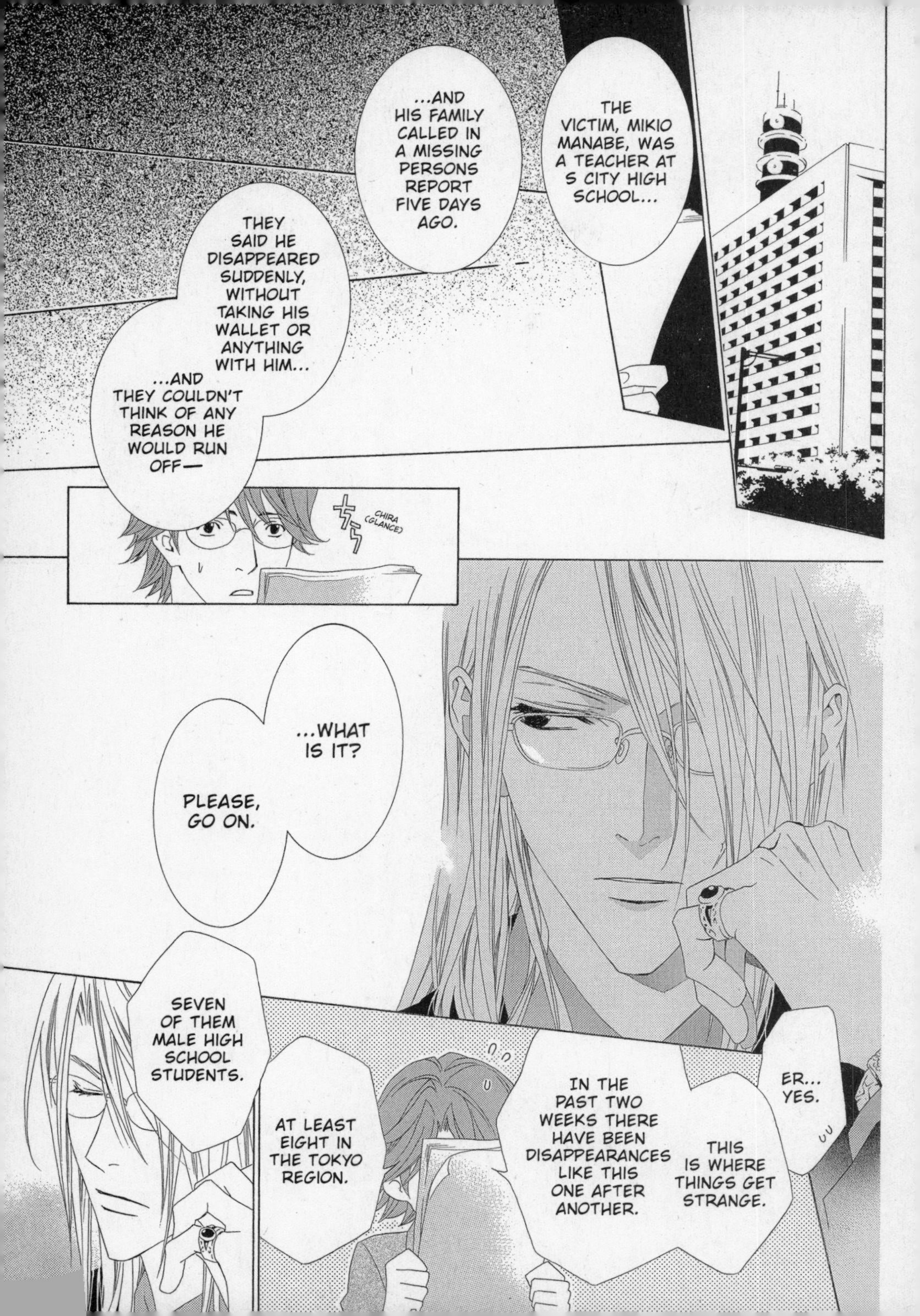
THE VICTIM, MIKIO MANABE, WAS A TEACHER AT S CITY HIGH SCHOOL...
...AND HIS FAMILY CALLED IN A MISSING PERSONS REPORT FIVE DAYS AGO.
THEY SAID HE DISAPPEARED SUDDENLY, WITHOUT TAKING HIS WALLET OR ANYTHING WITH HIM...
...AND THEY COULDN'T THINK OF ANY REASON HE WOULD RUN OFF—
CHIRA (GLANCE)
...WHAT IS IT?
PLEASE, GO ON.
ER... YES.
THIS IS WHERE THINGS GET STRANGE.
IN THE PAST TWO WEEKS THERE HAVE BEEN DISAPPEARANCES LIKE THIS ONE AFTER ANOTHER.
AT LEAST EIGHT IN THE TOKYO REGION.
SEVEN OF THEM MALE HIGH SCHOOL STUDENTS.

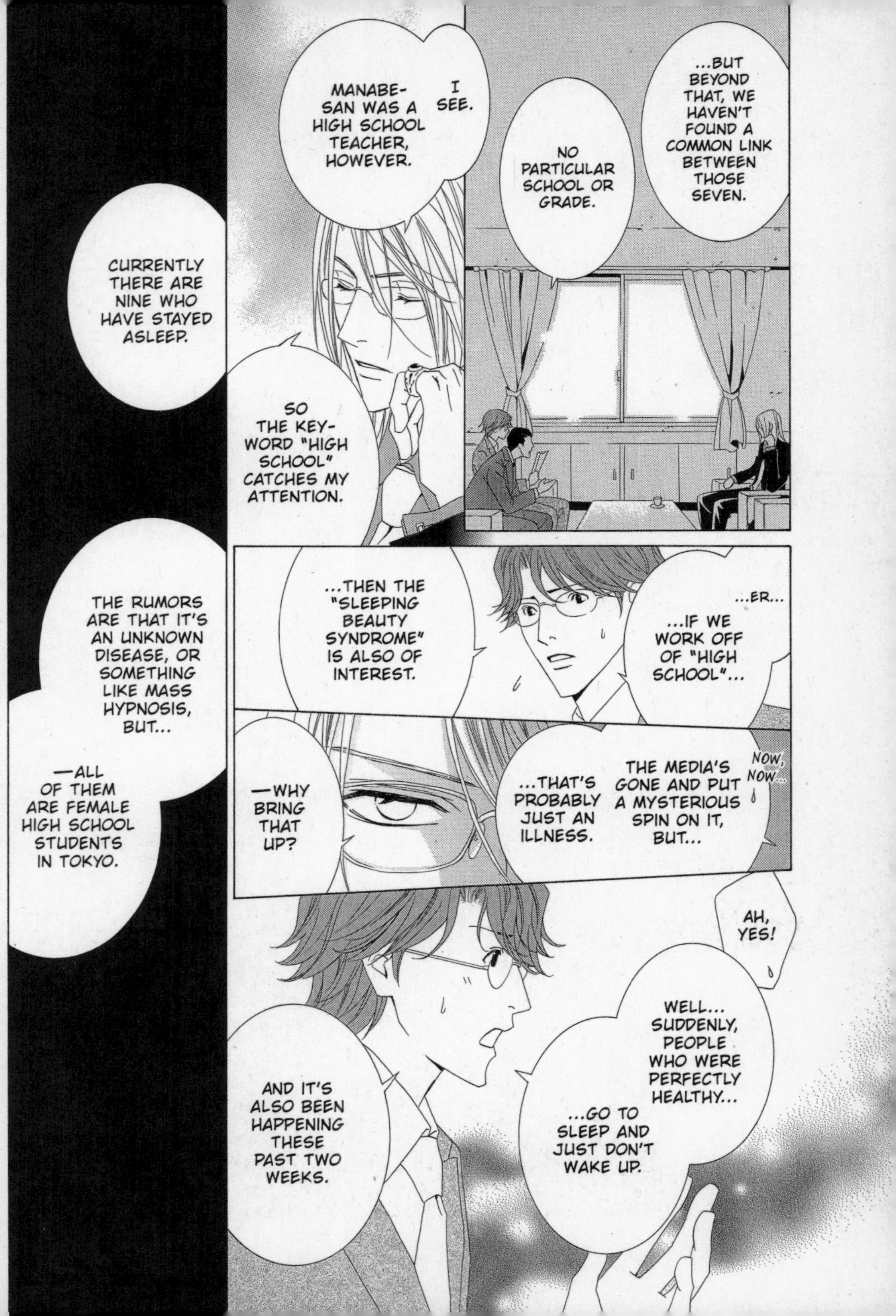
...BUT BEYOND THAT, WE HAVEN'T FOUND A COMMON LINK BETWEEN THOSE SEVEN.
NO PARTICULAR SCHOOL OR GRADE.
I SEE.
MANABE-SAN WAS A HIGH SCHOOL TEACHER, HOWEVER.
SO THE KEY-WORD "HIGH SCHOOL" CATCHES MY ATTENTION.
...ER...
...IF WE WORK OFF OF "HIGH SCHOOL"...
...THEN THE "SLEEPING BEAUTY SYNDROME" IS ALSO OF INTEREST.
NOW, NOW...
THE MEDIA'S GONE AND PUT A MYSTERIOUS SPIN ON IT, BUT...
...THAT'S PROBABLY JUST AN ILLNESS.
—WHY BRING THAT UP?
AH, YES!
WELL... SUDDENLY, PEOPLE WHO WERE PERFECTLY HEALTHY...
...GO TO SLEEP AND JUST DON'T WAKE UP.
AND IT'S ALSO BEEN HAPPENING THESE PAST TWO WEEKS.
CURRENTLY THERE ARE NINE WHO HAVE STAYED ASLEEP.
THE RUMORS ARE THAT IT'S AN UNKNOWN DISEASE, OR SOMETHING LIKE MASS HYPNOSIS, BUT...
—ALL OF THEM ARE FEMALE HIGH SCHOOL STUDENTS IN TOKYO.

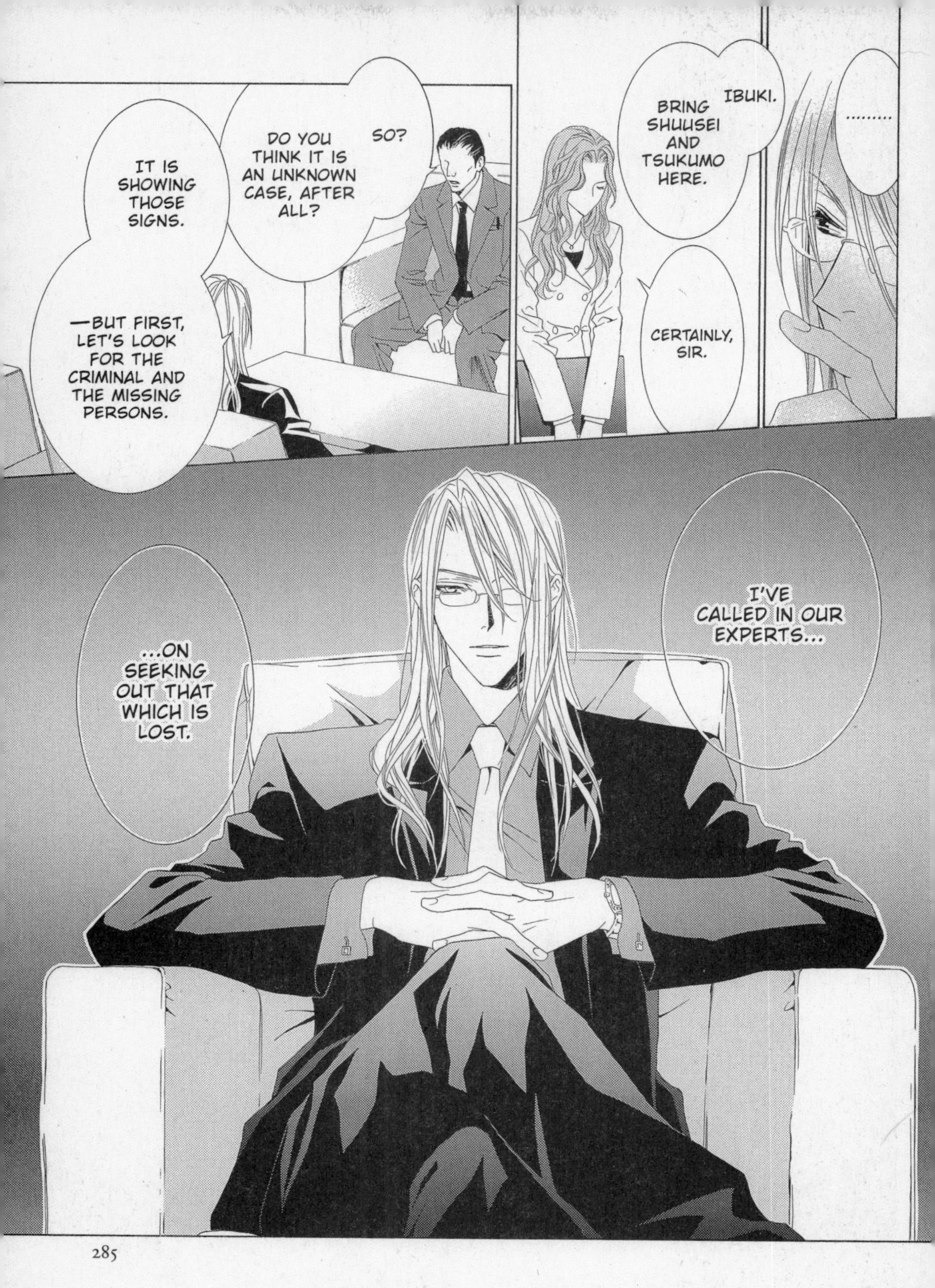
....
IBUKI.
BRING SHUUSEI AND TSUKUMO HERE.
CERTAINLY, SIR.
SO?
DO YOU THINK IT IS AN UNKNOWN CASE, AFTER ALL?
IT IS SHOWING THOSE SIGNS.
—BUT FIRST, LET'S LOOK FOR THE CRIMINAL AND THE MISSING PERSONS.
I'VE CALLED IN OUR EXPERTS...
...ON SEEKING OUT THAT WHICH IS LOST.

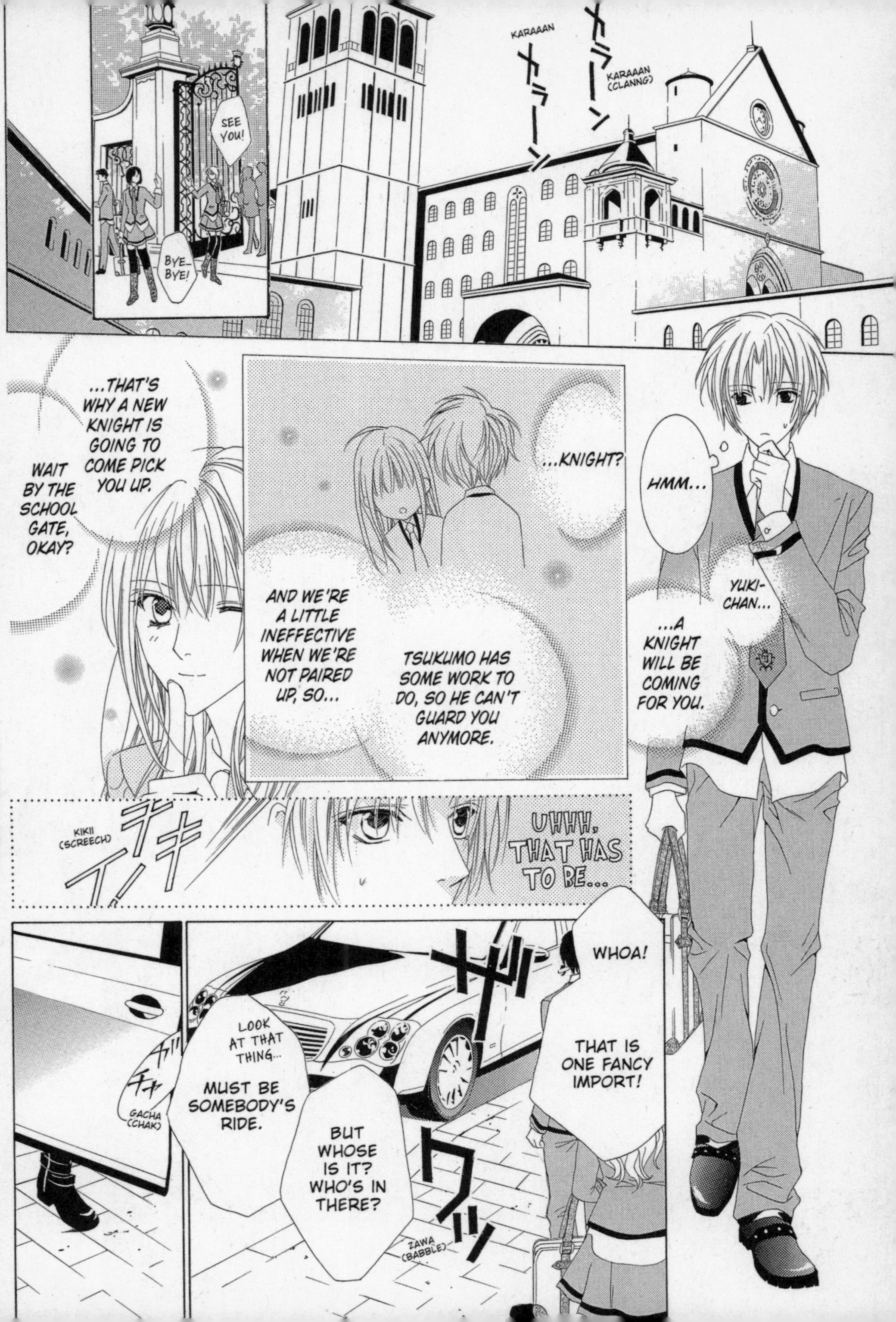

KARAAAN
KARAAAN (CLANNG)
SEE YOU!
BYE-BYE!
HMM...
...KNIGHT?
...THAT'S WHY A NEW KNIGHT IS GOING TO COME PICK YOU UP.
WAIT BY THE SCHOOL GATE, OKAY?
YUKI-CHAN...
...A KNIGHT WILL BE COMING FOR YOU.
TSUKUMO HAS SOME WORK TO DO, SO HE CAN'T GUARD YOU ANYMORE.
AND WE'RE A LITTLE INEFFECTIVE WHEN WE'RE NOT PAIRED UP, SO...
UHHH, THAT HAS TO BE...
KIKII (SCREECH)
WHOA!
THAT IS ONE FANCY IMPORT!
LOOK AT THAT THING...
MUST BE SOMEBODY'S RIDE.
BUT WHOSE IS IT? WHO'S IN THERE?
ZAWA (BABBLE)
GACHA (CHAK)

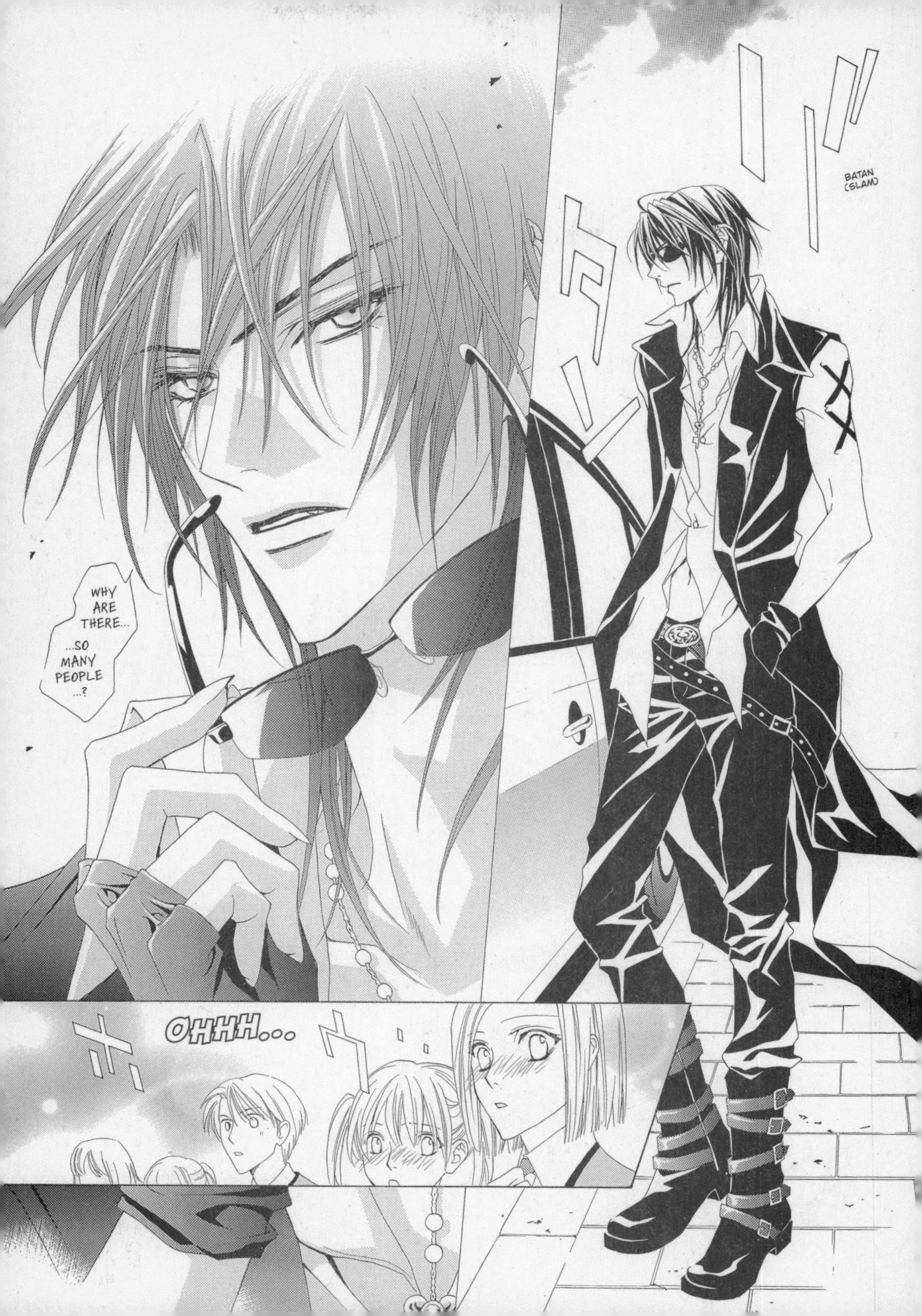

BATAN (SLAM)
WHY ARE THERE...
...SO MANY PEOPLE ...?
OHHH...

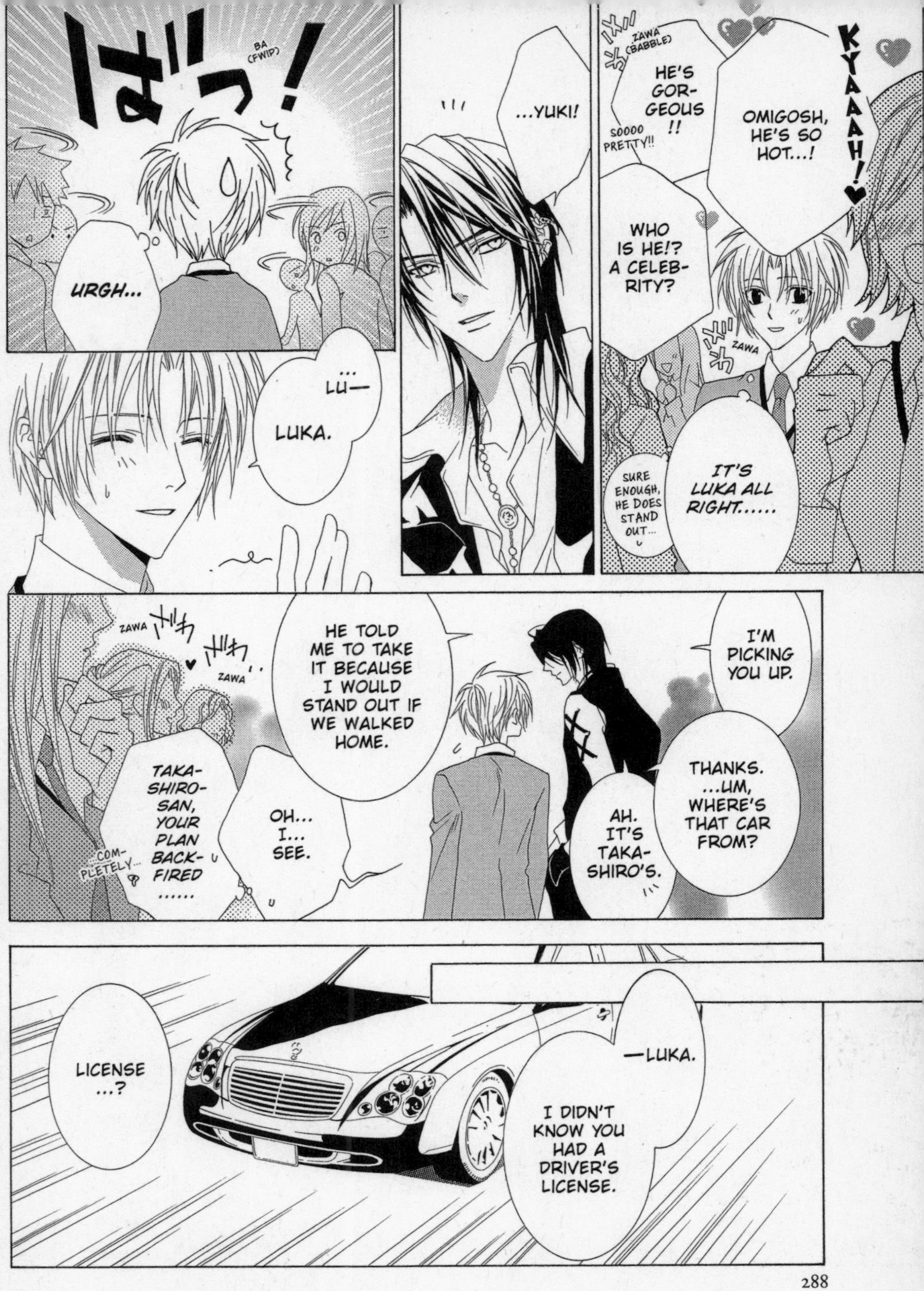
ZAWA (BABBLE)
KYAAAH!
OMIGOSH, HE'S SO HOT...!
HE'S GORGEOUS!!
SOOOO PRETTY!!
WHO IS HE!? A CELEBRITY?
ZAWA
...YUKI!
BA (FWIP)
URGH...
IT'S LUKA ALL RIGHT......
SURE ENOUGH, HE DOES STAND OUT...
...LU—
LUKA.
I'M PICKING YOU UP.
THANKS. ...UM, WHERE'S THAT CAR FROM?
AH. IT'S TAKASHIRO'S.
HE TOLD ME TO TAKE IT BECAUSE I WOULD STAND OUT IF WE WALKED HOME.
OH... I... SEE.
ZAWA
ZAWA
TAKASHIRO-SAN, YOUR PLAN BACKFIRED......
COMPLETELY...
—LUKA.
I DIDN'T KNOW YOU HAD A DRIVER'S LICENSE.
LICENSE...?

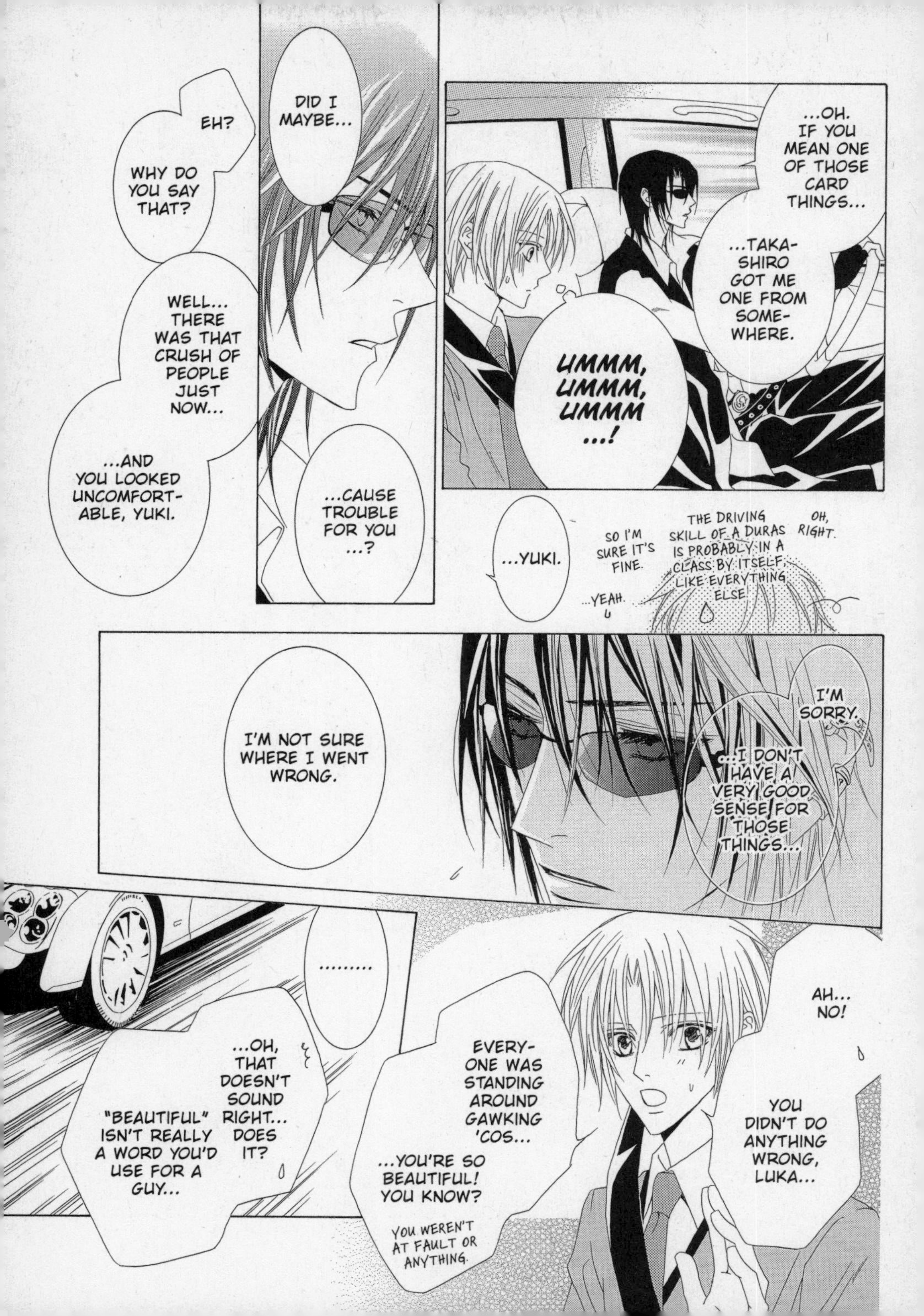

...OH. IF YOU MEAN ONE OF THOSE CARD THINGS...
...TAKASHIRO GOT ME ONE FROM SOMEWHERE.
UMMM, UMMM, UMMM...!
OH, RIGHT.
THE DRIVING SKILL OF A DURAS IS PROBABLY IN A CLASS BY ITSELF, LIKE EVERYTHING ELSE.
SO I'M SURE IT'S FINE.
...YEAH.
...YUKI.
DID I MAYBE...
...CAUSE TROUBLE FOR YOU...?
EH?
WHY DO YOU SAY THAT?
WELL... THERE WAS THAT CRUSH OF PEOPLE JUST NOW...
...AND YOU LOOKED UNCOMFORTABLE, YUKI.
I'M SORRY.
...I DON'T HAVE A VERY GOOD SENSE FOR THOSE THINGS...
I'M NOT SURE WHERE I WENT WRONG.
AH... NO!
YOU DIDN'T DO ANYTHING WRONG, LUKA...
EVERYONE WAS STANDING AROUND GAWKING 'COS...
...YOU'RE SO BEAUTIFUL! YOU KNOW?
YOU WEREN'T AT FAULT OR ANYTHING.
....
...OH, THAT DOESN'T SOUND RIGHT... DOES IT?
"BEAUTIFUL" ISN'T REALLY A WORD YOU'D USE FOR A GUY...

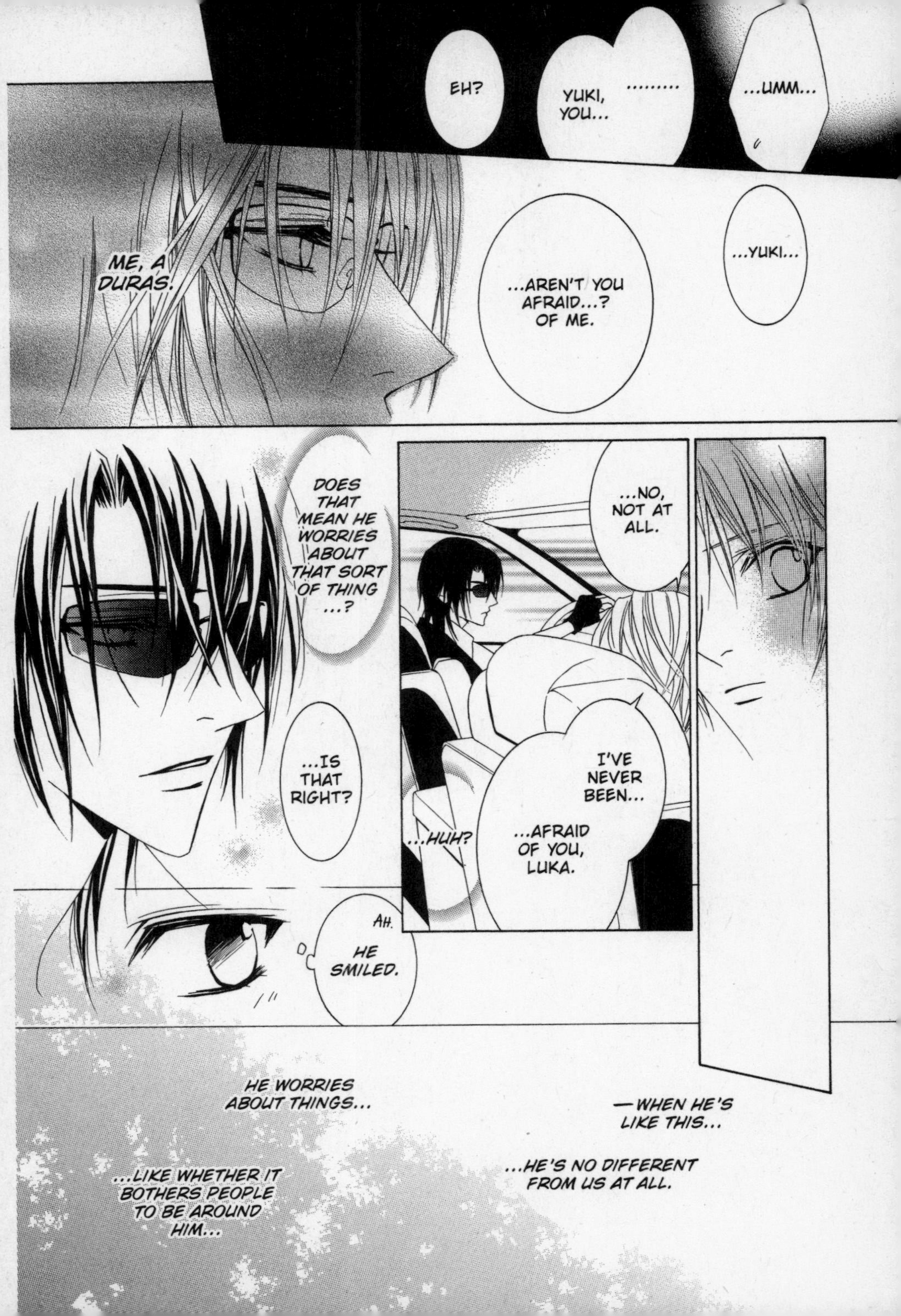
...UMM...
....
YUKI, YOU...
EH?
...YUKI...
...AREN'T YOU AFRAID...? OF ME.
ME, A DURAS.
...NO, NOT AT ALL.
I'VE NEVER BEEN...
...AFRAID OF YOU, LUKA.
...HUH?
DOES THAT MEAN HE WORRIES ABOUT THAT SORT OF THING ...?
...IS THAT RIGHT?
AH.
HE SMILED.
—WHEN HE'S LIKE THIS...
...HE'S NO DIFFERENT FROM US AT ALL.
HE WORRIES ABOUT THINGS...
...LIKE WHETHER IT BOTHERS PEOPLE TO BE AROUND HIM...

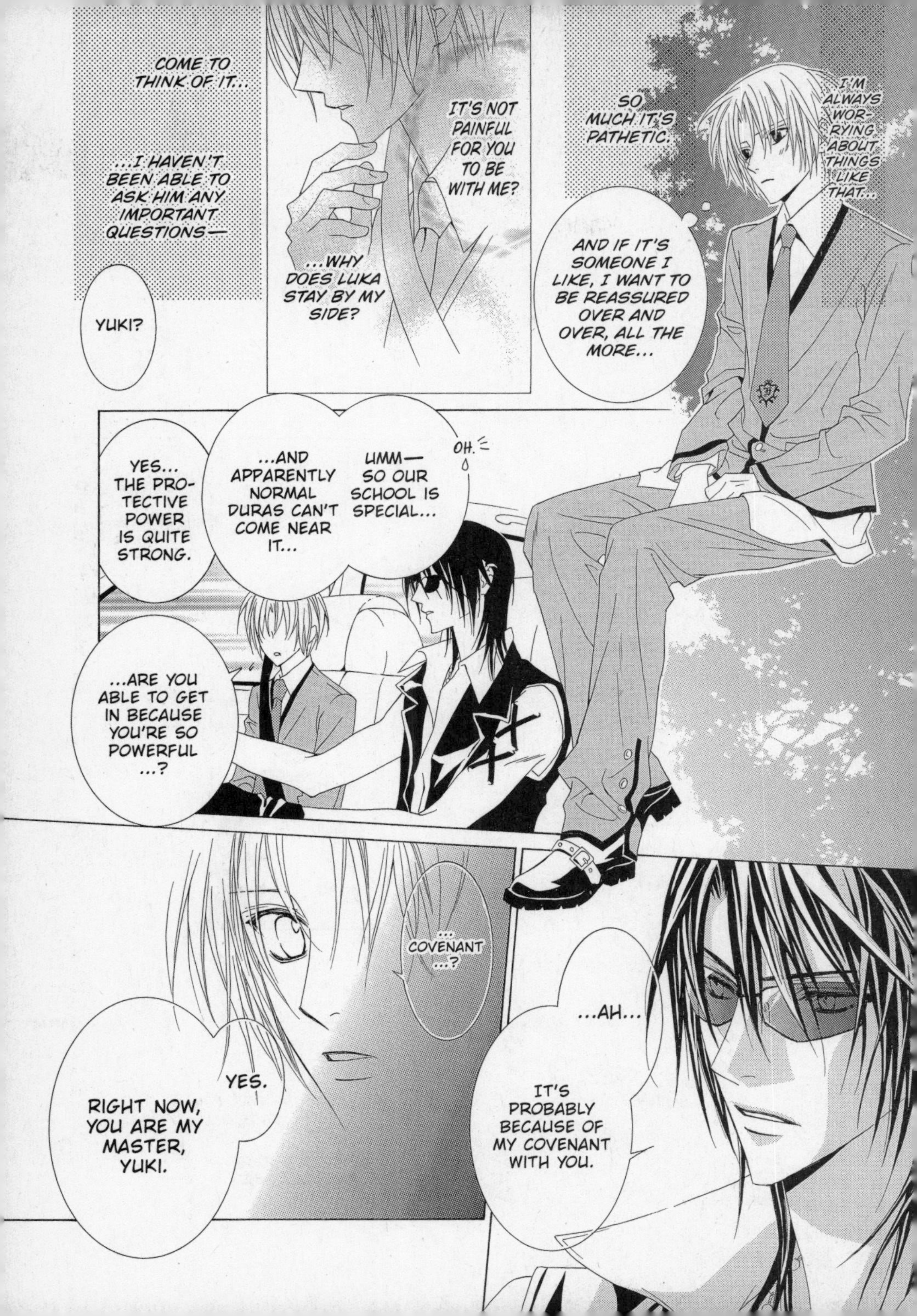
I'M ALWAYS WORRYING ABOUT THINGS LIKE THAT...
SO MUCH IT'S PATHETIC.
AND IF IT'S SOMEONE I LIKE, I WANT TO BE REASSURED OVER AND OVER, ALL THE MORE...
IT'S NOT PAINFUL FOR YOU TO BE WITH ME?
...WHY DOES LUKA STAY BY MY SIDE?
COME TO THINK OF IT...
...I HAVEN'T BEEN ABLE TO ASK HIM ANY IMPORTANT QUESTIONS—
YUKI?
OH.
UMM— SO OUR SCHOOL IS SPECIAL...
...AND APPARENTLY NORMAL DURAS CAN'T COME NEAR IT...
YES... THE PROTECTIVE POWER IS QUITE STRONG.
...ARE YOU ABLE TO GET IN BECAUSE YOU'RE SO POWERFUL ...?
...AH...
IT'S PROBABLY BECAUSE OF MY COVENANT WITH YOU.
... COVENANT ...?
YES.
RIGHT NOW, YOU ARE MY MASTER, YUKI.

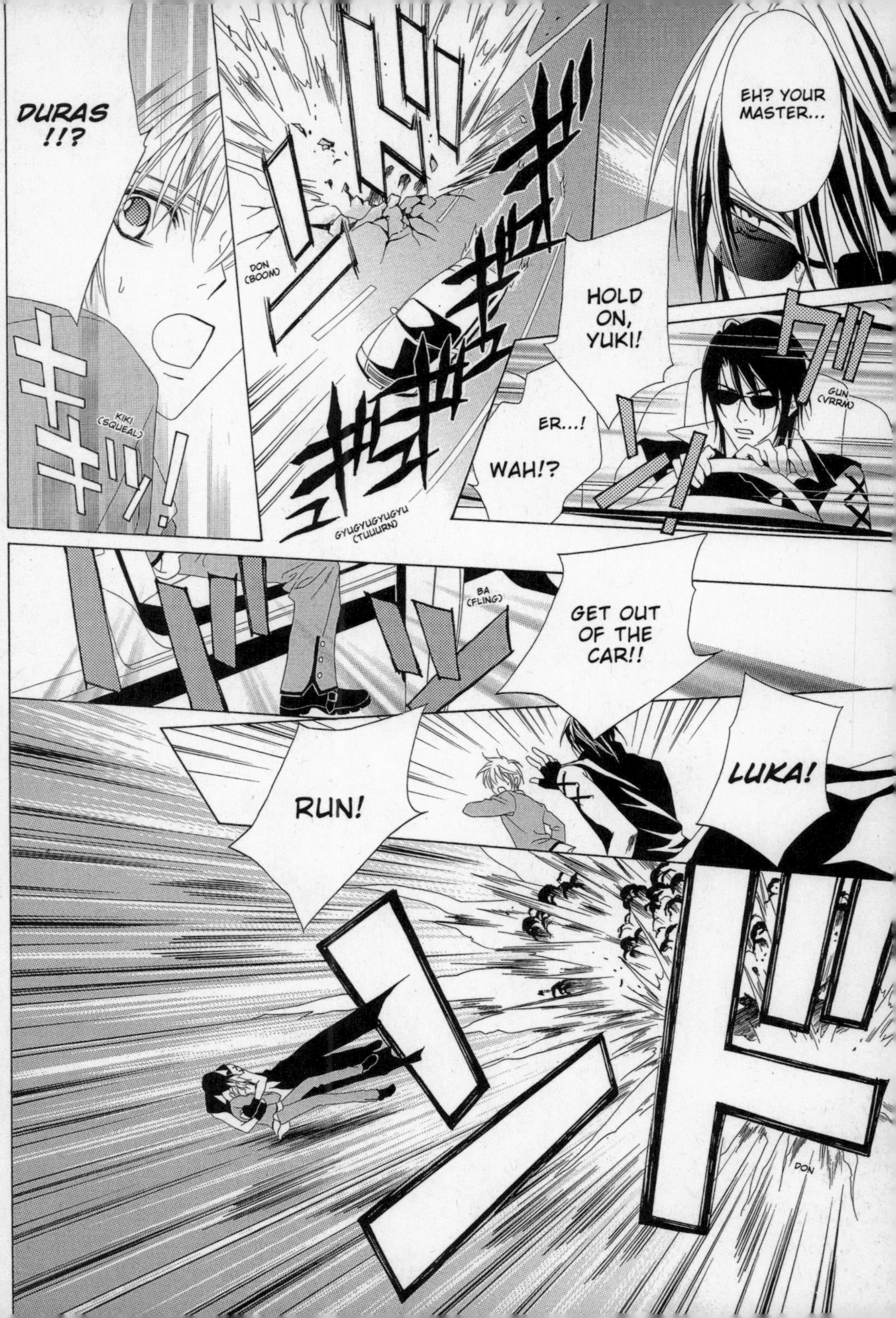

EH? YOUR MASTER...
DURAS !!?
DON (BOOM)
HOLD ON, YUKI!
GUN (VRRM)
ER...!
WAH!?
GYUGYUGYUGYU (TUUURN)
KIKI (SQUEAL)
GET OUT OF THE CAR!!
BA (FLING)
LUKA!
RUN!
DON

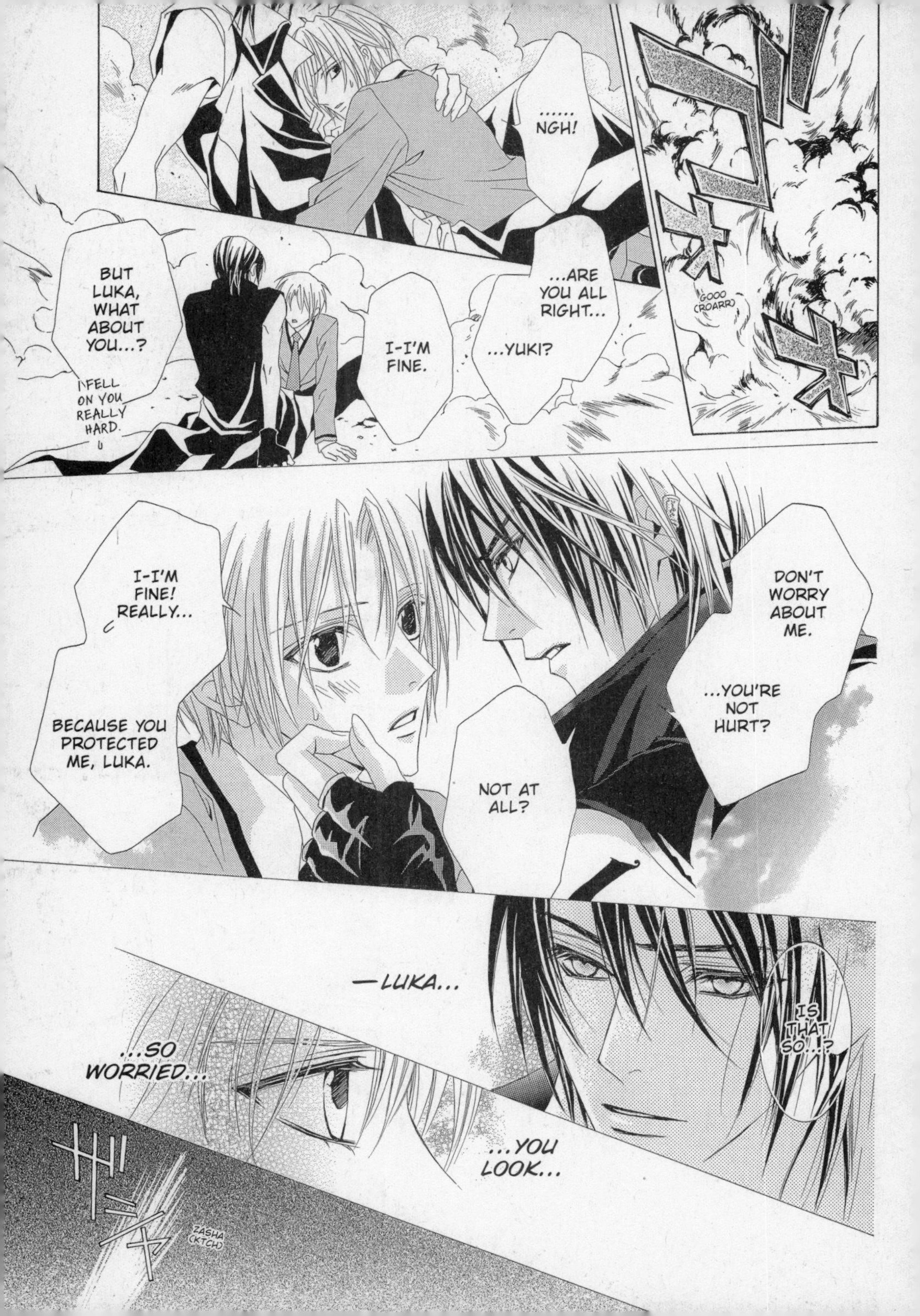
GOOO (ROARR)
......NGH!
...ARE YOU ALL RIGHT...
...YUKI?
I-I'M FINE.
BUT LUKA, WHAT ABOUT YOU...?
I FELL ON YOU REALLY HARD.
DON'T WORRY ABOUT ME.
...YOU'RE NOT HURT?
NOT AT ALL?
I-I'M FINE! REALLY...
BECAUSE YOU PROTECTED ME, LUKA.
IS THAT SO...?
—LUKA...
...YOU LOOK...
...SO WORRIED...
ZASHA (KTCH)

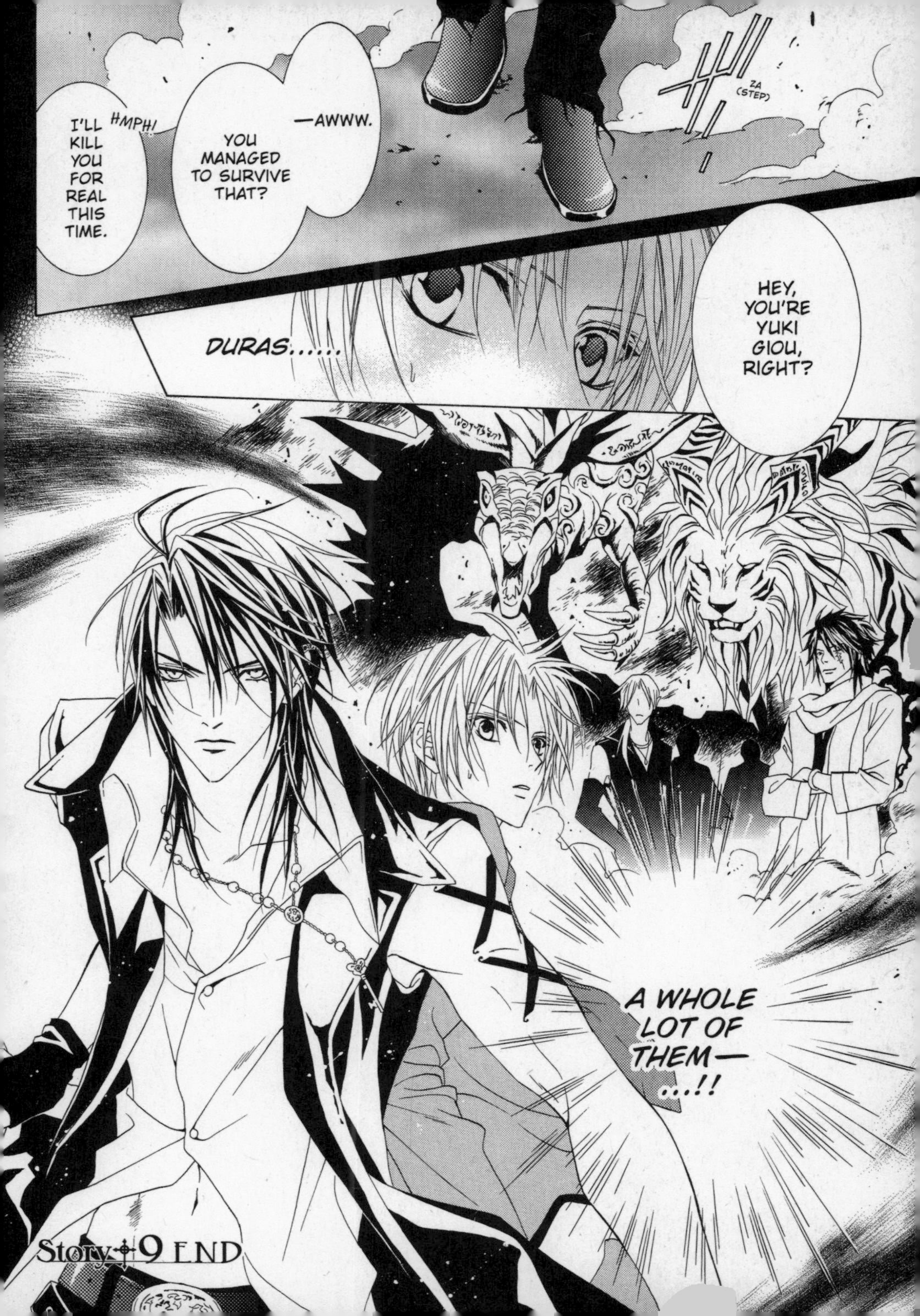
ZA (STEP)
—AWWW.
YOU MANAGED TO SURVIVE THAT?
HMPH!
I'LL KILL YOU FOR REAL THIS TIME.
HEY, YOU'RE YUKI GIOU, RIGHT?
DURAS......
A WHOLE LOT OF THEM—
...!!
Story 9 END

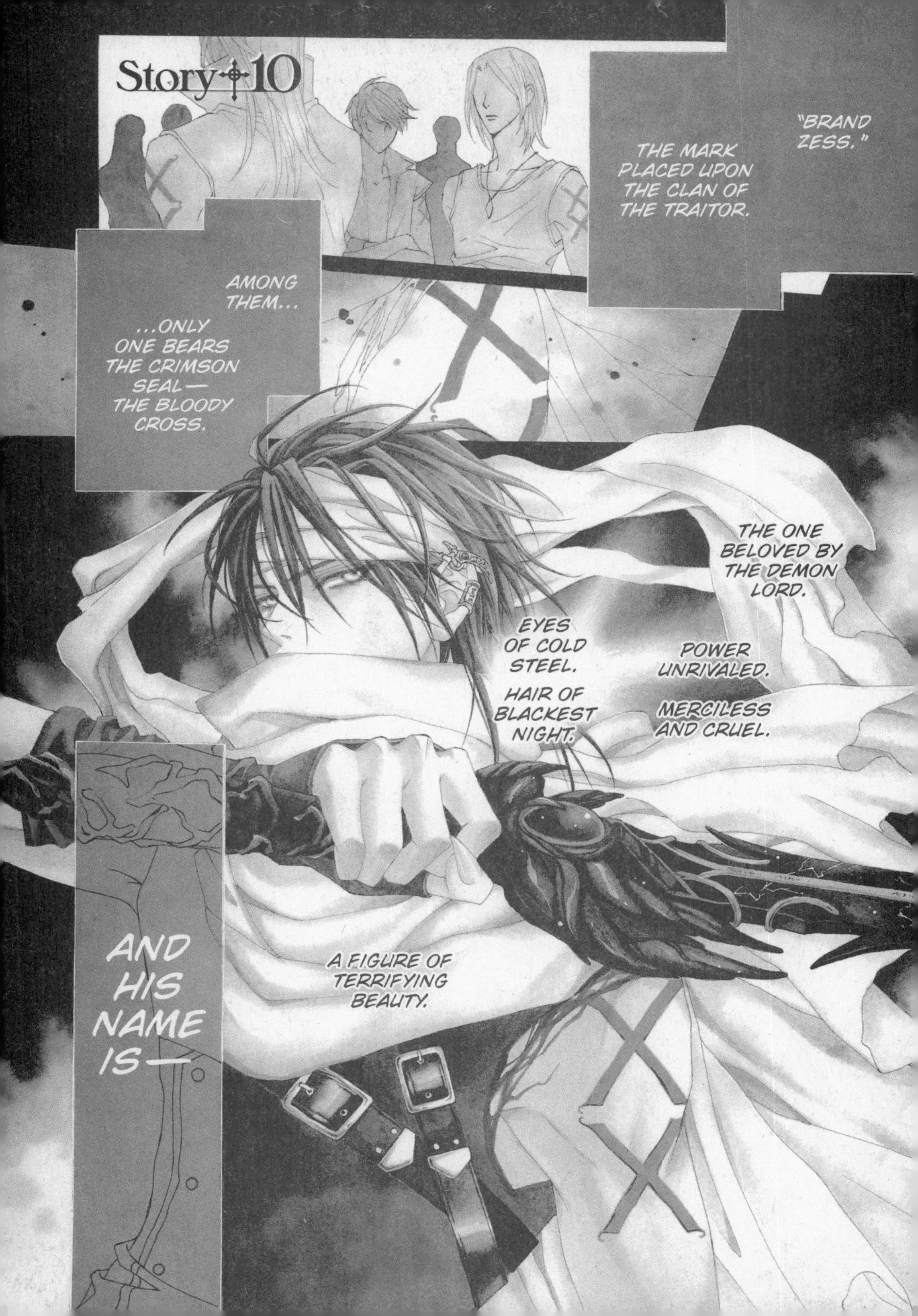
Story 10
"BRAND ZESS."
THE MARK PLACED UPON THE CLAN OF THE TRAITOR.
AMONG THEM...
...ONLY ONE BEARS THE CRIMSON SEAL— THE BLOODY CROSS.
THE ONE BELOVED BY THE DEMON LORD.
POWER UNRIVALED.
MERCILESS AND CRUEL.
EYES OF COLD STEEL.
HAIR OF BLACKEST NIGHT.
A FIGURE OF TERRIFYING BEAUTY.
AND HIS NAME IS—

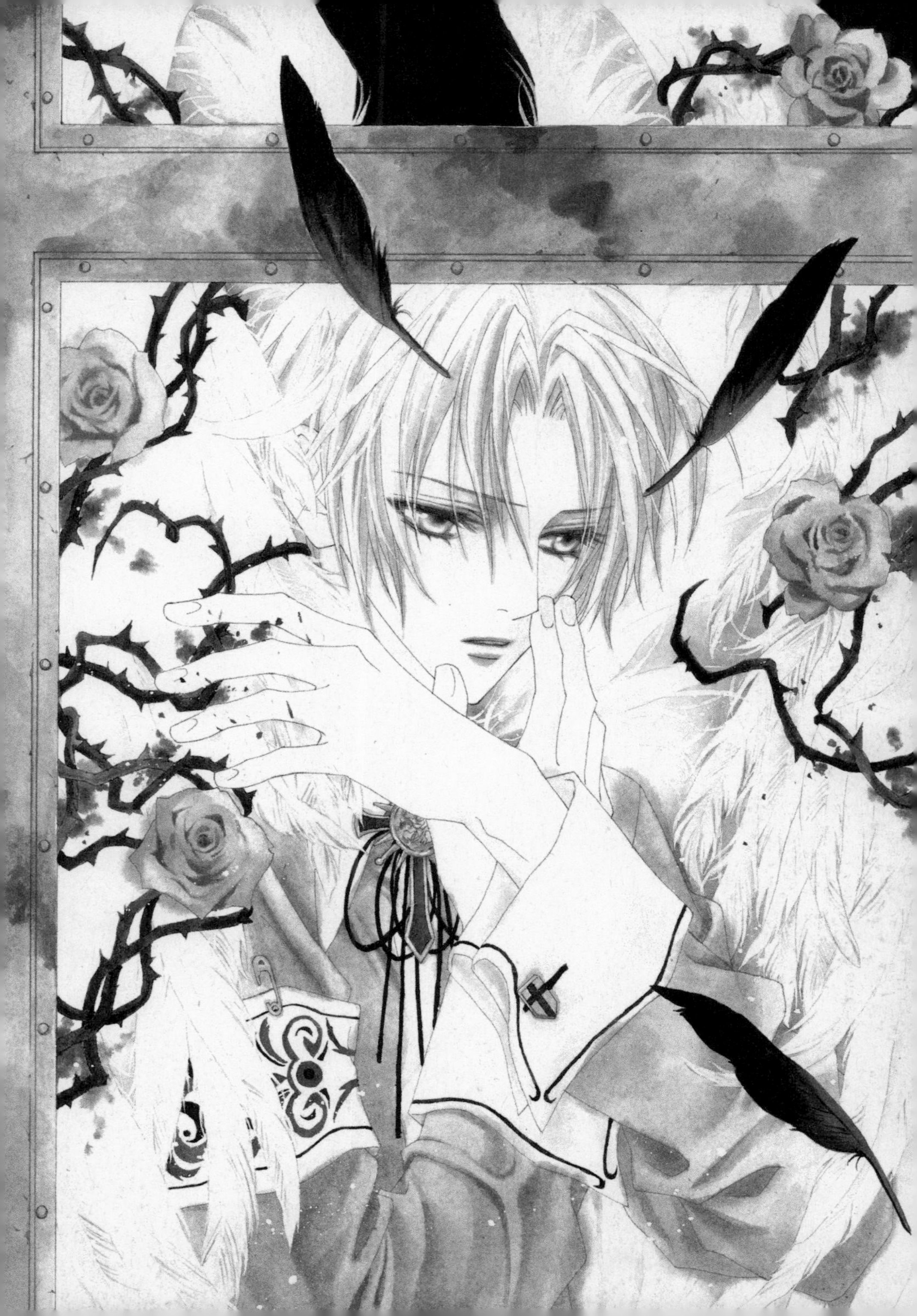

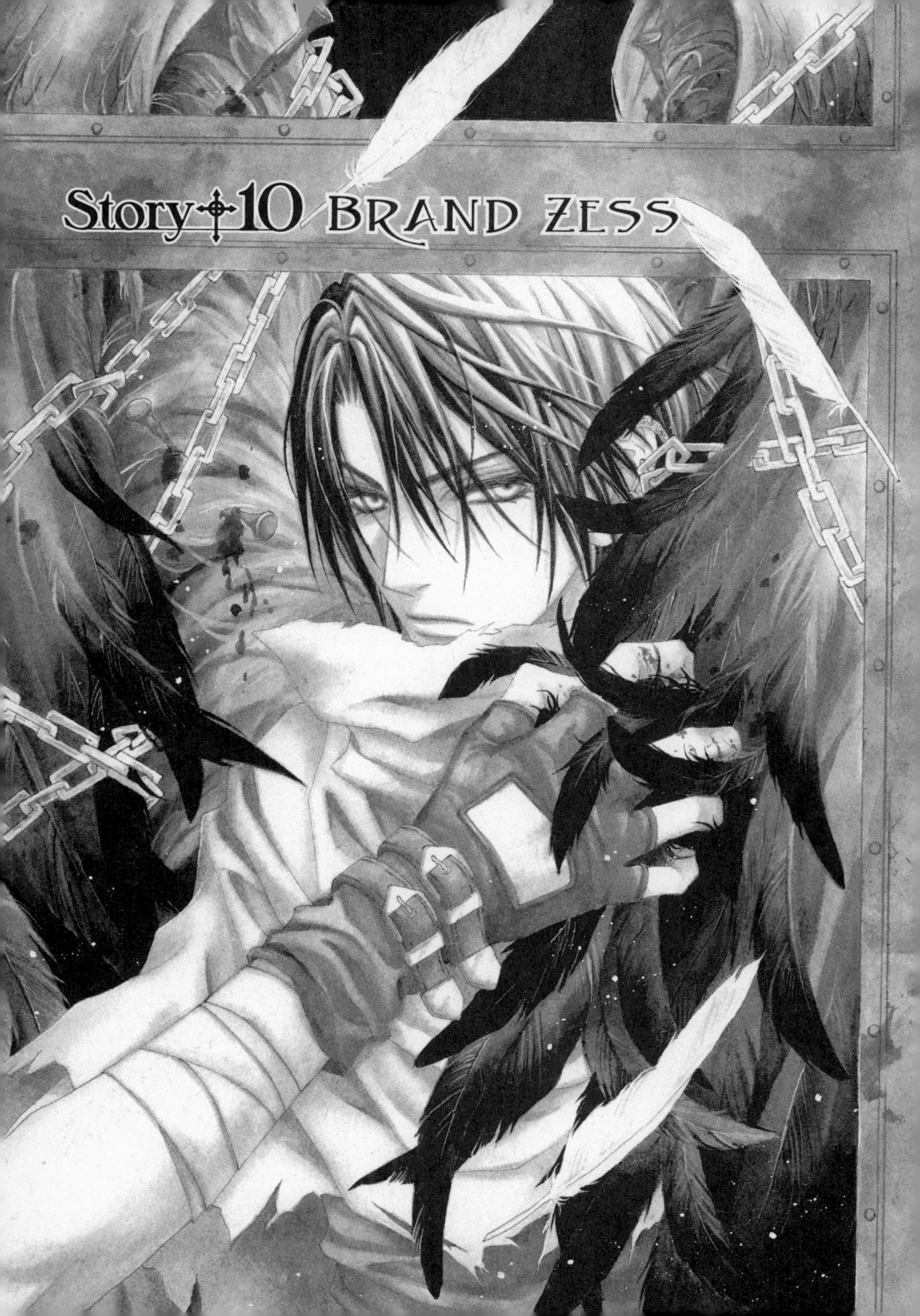
Story 10 BRAND ZESS

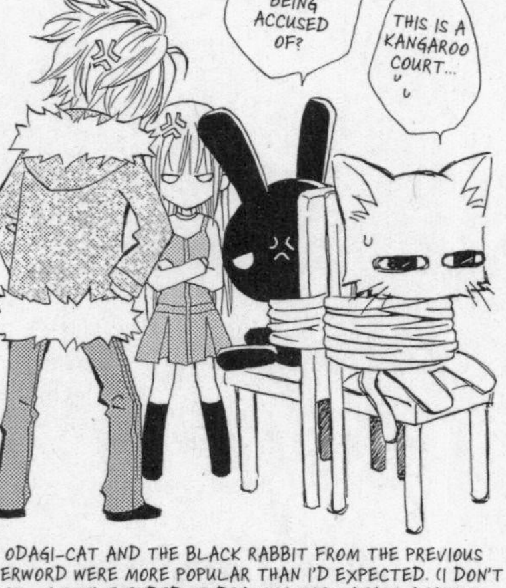
GRRR...
EXACTLY WHAT AM I BEING ACCUSED OF?
THIS IS A KANGAROO COURT...

THE ODAGI-CAT AND THE BLACK RABBIT FROM THE PREVIOUS AFTERWORD WERE MORE POPULAR THAN I'D EXPECTED. (I DON'T GET IT...) SO I'VE ENDED UP DRAWING THEM AGAIN, AGAINST MY BETTER JUDGMENT. IF YOU WANT TO KNOW WHY THEY'RE ON TRIAL IN A KANGAROO COURT, YOU SHOULD READ THE ORIGINAL COMIC AT THE END OF THIS VOLUME... (LOL)

▸HELLO, EVERYONE! HANGING ON BY A THREAD, I'VE SOMEHOW MANAGED TO BANG OUT THE SECOND VOLUME OF URABOKU—THANKS TO ALL OF YOUR VOICES CHEERING ME ON! THANK YOU! (WELL, IF THERE'S ANYONE WHO ONLY PICKED IT UP FROM VOLUME 2, OR ANYONE WHO'S BORROWING IT...GET THEE TO A BOOKSTORE!)

▸MEANWHILE...WITH THE SERIAL PUBLICATIONS IN THIS MAGAZINE, I'M WRITING THE STORY RIGHT NOW IN A STATE OF NERVOUS TENSION... PSYCHOLOGICALLY, IN FACT, I'M KIND OF AT MY LIMIT. THEN I REALIZED (TOO LATE) THAT "OH, MAYBE I'M THE KIND WHO TAKES ON THE PSYCHOLOGICAL STATES OF THE CHARACTERS OR SOMETHING..."
AND I FEEL LIKE I'VE CAUSED TROUBLE FOR A LOT OF PEOPLE, SO I REALLY WANT TO DO SOMETHING ABOUT IT, BUT I CAN'T DO MUCH, AND I FEEL KIND OF USELESS. (...)
OBVIOUSLY MY NUMBER ONE VICTIM IS MY EDITOR... PLEASE FORGIVE ME FOR ALWAYS THROWING YOU INTO SUCH CONFUSION! (÷CRIES÷) HMMM...YOU REALLY DO HAVE TO WORK HARDER, ODAGIRI.
THAT'S THE WAY IT IS WITH ASUKA MAGAZINE, BUT IF YOU BUY THE ISSUE ON SALE AT THE MOMENT (THE MAY ISSUE), IT'LL COME WITH A FREEBIE OVERSIZED POSTER OF LUKA (OR IT'S SUPPOSED TO), SO IT'S QUITE A DEAL. (÷GRIN÷) I WORKED HARD ILLUSTRATING THAT!♡ HEE- HEE...
OH YEAH, AND I WROTE IN THE AFTERWORD TO VOLUME 1 THAT MORE AND MORE CHARACTERS WOULD BE JOINING YUKI'S PARTY, BUT I HAVEN'T INTRODUCED A SINGLE NEW CHARACTER...... THEY'RE ON STANDBY, THOUGH, I SWEAR! IT HAS NO DIRECT BEARING ON THIS STORY, AND EVEN THE LITTLE TIDBITS GOT CUT, AND I DRAW AND DRAW BUT DON'T MAKE ANY PROGRESS... NO! I'M GOING TO FOLLOW THIS STORY AS FAITHFULLY AS POSSIBLE, SO IT'S BETTER THIS WAY. RIGHT.
...ALTHOUGH, IF YOU'RE READING IT IN THE MAGAZINE NOW, YOU'LL GET TO MEET THE NEW CHARACTERS... (SELF-PROMOTION!)♡
ANYWAY, IT'S UPSETTING THAT I DON'T GET TO DRAW THE TIDBITS THAT WERE CUT... SO I'LL DRAW THEM IN IF I SEE ANY CHANCES. LIKE THE ORIGINALS FOR THIS VOLUME. I CAN TAKE A BREATHER.

▸WELL, AS FOR THE... "PAST SAGA" WHEN YUKI AND LUKA FIRST MEET, WHICH SOME OF YOU ARE BEGGING ME TO GET TO ALREADY—OF COURSE, I DO WANT TO WRITE THAT SOMETIME, SO PLEASE HOLD ON! (WELL, IF THE SERIES CONTINUES.) I KNOW YOU AREN'T SATISFIED WITH WHAT I'VE PRESENTED OF YUKI'S PROFILE SO FAR, AND WHEN I GOT A LETTER THAT SAID "JUST WHO EXACTLY **IS** YUKI?" MY HEART SKIPPED A BEAT. NOW THAT IS A **VERY** GOOD QUESTION...

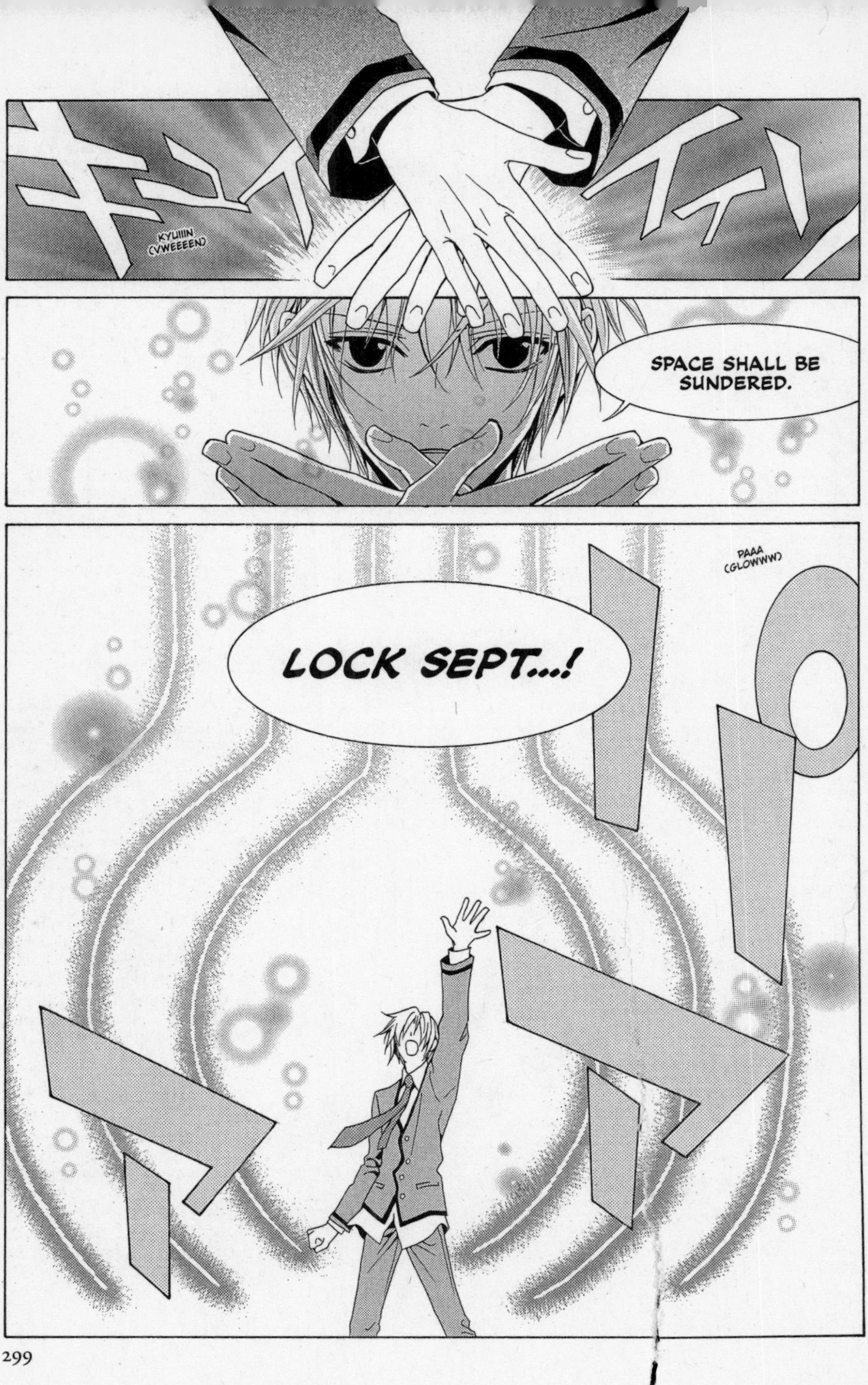
KYUIIIN
(VWEEEEN)
SPACE SHALL BE SUNDERED.
PAAA
(GLOWWW)
LOCK SEPT...!

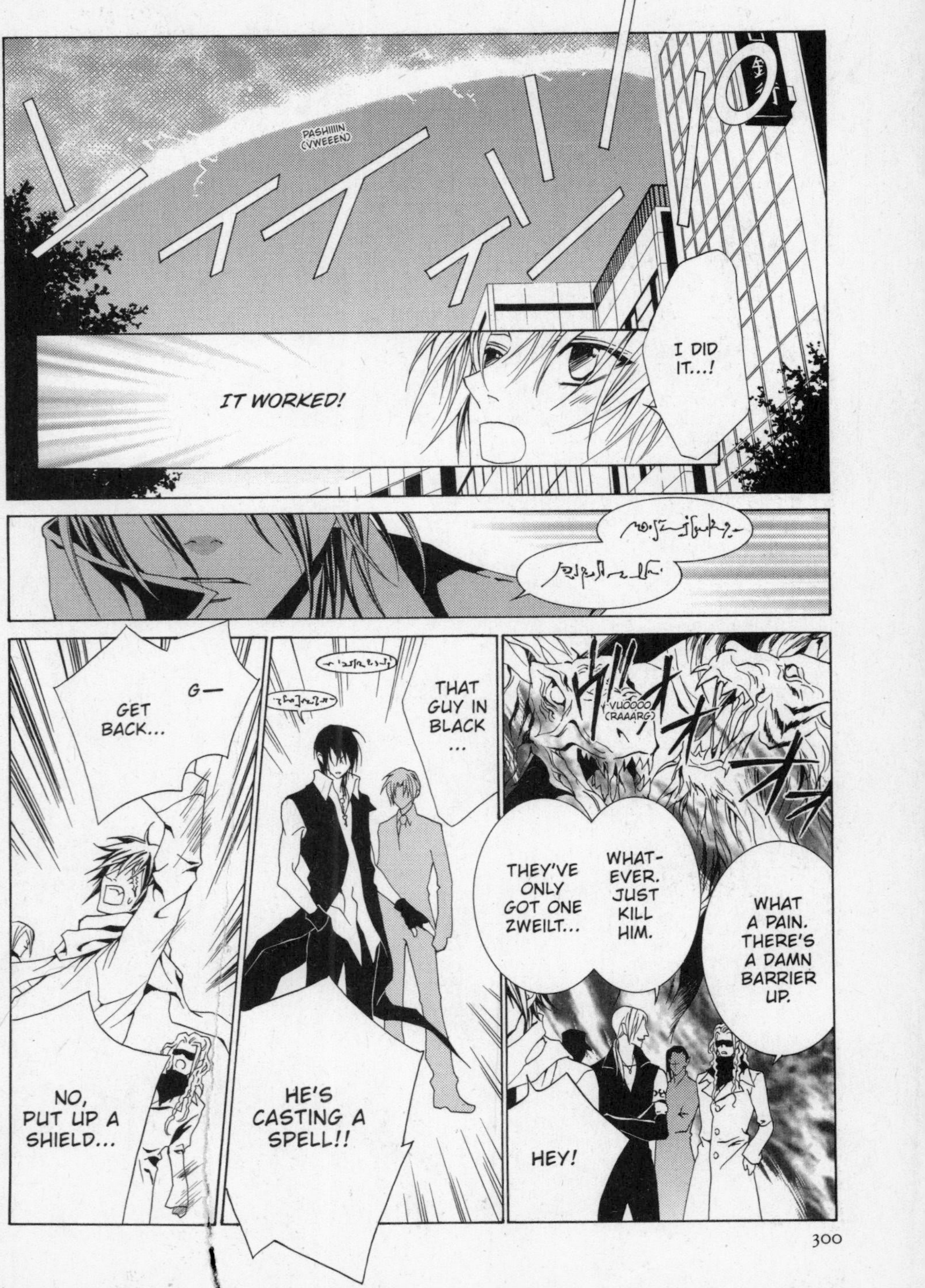

PASHIIIIN (VWEEEN)
I DID IT...!
IT WORKED!
WHAT A PAIN. THERE'S A DAMN BARRIER UP.
VUOOOO (RAAARG)
WHAT-EVER. JUST KILL HIM.
THEY'VE ONLY GOT ONE ZWEILT...
HEY!
THAT GUY IN BLACK ...
HE'S CASTING A SPELL!!
G—
GET BACK...
NO, PUT UP A SHIELD...

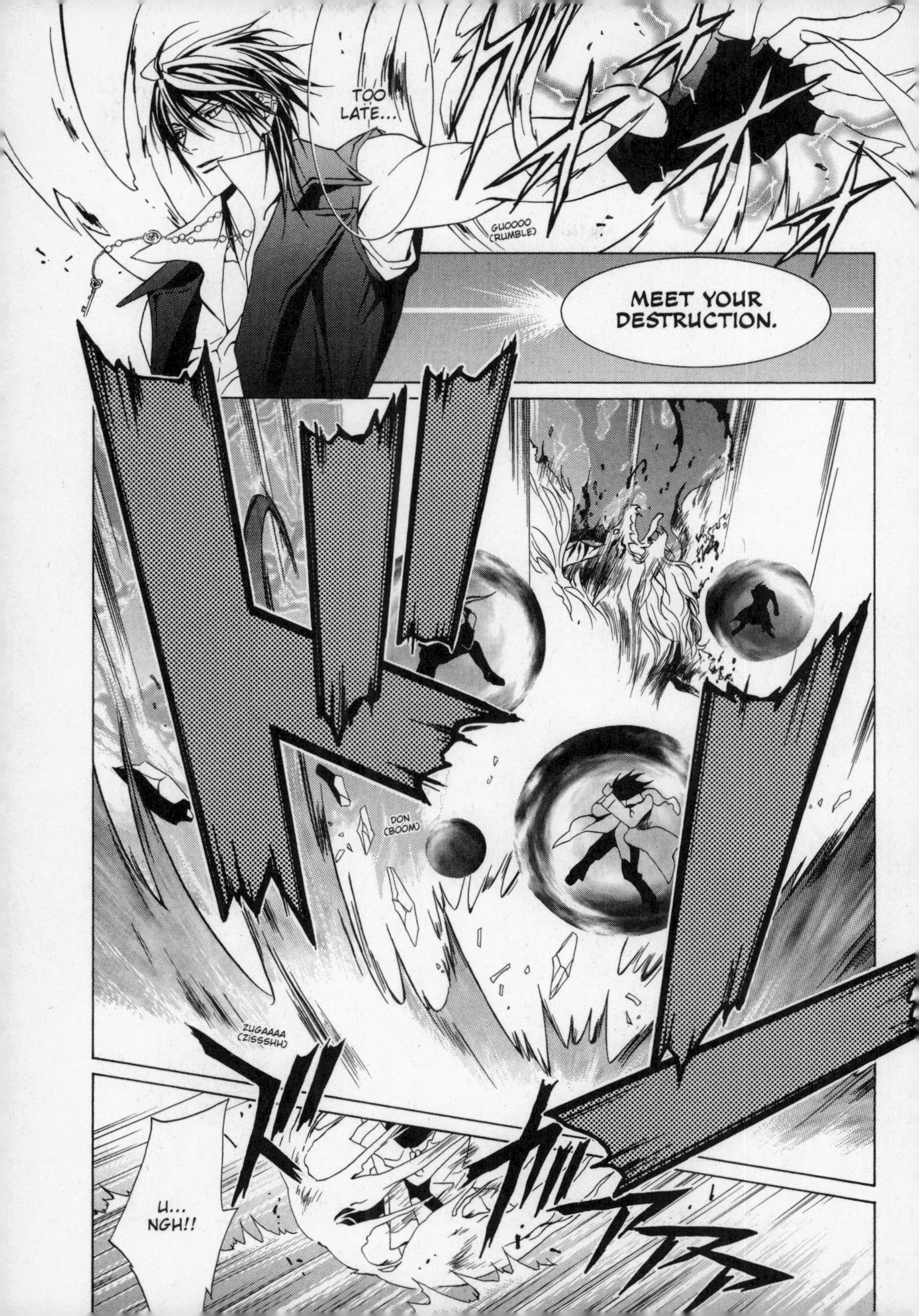
TOO LATE...
GUOOOO (RUMBLE)
MEET YOUR DESTRUCTION.
DON (BOOM)
ZUGAAAA (ZISSSHH)
U... NGH!!

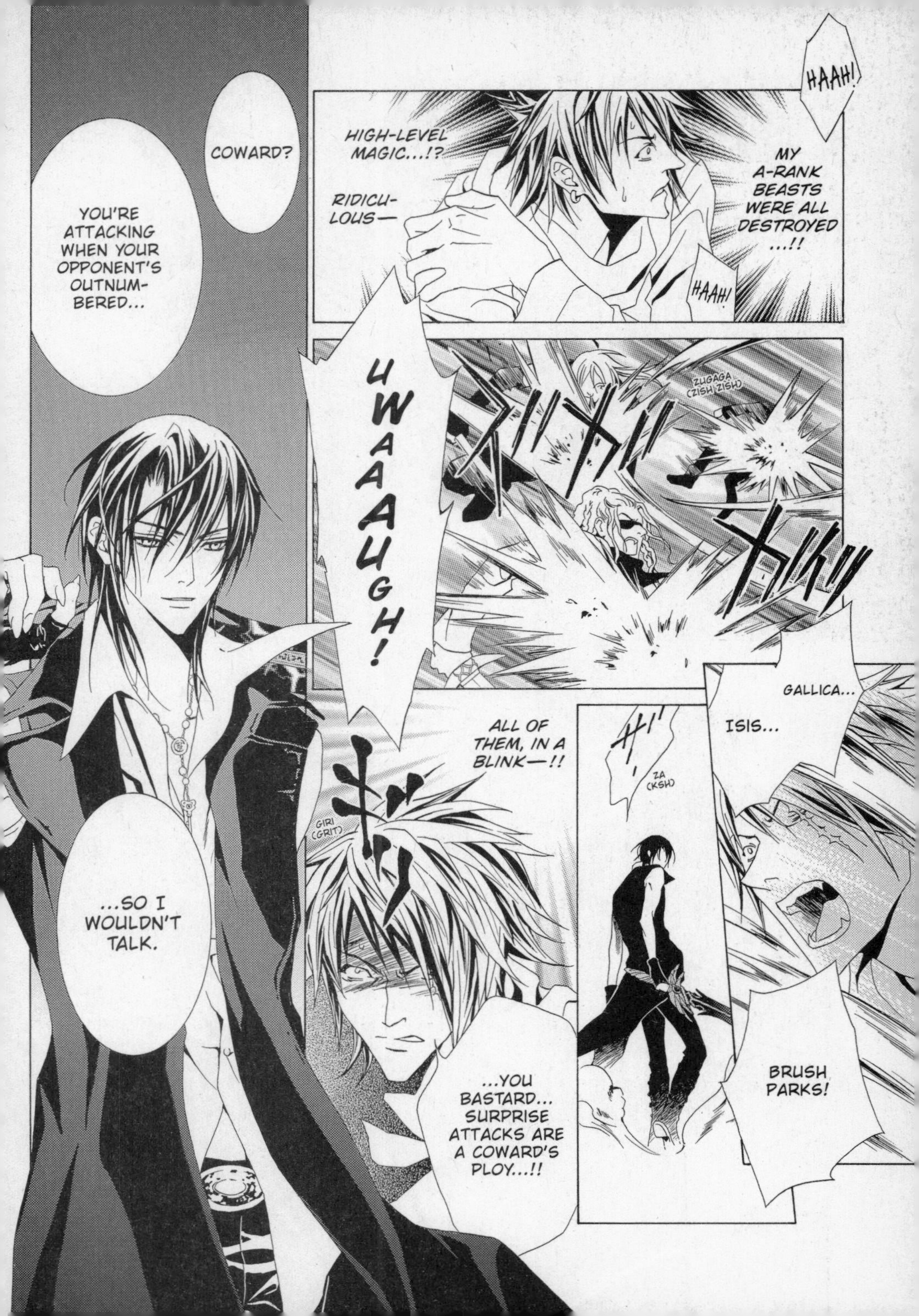

HAAH!
MY A-RANK BEASTS WERE ALL DESTROYED ...!!
HIGH-LEVEL MAGIC...!?
RIDICU-LOUS—
HAAH!
ZUGAGA (ZISH ZISH)
UWAAAAUGH!
GALLICA...
ISIS...
BRUSH PARKS!
ZA (KSH)
ALL OF THEM, IN A BLINK—!!
GIRI (GRIT)
...YOU BASTARD... SURPRISE ATTACKS ARE A COWARD'S PLOY...!!
COWARD?
YOU'RE ATTACKING WHEN YOUR OPPONENT'S OUTNUM-BERED...
...SO I WOULDN'T TALK.

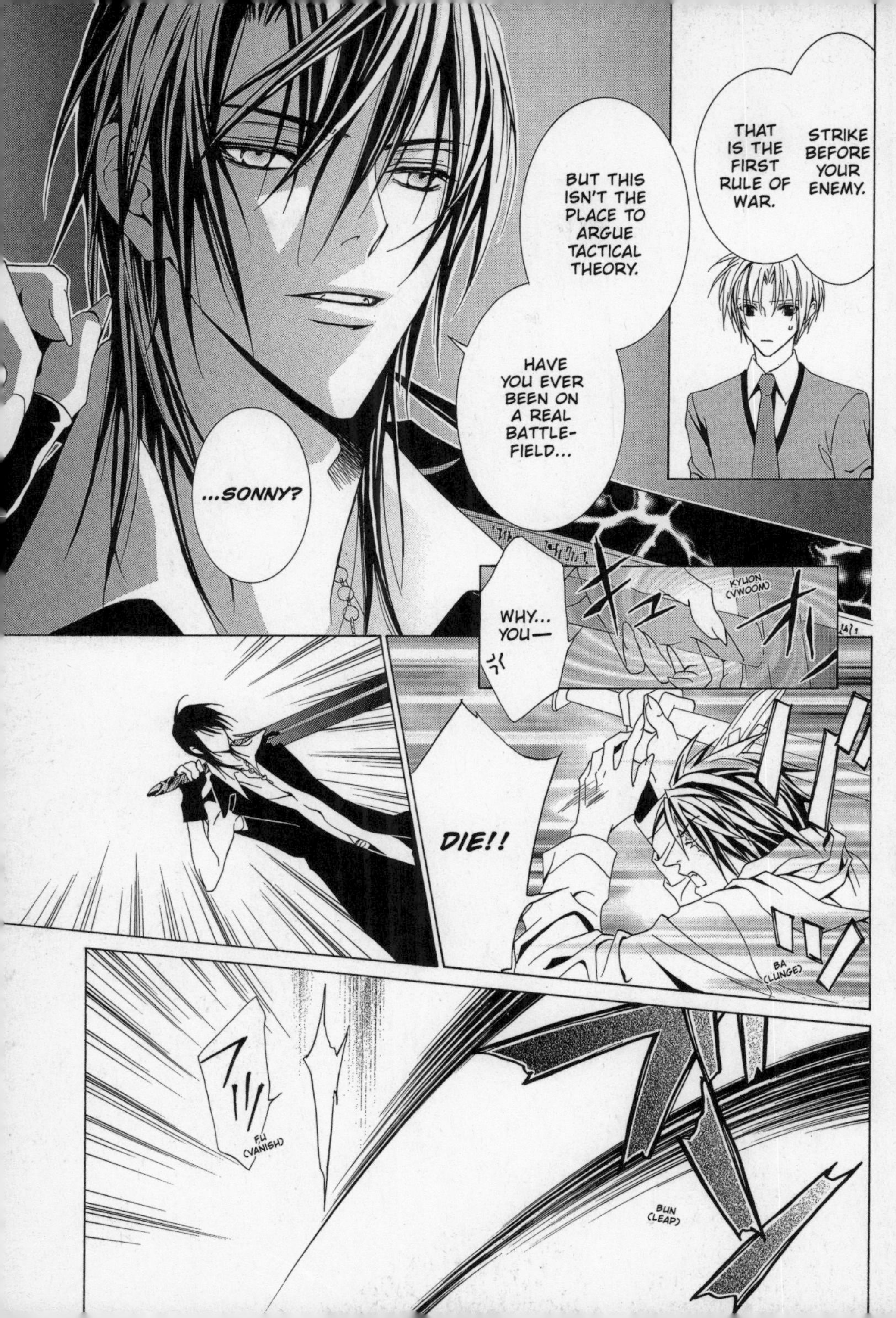
STRIKE BEFORE YOUR ENEMY.
THAT IS THE FIRST RULE OF WAR.
BUT THIS ISN'T THE PLACE TO ARGUE TACTICAL THEORY.
HAVE YOU EVER BEEN ON A REAL BATTLE-FIELD...
...SONNY?
KYUON (VWOOM)
WHY... YOU—
BA (LUNGE)
DIE!!
BUN (LEAP)
FU (VANISH)

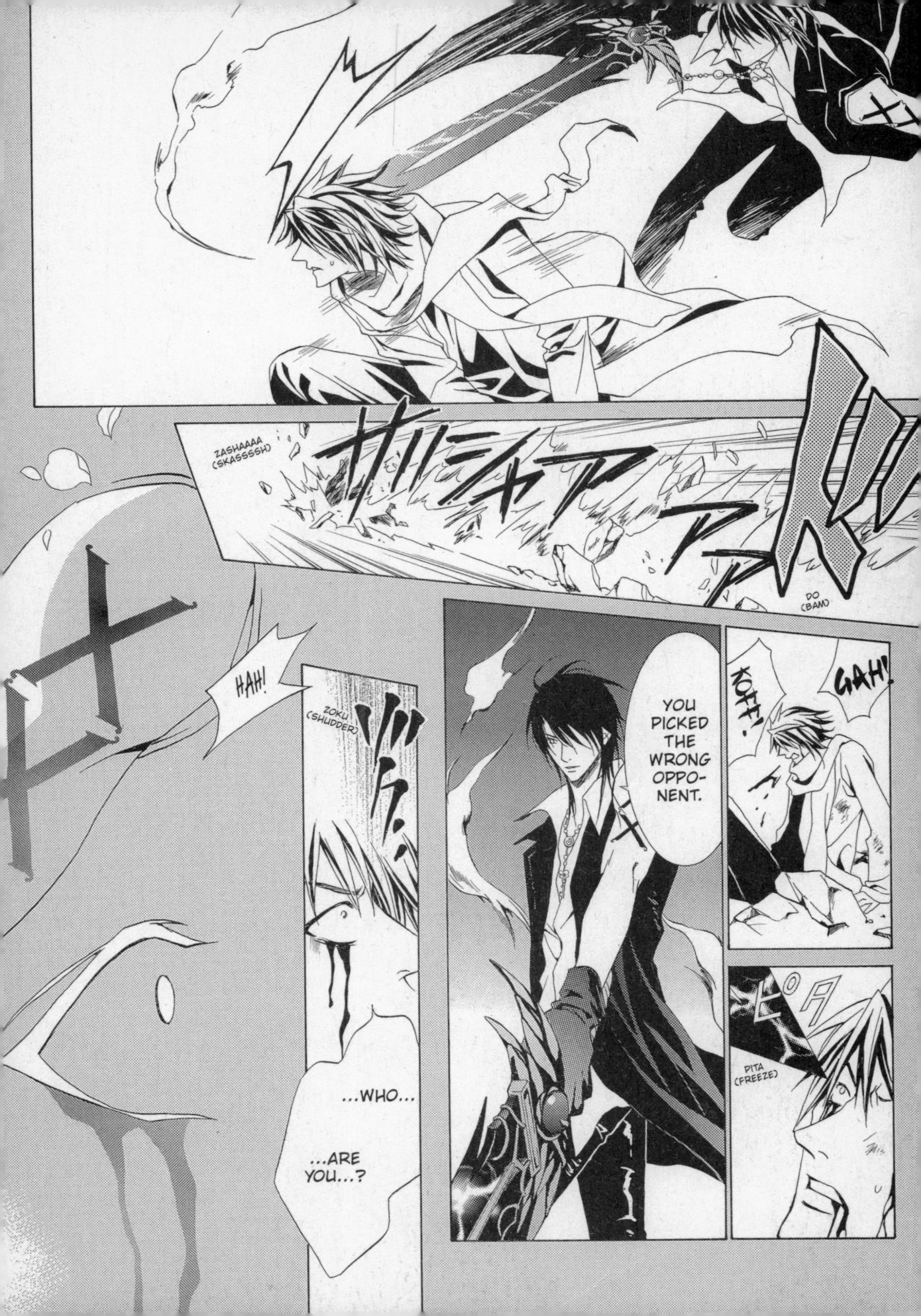
ZASHAAAA (SKASSSSH)
DO (BAM)
GAH!
KOFF!
PITA (FREEZE)
YOU PICKED THE WRONG OPPO-NENT.
HAH!
ZOKU (SHUDDER)
...WHO...
...ARE YOU...?

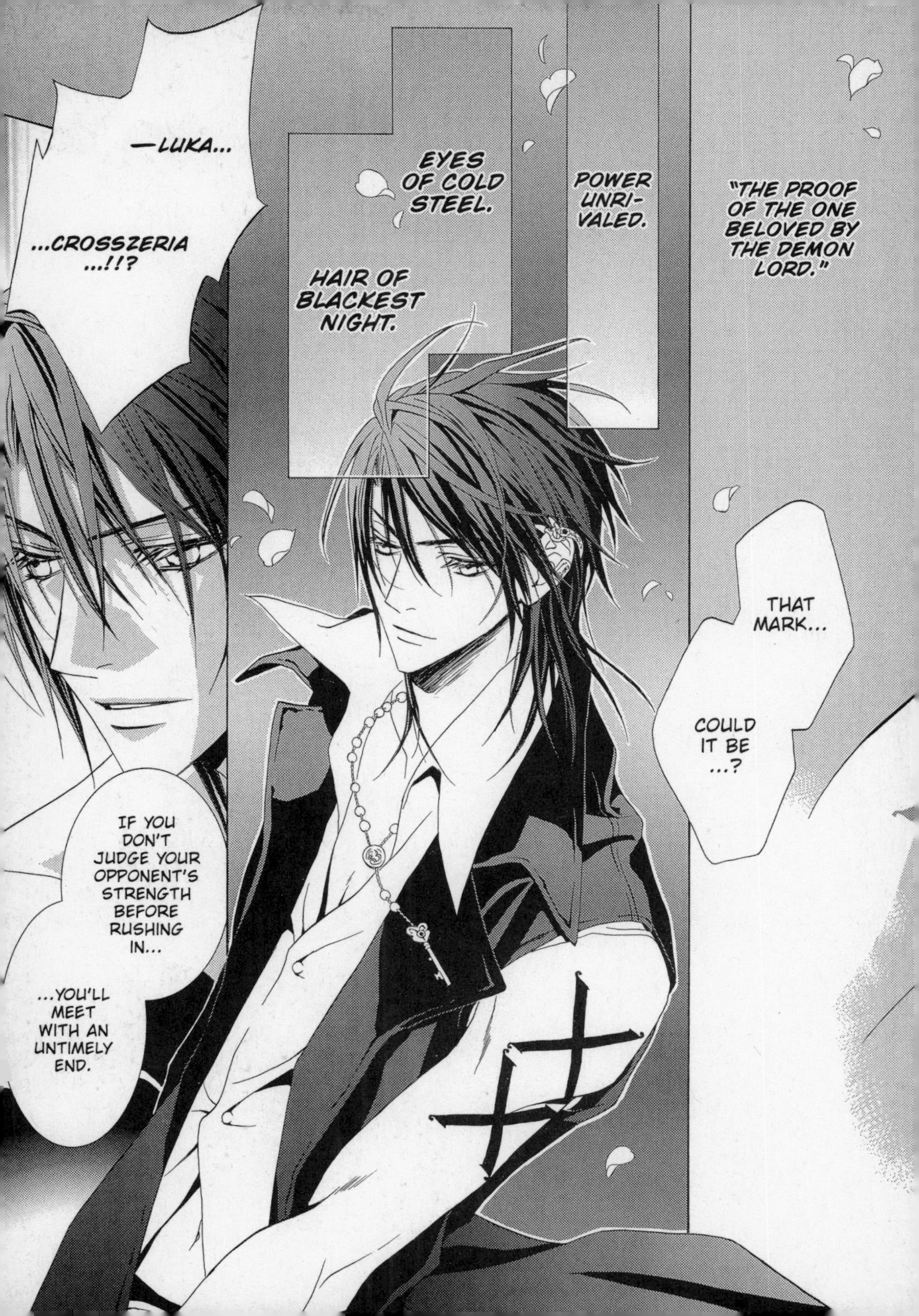
"THE PROOF OF THE ONE BELOVED BY THE DEMON LORD."
POWER UNRI-VALED.
EYES OF COLD STEEL.
HAIR OF BLACKEST NIGHT.
THAT MARK...
COULD IT BE ...?
—LUKA...
...CROSSZERIA ...!!?
IF YOU DON'T JUDGE YOUR OPPONENT'S STRENGTH BEFORE RUSHING IN...
...YOU'LL MEET WITH AN UNTIMELY END.

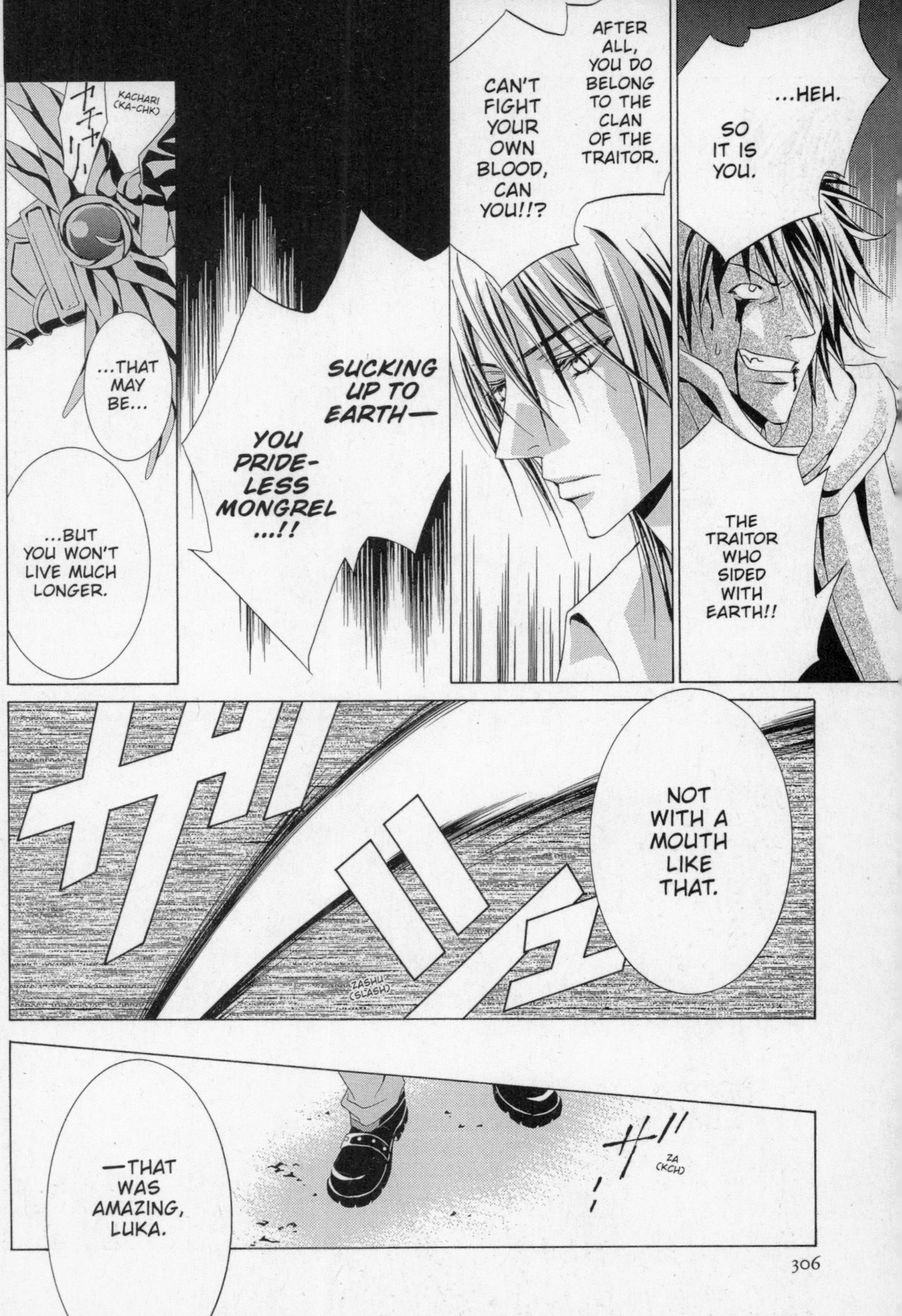
...HEH.
SO IT IS YOU.
THE TRAITOR WHO SIDED WITH EARTH!!
AFTER ALL, YOU DO BELONG TO THE CLAN OF THE TRAITOR.
CAN'T FIGHT YOUR OWN BLOOD, CAN YOU!!?
SUCKING UP TO EARTH—
YOU PRIDE-LESS MONGREL...!!
KACHARI (KA-CHK)
...THAT MAY BE...
...BUT YOU WON'T LIVE MUCH LONGER.
NOT WITH A MOUTH LIKE THAT.
ZASHU (SLASH)
ZA (KCH)
—THAT WAS AMAZING, LUKA.

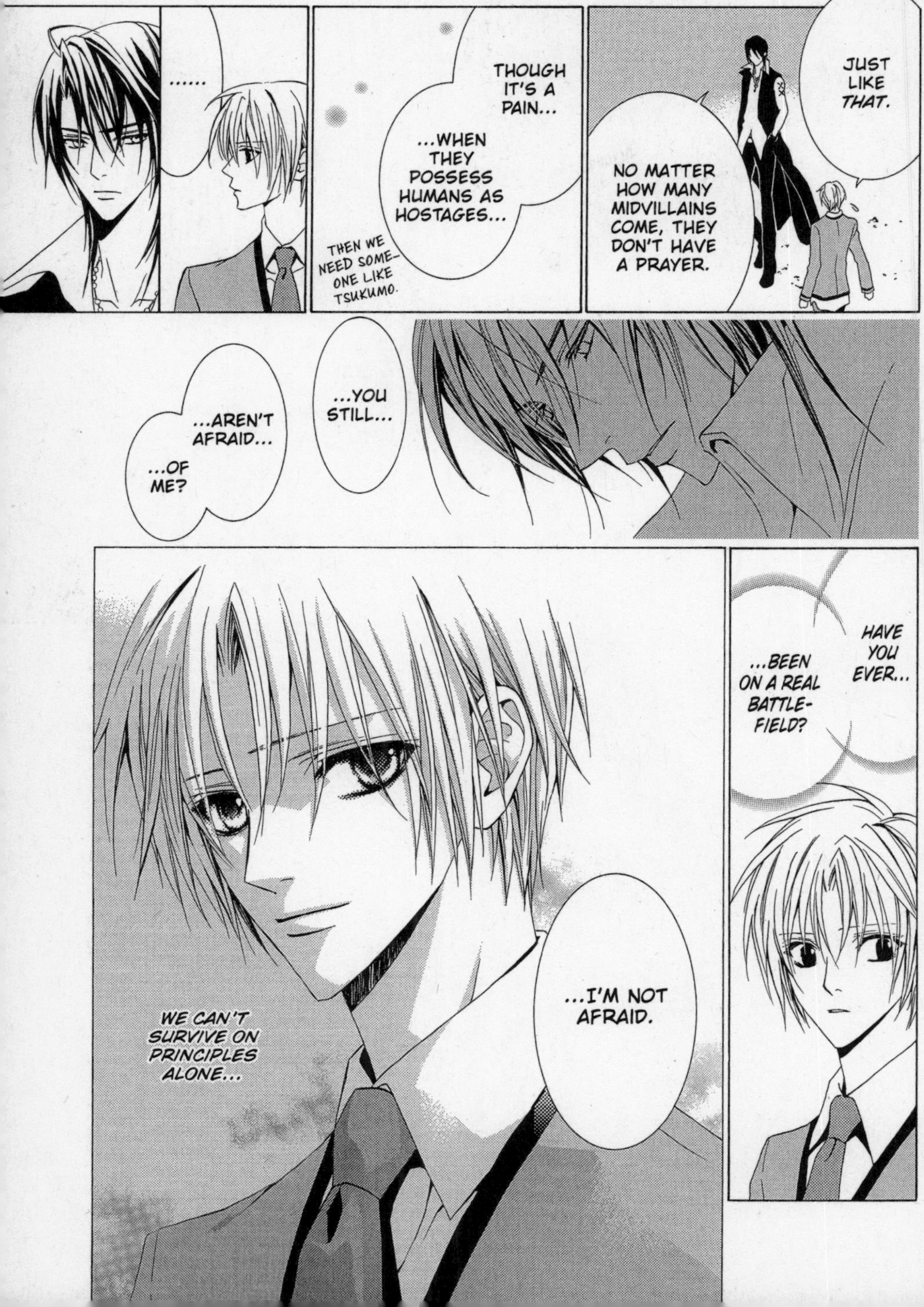
JUST LIKE THAT.
NO MATTER HOW MANY MIDVILLAINS COME, THEY DON'T HAVE A PRAYER.
THOUGH IT'S A PAIN...
...WHEN THEY POSSESS HUMANS AS HOSTAGES...
THEN WE NEED SOME-ONE LIKE TSUKUMO.
......
...YOU STILL...
...AREN'T AFRAID...
...OF ME?
HAVE YOU EVER...
...BEEN ON A REAL BATTLE-FIELD?
...I'M NOT AFRAID.
WE CAN'T SURVIVE ON PRINCIPLES ALONE...

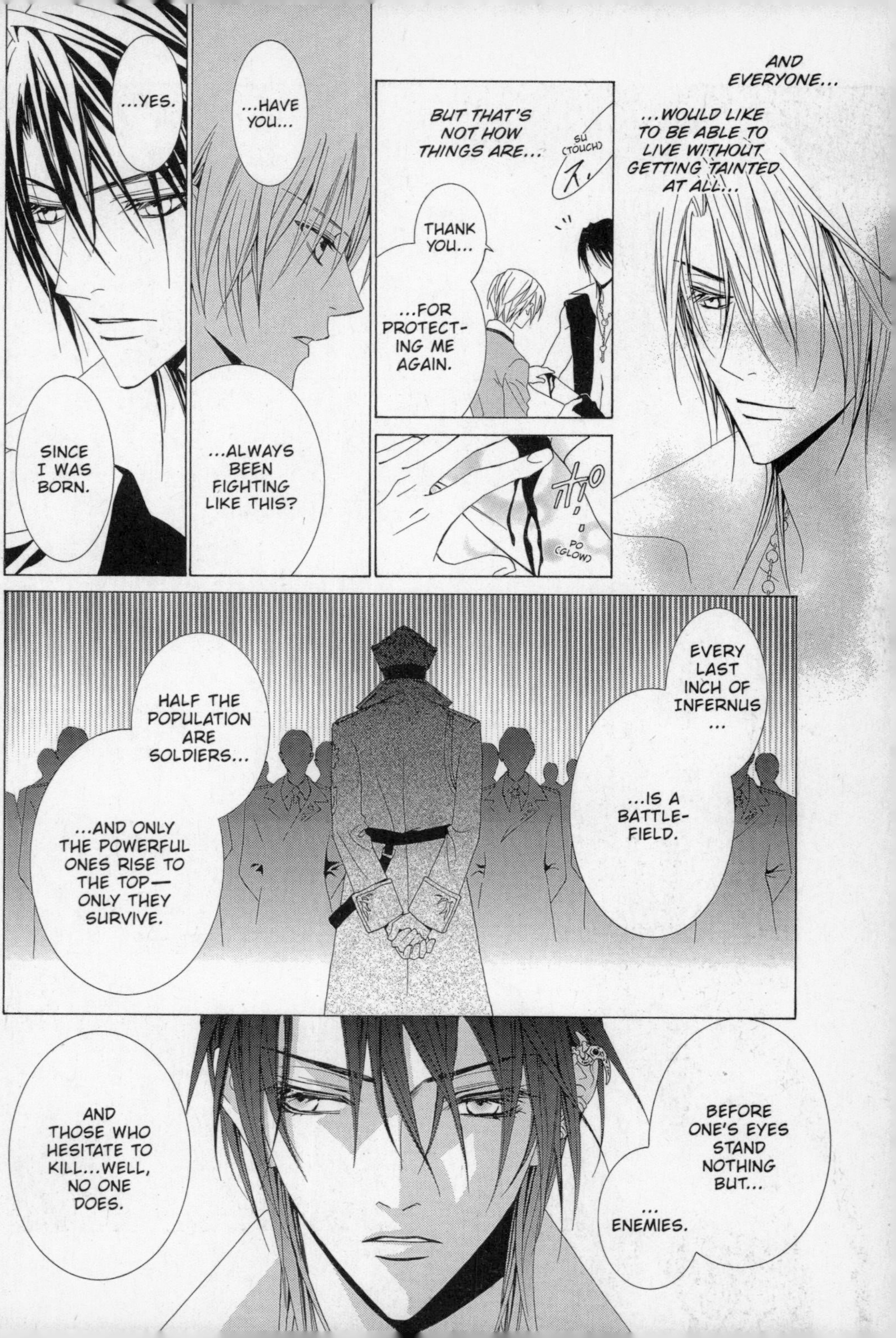
AND EVERYONE...
...WOULD LIKE TO BE ABLE TO LIVE WITHOUT GETTING TAINTED AT ALL...
BUT THAT'S NOT HOW THINGS ARE...
SU (TOUCH)
THANK YOU...
...FOR PROTECTING ME AGAIN.
PO (GLOW)
...HAVE YOU...
...ALWAYS BEEN FIGHTING LIKE THIS?
...YES.
SINCE I WAS BORN.
EVERY LAST INCH OF INFERNUS ...
...IS A BATTLEFIELD.
HALF THE POPULATION ARE SOLDIERS...
...AND ONLY THE POWERFUL ONES RISE TO THE TOP— ONLY THEY SURVIVE.
BEFORE ONE'S EYES STAND NOTHING BUT...
... ENEMIES.
AND THOSE WHO HESITATE TO KILL...WELL, NO ONE DOES.

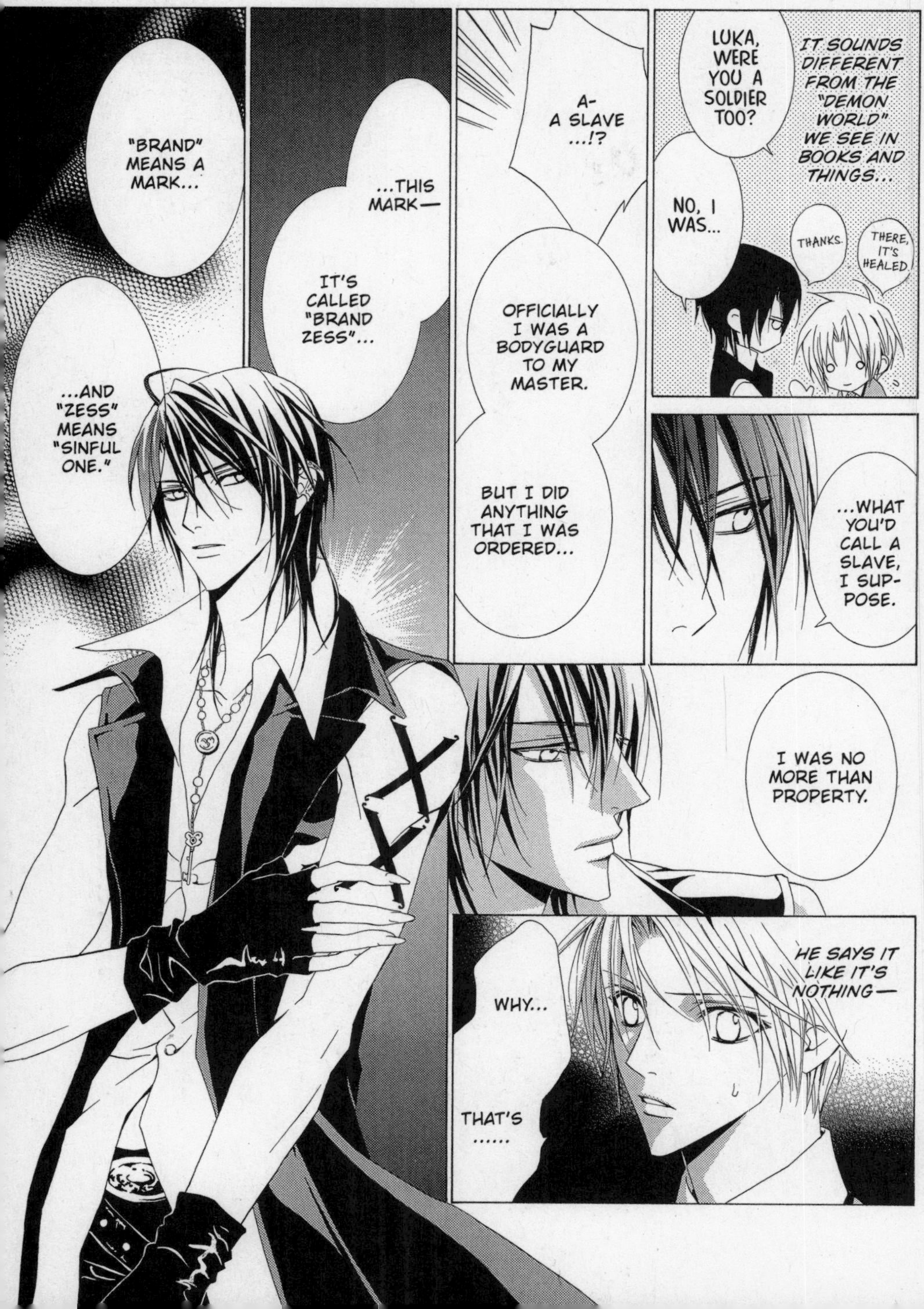
IT SOUNDS DIFFERENT FROM THE "DEMON WORLD" WE SEE IN BOOKS AND THINGS...
LUKA, WERE YOU A SOLDIER TOO?
NO, I WAS...
THERE, IT'S HEALED.
THANKS.
...WHAT YOU'D CALL A SLAVE, I SUPPOSE.
A- A SLAVE ...!?
OFFICIALLY I WAS A BODYGUARD TO MY MASTER.
BUT I DID ANYTHING THAT I WAS ORDERED...
I WAS NO MORE THAN PROPERTY.
...THIS MARK—
IT'S CALLED "BRAND ZESS"...
"BRAND" MEANS A MARK...
...AND "ZESS" MEANS "SINFUL ONE."
HE SAYS IT LIKE IT'S NOTHING—
WHY...
THAT'S ......

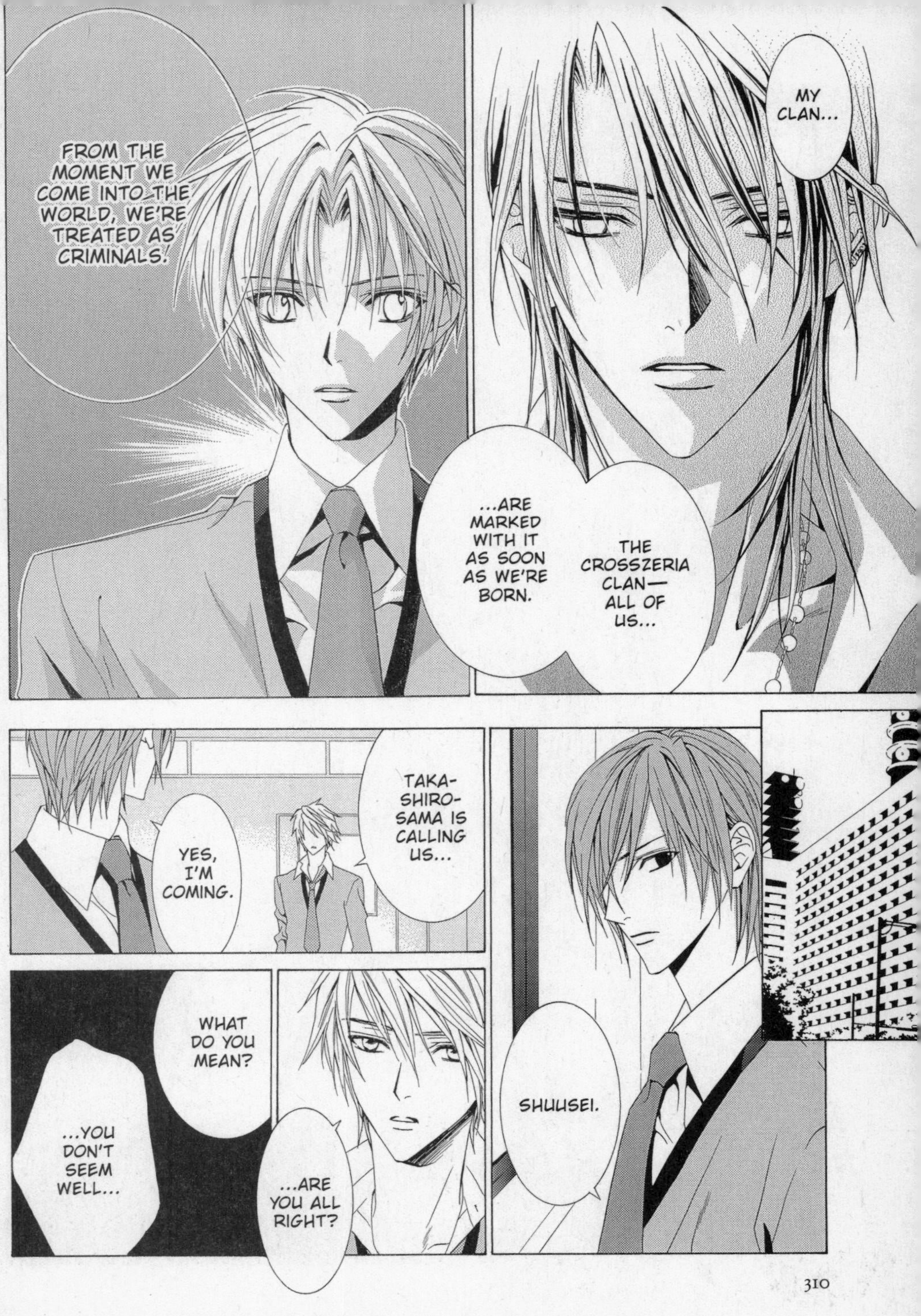
MY CLAN...
THE CROSSZERIA CLAN—ALL OF US...
...ARE MARKED WITH IT AS SOON AS WE'RE BORN.
FROM THE MOMENT WE COME INTO THE WORLD, WE'RE TREATED AS CRIMINALS.
SHUUSEI.
TAKA-SHIRO-SAMA IS CALLING US...
YES, I'M COMING.
...ARE YOU ALL RIGHT?
...YOU DON'T SEEM WELL...
WHAT DO YOU MEAN?

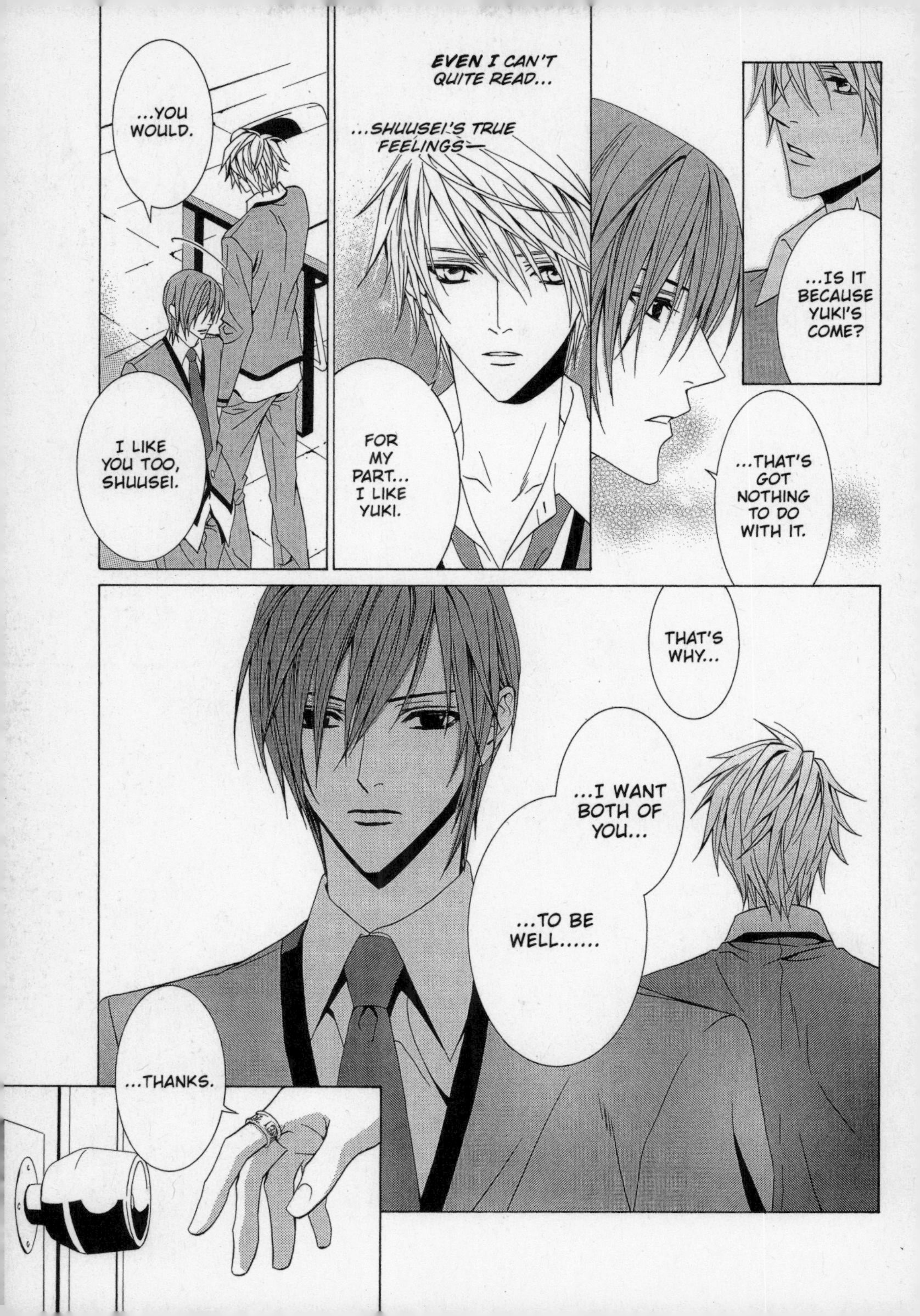

...IS IT BECAUSE YUKI'S COME?
...THAT'S GOT NOTHING TO DO WITH IT.
EVEN I CAN'T QUITE READ...
...SHUUSEI'S TRUE FEELINGS—
FOR MY PART... I LIKE YUKI.
...YOU WOULD.
I LIKE YOU TOO, SHUUSEI.
THAT'S WHY...
...I WANT BOTH OF YOU...
...TO BE WELL......
...THANKS.

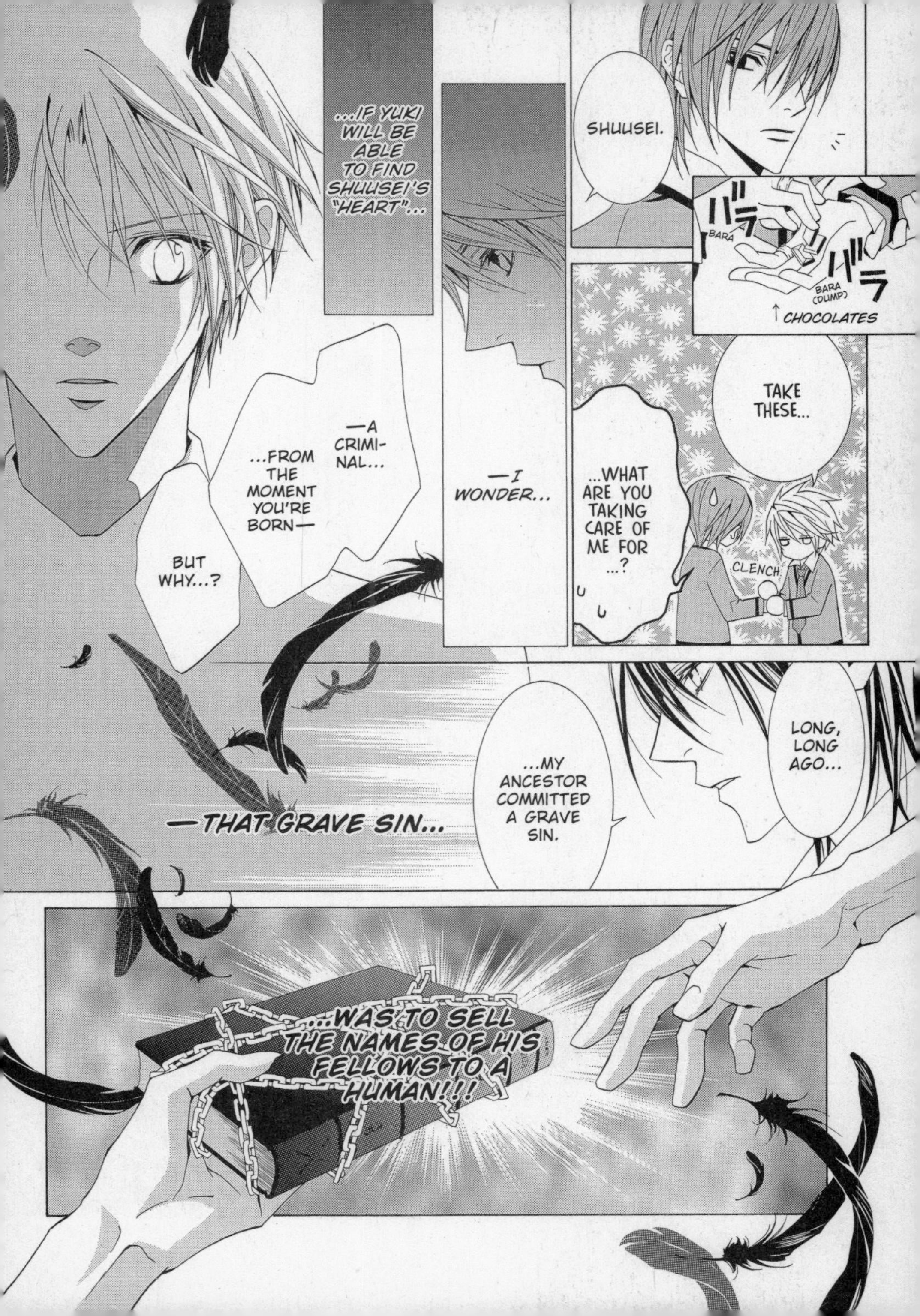
SHUUSEI.
バラ
BARA
バラ
BARA (DUMP)
↑ CHOCOLATES
TAKE THESE...
CLENCH
...WHAT ARE YOU TAKING CARE OF ME FOR ...?
...IF YUKI WILL BE ABLE TO FIND SHUUSEI'S "HEART"...
—I WONDER...
—A CRIMINAL...
...FROM THE MOMENT YOU'RE BORN—
BUT WHY...?
LONG, LONG AGO...
...MY ANCESTOR COMMITTED A GRAVE SIN.
—THAT GRAVE SIN...
...WAS TO SELL THE NAMES OF HIS FELLOWS TO A HUMAN!!!

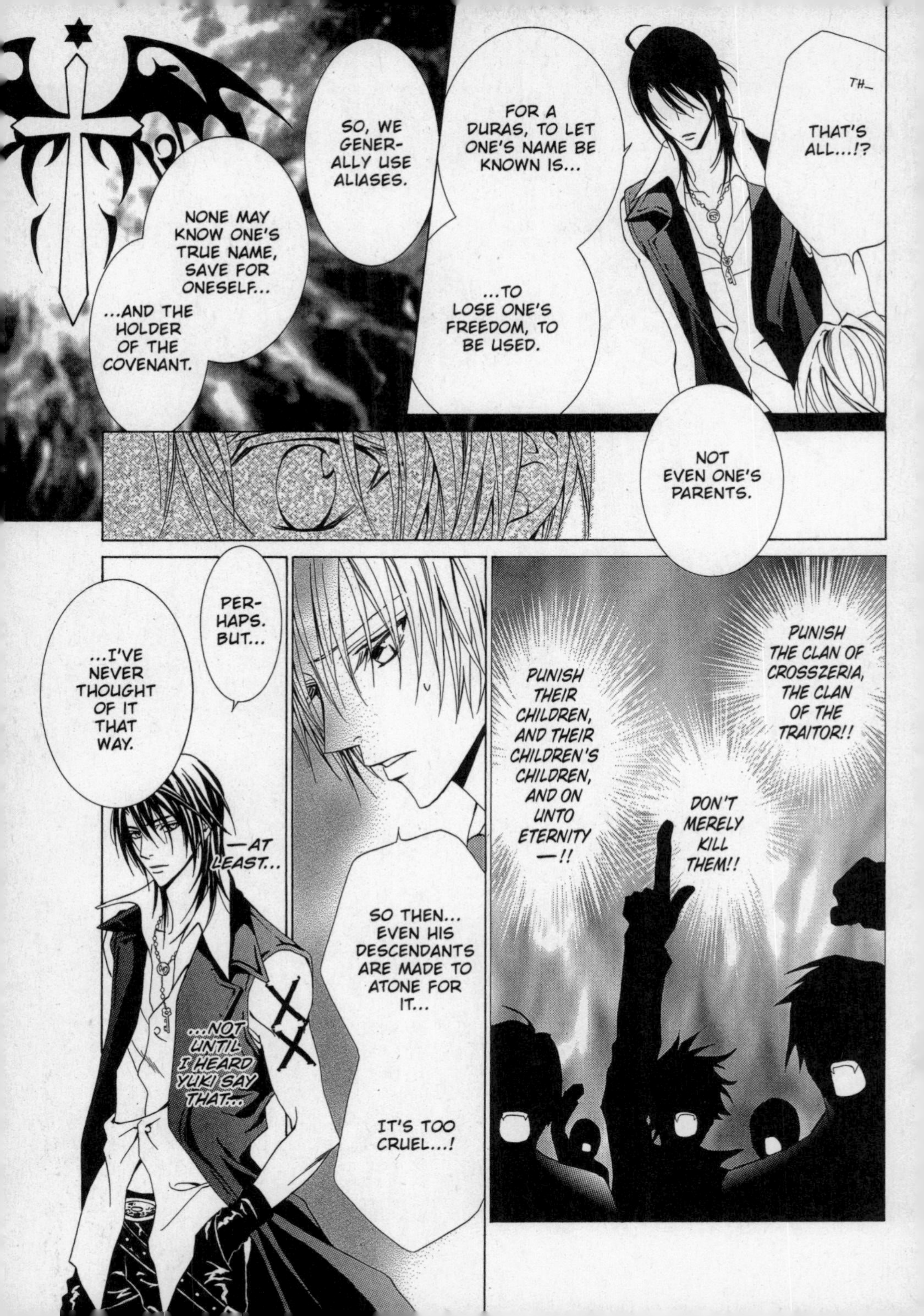

TH—
THAT'S ALL...!?
FOR A DURAS, TO LET ONE'S NAME BE KNOWN IS...
...TO LOSE ONE'S FREEDOM, TO BE USED.
SO, WE GENER-ALLY USE ALIASES.
NONE MAY KNOW ONE'S TRUE NAME, SAVE FOR ONESELF...
...AND THE HOLDER OF THE COVENANT.
NOT EVEN ONE'S PARENTS.
PUNISH THE CLAN OF CROSSZERIA, THE CLAN OF THE TRAITOR!!
DON'T MERELY KILL THEM!!
PUNISH THEIR CHILDREN, AND THEIR CHILDREN'S CHILDREN, AND ON UNTO ETERNITY—!!
SO THEN... EVEN HIS DESCENDANTS ARE MADE TO ATONE FOR IT...
IT'S TOO CRUEL...!
PER-HAPS. BUT...
...I'VE NEVER THOUGHT OF IT THAT WAY.
—AT LEAST...
...NOT UNTIL I HEARD YUKI SAY THAT...

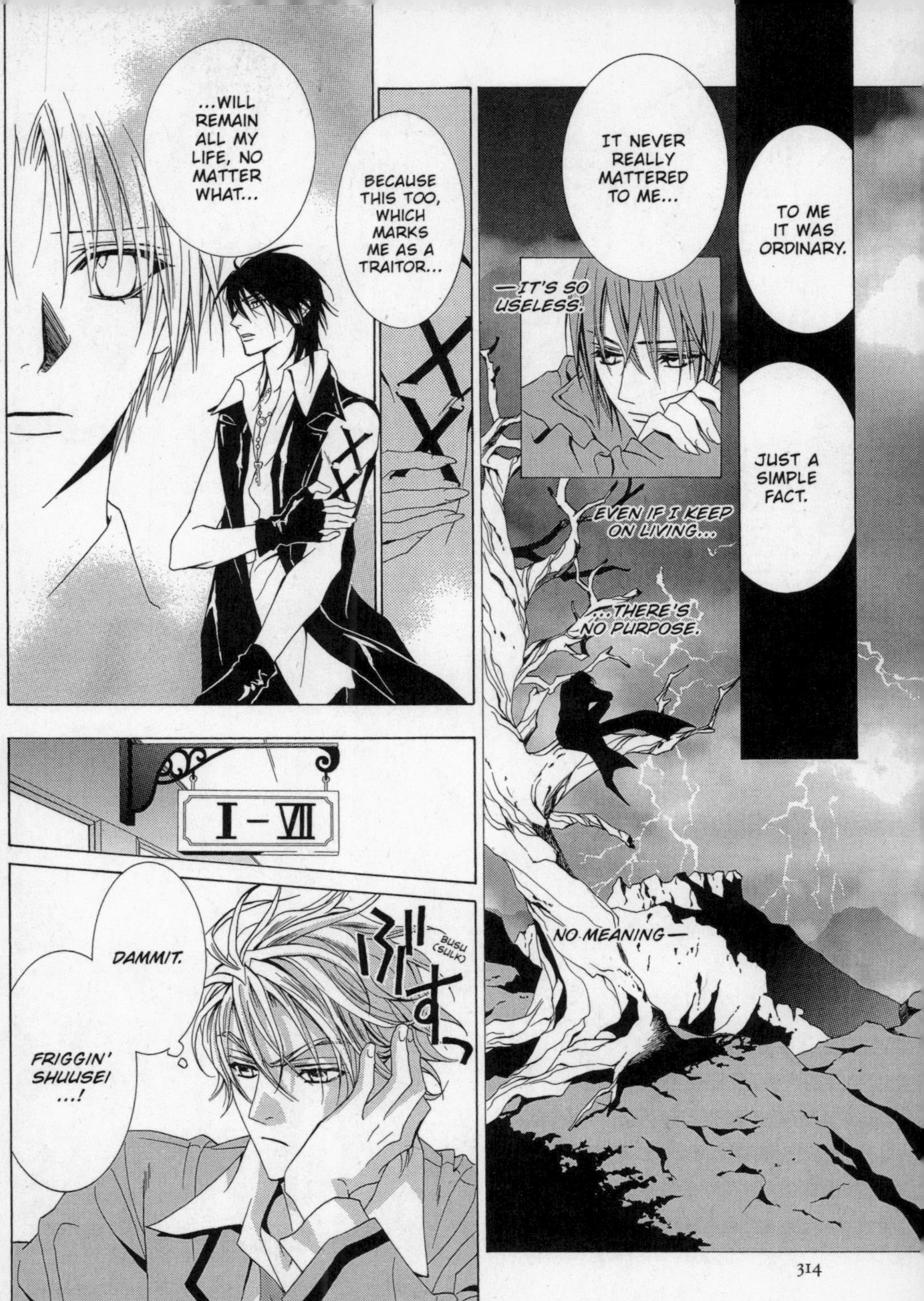
IT NEVER REALLY MATTERED TO ME...
TO ME IT WAS ORDINARY.
JUST A SIMPLE FACT.
—IT'S SO USELESS.
EVEN IF I KEEP ON LIVING...
...THERE'S NO PURPOSE.
NO MEANING—
BECAUSE THIS TOO, WHICH MARKS ME AS A TRAITOR...
...WILL REMAIN ALL MY LIFE, NO MATTER WHAT...
I – VII
ぶすっ
BUSU (SULK)
DAMMIT.
FRIGGIN' SHUUSEI ...!

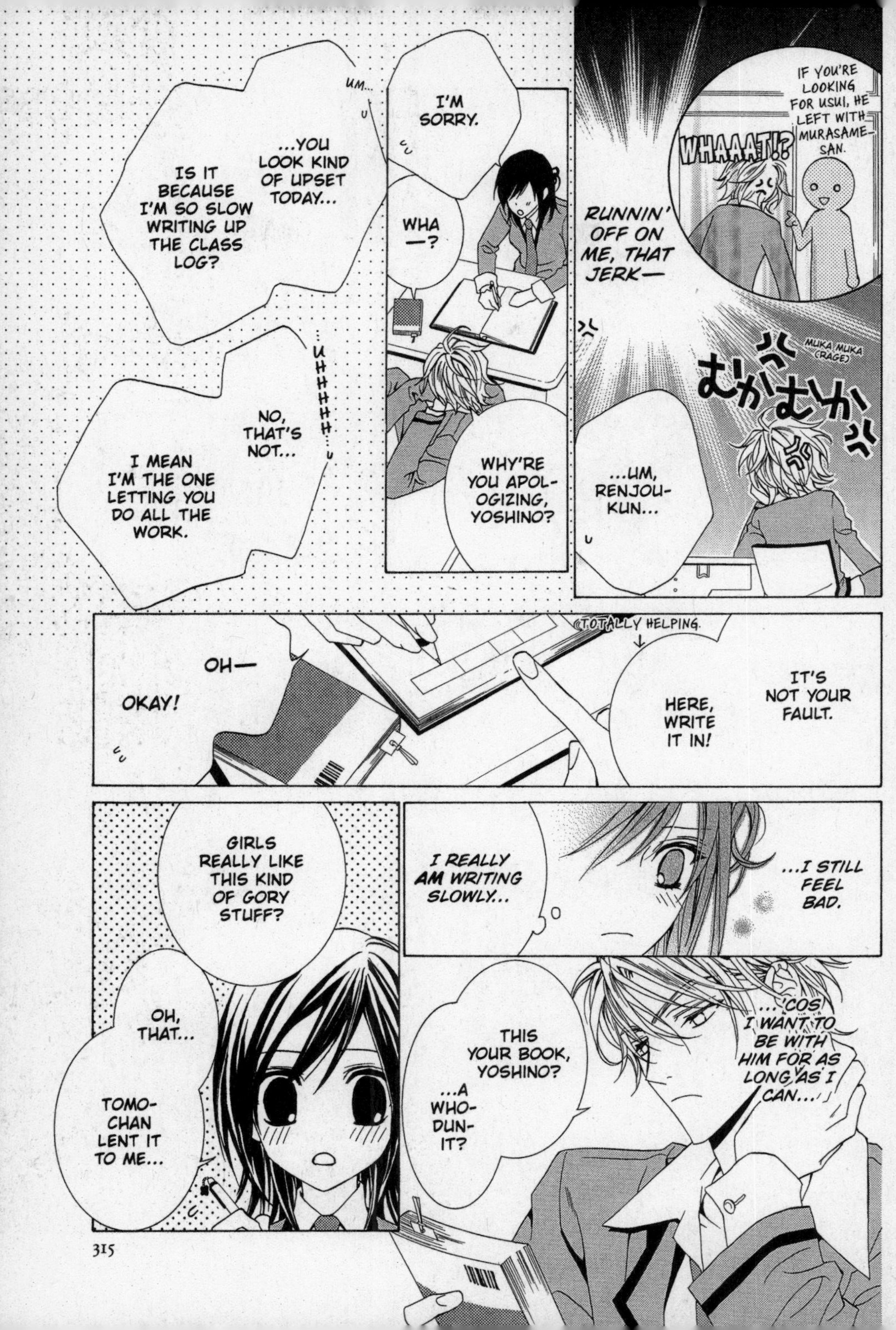
IF YOU'RE LOOKING FOR USUI, HE LEFT WITH MURASAME-SAN.
WHAAAT!?
RUNNIN' OFF ON ME, THAT JERK—
MUKA MUKA (RAGE)
...UM, RENJOU-KUN...
I'M SORRY.
WHA—?
WHY'RE YOU APOLOGIZING, YOSHINO?
UM...
...YOU LOOK KIND OF UPSET TODAY...
IS IT BECAUSE I'M SO SLOW WRITING UP THE CLASS LOG?
...UHHHHHH...
NO, THAT'S NOT...
I MEAN I'M THE ONE LETTING YOU DO ALL THE WORK.
IT'S NOT YOUR FAULT.
TOTALLY HELPING.
HERE, WRITE IT IN!
OH—
OKAY!
...I STILL FEEL BAD.
I REALLY AM WRITING SLOWLY...
...'COS I WANT TO BE WITH HIM FOR AS LONG AS I CAN...
THIS YOUR BOOK, YOSHINO?
...A WHODUNIT?
GIRLS REALLY LIKE THIS KIND OF GORY STUFF?
OH, THAT...
TOMO-CHAN LENT IT TO ME...

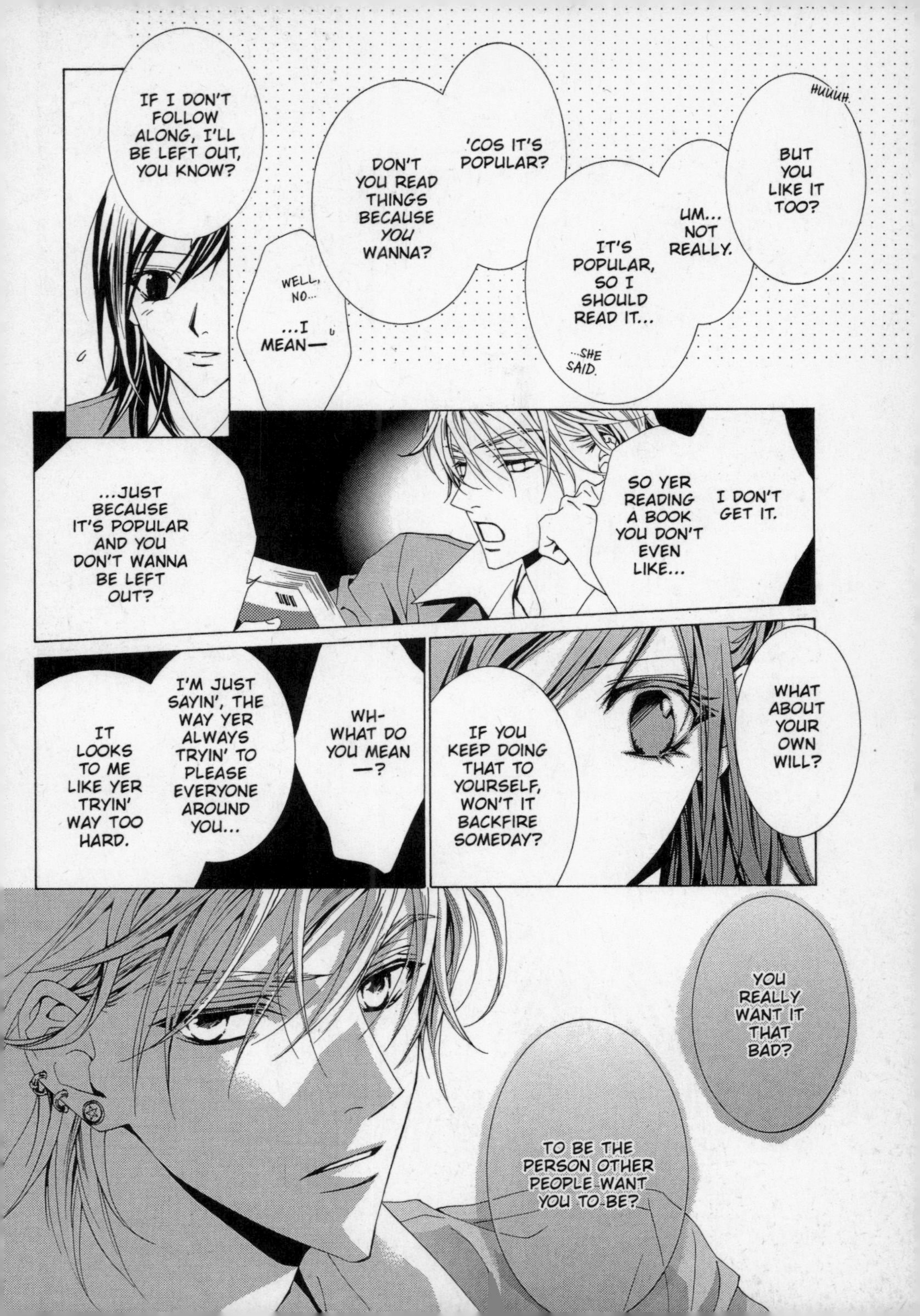
HUUUH.
BUT YOU LIKE IT TOO?
UM... NOT REALLY.
IT'S POPULAR, SO I SHOULD READ IT...
...SHE SAID.
'COS IT'S POPULAR?
DON'T YOU READ THINGS BECAUSE *YOU* WANNA?
WELL, NO...
...I MEAN—
IF I DON'T FOLLOW ALONG, I'LL BE LEFT OUT, YOU KNOW?
I DON'T GET IT.
SO YER READING A BOOK YOU DON'T EVEN LIKE...
...JUST BECAUSE IT'S POPULAR AND YOU DON'T WANNA BE LEFT OUT?
WHAT ABOUT YOUR OWN WILL?
IF YOU KEEP DOING THAT TO YOURSELF, WON'T IT BACKFIRE SOMEDAY?
WH- WHAT DO YOU MEAN—?
I'M JUST SAYIN', THE WAY YER ALWAYS TRYIN' TO PLEASE EVERYONE AROUND YOU...
IT LOOKS TO ME LIKE YER TRYIN' WAY TOO HARD.
YOU REALLY WANT IT THAT BAD?
TO BE THE PERSON OTHER PEOPLE WANT YOU TO BE?

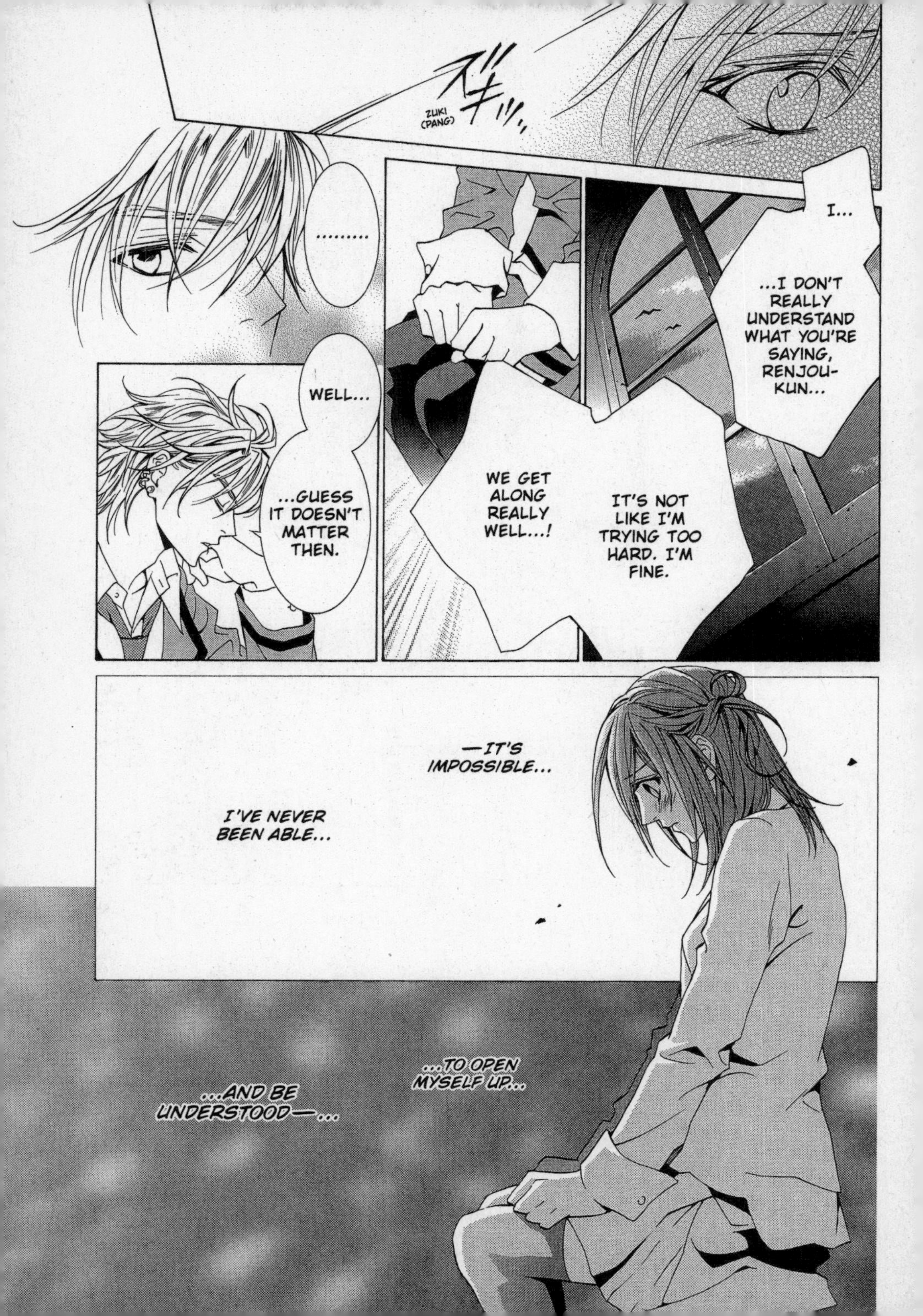
ZUKI (PANG)
I...
...I DON'T REALLY UNDERSTAND WHAT YOU'RE SAYING, RENJOU-KUN...
IT'S NOT LIKE I'M TRYING TOO HARD. I'M FINE.
WE GET ALONG REALLY WELL...!
....
WELL...
...GUESS IT DOESN'T MATTER THEN.
—IT'S IMPOSSIBLE...
I'VE NEVER BEEN ABLE...
...TO OPEN MYSELF UP...
...AND BE UNDERSTOOD—...

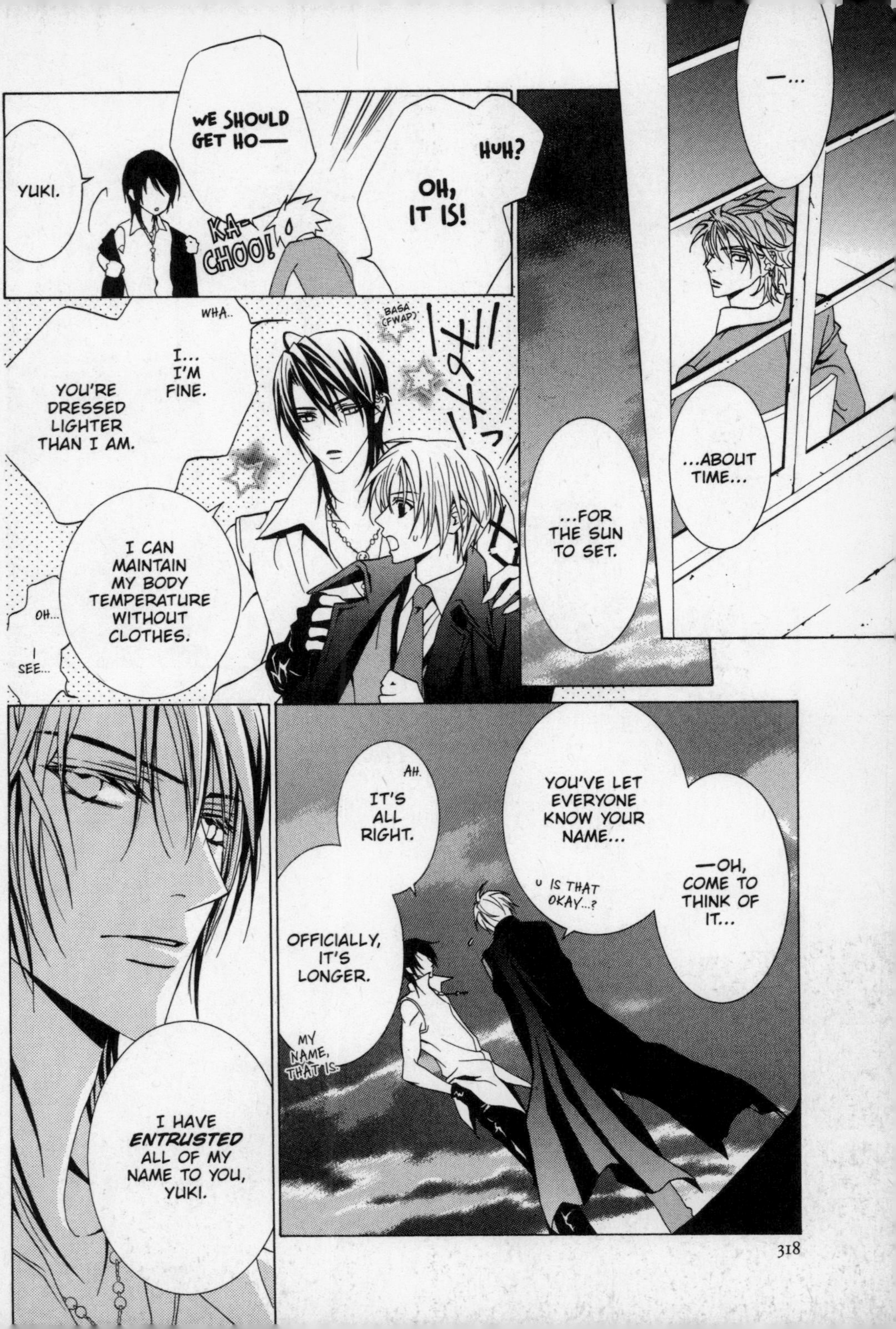
—...
...ABOUT TIME...
...FOR THE SUN TO SET.
HUH?
OH, IT IS!
KA-CHOO!
WE SHOULD GET HO—
YUKI.
BASA (FWAP)
WHA..
I... I'M FINE.
YOU'RE DRESSED LIGHTER THAN I AM.
I CAN MAINTAIN MY BODY TEMPERATURE WITHOUT CLOTHES.
OH... I SEE...
—OH, COME TO THINK OF IT...
YOU'VE LET EVERYONE KNOW YOUR NAME...
IS THAT OKAY...?
AH. IT'S ALL RIGHT.
OFFICIALLY, IT'S LONGER.
MY NAME, THAT IS.
I HAVE *ENTRUSTED* ALL OF MY NAME TO YOU, YUKI.

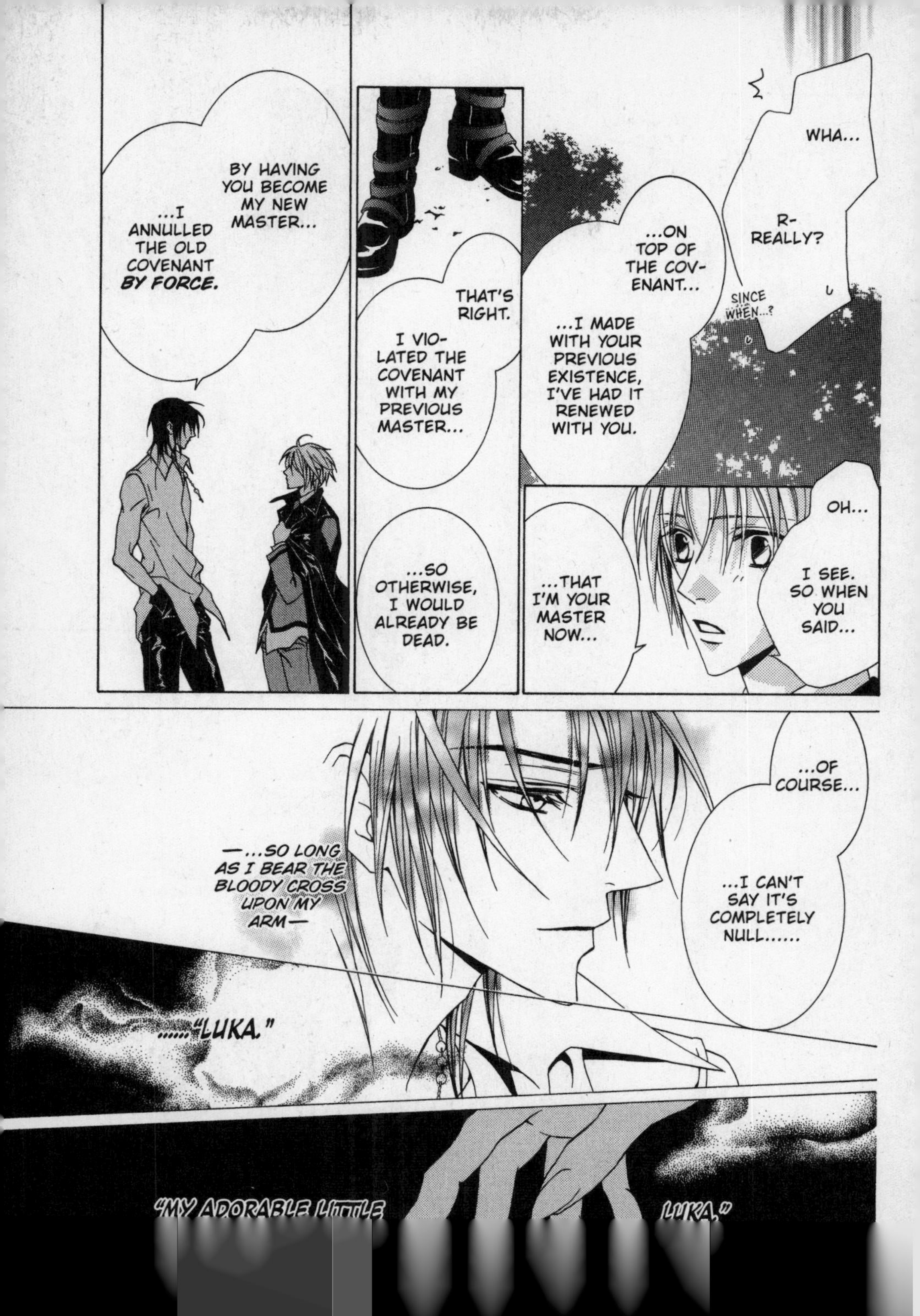
WHA...
R-REALLY?
SINCE WHEN...?
...ON TOP OF THE COVENANT...
...I MADE WITH YOUR PREVIOUS EXISTENCE, I'VE HAD IT RENEWED WITH YOU.
THAT'S RIGHT.
I VIOLATED THE COVENANT WITH MY PREVIOUS MASTER...
BY HAVING YOU BECOME MY NEW MASTER...
...I ANNULLED THE OLD COVENANT BY FORCE.
OH...
I SEE. SO WHEN YOU SAID...
...THAT I'M YOUR MASTER NOW...
...SO OTHERWISE, I WOULD ALREADY BE DEAD.
...OF COURSE...
...I CAN'T SAY IT'S COMPLETELY NULL......
—...SO LONG AS I BEAR THE BLOODY CROSS UPON MY ARM—
......"LUKA."
"MY ADORABLE LITTLE LUKA."

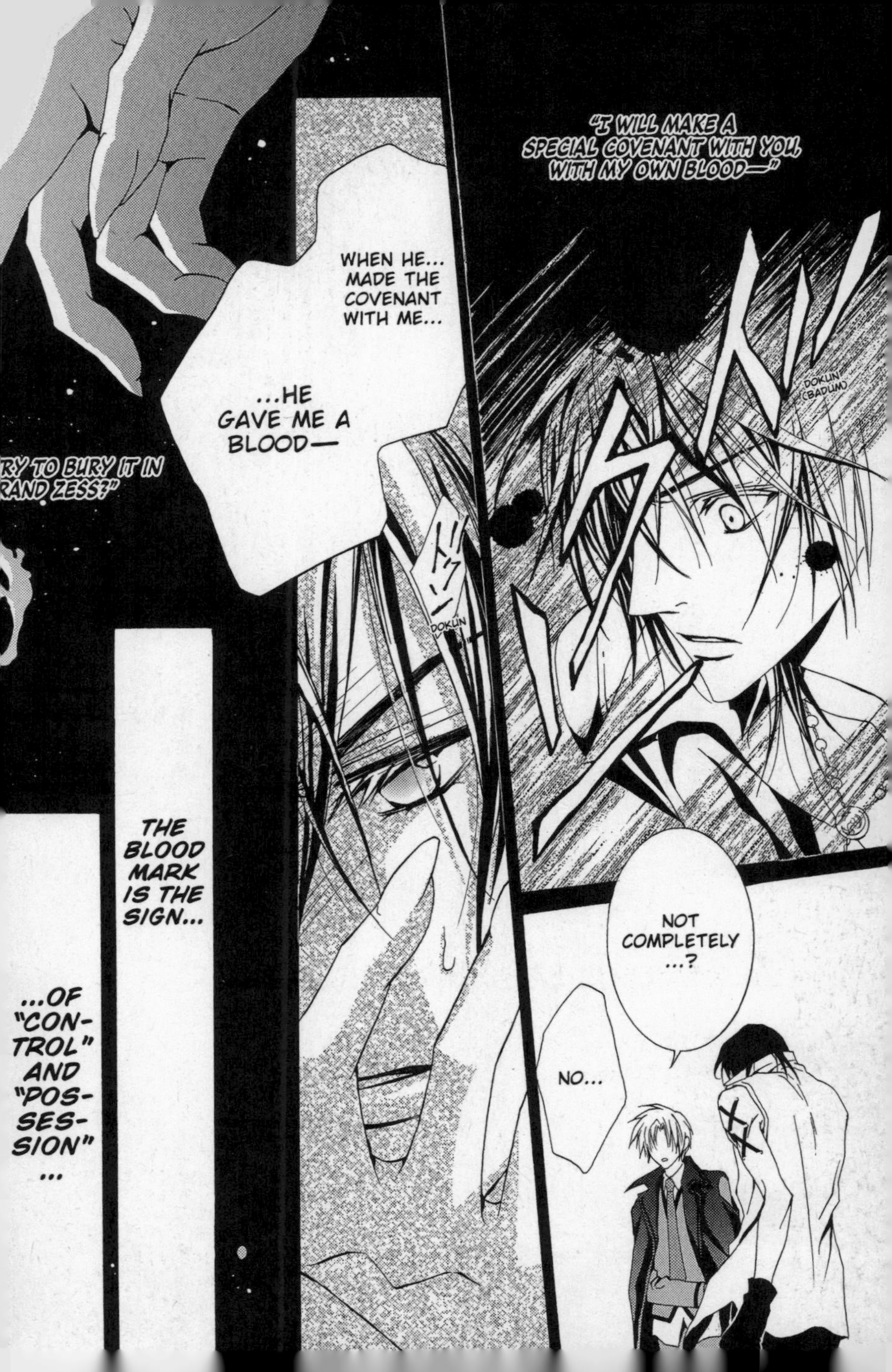
"I WILL MAKE A SPECIAL COVENANT WITH YOU, WITH MY OWN BLOOD—"
WHEN HE... MADE THE COVENANT WITH ME...
...HE GAVE ME A BLOOD—
DOKUN (BADUM)
DOKUN
RY TO BURY IT IN RAND ZESS?"
NOT COMPLETELY ...?
NO...
THE BLOOD MARK IS THE SIGN...
...OF "CON-TROL" AND "POS-SES-SION" ...

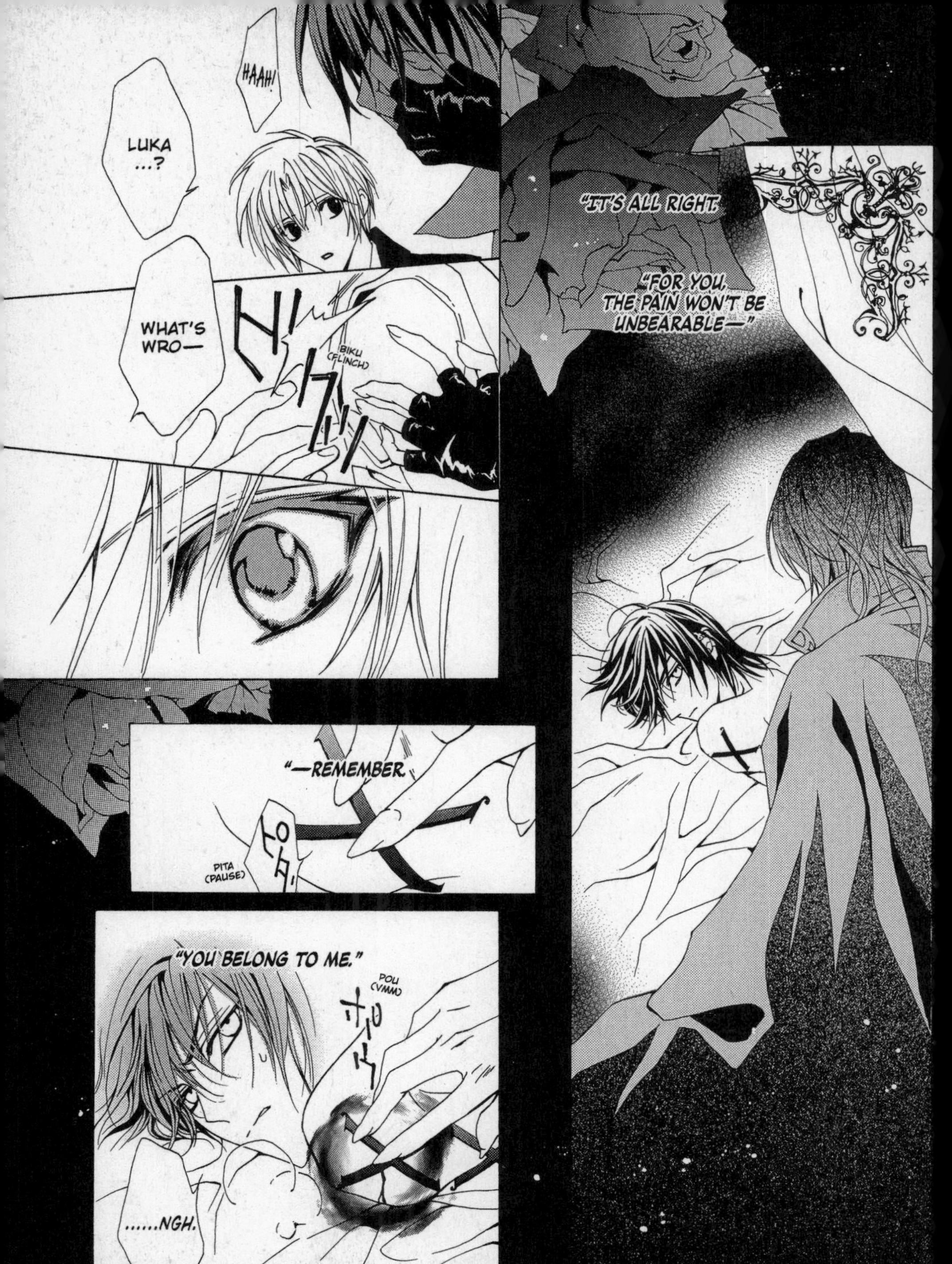
"IT'S ALL RIGHT.
"FOR YOU, THE PAIN WON'T BE UNBEARABLE—"
HAAH!
LUKA ...?
WHAT'S WRO—
BIKU (FLINCH)
"—REMEMBER
PITA (PAUSE)
"YOU BELONG TO ME."
POU (VMM)
......NGH.

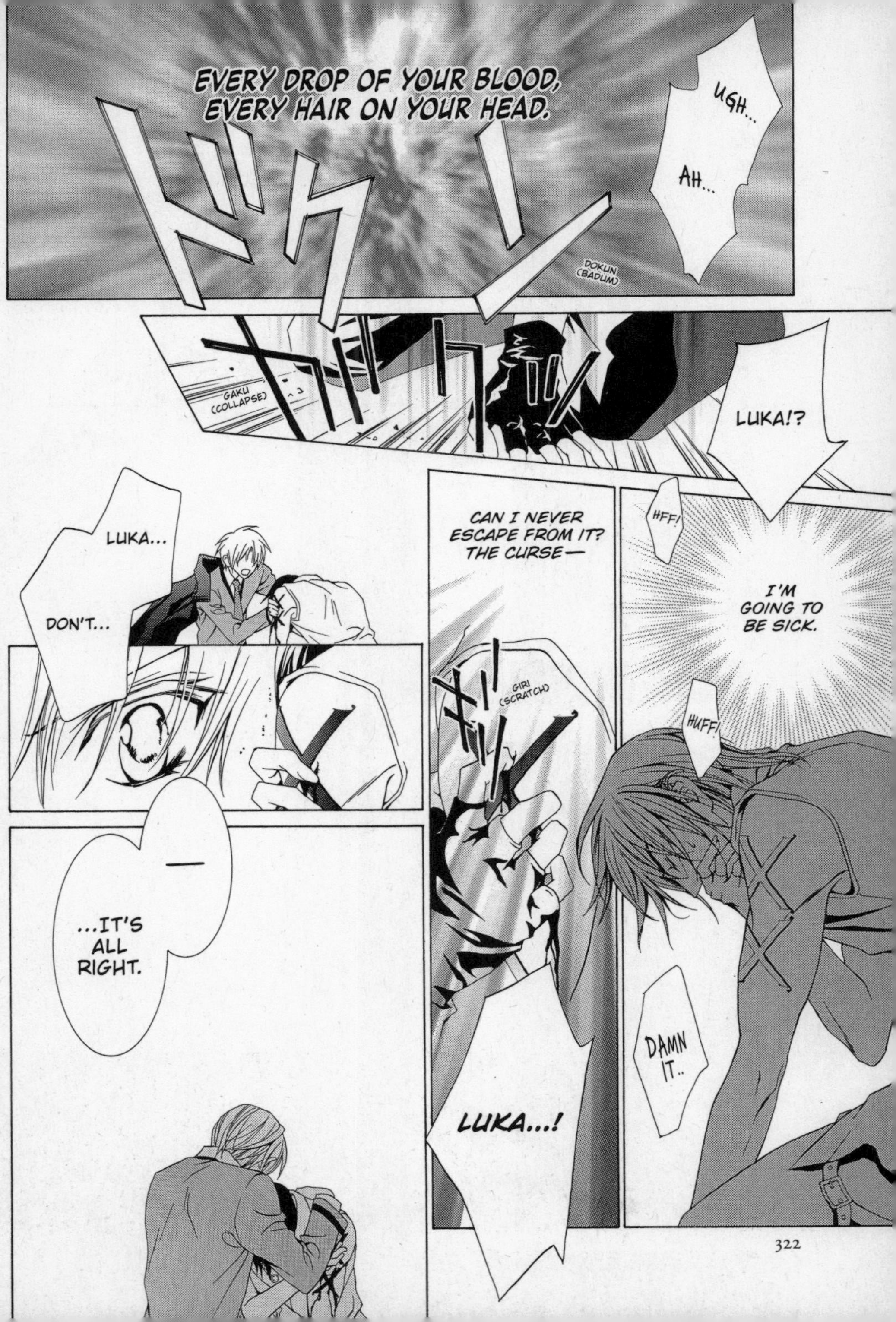

EVERY DROP OF YOUR BLOOD, EVERY HAIR ON YOUR HEAD.
UGH...
AH...
DOKUN (BADUM)
LUKA!?
GAKU (COLLAPSE)
HFF!
I'M GOING TO BE SICK.
HUFF!
CAN I NEVER ESCAPE FROM IT? THE CURSE—
GIRI (SCRATCH)
LUKA...
DON'T...
DAMN IT..
LUKA...!
—
...IT'S ALL RIGHT.

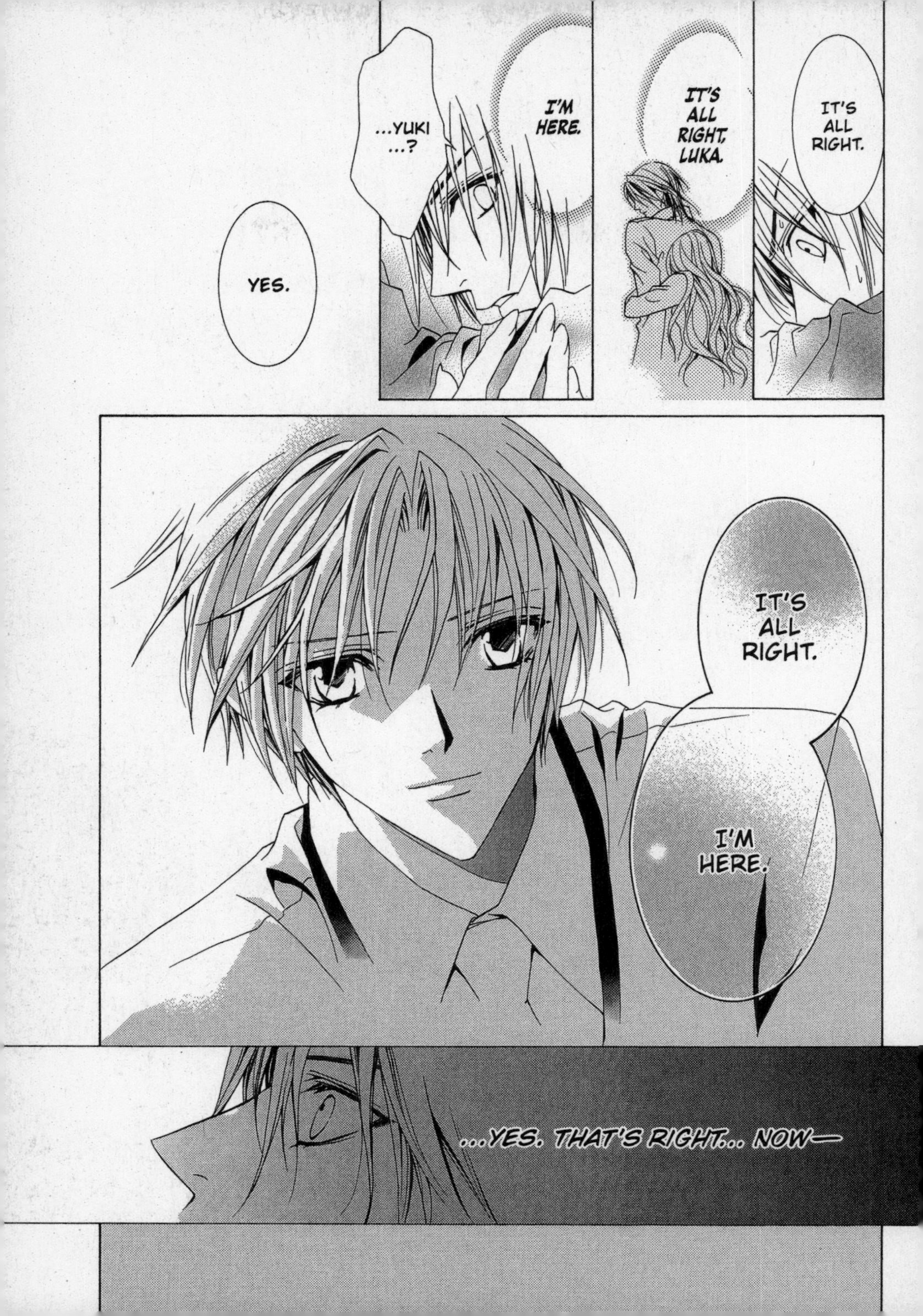
IT'S ALL RIGHT.
IT'S ALL RIGHT, LUKA.
I'M HERE.
...YUKI ...?
YES.
IT'S ALL RIGHT.
I'M HERE.
...YES. THAT'S RIGHT... NOW—

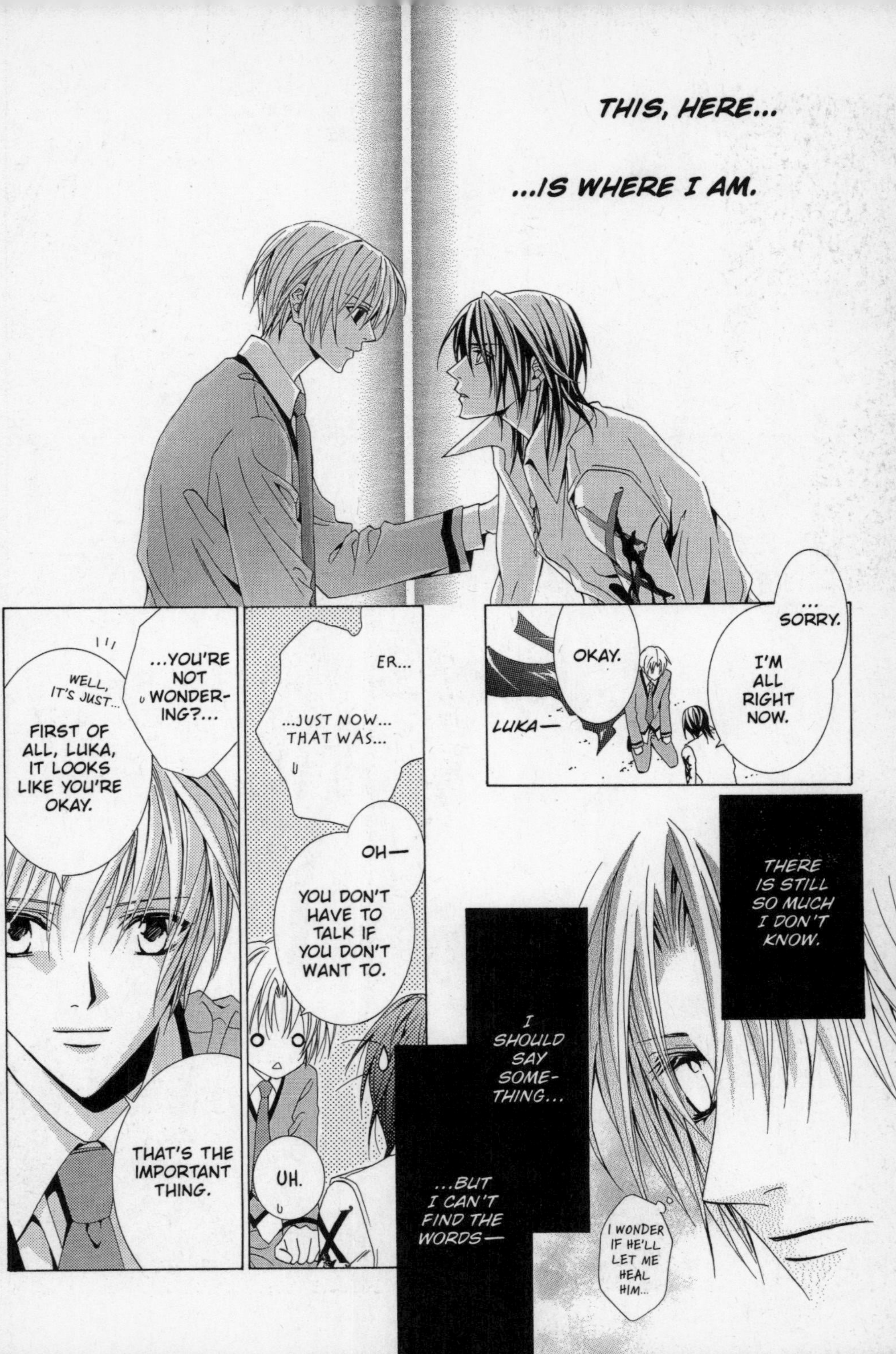
THIS, HERE...
...IS WHERE I AM.
...SORRY.
I'M ALL RIGHT NOW.
OKAY.
LUKA—
THERE IS STILL SO MUCH I DON'T KNOW.
I SHOULD SAY SOME-THING...
...BUT I CAN'T FIND THE WORDS—
I WONDER IF HE'LL LET ME HEAL HIM...
ER...
...JUST NOW... THAT WAS...
OH—
YOU DON'T HAVE TO TALK IF YOU DON'T WANT TO.
UH.
...YOU'RE NOT WONDER-ING?...
WELL, IT'S JUST...
FIRST OF ALL, LUKA, IT LOOKS LIKE YOU'RE OKAY.
THAT'S THE IMPORTANT THING.

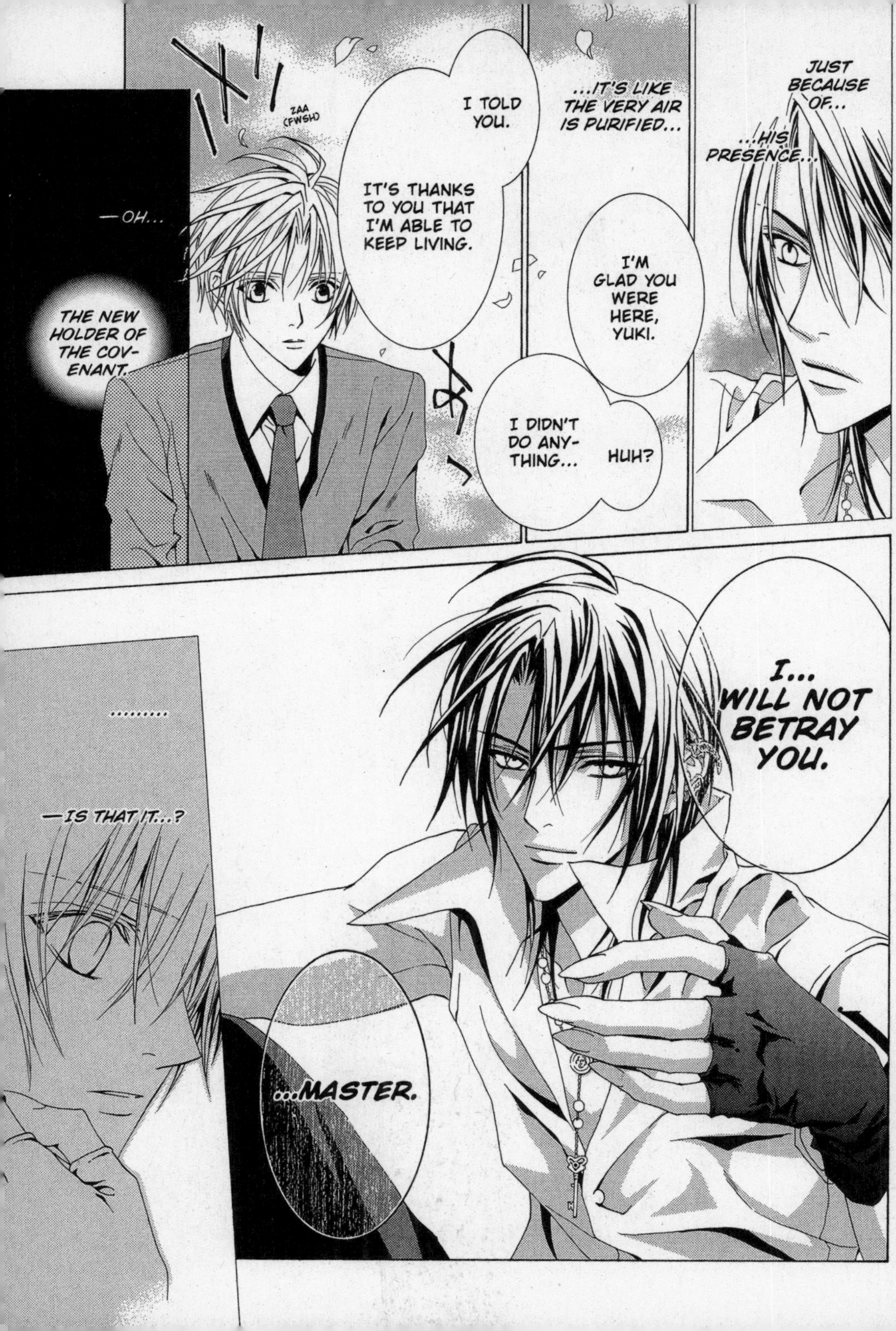
JUST BECAUSE OF...
...HIS PRESENCE...
...IT'S LIKE THE VERY AIR IS PURIFIED...
I'M GLAD YOU WERE HERE, YUKI.
HUH?
I DIDN'T DO ANYTHING...
I TOLD YOU.
IT'S THANKS TO YOU THAT I'M ABLE TO KEEP LIVING.
ZAA (FWSH)
—OH...
THE NEW HOLDER OF THE COV-ENANT.
I... WILL NOT BETRAY YOU.
...MASTER.
....
—IS THAT IT...?

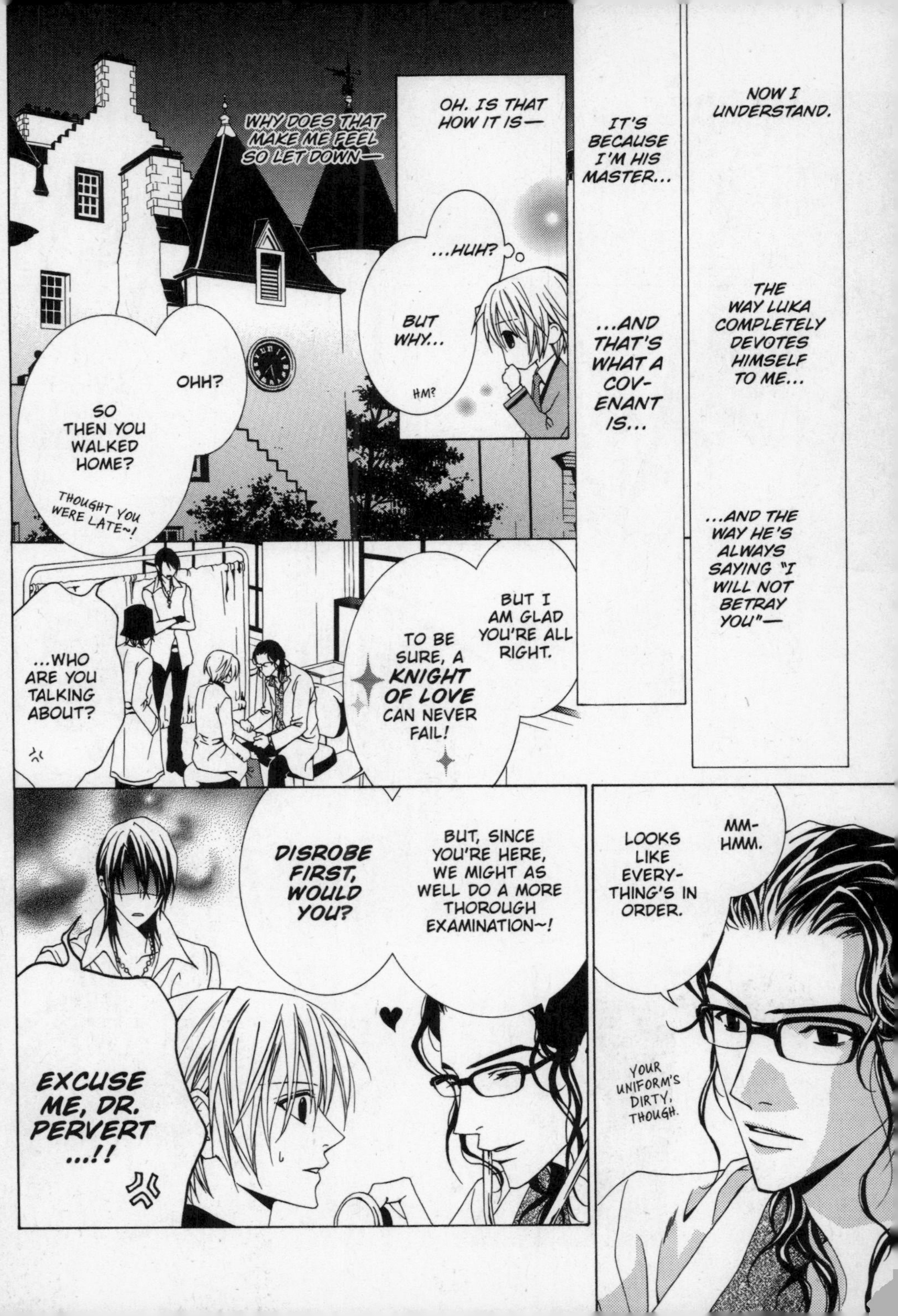
NOW I UNDERSTAND.
THE WAY LUKA COMPLETELY DEVOTES HIMSELF TO ME...
...AND THE WAY HE'S ALWAYS SAYING "I WILL NOT BETRAY YOU"—
IT'S BECAUSE I'M HIS MASTER...
...AND THAT'S WHAT A COV-ENANT IS...
OH. IS THAT HOW IT IS—
...HUH?
BUT WHY...
HM?
WHY DOES THAT MAKE ME FEEL SO LET DOWN—
OHH?
SO THEN YOU WALKED HOME?
THOUGHT YOU WERE LATE~!
BUT I AM GLAD YOU'RE ALL RIGHT.
TO BE SURE, A KNIGHT OF LOVE CAN NEVER FAIL!
...WHO ARE YOU TALKING ABOUT?
MM-HMM.
LOOKS LIKE EVERY-THING'S IN ORDER.
YOUR UNIFORM'S DIRTY, THOUGH.
BUT, SINCE YOU'RE HERE, WE MIGHT AS WELL DO A MORE THOROUGH EXAMINATION~!
DISROBE FIRST, WOULD YOU?
EXCUSE ME, DR. PERVERT...!!

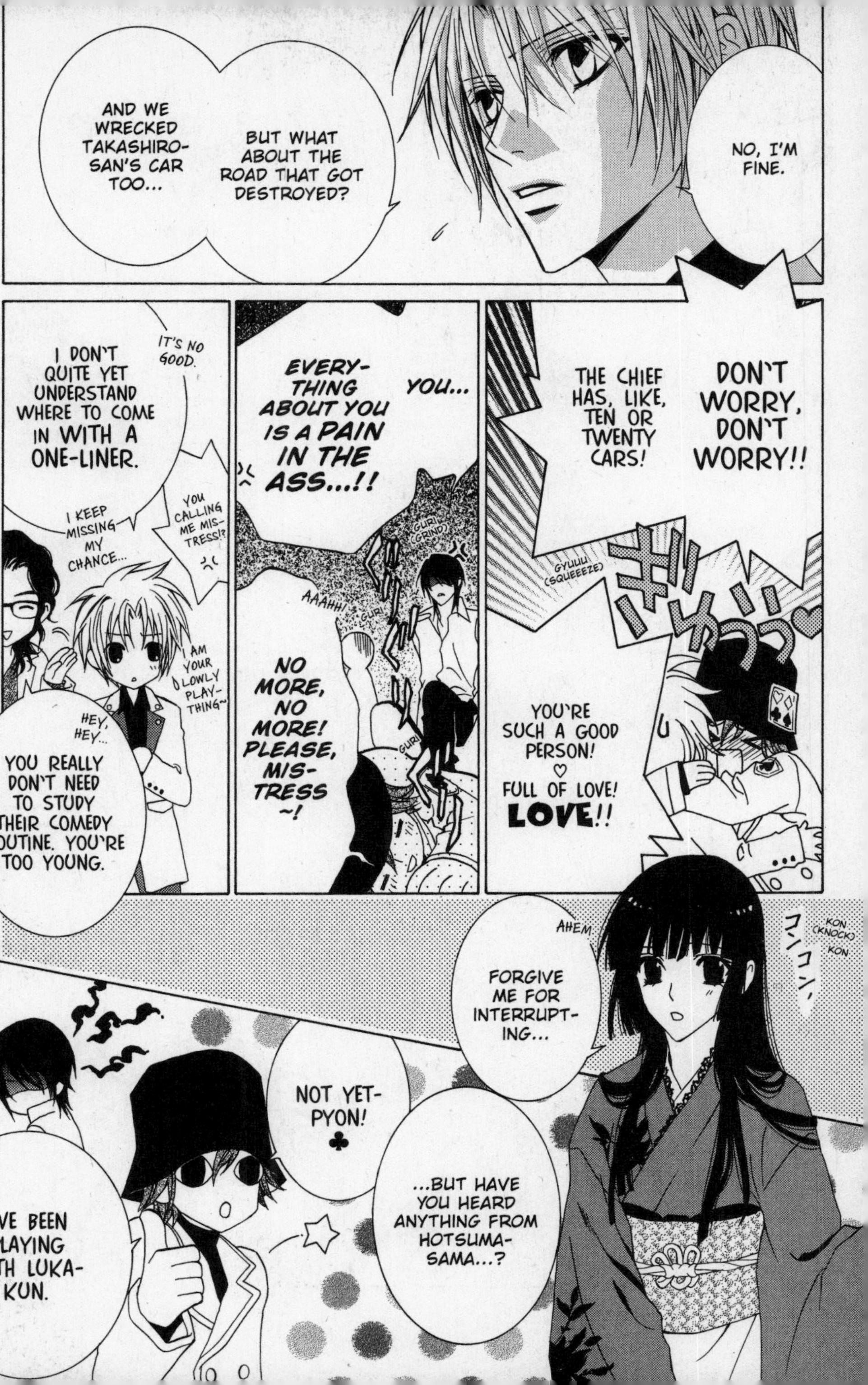
NO, I'M FINE.
BUT WHAT ABOUT THE ROAD THAT GOT DESTROYED?
AND WE WRECKED TAKASHIRO-SAN'S CAR TOO...
DON'T WORRY, DON'T WORRY!!
THE CHIEF HAS, LIKE, TEN OR TWENTY CARS!
GYUUU (SQUEEEZE)
YOU'RE SUCH A GOOD PERSON! ♡ FULL OF LOVE! LOVE!!
...
YOU...
EVERYTHING ABOUT YOU IS A PAIN IN THE ASS...!!
GURI (GRIND)
AAAHH!
GURI
NO MORE, NO MORE! PLEASE, MISTRESS ~!
GURI
IT'S NO GOOD.
I DON'T QUITE YET UNDERSTAND WHERE TO COME IN WITH A ONE-LINER.
YOU CALLING ME MISTRESS!?
I KEEP MISSING MY CHANCE...
I AM YOUR LOWLY PLAYTHING~
HEY, HEY...
YOU REALLY DON'T NEED TO STUDY THEIR COMEDY ROUTINE. YOU'RE TOO YOUNG.
KON (KNOCK) KON
AHEM.
FORGIVE ME FOR INTERRUPTING...
...BUT HAVE YOU HEARD ANYTHING FROM HOTSUMA-SAMA...?
NOT YET-PYON! ♣
I'VE BEEN PLAYING WITH LUKA-KUN. ♥

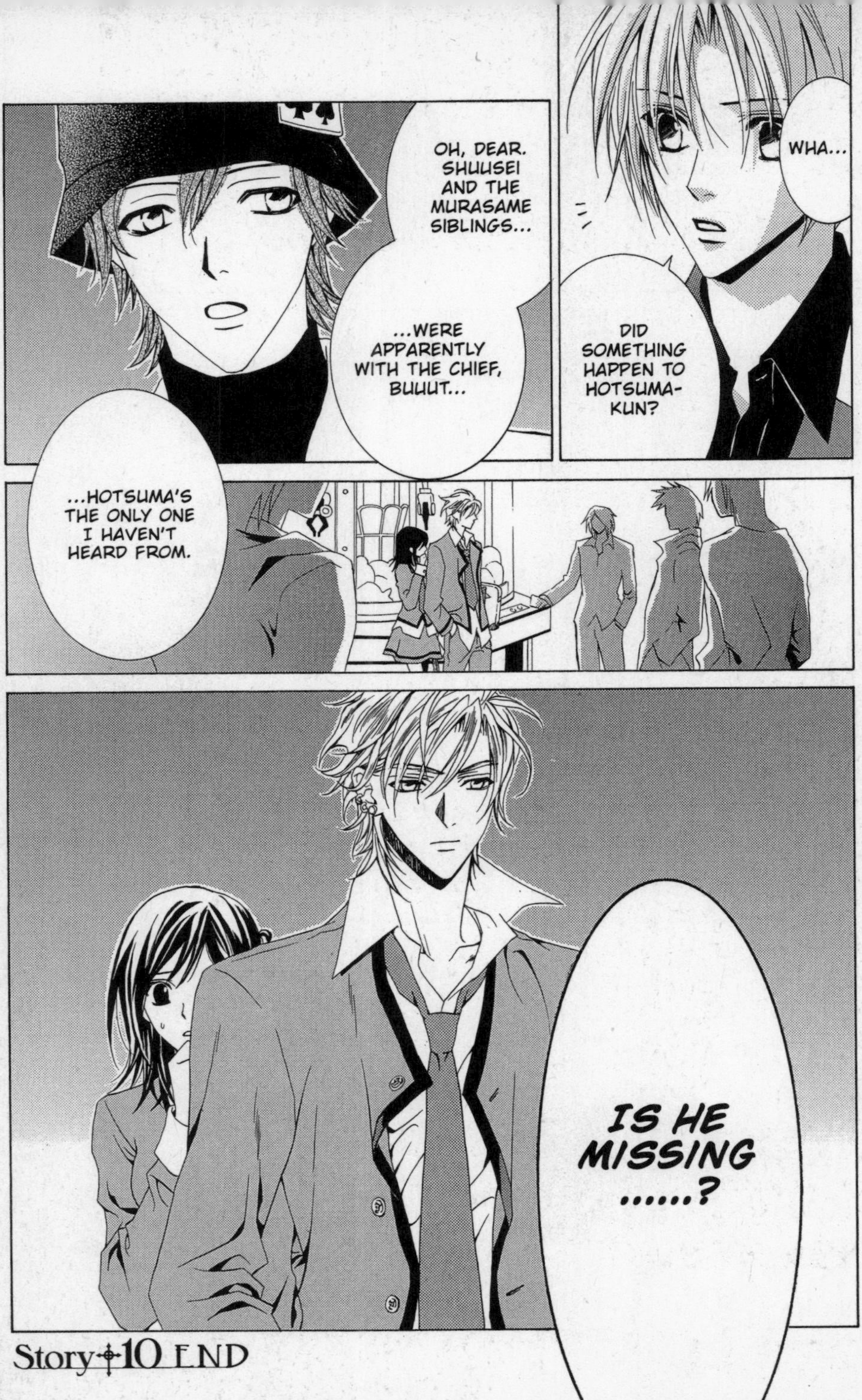
WHA...
DID SOMETHING HAPPEN TO HOTSUMA-KUN?
OH, DEAR. SHUUSEI AND THE MURASAME SIBLINGS...
...WERE APPARENTLY WITH THE CHIEF, BUUUT...
...HOTSUMA'S THE ONLY ONE I HAVEN'T HEARD FROM.
IS HE MISSING ......?

Story 10 END

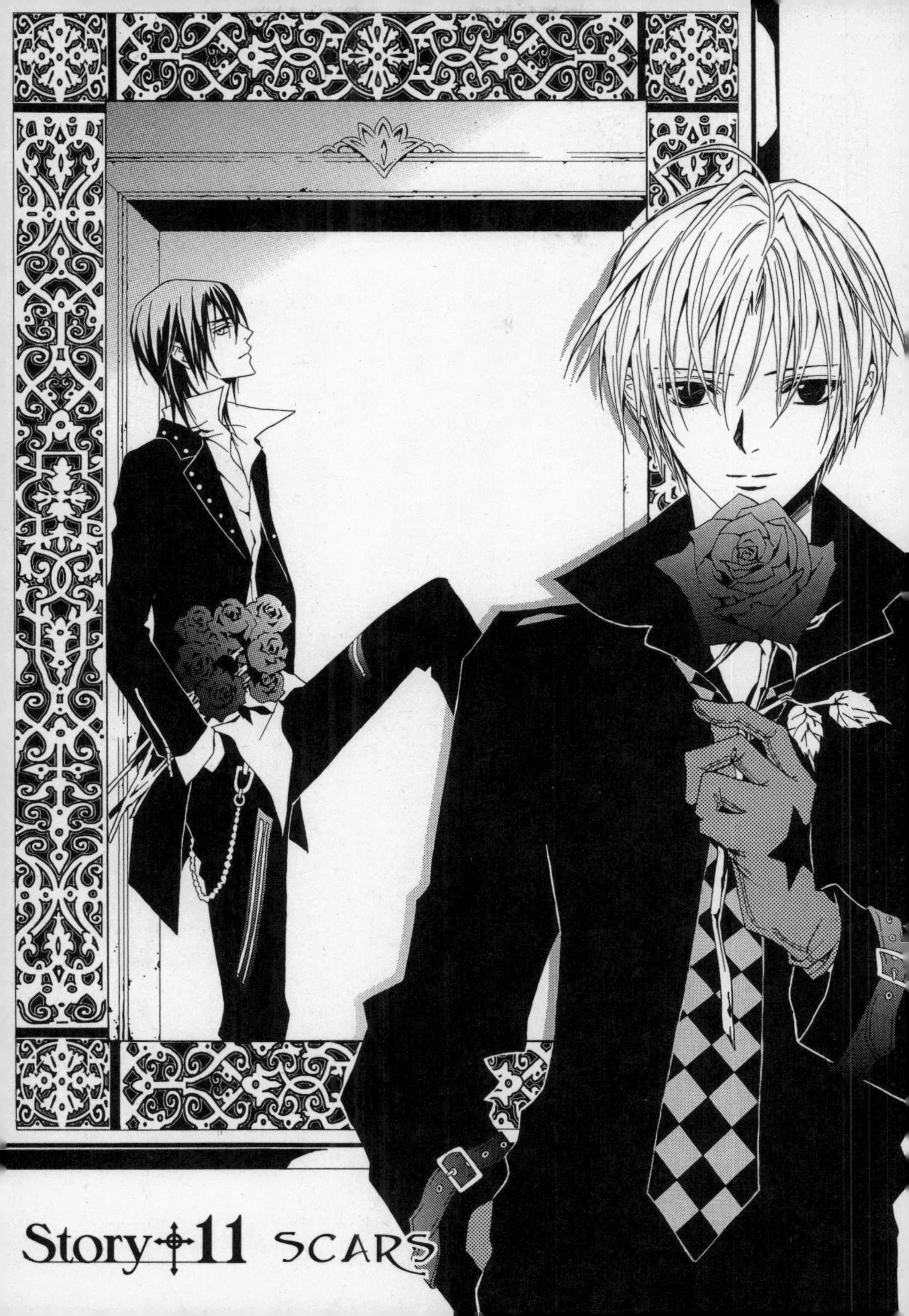

Story 11 SCARS

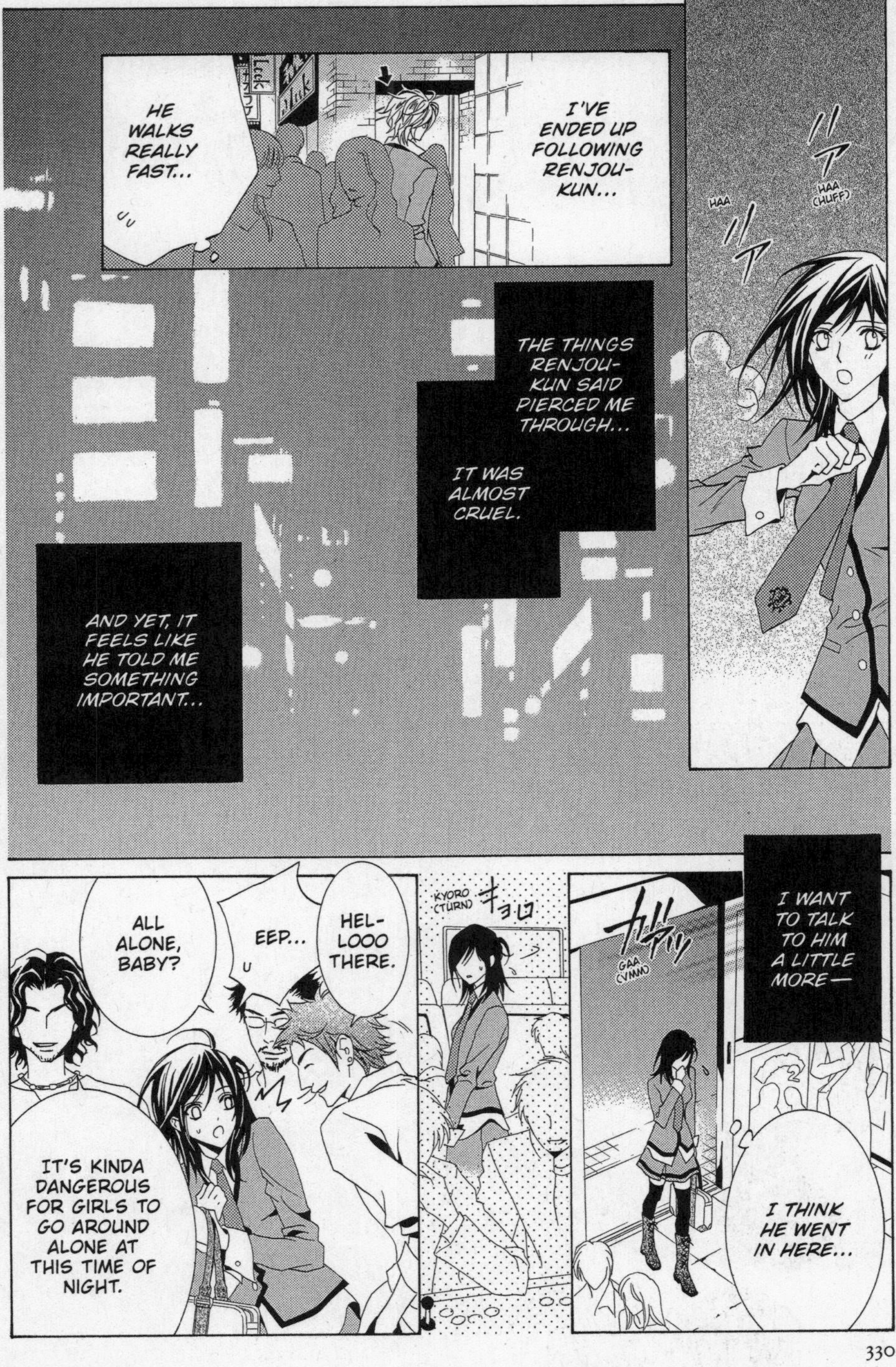
HAA (HUFF)
HAA
I'VE ENDED UP FOLLOWING RENJOU-KUN...
HE WALKS REALLY FAST...
THE THINGS RENJOU-KUN SAID PIERCED ME THROUGH...
IT WAS ALMOST CRUEL.
AND YET, IT FEELS LIKE HE TOLD ME SOMETHING IMPORTANT...
I WANT TO TALK TO HIM A LITTLE MORE—
GAA (VMM)
I THINK HE WENT IN HERE...
KYORO (TURN)
HEL-LOOO THERE.
EEP...
ALL ALONE, BABY?
IT'S KINDA DANGEROUS FOR GIRLS TO GO AROUND ALONE AT THIS TIME OF NIGHT.

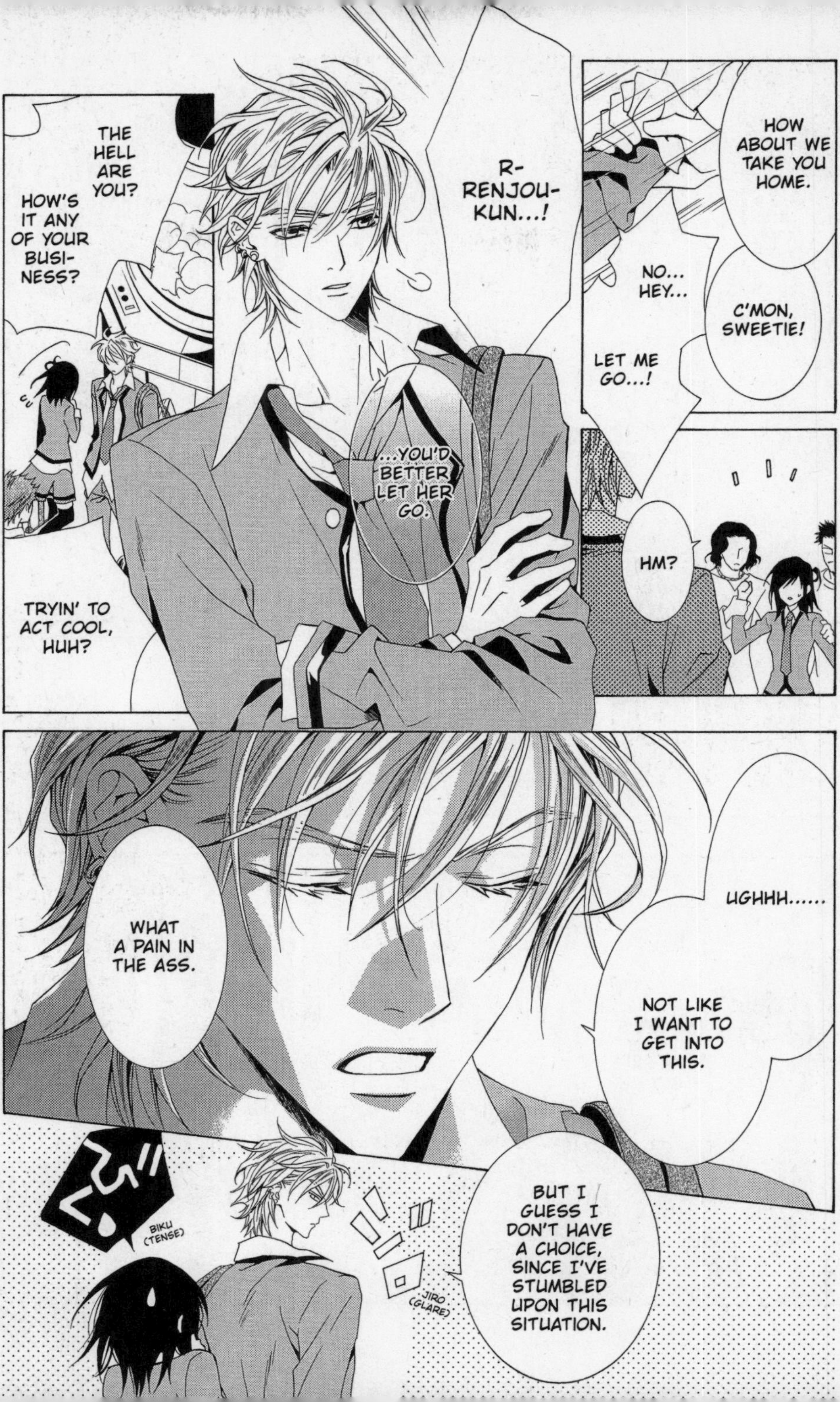
HOW ABOUT WE TAKE YOU HOME.
C'MON, SWEETIE!
NO... HEY...
LET ME GO...!
R-RENJOU-KUN...!
...YOU'D BETTER LET HER GO.
HM?
THE HELL ARE YOU?
HOW'S IT ANY OF YOUR BUSI-NESS?
TRYIN' TO ACT COOL, HUH?
UGHHH......
NOT LIKE I WANT TO GET INTO THIS.
WHAT A PAIN IN THE ASS.
BUT I GUESS I DON'T HAVE A CHOICE, SINCE I'VE STUMBLED UPON THIS SITUATION.
JIRO (GLARE)
BIKU (TENSE)

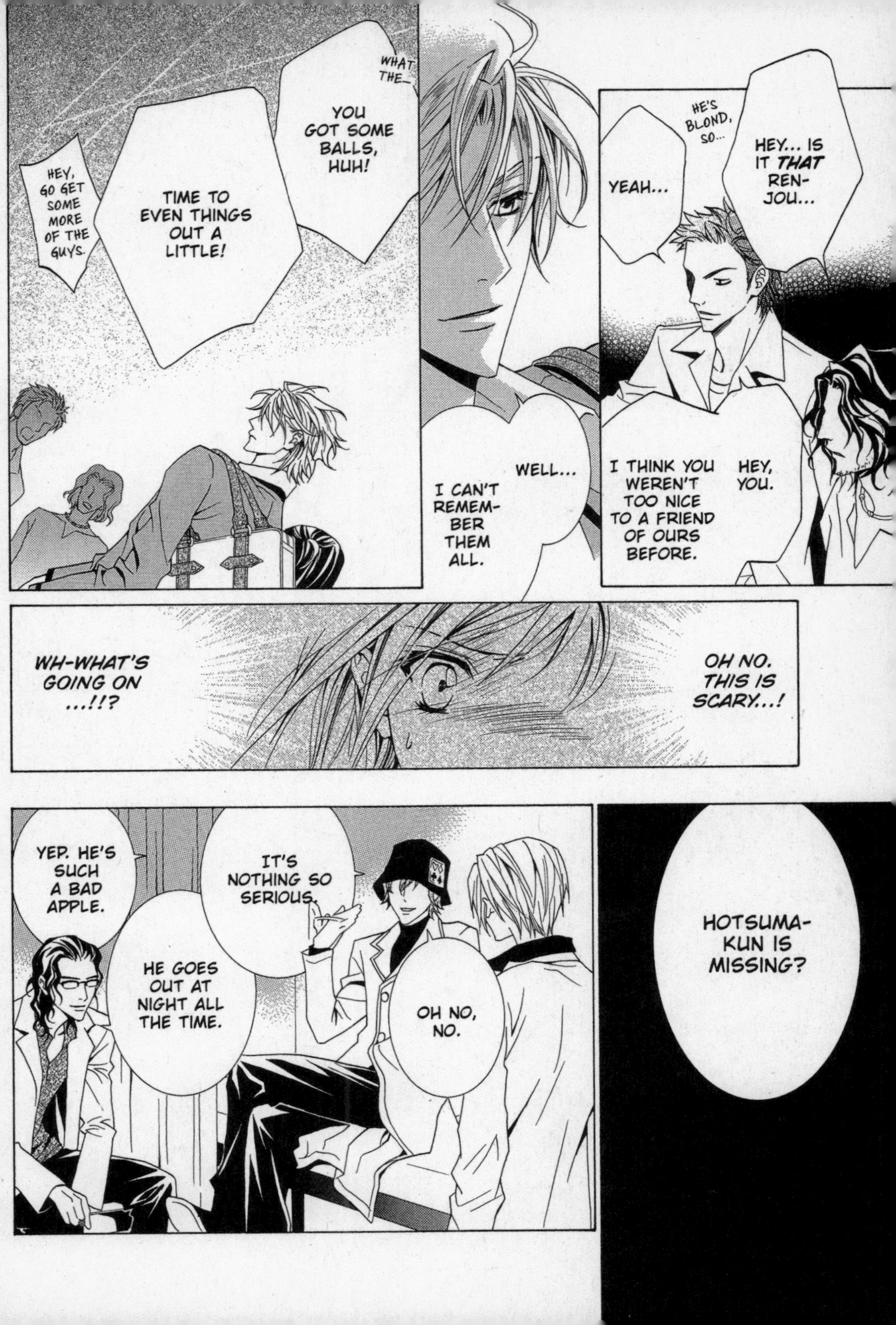
HEY... IS IT *THAT* RENJOU...
HE'S BLOND, SO...
YEAH...
HEY, YOU.
I THINK YOU WEREN'T TOO NICE TO A FRIEND OF OURS BEFORE.
WELL...
I CAN'T REMEMBER THEM ALL.
WHAT THE—
YOU GOT SOME BALLS, HUH!
TIME TO EVEN THINGS OUT A LITTLE!
HEY, GO GET SOME MORE OF THE GUYS.
OH NO. THIS IS SCARY...!
WH-WHAT'S GOING ON ...!!?
HOTSUMA-KUN IS MISSING?
OH NO, NO.
IT'S NOTHING SO SERIOUS.
HE GOES OUT AT NIGHT ALL THE TIME.
YEP. HE'S SUCH A BAD APPLE.

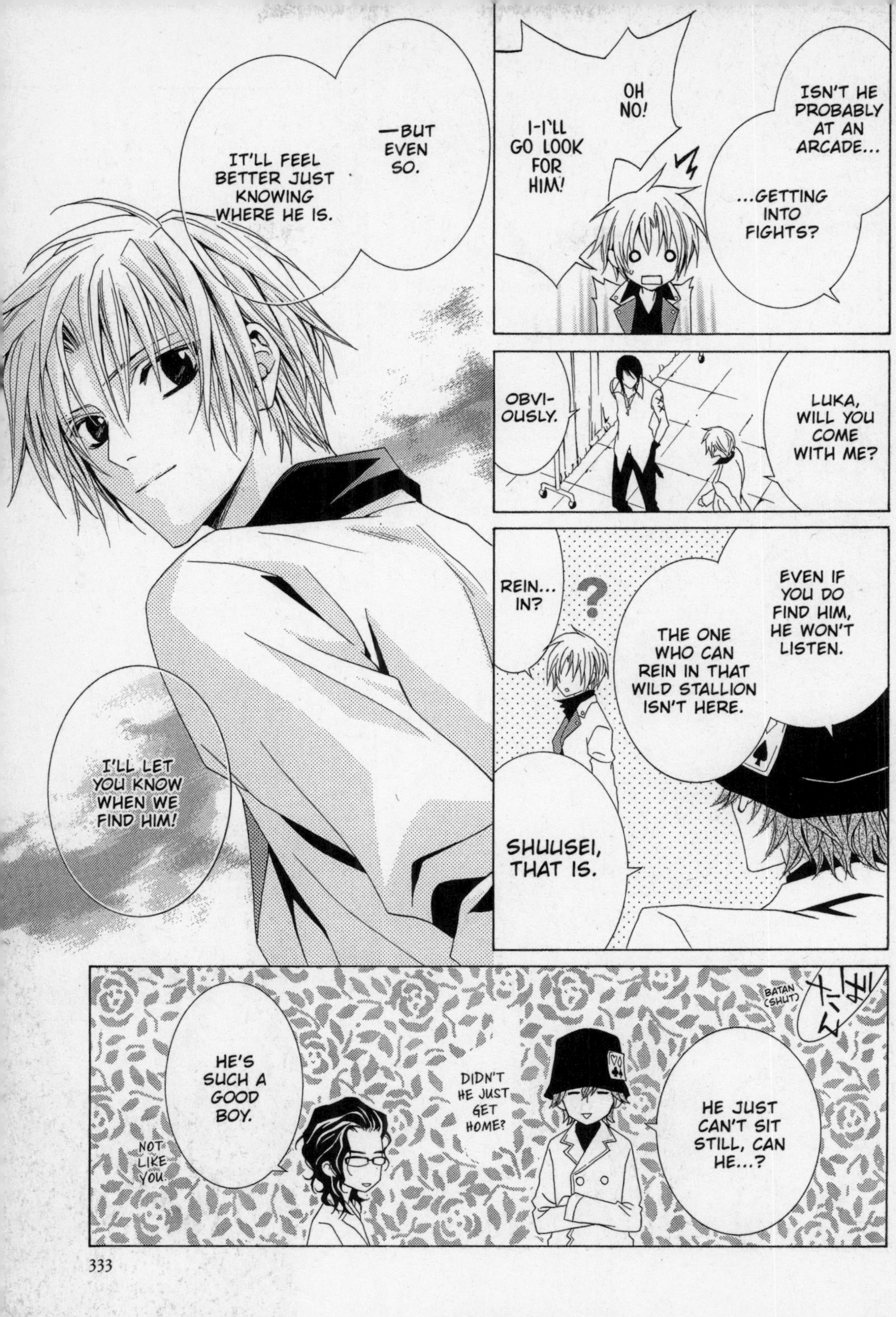
ISN'T HE PROBABLY AT AN ARCADE...
...GETTING INTO FIGHTS?
OH NO!
I-I'LL GO LOOK FOR HIM!
LUKA, WILL YOU COME WITH ME?
OBVI-OUSLY.
EVEN IF YOU DO FIND HIM, HE WON'T LISTEN.
THE ONE WHO CAN REIN IN THAT WILD STALLION ISN'T HERE.
REIN... IN?
?
SHUUSEI, THAT IS.
—BUT EVEN SO.
IT'LL FEEL BETTER JUST KNOWING WHERE HE IS.
I'LL LET YOU KNOW WHEN WE FIND HIM!
BATAN (SHUT)
HE JUST CAN'T SIT STILL, CAN HE...?
DIDN'T HE JUST GET HOME?
HE'S SUCH A GOOD BOY.
NOT LIKE YOU.

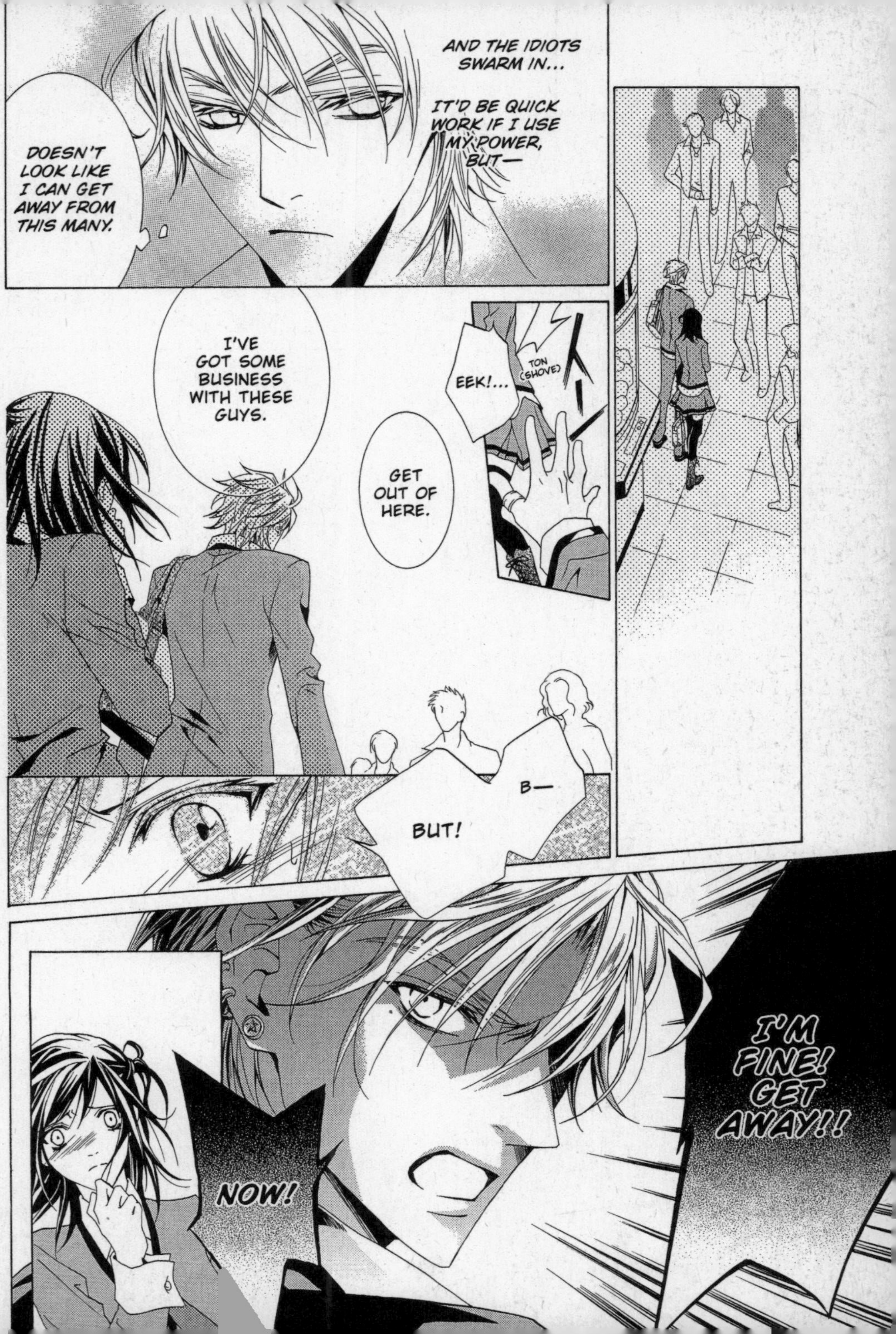
AND THE IDIOTS SWARM IN...
IT'D BE QUICK WORK IF I USE MY POWER, BUT—
DOESN'T LOOK LIKE I CAN GET AWAY FROM THIS MANY.
TON (SHOVE)
EEK!...
I'VE GOT SOME BUSINESS WITH THESE GUYS.
GET OUT OF HERE.
B—
BUT!
I'M FINE! GET AWAY!!
NOW!

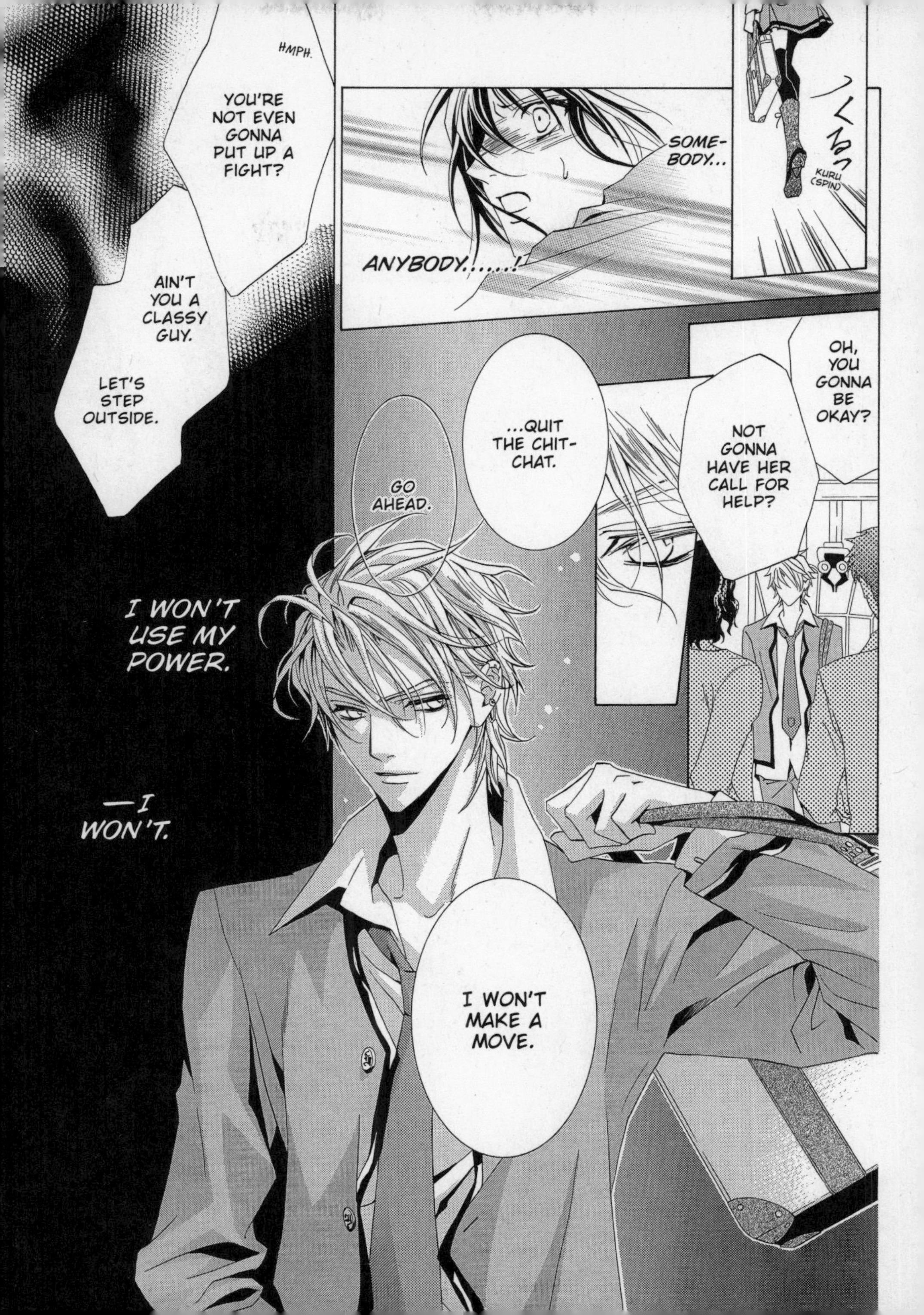
KURU (SPIN)
SOME-BODY...
ANYBODY......!
HMPH.
YOU'RE NOT EVEN GONNA PUT UP A FIGHT?
AIN'T YOU A CLASSY GUY.
LET'S STEP OUTSIDE.
OH, YOU GONNA BE OKAY?
NOT GONNA HAVE HER CALL FOR HELP?
...QUIT THE CHIT-CHAT.
GO AHEAD.
I WON'T MAKE A MOVE.
I WON'T USE MY POWER.
—I WON'T.

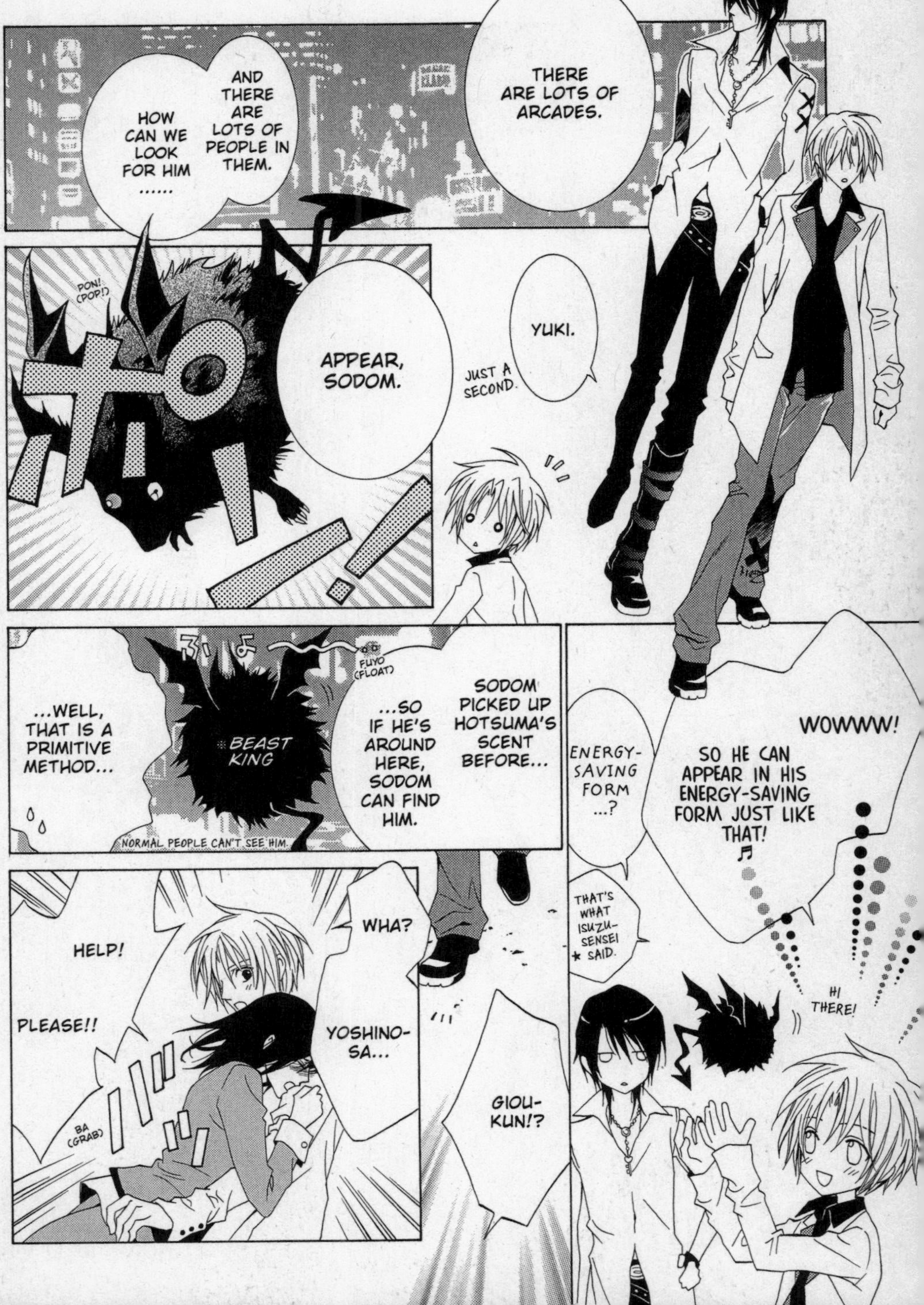
THERE ARE LOTS OF ARCADES.
AND THERE ARE LOTS OF PEOPLE IN THEM.
HOW CAN WE LOOK FOR HIM ......
YUKI.
JUST A SECOND.
APPEAR, SODOM.
PON! (POP!)
WOWWW!
SO HE CAN APPEAR IN HIS ENERGY-SAVING FORM JUST LIKE THAT! ♬
ENERGY-SAVING FORM ...?
THAT'S WHAT ISUZU-SENSEI * SAID.
HI THERE!
SODOM PICKED UP HOTSUMA'S SCENT BEFORE...
...SO IF HE'S AROUND HERE, SODOM CAN FIND HIM.
FUYO (FLOAT)
* BEAST KING
...WELL, THAT IS A PRIMITIVE METHOD...
NORMAL PEOPLE CAN'T SEE HIM.
GIOU-KUN!?
YOSHINO-SA...
WHA?
HELP!
PLEASE!!
BA (GRAB)

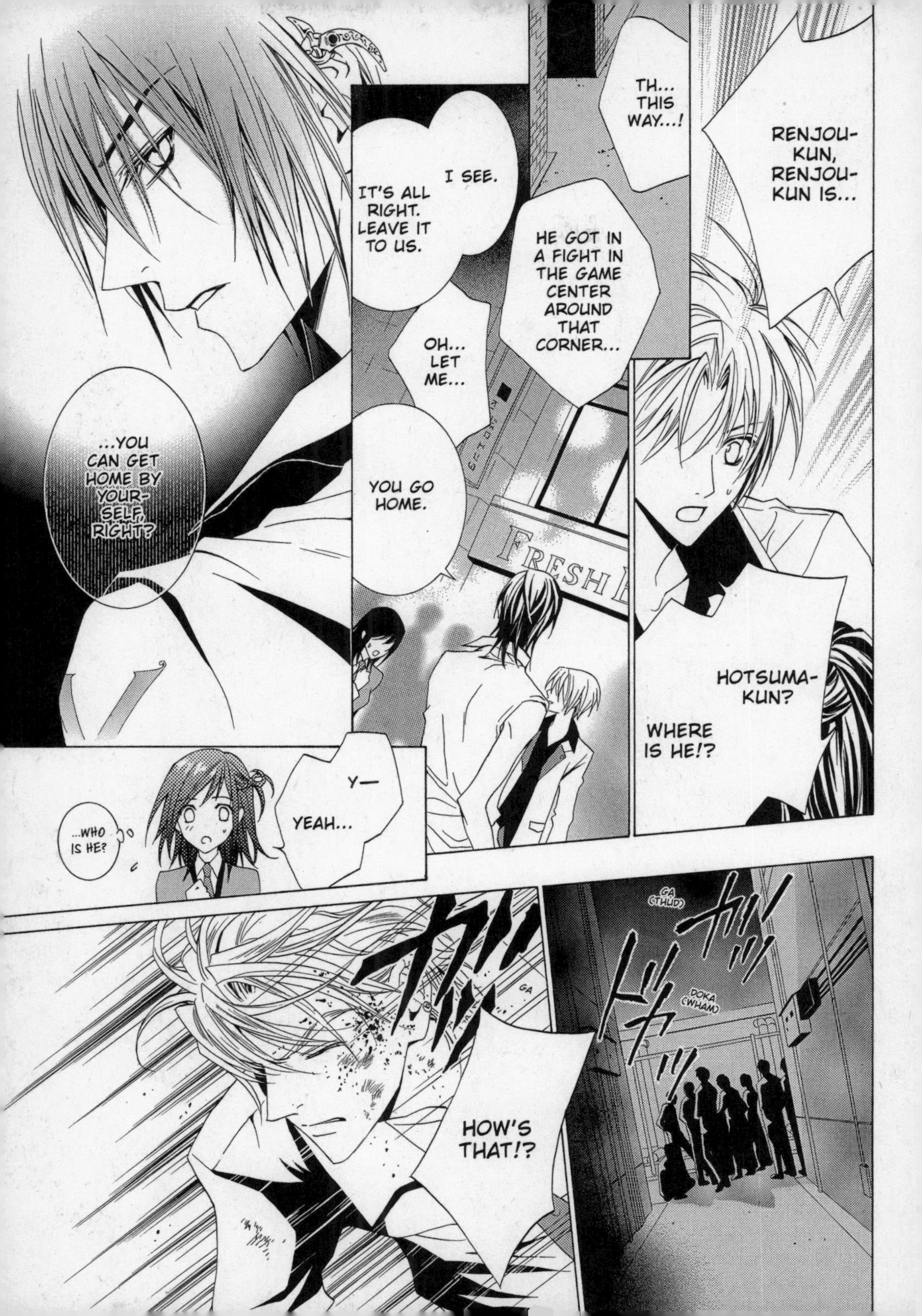
RENJOU-KUN, RENJOU-KUN IS...
TH... THIS WAY...!
HE GOT IN A FIGHT IN THE GAME CENTER AROUND THAT CORNER...
I SEE.
IT'S ALL RIGHT. LEAVE IT TO US.
OH... LET ME...
YOU GO HOME.
...YOU CAN GET HOME BY YOUR-SELF, RIGHT?
HOTSUMA-KUN?
WHERE IS HE!?
Y—
YEAH...
...WHO IS HE?
GA (THUD)
DOKA (WHAM)
GA
HOW'S THAT!?

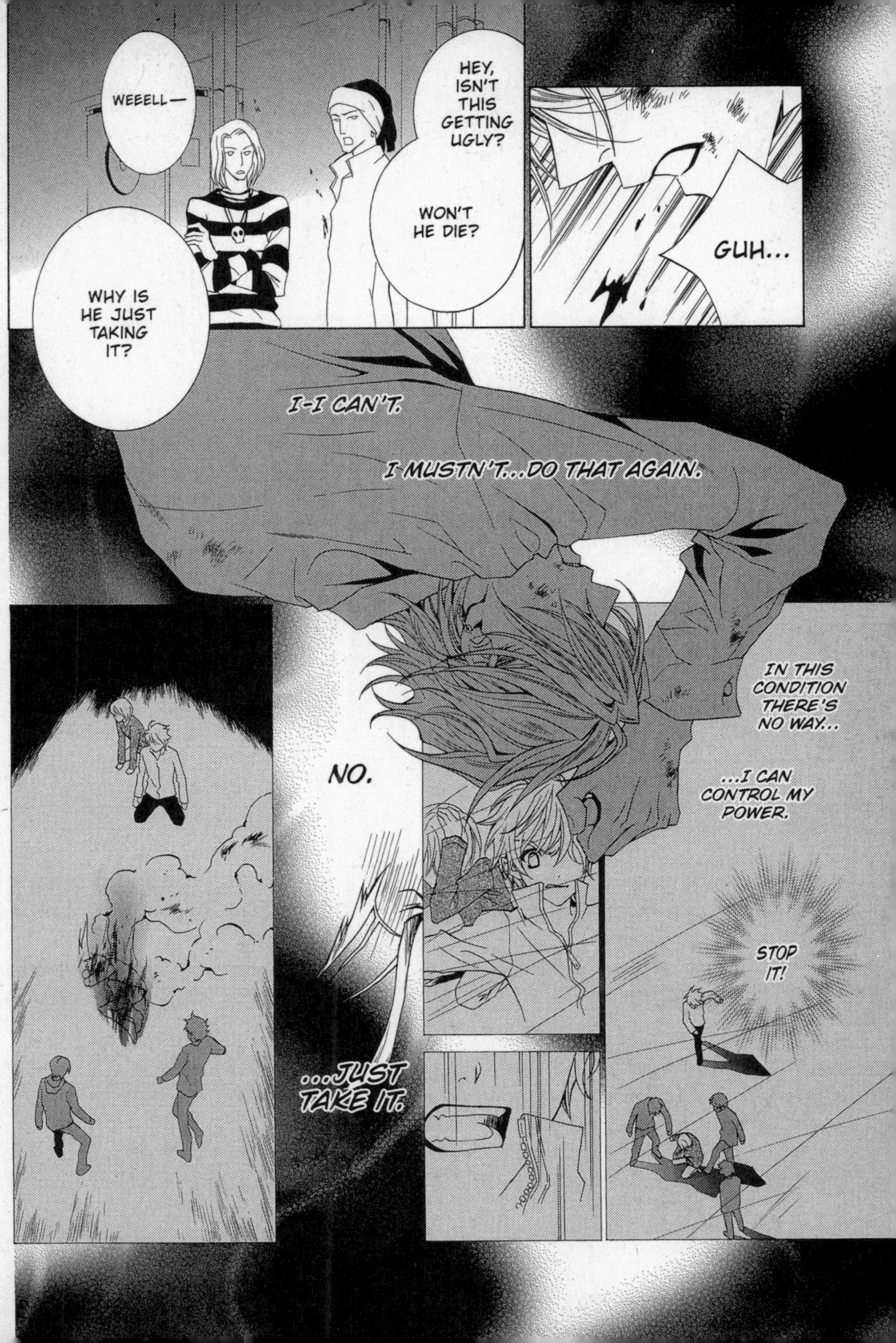
GUH...
HEY, ISN'T THIS GETTING UGLY?
WON'T HE DIE?
WEEELL—
WHY IS HE JUST TAKING IT?
I-I CAN'T.
I MUSTN'T...DO THAT AGAIN.
IN THIS CONDITION THERE'S NO WAY...
...I CAN CONTROL MY POWER.
STOP IT!
NO.
...JUST TAKE IT.

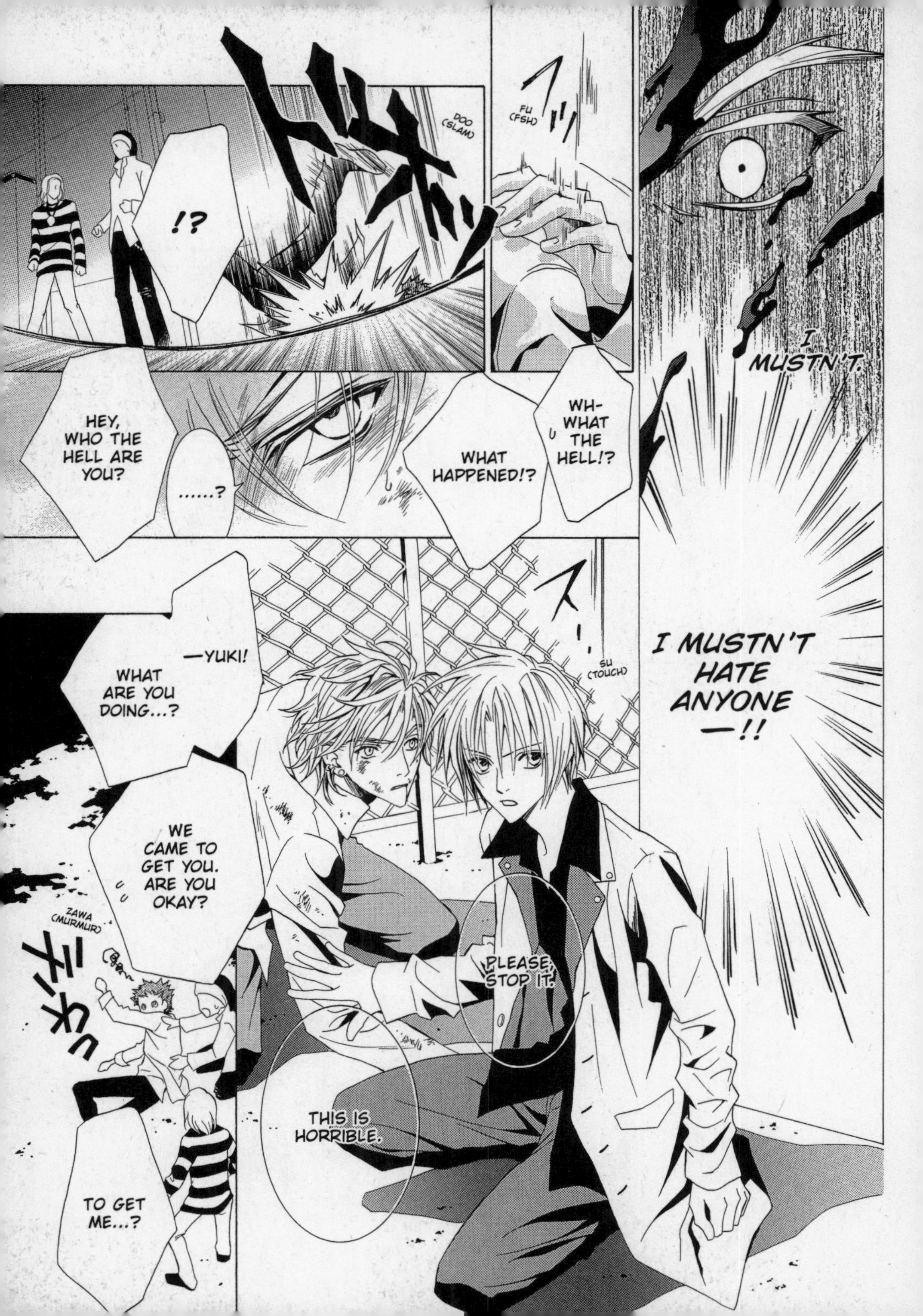
I MUSTN'T.
FU (FSH)
DOO (SLAM)
!?
WH- WHAT THE HELL!?
WHAT HAPPENED!?
......?
HEY, WHO THE HELL ARE YOU?
I MUSTN'T HATE ANYONE—!!
SU (TOUCH)
PLEASE, STOP IT.
THIS IS HORRIBLE.
—YUKI!
WHAT ARE YOU DOING...?
WE CAME TO GET YOU. ARE YOU OKAY?
ZAWA (MURMUR)
TO GET ME...?

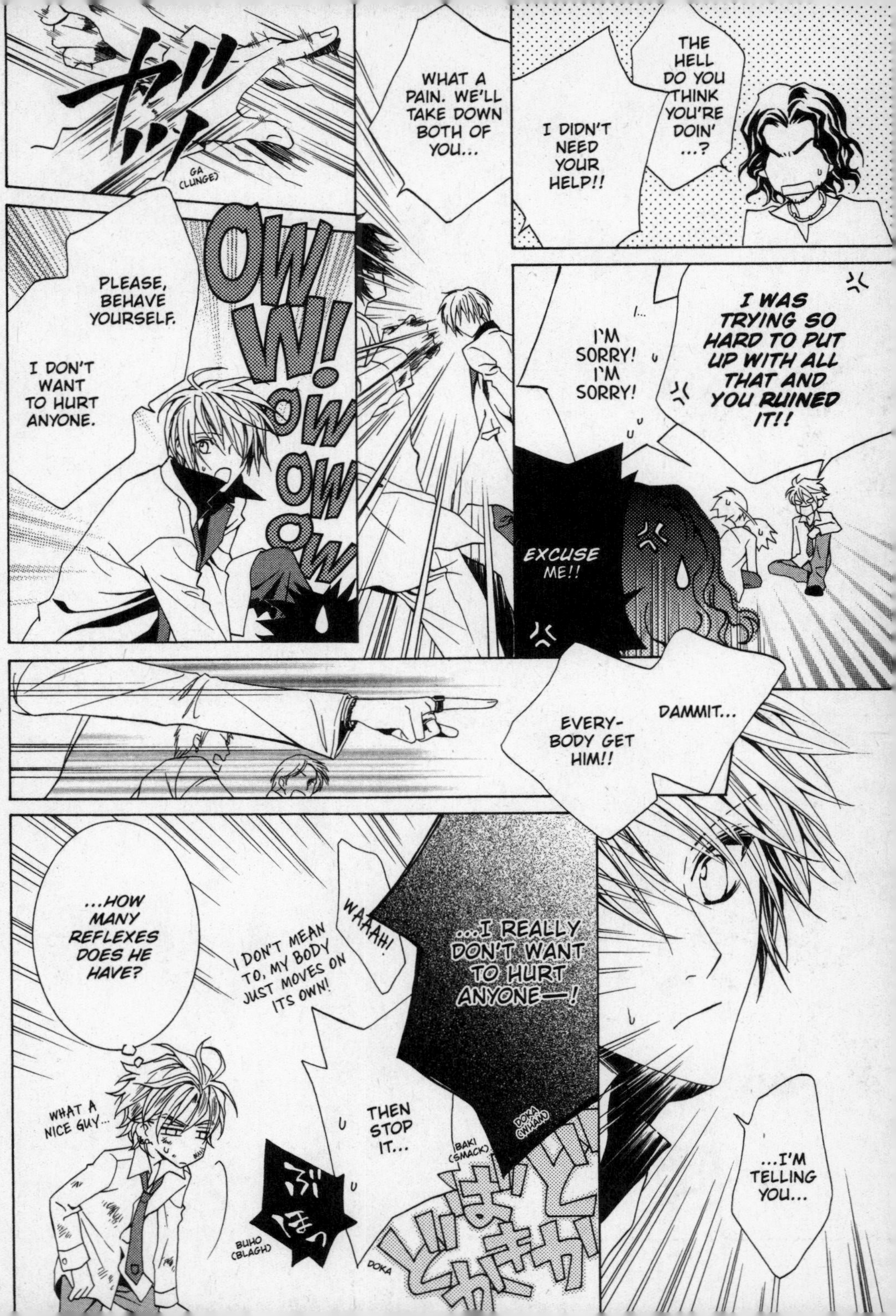
THE HELL DO YOU THINK YOU'RE DOIN' ...?
I DIDN'T NEED YOUR HELP!!
WHAT A PAIN. WE'LL TAKE DOWN BOTH OF YOU...
GA (LUNGE)
I WAS TRYING SO HARD TO PUT UP WITH ALL THAT AND YOU RUINED IT!!
I... I'M SORRY! I'M SORRY!
EXCUSE ME!!
OWWW! OW OW OW OW
PLEASE, BEHAVE YOURSELF.
I DON'T WANT TO HURT ANYONE.
DAMMIT...
EVERY-BODY GET HIM!!
...I'M TELLING YOU...
...I REALLY DON'T WANT TO HURT ANYONE—!
DOKA (WHAM)
BAKI (SMACK)
DOKA
WAAAAH!
I DON'T MEAN TO, MY BODY JUST MOVES ON ITS OWN!
THEN STOP IT...
BUHO (BLAGH)
...HOW MANY REFLEXES DOES HE HAVE?
WHAT A NICE GUY...

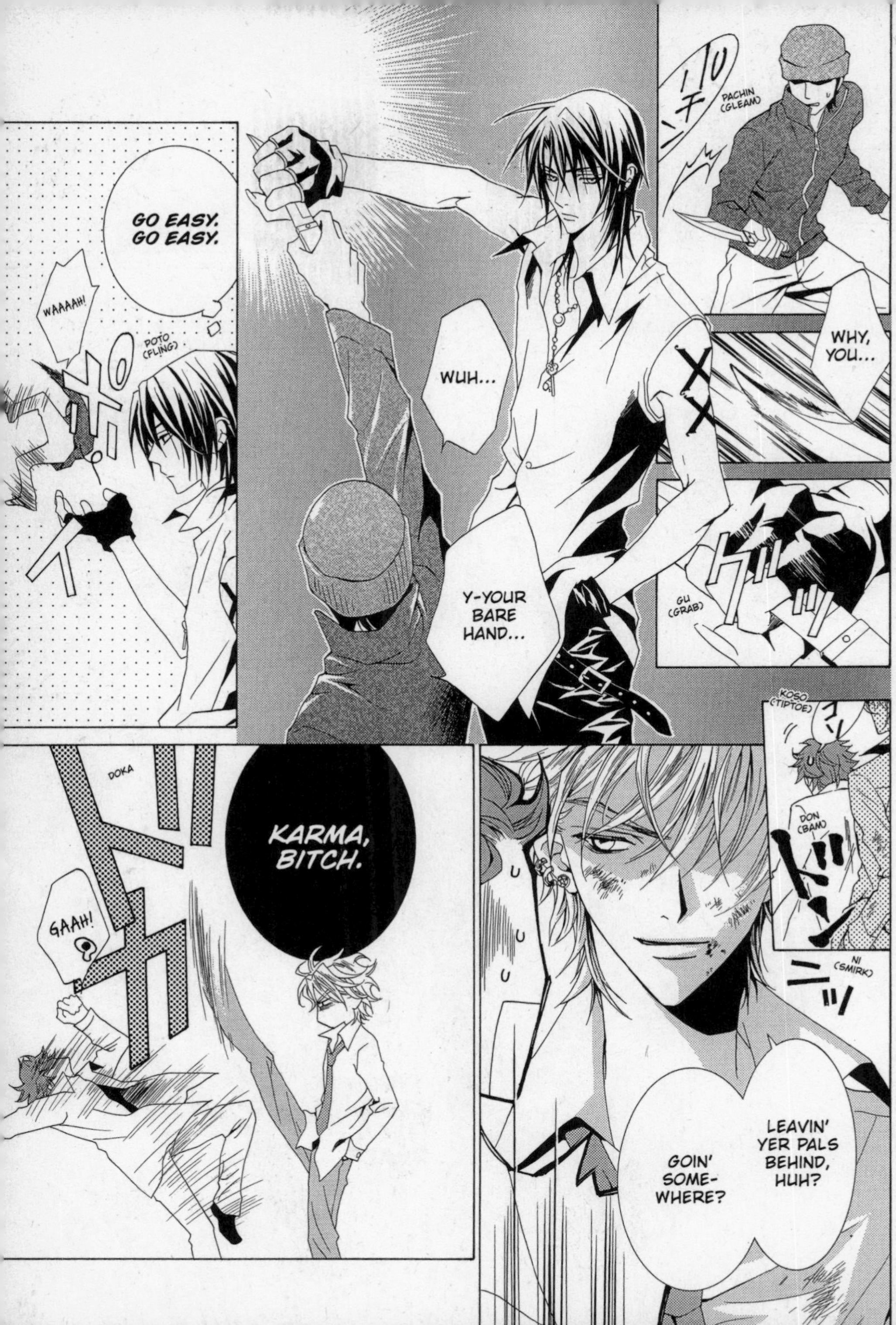
PACHIN (GLEAM)
WHY, YOU...
GU (GRAB)
WUH...
Y-YOUR BARE HAND...
GO EASY. GO EASY.
WAAAAH!
POTO (FLING)
KOSO (TIPTOE)
DON (BAM)
NI (SMIRK)
LEAVIN' YER PALS BEHIND, HUH?
GOIN' SOME-WHERE?
U
U
U
KARMA, BITCH.
DOKA
GAAH!

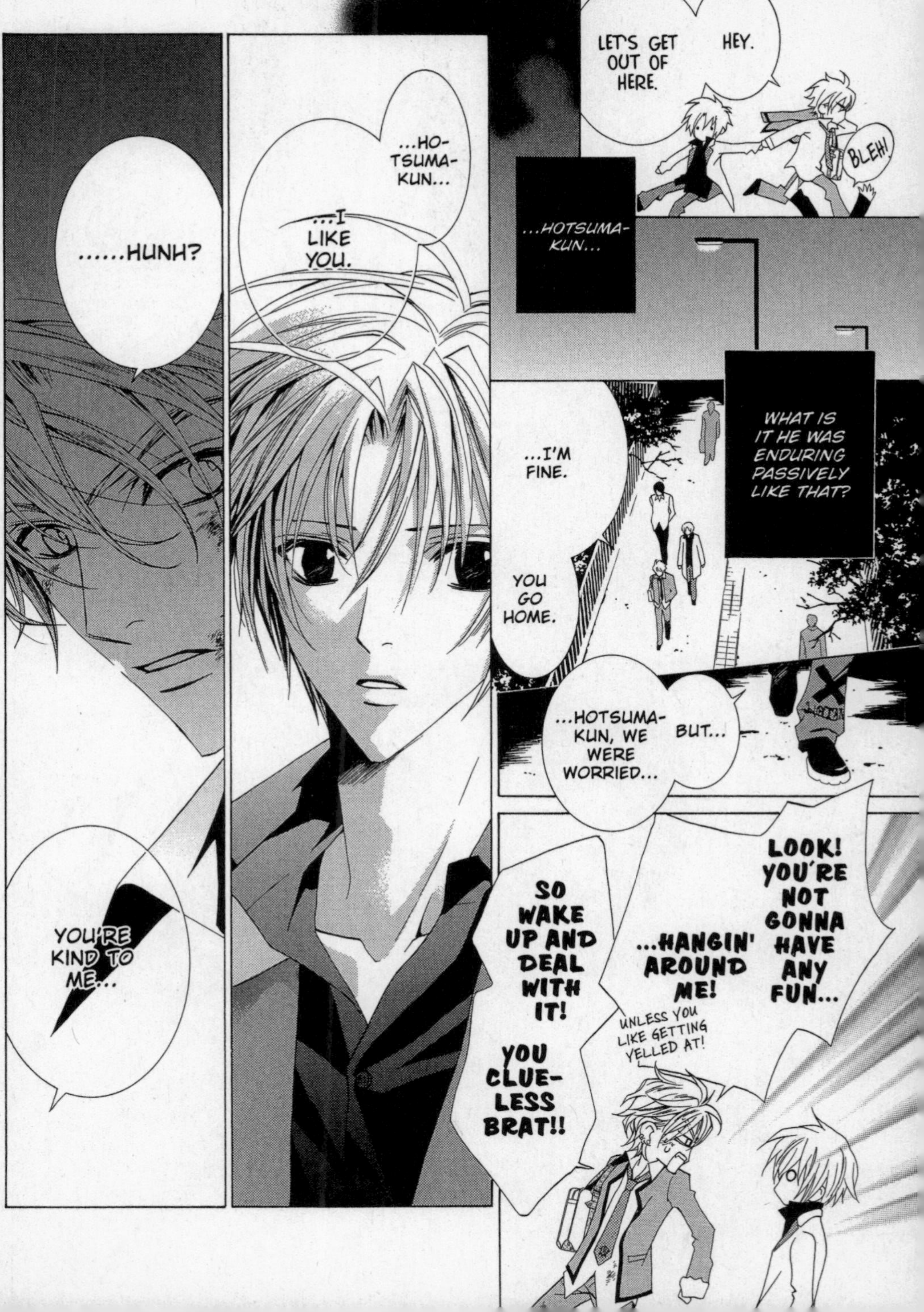
HEY.
LET'S GET OUT OF HERE.
BLEH!
...HOTSUMA-KUN...
WHAT IS IT HE WAS ENDURING PASSIVELY LIKE THAT?
...I'M FINE.
YOU GO HOME.
BUT...
...HOTSUMA-KUN, WE WERE WORRIED...
LOOK! YOU'RE NOT GONNA HAVE ANY FUN...
...HANGIN' AROUND ME!
UNLESS YOU LIKE GETTING YELLED AT!
SO WAKE UP AND DEAL WITH IT!
YOU CLUELESS BRAT!!
...HO-TSUMA-KUN...
...I LIKE YOU.
......HUNH?
YOU'RE KIND TO ME...

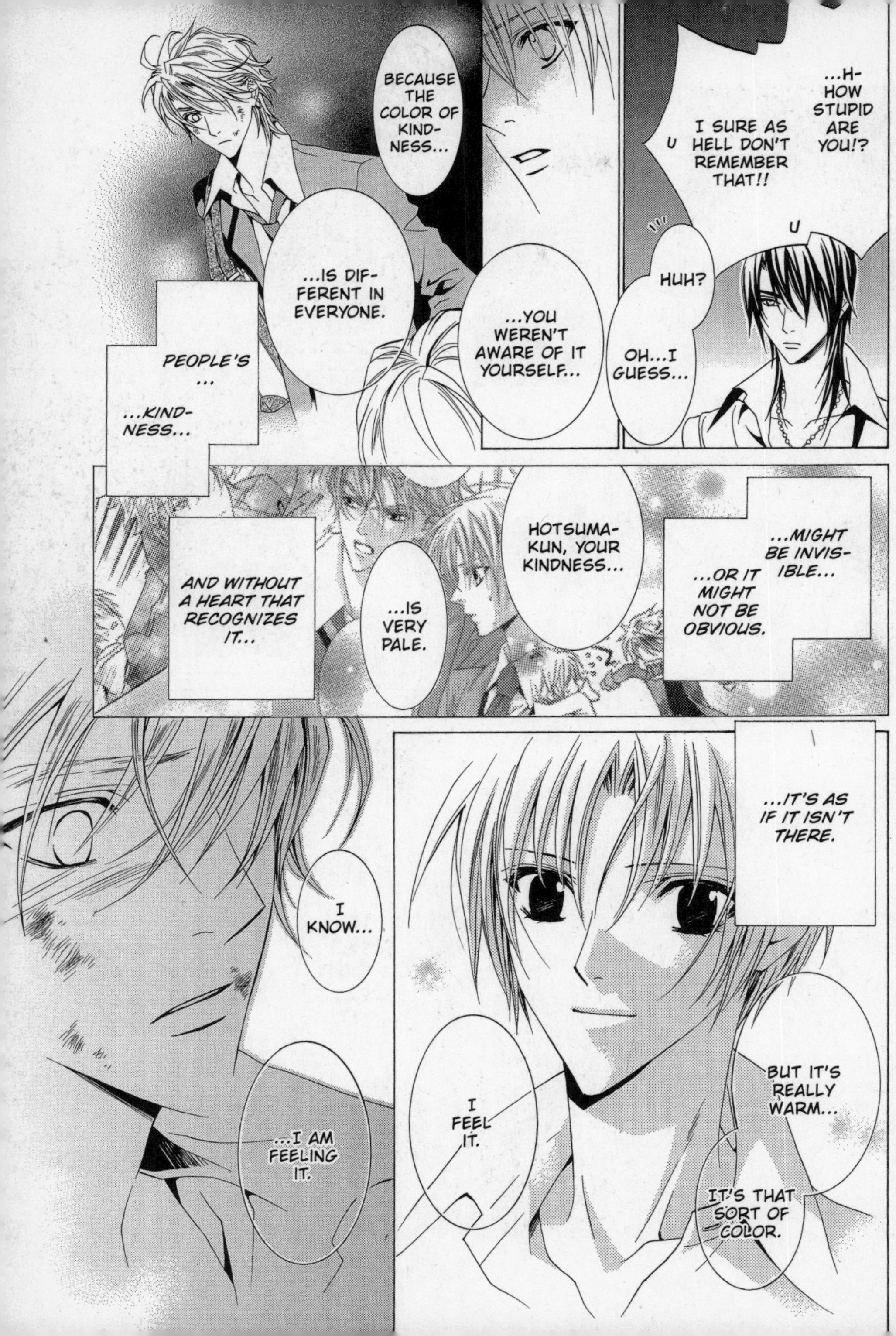
...H-HOW STUPID ARE YOU!?
I SURE AS HELL DON'T REMEMBER THAT!!
HUH?
OH...I GUESS...
...YOU WEREN'T AWARE OF IT YOURSELF...
BECAUSE THE COLOR OF KINDNESS...
...IS DIFFERENT IN EVERYONE.
PEOPLE'S ... ...KINDNESS...
...MIGHT BE INVISIBLE...
...OR IT MIGHT NOT BE OBVIOUS.
HOTSUMA-KUN, YOUR KINDNESS...
...IS VERY PALE.
AND WITHOUT A HEART THAT RECOGNIZES IT...
...IT'S AS IF IT ISN'T THERE.
BUT IT'S REALLY WARM...
IT'S THAT SORT OF COLOR.
I FEEL IT.
I KNOW...
...I AM FEELING IT.

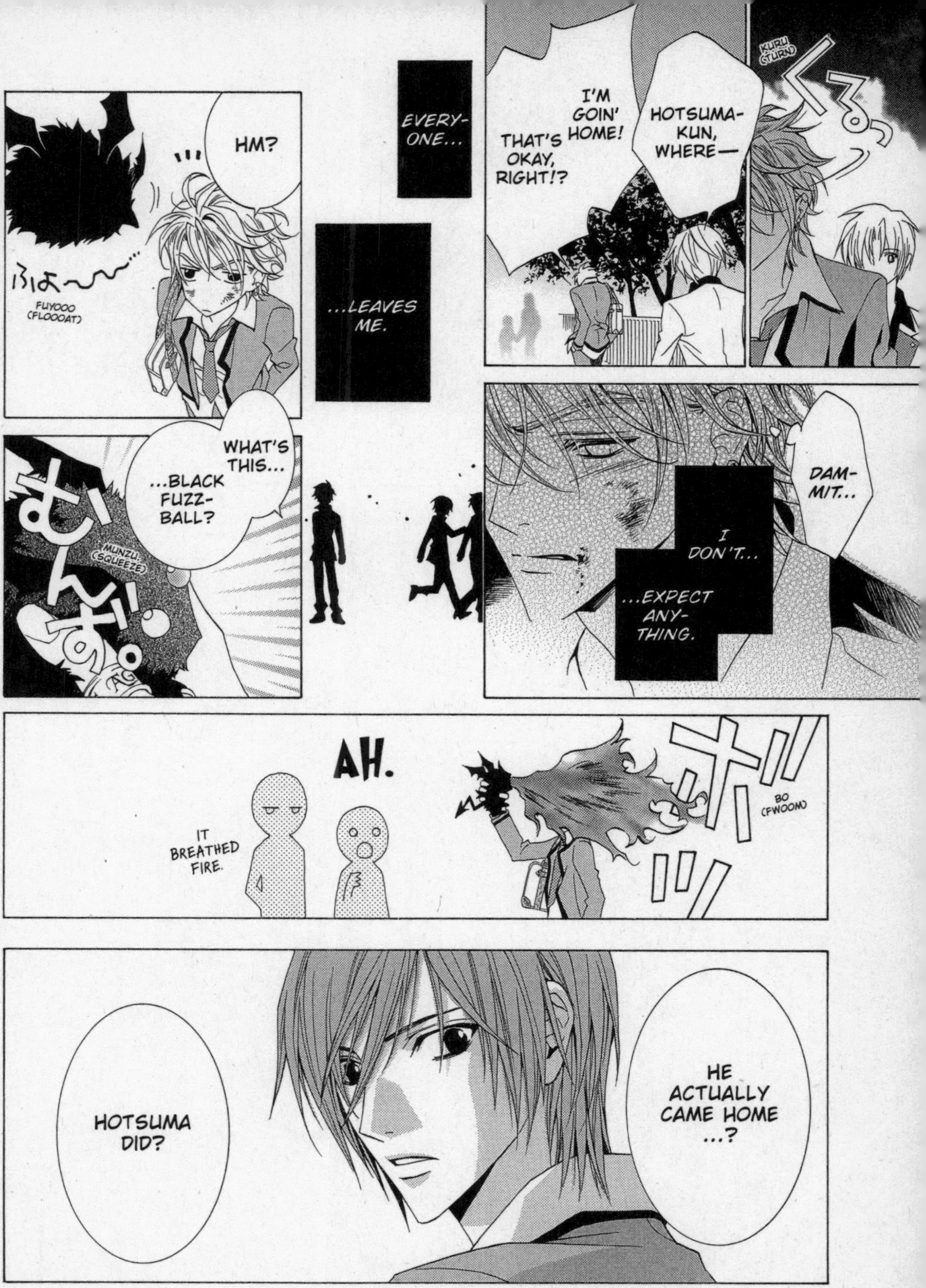

くるっ
KURU (TURN)
HOTSUMA-KUN, WHERE—
I'M GOIN' HOME! THAT'S OKAY, RIGHT!?
EVERY-ONE...
...LEAVES ME.
HM?
ふよ〜〜〜
FUYOOO (FLOOOAT)
DAM-MIT...
I DON'T...
...EXPECT ANY-THING.
WHAT'S THIS... ...BLACK FUZZ-BALL?
MUNZU (SQUEEZE)
BO (FWOOM)
AH.
IT BREATHED FIRE.
HE ACTUALLY CAME HOME ...?
HOTSUMA DID?

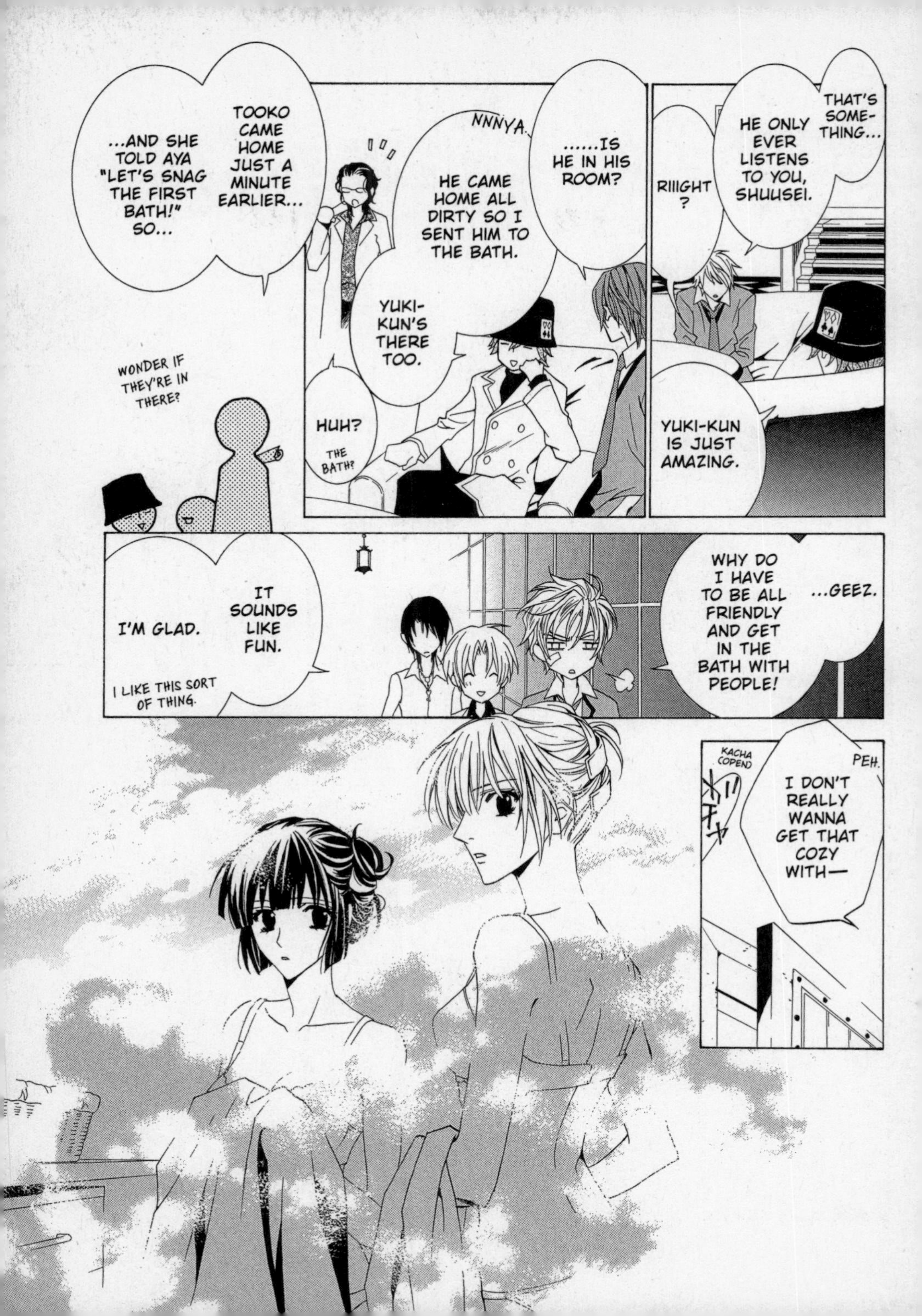
THAT'S SOMETHING...
HE ONLY EVER LISTENS TO YOU, SHUUSEI.
RIIIGHT?
YUKI-KUN IS JUST AMAZING.
......IS HE IN HIS ROOM?
NNNYA.
HE CAME HOME ALL DIRTY SO I SENT HIM TO THE BATH.
YUKI-KUN'S THERE TOO.
HUH?
THE BATH?
TOOKO CAME HOME JUST A MINUTE EARLIER...
...AND SHE TOLD AYA "LET'S SNAG THE FIRST BATH!" SO...
WONDER IF THEY'RE IN THERE?
...GEEZ.
WHY DO I HAVE TO BE ALL FRIENDLY AND GET IN THE BATH WITH PEOPLE!
IT SOUNDS LIKE FUN.
I'M GLAD.
I LIKE THIS SORT OF THING.
PEH.
I DON'T REALLY WANNA GET THAT COZY WITH—
KACHA (OPEN)

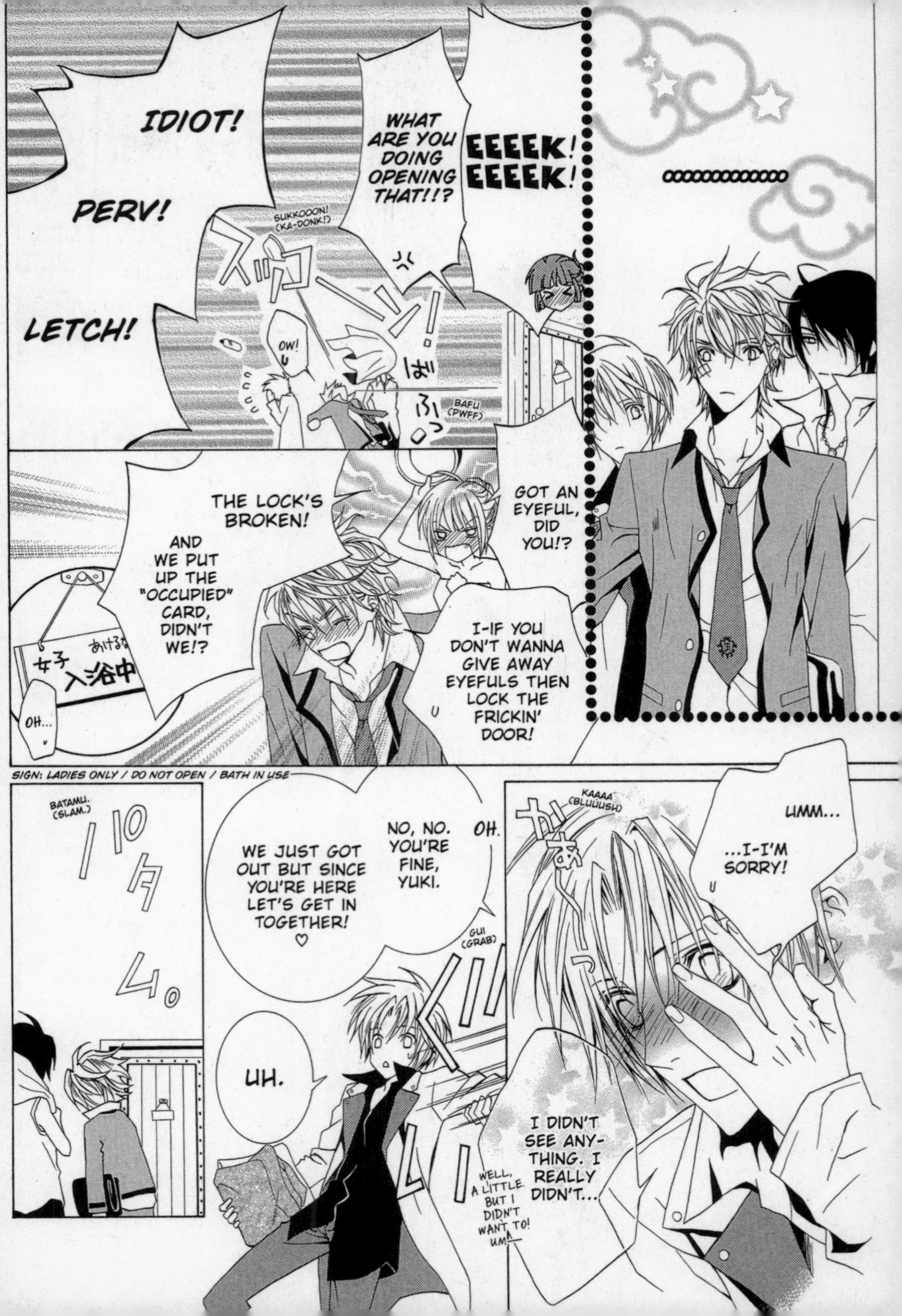
OOOOOOOOOOOOO
EEEEK! EEEEK!
WHAT ARE YOU DOING OPENING THAT!!?
IDIOT!
PERV!
LETCH!
SUKKOOON! (KA-DONK!)
OW!
BAFU (PWFF)
GOT AN EYEFUL, DID YOU!?
I-IF YOU DON'T WANNA GIVE AWAY EYEFULS THEN LOCK THE FRICKIN' DOOR!
THE LOCK'S BROKEN!
AND WE PUT UP THE "OCCUPIED" CARD, DIDN'T WE!?
女子 入浴中 あけるな
OH...
SIGN: LADIES ONLY / DO NOT OPEN / BATH IN USE
UMM...
...I-I'M SORRY!
KAAAA (BLUUUSH)
I DIDN'T SEE ANYTHING. I REALLY DIDN'T...
WELL, A LITTLE. BUT I DIDN'T WANT TO! UM!
OH.
NO, NO. YOU'RE FINE, YUKI.
WE JUST GOT OUT BUT SINCE YOU'RE HERE LET'S GET IN TOGETHER! ♡
GUI (GRAB)
UH.
BATAMU. (SLAM.)

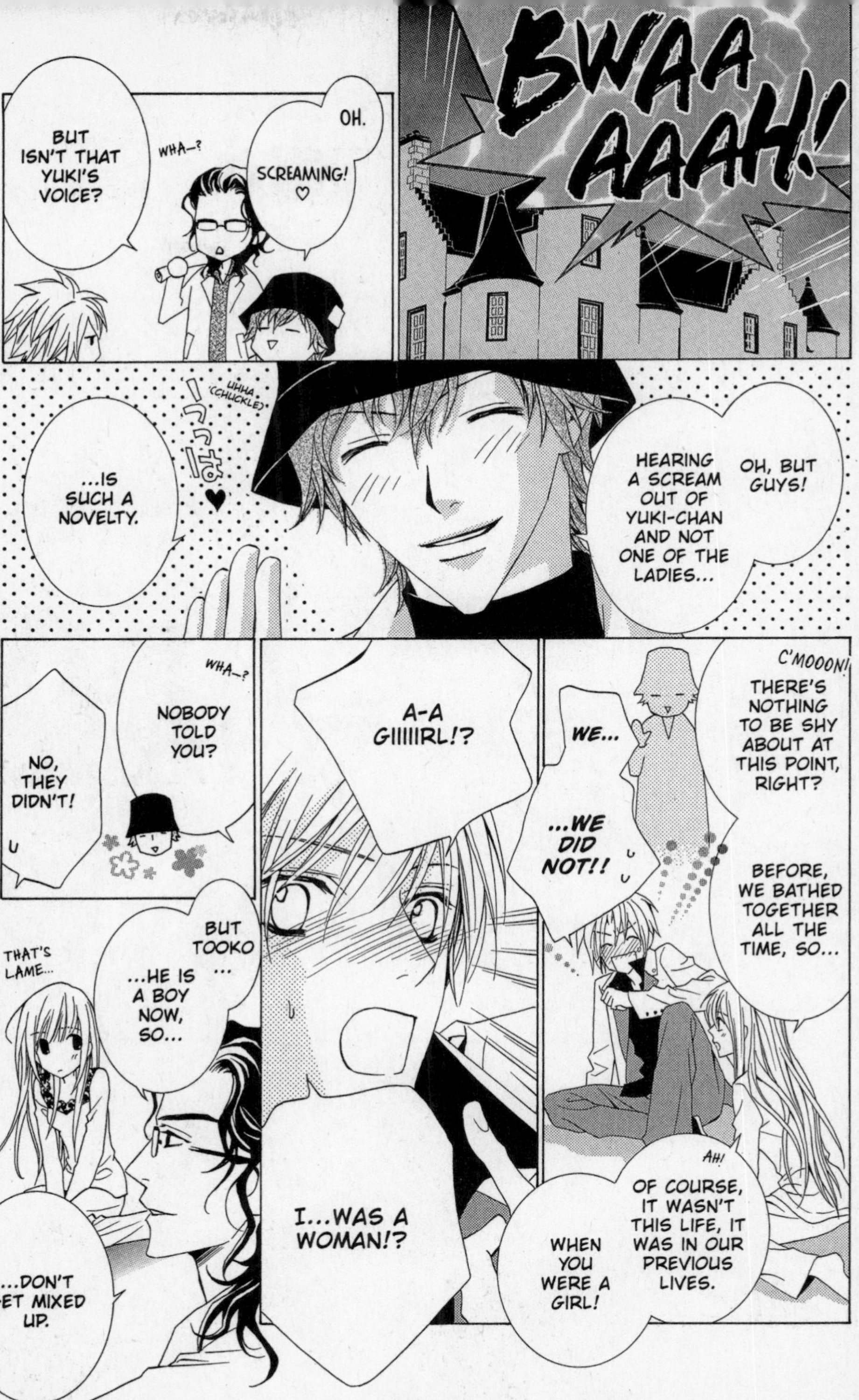
BWAA AAAH!
OH.
SCREAMING! ♡
WHA–?
BUT ISN'T THAT YUKI'S VOICE?
OH, BUT GUYS!
HEARING A SCREAM OUT OF YUKI-CHAN AND NOT ONE OF THE LADIES...
UHHA (CHUCKLE)
...IS SUCH A NOVELTY.
C'MOOON!
THERE'S NOTHING TO BE SHY ABOUT AT THIS POINT, RIGHT?
BEFORE, WE BATHED TOGETHER ALL THE TIME, SO...
WE...
...WE DID NOT!!
AH!
OF COURSE, IT WASN'T THIS LIFE, IT WAS IN OUR PREVIOUS LIVES.
WHEN YOU WERE A GIRL!
A-A GIIIIIRL!?
I...WAS A WOMAN!?
WHA–?
NOBODY TOLD YOU?
NO, THEY DIDN'T!
BUT TOOKO...
...HE IS A BOY NOW, SO...
THAT'S LAME...
...DON'T GET MIXED UP.

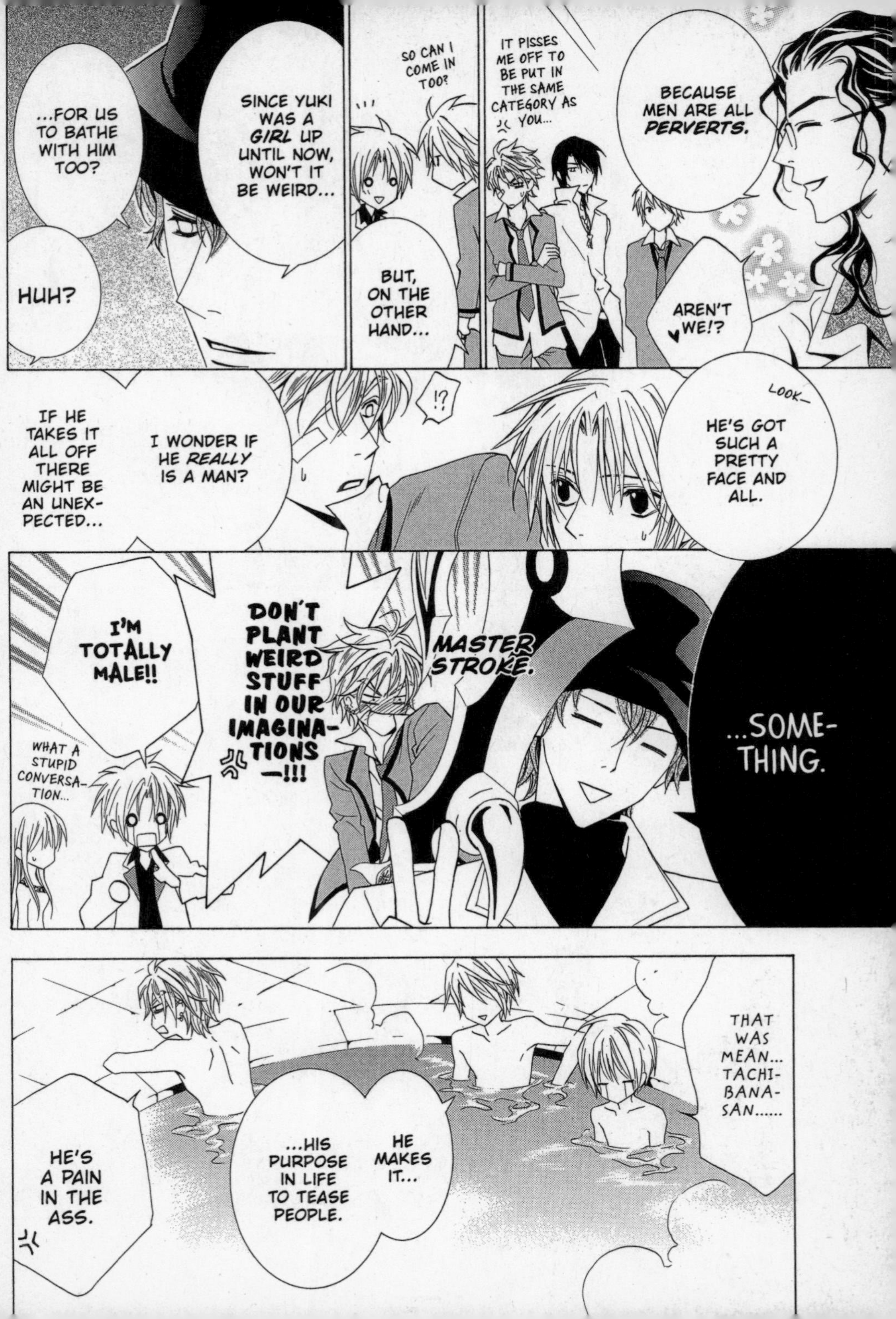

BECAUSE MEN ARE ALL PERVERTS.
AREN'T WE!?
IT PISSES ME OFF TO BE PUT IN THE SAME CATEGORY AS YOU...
SO CAN I COME IN TOO?
BUT, ON THE OTHER HAND...
SINCE YUKI WAS A GIRL UP UNTIL NOW, WON'T IT BE WEIRD...
...FOR US TO BATHE WITH HIM TOO?
HUH?
LOOK—
HE'S GOT SUCH A PRETTY FACE AND ALL.
!?
I WONDER IF HE REALLY IS A MAN?
IF HE TAKES IT ALL OFF THERE MIGHT BE AN UNEXPECTED...
...SOMETHING.
MASTER STROKE.
DON'T PLANT WEIRD STUFF IN OUR IMAGINATIONS—!!!
I'M TOTALLY MALE!!
WHAT A STUPID CONVERSATION...
THAT WAS MEAN... TACHIBANA-SAN......
HE MAKES IT...
...HIS PURPOSE IN LIFE TO TEASE PEOPLE.
HE'S A PAIN IN THE ASS.

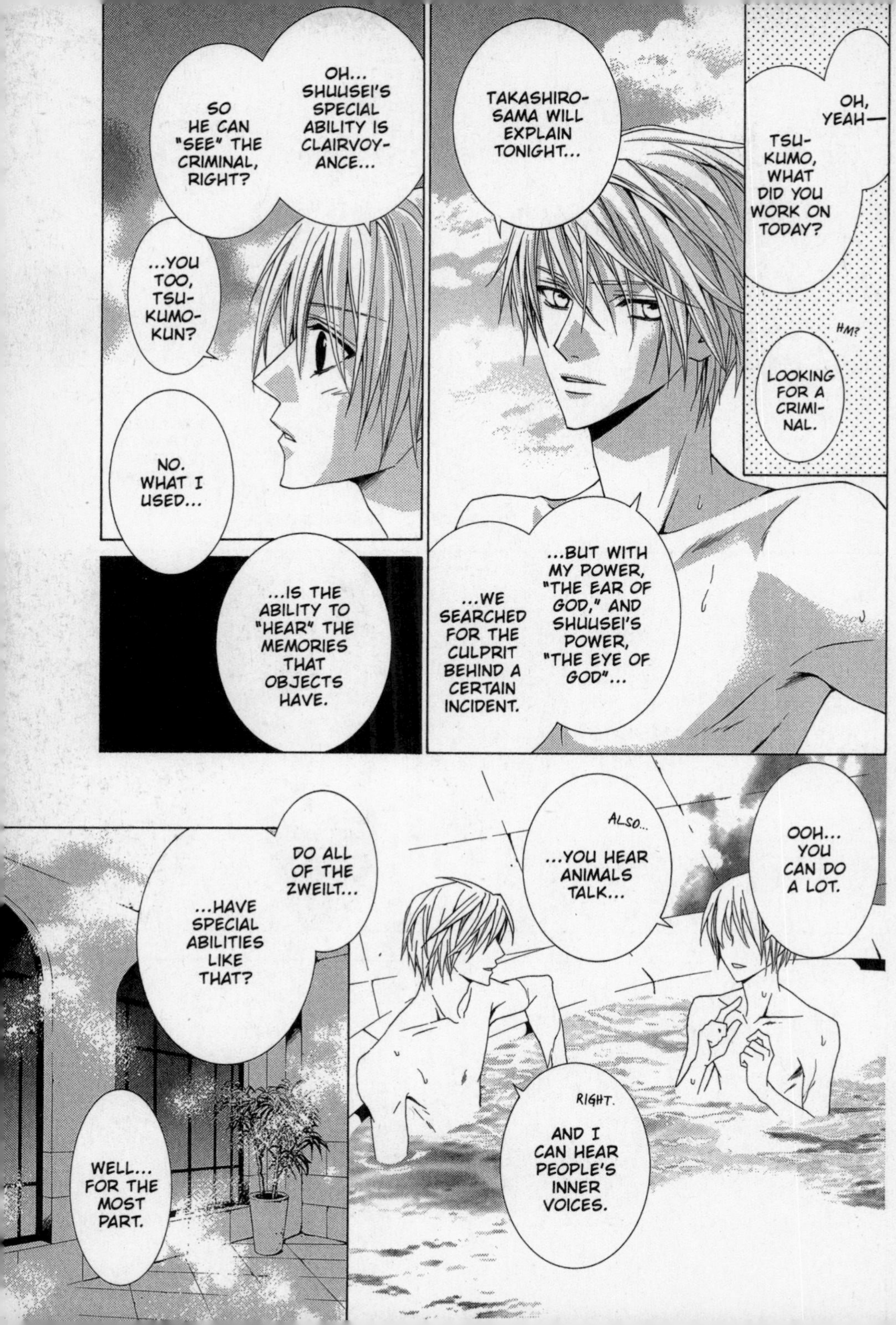
OH, YEAH—
TSUKUMO, WHAT DID YOU WORK ON TODAY?
HM?
LOOKING FOR A CRIMINAL.
TAKASHIRO-SAMA WILL EXPLAIN TONIGHT...
...BUT WITH MY POWER, "THE EAR OF GOD," AND SHUUSEI'S POWER, "THE EYE OF GOD"...
...WE SEARCHED FOR THE CULPRIT BEHIND A CERTAIN INCIDENT.
OH... SHUUSEI'S SPECIAL ABILITY IS CLAIRVOYANCE...
SO HE CAN "SEE" THE CRIMINAL, RIGHT?
...YOU TOO, TSUKUMO-KUN?
NO. WHAT I USED...
...IS THE ABILITY TO "HEAR" THE MEMORIES THAT OBJECTS HAVE.
OOH... YOU CAN DO A LOT.
ALSO...
...YOU HEAR ANIMALS TALK...
RIGHT.
AND I CAN HEAR PEOPLE'S INNER VOICES.
DO ALL OF THE ZWEILT...
...HAVE SPECIAL ABILITIES LIKE THAT?
WELL... FOR THE MOST PART.

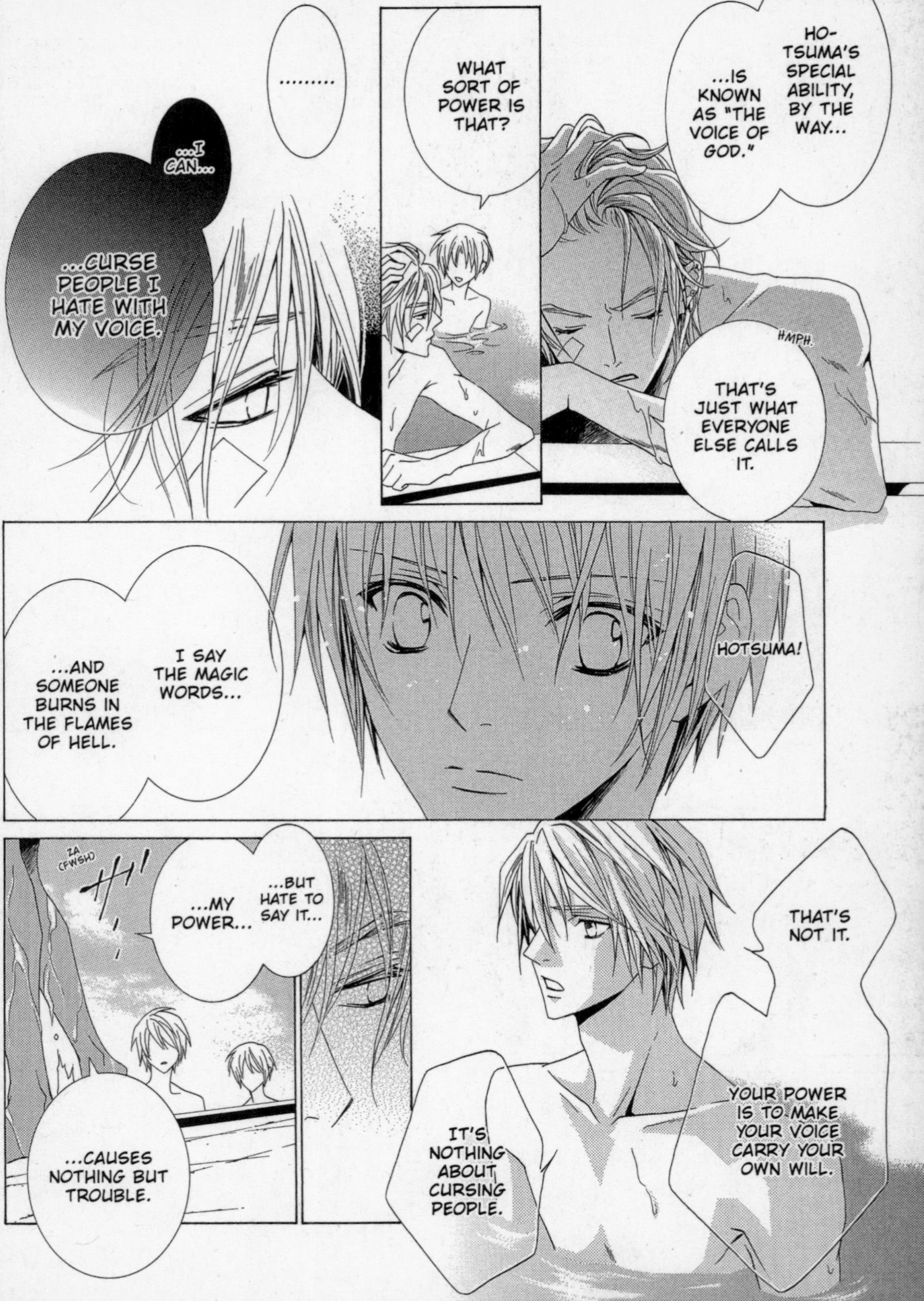

HO-TSUMA'S SPECIAL ABILITY, BY THE WAY...
...IS KNOWN AS "THE VOICE OF GOD."
HMPH.
THAT'S JUST WHAT EVERYONE ELSE CALLS IT.
WHAT SORT OF POWER IS THAT?
....
...I CAN...
...CURSE PEOPLE I HATE WITH MY VOICE.
HOTSUMA!
I SAY THE MAGIC WORDS...
...AND SOMEONE BURNS IN THE FLAMES OF HELL.
THAT'S NOT IT.
YOUR POWER IS TO MAKE YOUR VOICE CARRY YOUR OWN WILL.
IT'S NOTHING ABOUT CURSING PEOPLE.
...BUT HATE TO SAY IT...
...MY POWER...
ZA (FWSH)
...CAUSES NOTHING BUT TROUBLE.

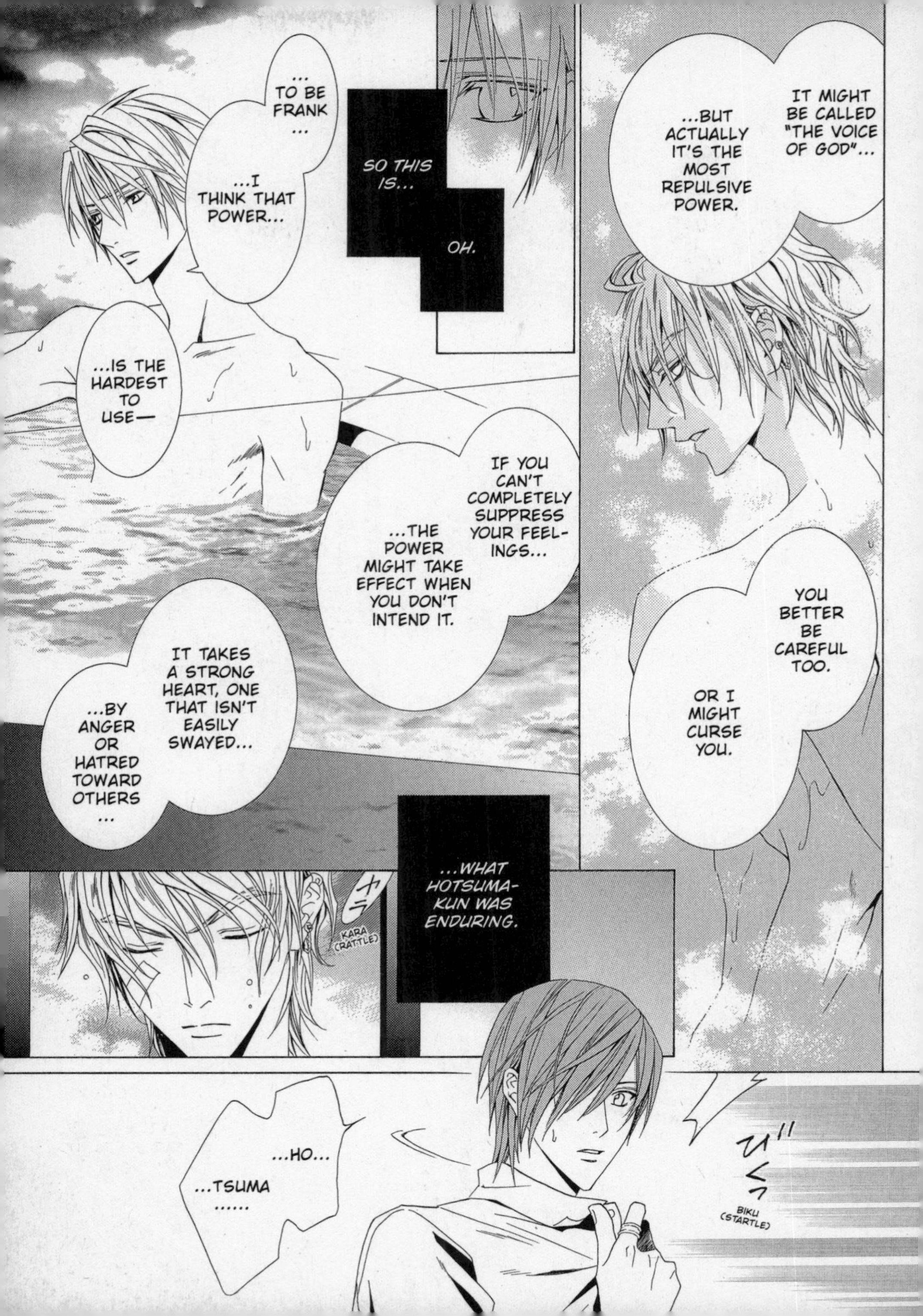
IT MIGHT BE CALLED "THE VOICE OF GOD"...
...BUT ACTUALLY IT'S THE MOST REPULSIVE POWER.
SO THIS IS...
OH.
... TO BE FRANK ...
...I THINK THAT POWER...
...IS THE HARDEST TO USE—
IF YOU CAN'T COMPLETELY SUPPRESS YOUR FEEL-INGS...
...THE POWER MIGHT TAKE EFFECT WHEN YOU DON'T INTEND IT.
IT TAKES A STRONG HEART, ONE THAT ISN'T EASILY SWAYED...
...BY ANGER OR HATRED TOWARD OTHERS ...
YOU BETTER BE CAREFUL TOO.
OR I MIGHT CURSE YOU.
...WHAT HOTSUMA-KUN WAS ENDURING.
KARA (RATTLE)
BIKU (STARTLE)
...HO...
...TSUMA ......

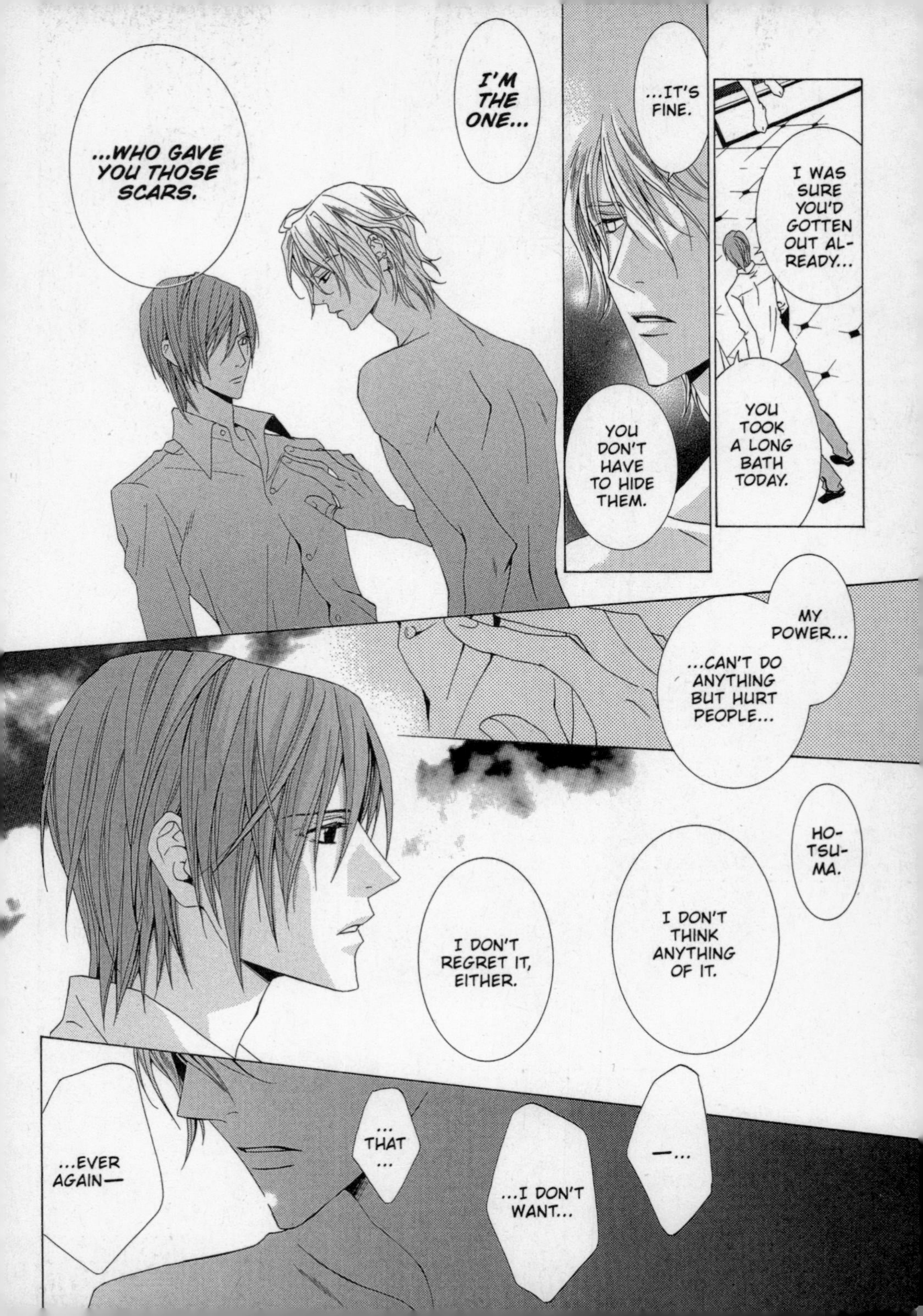
I WAS SURE YOU'D GOTTEN OUT AL-READY...
YOU TOOK A LONG BATH TODAY.
...IT'S FINE.
YOU DON'T HAVE TO HIDE THEM.
I'M THE ONE...
...WHO GAVE YOU THOSE SCARS.
MY POWER...
...CAN'T DO ANYTHING BUT HURT PEOPLE...
HO-TSU-MA.
I DON'T THINK ANYTHING OF IT.
I DON'T REGRET IT, EITHER.
—...
...I DON'T WANT...
...THAT...
...EVER AGAIN—

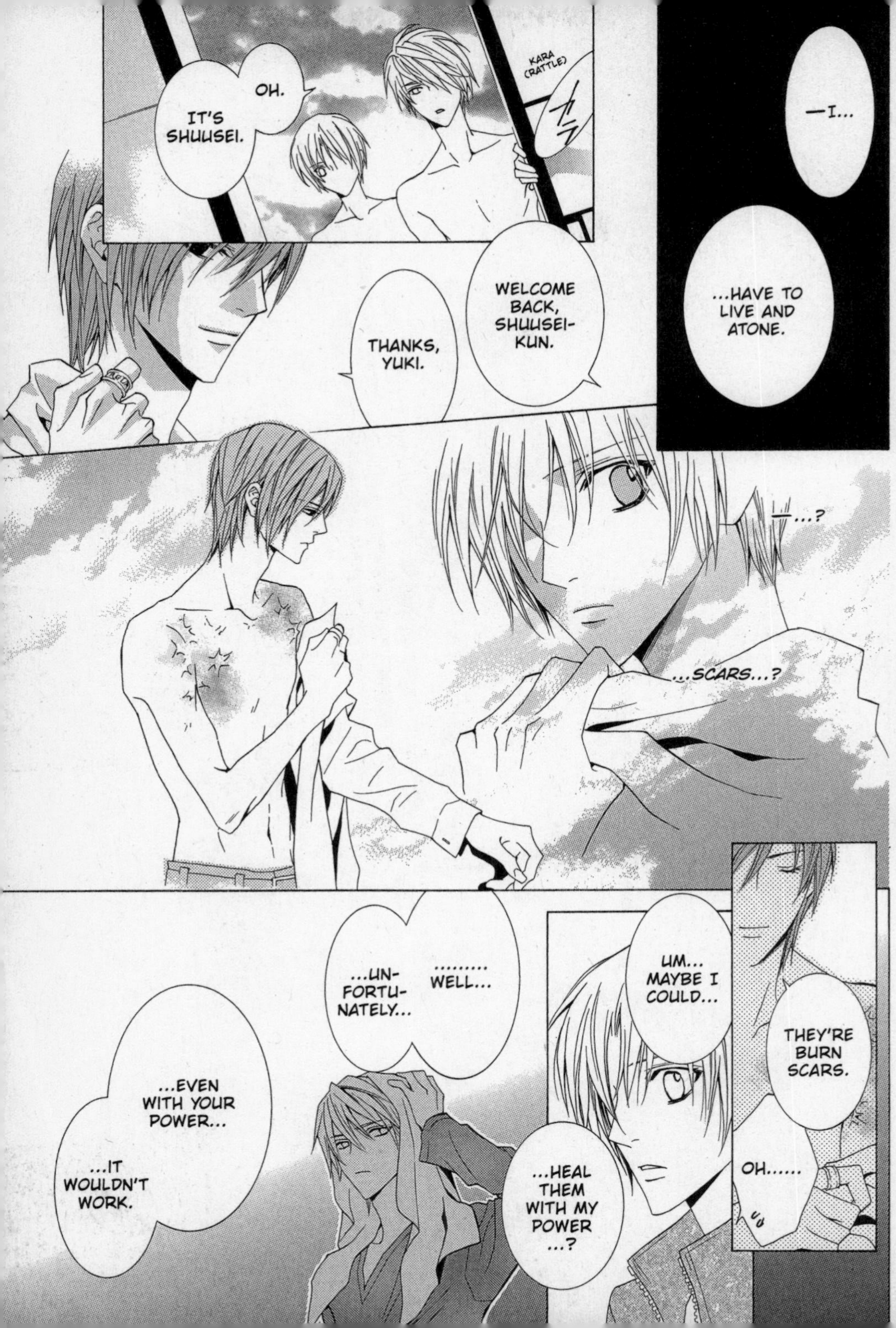
—I...
...HAVE TO LIVE AND ATONE.
KARA (RATTLE)
OH.
IT'S SHUUSEI.
WELCOME BACK, SHUUSEI-KUN.
THANKS, YUKI.
—...?
...SCARS...?
THEY'RE BURN SCARS.
OH......
UM... MAYBE I COULD...
...HEAL THEM WITH MY POWER ...?
.... WELL...
...UN-FORTU-NATELY...
...EVEN WITH YOUR POWER...
...IT WOULDN'T WORK.

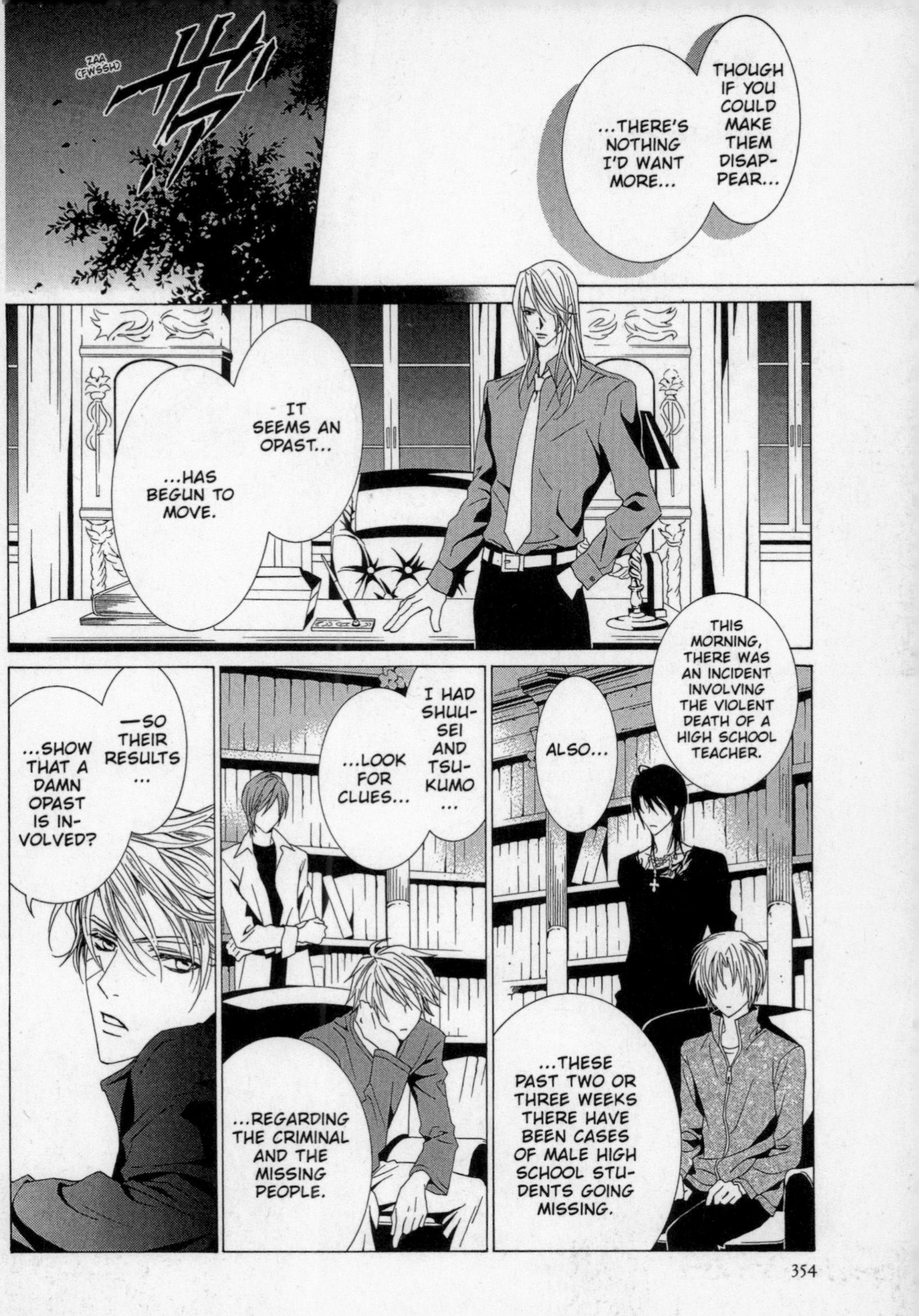
ZAA (FWSSH)
THOUGH IF YOU COULD MAKE THEM DISAP-PEAR...
...THERE'S NOTHING I'D WANT MORE...
IT SEEMS AN OPAST...
...HAS BEGUN TO MOVE.
THIS MORNING, THERE WAS AN INCIDENT INVOLVING THE VIOLENT DEATH OF A HIGH SCHOOL TEACHER.
ALSO...
...THESE PAST TWO OR THREE WEEKS THERE HAVE BEEN CASES OF MALE HIGH SCHOOL STU-DENTS GOING MISSING.
I HAD SHUU-SEI AND TSU-KUMO ...
...LOOK FOR CLUES...
...REGARDING THE CRIMINAL AND THE MISSING PEOPLE.
—SO THEIR RESULTS ...
...SHOW THAT A DAMN OPAST IS IN-VOLVED?

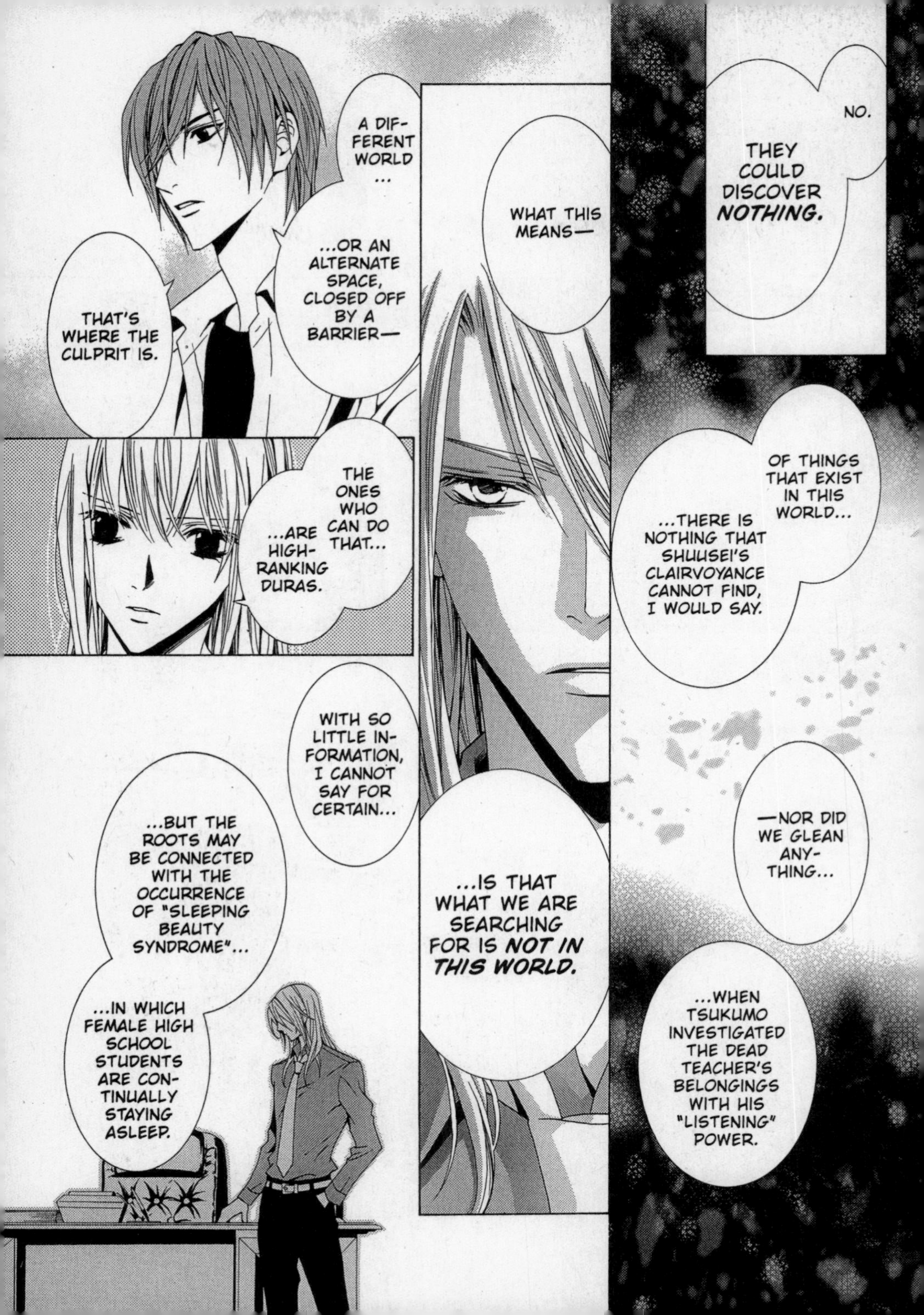
NO.
THEY COULD DISCOVER *NOTHING.*
OF THINGS THAT EXIST IN THIS WORLD...
...THERE IS NOTHING THAT SHUUSEI'S CLAIRVOYANCE CANNOT FIND, I WOULD SAY.
—NOR DID WE GLEAN ANYTHING...
...WHEN TSUKUMO INVESTIGATED THE DEAD TEACHER'S BELONGINGS WITH HIS "LISTENING" POWER.
WHAT THIS MEANS—
...IS THAT WHAT WE ARE SEARCHING FOR IS *NOT IN THIS WORLD.*
A DIFFERENT WORLD...
...OR AN ALTERNATE SPACE, CLOSED OFF BY A BARRIER—
THAT'S WHERE THE CULPRIT IS.
THE ONES WHO CAN DO THAT...
...ARE HIGH-RANKING DURAS.
WITH SO LITTLE INFORMATION, I CANNOT SAY FOR CERTAIN...
...BUT THE ROOTS MAY BE CONNECTED WITH THE OCCURRENCE OF "SLEEPING BEAUTY SYNDROME"...
...IN WHICH FEMALE HIGH SCHOOL STUDENTS ARE CONTINUALLY STAYING ASLEEP.

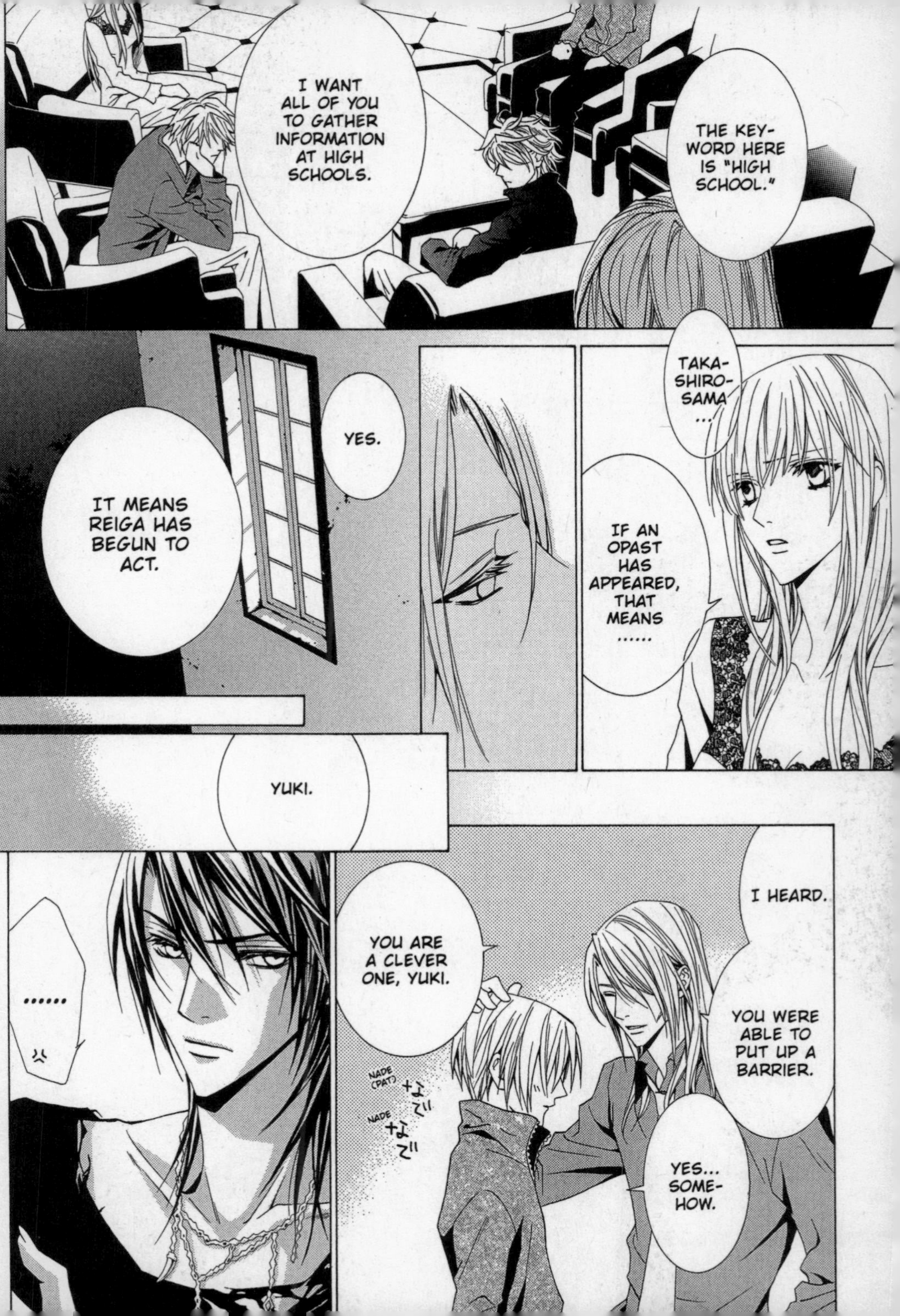
THE KEY-WORD HERE IS "HIGH SCHOOL."
I WANT ALL OF YOU TO GATHER INFORMATION AT HIGH SCHOOLS.
TAKA-SHIRO-SAMA...
IF AN OPAST HAS APPEARED, THAT MEANS......
YES.
IT MEANS REIGA HAS BEGUN TO ACT.
YUKI.
I HEARD.
YOU WERE ABLE TO PUT UP A BARRIER.
YOU ARE A CLEVER ONE, YUKI.
YES... SOME-HOW.
NADE (PAT) なで
NADE なで
......

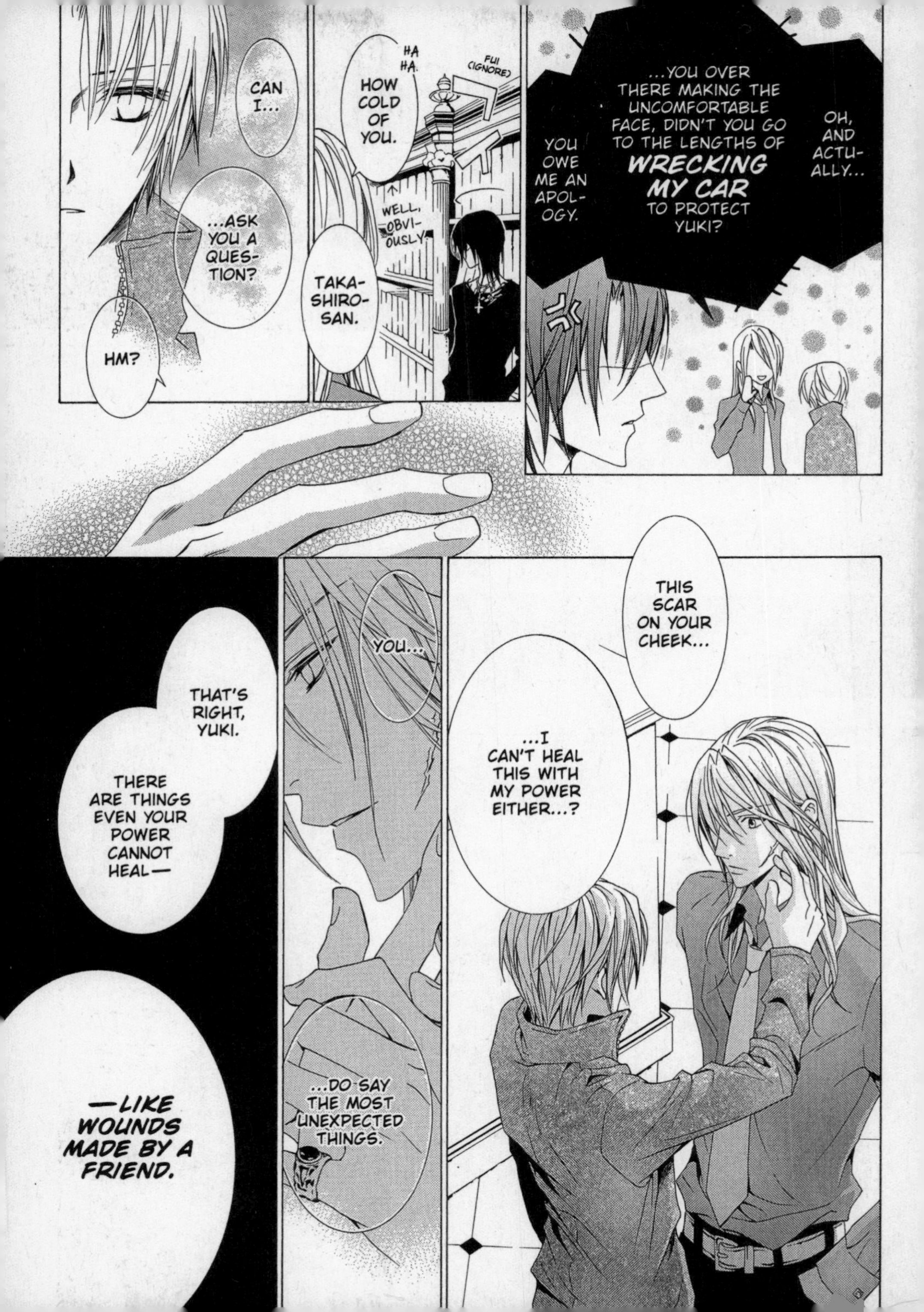
OH, AND ACTUALLY...
...YOU OVER THERE MAKING THE UNCOMFORTABLE FACE, DIDN'T YOU GO TO THE LENGTHS OF WRECKING MY CAR TO PROTECT YUKI?
YOU OWE ME AN APOLOGY.
FUI (IGNORE)
HA HA.
HOW COLD OF YOU.
↑ WELL, OBVIOUSLY.
TAKASHIRO-SAN.
CAN I...
...ASK YOU A QUESTION?
HM?
THIS SCAR ON YOUR CHEEK...
...I CAN'T HEAL THIS WITH MY POWER EITHER...?
YOU...
...DO SAY THE MOST UNEXPECTED THINGS.
THAT'S RIGHT, YUKI.
THERE ARE THINGS EVEN YOUR POWER CANNOT HEAL—
—LIKE WOUNDS MADE BY A FRIEND.

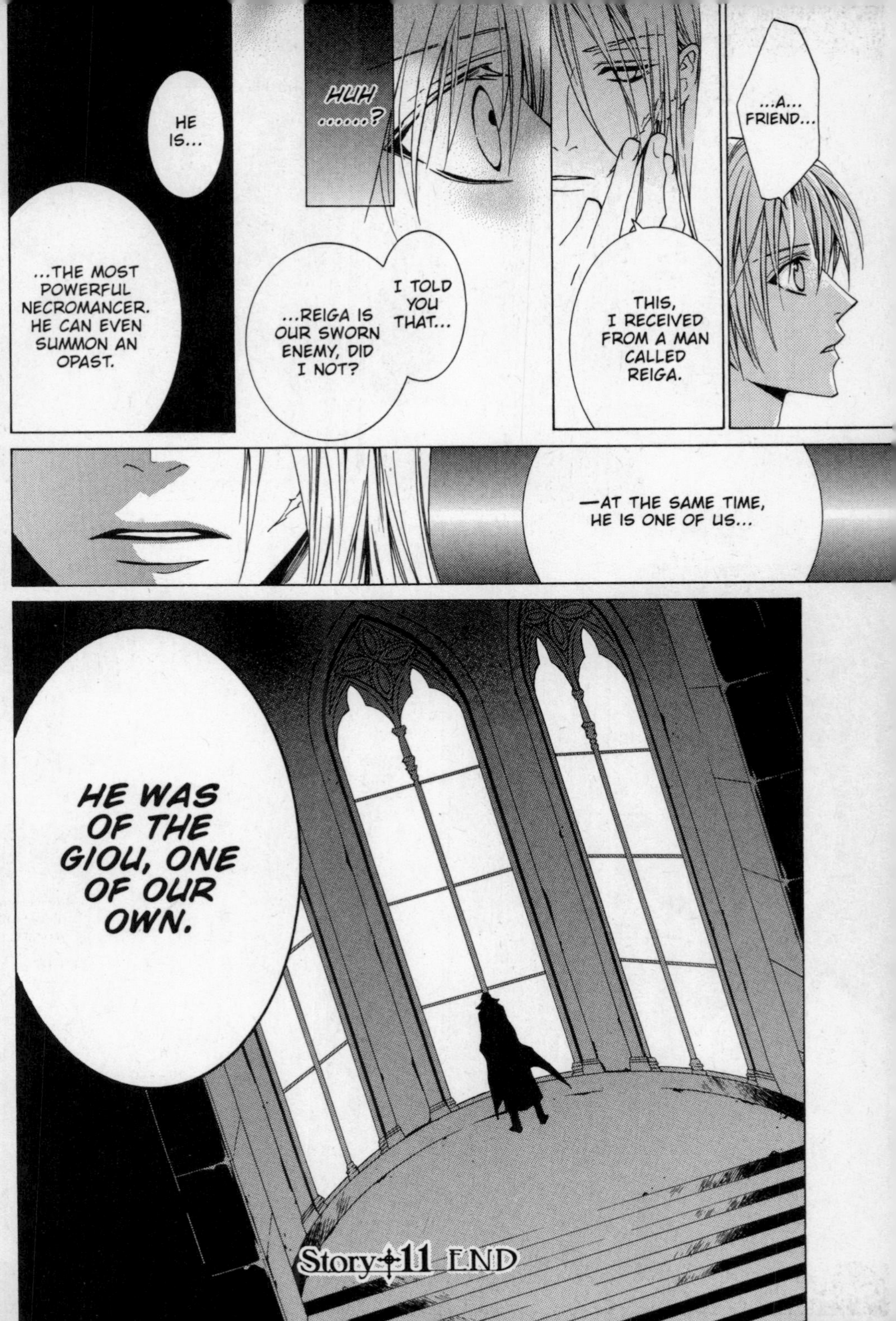
...A... FRIEND...
HUH ......?
THIS, I RECEIVED FROM A MAN CALLED REIGA.
I TOLD YOU THAT...
...REIGA IS OUR SWORN ENEMY, DID I NOT?
HE IS...
...THE MOST POWERFUL NECROMANCER. HE CAN EVEN SUMMON AN OPAST.
—AT THE SAME TIME, HE IS ONE OF US...
HE WAS OF THE GIOU, ONE OF OUR OWN.
Story 11 END

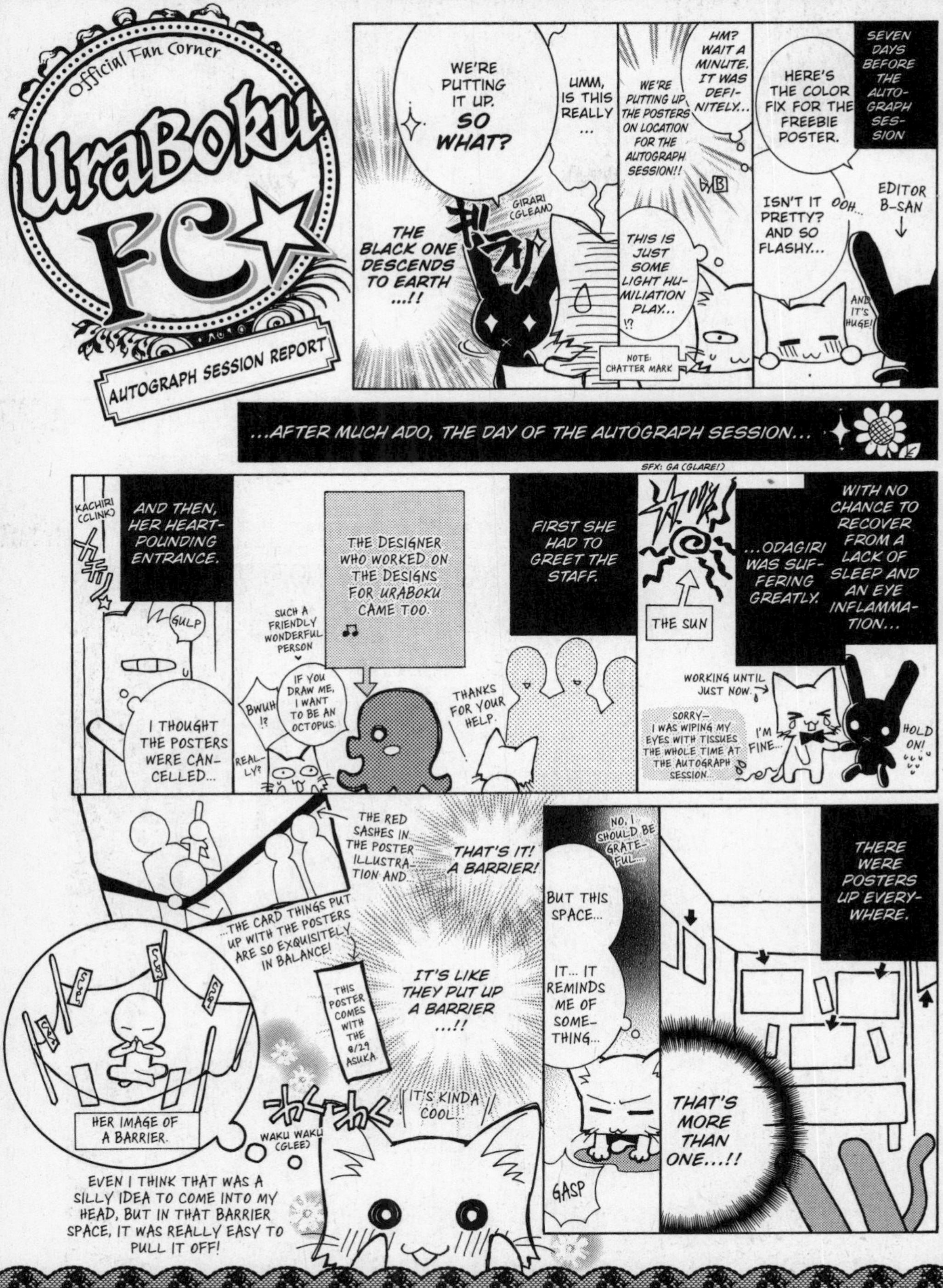
Official Fan Corner
UraBoku FC
AUTOGRAPH SESSION REPORT
SEVEN DAYS BEFORE THE AUTOGRAPH SESSION
HERE'S THE COLOR FIX FOR THE FREEBIE POSTER.
EDITOR B-SAN
OOH...
ISN'T IT PRETTY? AND SO FLASHY...
AND IT'S HUGE!
HM? WAIT A MINUTE. IT WAS DEFINITELY...
WE'RE PUTTING UP THE POSTERS ON LOCATION FOR THE AUTOGRAPH SESSION!!
by B
THIS IS JUST SOME LIGHT HUMILIATION PLAY...
!?
NOTE: CHATTER MARK
UMM, IS THIS REALLY ...
WE'RE PUTTING IT UP. SO WHAT?
GIRARI (GLEAM)
THE BLACK ONE DESCENDS TO EARTH ...!!
...AFTER MUCH ADO, THE DAY OF THE AUTOGRAPH SESSION...
SFX: GA (GLARE!)
WITH NO CHANCE TO RECOVER FROM A LACK OF SLEEP AND AN EYE INFLAMMATION...
...ODAGIRI WAS SUFFERING GREATLY.
THE SUN
WORKING UNTIL JUST NOW.
SORRY— I WAS WIPING MY EYES WITH TISSUES THE WHOLE TIME AT THE AUTOGRAPH SESSION...
I'M FINE...
HOLD ON!
FIRST SHE HAD TO GREET THE STAFF.
THANKS FOR YOUR HELP.
THE DESIGNER WHO WORKED ON THE DESIGNS FOR URABOKU CAME TOO.
SUCH A FRIENDLY WONDERFUL PERSON
IF YOU DRAW ME, I WANT TO BE AN OCTOPUS.
BWUH!?
REALLY?
AND THEN, HER HEART-POUNDING ENTRANCE.
KACHIRI (CLINK)
GULP
I THOUGHT THE POSTERS WERE CANCELLED...
THERE WERE POSTERS UP EVERYWHERE.
THAT'S MORE THAN ONE...!!
NO, I SHOULD BE GRATEFUL...
BUT THIS SPACE...
IT... IT REMINDS ME OF SOMETHING...
GASP
THAT'S IT! A BARRIER!
THE RED SASHES IN THE POSTER ILLUSTRATION AND...
...THE CARD THINGS PUT UP WITH THE POSTERS ARE SO EXQUISITELY IN BALANCE!
IT'S LIKE THEY PUT UP A BARRIER ...!!
THIS POSTER COMES WITH THE 8/29 ASUKA.
IT'S KINDA COOL...
WAKU WAKU (GLEE)
HER IMAGE OF A BARRIER.
EVEN I THINK THAT WAS A SILLY IDEA TO COME INTO MY HEAD, BUT IN THAT BARRIER SPACE, IT WAS REALLY EASY TO PULL IT OFF!

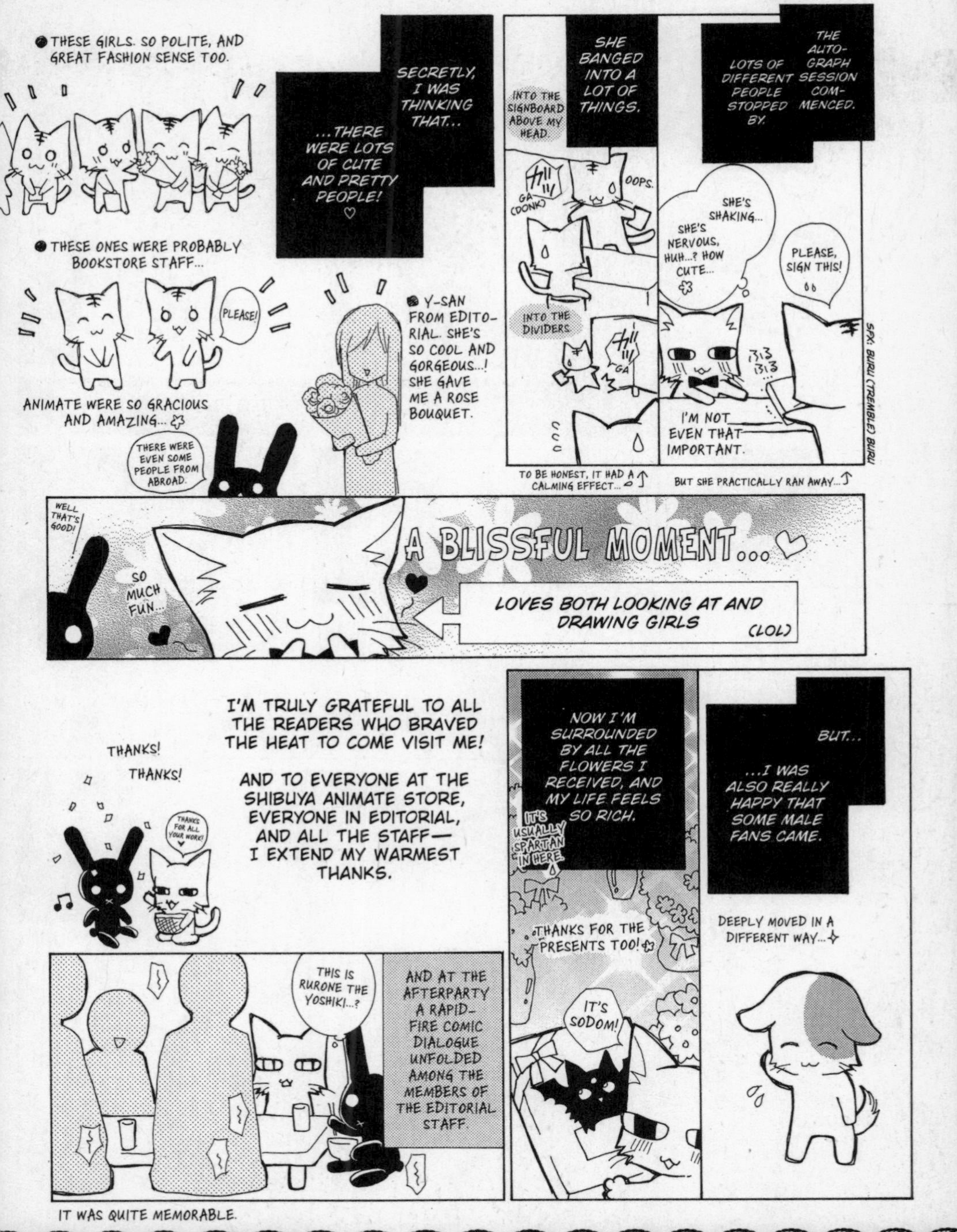

THE AUTOGRAPH SESSION COMMENCED.
LOTS OF DIFFERENT PEOPLE STOPPED BY.
PLEASE, SIGN THIS!
SHE'S SHAKING...
SHE'S NERVOUS, HUH...? HOW CUTE...
I'M NOT EVEN THAT IMPORTANT.
SFX: BURU (TREMBLE) BURU
BUT SHE PRACTICALLY RAN AWAY...
SHE BANGED INTO A LOT OF THINGS.
INTO THE SIGNBOARD ABOVE MY HEAD.
GA (DONK)
OOPS.
INTO THE DIVIDERS
GA
TO BE HONEST, IT HAD A CALMING EFFECT...
SECRETLY, I WAS THINKING THAT...
...THERE WERE LOTS OF CUTE AND PRETTY PEOPLE! ♡
THESE GIRLS. SO POLITE, AND GREAT FASHION SENSE TOO.
THESE ONES WERE PROBABLY BOOKSTORE STAFF...
PLEASE!
ANIMATE WERE SO GRACIOUS AND AMAZING...
Y-SAN FROM EDITORIAL. SHE'S SO COOL AND GORGEOUS...! SHE GAVE ME A ROSE BOUQUET.
THERE WERE EVEN SOME PEOPLE FROM ABROAD.
A BLISSFUL MOMENT...
LOVES BOTH LOOKING AT AND DRAWING GIRLS (LOL)
WELL THAT'S GOOD!
SO MUCH FUN...
BUT...
...I WAS ALSO REALLY HAPPY THAT SOME MALE FANS CAME.
DEEPLY MOVED IN A DIFFERENT WAY...
NOW I'M SURROUNDED BY ALL THE FLOWERS I RECEIVED, AND MY LIFE FEELS SO RICH.
IT'S USUALLY SPARTAN IN HERE.
THANKS FOR THE PRESENTS TOO!
IT'S SODOM!
I'M TRULY GRATEFUL TO ALL THE READERS WHO BRAVED THE HEAT TO COME VISIT ME!
AND TO EVERYONE AT THE SHIBUYA ANIMATE STORE, EVERYONE IN EDITORIAL, AND ALL THE STAFF— I EXTEND MY WARMEST THANKS.
THANKS!
THANKS!
THANKS FOR ALL YOUR WORK!
AND AT THE AFTERPARTY A RAPID-FIRE COMIC DIALOGUE UNFOLDED AMONG THE MEMBERS OF THE EDITORIAL STAFF.
THIS IS RURONE THE YOSHIKI...?
IT WAS QUITE MEMORABLE.

Extra ✝ FUN FOR TAKASHIRO-SAMA

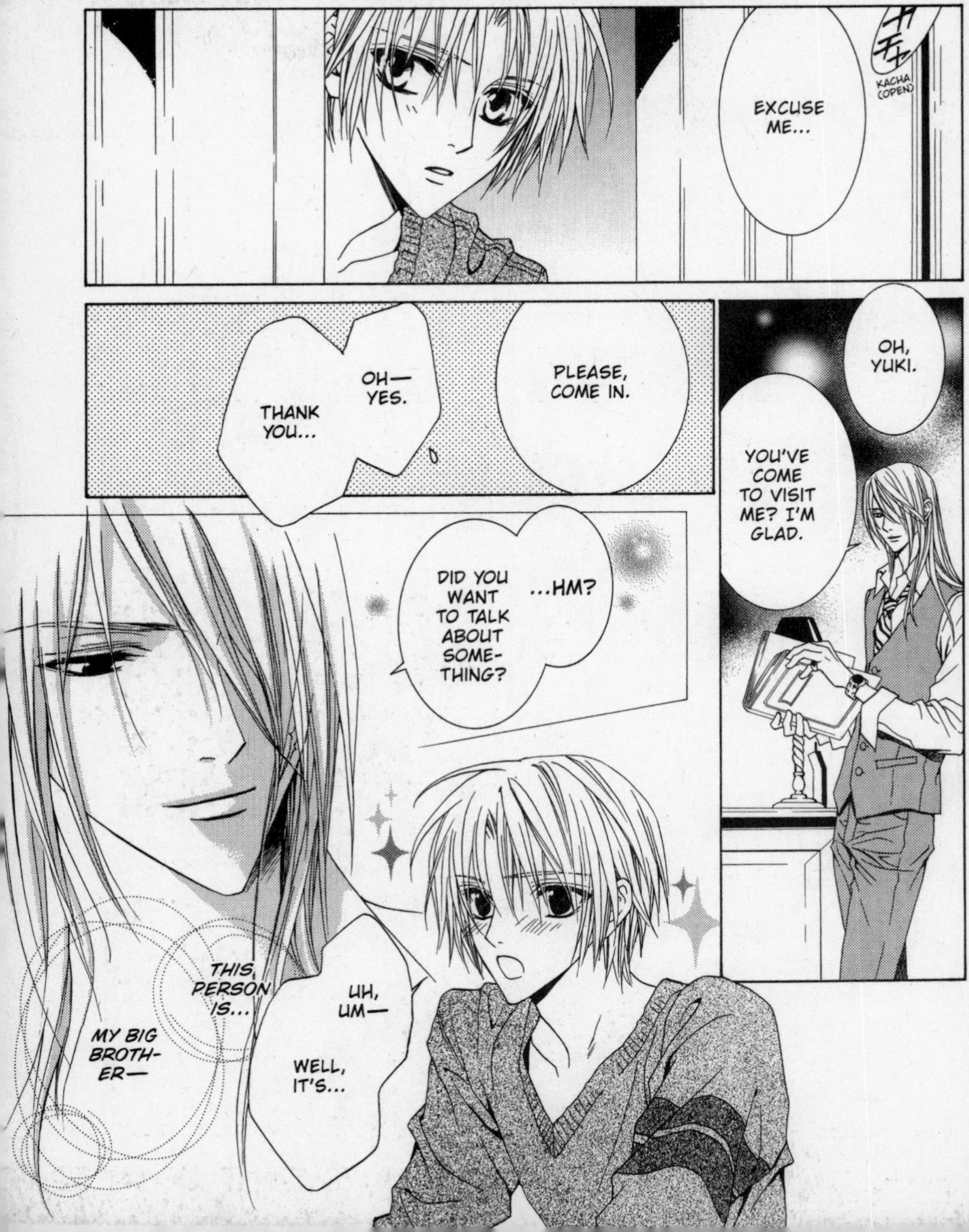
KACHA (OPEN)
EXCUSE ME...
OH, YUKI.
YOU'VE COME TO VISIT ME? I'M GLAD.
PLEASE, COME IN.
OH— YES.
THANK YOU...
...HM?
DID YOU WANT TO TALK ABOUT SOME-THING?
UH, UM—
WELL, IT'S...
THIS PERSON IS...
MY BIG BROTH-ER—

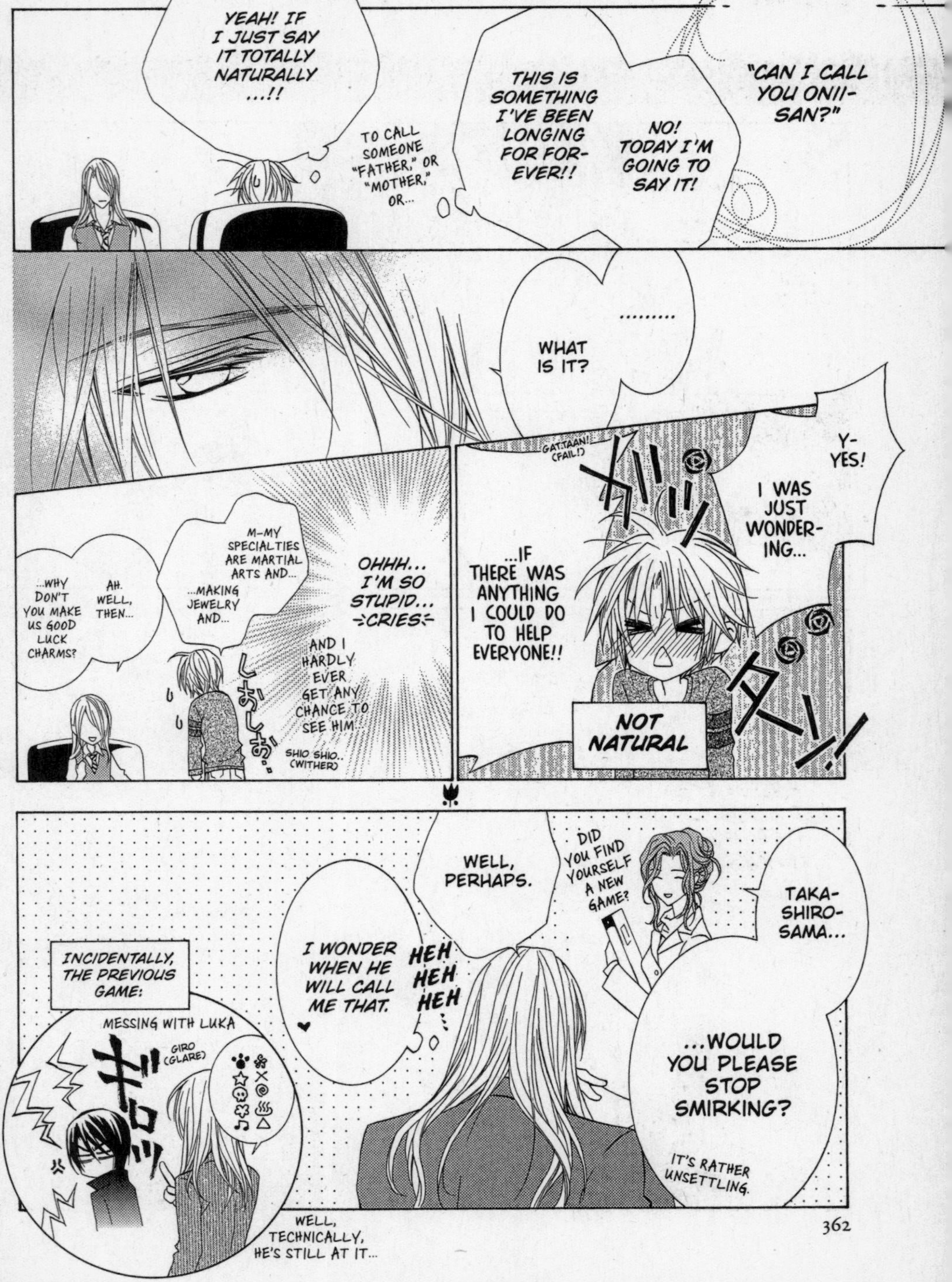
"CAN I CALL YOU ONII-SAN?"
NO! TODAY I'M GOING TO SAY IT!
THIS IS SOMETHING I'VE BEEN LONGING FOR FOR-EVER!!
TO CALL SOMEONE "FATHER," OR "MOTHER," OR...
YEAH! IF I JUST SAY IT TOTALLY NATURALLY ...!!
....
WHAT IS IT?
Y-YES!
I WAS JUST WONDER-ING...
...IF THERE WAS ANYTHING I COULD DO TO HELP EVERYONE!!
GATTAAN! (FAIL!)
NOT NATURAL
OHHH... I'M SO STUPID... =CRIES=
AND I HARDLY EVER GET ANY CHANCE TO SEE HIM
SHIO SHIO.. (WITHER)
M-MY SPECIALTIES ARE MARTIAL ARTS AND...
...MAKING JEWELRY AND...
AH. WELL, THEN...
...WHY DON'T YOU MAKE US GOOD LUCK CHARMS?
TAKA-SHIRO-SAMA...
DID YOU FIND YOURSELF A NEW GAME?
WELL, PERHAPS.
...WOULD YOU PLEASE STOP SMIRKING?
IT'S RATHER UNSETTLING.
I WONDER WHEN HE WILL CALL ME THAT.
HEH HEH HEH
INCIDENTALLY, THE PREVIOUS GAME:
MESSING WITH LUKA
GIRO (GLARE)
WELL, TECHNICALLY, HE'S STILL AT IT...

Extra ✝ I HAVE AN OBJECTION TO THE SCRIPT

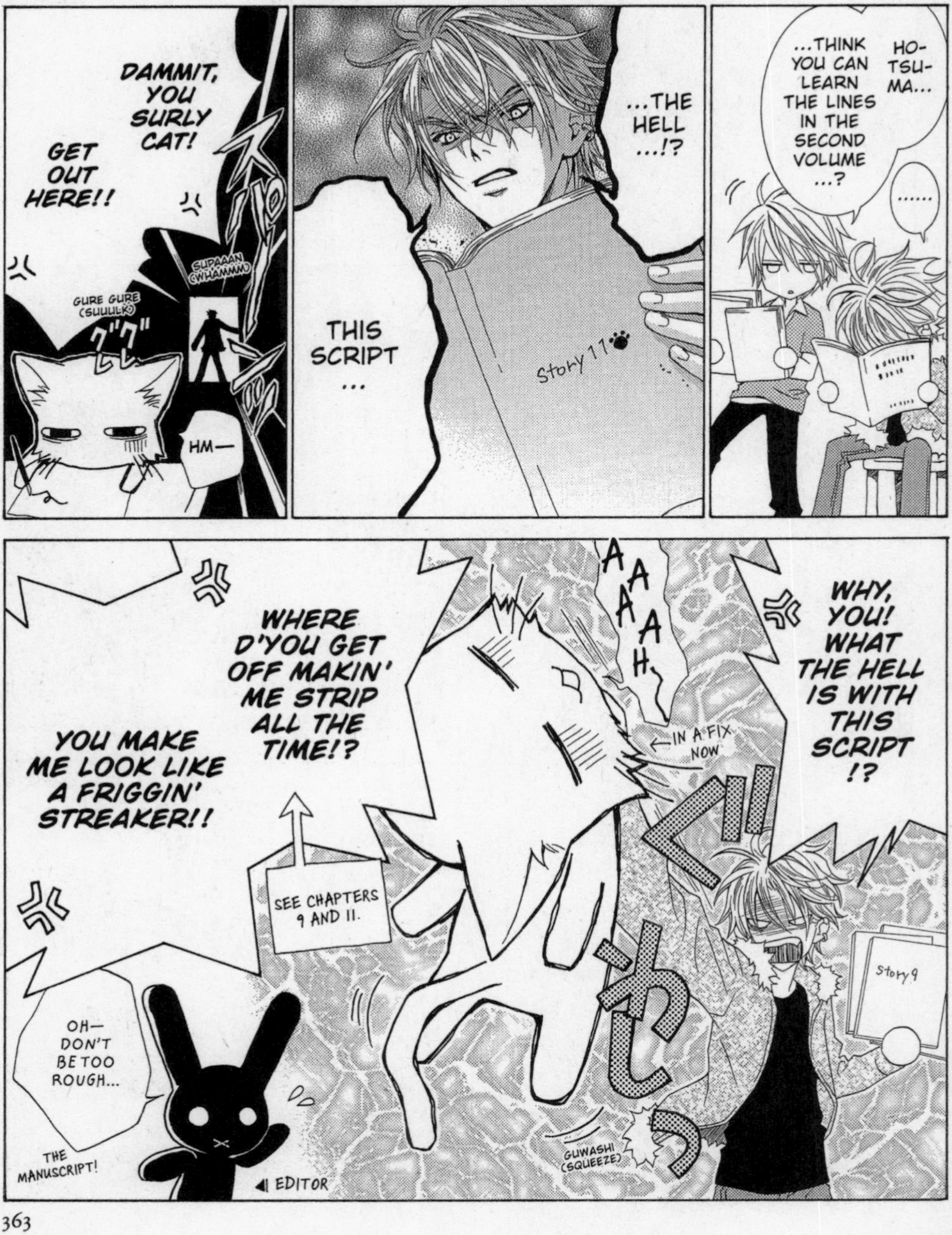
HO-TSU-MA...
...THINK YOU CAN LEARN THE LINES IN THE SECOND VOLUME ...?
......
...THE HELL ...!?
THIS SCRIPT ...
Story 11
DAMMIT, YOU SURLY CAT!
GET OUT HERE!!
SUPAAAN (WHAMMM)
GURE GURE (SUUULK)
HM—
ODAGI
WHY, YOU! WHAT THE HELL IS WITH THIS SCRIPT !?
AAAAH
IN A FIX NOW
WHERE D'YOU GET OFF MAKIN' ME STRIP ALL THE TIME!?
YOU MAKE ME LOOK LIKE A FRIGGIN' STREAKER!!
SEE CHAPTERS 9 AND 11.
Story 9
GUWASHI (SQUEEZE)
OH— DON'T BE TOO ROUGH...
THE MANUSCRIPT!
EDITOR

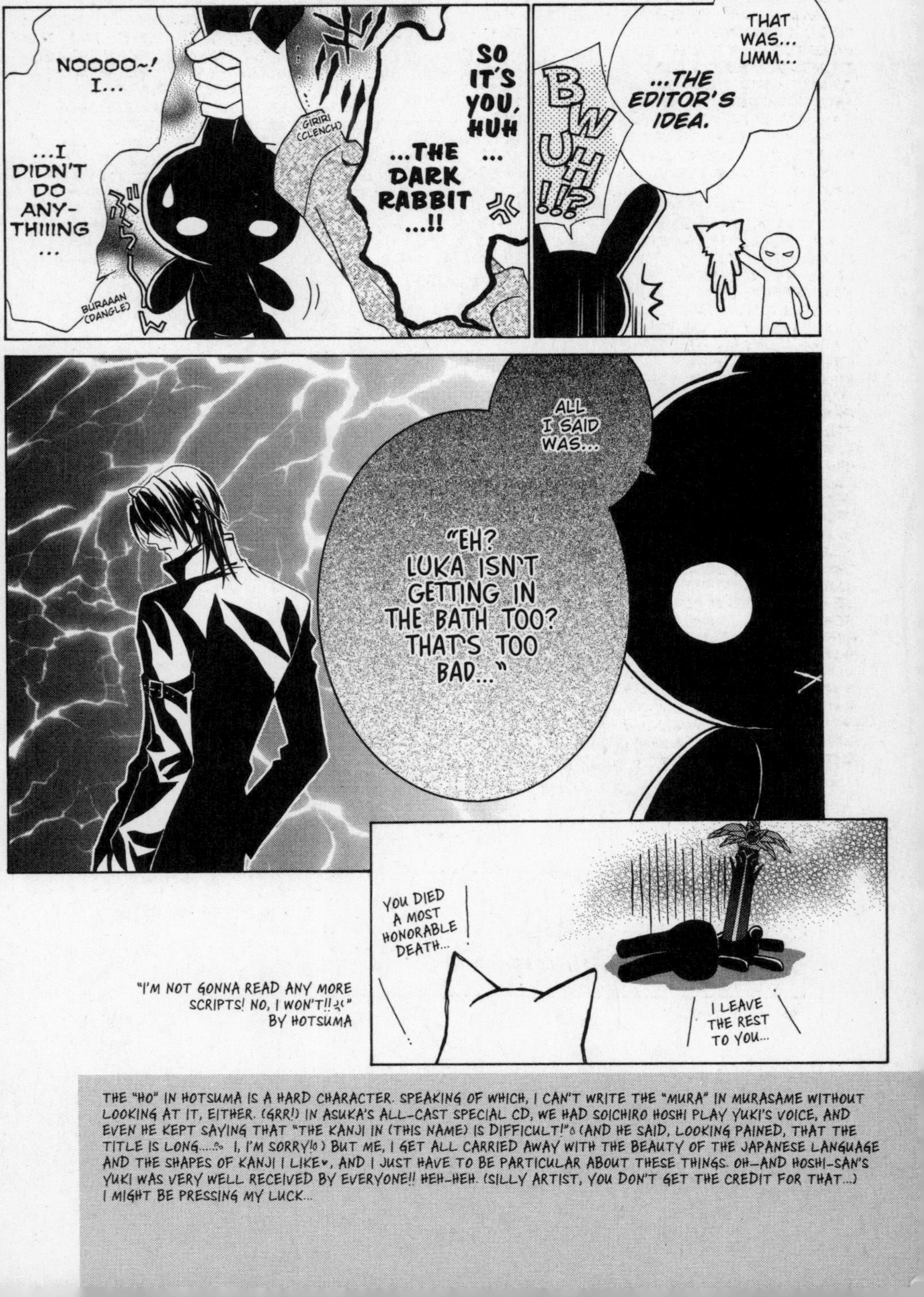
THAT WAS... UMM...
...THE EDITOR'S IDEA.
BWUH!!?
SO IT'S YOU, HUH ...
...THE DARK RABBIT ...!!
GIRIRI (CLENCH)
NOOOO~! I...
...I DIDN'T DO ANY-THIIING ...
BURAAAN (DANGLE)
ALL I SAID WAS...
"EH? LUKA ISN'T GETTING IN THE BATH TOO? THAT'S TOO BAD..."
I LEAVE THE REST TO YOU...
YOU DIED A MOST HONORABLE DEATH...
"I'M NOT GONNA READ ANY MORE SCRIPTS! NO, I WON'T!!"
BY HOTSUMA

THE "HO" IN HOTSUMA IS A HARD CHARACTER. SPEAKING OF WHICH, I CAN'T WRITE THE "MURA" IN MURASAME WITHOUT LOOKING AT IT, EITHER. (GRR!) IN ASUKA'S ALL-CAST SPECIAL CD, WE HAD SOICHIRO HOSHI PLAY YUKI'S VOICE, AND EVEN HE KEPT SAYING THAT "THE KANJI IN (THIS NAME) IS DIFFICULT!" (AND HE SAID, LOOKING PAINED, THAT THE TITLE IS LONG.... I, I'M SORRY!) BUT ME, I GET ALL CARRIED AWAY WITH THE BEAUTY OF THE JAPANESE LANGUAGE AND THE SHAPES OF KANJI I LIKE, AND I JUST HAVE TO BE PARTICULAR ABOUT THESE THINGS. OH—AND HOSHI-SAN'S YUKI WAS VERY WELL RECEIVED BY EVERYONE!! HEH-HEH. (SILLY ARTIST, YOU DON'T GET THE CREDIT FOR THAT...) I MIGHT BE PRESSING MY LUCK...

TO BELIEVE THAT WAS A LITTLE JOKE. (BUT REALLY, MR. EDITOR-IN-CHIEF, THANKS FOR TAKING CARE OF ME~~~!)

▸I REALLY WANT TO SEND REPLIES TO MY LETTERS, AND THANK-YOU NOTES FOR THE PRESENTS TOO, BUT I JUST DON'T HAVE A MINUTE TO SPARE... SO I'LL HAVE TO ASK EVERYONE TO WAIT UNTIL I CAN GET A NICE LONG BREAK. ABOUT THE REPLIES, THOUGH, I CAN'T REALLY SAY "WHEN" OR "DEFINITELY," AND WHETHER IT WILL BE A QUICK POSTCARD OR A PROPER LETTER WILL DEPEND ON HOW I FEEL AT THE TIME, SO PLEASE DON'T SEND ME AN SASE OR ANYTHING.

AND THE PEOPLE WHO **DON'T** WANT A REPLY, WHOSE FAMILIES WILL BE HORRIBLY SHOCKED IF THEY RECEIVE ONE—PLEASE DO MENTION THAT. BUT WHATEVER IT IS, OPINIONS OR IMPRESSIONS OR QUESTIONS OR ANYTHING ELSE, I'M SO HAPPY TO RECEIVE LETTERS! ♡ DRAWING MANGA ISN'T A NONSTOP PARTY—ACTUALLY THERE IS PLENTY OF PAIN AND HARDSHIP TOO. (IN FACT, I'M ON THE VERGE OF THROWING MY HANDS UP IN DESPAIR.) AND WHAT PLUCKS THIS SULKY HEART OF MINE UP FROM THE DEPTHS ARE EVERYONE'S KIND LETTERS! TO EVERYONE WHO GIVES ME THE COURAGE TO DRAW, I'M TRULY GRATEFUL. (THERE ARE EVEN FANS WHO WRITE ME FROM ABROAD...!) ALSO, I'M SIMPLE-MINDED, SO IF YOU SAY YOU LIKE WHOEVER, I'LL TRY TO GIVE THAT CHARACTER MORE PAGE TIME. (LOL) (THE DOCTOR HAS BEEN SHOWING UP MORE. HE'S REALLY GETTING SOME SERIOUS LOVE FROM THE FANS.)

▸OF COURSE, I CAN'T GET THIS MANGA OUT TO THE WORLD ALL BY MYSELF! TO K-SAN, WHO'S ALWAYS HELPING ME (I THINK I'D HARDLY EVEN BE ABLE TO DRAW MANGA WITHOUT THIS PERSON...), AND ALL MY STAFF, AND MY EDITOR WHO WORKS SO HARD AND WITH SUCH PASSION... THANK YOU FOR ALWAYS HOLDING ME UP.

▸I REALLY FEEL EVERYONE'S LOVE AND SUPPORT, AND I'M BRINGING ALONG THE STORY AS FAITHFULLY AS I CAN, AND I'M WORKING HARD SO YOU'LL WANT TO KEEP READING IT. I'M HOPING I CAN EVEN GET OUT THE THIRD VOLUME A LITTLE EARLY... MAYBE I'LL SEE YOU LATER! ☆

▸SO THERE ARE SOME THINGS IN HERE LIKE THE AUTOGRAPH SESSION REPORT...I WAS KINDLY ALLOWED TO HAVE IT WHEN THE FIRST VOLUME CAME OUT. I'M GRATEFUL TO PEOPLE JUST FOR COMING, BUT ON TOP OF THAT THEY GAVE ME **SO** MANY THINGS...THANK YOU SO MUCH! ♪ BY THE WAY, THE POTTED PLANTS AND THE CACTUS I RECEIVED ARE GROWING HEALTHILY EVEN NOW...WHICH IS UNUSUAL FOR ME. ACTUALLY, I'M FAMOUS FOR MAKING EVEN THE HARDIEST OF HOUSE PLANTS WITHER UP... (AMONG MY FAMILY.) IT'S KIND OF A SHOCK WHEN THEY DIE, SO I'M GLAD THAT THIS TIME THEY'RE REALLY STAYING HEALTHY! ♡

▸WHEN I MEET READERS, MOST OF THEM SAY "YOU LOOK JUST LIKE I PICTURE YOU FROM YOUR MANGA!" AND I WONDER, THEN WHAT DO PEOPLE THINK I'M LIKE......? (LOL) ONE THING I HEAR A LOT FROM PEOPLE AROUND ME IS "YOU'RE MORE MASCULINE THAN I THOUGHT." ...YEAH. (UM, I'M A LADY, SO WHAT'S THAT MEAN FOR ME? LOL) MAYBE IT'S BECAUSE I'M SPIRITED?

AND YET I SEEM TO BE LACKING IN LIFE SKILLS...

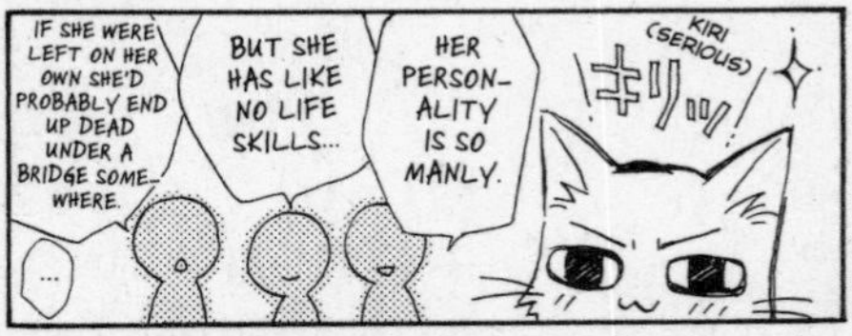
KIRI (SERIOUS)
キリッ!
HER PERSONALITY IS SO MANLY.
BUT SHE HAS LIKE NO LIFE SKILLS...
IF SHE WERE LEFT ON HER OWN SHE'D PROBABLY END UP DEAD UNDER A BRIDGE SOMEWHERE.
...

ANOTHER THING I HEAR A LOT IS "IF YOU WERE A SWEET YOU'D BE A COOKIE, IF YOU WERE A TEA YOU'D BE BLACK TEA." MAYBE IT'S BECAUSE OF THE NAME "HOTARU" (FIREFLY). (← NOT MY REAL NAME.)

ACTUALLY WHAT I LIKE TO DRINK IS JAPANESE TEA, AND I HARDLY EVER EAT SWEET THINGS. IF I HAD TO PICK A FAVORITE FOOD IT WOULD BE SCALLIONS, OR ONIONS, OR NORI SEAWEED.

↑ PEOPLE ARE ALWAYS WEIRDED OUT WHEN I SAY THAT. (LOL)

▸AND THEN, AT THE LAUNCH PARTY, IT WAS THE EDITOR-IN-CHIEF WHO SAID TO ME, "THE AUTOGRAPH SESSION WAS FUN—MAYBE WE COULD DO A TOUR NEXT TIME." SO I SAID, "WELL, WHEN WE DO, PLEASE GIVE ME SOME TIME OFF!" AND HE SAID, "NO...WE'D HAVE YOU WORKING ON THE MANUSCRIPT IN YOUR HOTEL." ....SILENCE. I'M CHOOSING

SPECIAL THANKS

K-SAN · A. FUJISAKI · H. MATSUO
K.O · E.Y · S.K
Y. SUZUKI ...AND EVERYONE IN EDITORIAL

SEND LETTERS TO:
GEKKAN ASUKA EDITING DEPARTMENT
C/O HOTARU ODAGIRI
KADOKAWA SHOTEN KK
102-8078

➡ TO BE CONTINUED

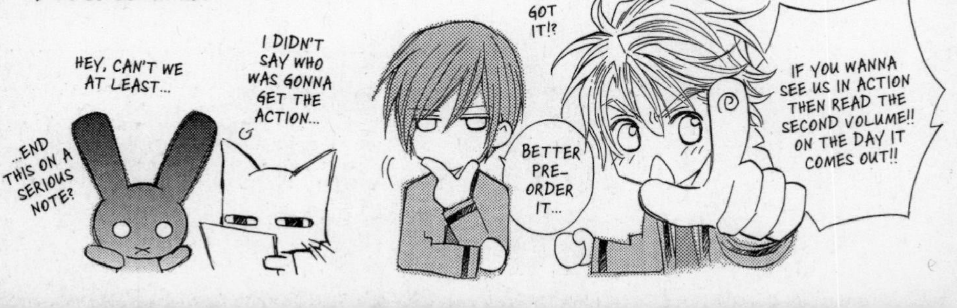
IF YOU WANNA SEE US IN ACTION THEN READ THE SECOND VOLUME!! ON THE DAY IT COMES OUT!!
GOT IT!?
BETTER PRE-ORDER IT...
I DIDN'T SAY WHO WAS GONNA GET THE ACTION...
HEY, CAN'T WE AT LEAST...
...END THIS ON A SERIOUS NOTE?

Hotaru odaqiti

The eternal ideal
is to "be yourself," but
I still haven't the faintest
idea what "myself" is. So,
along with the characters
in this story, I'm setting
out on a journey in search
of myself. Won't you
come along too?

Message from Volume 1
(Japanese edition)

Hotaru odaqiti

The characters
have started to act
however they please...
in both promising and
frightening ways. I really
wonder what will
happen next...
(*grin*)

**Message from
Volume 2**
(Japanese edition)

The Phantomhive family has a butler who's almost too good to be true...

...or maybe he's just too good to be human.

Black Butler

YANA TOBOSO

VOLUMES 1 THROUGH 5 IN STORES NOW!

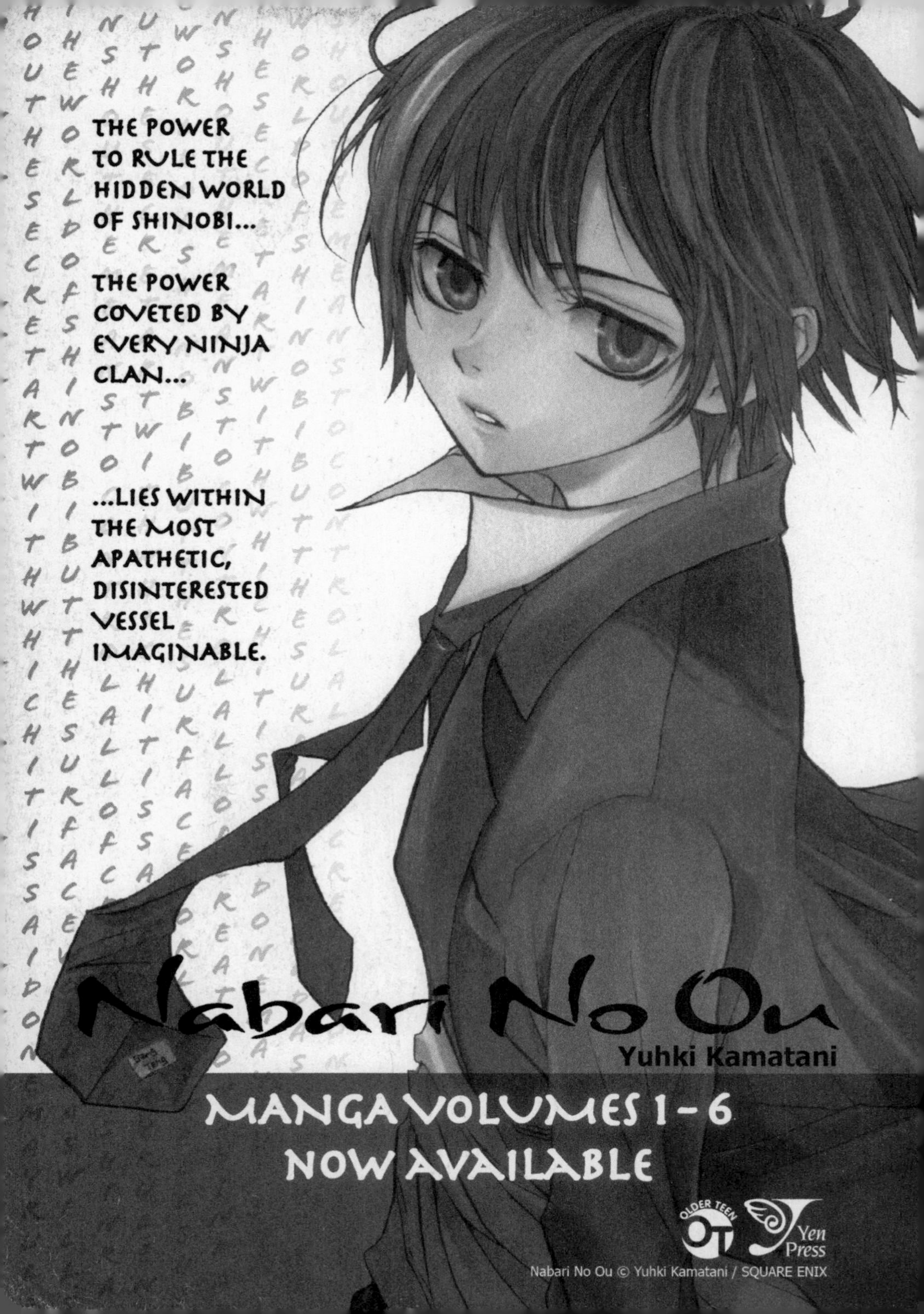
THE POWER TO RULE THE HIDDEN WORLD OF SHINOBI...
THE POWER COVETED BY EVERY NINJA CLAN...
...LIES WITHIN THE MOST APATHETIC, DISINTERESTED VESSEL IMAGINABLE.
Nabari No Ou
Yuhki Kamatani
MANGA VOLUMES 1-6 NOW AVAILABLE
OLDER TEEN OT
Yen Press
Nabari No Ou © Yuhki Kamatani / SQUARE ENIX

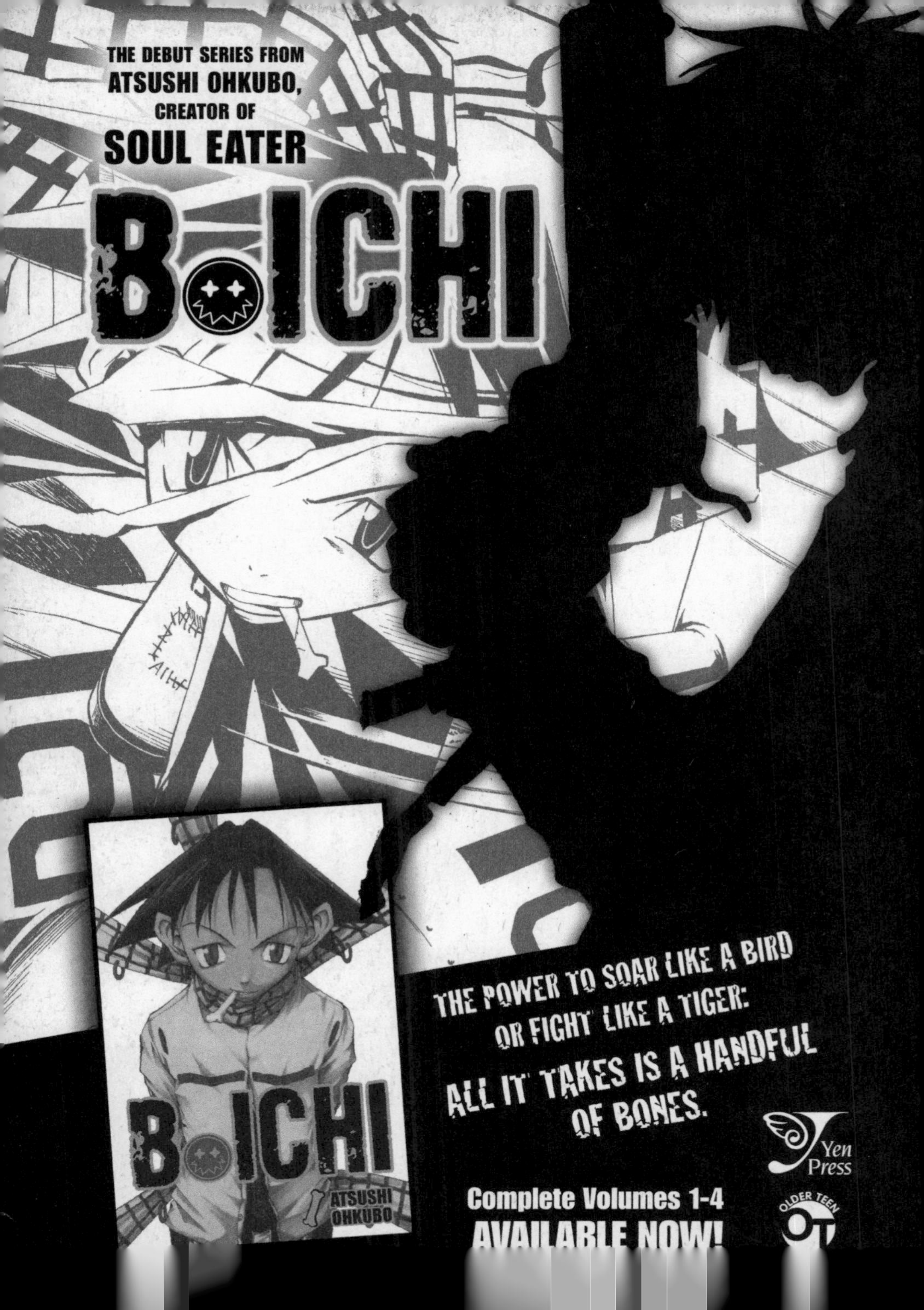
THE DEBUT SERIES FROM
ATSUSHI OHKUBO,
CREATOR OF
SOUL EATER
B ICHI
B ICHI
ATSUSHI OHKUBO
THE POWER TO SOAR LIKE A BIRD
OR FIGHT LIKE A TIGER:
ALL IT TAKES IS A HANDFUL
OF BONES.
Yen Press
Complete Volumes 1-4
AVAILABLE NOW!
OLDER TEEN
OT

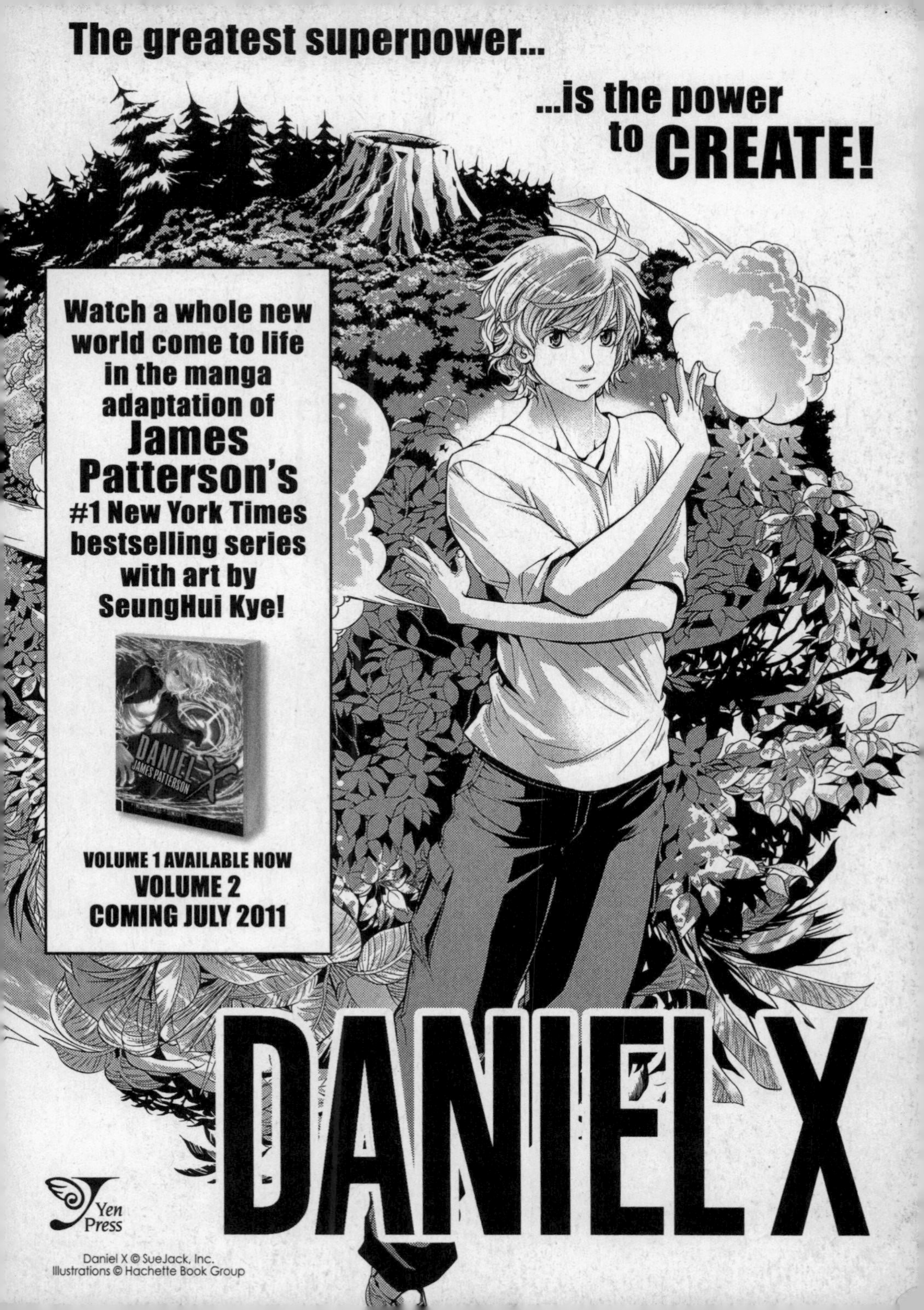
The greatest superpower...
...is the power to CREATE!
Watch a whole new world come to life in the manga adaptation of James Patterson's #1 New York Times bestselling series with art by SeungHui Kye!
DANIEL X
JAMES PATTERSON
VOLUME 1 AVAILABLE NOW
VOLUME 2 COMING JULY 2011
DANIEL X
Yen Press
Daniel X © SueJack, Inc.
Illustrations © Hachette Book Group

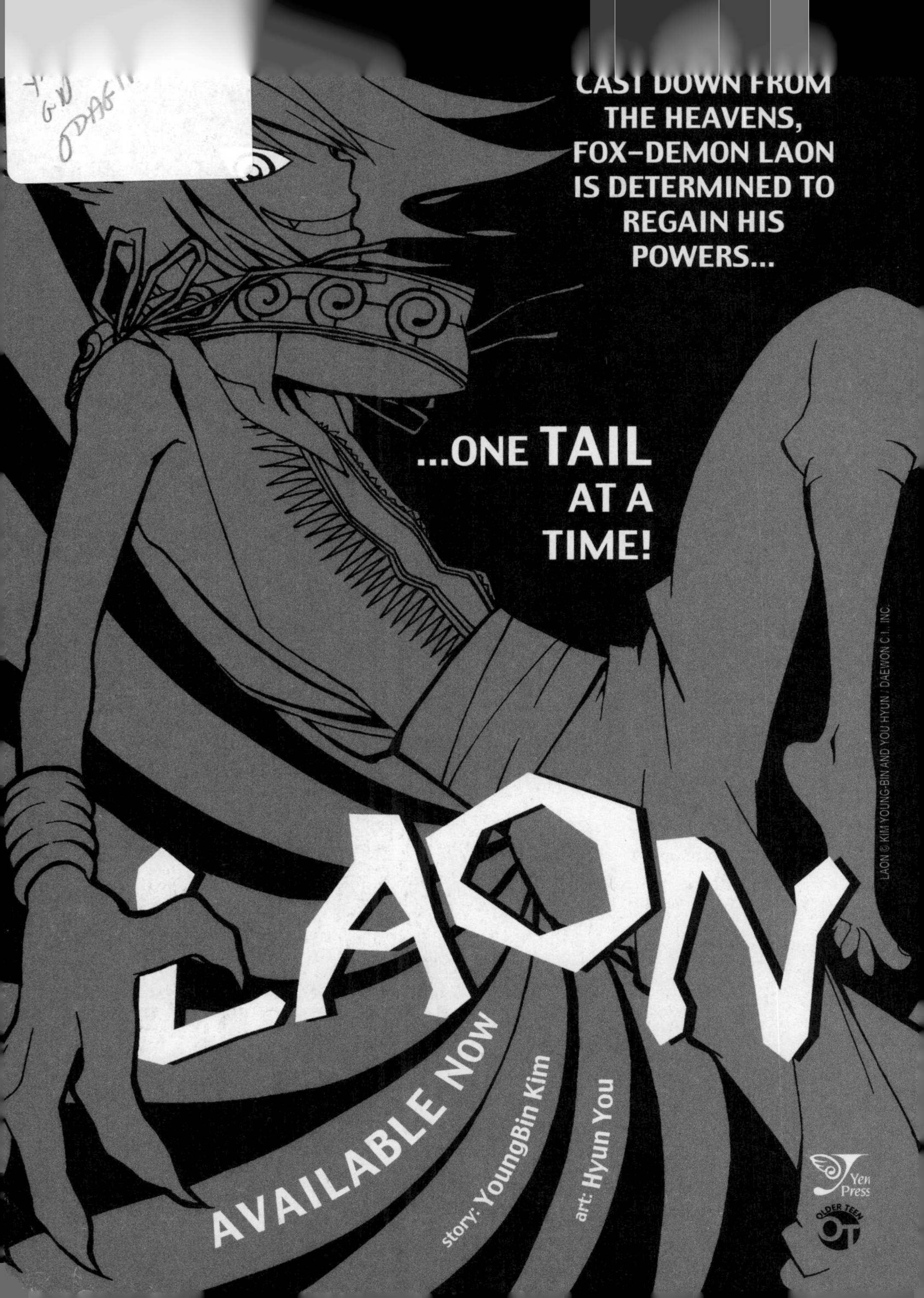

CAST DOWN FROM
THE HEAVENS,
FOX-DEMON LAON
IS DETERMINED TO
REGAIN HIS
POWERS...
...ONE TAIL
AT A
TIME!
LAON
AVAILABLE NOW
story: YoungBin Kim
art: Hyun You
LAON © KIM YOUNG-BIN AND YOU HYUN / DAEWON C.I. INC.
Yen Press
OLDER TEEN
OT

A totally new Arabian nights, where Scheherazade is a guy!

Everyone knows the story of Scheherazade and her wonderful tales from the Arabian Nights. For one thousand and one nights, the stories that she created entertained the mad Sultan and eventually saved her life. In this version, Scheherazade is a guy who disguises himself as a woman to save his sister from the mad Sultan. When he puts his life on the line, what kind of strange and unique stories will he tell? This new twist on one of the greatest classical tales might just keep you awake for another ONE THOUSAND AND ONE NIGHTS!

Yen Press
www.yenpress.com

Available at bookstores near you!

One thousand and one nights 1~11 Final

Han SeungHee · Jeon JinSeok

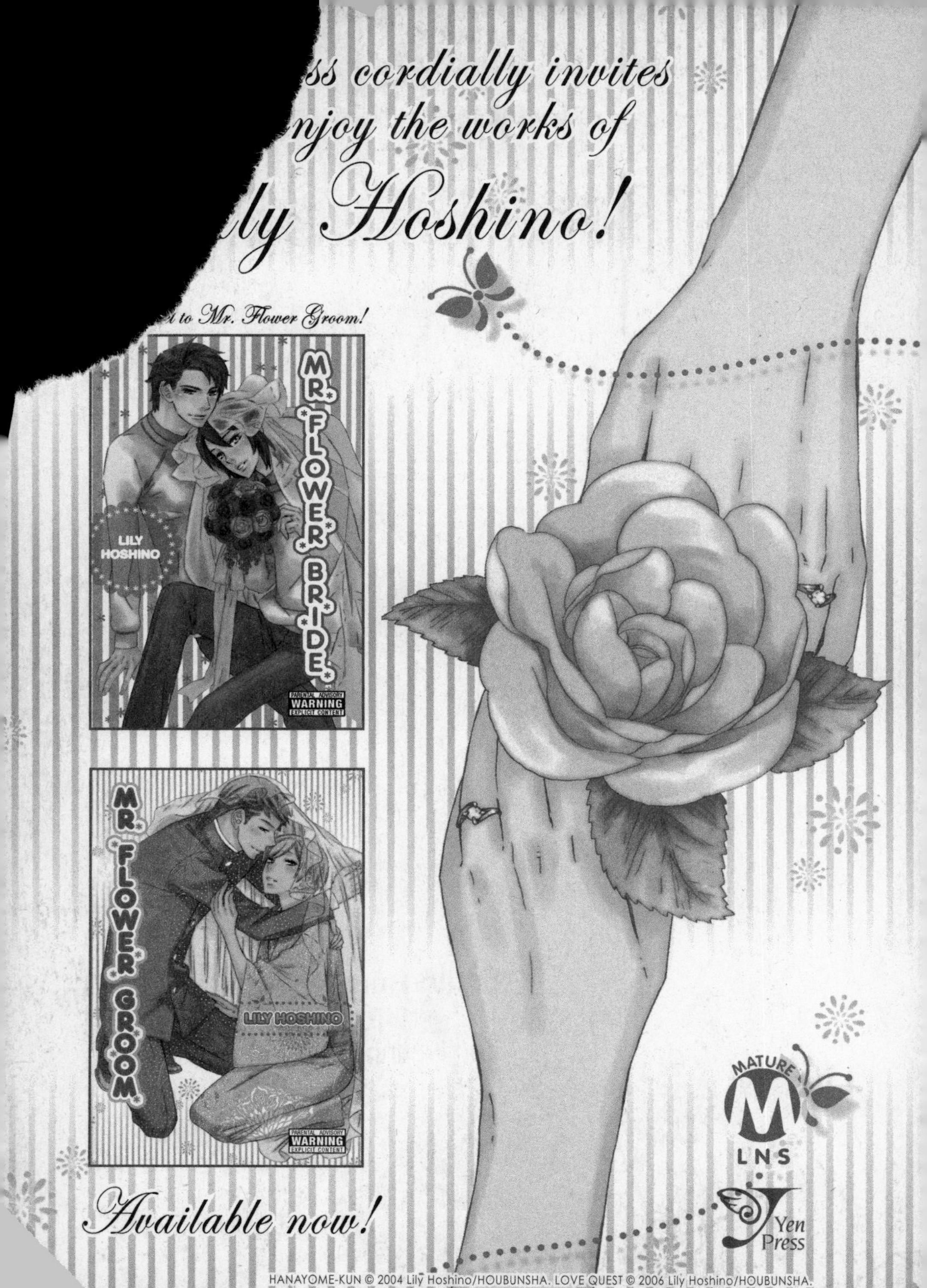

...ss cordially invites
...njoy the works of
...ily Hoshino!
...to Mr. Flower Groom!
MR. FLOWER BRIDE
LILY HOSHINO
PARENTAL ADVISORY WARNING EXPLICIT CONTENT
MR. FLOWER GROOM
LILY HOSHINO
PARENTAL ADVISORY WARNING EXPLICIT CONTENT
Available now!
MATURE M LNS
Yen Press

THE BETRAYAL

kNoWS MY NAME

Hotaru Odagiri

Translation: Melissa Tanaka † Lettering: Lys Blakeslee

URAGIRI WA BOKU NO NAMAE WO SHITTEIRU Volumes 1 and 2 © Hotaru ODAGIRI 2006, 2007. First published in Japan in 2006, 2007 by KADOKAWA SHOTEN Co., Ltd., Tokyo. English translation rights arranged with KADOKAWA SHOTEN Co., Ltd., Tokyo through TUTTLE MORI AGENCY, INC., Tokyo.

Translation © 2011 by Hachette Book Group, Inc.

Yen Press
Hachette Book Group
237 Park Avenue, New York, NY 10017

www.HachetteBookGroup.com
www.YenPress.com

Yen Press is an imprint of Hachette Book Group, Inc. The Yen Press name and logo are trademarks of Hachette Book Group, Inc.

First Yen Press Edition: June 2011

ISBN: 978-0-316-11941-2

10 9 8 7 6 5 4

BVG

Printed in the United States of America